PROPHET OF INNOVATION

PROPHET OF INNOVATION

Joseph Schumpeter and Creative Destruction

THOMAS K. MCCRAW

THE BELKNAP PRESS OF HARVARD UNIVERSITY PRESS

Cambridge, Massachusetts, and London, England

2007

Cataloging-in-Publication Data available from the Library of Congress
Library of Congress catalog card number: 2006050887
ISBN-13: 978-0-674-02523-3 (alk. paper)
ISBN-10: 0-674-02523-7 (alk. paper)

To Susan, with love

CONTENTS

PREFACE

This biography, by necessity, has two protagonists: Joseph Alois Schumpeter (1883–1950) and the phenomenon of capitalist innovation. Schumpeter was one of the greatest economists who ever lived, and an electrifying personality besides. The study of capitalism obsessed him. His insights, in turn, were shaped by his own tumultuous experiences amid wars, economic upheavals, and personal misfortunes.

Schumpeter's work was so powerful that today's thinking about capitalism is in large part his—specifically, his emphasis on innovation, entrepreneurship, business strategy, and "creative destruction." Specialists in the analysis of business identify him closely with the first two of these terms. He helped to popularize the third, and he coined the fourth himself. Schumpeter was to capitalism what Freud was to the mind: someone whose ideas have become so ubiquitous and ingrained that we cannot separate his foundational thoughts from our own. My intention in this book is to recover his life and work, so that we can better take the measure of the man and his influence.

Despite Schumpeter's own attraction to numbers, this will not be a book heavy on statistics. But before we meet the man, let us consider the object of his study—capitalism—in the sort of quick statistical overview he would have relished.[1]

The cash income of the average American is now more than twenty times what it was in 1800. If you're an American, imagine trying to live on one-twentieth of what you now earn. Among other changes in your way of life, you'd probably have to grow your own food, as most of your predecessors did in 1800.

Today, in the twenty-first century, about 80 percent of the world's population is still very poor. Many people in the rich countries know this, but the gruesome reality of mass poverty is nonetheless hard to imagine—especially the plight of the desperately poor. Almost half of the global population struggles to survive on less than two dollars a day, compared to about a hundred dollars in the United States. Per capita income in the twenty richest countries is thirty-seven times that in the twenty poorest. Despite big gains in sections of China and India, most countries still have not succeeded in making capitalism work for their people.

But some have, and in grand fashion. Recall how quickly Japan and West Germany recovered from the chaos of World War II—vivid examples of innovation driven by local entrepreneurship and national growth policies. The United States helped because the Americans wanted both Japan and Germany to become strong allies in the Cold War against the Soviet Union.

Another example: the Czech Republic, the land of Schumpeter's birth, lies between Germany and Austria, two countries where he also lived before he moved to the United States. The Czechs have a lengthy history of prosperous industrialization. But when the Nazis and then the Soviets imposed their political and economic systems, they inflicted grievous damage that lasted long after the advent of democracy in 1990. In 1995 the per capita income of Czechs was only one half that of Germans and Austrians. By 2005 it had risen to two thirds.

Most of these numbers reflect the *cumulative* power of capitalism. In the very long term—say, the thousand years preceding the eighteenth century—personal incomes in Western Europe doubled at the rate of once every 630 years. But after the spread of modern capitalism, they began to double every fifty or sixty years. They doubled every forty years in the United States, and every twenty-five in Japan, which got a later start and profited from the European and American examples. Even Karl Marx and Friedrich Engels conceded in *The Communist Manifesto* that a scant hundred years of capitalism had "created more massive and more colossal productive forces than have all preceding generations together." And when *The Communist Manifesto* first appeared in 1848, the "capitalist engine," as Schumpeter called it, was just warming up. Marx and his followers were the first to use the word capitalism, which they invented as an antonym for socialism. But it took Schumpeter to tell us what the word really meant.[2]

This book is not concerned with Schumpeter's economic thinking, narrowly construed. Instead, it is about his turbulent life and his compulsive drive to understand capitalism—its yeasty mix of economic, social, cultural, and political elements; its good and bad qualities (both very strong); and its impact on individuals, families, and nations.

Schumpeter pierced the veil of capitalism by defying one of the strongest intellectual trends of his time, and of ours as well—the trend toward narrow specialization. Rather than concentrate on economic theory alone, he also immersed himself in history, law, literature, business, sociology, psychology, mathematics, and political science. Because capitalism is more than an economic system, he made himself more than an economist. As one of his contemporaries put it, he was "perhaps the last of the great polymaths."[3]

During his otherwise continuous intellectual odyssey, three subtle shifts occurred, and the three parts of this book correspond to those intellectual shifts. First, he focused on the economics of capitalism; second, on its social structure; third, and most satisfying to him, on its historical record. The pleasure he took in solving so many riddles in so many fields sometimes bordered on exultation, and here I try to convey the reasons why.

Without innovations, no entrepreneurs; without entrepreneurial achievement, no capitalist returns and no capitalist propulsion. The atmosphere of industrial revolutions—of "progress"—is the only one in which capitalism can survive.

JOSEPH SCHUMPETER, *Business Cycles,* 1939

PART I

L'Enfant Terrible, 1883–1926:

Innovation and Economics

PROLOGUE

Who He Was and What He Did

There is nothing stable in the world; uproar's your only
music.

JOHN KEATS, letter to his brother, 1818

SCHUMPETER FIRST USED the phrase creative destruction in
1942, to describe how innovative capitalist products and methods continually
displace old ones. He gave abundant examples. The factory wiped out the
blacksmith shop, the car superseded the horse and buggy, and the corporation
overthrew the proprietorship. "Creative destruction is the essential fact about
capitalism," he wrote. "Stabilized capitalism is a contradiction in terms."[1]

The notion of creative destruction expresses two clashing ideas, not surprising for someone whose personal life embodied so many paradoxes.
Schumpeter epitomized F. Scott Fitzgerald's test of a first-rate intelligence: the
capacity "to hold two opposed ideas in the mind at the same time, and still retain the ability to function." Schumpeter's native Austria has been described as
a "techno-romantic" civilization at the time when he was growing up, and this
adjective applies as aptly to the man as to the country.[2]

An English critic once wrote that Schumpeter "was a bravura character
whose life history could have been specially scripted for a T.V. mini-series." He
liked to play the part of an aristocrat, even though his origins were middle-class
and his eminence self-made. Starting as an academic boy wonder, he aston-

ished his elders with books he wrote in his twenties. In his thirties, he had a brief public career as Austria's finance minister. He next reinvented himself as a banker and made a fortune that he promptly lost in a stock market crash. After returning to academics, he moved to the United States to become a Harvard professor. World-famous by this time, he was also penniless. He had to make paid speeches to raise the money for his transatlantic ticket.[3]

During these adventures, he suffered crushing misfortunes that would have destroyed lesser people. But—in the brutal language of boxing—he could take a punch. Regardless of his troubles, he always behaved in public like a Continental *bon vivant,* the sort of charming rogue played by Cary Grant in old movies. Musing on his own reinventions, Cary Grant once said, "I pretended to be someone that I wanted to be, and I finally became that person. Or he became me."

So with Schumpeter. He overflowed with witty conversation—his prominent chin wagging in exuberant motion, his olive-skinned face quickly changing expressions, his lively brown eyes fixing his listener with close attention. He liked to flaunt his brilliance while at the same time making fun of himself. In the midst of his youthful triumphs, he reported having acquired "some local popularity and reputation which the years will doubtlessly reduce to its proper level of zero." He wore expensive tailored clothes and confessed that "it takes me an hour to dress." Numerous women loved Schumpeter, and he loved them back. "OK, I have a gift for women," he wrote in his diary. He regarded valor as the better part of discretion and enjoyed saying that he aspired to become the greatest economist, horseman, and lover in the world. Then came his punch line: things were not going well with the horses.[4]

But he was never flippant about his work. He became obsessed with it, as often happens with people of genius. Like Benjamin Franklin, he set down numerical scores for his daily and weekly accomplishments, his system ranging from zero for failure to 1.0 for what he called a good intellectual "performance." He judged himself harshly, setting down zeroes even for many days when he worked into the night. He frequently recorded one half and occasionally two thirds but seldom a one.

Beneath a veneer of ebullience, Schumpeter hid his passionate and dark—sometimes very dark—emotional side. Throughout his life, he fought a fierce internal wrestling match with himself, often holding not just two opposing ideas at the same time but half a dozen. He believed, for example, that Karl Marx had been profoundly correct on many issues but wrong on others because of an unyielding ideology—or, as Schumpeter came to call it, "vision." He made the same kind of judgment about John Maynard Keynes, his own contemporary. Schumpeter himself aspired to be a value-neutral social scientist whose work remained pristine and untainted by ideology. He thought he could avoid the trap that had ensnared Marx and Keynes.

But as it turned out, he had his own distinctive vision. His deepest analytical tension was the strain between determinism on the one hand and contingency on the other. This tension ran throughout his life's work, eluding resolution until he reached his sixties. In the meantime, the more he studied different economic systems, the more convinced he became of the unique advantages of capitalism for productivity and growth.

Schumpeter dreamed of developing what he called an "exact economics"—a hard science like physics, with determinate predictive power. He believed that he could reconcile stripped-down mathematical models of abstract theory with the full record of historical and sociological evidence. But his drive for technical exactitude was an essentially romantic mission, unattainable on a broad scale by Schumpeter or anyone else. Even so, his struggle to work out the problems of value neutrality, scientific precision, and fidelity to historical experience paid tremendous dividends for his analysis of capitalism.[5]

Questions about capitalism—what it is, how and why it has worked well in some places and not others—are among the most important that people and governments have faced. This has been true for about three hundred years, and seldom more so than in the present and the recent past. Recall the turbulent transition from the last decade of the twentieth century to the initial one of the twenty-first: the sudden collapse of communism, for seventy years a serious challenger to capitalism; the riotous prosperity of the 1990s, when entrepreneurs became folk heroes; the ensuing epidemic of corporate scandals, which bankrupted shareholders and employees and disgraced capitalism itself; then the scourge of international terrorism, portending warfare without end; and finally the spectacular economic gains in many parts of the world—most notably China, which combined a new capitalist economic system with an old communist political regime.

How can one understand these issues? Why, after seven decades of struggle, did capitalism triumph over communism? Are exorbitant executive pay schemes and continual accounting frauds corruptions of capitalism or its natural state? When people ask about terrorists "Why do they hate us so much?" what part does capitalism play in the definition of "us"? How long can China and other countries sustain their economic progress without granting more political liberties to their people?

Some of the clearest guides to these kinds of questions come from Schumpeter, who assessed capitalism as an expression of innovation, human drama, and sheer havoc—all going on at once. He told of capitalism in the way most people experience it: as consumer desires aroused by endless advertising; as forcible jolts up and down the social pecking order; as goals reached, shattered, altered, then reached once more as people try, try again. For capitalism, and for Schumpeter personally, nothing was ever stable. Uproar was their only music.

Like nearly everyone who has thought deeply about capitalism, Schumpeter came away with mixed feelings. He regarded himself as a conservative and planned to write a book on the meaning of conservatism. But, as he told his fellow economist John Kenneth Galbraith, "I am pretty sure that no conservative I have ever met would recognize himself in the picture I am going to draw." Schumpeter abhorred some of the banalities of business culture and revered the artistic attainments of the Old World. He knew that creative destruction fosters economic growth but also that it undercuts cherished human values. He saw that poverty brings misery but also that prosperity cannot assure peace of mind.[6]

A steep rise in living standards would seem to be a prize of supreme value for any society. Yet capitalism has a dreadful reputation for robbing the poor to profit the rich, and it has never achieved what most people regard as a fair distribution of its bounties. In some countries it still represents a curse to be resisted and overcome. Even its fortunate beneficiaries in rich countries often have a guilty feeling that capitalism is an unworthy pursuit—something to be accepted but not celebrated. As Schumpeter himself put it, "The stock exchange is a poor substitute for the Holy Grail."[7]

He applied his immense energy to analyzing and explaining capitalist innovation not only for other experts but sometimes for the nonspecialist. From the compelling story of his life and work, a reader can grasp the basic mechanism of the capitalist engine about as well as from a whole shelf of textbooks. The subject is momentous, and its full social mechanism quite intricate. But its *economic* essence is not very complicated. As Schumpeter himself wrote in 1946, at the beginning of his long article on capitalism for the *Encyclopaedia Britannica*, "A society is called capitalist if it entrusts its economic process to the guidance of the private businessman. This may be said to imply, first, private ownership of nonpersonal means of production . . . second, production for private account, i.e., production by private initiative for private profit." He went on to say that a third element is "so essential to the functioning of the capitalist system" that it must be added to the other two.[8]

This third element is the creation of credit. The core ethos of capitalism looks constantly ahead and relies on credit in launching new ventures. From the Latin root *credo*—"I believe"—credit represents a wager on a better future. The entrepreneurs and consumers who make these bets often care little about the past and have scant patience with the present. They undertake innovative projects and make expensive purchases (houses, for example) that require far greater resources than those lying at hand. In the absence of credit, both consumers and entrepreneurs would suffer endless frustrations.

The entrepreneur, Schumpeter once wrote, is "the pivot on which everything turns." Entrepreneurs—whether they operate in big firms or small ones, old companies or startups—are the agents of innovation and creative destruction. Their projects are the wellsprings of new jobs, higher incomes, and general economic progress. But in releasing their creative energies, rising entrepreneurs shove older ones aside, destroying their dreams and often their fortunes. The majority of people, even in rich countries, will never become entrepreneurs. Some will not even find employment in successful enterprises. And sooner or later, most businesses will fail, sometimes damaging whole communities as well as individuals.[9]

At its worst, capitalism reduces all human relationships to crass calculations of personal costs and benefits. It elevates material values over spiritual ones, despoils the environment, and exploits the foulest aspects of human nature. In a setting where everything is for sale, businesses can turn a profit on anything—including all of the seven deadly sins with the possible exception of sloth. "I often wonder," Schumpeter wrote in his diary, "if there is any cause that ever arose and had success that was not business for somebody."[10]

But if capitalism can somehow be brought into balance with nobler human purposes, it becomes the economic equivalent of Churchill's famous definition of democracy: the worst possible system except for all the others. For despite its flaws, capitalism alone has fostered the scientific, technical, and medical innovations necessary to lift humanity out of a Hobbesian state of nature, where life is solitary, poor, nasty, brutish, and short.

Hundreds of first-rate thinkers have grappled with these issues. Two of the very greatest, Adam Smith and Karl Marx, came to opposite conclusions. Smith (1723–1790) saw the market economy as a nearly ideal system, whereas Marx (1818–1883) denounced it as an unpleasant interval on the inevitable path to socialism. Schumpeter, born late enough to study capitalism in its twentieth-century maturity, surpassed both of his more famous predecessors in analytical sophistication.[11]

Events during his lifetime showed that capitalism can take very diverse forms in different settings. He once wrote of "the infinitely complex organism of capitalist society." A social and cultural system as much as an economic one, capitalism can work for either good ends or bad. It can be moral, immoral, or—most often—amoral. Everything depends on the context, mainly the degree to which a group or a nation can maximize the creative components while mitigating the destructive side effects.[12]

Many people of Schumpeter's generation grew up with too hopeful a view of capitalism. Imbued with the nineteenth century's faith that democracy and technology would bring long-lasting peace and prosperity, they witnessed in the twentieth century something very different: wars, depressions, totalitarianism, and genocide. The carnage of World War I killed their optimism. The Great Depression of the 1930s shook their faith in both democracy and capitalism. For many, the Depression and the start of World War II confirmed the failure of markets and the superiority of socialism.

Not so for Schumpeter. In peacetime and war, he watched as economic systems and political ideologies battled to the death for supremacy. He saw families and communities career back and forth between wealth and poverty. He had no illusions about capitalism but also no doubt about his own verdict: its economic bounties so enhanced the life of the average person that they far offset its negative effects. What was the bankruptcy of an individual entrepreneur, or the obsolescence of a few thousand craftsmen, compared to the greater freedom and comfort of millions of people with access to new and inexpensive goods?[13]

At a high tide of anti-capitalist feeling just after the Great Depression, Schumpeter wrote: "It is the cheap cloth, the cheap cotton and rayon fabric, boots, motorcars and so on that are the typical achievement of capitalist production, and not as a rule improvements that would mean much to the rich man. Queen Elizabeth owned silk stockings [in the 16th century]. The capitalist achievement does not typically consist in providing more silk stockings for queens but in bringing them within the reach of factory girls in return for steadily decreasing amounts of effort . . . the capitalist process, not by coincidence but by virtue of its mechanism, progressively raises the standard of life of the masses."[14]

But capitalism is not the natural state of human existence. If it were, it would have emerged much earlier in history and would now prevail almost everywhere. Instead, it is an uncommonly difficult system to construct and sustain. Adam Smith's "invisible hand" is still essential, but it is no longer sufficient, any more than are the eighteenth-century waterwheels Smith so admired. *Modern* capitalism must be actively nurtured and controlled, with sophistication and resolve. Without constant promotion by entrepreneurs and careful monitoring by regulators (a necessity much underestimated by many advocates of the free market, including Schumpeter himself), it cannot achieve or maintain its full potential. Like the actual engines that loom so large in creative destruction—steam, electric, diesel, gasoline, jet—the capitalist engine can slow down, sputter, overheat, explode, or die.

Schumpeter believed that the world could fully benefit from capitalism only if people understood how it works. That is one reason why he spent so much of his time figuring it out and explaining it. The capitalist engine can hum along at full throttle and do wondrous things for humanity, if—but only if—it is well understood.

I

Leaving Home

> After a little I am taken in and put to bed. Sleep, soft smil-
> ing, draws me unto her: and those receive me, who quietly
> treat me, as one well-beloved in that home: but will not,
> oh, will not, not now, not ever; but will not ever tell me
> who I am.

JAMES AGEE, A Death in the Family, 1957

THE YEAR IS 1887. Joseph Schumpeter, whose family calls him Jozsi
(YO-shee), is four years old. Since his birth he has lived in the small town
where his father's family operates a textile factory. Everyone in the town knows
who Jozsi is. He has no reason to worry about the present or think much about
the future.

But then his father dies in an apparent hunting accident, at the age of thirty-
one. His mother, Johanna, a proud and striking woman, is stunned. Within a
year, both of her own parents also die.

In 1888, shortly after these traumas, Jozsi and his mother leave the town, to
begin an unimaginable adventure. They board a train for a long trip to a city
they have never seen. There, they settle as strangers and start a very different
life. Jozsi begins to grow up to be a man that the milieu of his home town
could neither have produced nor envisioned. That train trip permanently sev-
ers his connection with the extended families of both his mother and father.
And the separation starts to create doubts in his mind about who he is.

For approximately four hundred years—equal to the time from the first English settlement in North America to the present day—succeeding generations of the Schumpeter family had lived in one place. That place was Triesch, a hamlet nestled in a river valley seventy-five miles south of Prague, in the province of Moravia. In the twenty-first century, the town remains tiny and mostly unchanged. Visitors receive a handout saying that if his father had not died young, Schumpeter might "with the greatest probability" have remained there all of his life.

The large stone house where he was born still adorns the town's main street, pointed out with pride by the staff of the visitors' bureau. The handout this office distributes describes him as "one of the most important economists of the twentieth century, first Austrian minister of finance, professor at Harvard University," and "creator of the Japanese economic miracle." The word "creator" is too strong, of course. But the Japanese achievement did proceed on Schumpeter's principles of entrepreneurship, credit, and creative destruction. To this day he remains better known in Europe and Japan than in the United States.[1]

The Schumpeters had long ranked among Triesch's leading families. Jozsi's grandfather and great-grandfather were bourgeois Catholics descended from German-speaking forebears, and both had served as mayor of the town. They had also made their living in business, and their innovations likely influenced the mature Schumpeter's emphasis on entrepreneurship. In a quiet rural setting, his great-grandfather had founded the family textile business. His grandfather and father had continued to manage and improve it, installing the first steam engine in Triesch.[2]

They and other family members are now buried on a high hill in a mausoleum, the only one in the town's cemetery. The local government keeps this elegant little neoclassical building in pristine condition, often repainting it in the gold color of royal palaces in Vienna, known as Habsburg yellow after the name of the imperial dynasty. The tranquil scene strikes the interested visitor as a small shrine to the family's prominence—and to its greatest member's intellectual renown.

At the time of Jozsi's birth, the great majority of the 4,400 people in Triesch were Czech-speakers. Most of them belonged to the working class or the peasantry and were looked down upon by the German-speaking elite, who made up only 9 percent of the town's population. Many of the German-speakers, including the Schumpeters, had Czech-speaking servants. A few of the Germans were Jews and the rest Catholics, who generally did not mix socially with Jews and only on a modest scale with Czechs. Even so, there was significant intermarriage between German-speakers and Czechs, and both of Jozsi's grandfathers had married Czech women. The German-speaking Catholics held the best jobs and enjoyed disproportionate voting power because they owned property.[3]

Jozsi's maternal ancestors, who were also Catholics, stood alongside the Schumpeters at the top of the region's social ladder. His mother, Johanna, came from the nearby and mostly German-speaking town of Iglau, where her father and grandfather were prominent doctors.[4]

In Triesch, as in most of the Austro-Hungarian Empire at that time, German-speakers were straining to hold on to their privileged position. They disparaged the many other ethnic groups within the empire's borders: Czechs, Croats, Slovenes, Poles, Ukrainians, and so on. As the forces of democracy, capitalism, and nationalism began to intensify, the situation became less and less stable. This was the climate into which Jozsi was born in 1883.

When his father died, Johanna found herself alone in an isolated town full of prominent in-laws. Then twenty-six, she could have remained under the care and comfort of the Schumpeter family for the rest of her life. But she could see that this would be a dead end for her, and she also began to develop lofty ambitions for her only child, ambitions that humble Triesch could never satisfy. After careful thought, she decided to move to Graz, an attractive Austrian city of 150,000 German-speaking people, located 300 miles south of Triesch and 140 miles southwest of Vienna. Graz was home to one of the empire's few universities, and Johanna believed that this new environment offered opportunities for herself and a chance for her son to blossom.

For a widowed young mother to uproot herself in this way was unusual— very unusual—for that time and place. Johanna possessed no real wealth, but she was not destitute. She had inherited part of her parents' estate and some of her husband's interest in the family business. She now installed herself and Jozsi in the center of Graz, renting first a tiny apartment, then a larger one on Mozart Lane near the university.[5]

German-speaking provinces of the Austro-Hungarian Empire had better educational systems than most other parts of Europe did, and in Graz Jozsi attended a good primary school. Because Johanna had moved him at age five to a German-speaking region of Austria, he always regarded himself as an Austrian, and never a Czech. Still, he had questions about his identity.[6]

As he grew older, his resourceful mother began to devise ways in which the two of them might rise to higher levels in Austria's stratified society. Part of her motivation was on her own behalf. But she was also determined to gain for Jozsi advantages she thought he deserved but could never obtain as the orphaned son of a provincial businessman.

When Jozsi was about nine, Johanna set her sights on a man named Sigmund von Kéler, a three-star general more than thirty years her senior. Kéler had served for nearly four decades in the Austro-Hungarian army. He had then retired to Graz—nicknamed "Pensionopolis" because it was a favorite haven for high-ranking former military officers, much like Florida and southern California in the United States today. A lifelong bachelor, he was not an extremely rich man, but he had a generous annuity from his long military service. More importantly for Johanna, Kéler belonged to the Austrian nobility. He could hardly have been a better instrument for her objectives.[7]

She married him in 1893. He was sixty-five, she thirty-two, Jozsi ten. Whatever the motivations of bride and groom, the marriage had profound consequences for the young Schumpeter. Because of his new stepfather's social standing, he might now pursue his education in the empire's finest schools, a privilege he could have gained in no other way. Most boys in Austria dropped out at an early age and did not go to *gymnasium,* the equivalent of an American college preparatory school.[8]

Many great thinkers have written about mother-son relationships, over the millennia. "Sons are the anchors of a mother's life," Sophocles wrote in 400 B.C., and Emerson observed in 1860 that "men are what their mothers made them." Obviously, there are many exceptions, but the attachment between Johanna and Jozsi was not one of them. They remained extraordinarily close. She became a kind of stage mother, forever seeking larger venues in which Jozsi might display his abilities. In the broad sense of the word "entrepreneur," Johanna was one of the most effective her son ever knew. She fit the type perfectly. As a young widow lacking opportunities in Triesch, she moved to a much bigger city. When family members objected to the move, she ignored them. When she thought her son needed a titled stepfather, she married one. When she wanted an even larger stage for her talents and her son's, she found it.

Not long after Johanna's wedding, she arranged for the new family to move to Vienna, a city approaching two million in population—a far cry from Graz, let alone Triesch. In Vienna she entered Jozsi in a renowned preparatory school founded by and named for the eighteenth-century empress Maria Theresa. The Theresianum was one of the best and most demanding schools of its kind anywhere. When he enrolled, Jozsi was not only entering a prestigious academy. Like John Maynard Keynes (also born in 1883) at Eton and Franklin D. Roosevelt (born in 1882) at Groton, which was modeled on Eton, Jozsi was stepping into a patrician social world. As one of his Harvard friends later wrote, he acquired at the Theresianum "the agreeable, sometimes quaintly overpolite old-world manner, which, together with his natural charm, friendliness, and vitality, produced the man Schumpeter as we knew him."[9]

Unlike Keynes and Roosevelt, Schumpeter did not board at his new school but continued to live at home. His status as a day student implied slightly less social cachet, but in his case it carried real advantages. The Theresianum, unlike rural Eton and Groton, lies in the heart of a great capital city and cultural center. Day after day, the young Schumpeter walked among some of Vienna's most magisterial buildings on his way to the new electric trolley, which took him to school.

His family had leased an entire floor of one of the luxurious apartments situated near the famous Ringstrasse. One of the grandest avenues in Europe, the Ring is a two-and-a-half-mile semicircular boulevard lined with imposing structures that house Austria's leading institutions. Among them are Parliament, city hall, the University of Vienna, and the main theater and opera house. The six-story building that contained the Kélers' apartment stands only about a hundred feet from Parliament's rear façade. Schumpeter's daily walks took him past places steeped in history, and where history was still being made.

It was as if he were living a hundred feet from the U.S. Capitol in Washington, or beside Parliament in London, or near the Vatican in Rome—and routinely passing by them every day. He did this from the ages of ten to twenty-three. Whatever his other diversions, no young man so sensitive and ambitious could easily avoid absorbing lessons about architecture, art, and politics just from the effects of proximity. He grew to love both the empire and its capital city. For the rest of his life he never felt as much at home as he did during these years in Vienna.

The Theresianum required far more rigorous work than most high schools do today. Like aristocratic British academies at the time, it offered courses in mathematics, science, history, and literature, and relied on the ancient classics. Schumpeter studied Latin daily for eight years and Greek for six. He also spent a tremendous amount of time on English, Italian, and French, as well as his native German.

As at high schools everywhere, then and now, many students tried to idle their way through, doing as little work as possible. But Schumpeter—playful and outgoing as he was—had the true intellectual's curiosity about the world. These characteristics, along with his ambitious mother's urgings that he shine academically, made him one of the school's best students. By the end of his time at the Theresianum, he had gained a superb secondary education, including fluent knowledge of six languages. Because of his continued wide reading and remarkable memory, this knowledge stayed with him for the rest of his life. On the night in 1950 when he died, a copy of Euripides' plays in their original Greek lay on his bedside table.[10]

Among its other missions, the Theresianum trained young men to administer the far-flung Austro-Hungarian Empire. As at Keynes's Eton, a sense of imperial responsibilities pervaded the school's curriculum and social structure. This was true not only of the Theresianum but also of the University of Vienna, where Schumpeter next enrolled. A first-class university, Vienna was the Austrian version of Oxford and Cambridge.

For a diligent student like Schumpeter, an education at the Theresianum followed by a degree at the University of Vienna conferred priceless intellectual assets. He and his peers were trained to emulate the abstract thinking of the ancient Greeks and Romans. They learned to speak extemporaneously on a broad range of topics. They also endured intense pressures from difficult examinations. One of Sigmund Freud's most famous books, *The Interpretation of Dreams,* describes the terror of failure in "examination dreams" that can persist into adulthood. This book appeared in 1900, when Schumpeter was seventeen years old and Freud was practicing psychoanalysis in Vienna.[11]

Both the Theresianum and the University of Vienna emphasized what today would be called "networking." Many students—especially the native German-speakers—saw themselves as members of a select group preparing for imperial duty. They took for granted their own intellectual, social, and sometimes "racial" superiority. Schumpeter's years in Vienna occurred during a period when the word "race" was used more loosely than at any time since. People throughout Europe and the United States spoke casually of the German race, the Slavic race, the Jewish race, and others—in addition to color-based races throughout the world. So, along with his other lessons, Schumpeter absorbed some of the prejudices of his day.

Sometimes he found these prejudices directed against himself. He was often thought to be Jewish, apparently because of his looks, and throughout his life people commented on what they called his exotic "Eastern" appearance. The first known photograph of him was taken when he was fifteen, and from this picture alone it would be hard to know much about his ethnicity. The photo could be of a young Indian, Lebanese, or member of any number of other "races."[12]

In the Habsburg Empire, university students enjoyed the privilege of reduced military obligations, and many knew that after graduation they would try out for the higher civil service. But social connections remained crucial. Sponsorship by a member of the nobility or aristocracy often tipped the balance in competitions for the best jobs. This was true even for university professors, who were themselves members of the civil service. In the early stages of his career, Schumpeter was to discover that he too needed noble patronage.[13]

Johanna pushed him hard. She introduced him into the highest circles she could reach, and he was glad enough to play the role of upper-class gentleman. Sometimes he copied his mother's arrogant airs. Johanna insisted on being addressed as "Excellenz" in recognition of Sigmund von Kéler's status, even after she secured a separation from him. That event occurred, coincidentally or not, during the year her son graduated from the University of Vienna. Kéler was then seventy-eight and willing to go his independent way.

Years later, Schumpeter worked intermittently on an autobiographical novel. In this fragmentary work he appears as an Englishman named Henry, whose father had come from the Adriatic city of Trieste. Schumpeter loved England, and the similarity of the name Trieste to Triesch is obvious. The fragment is worth quoting at length for what it reveals about his sense of identity:

Now backgrounds, racial and social, are essential to understand what a man is . . . [Henry's] family belonged to the fringe end of the commercial and financial set of Trieste which racially was a mixture defying analysis. Greek, German, Serb, and Italian elements . . . [As an only child, Henry] was four years old when, well on the way to a considerable financial position, the father was killed in the hunting field. And the mother was thenceforth the one great human factor in Henry's life. She was an excellent woman, strong and kind and amply provided him with the delightful blinders of English society. She did her duties in a way which can only be called manful though it was truly womanly when I come to think of it. To make him an English gentleman was her one aim in life . . . She had not much money—her husband had been on the path to wealth, but had not traveled far on it. But she had connections which she resolutely exploited for her darling . . . he was seen on terms of equality in houses that rank much above what is referred to as the smart set . . . But I want to make this quite clear—the social world was open from the beginning and shut only when he did not trouble to go & that meant much. No complexes. No fake contempt. No hidden wistfulness.[14]

Schumpeter seldom wrote about himself, and he composed this fragment a few years after Johanna's death, by which time he had traveled all over the world. Perhaps better than any other single piece of evidence, it shows his persistent sense of rootlessness:

Where was he at home? Not really in England! Often he had thought so but ancestral past had asserted itself each time! But neither in France or Italy though he found himself drifting to both whenever he had a week to spare or a month. Certainly not in Germany or what had been the Austro Hungarian Emp[ire].

But that was not the salient point. More important than country means class—but he did not with subconscious allegiance belong either to society or the business class or the professions or the trade union world, all of which provided such comfortable homes for anyone he knew. Yes—his mother's corner of society had been his as long as she lived . . . Oh mother, mother.[15]

Wherever he found himself, Schumpeter never felt that he quite belonged. Many years later, his brilliant Harvard student Paul Samuelson saw "an insecurity in his nature, perhaps typical of a precocious only child." With the disappearance of the ordered Viennese society of his youth, "he became completely qualified to play the important sociological role of the alienated stranger."[16]

Over the years, he reinvented himself many times, building on what Johanna had begun. Thinking not of where he started but of how he might move forward, he was well suited to grasp the mindset of the entrepreneur. With his own tenacity, opportunism, and flexibility, he learned to excel in diverse circumstances—much like successful economic players in the capitalist system. His most important goal remained his mother's approval, even after her death. The grades he gave himself seem addressed implicitly to her—report cards from a dutiful son.

"I know who I am," said Don Quixote, in one of his many self-delusions. Schumpeter never felt any such assurance. By the time he reached Vienna at the age of ten, he was a twice-transplanted heir of Moravian entrepreneurs whose forebears had lived for four centuries in a tiny remote town. Once uprooted from that town, he had only his abilities and his mother's compelling love to guide him. For the rest of his life he lived strictly by his wits and talent, like a trapeze artist performing without a net.

Regardless of his roots, what he *became* derived from his intellect, his upbeat temperament, and his driving energy. It also depended on his mother's piloting of their little two-person boat through the treacherous shoals of Vienna and the empire. There, he learned that one's identity in a rapidly changing world might come more from innovation than from inheritance; that exchanging security for opportunity could bring great rewards; and that for someone with his gifts almost anything was possible.

Top: The house in Triesch (now Třešť, Czech Republic) where Schumpeter was born in 1883. This is the way it looked in the early twenty-first century, after some restoration.

Bottom: The mausoleum in Třešť where Schumpeter's paternal ancestors are buried. This graceful building is only three meters wide and three-and-a-half deep.

Left: In 1888 Johanna and Jozsi moved from Triesch into a tiny apartment in this modest building near the center of Graz. Johanna was twenty-seven years old, Jozsi five.

Below: From 1889 to 1893, they lived here, on part of the top floor, in the building's least expensive apartment. Today this building houses the German language department of the University of Graz.

Top: The Theresianum in Vienna, which Schumpeter attended from 1893 to 1901. The building and grounds occupy an entire city block.

Bottom: The main entrance to the Theresianum, as it appeared in both Schumpeter's time and in the early twenty-first century.

Joseph Schumpeter at age fifteen. Here he looks not unlike the young Mohandas Gandhi or
W. E. B. DuBois, both of whom were about fourteen years his senior.

2

Shaping His Character

If a man has been his mother's undisputed darling he retains
throughout life the triumphant feeling, the confidence in
success, which not seldom brings actual success with it.

SIGMUND FREUD, *A Childhood Memory of Goethe's,* 1917

WHEN HE FIRST arrived in Vienna, the young Schumpeter had
moved with his mother and stepfather into an elegant new apartment near the
city's central boulevard, the Ringstrasse. To encourage occupancy of these
apartments by the "right" sort of people, the Austrian and Viennese governments had granted a thirty-year exemption from property taxes. Beginning in
the 1860s, the two governments had also sponsored a series of new public
structures along the Ringstrasse, using land prepared by leveling fortifications
that had protected the city from a siege by the Turks in 1683. The varied designs and uses of the new buildings reflected the ideals of both the city and the
empire.[1]

In an old city like Vienna, fresh architecture usually brings a type of creative
destruction, but that did not happen along the Ringstrasse. The architects
looked backward, not forward. The University of Vienna, founded in 1365, was
reconstructed in 1884 in the Italian Renaissance style of the 1400s. Other new
Ringstrasse buildings imitated the Baroque mode of the sixteenth century.
Their collective impact amounted to a kind of institutionalized nostalgia—an

attempt to link designs to the periods when the ideals each building represented had reached an apex: classical Greek architecture for the Parliament, Gothic for the city hall, and so on.[2]

Although Vienna's outward appearance might seem frozen in time, its culture was moving forward very fast under the forces of Modernism. Perhaps no other city in the world was the scene of so much intellectual ferment—in the arts (the paintings of Egon Schiele and Gustav Klimt, the architecture of Otto Wagner and Adolph Loos, the writings of Karl Kraus and Robert Musil) and also the social sciences, most notably Freudian psychology and "Austrian economics," a movement in which Schumpeter was to play a significant role. All kinds of change were in the air. A perceptive historian has written that in Austria (and Germany as well), the transition from the old ways to the new did not evolve over a two-hundred-year period, as it did in England, thereby providing time for people to adjust gradually and avoid social disruption. Instead, the process occurred "within a single lifetime, and the medieval and modern orders collided head-on."[3]

That single lifetime was Joseph Schumpeter's. He grew up not only in the midst of cultural ferment but also at a time when the engine of modern capitalism was transforming the Habsburg Empire. Most of its people still lived on farms, and its commercial and industrial economy consisted mainly of small businesses whose methods were rapidly becoming obsolete. Vienna itself was a patchwork of competing ethnic groups and economic interests, many of them fighting to resist modernization. These tensions in Vienna and the empire molded Schumpeter's character and outward bearing into a form that no subsequent influence would alter. Their cultures affected his likes and dislikes, his beliefs about human behavior, his ideas about business and government, and—above all—his ambitions.

By the time Johanna von Kéler arranged the move from Graz, Vienna had long since become a place of public spectacles and entertainments where people went to have a good time. There were the city's outdoor gardens, its nearby Vienna Woods, and its grand municipal parks. The Spanish Riding School, adjacent to the Imperial Palace and a gem of Vienna's tourist industry even today, was already more than two centuries old when Schumpeter and his mother arrived in 1893. One amusement park, the Prater, showcased a two-hundred-foot-high Ferris wheel, built in 1897 and still operating today, making a stately revolution every ten minutes and offering passengers matchless views of the cityscape.[4]

Vienna also proudly claimed to be the world capital of classical music. Some of the most brilliant composers and performers who ever lived had worked in and around the city: the Austrians Haydn, Mozart, Schubert, and Johann Strauss (who, together with his three sons, composed the most renowned Viennese waltzes), plus Beethoven, Brahms, and other German composers. In Schumpeter's time, the operettas of Johann Strauss the younger, whose masterpiece *Die Fledermaus* debuted in 1874, competed with efforts by other composers who carried this popular genre forward. Meanwhile, Modernist musicians such as Gustav Mahler and Arnold Schönberg were challenging the old order altogether.[5]

"It was the particular genius of this city of music," recalled the writer Stefan Zweig, to dissolve "all the contrasts harmoniously." Arriving in Vienna as a boy at about the same time as Schumpeter, Zweig went on to become a prominent biographer and novelist. "It was sweet to live here, in this atmosphere of spiritual conciliation, and subconsciously every citizen became supranational, cosmopolitan, a citizen of the world."[6]

Even so, despite its gaiety and modernism, Vienna remained the capital of a semifeudal assemblage of quarreling provinces, governed by a decaying dynasty six centuries old. Much of the innovation of the age directly rebelled against the stagnation of old Vienna. One prominent group underscored their attack by calling themselves Secessionists and building an ultra-modern museum where they could display their work.[7]

Elsewhere in Europe, nationalism and democracy were challenging traditional regimes, as industrialization sped forward. But many of the small-scale shops of Vienna and other Habsburg cities continued to manufacture goods that were losing out to less expensive products from Germany, Britain, and France. In some parts of the Habsburg Empire, entrepreneurs prospered and did not lag behind their counterparts in more advanced countries. But the government itself showed little inclination to change its policies.

How long could the old culture hold the forces of modernity at bay? This was the question, above all others, that Schumpeter and his fellow Viennese debated endlessly in the city's many coffeehouses, with their broad offerings of newspapers from all over Europe. The coffeehouses provided congenial surroundings for the new cosmopolitans to exchange ideas about politics, business, and the fine arts—often all at once.[8]

Some of the fiercest debates about politics and art concerned not only established canons but also the ways in which Modernism contested tradition. As Vienna began to idealize its writers, musicians, and actors, a new atmosphere of celebrity emerged. That ambience proved very seductive to Schumpeter, and before long he began to aspire to celebrity himself.[9]

In 1897 Mark Twain was touring Europe and sending articles back to the United States for *Harper's New Monthly Magazine.* "In countries like England and America," he wrote from Vienna, "where there is one tongue and public interests are common, the government must take account of public opinion; but in Austria-Hungary there are nineteen public opinions—one for each state. No—two or three for each state, since there are two or three nationalities in each." The 425 members of the Imperial Parliament spoke eleven different languages. Restrictions on voting gave lopsided power to property owners, most of whom were German-speakers.[10]

The Habsburg dominions had evolved in haphazard fashion for several centuries, mostly through treaties and royal marriages. Aspiring to become "an empire of seventy millions" and actually reaching fifty-six million, it had become one of the most eclectic assemblages the world has ever known. Physically, it was as big as England and France combined. It included all of today's Austria, Hungary, the Czech Republic, Slovakia, Slovenia, and Croatia, plus parts of Poland, Ukraine, northern Italy, and Romania. Read all together, Emperor Francis Joseph's dozens of royal titles appear to be some sort of historical joke. Like Schumpeter, the empire seemed to be searching for a stable identity.[11]

Mark Twain wrote of the Imperial Parliament that he had never seen a chamber so "sumptuously gilded," yet wracked by such constant turmoil within. The warring deputies "come from all the walks of life and from all the grades of society. There are princes, counts, barons, priests, peasants, mechanics, laborers, lawyers, judges, physicians, professors, merchants, bankers, shopkeepers."[12]

Outside Vienna, in other major cities such as Prague, Crakow, and Budapest, local issues overshadowed imperial interests. But the empire commanded its members' armed forces and administered their foreign affairs. The emperor held authority over a broad range of other matters as well. If he chose, he could rule without Parliament, and often he had to issue "emergency" decrees to keep the government running.

What kept this jigsaw-puzzle of an empire from breaking apart? For one thing, the military strategies of ambitious neighbors. The Great Powers of Europe wanted to keep the Habsburg monarchy intact as a check on one another's ambitions. On its borders lay Germany to the north, Russia to the northeast, Serbia and the Ottoman Empire to the southeast, and Italy to the south. To the west, Switzerland served as something of a buffer against France—but even the Alps had not prevented Napoleon's invasion decades earlier (he took a mostly northward route around the mountains).

Within the empire itself, the smoldering embers of ethnic nationalism often threatened to flare into open conflict. From Vienna a set of skilled civil servants, behaving like a corps of elite firefighters, dealt constantly with this problem. When a blaze erupted in one of the provinces, they doused it through political compromise, military action, or economic bribery in the form of public works. The large Joint Army of Austria-Hungary maintained small garrisons of troops in the cities and towns of every province, and their visibility helped to create a common feeling of imperial cohesion without a commensurate sense of coercion.[13]

A second unifying element was the Roman Catholic Church, to which most people belonged, including the Schumpeters. A network of clerical connections stretched from local parishes all the way to the Vatican. Emperor Francis Joseph was called His Apostolic Majesty, and he deeply believed that the hand of Providence guided his earthly affairs. In general, the Church tended toward a moderate opposition to nationalism, modernism, liberalism, and wider democracy. Sometimes it indirectly hindered industrialization as well. During the eighteenth and nineteenth centuries, its control over education and other affairs had declined, but its influence never died. Even today, the spires of churches dominate the cities and towns of the old empire, although the pews below are often empty.

A third force, closely allied with the Catholic Church, was the cult of royal personality embodied in the Habsburgs. For centuries they had ruled large parts of Europe, including areas widely separated from one another. Much of the land in these areas belonged to the Habsburg family itself. The emperor could confer influence on anyone he chose, and he and his ministers welcomed persons of talent into the imperial civil service, often without regard to nationality. But Emperor Francis Joseph socialized almost exclusively with members of the upper nobility who were related to him and deemed "court worthy."[14]

Most nobles still behaved as if history were stuck in a pre-capitalist feudal mold. The "first society" amused themselves by constant rounds of dances, parties, gaudy sexual escapades, mountain-climbing, and game-shooting. One imperial count said on his deathbed, "And when the Lord enquires of me, 'What hast thou done with thy life?' I must answer 'Oh! Lord. I have shot hares, shot hares, shot hares.'" Many aristocrats had a special fondness for gambling, and the sport of betting on snail races was popular at one of their stylish clubs in Vienna.[15]

Yet somehow, despite the decadence of the Austrian nobility, Francis Joseph held his empire together through the force of his personality and the rigor of his personal habits. He reigned for sixty-eight years, from 1848 until his death in 1916 at the age of eighty-six. He lived in vast palaces but was inclined to a spartan routine of iron cots and cold baths. He rose at 4:00 a.m., to begin at 5:00 his long day of signing papers, conferring with ministers, and receiving visitors. When he appeared in public, he wore his military uniform, covered with medals. This attire, accented by his elaborate white muttonchop whiskers, gave a certain gravity to his presence, and he performed his duties with the utmost seriousness.

Even so, in an era of constant innovation he had little interest in economic advances. He wanted nothing to do with telephones, trains, typewriters, automobiles, and electric lights. But he was not a mean-spirited ruler, and he showed his humane side in many ways. Respected and, as he grew older, revered as a royal symbol, he labored with his ministers to keep his motley provinces and kingdoms intact. By and large he succeeded. Until 1914, when Schumpeter was thirty-one, the empire remained whole, reasonably prosperous, and peaceful.[16]

Schumpeter, like many of his fellow intellectuals whose politics lay to the left of his own, felt a sense of dislocation and grief when the empire finally came to an end. Given his own attraction to capitalism as a future-oriented vehicle of change, his nostalgia reflected the tensions within his soul. Certainly nobody knew better than he that the empire had clung to the past during one of the most vibrant periods of human history.

THE LATE NINETEENTH century and early twentieth were times of radical change in science, business, the arts, and society itself. In the United States and Western Europe, hordes of people flocked from farms to cities, as the pace of industrialization raced forward. Between 1850 and 1900 the population of Vienna itself increased four-fold, to about two million. The flood of newcomers included middle-class people like the Schumpeters but much larger numbers of impoverished Poles, Romanians, Russians, and especially Czechs. All converged on the imperial capital in quest of a better life. In its rich mix of ethnicities, Vienna came to resemble New York and Chicago as much as it did any European city. During the 1890s, while Schumpeter and his family lived in their comfortable apartment, most other new arrivals had to make do with cramped tenements. Slum-dwelling increased markedly, and with it political unrest.

One conspicuous change was the growing presence of Jews, in an environment otherwise strongly Catholic. As Vienna's population quadrupled, the number of its Jewish citizens grew by a factor of twenty-seven, to over 175,000. This influx of Jews comprised a very diverse group. Some were wealthy, but many more were poor farmers fleeing persecution in the Russian Empire, Romania, and other areas. Their arrival was greeted with hostility by many Christians. To his credit, Emperor Francis Joseph did what he could to safeguard the rights of Jews. During the 1890s he instructed his Austrian prime minister that "every anti-Semitic movement must be nipped in the bud at once . . . You will immediately have any anti-Semitic assembly dissolved. The Jews are brave and patriotic men who happily risk their lives for emperor and fatherland."[17]

In 1897, when Schumpeter was fourteen, the charismatic Karl Lueger took office as mayor. Like Schumpeter, Lueger had attended the Theresianum, having been admitted because his working-class father served as a porter at the school. A very skillful politician, he had already won the mayoral election four times, but the emperor had vetoed his victories because of his anti-Semitic political tactics. In the face of Lueger's overwhelming popularity, Francis Joseph finally relented. Much as contemporary politicians in the United States were lambasting African Americans to win the votes of poor whites, Lueger cynically scapegoated Jews to get elected.[18]

He became an effective spokesman for small manufacturers and shopkeepers, and also for the masses of people moving into Vienna from the countryside, provided they were not Jews. Conscious of Vienna's economic problems, Lueger sought to modernize the city through public works programs, one of the few means available to him. Among other initiatives, he built new parks and opened new beaches along the Danube. But in the long run, his conduct had some dire consequences. Adolf Hitler happened to be living in Vienna at this time, and he later mentioned in *Mein Kampf* how much he learned about mass movements from observing Lueger's political techniques. Hitler went on to say that the mixture of ethnic groups in Vienna disgusted him, especially after he left the Austrian capital for Munich: "A *German* city! What a difference from Vienna! I grew sick to my stomach when I even thought back on this Babylon of races."[19]

The effect of migration within the Habsburg lands contrasted with that in the United States and the nations of Western Europe. Urban poverty plagued those countries as well, but overall economic progress was accelerating so quickly that historians today speak of a second industrial revolution. What the steam engine had been for the first industrial revolution, the electric motor and internal combustion engine was doing for the second. The invention of these machines, along with the telephone and a burst of railroad construction, hastened economic growth and replaced old ways of doing business.

As Schumpeter grew to manhood, his interest in economic change began to border on obsession. He knew that portions of the Habsburg Empire were falling behind, and he read zealously of innovations in more industrially advanced countries. First at the Theresianum and then at the University of Vienna, he soaked up news from the United States, Germany, and Britain.

The scale of business operations driven by capitalism was becoming immense not only in those national economics but even within individual companies. In 1901, the year when Schumpeter entered the University of Vienna, the world's three largest industrial firms were United States Steel, American Tobacco, and Standard Oil. U.S. Steel alone employed 170,000 workers, more than any other corporation on earth and at least twenty times any in Austria-Hungary.

Closer to home, German companies such as Krupp and Thyssen in steel, Siemens in electrical equipment, and the chemical giants Bayer, Hoechst, and BASF had become industrial powerhouses. These German firms prospered in nearby Habsburg lands and other export markets. Historians differ in their estimates of Habsburg economic growth, but it is now clear that most of Francis Joseph's domains were not quite the severe laggards they were once thought to be. Parts of the empire made substantial economic progress, particularly the provinces of Bohemia and Moravia. The empire's eventual breakup derived primarily not from economic weakness but from intense nationalisms and World War I.[20]

Despite some economic gains, German Austria's per capita income in 1913 was only about half that of Britain (yet still twice that of Hungary). Most of the empire's people, and a majority of Vienna's new arrivals, had no easy access to indoor plumbing, uncontaminated water, or mass-produced shoes and clothing. Telephones were rare, and central heating was available only in the most expensive dwellings. Within the government, clerks scrawled out by hand the reams of paperwork necessary to administer the imperial bureaucracy. Elsewhere, typewriters had been in common use for twenty years. The Habsburg province of Galicia contained the world's third-largest known deposits of oil, ranking behind only the United States and the Russian Empire. But both the provincial and imperial governments, and most of the companies involved, ineptly managed the extraction and refining of this "black gold."[21]

Meanwhile, in Britain, Germany, and the United States, the mass production and mass marketing of all kinds of products shot ahead, stimulated by new industrial technology, fast railroad transportation, and an explosion in advertising. Standard-sized dresses and shirts suddenly appeared in department stores. In local groceries, consumers encountered wide choices of branded and individually packaged soaps, soups, canned vegetables, and cigarettes. Big electric signs began to appear in London, Berlin, and New York, proclaiming the virtues of Cadbury's chocolates, Bayer aspirin, Heinz pickles, and a host of other consumer products. Capitalism was starting to raise the living standards of almost everybody, even though enormous disparities of income persisted.

Schumpeter never forgot the lessons he learned during this period of Habsburg stagnation amid economic tumult. In his later years, he liked to speak of an economist's "vision"—a sort of pre-analytic intuition of the way the world worked. Having seen how his entrepreneurial mother engineered their own series of moves from Triesch to Graz to Vienna, he understood how quickly circumstances could alter and what kinds of social and economic mechanisms came into play. During his own youth and early adulthood, he saw rapid cultural and economic change at first hand in Vienna and read about its progress elsewhere. He understood it uncommonly well and began to write about it at an early age.

Because the maturing Schumpeter sensed that creative destruction in the *economic* sphere could be violently disruptive, he began to place a high premium on political order. He became convinced that the supplanting of one set of entrepreneurial elites by another could bring social turmoil that might stall the capitalist engine. Thus, economic growth demanded a steady hand of government, and Schumpeter saw that capitalist progress required enforceable rules of law and private property. In his judgment, the best kind of oversight was embodied in a nonpartisan civil service and a symbolic leader whose legitimacy the masses were unlikely to question. The empire had all these advantages, but it still struggled with continuing nationalist movements within its borders and with resistance to economic modernization.

Nor did the empire benefit from the overt chaos going on in Parliament, thirty yards down the street from where Schumpeter lived. There, the legislature had taken on the tenor of a vaudeville show or, as one historian has described it, "an insane asylum." A visitor from Berlin commented that anybody could go to Parliament and "get entertainment for free. The representatives personally 'jumping on' each other compensates the Viennese entirely for theater performances."[22]

Day after day, year after year, parliamentary debates dragged on without resolution. Delegates spent much of their time flinging insults at one another across the legislative floor. Mark Twain recorded many of these barbs during his 1897 visit: "You belong in a gin mill." "You Judas!" "Brothel-knight!" "East-German offal-tub!" "Infamous louse-brat!" "Street arab!" "Contemptible cub!" "Pimp!" "Blatherskite!" "You Jew, you!" "Drunken clown!" "Brothel-daddy!" "Which is the hardest, a Pole's skull or a German's?" "Polish dog!" (this last epithet addressed to the nobleman whom the emperor had appointed head of Parliament).[23]

The uproar of constant nationalist quarrels was also evident in frequent student fistfights at the University of Vienna. Dueling was commonplace, the object being not to kill one's opponent but to draw blood, preferably from the face so as to leave a visible scar. In the courts, meanwhile, libel trials began to multiply. They usually ended in the acquittal of journalists who had printed anti-Semitic material or stories attacking the Catholic Church. One defense counsel explained that all the sound and fury meant nothing. Feverish bombast in Vienna was just a way to let off steam, and everyone knew it.[24]

Many years later, Schumpeter's American friends wondered why he sometimes tossed off outrageous statements that were certain to offend his listeners. His private diaries also contain inflammatory comments on a variety of subjects. It was almost as though he were back in Vienna, venting his feelings in meaningless rhetoric.

Even as a young man, Schumpeter became known as a wonderful conversationalist with a keen wit. Like other great talkers—Samuel Johnson in the eighteenth century, Oscar Wilde in the nineteenth, H. L. Mencken and Dorothy Parker in the twentieth—he found the line between prudence and sarcasm hard to draw. One of Schumpeter's professors called his too-clever tongue "a dangerous gift by the gods." His friend and classmate Felix Somary recalled that "he could be extremely irritating to one's self-esteem." People mistakenly thought of him as a cynic, and this, said Somary, "cost him many a defeat throughout his life." By no means all of the habits he picked up in Vienna worked to his advantage.[25]

Watching the chaos in Parliament year after year, Schumpeter came to distrust mass politics. Like many German and Austrian intellectuals, he especially detested bolshevism, which he regarded as a complete fraud. But he did not stop there. He believed that even in democratic governments, politicians of all stripes pandered to electorates. They purchased office by promising to enact measures that brought quick benefits to voters, even if these same measures injured the country over the long run.

Schumpeter had an elitist streak that longed for electoral peace, if only as an alternative to chaos. Of all political systems, he most admired the British. Its constitutional monarchy and bicameral Houses of Commons and Lords seemed to him the optimal way to organize a government. He admired Benjamin Disraeli, but his special hero was William E. Gladstone, the anti-imperialist statesman who favored low taxation combined with proper care for the poor. Schumpeter much esteemed Britain's well-trained and apolitical civil service, and the whole British system appealed to his sense of order and stability. He agreed with the Conservative Edmund Burke's statement that "good order is the foundation of all good things."[26]

But there was a big difference between the British Empire and the Austro-Hungarian, with its multiple ethnicities. Most British possessions lay overseas, far from the homogeneous motherland. Jealous ethnic groups crammed into narrow spaces did not bump up against one another in constant collision, like marbles jangling in a bag.[27]

Schumpeter himself was part of the vast stream of people who had poured into Vienna, and some of his friends knew him better than to take his outward nonchalance at face value. Felix Somary surmised that it came especially from his prep school, "the Vienna Theresianum, where the pupils were taught to stick to subjects, and not get personally involved. The rules of the game in every party and ideology were to be learned thoroughly, but nobody should join a party or subscribe to a dogma. And Schumpeter was a virtuoso at playing any political game, from the extreme left to the extreme right." As he grew older, Schumpeter began to carry himself in a genial, courtly manner that conveyed as little as possible about what he was really thinking.[28]

By the time he enrolled at the University of Vienna, he had made up his mind to become a celebrity himself, like the new breed of musicians and artists he was watching and reading about. Exactly how he might do this was far from clear, since he had little talent as an artist and less as a musician. But within a few years the answer began to take shape with his vision of how capitalism was changing the world. He would become an *intellectual* artist, recognized as best in his class—the Michelangelo of economics, or the even more versatile Leonardo da Vinci of social science. As his student Paul Samuelson later put it, the adult Schumpeter "strove to be number one, and number one forever." That ambition began in his late teens, in the techno-romantic, celebrity-soaked culture of Vienna.[29]

Emperor Francis Joseph, who reigned for sixty-eight years until his death in 1916, at the age of eighty-six.

The Imperial Parliament in Vienna. Next to it on the Ringstrasse is the even more ornate city hall, with its tall towers, and farther down the University of Vienna. In front of these buildings one can see the trolleys and tracks on which the young Schumpeter rode to and from the Theresianum.

Right: The von Kéler family occupied an entire floor of this large building, one of the tax-free "rental palaces" constructed in Vienna late in the nineteenth century.

Below: Parliament's rear façade as seen from directly in front of the von Kélers' apartment building.

3

Learning Economics

Give me the political economist, the sanitary reformer,
the engineer; and take your saints and virgins, relics and
miracles.

CHARLES KINGSLEY, *Yeast,* 1848

NO CITY COULD HAVE suited the young Schumpeter's intellectual obsessions better than Vienna. After completing his eight years at the
Theresianum in 1901, he entered the University of Vienna, located just a few
blocks from the apartment where he continued to live with his mother and
stepfather. The remodeled university had opened in 1884, a year after Schumpeter's birth, and architects had decorated the huge structure with elaborate
ornamentation. In the decades since then, modern buildings have been added,
but the halls where Schumpeter moved from class to class remain mostly
unchanged. Statues and busts of Habsburg rulers and academic luminaries
adorn these spaces. Bas-relief plaques set into columns along the interior courtyard memorialize distinguished professors, including several of Schumpeter's own
teachers.

As at the Theresianum, he and his classmates encountered a far more difficult curriculum than most students do today. Whereas the average student
load is now between twelve and fifteen hours in the classroom per week,
Schumpeter typically spent between twenty-five and thirty-five. Lectures

Top: The University of Vienna, founded in the fourteenth century and rebuilt in 1884 in the Italian Renaissance style its planners thought appropriate for a great center of learning. Schumpeter attended from 1901 to 1906, walking the short distance from his family apartment behind Parliament.

Bottom: One side of the university's interior courtyard arcade, as it appears today. The bronze tablets in the columns on the left memorialize Schumpeter's teachers Friedrich von Wieser and Eugen von Böhm-Bawerk, as well as their own mentor Carl Menger. The busts on the right are mostly of natural scientists.

began at 7:00 a.m., and sometimes as early as 6:15. The last classes ended at 8:00 p.m. Students were a privileged group, but serious ones like Schumpeter worked very hard. Emphasis in his courses fell on law, economics, and history.[1]

The university's site among great public buildings along the Ringstrasse underscored its primary function: training people to administer the empire. More than half of the Law Faculty's students entered the imperial civil service, and all university professors were themselves civil servants whose selection required the approval of the emperor. On the occasion of their appointment to office, they appeared in uniform for an audience with him. (As an adult, Schumpeter himself went through this interesting experience.) Professors enjoyed a higher rank in society than they do today, and there was less of the ivory tower separation. Besides academic work, many wrote articles for the popular press and held public office while on leave from teaching.[2]

In the custom of other European universities, Vienna's economics professors were part of the Faculty of Law. Schumpeter's degree, which he received in 1906, was therefore not in economics but in civil and Roman law—a type of training that deepened his sense of both politics and history. Later on, he practiced briefly as an attorney, and that experience broadened his sense of the way business actually works.

As the twentieth century began, German-speaking universities led the world in most of the physical and social sciences. The University of Vienna was one of the three or four best places on earth to study economics, and it did not take Schumpeter long to find that he had a special gift for the subject. Although he had preferred history and sociology, he now saw that economics held the possibility of integrating other areas of knowledge and bringing order to confusion. Even so, as he himself put it, "One has to remember that economics is a very young discipline which has hardly outgrown its baby shoes." Practitioners did not yet define themselves as technical specialists, as most do today. Instead, they marched under the broad banner of "political economists" intent on reforming society.[3]

Knowledge of economics lagged far behind that of law, which many great scholars had analyzed over thousands of years. Sir William Blackstone, author of the famous *Commentaries* on law, happened to be a perfect contemporary of Adam Smith, both men having been born in 1723. But Blackstone's *Commen-*

taries represented something of an intellectual climax, whereas Smith's *Wealth of Nations* was only a beginning—the first great synthesis of its field. Smith's book appeared in 1776, but he had been a professor of rhetoric and moral philosophy, not of economics (there were few anywhere at the time). And Smith described a world of small factories and shopkeepers, not of highly mechanized industry and big business, which had yet to appear.

After *The Wealth of Nations* was published, the study of economics began to accelerate. Throughout the nineteenth century, political economists wrote about government, the welfare of society, and the nature of its institutions. They argued for or against socialism ("the labor question"), the gold standard ("the money question"), and free trade versus protectionism. This emphasis on current controversies continued even after economics became an established academic profession during the 1880s. But at the University of Vienna, concern with policy prevailed much less than it did elsewhere. In Vienna, members of the "Austrian School" were trying to make the discipline more rigorous by reducing its fixation on political issues.[4]

This was not easy. The practice of mixing economics with politics—often in service to some preconceived ideology—continues today, when the world contains about thirty thousand Ph.D. economists in academics, business, and government. Yet a preoccupation with policy clashed with Schumpeter's concept of economics as a "science"—a discipline which could enlighten public debates by producing knowledge free from particular interests but which itself should aspire to neutrality. Throughout his life Schumpeter believed that when economists injected politics into technical discussions, they tainted their scientific integrity.

During Schumpeter's university years, the work of Karl Marx and his socialist apostles hovered in the background almost everywhere, even though it prevailed almost nowhere. More than any other economist before Schumpeter himself, Marx had emphasized the *dynamics* of capitalism—its ever-changing nature whose only music was uproar. That was Marx's greatest contribution, and it had a potent influence on Schumpeter. But Marx went on to draw groundless conclusions about what he called the "inevitable" results of capitalism. His predictions about "the dictatorship of the proletariat" and the "withering away of the state" never came to pass. Even so, Marxism exerted a check on more orthodox theories. It posed a body of doctrine against which to measure rival approaches.

WHEN SCHUMPETER ENTERED the University of Vienna, he confronted three leading methods for the study of economics. The first, the Classical School, was founded by Adam Smith and developed by David Ricardo and others. Its fullest expression came in John Stuart Mill's *Principles of Political Economy* (1848). Most classical economists were British and were deeply concerned with questions of public policy.

Schumpeter found much to admire in the Classical School. He did not regard Adam Smith as very original, but he esteemed him as a literary artist, later declaring *The Wealth of Nations* to be "the most successful not only of all books on economics but, with the possible exception of Darwin's *Origin of Species,* of all scientific books that have appeared to this day." Smith's long experience as a professor of rhetoric served him well, and no economic metaphor has ever surpassed the "invisible hand"—Smith's way of saying that millions of simultaneous decisions by individual consumers automatically serve "the public interest." Smith argued in *The Wealth of Nations* against governmental interference in the marketplace; and for the heavily regulated national economies of 1776, this was the right message.[5]

Like Adam Smith, Schumpeter believed fully in the virtues of the market. But in addition to objecting to the classicists' fixation on public policy, he believed that they took too little notice of industrialization. Smith's *Wealth of Nations,* for all its virtues, described a mostly preindustrial economy. And in the work of David Ricardo, published in the 1820s, Schumpeter and others detected a potentially misleading principle. Ricardo, in what became a famous analysis of agriculture, pointed out that farmers till their best lands first, their next-best second, and their worst lands last—because only in that way can they get their best yield of crops. From this valid principle he went on to infer a general doctrine of "diminishing returns" as the volume of production increased. That insight has shaped the teaching of economics from Ricardo's time to the present day.[6]

But for many products, Ricardo's principle was completely backwards and wrong. Just as he was making his argument, the industrial revolution was gathering speed, and instead of *de*creasing returns to scale, most industrialists enjoyed *in*creasing returns. The more yards of cloth a modern textile mill turned out, the cheaper each yard was to produce and the lower the price to consumers. Later on, Schumpeter liked to speak of the "Ricardian vice" of hewing to one valid principle in the face of wholly differing contexts and of applying that principle indiscriminately to public policies. Sometimes he even used the word "sin."[7]

Schumpeter criticized mid-nineteenth-century British economists of the classical tradition for a "complete lack of imagination" in their vision of capitalism. "Those writers lived at the threshold of the most spectacular economic developments ever witnessed. Vast possibilities matured into realities under their very eyes. Nevertheless, they saw nothing but cramped economies, struggling with ever-decreasing success for their daily bread." At bottom, "they were all stagnationists." Even Mill, the most optimistic of them, "had no idea what the capitalist engine of production was going to achieve."[8]

A second leading approach to economics, that of the German Historical School, also affected Schumpeter's thinking. This method consisted mainly of writing detailed histories of various industries and institutions. Centered in Berlin, the Historical School's influence derived partly from the vigor of its brightest star, Gustav von Schmoller. As Schumpeter put it, Schmoller "brought to bear on his task of leadership not only energy, fighting spirit, and a tremendous capacity for work, but also considerable strategic and organizing ability." He founded a journal to serve as an outlet for research papers and also sponsored the publication of a series of historical books. Schmoller and other members of the Historical School, like the classicists, emphasized the role economists should take in the making of public policy.[9]

Schumpeter himself loved history, but he had one big problem with Schmoller's school: it shortchanged economic theory. No number of historical monographs, however well done, could add up to a coherent theory. For that to occur, general hypotheses and propositions had to be formed and tested— and then kept, adjusted, or discarded. The reluctance of the Historical School's members to do this meant that they were sometimes engaging in trivial tasks.[10]

By no means did their efforts go for naught, however. One of the greatest figures in all of social science emerged in part from the German Historical School. This was Max Weber, author of many seminal works, most notably

The Protestant Ethic and the Spirit of Capitalism (1904–1905). Weber *was* willing to theorize. A prodigious scholar, he put forward numerous broad propositions supported by empirical data. Schumpeter admired Weber, who was nineteen years his senior, and on occasion worked with him directly. But Weber was a sociologist, not an economist, and he did not involve himself in the bitter struggle over methods that developed between the German Historical School and the Austrian School of economists, led by Schumpeter's own professors in Vienna.[11]

This third prominent group of economists had the strongest influence on Schumpeter's thinking during his university years. Among other things, they taught him the revolutionary new doctrine of marginalism, which addresses the range of choices consumers and producers make in everyday life. Rather than emphasizing public policy, marginalism shows how individuals optimize their own particular mix of consumer goods or production methods. And during the final three decades of the nineteenth century, this new doctrine began to shake the very foundations of economics, ushering in an early phase of the so-called neoclassical revolution.[12]

The chief progenitors of the new thinking were three economists from different countries: the French-Swiss Léon Walras, the Englishman W. Stanley Jevons, and the Austrian Carl Menger. Of the three pioneers, Menger gained the greatest influence during his own lifetime, though Walras was far more influential over the long term. Menger's ideas and those of his disciples dominated this new branch of economics while Schumpeter was a student in Vienna, though Menger had already retired from the university in 1893.[13]

Schumpeter considered Léon Walras to be a more important economist than Menger, because of Walras's pathbreaking work on equilibrium theory. One of the overarching principles of economic reasoning is that everything is connected to everything else—if prices rise, for example, then fewer consumers will buy (that is, demand will fall), and a new equilibrium will emerge. Walras greatly expanded this idea and worked it out mathematically. "For the first time in the history of our science," Schumpeter later wrote, Walras gave the world a coherent blueprint embracing "the pure logic of the interdependence between economic quantities." His system of equations on equilibrium "is the Magna Carta of economic theory." And without marginalism, the full development of equilibrium theory would have been extremely difficult, if not impossible.[14]

Overall, marginalism became a completely different way of analyzing economic issues: theories of value, prices, costs of production, and relationships between producers and consumers. Menger was especially perceptive on this last question, bringing psychological insights to his analysis of consumers' preferences ("utilities"). A pre-eminent theorist and—with his tall frame and dramatic black beard—an unforgettable teacher, Menger launched the Austrians' bitter, decades-long fight against the German Historical School.[15]

Menger's thinking shaped Schumpeter's work because he had inspired Schumpeter's own professors at the university. One of Schumpeter's favorite teachers was Menger's successor, Friedrich von Wieser, whose approach to economics he once said most resembled his own. Wieser used a term very similar to the modern phrase "marginal utility" to express the essence of Menger's ideas. Wieser was also one of several pioneers in the theory of opportunity cost, a core principle of economics. (If you spend a dollar—or an hour of your time—on one thing, then you lose the opportunity to spend it on something else.)[16]

The most important of all Schumpeter's teachers was another former student of Menger: Eugen von Böhm-Bawerk, who served as imperial Austria's finance minister on three occasions before joining the faculty at Vienna. A formidable presence in any controversy, Böhm-Bawerk wielded what Schumpeter called a "sharp scalpel." Having been on the receiving end of Böhm-Bawerk's incisions, Schumpeter extolled him as "a redoubtable debater to whom many an adversary paid the highest compliment that man can pay to man, that of shying from giving him battle."[17]

During the 1880s, Böhm-Bawerk had published two books, both critical of Karl Marx, that made him famous throughout Europe. The single experience most crucial to the maturation of Schumpeter's own vision of capitalism came during 1905, when he enrolled in Böhm-Bawerk's seminar on Marx. There, he became a member of a remarkable class that included four other students who also went on to careers of genuine distinction: Otto Bauer, Rudolf Hilferding, Emil Lederer, and Ludwig von Mises. All four were Jews. Bauer, Hilferding, and Lederer were Marxists. Mises, by contrast, became the most influential free-market fundamentalist of the twentieth century, both through his own prolific writings and those of his great pupil, Friedrich von Hayek. Schumpeter's own position was that of a self-styled conservative, with a very clear view of what conservatism meant. As he remarked years later, it was "the bringing

Left: Karl Marx (1818–1883), a major inspiration for Schumpeter's work and a perennial foil for his thinking about capitalism and social classes. Right: Carl Menger (1840–1921), founder of the Austrian School of Economics, a prime mover in the marginalist revolution, and—as this picture suggests—a very powerful personality.

about of transitions from your social structure to other social structures with a minimum of loss of human values."[18]

The back-and-forth discussions by these five brilliant students in Böhm-Bawerk's seminar, led by a teacher who himself was one of the world's leading authorities on Marx, turned out to be a transforming experience for Schumpeter. In the coming years, he conducted a continuous inner dialogue with Marx's work, and he wrote some of the most thoughtful criticisms of Marx ever put to paper. As Paul Samuelson later expressed it, Schumpeter's unembarrassed praise of Marx for "being learned, bold to speculate, and broad in his dynamic vision" actually describes Schumpeter himself. Yet Samuelson well understood that, politically, Schumpeter was no left-winger, and "of all my teachers the one whose *economics* was essentially farthest from Marx's."[19]

The Austrian School as a whole later became known for its spirited opposition to socialism and other forms of government interference in economic affairs. Schumpeter always regarded himself as a conservative, but he never op-

Left: Friedrich von Wieser (1851–1926), successor to Menger's chair at the University of Vienna, one of Schumpeter's most important teachers, and the economist whose way of thinking most resembled his own. Right: Eugen von Böhm-Bawerk (1851–1914), Schumpeter's mentor, patron, and role model. He was also Wieser's brother-in-law. Three times imperial minister of finance, he appears here in his standard civil service uniform.

posed public interventions to the extreme degree of Mises, Hayek, and other members of the Austrian School. Instead, he soaked up insights from all leading approaches: the Classical School, the German Historical School, the Austrian School, and the analysis of capitalism by Marx. And in the end, it was not the classical economists who developed the most thorough and accurate analysis of capitalism. Nor was it Karl Marx, nor members of the German Historical School, nor Carl Menger, nor the British neoclassicists. The key figure was Schumpeter himself.[20]

He rooted his own theories in the overriding fact that capitalism is more than just an economic system. As he wrote in 1914, "The reality of which we think when using this term [capitalism] has of course been the subject of very different interpretations: not only scientific, political, and ethical, but different

Schumpeter's classmates in Böhm-Bawerk's Seminar on Marx (clockwise from top left):
Ludwig von Mises (1881–1973), the leading "free-market" economist of the twentieth century, through his own works and those of his student Friedrich von Hayek; Otto Bauer
(1881–1938), socialist theorist, author, and first foreign minister of the Republic of Austria;
Rudolf Hilferding (1877–1941), economist, socialist scholar, and finance minister of Germany
in 1923 and 1928–1929; Emil Lederer (1882–1939), economist, socialist, and eminent professor
at universities in Japan, Germany, and the United States.

interpretations even within the realm of science, flowing from sociology, social psychology, analysis of culture, and history." Schumpeter managed to synthesize broad lessons from all these disciplines into a coherent, full-fledged theory of capitalism. But that task took him many years to complete; and in the meantime he continued his ambitious but impossible struggle to achieve "exact economics," primarily through the use of mathematics.[21]

SCHUMPETER HAD BEEN fortunate to get in on the ground floor of the new doctrine of marginalism, because its novel (and partly mathematical) approach came at a pivotal moment in the rise of industrial capitalism. Menger, for example, had carefully studied the profound new shifts in international commodity trading and the rapid changes of share prices on stock exchanges. In the preface to his seminal book of 1871, Menger wrote: "Never was there an age that placed economic interests higher than does our own. Never was the need of a scientific foundation for economic affairs felt more generally or more acutely. And never was the ability of practical men to utilize the achievements of science, in all fields of human activity, greater than in our day."[22]

Menger, Jevons, and Walras—the pioneers of marginalism—were close contemporaries of rising business titans in Europe and especially the United States—entrepreneurs such as Andrew Carnegie, John D. Rockefeller, Marshall Field, J. P. Morgan, Jay Gould, James J. Hill, and Gustavus Swift. In a remarkable confluence of parallel genius, all ten of these men—the three economists and the seven entrepreneurs—were born during the period 1834–1840. Little evidence exists of reciprocal influences between the theorists and the business titans, but, as Schumpeter later wrote, "Theory grows out of the observation of business practice."[23]

One of the best examples of how both economists and businessmen used the principle of marginalism has to do with the theory of value, one of the most important subjects in all of economics. It is also, of course, a crucial question in daily business operations. What, exactly, is the *value* of a particular good or service? What is it worth? For what price should it sell?[24]

Should there be a "just price" for everything, to be determined not only by market forces but also by community leaders, the clergy, and craft guilds?

As odd as it may seem today, that kind of solution—as defined somewhat loosely by Thomas Aquinas and other great thinkers of the Middle Ages—had considerable influence for hundreds of years, especially in Christian countries, whether Catholic or Protestant. Civil authorities actually set the prices of some items, and excessive deviations from less formal just prices sometimes brought down the wrath of church authorities and made pariahs out of merchants who charged too much or too little.[25]

But by the seventeenth and eighteenth centuries, the notion of a just price began to yield to commercial reality, especially for goods traded in very competitive markets. As a result, more practical ways of thinking about price and value started to evolve. One apparently fruitful approach was to add up the cost of all the labor and materials that went into an item's production and tack on some appropriate percentage for profit: the result is the appropriate price.

This labor theory of value, as it was called, became a doctrine of many members of the Classical School. Later, it connected aspects of their economics with those of Karl Marx, who was practically obsessed with the labor theory. With eloquence born of outrage, Marx denounced the lavish profits taken by producers who priced goods far above their value as calculated using the labor theory. Here matters stood when Walras, Jevons, and Menger came onto the intellectual stage. Working individually, each of the three uncovered a much better definition of value. They did this by the simple step of shifting the spotlight from producers to consumers. The value of anything was "subjective" (Menger's word), because it depended on particular circumstances. The appropriate price for everything was whatever an individual consumer would pay for it at a specific time: no more, no less.[26]

This insight provided, at long last, a way to make sense of why a consumer might pay the same price for widely diverse goods and services: a theater ticket, a room at an inn, a bottle of perfume, a ride in a hansom cab, or a box of nails. These items have no "just price." Nor can they possibly have the same value as defined by the labor theory. But they might well have about the same desirability to an individual consumer at a particular time.

Menger demonstrated that consumers would alter the value they assigned to each item as their own stock of possessions changed. Though not inclined toward mathematics, he devised a simple but ingenious numerical table showing how, once a consumer had enough food for daily sustenance, the value which he attached to still more food would gradually diminish. Meanwhile, the same consumer might also want to buy tobacco, which would be less valuable relative to food at the beginning but more so once sufficient food was in hand. "The individual will therefore endeavor, from this point on, to bring the satisfaction of his need for tobacco into equilibrium with satisfaction of his need for food."[27]

Menger went on to show how his principle held when multiple consumers confronted multiple products. Consumers' tenth shirts or tenth dresses were obviously less useful than their first ones, and therefore less valuable to them. So, instead of acquiring a tenth shirt or dress, they would spend their available money on something else. Consumers' choices of what goods or services to buy would depend on their relative needs and wishes at the time and place of their purchases—that is, on the marginal utility of the goods or services under consideration.[28]

As Schumpeter himself put it in 1909, "Marginal utilities do not depend on what society as such has, but on what individual members have. Nobody values bread according to the quantity of it which is to be found in his country or in the world, but everybody measures the utility of it according to the amount that he has himself." All consumers, given the freedom of choice, would make their choices so as to obtain the desired mix of things they wanted to buy. Prices would follow their preferences and would be determined by what consumers as a group were willing to pay.[29]

Socialist and communist regimes totally rejected this idea. They opted instead for price-setting by central authorities. But capitalist economies fell in love with the new thinking. Millions of individual consumers, liberated from the shackles of just prices and labor theories, could now vote with their pocketbooks. The value of everything began to depend on their choices of how to spend their money. Schumpeter coined the term "methodological individualism" to express this way of looking at things, and that term is still used today.[30]

The same type of analysis applied as strongly to producers as to consumers. The theory of marginal productivity provided a new way for economists to think about the quantities of products manufacturers should make and how they should use different blends of capital, raw materials, and labor to best advantage. The new technique proved especially useful in analyzing industries that required large amounts of capital.[31]

Imagine, for instance, the difference between a small hand laundry and a large steel mill. Most of the laundry's costs are for workers' wages, since soap, water, tubs, and scrub boards are not expensive. When the demand for laundry services slackens—as it does in the winter, when people perspire less—then the owners can cut their expenses simply by laying off workers. For the steel mill, by contrast, the huge costs of constructing the plant and buying raw materials cannot easily be reduced when business is bad. Much of the capital needed to build the mill is likely to be borrowed money, and the mill's owners cannot lay off creditors in the way that the laundry's owners can lay off workers.

The upshot is that the laundry owners' total cost of doing business parallels their labor costs very closely. The cost of hand-washing a shirt is about the same regardless of how many shirts are washed. But for steel, the more pounds a mill turns out, the less it costs the operator to produce each additional (marginal) pound. So the logic of the steel industry is to build large plants and run them with minimal interruption. This principle is related to the more familiar idea of economies of scale: the bigger the mill (within reason) the more pounds of steel it can produce and the cheaper the last units produced will become. The lower the cost to producers, the lower the price they can charge consumers for a pound of steel.[32]

In 1890 the great British economist Alfred Marshall of Cambridge University had synthesized the doctrines of the Classical School with the new idea of marginalism. In his "scissors" metaphor, which became a famous staple of economics education for the next two generations, Marshall showed how prices are determined both by consumers' utilities (the demand blade of the scissors) and by the production cost of particular goods (the supply blade).

Despite its powerful logic for both consumers and producers, the idea of marginalism, so intuitive to Schumpeter, proved to be a difficult intellectual sale to make. For one thing, it lacked the moral appeal of both the just price and the labor theory. And in business practice, it directly challenged the time-honored method of computing production costs. Before the industrial revolution hit its full stride, most businesspeople had only a vague notion of the difference between "fixed" costs (the construction of a steel mill) and "variable" ones (wages for hand launderers). They relied on common sense and those few elements of doing business that they *could* calculate. One of these was average costs.

Let us assume that a steel mill turns out ten pounds per day. Because the mill's furnace must use a great deal of fuel to generate the heat needed to produce any steel at all, the cost of producing the first pound might be, say, $10. But once the furnace is sufficiently hot, the mill's operator can make additional steel by using just a little more fuel. So the average cost of producing the second pound might fall to $9, the third to $8, and so on, until the cost of the tenth pound is only $1. The average cost of all ten pounds would then be the sum of $10 + $9 + $8 + $7 + $6 + $5 + $4 + $3 + $2 + $1 (which equals $55), divided by 10—that is, $5.50. So the producer would charge $5.50 for each pound of steel. Most manufacturers of all kinds of items had followed this kind of average-cost pricing logic for hundreds of years.[33]

After the industrial revolution, however, average-cost pricing made less sense for either the makers or consumers of mass-produced goods. Using the average-cost method, manufacturers would make less of their product than consumers wanted to buy, and would set prices too high. Consumers could afford only a fraction of what they might purchase under a better pricing system. Under that new system, based on marginal costs, the appropriate price for steel should be closer to $1, the cost of production for its final unit, than to the average cost of $5.50 for the whole batch. Of course, if a producer actually priced all ten pounds of steel in the whole batch at $1 per pound, the company would lose an average of $4.50 on every pound sold. So the whole idea seemed insane—a formula for quick bankruptcy.

But that view ignored one vital fact: in a dynamic, changing economy containing vastly more consumers, demand would grow enormously if prices were cut. A steel manufacturer would produce far, far more than ten pounds to meet this unprecedented demand, and the marginal cost of each additional pound would continue to fall. The steel manufacturer would then make larger profits by pricing *below* the old average costs. Granted, the manufacturer had to gamble on just how much consumer demand would grow in response to lower prices. But it quickly became obvious that consumers would buy much more steel at prices tending toward $1 per pound than at the old price of $5.50. (By contrast, for habituating items such as liquor and cigarettes, consumers will keep buying even at extremely high prices. Governments had long understood the rudiments of this principle and had taxed liquor and cigarettes very heavily, as they still do today.)[34]

Steel is a key input for critical industries such as railroads, automobiles, and building construction. So the availability of large volumes of steel at lower prices benefits any nation's economy. During the very year when Schumpeter entered the University of Vienna, Andrew Carnegie's giant company in the United States turned out such immense quantities of steel that it cut its own costs to about one cent per pound! This meant that steel was now cheap enough to use in all sorts of ways never before imagined.[35]

By the twenty-first century, the biggest cost reductions in the history of business had appeared in industries based on information technology. The extremely high cost of producing the first semiconductors, disk drives, data transmission cables, and computers dropped by unbelievable amounts as the underlying science and engineering leaped forward and volumes of production skyrocketed. Because of falling prices, the use of chips, microprocessors, and software rapidly migrated to a host of products whose low cost people now take for granted: thermostats, engine regulators, consumer electronics—almost any item that contains semiconductors.[36]

These illustrations from everyday price declines reveal not only the power of marginalism as a way of thinking but also the nature of capitalism as an economic and social system. For many kinds of products, a key ingredient in that system encourages entrepreneurs to pursue profits through *future* expectations of high volume. It therefore promotes and depends on mass consumption. This means, in turn, that consumers often must be persuaded that they need new products, when that need may be true only in the psychological sense.[37]

Setting consumer prices and industrial production schedules under the influence of marginal costs constituted an authentic intellectual revolution. It directly addressed economic change, which Schumpeter always insisted was the essence of capitalism. It reoriented business thinking away from the past and toward the future and yielded vastly expanded outputs of steel, cars, and a host of other products. Because masses of consumers could now buy products at far cheaper prices, their living standards could improve markedly—even out of proportion to increases in their earnings or accumulated wealth. And that is exactly what happened in advanced capitalist economies during Schumpeter's lifetime.

WHEN HE FINISHED his degree at the University of Vienna in 1906, Joseph Schumpeter was in a state of high intellectual enthusiasm, and he seethed with ambition. The new graduate dressed like a dandy, spent money freely, and carried on frequent liaisons with willing women. He held his head high and tilted slightly backward, accentuating his prominent chin and making his 5'8" 145-pound frame look a little bigger than it was. Still buoyant and playful, he had also become a bit arrogant and officious. He often comported himself like a member of the nobility, though his bourgeois origins in Triesch remained an open secret, and he was too dark-skinned to look much like an Austrian aristocrat.

The imperial civil service was receptive to fresh talent, its ministers comprising a group whose main qualification was sheer ability. Otherwise the empire could not have prospered for so long. But Schumpeter was too free-spirited for bureaucratic routine and too impatient to spend decades rising through the ranks. With his degree in law, he could become a member of the Austrian bar, but admission would require seven years of apprenticeship. Would that be the best use of his time?

By the end of his five years at the University of Vienna, Schumpeter had benefited from some of the best teaching of economics available anywhere. Now twenty-three years old, he had formed his vision of how the world works. He understood how economic analysis could clarify many aspects of this vision, but not all. While economics stood first, it could not stand alone. Schumpeter knew that law, mathematics, and history mattered mightily, as did the newer fields of sociology, psychology, and political science.

As an undergraduate he had already published three articles, each of them statistical in nature. They appeared in 1905, when he was twenty-two, and he had written two of them at the age of twenty. He also published a piece on the importance of mathematics in economics, even though he possessed no special gift for math. He could perform the necessary computations, but he had to work hard at it. Yet from this point onward he crusaded for more use of calculus and advanced algebra. And so began, at this early date, Schumpeter's wrestling match with himself in quest of "exact economics." It was one of the enduring paradoxes of his life and work that someone so broad-minded as to appreciate, ahead of his time, all that was fluid and psychological in economic behavior would also become preoccupied with ever-greater levels of mathematical determinacy and precision.[38]

With his articles on statistics, his piece on math, and a short research note on the great American economist John Bates Clark (a pioneer of marginal productivity theory), Schumpeter had dipped his toe into the waters of academic publication. The positive response of readers suggested that he might do well as an economist. And the chance to combine a career as an economics professor with a high-level position in public service seemed a good fit with his talents. His mentor Eugen von Böhm-Bawerk had followed just this path. As a professor and finance minister, he had become the kind of public intellectual and celebrity that Schumpeter wanted to be.

But such a plan raised serious problems. Only a few universities existed in the Habsburg Empire, and professorships in any field were hard to come by. Nor did Schumpeter wish immediately to start the long "habilitation" that would qualify him for a job as a professor. Habilitation was a credential roughly equivalent to a modern Ph.D. It required the writing of a substantial treatise, an examination by senior professors, and the delivery of several public lectures. Then, too, there was the issue of money. During his thirteen years in Vienna he had acquired expensive tastes, and, as a friend later put it, he "wanted an academic job but not an academic salary."[39]

The question of self-identity lingered, and despite his gifts he was not ready to decide on a career. Heredity and class still meant a great deal in Vienna. Böhm-Bawerk was higher-born than he was, and Schumpeter knew that being an intellectual prodigy did not, by itself, suffice for the kind of prosperous and exciting life he sought.

So what should he do now?

4

Moving Out

Fame is the thirst of youth.

BYRON, *Childe Harold's Pilgrimage,* 1816

WITH HIS FUTURE up in the air, Schumpeter decided to do what young men with aristocratic pretensions often did. He took a Grand Tour. He wanted not only to visit other parts of the world but also to meet the European economists whose works he had been reading. As it turned out, the next three years became a whirlwind for him. He traveled to Germany, France, England, and Egypt, trying on different identities and deciding on a vocation.[1]

Soon after graduating from the University of Vienna, he went to Germany. For the next few months, he studied at the University of Berlin and took part in its seminar on political economy. There, at the center of the German Historical School, he became acquainted with Gustav von Schmoller, Werner Sombart, and other luminaries. He also began to think about writing a book that might somehow reconcile the Historical School with the more theoretical Austrian School he himself preferred. Given the acrimonious history of warfare between these two branches of the discipline, this was a near-impossible mission. But the young Schumpeter seems to have believed that he could do anything.

After absorbing what he thought Berlin had to offer, he left for France and spent several weeks immersed in the culture of Paris and the Sorbonne. Then he set out for England, where he was to remain for more than a year. To the English people he met, in academia and society, he spoke in an upper-class Viennese accent and acted the part of an Austrian aristocrat. He took an apartment in the center of London and bought a horse for regular rides in Hyde Park. Making use of the social-climbing skills his mother had taught him, he conversed with wit and facility, and finessed his way into ever-higher circles. And the longer he lingered in London, the more ardent an Anglophile he became. Reveling in English culture during the heady decade before the First World War, he found little to dislike.

His contemporary John Maynard Keynes wrote a memorable description of this milieu and the bounties it held "for any man of capacity or character at all exceeding the average." Once a person escaped the routine of dull work and entered a higher social class, life in London

> offered, at a low cost and with the least trouble, conveniences, comforts, and amenities beyond the compass of the richest and most powerful monarchs of other ages. The inhabitant of London could order by telephone, sipping his morning tea in bed, the various products of the whole earth, in such quantity as he might see fit, and reasonably expect their early delivery upon his doorstep . . . He could secure forthwith, if he wished it, cheap and comfortable means of transit to any country or climate without passport or other formality, could despatch his servant to the neighboring office of a bank for such supply of the precious metals as might seem convenient, and could then proceed abroad to foreign quarters, without knowledge of their religion, language, or customs, bearing coined wealth upon his person, and would consider himself greatly aggrieved and much surprised at the least interference. But, most important of all, he regarded this state of affairs as normal, certain, and permanent, except in the direction of further improvement, and any deviation from it as aberrant, scandalous, and avoidable.

As a friend of Schumpeter's later wrote, "Prewar England was to him the apotheosis of the civilization of capitalism." Following a lifelong pattern, he took it for granted that servants and others would look after his needs. Neither then nor later did he live within his means. He never learned to cook, do his laundry, fix a faucet, drive a car, or type his own manuscripts.[2]

Yet he was very seldom idle. He followed the daily routine of an obsessive scholar and absorbed knowledge at an extraordinary rate. He set up a good academic base as a special student at the new London School of Economics, founded in 1895, and he also spent time at the Inns of Court, the ancient training ground for English lawyers. Most of all, he put in long hours doing research in the library of the British Museum, as Marx had done a half-century before. He made detailed notes on what he read, and these notes, together with his remarkable memory, enabled him to retain for many years most of what he learned. In particular, he studied items published in Britain and the United States but not available on the Continent. Submerging himself in this literature, he wrote with some prescience that "I cannot help thinking that it is the U.S. where the future of our science is to be."[3]

During evenings and holidays, he shed his scholar's skin and took on the guise of a worldly socialite. He enjoyed many weekends at country houses, attended numerous parties, and exploited his puckish charm and "Eastern" appearance to full advantage. Playing the part of "a great snob" (his own words), he gave no hint that he was spending his days sequestered in libraries. He tailored his persona to fit the English ideal of the gifted amateur, effortlessly digesting reams of information about all kinds of subjects.[4]

As in Berlin, he met every important economist within reasonable traveling distance. After absorbing what the best brains at the London School of Economics had to offer, he took the train to Cambridge. There, he had breakfast with Alfred Marshall, who was forty years his senior and the best-known economist in the world—"a masterful man," Schumpeter later wrote. "To some he looked pontifical." He debated with Marshall whether economics should be studied for its own sake (Schumpeter's view) or whether its practitioners should help guide businesspeople and public servants (Marshall's position, as Schumpeter well knew). He also spent an hour with Philip Wicksteed, a theologian whose contributions to economic theory took many years to win their deserved appreciation.

At Oxford he very much enjoyed meeting the sixty-two-year-old Francis Y. Edgeworth, editor of the *Economic Journal,* the most important periodical in the field. In Schumpeter's opinion, Edgeworth's advances in scientific economics were as important as Marshall's, but Edgeworth himself was "personally in-effective . . . absent-minded to a pathological degree, the worst speaker and lec-turer imaginable." Yet Edgeworth dearly loved economics for its own sake, and his approach to theory was closer to Schumpeter's than was Marshall's.[5]

Although British society and government attracted Schumpeter almost irre-sistibly, he faulted the work of many British economists on the grounds that it was too policy-oriented. Edgeworth and Marshall were partial exceptions—Edgeworth because he relished economics as a playful intellectual exercise as well as a tool of policy, and Marshall because he fused the new marginalism with earlier theoretical insights and understood the ways of business.[6]

Meanwhile, as was his habit, Schumpeter charmed his way into intimacies with young women. And at this unlikely juncture, he actually married one of them. In August 1907 he became engaged to Gladys Ricarde Seaver, the thirty-six-year-old daughter of an official of the Church of England. "We beg respect-fully to inform you," a London jeweler wrote him, enclosing a price list, "that we have today forwarded 8 Rings [sic] to Miss Ricarde Seaver in accordance with your instructions." On November 5, 1907, eighteen months after he left Vienna and shortly before his own twenty-fifth birthday, he and Gladys were wed. She was beautiful, well-connected, and—as time would soon reveal—an adventurous woman. Johanna von Kéler took no pleasure in this turn of events and did not attend the ceremony. Having long monopolized her son's affec-tions, she did not welcome a serious rival, and certainly no daughter-in-law from England.[7]

Why Schumpeter would choose to take such a serious step at this time re-mains a mystery. He was not madly in love with Gladys, who was nearly twelve years his senior, and he was in no position to support a family. He had yet to settle on a vocation, let alone find a job. Perhaps it was again an issue of iden-tity, of trying to reinvent himself as a continental aristocrat and an English gentleman. Gladys, as a member of the upper class, could help in that effort. Whatever the impulse behind his marriage, he now needed employment. He had a law degree but no experience, and his credentials did not qualify him to practice in Vienna or London. But he discovered that he could do so in Cairo, and he arranged for a position with a law firm there. He and Gladys then sailed for Egypt—at that time a de facto protectorate of Britain but nominally ad-ministered by the Khedive, an Egyptian functionary of the Ottoman Empire.[8]

Schumpeter in England at age twenty-six, shortly after he married Gladys Ricarde Seaver.

Once in Cairo, Schumpeter represented clients in cases before the International Mixed Tribunal, a court established by Britain and Egypt. His law practice brought in a very good income, which he supplemented by handling some of the finances of the Khedive's daughter, an Egyptian princess. This role gave him further opportunities to indulge his aristocratic predilections. More important, his work for the princess brought him extra compensation when his investments on her behalf earned good returns. During his ten months in Cairo, he made a substantial amount of money, on which he and Gladys lived well for the next six years.[9]

Even before going to Cairo, Schumpeter had tentatively decided to become an economist. During his tour of Europe and his year in England he had begun to write a treatise about the theory and methods of economics, and his manuscript kept growing. He intended to rethink the field as broadly as he could and to reconcile the German Historical School with the Austrian marginalists. After all, Alfred Marshall had made noteworthy progress in combining the new marginalism with the old classical tradition of Smith and Ricardo. Why should Schumpeter not do something similar for Continental economics and thereby bring the *Methodenstreit* to an end?

By the time he put down his pen, his manuscript had grown to prodigious length, and the printed book reached 626 pages. He published it in 1908 under the title *The Nature and Content of Theoretical Economics* and dedicated it to Johanna. He had written the entire book in only eighteen months, finishing it when he was still just twenty-five years old. He now felt ready to leave Cairo and return to Vienna.[10]

This first book of Schumpeter's did not succeed in the way he had hoped. His purpose in writing it was not so much to carve out a bold new path as it was to reconcile existing schools, a step that would introduce advanced theory to German-speaking economists. He believed he might thereby transform economics in Central Europe and achieve instant fame for himself. From this dual drive came the energy to produce so long a book in so short a time.

But, as almost anyone familiar with the workings of academic life might have predicted, neither of his aims met quick success. He had been living in something of a fool's paradise all along, and now he was deeply disappointed. His book sold fewer than a thousand copies, and the German scholars he was trying to impress took little notice. No youthful economist associated with the Austrian School, no matter how brilliant, was likely to redirect the German Historical School toward abstract theory. Then, too, as Schumpeter later remembered, his own mentor, Eugen von Böhm-Bawerk, "once told a restless and recalcitrant young man" (Schumpeter himself) that science progresses not necessarily through bright new insights but "through the old professors' dying off."[11]

Yet in many ways *The Nature and Content of Theoretical Economics* was an impressive performance, and it has several characteristics that were to reappear in Schumpeter's more successful later works. As he writes in his preface, "I hold aloof from practical politics and recognize no purpose other than knowledge," a disclaimer he was to make many times in the future. In the text of his book, the writing is straightforward, its terms defined with care. Schumpeter explores production and consumption, the determination of price, the importance of marginal utility, the necessity of mathematics (though the book contains little math), and the usefulness of equilibrium as a way of thinking.[12]

Most of what he wrote pertains to static equilibrium. He describes a purely theoretical cosmos, not the constantly changing world of actual business. The book makes no recommendations for public policy, in contrast to the work of Mill, Marshall, and other British economists. Nor does it take significant note of the psychological insights of the Austrians Menger and Wieser.

Its approach owes more to Léon Walras than to anyone else, because of Walras' pathbreaking work on general equilibrium. Schumpeter sent a copy of the book to the aged Walras and then—again taking care to meet the great figures of his discipline face to face—traveled to Switzerland to see him. Surprised by his visitor's youth and confused about exactly who had written the book, Walras proceeded to compliment Schumpeter on the superb work produced by his father. Walras then said, as Schumpeter recalled, "that of course economic life is essentially passive," merely adapting itself to outside influences. Therefore, "the theory of a stationary process constitutes really the whole of theoretical economics." Despite his admiration of Walras, Schumpeter emphatically disagreed. "I felt very strongly that this was wrong."[13]

Even so, Schumpeter lays little emphasis in his first book on the themes of change and innovation that dominate his subsequent work. Entrepreneurs take the stage from time to time but not as often as might be expected. Overall, the book amounts to a ground-clearing exercise, an analysis of what Schumpeter calls "the steady state": the economic system as a "circular flow" in which buyers and sellers exchange goods without altering anything basic to the system.[14]

He does take some note of what became known as comparative statics, which had been foreshadowed by Alfred Marshall and others. This method presents a before-and-after photograph of what will happen if one element in an equilibrium is altered. But comparative statics says nothing about the *process* of change, and Schumpeter's text communicates little sense of a capitalist economy as an engine of creative destruction. Although the analysis has some traits in common with his later writings, it is not a typically "Schumpeterian" performance.

Even on its own terms, the book is far too long and repetitive, making unnecessary demands on the reader. In part, this was because of its topical organization, which required the author to lay out his basic arguments again and again. Its length also owed something to Schumpeter's youthful reading of massive tomes from Hegel, Marx, and other great German scholars he was trying to emulate.

As a magnum opus from a boy wonder, the book failed. But it did bring Schumpeter respectful attention from many important economists. Friedrich von Wieser gave his former student's book a good review in a German-language journal, as did an English scholar writing in a prominent British quarterly. John Bates Clark, one of the most influential American economists, wrote in the *Political Science Quarterly* that "this work is both critical and constructive, and in each direction it contributes distinctly to the progress of economic science. One of its purposes is to indicate the weak points in current theories, and to this extent it is controversial; but it aims to reduce the amount of controversy in progress rather than to increase it, and the candor with which it treats other men's work gives ground for hoping that this end may be attained. The work holds aloof from entangling controversies as to method and uses whatever method is best adapted to the purpose at any time in view."[15]

Here Clark identified a characteristic that became a hallmark of Schumpeter's writings: his magnanimity toward the work of others. In the preface to this very first book, Schumpeter makes a strong plea for intellectual patience and mutual learning: "We want to understand and not to fight; to learn, not criticize; to analyze and draw out from every principle what is right, not simply to approve or reproach." This kind of intellectual generosity is not typical of great scholars. Schumpeter had many faults, but pettiness was not one of them.[16]

Above all, he could not countenance anyone's dogmatic insistence on a single approach to the study of economics. In 1911, three years after his book appeared, he wrote that head-of-a-pin arguments are usually pointless, even in academic discourse: "People can have various opinions on the value of general discussions of questions of method . . . But to work on problems, not so many methodological principles are needed as there might seem. Rather, discussions of them are a sign of unfruitfulness concerning concrete achievements." In a short piece published in 1913 he warned against mixing value judgments with science. Instead, he advocated value-neutral analyses that took multiple perspectives into account.[17]

In 1914, reviewing a collection of essays by a prominent French sociologist, Schumpeter reported with regret that the author exhibited "that almost childish small-mindedness that holds only its own way of working possible . . . and considers it the first task to annihilate all others in holy rage." Because economics and capitalism were so multifaceted, he wrote, they required approaches from many directions. He concluded his review of the French sociologist's work as follows: "When at long last will the day come that will bring home the realization to all of us that weapons to cope with the vast mass of facts must first be forged, each by itself?—that this vast mass possesses countless different aspects, demanding countless different approaches? When at long last shall we have learned our scientific craft to the point where we can grasp what our neighbor is doing and calmly till our own field rather than attack him?" Schumpeter himself somehow remained immune to the faddishness that characterized academic life at that time (and still does today).[18]

When he returned to Austria from Egypt in 1908, his new book became the centerpiece of his habilitation at the University of Vienna. He submitted the book to the Faculty of Law, which assigned it to Böhm-Bawerk and Wieser for evaluation. Schumpeter's praise of mathematics took issue with the approaches favored by both of his former professors, but the book was so obviously the work of a superior young scholar that they had no trouble approving it. After receiving their endorsement, Schumpeter completed his examination in economics and delivered the standard series of lectures required of habilitationists. He thereupon gained full certification to teach at any university in the Austro-Hungarian Empire.[19]

By no means did a successful habilitation guarantee a job, however. Schumpeter wanted and likely expected to stay at the University of Vienna as a junior professor. For a brief period he did a small amount of teaching there, but he was so mercurial that there was little inclination to invite him to join the faculty. Nor did a permanent opening exist at any other imperial university.

Fortunately, his mentors were able to secure a temporary job for him as an associate professor at the University of Czernowitz. This was a relatively new school in a city of eighty-five thousand located at the extreme eastern boundary of the empire, more than four hundred miles from Vienna. The capital of the small Habsburg province of Bukovina, Czernowitz lay near the Russian and Romanian borders, a part of the world formerly governed by the Ottoman Empire. It was populated mostly by Ukrainians, Romanians, and Hungarians. About a third of Czernowitz's population was Jewish, and it also contained a substantial number of German-speaking Catholics.[20]

Today Czernowitz, renamed Chernivtsi and part of Ukraine, continues somewhat as it was when Schumpeter moved there: a very remote city but now, because of World War II and the Holocaust, with a much reduced population of German-speakers and Jews. In 1909 it was hardly the kind of place where Schumpeter expected to launch his academic career. But success at his chosen profession was not far off at all.

5

Career Takeoff

Towering genius disdains a beaten path. It seeks regions
hitherto unexplored . . . It thirsts and burns for distinction.

ABRAHAM LINCOLN, Lyceum speech, Springfield, Illinois, 1838

LINCOLN, ONLY twenty-nine at the time and himself extremely ambitious, went on to say that in their quest for "celebrity and fame," singularly talented people almost always strike out in bold new directions. This is what the twenty-six-year-old Schumpeter did in Czernowitz, and he did it deliberately. The book he wrote there, *The Theory of Economic Development*, is a full reflection of his genius. It launched his rise to stardom and became one of the classic economics texts of the twentieth century.[1]

Schumpeter's very acceptance of the Czernowitz post underscored his resolve to try for academic celebrity at any cost. His decision was the equivalent of a bright British Ph.D.'s taking a first job at, say, the University of Singapore prior to World War II. Like Singapore, Czernowitz was a faraway, exotic, and multi-ethnic city located at the juncture of hostile empires. It had a lively local culture but no university of international standing. Yet Schumpeter embraced this challenge with great vigor and made the most of an unpromising situation.

He also seems to have enjoyed his life in Czernowitz. For years afterward, he regaled his friends with scandalous tales of orgies and lessons in advanced sexuality that he learned from women in and around the city. It is hard to know what to make of these stories, since Schumpeter was their source and corroboration is impossible. But he often said that neither he nor Gladys put much restraint on their libidinous impulses. And certainly his reputation as a womanizer persisted for many decades, until he reached his mid-fifties.[2]

One of the most colorful anecdotes of his time in Czernowitz, however embellished, was the story of a duel between two men employed by the university. On a morning in the early fall of 1909 each took the field of honor accompanied by a second, as the *code duello* required. Neither had great skill with swordsmanship. But after much clumsy clashing of metal on metal, the blade of one hacked a small slice in the shoulder of the other. The appearance of blood brought quick intervention from the seconds, who declared an end to the duel.

Were these men rival suitors contending for the hand of a woman? Military officers settling an affair of honor? No. One was a professor, the other a librarian. They were fighting over students' access to books. The professor, who won the duel, was Schumpeter himself. He had arrived in Czernowitz just weeks before, but news of his precocious intelligence had spread quickly, along with accounts of his self-dramatizing. (He liked to disrupt faculty meetings by showing up late, still clad in jodhpurs and helmet from his daily horseback rides.) In the classroom, he was a demanding teacher who handed out heavy homework. When his students complained that the librarian forbade them to check out books he had assigned, he rushed over and confronted the offender. The argument escalated, and Schumpeter began to roar out insults.

The librarian, his personal integrity now in question, abruptly raised the stakes and challenged Schumpeter to a duel. Though taken aback, Schumpeter accepted. For the principle of book-borrowing, he was willing to risk injury, though probably not his life, since such affairs seldom ended in dangerous wounds. At the end of the duel, the librarian left the field with a cut on his shoulder and the satisfaction of having defended his honor. Schumpeter had made his point as well—the students would now get access to the books. And despite this inauspicious start, he and the librarian went on to become good friends.[3]

Sexual escapades and duels aside, the real story of Schumpeter's two years in Czernowitz was the writing of his brilliant *Theory of Economic Development*. Full of insight and originality, it set the foundation for his own analysis of capitalism and for an immense amount of research by other writers. Among

The University of Czernowitz.

other new interpretations, Schumpeter turned Karl Marx on his head. Hateful gangs of parasitic capitalists become, in Schumpeter's hands, innovative and beneficent entrepreneurs.[4]

Schumpeter begins the book by reviewing conventional economic doctrine: the hypothetical circular flow of production and consumption. This idea, first developed in the eighteenth century, describes in simple terms the way an economy works. Employers produce goods and services and pay their workers. Next, the workers, in their roles as consumers, buy these goods and services. Then the employers use the consumers' money for investment, further production, wage payments, and profits—thereby starting the cycle again. The circular flow is like a constantly running river that can rise or fall slightly. But real floods or droughts do not take place, and the river can never go off its course.

This steady-state economy, which Schumpeter had described in his first book, reappears in *The Theory of Economic Development* as a starting point for his real interest: continual economic change under capitalism. Whereas his purpose in the first book had been to reconcile warring economic schools, he now broke entirely fresh ground. In his new theory, the circular flow becomes highly irregular. Floods and droughts become commonplace, and entrepreneurial adventurers routinely cut new channels into the economic landscape.[5]

This key insight, even though it resonates with the experience of nearly all businesspeople, has seldom been embraced by academic economists. The reason for its rejection is that, unlike the idea of equilibrium, the phenomenon of entrepreneurship is almost impossible to "model" through the use of equations yielding mathematical proof. Thus, even though academic economists have moved beyond the steady state, they have paid little attention to the entrepreneur, even to this day.[6]

But in *The Theory of Economic Development,* Schumpeter fearlessly elaborates the crucial role that entrepreneurs play in the real world of capitalism. In his definition, the entrepreneur is not a run-of-the-mill business executive, or even the owner or chief executive of a successful firm. The entrepreneur is "the modern type of 'captain of industry'"—obsessively seeking an innovative edge.[7]

Warming to his theme, Schumpeter explores not only the economics but also the sociology of entrepreneurship—its role in undermining traditional class structures and the perennial scarcity of truly high-level ability: "We can assume that every healthy man can sing if he will. Perhaps half the individuals in an ethnically homogeneous group have the capacity for it to an average degree, a quarter in progressively diminishing measure, and, let us say, a quarter in a measure above the average; and within this [upper] quarter, through a series of continually increasing singing ability and continually diminishing number of people who possess it, we come finally to the Carusos."[8]

Moving into psychological speculations—and beyond the disciplinary boundaries of almost all prior work in economics—Schumpeter next turns to the motivation of entrepreneurs. Here again he shows the kind of insight that, however imaginative, is not amenable to mathematical measurement: "The typical entrepreneur is more self-centered than other types, because he relies less than they do on tradition and connection and because his characteristic task—theoretically as well as historically—consists precisely in breaking up old, and creating new, tradition."[9]

Breaking up old traditions and creating new ones could just as well describe what Schumpeter himself was doing to the discipline of economics. In passages such as these, he is defining the behavioral profile of the entrepreneur as a type. He is arguing that the entrepreneur, in contrast to the ordinary manufacturer or merchant, is not merely overseeing the daily flow of production and consumption but is actually crafting the future.

Schumpeter's entrepreneur is not driven solely by a wish to grow rich or by any other "motivation of the hedonist kind." Instead, he or she feels "the dream and the will to found a private kingdom"—usually a family business dynasty. "Then there is the will to conquer: the impulse to fight, to prove oneself superior to others, to succeed for the sake, not of the fruits of success, but of success itself . . . Finally, there is the joy of creating, of getting things done, or simply of exercising one's energy and ingenuity . . . Our type seeks out difficulties, changes in order to change, delights in ventures." The Schumpeterian entrepreneur has some characteristics in common with Max Weber's "charismatic" leader but falls short of the "superman" portrayed by Friedrich Nietzsche.[10]

In the rise of one set of entrepreneurs and concurrent decline of others, Schumpeter sees profound social implications. "The upper strata of society are like hotels which are indeed always full of people, but people who are forever changing." Just as businesses go up and down, so too do entrepreneurs and their families. "This represents the most important factor of rise in the social scale in the capitalist world. Because it proceeds by competitively destroying old businesses and hence the existences dependent upon them, there always corresponds to it a process of decline, of loss of caste, of elimination." In many of his writings, Schumpeter attached great importance to families—both for the entrepreneurs who founded new firms and in the gradual dissipation of business energy that typically followed in succeeding generations. (Thomas Mann exploits this theme in *Buddenbrooks,* published in 1901 and one of the best novels about business ever written.)[11]

In *The Theory of Economic Development,* Schumpeter takes note of the difficulty of overthrowing established ways of thinking, and then draws a parallel between this intellectual barrier and similar impediments in business. "The history of science is one great confirmation of the fact that we find it exceedingly difficult to adopt a new scientific point of view or method . . . So it is also in the economic world." The barriers in business are social as well as economic, and those who feel their interests threatened will battle fiercely against innovation.[12]

Perhaps with his own trailblazing in mind, Schumpeter goes on to describe a sequence of stubborn opposition against anyone who wants to do anything new. "This resistance manifests itself first of all in the groups threatened by the innovation, then in the difficulty in finding the necessary cooperation, finally in the difficulty in winning over consumers." In business, the development of a large-scale corporation is especially challenging, because few useful patterns exist. "All the necessary conditions are wanting—workers, trained personnel, the necessary market conditions. Innumerable resistances of a social and political character work against it." To overcome all these barriers requires a "special aptitude." The same could be said for remaking an academic discipline, as Schumpeter was trying to do.[13]

In business, it took the supreme organizational talents of entrepreneurs such as John D. Rockefeller (oil), August Thyssen (steel), George Eastman (photography) and H. J. Heinz (processed food) to conceive how a large and complex company might work. They were the Carusos of big business when Schumpeter, the would-be Caruso of economics, was writing his book. And it took their constant vigilance to ensure that the designs they worked out not only materialized but also continued to function.[14]

Schumpeter then argues that entrepreneurial interventions make the notion of the steady state a mere fiction, nothing more than a hypothetical teaching device. The idea of equilibrium itself becomes problematical, since continual disruption is the basis for economic development and embodies the essence of capitalism.

Part of that essence is the creation of new markets. After discussing the crucial importance of innovation, Schumpeter suggests that firms often must take steps to build demand for their products. "The spontaneity of [human] wants is small." Thus, it is "the producer who as a rule initiates economic change, and consumers are educated by him if necessary; they are, as it were, taught to want new things, or things which differ in some respect or other from those which they have been in the habit of using. Therefore, while it is permissible and even necessary to consider consumers' wants as an independent and indeed the fundamental force in a theory of the circular flow, we must take a different attitude as soon as we analyze *change*."[15]

Although this statement seems natural enough in the twenty-first century, it was quite a strong assertion to make in 1911. It says that the list of human desires is not inherently large but, if properly stimulated, can become insatiable. At about the same time, the French sociologist Emile Durkheim was saying something quite similar: "Our needs are unlimited. The more one has, the more one wants." The foundation of capitalism, both economically and socially, is, therefore, the insatiability of wants that entrepreneurs have managed to induce consumers to see as needs.

Schumpeter goes on to set forth his definitions of innovation and development, and here he takes special pains to be precise—revising, condensing, numbering, and clarifying thoughts that had been obscure in his initial drafts. He specifies five types of innovation that define the entrepreneurial act. To quote his list directly:

(1) The introduction of a new good—that is one with which consumers are not yet familiar—or of a new quality of a good.

(2) The introduction of a new method of production, that is one not yet tested by experience in the branch of manufacture concerned.

(3) The opening of a new market, that is a market into which the particular branch of manufacture of the country in question has not previously entered, whether or not this market has existed before.

(4) The conquest of a new source of supply of raw materials or half-manufactured goods, again irrespective of whether this source already exists or whether it has first to be created.

(5) The carrying out of the new organization of any industry, like the creation of a monopoly position (for example through trustification) or the breaking up of a monopoly position.[16]

This passage has been quoted many times by economists, historians, and others studying the anatomy of innovation. If some elements of the list seem trite, this is because they have become conventional wisdom—which they most certainly were not when Schumpeter assembled them in 1911. In his own future books, he himself provided scores of examples from each category of innovation.

In *The Theory of Economic Development,* Schumpeter especially emphasizes the role of *new* companies in making innovations that interrupt the circular flow. New firms "do not arise out of the old ones but start producing beside them." In transportation, for example, "it is not the owner of stage-coaches who builds railways." Schumpeter also argues that "the entrepreneur is never the risk bearer. The one who gives credit [that is, provides the necessary capital] comes to grief if the undertaking fails . . . Even though [the entrepreneur] may risk his reputation, the direct economic responsibility of failure never falls on him."[17]

Here, Schumpeter seems to be clarifying the role of capital in capital*ism*. The *Oxford English Dictionary* defines capital as "accumulated wealth reproductively employed." That is a wonderful definition. But capital*ism* is something else again, because it relies so heavily on credit—wealth that has not yet been accumulated. Credit must be created out of nothing but future expectations, which is a basic reason why capitalism, of all economic systems, is so distinctly oriented toward the future.

"The headquarters of the capitalist system," says Schumpeter, is the money market—the place where credit is allocated. Investors clustered in money centers such as New York, London, and Berlin (and, today, also Tokyo, Shanghai, Silicon Valley, and other places) decide on which entrepreneurial projects deserve financial backing and which do not.[18] "All kinds of credit requirements come to this market; all kinds of economic projects are first brought into relation with one another, and contend for their realization in it."[19]

Schumpeter goes on to argue that "in carrying out new combinations, 'financing' as a special act" is critical to successful innovation. "By far the greater part of it does not come from thrift in the strict sense, that is from abstaining from the consumption of part of one's regular income, but it consists of funds which are themselves the result of successful innovation and in which we shall later recognize entrepreneurial profit." In other words, the financial basis of development comes not from penny-pinching but rather from new sources of funds, including money created by banks when they finance new ventures. The important players in this process are entrepreneurs and investment bankers, who generate "new purchasing power out of nothing." The investment banker is not just a middleman standing between savers and users of capital; he is instead "a *producer*" of money and credit, "the capitalist par excellence."[20]

Many times throughout his career, Schumpeter hammered home the necessity for credit and the function of banks in creating money. This fact of economic life—that banks create money—often seems questionable even to very intelligent people, and it was denied by some theorists well into the twentieth century. Schumpeter once told a group of Japanese economists that Keynes had said to him "there were not more than five people in the world who understood monetary theory," adding that he, Schumpeter, assumed himself to be one of the five.[21]

The Theory of Economic Development is an exemplary book, but the timing of its appearance was inopportune. Soon the First World War completely diverted readers' attention from peacetime economic development. And Germany's loss of the war diminished the book's intended audience. The English-language edition did not appear until 1934, and by then Schumpeter's emphasis on entrepreneurship was again out of phase with contemporary problems. In the midst of the worldwide Great Depression, there was hardly enough entrepreneurial energy to feed people, let alone to establish dynamic new businesses.[22]

Even so, reviews of the book were uniformly enthusiastic, both at the time of its first publication and later in the English-language edition.[23] Reviewing the original version, a Harvard professor praised its revision of Adam Smith's doctrine that economic self-interest is always the prime motivator of human behavior. "The psychology of Schumpeter's entrepreneur includes such elements as love of activity for its own sake, love of creative activity, love of distinction, love of victory over others, love of the game, and other traits which the newer psychology has been emphasizing." In another review of the original German edition, the Columbia economist John Bates Clark endorsed Schumpeter's connections between theory and fact. Economic theory, Clark wrote, was making a new kind of progress: "It is theory still, but it studies facts in their causal connection and the causes as well as the facts are of vital interest to humanity."[24]

In a review of the English translation published in 1934, Alvin Hansen, then of the University of Minnesota and later Schumpeter's colleague at Harvard, lavished praise on the book: "Nowhere else does one find so penetrating a treatment as here of the significant characteristics of the process of development, of economic dynamics, in contrast with the 'circular flow' of an essentially static society." Equally important, Schumpeter's analysis was "one of the first to elucidate the effect of credit expansion upon the distribution of income and upon capital formation."[25]

The Theory of Economic Development impresses even more with the passage of time. As an analytical performance, it is an obvious *tour de force,* all the more noteworthy for having come from a twenty-eight-year-old reporting from Czernowitz, which seemed to be the middle of nowhere. Schumpeter had laid a solid keel for the great ship of his future work. *The Theory of Economic Development* foreshadowed a long series of penetrating essays by Schumpeter on economic, social, and historical topics. It also formed the core of ideas he fleshed out in *Business Cycles* (1939) and in the most popular of all his works, *Capitalism, Socialism and Democracy* (1942).[26]

IN 1911 SCHUMPETER left Czernowitz for a more prestigious position at the University of Graz, in the city of his boyhood home. When the faculty at Graz was considering him for its chair in political economy, *The Theory of Economic Development* was still in the process of publication, so it played little role in the discussion. Had the professors at Graz been exposed to this great work, their task would have been easy. But they took no account of the book, and the hiring decision turned into a petty academic squabble.

Schumpeter's predecessor at Graz was a man named Richard Hildebrand, who had been a pillar of the faculty for forty years and now headed the three-person committee to choose his own successor. As a disciple of the German Historical School (of which his father had been a prominent member), Hildebrand wanted no part of modern theory. His committee's list of acceptable candidates excluded the names of Schumpeter and all other serious theorists. Nor did the report mention a single Austrian economist.[27]

Hildebrand went out of his way to denigrate Schumpeter's work: "He adheres to an entirely barren, abstract, and formalistic approach only toying around with mathematical or mechanistic concepts and analogies without any relation to real life. His [first] book on [*The Nature and Content of Theoretical Economics*] contains nothing but empty commonplaces and trivialities presented, however, with great self-complacency and emphasis as if they were important findings."[28]

The committee's report, which recommended three mediocre candidates while denouncing Schumpeter and two other theorists, won the endorsement of a majority of Graz's Faculty of Law. But the gratuitous attacks on theory aroused the suspicions of four members of the Law Faculty, who proceeded to vote against Hildebrand's recommendations. Two of the four then took the unusual step of preparing minority reports proposing additional candidates, and Schumpeter's name appeared on both lists. The senior dissenter, a distinguished professor of commercial and Roman law, described Schumpeter as "a man of outstanding talent and original power," adding that "an author of his prominence must not be ignored." These comments and others, accompanied by a rejoinder from committee chairman Hildebrand, then went to the Ministry of Culture and Instruction in Vienna.[29]

What happened next has never become clear because of the absence of written records; but speculation has fixed on the likely role that Eugen von Böhm-Bawerk played in sponsoring his former pupil. One of the world's most famous economists, Böhm-Bawerk was also the incoming president of the Imperial Academy of Sciences. He knew Emperor Francis Joseph personally, having served on three occasions as the country's finance minister. In the Austrian tradition of patronage, any recommendation from Böhm-Bawerk would carry enormous weight—not only with the ministry but also with the emperor, who had the authority to make all professorial appointments.

In the end, the ministry chose Schumpeter, and the emperor received him in a formal ceremony. The new appointee appeared in the standard civil servant's uniform, which included a cocked hat of the type worn by eighteenth-century military officers. At age twenty-eight, Schumpeter thus became the youngest full professor of political economy in the empire, and one of the youngest in any field. Meanwhile, back in Graz, the humiliated Hildebrand began to plot his revenge even before Schumpeter left Czernowitz for the long trip to his new post.[30]

After arriving in Graz, Joseph and Gladys leased an apartment in a narrow building at the end of a tapered block, with light coming in from three sides. Their living room overlooked Graz's beautiful municipal park, the main attraction of which is a hill so steep that, even today, cable cars ascend it at a sixty-one-degree angle, the trip taking about ten minutes. The apartment was only a few blocks from the lodging on Mozart Lane where Johanna and the five-year-old Jozsi had lived after their move from Triesch twenty-three

The University of Graz (technically, Karl-Josef University, after two Habsburg emperors), founded as a Jesuit school in 1585 as part of the Counter-Reformation, then reconstituted in 1827. The impressive building pictured here opened in 1885 and is still in use.

years earlier. In the opposite direction, Professor Schumpeter could now walk four blocks to his new office at the university. "I like this pretty town surrounded by woody hills," he wrote an American friend. Graz lies in a river valley just below the Alps, "and my wife feels very *well* in its damp and English climate."[31]

During his first year of teaching, which began in the fall of 1911, Schumpeter worked very hard as the only economist on the faculty. In his second year he agreed to lecture also at the Graz University of Technology, a nearby engineering school. In addition, he began to accept numerous invitations to address local civic and business groups, who knew him to be a colorful speaker. He therefore had little time for research, and no time at all to coddle his pupils at the university. He quickly earned the reputation of a tough taskmaster.

The main auditorium at the University of Graz, as it still appears today. The very large statue at the center front is of Emperor Francis Joseph.

Unfortunately for him, students at Graz proved to be less diligent than those in Vienna and Czernowitz. Under the lenient hand of Richard Hildebrand, they had grown accustomed to doing little work in their economics courses. They were also a more ingrown group than their counterparts in Czernowitz and Vienna and therefore easier to organize. So when the youthful Schumpeter imposed a hard regimen of reading, gave difficult examinations, and made no secret of his low opinion of the popular Hildebrand, the students responded with open rebellion.

One morning at the start of his 9:30 class they simply drowned out their new professor in an uproar of protest. Astounded by this show of disrespect, Schumpeter tried to pacify them, but to no avail. On October 14, 1912, the students began a boycott of Schumpeter's classes and called on university officials to dismiss him. All of this was virtually unprecedented at any university in the

Habsburg Empire. Schumpeter's fellow professors rallied in support, but the episode was a nightmare for him.[32]

It became worse when the controversy spilled over into local, provincial, and even national politics, as university authorities informed the minister of culture and instruction in Vienna. The governor of Styria, the Austrian province of which Graz is the capital, called on the university's rector for a report, and the rector began a mediation between professor and students. Schumpeter resisted, arguing that his course delivered to students the best economics the world had to offer. But in fact he was a chastened man, and after three weeks of negotiation the rector and dean brought the boycott to an end.[33]

The whole ordeal led Schumpeter to rethink his role as a teacher and colleague. As at Czernowitz, he was not a favorite of other professors, who were put off by his brashness. Then, too, despite their outward support during the boycott, a majority of the Law Faculty had voted against his appointment in the first place. From this time forward, Schumpeter assumed a less arrogant attitude. He became more gracious toward his colleagues at Graz and later at other universities. He kept giving students hard assignments, but he began to grade their performances less sternly.

He also paid closer attention to what was happening in his classrooms. He dropped none of his showmanship, but—always a superb actor—he now took on the role of kindly mentor. He extended his office hours and patiently guided his charges through the thicket of economics. In the years ahead he never mentioned this episode to his fellow professors at Harvard and elsewhere. As talkative as he was about other adventures in Europe—the duel at Czernowitz, his numerous sexual exploits—he kept silent about any student rebellion.[34]

Graz was a very pleasant city, but it was not Vienna, which remained the center of Schumpeter's universe. Trips from faraway Czernowitz had been impractical, but from Graz trains could reach the capital in three or four hours, the tracks curving through beautiful hills. The Schumpeters made frequent visits to see Johanna and old friends and to bask in Vienna's bounties of art, architecture, and coffeehouse culture.

Toward the end of his second year at Graz, in 1913, Columbia University invited Schumpeter to spend the next two semesters as an exchange professor in New York. Austria had never sent a professor to Columbia, and Schumpeter's selection was a signal honor, especially for a person so young. The invitation likely originated with John Bates Clark, the eminent marginalist who held a chair in Columbia's Political Science Department, which was responsible for teaching economics. He and Schumpeter had corresponded, and their mutual respect was evident in the reviews they wrote of each other's books. Clark had just published his favorable notice of Schumpeter's *Theory of Economic Development,* and this review provided a glowing introduction of the young Austrian to American economists.[35]

In October 1913 a delighted Schumpeter boarded the *Lusitania* in Liverpool for the six-day trip to America. Significantly, Gladys chose neither to remain in Graz nor to accompany her husband to New York. Instead, she returned to her home in England.

Throughout his months in New York, Schumpeter stayed at the large Hotel Marseilles, located on the corner of Broadway and 103rd Street near the Columbia campus. At his inaugural lecture, in an auditorium packed with students and faculty, he gave a stunning presentation. Professor E. R. A. Seligman, another well-known Columbia economist, reported to the university's president on "the unusual character of the event":

> Professor Schumpeter held the close attention of this audience to
> the very end of his lecture. It was a remarkable performance from
> many points of view. His command of English is phenomenal. He
> spoke without a note, in language that was not only fluent but
> choice and elevated; and he displayed a familiarity with the finer
> points of the language which I am sure had not been equalled by
> any exchange professor hitherto.

Schumpeter's talk covered not only economic theory but also, as Seligman described it, "the relation of economics to psychology and sociology. He was— what is very unusual—both brilliant and profound; his choice of novel illustrations taken from a great variety of different fields, shows a surprising breadth of culture, which is unusual in a specialist . . . The Faculty of Political Science deems itself very fortunate in being able to present to the students under its charge so brilliant an exponent of economic doctrine. It is easy to predict for Professor Schumpeter a highly successful stay in this country."[36]

The more lectures Schumpeter gave, the wider his reputation spread, and he soon received requests to speak at other major universities. Columbia itself awarded him an honorary degree, even though he was still only thirty. All of this praise and attention contrasted with his lukewarm reception at Graz, which was a fine university but hardly in the same league with Columbia. Schumpeter could not have been more pleased.

Seligman asked him for additional details about his academic background, and his handwritten response shows just how self-deprecating he could be—while at the same time cognizant of his growing importance:

> All I have to say is that after having survived what was a most con-
> ventional education . . . I spent some years travelling until, after
> the publication of a few papers and my first book, which locally
> made something of a hit (undeservedly of course), I was invited to
> get a docent [qualification as teacher] of Political economy in Vi-
> enna, which I did in 1909 . . . [I then became] the youngest pro-
> fessor in Austria and Germany by being promoted to the chair of
> political economy in the University of Czernowitz at the age of 26.
> There I published a few other studies on points of theory and my
> second big (in size) book, which seems to enjoy the most wide-
> spread obscurity though I myself thought some of the results it
> aimed at explaining new and not entirely void of importance—
> evidently a case of the proverbial love of a mother for a monster.
> In 1911 I was appointed to the chair of political economy in the
> university in Graz, the most agreeable university in Austria and
> second in size, Vienna being the first.[37]

Schumpeter made the most of his time in America. Ever curious, he decided to take a train trip to California and back. This six-thousand-mile journey showed him the immense size and variety of the United States. It also con-firmed—emphatically—his beliefs about the importance of entrepreneurship and credit creation in promoting business growth. He was astonished at the rapid pace of American industrial development. He saw at first hand how the unfettered release of entrepreneurial energy, much of it financed with bor-rowed money, had made the United States the richest country in the world. As he later put it, the nation's "scheme of values" during the nineteenth century "drew nearly all the brains into business and impressed the businessman's attitudes upon the soul of the nation." (His Vienna classmate Felix Somary once observed that "assimilating a new invention or a modern process took as many years in Austria as it did months in America.") Schumpeter's sojourn in the United States gave him ample reason to think that his analysis of capitalism in *The Theory of Economic Development* had hit the bull's-eye.[38]

Much as he had done earlier in Europe and Britain, Schumpeter took pains to meet as many important economists as possible. "My mission," he wrote Jacob Hollander of Johns Hopkins, "is to see as much of American universities and men of eminence as I can." In Minneapolis he attended the annual meeting of the American Economic Association. In New Haven he had Thanksgiving dinner with Irving Fisher of Yale, one of the world's leading mathematical economists. In Cambridge he visited Frank Taussig, beginning a long friendship that would be pivotal in his eventual move to Harvard. At Princeton he stayed overnight at the home of Frank Fetter, who chaired that university's Economics Department.[39]

After five months of intense activity, he returned to Austria. In a farewell note to Fetter, he wrote: "I have seen, and given addresses at, seventeen American universities and am taking with me the pleasantest possible impressions of men and institutions. Truly this is a great country and I am awfully sorry to have to leave it. I always felt that in the inspiring company of American colleagues I could turn out much better things than I shall be able to over there. And the personal charm of many of them makes it really hard to leave."[40]

Economics in the United States was now on a par with that in Oxford and Cambridge. It had moved ahead of anything taught on the European Continent except in Vienna. And the sheer number of first-class universities amazed Schumpeter. Meanwhile, his own international reputation was rising like a rocket. By 1914, when he returned to Europe, he was sitting on top of the world.

But there was one very big problem. The world itself was about to explode. The event that affected Schumpeter most during the next ten years had nothing to do with academics, either in Austria or the United States. That event was the First World War. For masses of people, the war and its aftermath transformed almost everything. For Schumpeter, it changed his marriage, his job, his finances, his reputation, and ultimately the country in which he chose to live.

6

War and Politics

The lights are going out all over Europe;
we shall not see them lit again in our lifetime.

BRITISH FOREIGN SECRETARY EDWARD GREY, 1914

THE GREAT WAR, as it was called, proved catastrophic for the entrepreneurial, future-oriented capitalism Schumpeter had portrayed in *The Theory of Economic Development.* It also marked a defeat for Schumpeter personally, for the more he tried to inject himself into affairs of state, the more he
displayed his own political ineptitude.

The war interrupted the trading of goods across national borders, the migration of people, and the easy transfer of money. The advance toward freer markets went into reverse gear. Nobody had yet coined the word "globalization,"
but that phenomenon stood closer to fulfillment in 1914 than it would for the
next seventy-five years.

Ten million soldiers, sailors, and airmen were killed in the Great War, and
twenty million wounded. In addition, about twenty million civilians lost their
lives. The war created the conditions that led to Soviet communism, German
fascism, and World War II. No creative destruction here, just sheer wreckage.[1]

The Great War had been brewing for twenty-five years. It had many causes,
the most conspicuous being a web of alliances designed to protect European
countries from one another. Thus, the Triple Entente (France, Russia, Britain)

was formed as a counterpoise to the Triple Alliance (Germany, Italy, Austria-Hungary). The swift rise of Germany as the strongest nation in Europe had troubled many thoughtful people, including Schumpeter.

Prior to Germany's ascent, Britain had been the world's leading industrial power. In 1870 the British had produced more than half the world's pig iron, a key product of heavy industrialization. But by 1914 Germany's output of pig iron was 1.5 times Britain's, and Germany was exporting more iron and steel than any other country. German firms also exported 35 percent of the electrical goods traded on world markets, 27 percent of the chemicals, and 90 percent of the dyestuffs. A frenzied arms race had developed between Germany and Britain, and a series of deadly new weapons—the submarine, the giant battleship, the tank, the machine gun, poison gas, long-range artillery, and the then-primitive airplane—had brought warfare to a level more lethal than ever.[2]

The spark that ignited the conflagration was the assassination of Emperor Francis Joseph's heir-apparent, Archduke Francis Ferdinand, together with the archduke's wife, Sophie. The killings occurred during the archduke's ill-advised visit to Sarajevo in Bosnia, which Austria-Hungary had annexed in 1908. The shooter, an eighteen-year-old Bosnian Serb named Gavrilo Princip, was the agent of an organized movement for the independence of Balkan Slavs. Following the assassination, diplomats in Vienna invoked the terms of the Triple Alliance. They requested from Kaiser Wilhelm II of Germany what became known as a "blank check" to invade Serbia—and, to their surprise, received it.

The Serbs, rebuffed in all their efforts to placate Vienna, then appealed to their fellow Slavs, the Russians. Each member of the Triple Alliance then proceeded to declare war on each member of the Triple Entente (the "Allies"), and vice versa. Meanwhile, Turkey and Bulgaria joined Germany and Austria-Hungary to form the Central Powers. Thus began in Sarajevo the least justifiable major war ever fought, and by far the bloodiest up to that time.[3]

The first shot was fired only three months after Schumpeter's return from his exhilarating tour of the United States. Neither he nor anyone else then expected that the conflict would persist not for a few months but for four years. In all of human history, the cataclysm of the First World War has been surpassed only by that of the Second, which grew directly out of the First. And despite the unspeakable butchery of 1914–1918, neither side gained or lost much territory during the fighting.[4]

But aggressive diplomatic maneuvering after the war accomplished what military strength alone could not. The peace treaties redrew the boundaries of Central Europe, parts of Africa, and most of the Middle East. They created unstable new countries such as Iraq, Syria, and Jordan. The Allied victory also split the Habsburg Empire into a half dozen pieces. Mercifully, Francis Joseph did not live to see the disintegration, having died in 1916, during the sixty-eighth year of his reign. The treaties reduced Austria, once the core of the vaunted "empire of seventy millions," to an insignificant country of six million—"too small to live and too big to die," as Austrians themselves put it. Whereas the old empire had been about the size of England and France combined, the new Austria was smaller than Portugal.[5]

During the war itself, little fighting occurred in the empire's German-speaking territories, and its forces won a few victories. But the imperial army suffered horrendous losses on the Russian, Romanian, Serbian, and Italian fronts. The final accounting bordered on the incredible: 90 percent of the empire's 7.8 million soldiers were either killed (1.2 million), wounded (3.6 million), or captured/missing (2.2 million). No other army sustained such a high rate of casualties, and for so large a force the percentage is unmatched in the history of warfare itself. The same problems that had plagued the imperial government now disabled its army. Most of the officers were German-speakers, but only a fourth of the enlisted men understood German.[6]

In the months before and after the Allies' armistice with Germany in November 1918, much of Central Europe drifted into left-wing revolution. After the abdication of Francis Joseph's successor, Emperor Charles I, Austria set up its First Republic, which was soon dominated by Socialists elected by a disgruntled populace. Of the six million people in the new Republic, a disproportionate one third lived in the capital city. An ideological split opened between "Red Vienna" and the rest of Austria, which was reluctant to accept the sudden removal of the Habsburgs from the throne—as well as the throne itself. Most of the country's population wanted Austria to become part of Germany. Some people in the mountainous west wished to secede and start new lives as citizens of Switzerland. Meanwhile, the Russian Revolution inaugurated a bloody civil war in Eurasia, which was followed by seventy years of totalitarian dictatorship.[7]

During its first two years, from 1914 to 1916, the war had few consequences for Joseph Schumpeter, who went about his routine as a professor at the University of Graz. He even served briefly as dean of the Law Faculty. But wartime restrictions had a powerful indirect effect on his personal life. Gladys Schumpeter, who had chosen to remain in England during her husband's sojourn in the United States and the months after his return, now found herself cut off from Austria. Joseph wrote her many letters from Graz, all of which she evidently received. But few of her letters to him made it through the Austrian postal system, probably because of censorship.

In November 1915, Gladys—now in her mid-forties—tried to reach her husband through Professor Jacob Hollander of Johns Hopkins University, a German-speaking economist who had been visiting Europe when the war broke out. The two economists had become friendly when Schumpeter had given seminars at Hopkins. Gladys, believing that letters from the neutral United States might find their way through war-torn Europe, wrote Hollander:

> I hope you won't mind my troubling you in these sad times. I am
> the wife of Professor J. A. Schumpeter Graz University Austria—
> who visited you in Feb 1914. Altho' I have written him any
> amount of letters from time to time he has not received any news
> of me since last March. I often receive letters from him urging me
> to let him know how I am. So it has occurred to me that perhaps
> you would be more fortunate in getting a letter through to Austria
> especially if it were written in German. If you would be so kind as
> to tell him that you have heard from me and that I am quite all
> right and as happy as one can be under such sad circumstances—
> that I have constantly written him and that I have received many
> letters from him.[8]

Hollander forwarded Gladys's news to Schumpeter, who thanked him for acting "as messenger of conjugal affection . . . as I have indeed not heard for months from my wife, your kindness has relieved me from considerable anxiety." Hollander then wrote Gladys, enclosing Schumpeter's letter to him. She responded warmly, thanking him also for his offer of financial help. "Fortunately, this is not my trouble, but I feel just as touched and grateful as if I had accepted your most thoughtful and generous offer." Schumpeter likely sent Gladys what money he could during the war, along with his many letters.[9]

But lines of communication continued in a disrupted state. The war lasted four years, and the postwar situation remained chaotic for about three more. Contact between husband and wife gradually dwindled. By 1920, not having laid eyes on Gladys since 1913, Schumpeter began to list himself as "unmarried." In this way, the marriage came to a de facto end without any formal breakup. Schumpeter did not take the trouble to get a divorce, and that oversight would cause him serious problems in the future.[10]

He had resumed teaching at Graz in the summer of 1914. In December he received his notice of conscription into the army but was exempted from service because he was the university's only economics professor. He continued his academic work and, despite a heavy teaching load, produced a substantial body of writing. He also began to plan for the establishment of a new economics journal. Frustrated by his solitude in Graz, he corresponded with the many scholars in Europe, Britain, and America whom he had taken such trouble to meet. Meanwhile, he published dozens of reviews and articles, a brief treatise on "The Past and Future of Social Science," and a third book, which was an excellent short history of economic thought from 1750 to 1900. In several of these works he continued to plead for a broad, methodologically tolerant approach to economics.[11]

In 1916 he wrote a long and very revealing letter to his friend Paul Siebeck, a prominent German publisher. He proposed to go forward not only with the new economics journal but with several other ventures as well. He described two big projects he was working on and outlined a series of six shorter books that would incorporate the results of his recent research, teaching, and public lecturing. Siebeck responded with enthusiasm, tempered only a bit by the uncertainties of the war.[12]

Schumpeter's plan for so many projects was typically bold and ambitious. Yet he was quite serious, and his prospectus to Siebeck was not unrealistic. By 1915, the year he turned thirty-two, he had already written three significant books, twenty articles appearing in six journals based in four countries, and over sixty book reviews. But because of the war, most of his joint plans with Siebeck never came to fruition. From 1916 through the end of the war in November 1918, he continued to write articles and reviews, but at a slower pace because he began to involve himself heavily in public affairs. Even so, two of the articles he did manage to produce became classics.[13]

Meanwhile, Schumpeter's move into the public arena again raised the question of personal identity. Was he married? Yes and no. He was not unmarried, but he had not seen his wife since the war began. Was he a professor at Graz? Yes and no. He continued to teach there, but he traveled to Vienna whenever he could. And even if his mind had been completely clear about how he wanted to live his life, the overwhelming reality of the war pulled his emotions in several different directions.

At heart, Schumpeter was a pacifist who saw no good reason why Austria should even be involved in the war. He had no taste for the bellicose "German-national beer-house" mentality, as he called it. An unabashed Anglophile, he remained at the same time a loyal Habsburg subject, and in this sense he wanted neither side to win or lose. He wished to do what he could to minimize the war's horrors, but in Graz he felt "pretty much isolated . . . totally cut off from any possibility of being effective." And he was exceedingly wary of the motives and methods of Germany, Austria's ally.[14]

As the war ground on, with battle deaths reaching into the millions, shortages of food and fuel became common, and prices rose in an inflationary spiral. By 1916 it became clear to Schumpeter that no matter who won the war, things would never be the same. "The signs of the times are grim," he wrote, and opportunities for peace were going by the board. His own government paid no attention to offers of mediation coming from the United States, a neutral country about which Schumpeter had learned much during his recent visit. "Financially as well as politically," he wrote, "America could now become of the greatest significance for us." As the government in Vienna dithered, Schumpeter accurately predicted that Germany's "escalation of submarine warfare must alienate the United States as well as strengthen the military sentiment in England."[15]

He soon became obsessed with the war's potential consequences, and three in particular: the fate of the Habsburg monarchy, the viability of the Austro-Hungarian economy, and the future relationship between Austria and Germany. This last issue had been festering for more than two hundred years. During all of the eighteenth century and most of the nineteenth, Austria had contended with Prussia for influence among the scores of other German-speaking principalities. Some of these were large, some small. Some were governed as free cities, others as tiny remnants of the Holy Roman Empire. As the nineteenth century wore on, a customs union of about forty German-speaking states evolved that did not include Austria. That arrangement presaged a Prussian-led drive for a unified Germany.

Though much smaller in population than the Habsburg monarchy, Prussia in 1866 defeated Austria in a short war. Then, under the direction of its great leader Otto von Bismarck, Prussia welded numerous independent states into the North German Federation and defeated France in the Franco-Prussian war of 1870–1871. In 1871 Bismarck established the new German Empire, with its capital in Berlin. With extraordinary political skill, he brought Germany to a position of European supremacy. In 1890 the impulsive young Emperor Wilhelm II forced Bismarck out of office, but by that time his work was done.

Bismarck had not wanted to include the German-speaking regions of Habsburg Austria in the German Empire, preferring instead to use Francis Joseph's domains as a buffer whose foreign policy he himself would guide from Berlin. Nor did the Habsburg monarchy itself embrace the idea of unification. About 97 percent of German Austrians were Catholics, and they distrusted the Protestant Prussians. Habsburg ministers knew that in any showdown Berlin would dominate Vienna, Austria would lose its independence, and the Austro-Hungarian Empire would come to an end.[16]

Yet once the Great War started, the prospect of unification appealed to many German-speaking citizens of Austria's western provinces. Union with Germany might split the Habsburg monarchy, but it would thereby liberate German-speaking Austrians. No longer would they have to bicker with Hungarians, Czechs, Balkan Slavs, and others who had reduced imperial affairs to bedlam. However the war turned out, the empire's relationship to Germany was certain to change. And in 1916, Austrian advocates of unification began to press their case. Some did so from right-wing premises of a "Greater Germany." Others saw an opportunity to combine both countries' working classes into a left-leaning social-democratic majority that could usher in a more just and modern society.

It was against this convoluted background that Schumpeter decided to enter politics. Like many other Austrian intellectuals, he was disillusioned by the ongoing war and appalled by the prospect of unification with Germany. He thought it might be possible for the Habsburg Empire to negotiate a separate

peace with the Allies and thereby preserve the monarchy while fending off se-
ducers from Germany. As he wrote to a friend in 1916, the Austro-Hungarian
government might actually take the lead and "speak an authoritative word of
reconciliation." Certainly it had "no part in the great confrontation between
Germany and England."[17]

In the spring of 1915 a member of Germany's Parliament had published a
book proposing a customs union with the German-speaking regions of the
Habsburg Empire. Later in that year the German government sent a confidential note to the Foreign Ministry in Vienna suggesting a new customs arrangement that would include a common external tariff. This plan would enhance
the economic security of all German-speaking peoples against future enemies,
no matter who won the Great War.

Schumpeter knew that the consolidation of Germany itself had begun in
just this way, decades earlier. Fearing a similar fusion between Germany and
Austria, he sent a letter to Heinrich Lammasch, one of his former teachers at
the University of Vienna. Lammasch was a member of Parliament, an inter-
nationally known constitutional lawyer, and a pacifist. "Consider what all this
means," Schumpeter wrote. "A Prussian-Lutheran-militaristic Mitteleuropa
would from now on confront the rest of the world like a predatory animal."
The nature of "*that* Austria which we know and love would cease to exist."[18]

For Lammasch's private use within the government, Schumpeter prepared a
memorandum warning against the danger of a closer relationship with Germany. In vehement language, he suggested several steps to prevent it, beginning with the recall of Parliament, which the emperor had temporarily dismissed at the start of the war. Working with the civil service, Parliament might
design a new federated empire, to be governed by a "tory democracy" of the
British type that Schumpeter so admired (he used those very words).[19]

Later in 1916 he sent a second memo to Lammasch and other associates in
Vienna. He noted how badly the diplomatic position of Austria-Hungary had
deteriorated and hinted that it should now make a separate peace with the
Allies. Otherwise, "we will be economically conquered by Germany and politically dominated by Hungary." In addition, the empire will fall into "a precarious position vis-à-vis Russia." It will encounter "total uncertainty in the position towards Italy" and "the permanent enmity of the Western powers." The

Habsburg monarchy would therefore be the greatest loser of all participants in the Great War.[20]

The new emperor Charles I, only twenty-nine years old in 1916, was less inclined to continue fighting than Francis Joseph had been, and Charles's advisers did take tentative steps toward a separate peace. This activity, Schumpeter wrote in still another letter, "has roused the imperial German sensibilities," creating "an exceedingly delicate situation." Austria-Hungary was now trapped between the enormous power of Germany on the one hand and the growing strength of the Allies on the other. In Vienna, the numerous factions contending for influence were beginning to harden their positions, and the level of political intrigue was ratcheting steadily upward.[21]

By this time Schumpeter had become thoroughly immersed in politics and had started to imagine for himself an active role in the government. This was natural enough for a patriot who could see where the war was taking his country. But his new ambitions drew him into the kind of political alliance-building for which he had no talent. What he wanted, as a friend of his once put it, "was the gradual conversion of an absolute [monarchy] into a constitutional monarchy" of the British type. Yet he had no experience with vicious infighting for truly high stakes. He had spent his career in cloistered universities; playing international politics during a deadly world war was a far cry from dueling with librarians and dealing with student boycotts. "I do not feel completely at ease in this milieu, to put it mildly," he wrote in 1917.[22]

Caught up in the excitement of public affairs, he had again become uncertain about his proper role. Still, one never knows until one tries, and Schumpeter had ample reason to believe in himself. He had traveled the world and measured his abilities against brilliant people everywhere. Thirty-four years old in 1917, he was not prepared to watch great events pass him by. He wanted to take some influential role in public affairs, preferably as a government minister or perhaps as a newspaper columnist. Many of his letters argue for setting up a paper in Vienna to promote the policies he favored.[23]

Here, Schumpeter's personal quandary reflected the dilemmas of his generation. It was very difficult for Europeans who lived through the Great War to reconcile its horrors with the culture they thought they knew. They had grown up believing that science, capitalism, and the spread of "European civilization" would bring continuous progress. Yet from 1914 to 1918 they witnessed, year after year, an endless pageant of senseless slaughter—the antithesis of progress. In the midst of an apocalypse, it seemed unthinkable to sit by and do nothing.

IN APRIL 1917, the month when the United States entered the war because of Germany's unrestricted use of submarines against ships of neutral as well as enemy countries, Schumpeter sent still a third memorandum to Vienna. In thirty strongly worded pages, he denounced the new level of submarine warfare as a horrible mistake "in whose consequences the [Austro-Hungarian] Monarchy . . . had unfortunately become entangled"—just as he had predicted more than a year earlier. He hoped that the Americans' attention might be confined to the naval war in the Atlantic and to land battles on the Western Front, where the opposing armies continued to massacre each other. He implied that Austria could survive only by making a separate peace while there was still a window of opportunity. The Americans had declared war on Germany in April 1917 but not yet on Austria-Hungary.[24]

They did so the following December, eight months after Schumpeter sent his third memorandum. To his great disappointment, the window of mediation was now closed. He later wrote that the United States had declared war on Germany in April not because of its own national or economic interest but because "moral forces have real power among the people there. Whether right or wrong, the World War appears to the American people as an illegal act of aggression—one that every civilized people is obliged to repel, just as it is every man's obligation to rush to aid when he observes that someone is suddenly mugged on the street."[25]

Schumpeter was very pleased when Heinrich Lammasch, to whom he had been sending his memoranda, became the new prime minister in 1917. He now composed a fourth memo, this one on rising Czech nationalism. He respected the Czechs, and he believed that the Habsburg Empire might be preserved by making it a more democratic Triple Monarchy, with a third capital at Prague in addition to the two at Vienna and Budapest. "All nationalist groups," he wrote, "have of late become too radicalized." This was dangerous in itself, and Schumpeter sought a policy "which in essence pacifies them and eliminates the worst sources of friction. Otherwise the monarchy will perish."[26]

At this point Schumpeter began to envision a cabinet post for himself, perhaps as minister of commerce. In June 1918 he angled for this position with Joseph Redlich, who became a minister in the Lammasch government. The record of this conversation, preserved in Redlich's diary, reveals Schumpeter's political ineptitude: "Yesterday morning Professor Schumpeter paid a visit for two hours. I gathered from his talks that I am supposed by 'conservative' circles, whose advisor Schumpeter likes to regard himself, to become a minister . . . but that these circles distrusted me. He, however, had successfully used his influence that they would not oppose me . . . Bubbles! Nothing to it! . . . His mixture of praise, flattery, and bold disclosure of his distrust against me represents a peculiar medley. This man really believes that I am intriguing in order to attain power."[27]

During the war Schumpeter never got the position he wanted, even though he became much better known in government circles and no one doubted his intellectual abilities. He simply lacked the tact and discretion necessary to succeed in public life. Late in 1918, for example, he and his friend Felix Somary had a long discussion with Max Weber, whose work Schumpeter much admired. Their meeting took place in a coffeehouse just across from the University of Vienna, where Weber had recently become a professor. Soon the conversation turned to the Russian Revolution, and Schumpeter said that at last Marxism would have a practical test. Weber replied that the result was likely to be catastrophic, because the Bolsheviks were so brutal. "That may well be," Schumpeter said, "but it would be a good laboratory to test our theories." "A laboratory heaped with human corpses!" said Weber. "Every anatomy classroom is the same thing," replied Schumpeter.

As the conversation went on, Somary recalled, "Weber became more vehement and raised his voice, as Schumpeter for his part became more sarcastic and lowered his. All around us the café customers stopped their card games and listened eagerly, until the point when Weber sprang to his feet and rushed out into the Ringstrasse, crying 'This is intolerable!'" Meanwhile, "Schumpeter, who had remained behind with me, only smiled and said 'How can someone carry on like that in a coffeehouse!'"[28]

In 1918 Schumpeter delivered a lecture in Vienna that he turned into an article on Austria's prospects during and after the war. His arguments anticipate the issues he himself was soon to face as a high-ranking cabinet minister. And his analysis is so broad and insightful that the essay is still required reading in many university courses today. Titled "The Crisis of the Tax State," it examines the connections among war, taxation, and capitalism. (By the term "tax state," Schumpeter meant the government of a capitalist country.) The essay's contents range over history, economics, and sociology, displaying in full the author's learning and originality.[29]

Taking his characteristic long-term view, Schumpeter begins by referring to pre-capitalist times. He says that someone who analyzes a state's fiscal history—that is, how it chooses to spend its revenues—"discerns the thunder of world history more clearly than anywhere else." He argues that of all forces, war was the most important in the rise of large nation-states. Once a major war started, national survival required a modern tax system to pay for military expenditures. Historically, the challenges posed to Britain by France, to Austria by Turkey, and to Germany by Russia and France played key roles in the tighter unification of all six countries, on both sides.[30]

For the nation-builders at that time, it had proved fortuitous that their military adventures coincided with the rise of entrepreneurial capitalism. Only such a productive economic system made it possible for national governments to collect sufficient taxes to fight their wars without at the same time destroying individuals' incentives to work. If taxes ever rose high enough to compromise those incentives, then entrepreneurship would falter and the tax state might collapse.

But assuming that this did not happen, the state would become an entity whose functions reached far beyond military action. In this new setting, "Taxes were no longer raised merely for the purposes for which the prince had asked them" but also for nonmilitary functions such as free public education. Under wise management, the state could even reduce tax *rates* in such a way that tax *revenues* increased—entrepreneurial profit being "the premium which capitalism attaches to innovation." Ever the Anglophile, Schumpeter cited William E. Gladstone and the younger William Pitt as exemplars in shaping good tax policies.[31]

In the case of Habsburg Austria, excessive taxes had reduced innovation by causing entrepreneurs "to migrate to countries of lower taxation." Generalizing broadly, Schumpeter went on to argue that excessive demands for social services in any country could stop the flow of golden eggs by killing the capitalist goose.[32]

But capitalism is such a uniquely powerful system that it can withstand immense pressures. Referring to the Great War, Schumpeter pointed to the ability of strong tax states such as Britain, France, and Germany to finance "the murderous insanity which devastates Europe." Weaker states such as the Habsburg Empire were also managing to do it, but only by mortgaging their futures.[33]

Was it possible for his own country to survive economically after 1918? Yes, says Schumpeter, but only with great difficulty. The proper path to recovery would be simple enough: first a "capital levy" (tax on liquid assets) to control inflation; next a plan for gradual discharge of the war debt; then measures to attract flows of capital from abroad; and above all the encouragement of entrepreneurial ventures at home.

Entrepreneurship, credit, and innovation must be strengthened by any means possible. "I am not in the habit of crowning our bourgeoisie with laurel wreaths," Schumpeter wrote. "However, it can do *exactly* what is needed now . . . Marx himself, if he lived today, could not be of a different opinion. And he would laugh grimly at those of his disciples who welcome the present administrative [state-directed] economy which is the most undemocratic thing there is." A widespread socialization of industry might be necessary as a means of achieving political fairness; but any such movement must be preceded for many years by the kind of "competitive economy" that alone can generate enough material wealth to rescue Austria from ruin.[34]

Thus, policy makers *could* accomplish the "salvation of the state from shame and evil." Certainly they "need not fail from technical difficulties." The question was whether they had the courage to carry out appropriate measures. "The man who is to solve this task needs real political and fiscal ability—and he needs that brilliance of willpower and word which nations trust."[35]

When he delivered the lecture that became "The Crisis of the Tax State," Schumpeter might or might not have had himself in mind as the man to resolve the economic crisis. But a few months later, he joined the cabinet, becoming state secretary of finance in Austria's First Republic—the equivalent of the secretary of the treasury in the United States, the chancellor of the exchequer in Britain, and the minister of finance in Germany, France, and other countries.

Schumpeter's route to this high office was extremely circuitous. It led through Berlin and was laid out not by his fellow conservatives but by the Marxists Rudolf Hilferding, Emil Lederer, and Otto Bauer. All three had been his friends and classmates in Böhm-Bawerk's 1905 seminar at the University of Vienna. After graduation, Hilferding had become active in politics and was destined for a key role in the Finance Ministry of postwar Germany. Lederer had embarked on a productive career in university teaching. And Otto Bauer, after serving in the army and being wounded on the Russian front, had returned to Vienna to become a leader of the Austrian socialist movement. Unlike Schumpeter, Bauer favored unification with Germany. He dreamed of promoting human rights in a postwar socialist republic comprising all German-speaking peoples.

Early in 1919 Hilferding and Lederer arranged for Schumpeter to join Germany's Socialization Commission, an eleven-member body meeting in Berlin. Its task was to recommend improvements in the structure of the German coal industry, whose workers included numerous left-wing revolutionaries. Hilferding and Lederer were themselves members of the Socialization Commission, and their own politics lay to the left of Schumpeter's. But they knew their friend to be an astute economist, and in any case the commission's assignment was more technical than political.

Schumpeter accepted the invitation and moved to Berlin, taking another leave from the University of Graz. During two months of work on the commission, he argued that any policy toward the coal industry should be guided by the principle of economic efficiency. He recommended a public corporation that might turn into a profit-making entity and create funds to alleviate food shortages. In the end, the commission proposed to "socialize" the industry (make it more responsible to the country's interests), without actually nationalizing it. Schumpeter signed the final report with no regret that he seemed to be endorsing quasi-socialist principles. Short-term settlements of this kind were mere details to him.[36]

In February 1919, while he was still in Berlin, the Austrian republic held its first elections. Schumpeter's friend Otto Bauer, parliamentary leader of the Social Democratic Party, became foreign minister in the new coalition government headed by Chancellor Karl Renner, another socialist. Along with proclaiming the First Republic, Parliament declared Austria's intention to become part of Germany, a step that had been one of Otto Bauer's primary goals. Bauer then put forward Schumpeter's name for the Finance Ministry, on the recommendation of Rudolf Hilferding.[37]

By this unusual route Schumpeter, a conservative who had no party affiliation and no independent power base, became a high cabinet minister in a Socialist Austrian government. The food rationing begun during the war was still in effect, inflation ran wild, and no one knew how long Austria would exist as a nation independent of Germany. There was real potential for a Communist revolution, as had happened not only in Russia but also in Munich and Budapest. Schumpeter's acceptance of a job that any person with his knowledge should have seen to be impossible was testimony to his patriotism, ambition, or naïveté—and perhaps all three. He had achieved his goal of becoming a celebrity, but at a moment when success could hardly have been less likely.[38]

He now moved into the grandiose Baroque headquarters of the Finance Ministry and set to work. Consulting almost nobody, he worked to devise a program for Austria's economic rescue. As always, he looked to the long term and to the central roles of entrepreneurship and credit. His plan aimed at opening markets abroad for Austrian products and at attracting foreign investment in Austrian firms. His program for freer trade and international loans anticipated in many respects the Marshall Plan of 1947.

Technically, Schumpeter's *Finanzplan* had a number of merits. As one of his students later described it, "The plan [was] the only one which could possibly have saved the situation." But the likelihood of its adoption was close to zero, because of the vengeance with which the Allies were drafting the peace treaties. The harsh terms of those accords meant that Schumpeter and his cabinet colleagues were engaging in an almost meaningless task. The victorious Allies were not going to grant them either the latitude or the resources to govern effectively.[39]

And even if that had not been so, the *Finanzplan* might have failed on purely domestic terms. For one thing, it required that inflation be brought under control through a capital levy under which the government would confiscate a percentage of all liquid assets held by companies and citizens. Through this process, enough money would be taken out of circulation to stop the inflationary spiral. The idea of imposing such a levy had been the focus of many discussions during the war, but there were formidable obstacles to carrying it out.

Schumpeter in 1919, as the new Austrian Republic's secretary of state for finance. He was now thirty-six years old, and this official photograph reflects his sense of the daunting tasks he faced.

The same was true of Schumpeter's proposal to sell shares in Austrian companies to foreigners, as a way of drawing new capital into the country. Again, the policy had much merit but was certain to create vehement opposition. Many voters viewed it as a fire sale of Austria's few remaining assets, and Schumpeter's reputation suffered for years afterward because of one large transaction that actually took place.[40]

Overall, his *Finanzplan* was doomed almost from the start. Not only was he himself a nonsocialist member of a Socialist government, but he showed no skill in pushing his proposals forward. He made numerous public speeches but presented his ideas much too bluntly. After an interview with Schumpeter on the capital levy, a leading Vienna newspaper reported that people would be responsible for registering with the government most of their "movable property"—cash, stocks and bonds, gold, silver, and jewelry above a certain value. The Finance Ministry would then assign an appropriate capital tax for each citizen. As Schumpeter himself tactlessly put it, "The operation ends in the furnace in which all cash and titles which fall into the hands of the state must be burned." Metaphorically charged statements like these could only confuse and alarm Austria's people.[41]

Schumpeter's colleagues in the cabinet, few of whom knew him well, could hardly be expected to support know-it-all pronouncements by a young professor from Graz, no matter how brilliant he was supposed to be. Nor did they appreciate Schumpeter's intrigues with foreign diplomats, and sometimes even with their own political enemies. His habit of vetting proposals with the press before clearing them with members of Parliament also did not sit well. Nor did his conversing freely with journalists about financing the overthrow of the Communist regime in Budapest.[42]

Foreign Minister Otto Bauer, who evidently knew nothing of Schumpeter's memoranda denouncing unification with Germany, became very angry with him over that issue. Joining with Germany was not just a personal goal of Bauer's, it was the official policy of the new government and, as Schumpeter himself later estimated, the wish of "at least three quarters of the population." Bauer also wanted to socialize Austria's industries, and he opposed Schumpeter's plan for the full payment of all state debts. Soon it became clear that Schumpeter's incumbency was going to be brief. In the end, his ministry lasted from March to October 1919, a time of complex political maneuvering, violence in the streets of Vienna, and near-starvation for thousands of the city's people.[43]

In addition to all this complication, the postwar settlements were being worked out by the war's victors while Schumpeter was still in office, and his conduct had an awkward effect. As a prominent journalist in Vienna wrote privately in December 1919: "What made his continued membership in the Cabinet impossible was above all his objective opposition to the policy of the Government . . . While the Government and [its] peace negotiators did everything in their power to prove the [economic] impossibility of the peace treaty, Schumpeter gave one optimistic speech after another in which he explained that he could restore the economic health of Austria in three to four years."[44]

These speeches were predicated on the resilient power of capitalism and on Austria's willingness to pay the price necessary for recovery. Yet Schumpeter gave pessimistic speeches as well. Watching his overall performance, his former teacher Friedrich von Wieser wondered why such a "friend of England and hater of the Germans" had entered the cabinet in the first place. Even so, Wieser could not help admiring him. "He is not misled by prevalent sentiment," the professor wrote in his diary. "Schumpeter has courage, an asset which cannot be over-praised."[45]

CENTRAL EUROPE CONTINUED in turmoil long after the war ended, partly because the treaties of Versailles (which addressed the German Empire) and St. Germain (which dealt with the Austro-Hungarian) were so merciless. In November 1918, when Germany had asked for peace, it had already begun to lose the war, but its own army was still deep inside France. Germany itself had not been invaded, though severe hardships on the home front were beginning to foment revolution. In the eyes of the German and Austrian negotiators, the peace was to be based on Woodrow Wilson's Fourteen Points—acceptable terms, but a very far cry from what actually ensued. Rather than Wilson's dream of "a war to end all war," the reality turned out to be "a peace to end all peace."[46]

Schumpeter never forgot the terms of these treaties and what he regarded as the Allies' fundamental dishonesty toward Germany and Austria. And twenty-five years later, during World War II, he found himself impossibly conflicted over the prospect of another 1919—if not something much worse. By 1943 the Americans were offering nothing like Wilson's Fourteen Points or any other negotiated settlement. Instead, they were demanding the "unconditional surrender" of both Germany and Japan, a prospect that made Schumpeter shudder. The difference in Americans' own perceptions of 1918 and 1945 can still be read in the language of the nation's remembrance: November 11, 1918, is called Armistice Day or Veterans' Day, in contrast with V-E Day and V-J Day in 1945, commemorating not peace or personal sacrifice but victory in Europe and Japan.

In 1919, as John Maynard Keynes was advising the British negotiators at Versailles, he proposed some of the same economic provisions for Germany contained in Schumpeter's *Finanzplan* for Austria. But when Keynes saw what was happening—that the treaty was instead going to require huge financial reparations while at the same time depriving Germany of the resources to pay them—he abruptly left Versailles and returned to England. There, with an eloquence born of fury, he wrote *The Economic Consequences of the Peace,* a book that made him famous throughout the world.

Meanwhile, the Treaty of St. Germain matched that of Versailles in its ruthlessness. It dissolved the Habsburg Empire, setting the stage for the economic ruin of Austria. When the draft of this document appeared during the summer of 1919, Schumpeter, still in office, publicly denounced it as a "death sentence" for his country. The treaty was "totally senseless" in its economic provisions: "With this, Austria has lost all possibility to live. No credit institution, no bank, no savings institution could survive if this decision becomes effective. The masses of Vienna must become poorer and poorer." Schumpeter added that the treaty "need only be ratified to make a catastrophe inevitable." It even imposed unfavorable prices on the export of timber, one of the few products Austria could sell abroad at a profit. As an aphorism of the time put it, the victorious Allies had given the industry of the old empire to the Czechs and its agriculture to the Hungarians. They had left German-speaking Austrians with some alpine scenery, the Viennese bureaucracy, and the imperial war debt.[47]

The treaty severed all ties between Austria and Hungary and awarded the province of Transylvania to Romania. It ceded the large northeastern province of Galicia to the new Polish Republic. To the west, other territories went to Italy. To the south, the Habsburg provinces of Slovenia, Bosnia, and Croatia joined Serbia to form what eventually became Yugoslavia.[48]

Most painfully for German Austria, the treaty merged the industrialized Czech areas of Bohemia and Moravia with the Slovakian parts of Hungary and Ruthenia to create the new country of Czechoslovakia. Nearly four million German-speaking Austrians who might have been placed within either Austria or Germany now found themselves inside Czechoslovakia. Twenty years later, in October 1938, this situation furnished a pretext for Adolf Hitler's invasion of the *Sudetenland* just across Germany's southeastern border, "freeing" German-speakers from alien control by the Czechs.

Except for the ban on unification with Germany, the treaties of 1919 enacted Schumpeter's worst nightmares. Now there was no possibility for an Austrian recovery led by local entrepreneurship. Instead, Schumpeter's successors in the Finance Ministry, most of whom also served brief terms, had to rely on the United States and Britain for relief shipments. By this time, the citizens of Vienna were subsisting on about 1,300 calories per day—about two thirds of the nourishment they needed. And as in Germany, wartime inflation turned into peacetime hyperinflation. By 1922 the proverbial wheelbarrows of currency necessary to buy a loaf of bread had become a reality. As Schumpeter said, the treaties might have been somewhat defensible on political terms but not at all on economic ones. They blew to smithereens the economic unity and trading patterns of the Danube River basin, of which Vienna was the center.[49]

With these measures, the "Carthaginian Peace," as Keynes called it, was complete. He was referring to the ancient Romans' salting of the farms of conquered Carthage to prevent the growth of new crops. But what had now been effectively sown were the seeds of a second world war.

For Schumpeter personally, thirty years of relatively good luck ran out in 1918. The odyssey that took him from Triesch to Graz to Vienna—then on to England and Egypt, to Czernowitz, back to Graz, then to America, and finally to celebrity as Austria's finance minister—was now just a set of memories, artifacts of a bygone world. In 1920, at the age of thirty-seven, he faced a very uncertain future.

7

Gran Rifiuto

A man must learn from his mistakes . . .
from MAKING THEM, not from being saved from them.

SHELBY FOOTE, letter to Walker Percy, 1952

SCHUMPETER LIKED TO speak of the years during and after his time at the Finance Ministry as his *gran rifiuto*—an Italian phrase meaning great waste. During these years he took active roles in both government and business. He learned about the perils of starting new companies, the hazards of commerce and industry, and the fickleness of finance. He made many mistakes, but his first-hand lessons about the nature of capitalism proved priceless when he returned to his true calling in the academy.

In 1922, three years after his departure from the Finance Ministry, Austria was still in deep economic trouble. Conditions had seemed to improve, only to decline once more. In a newspaper article Schumpeter summed up the situation: "Austria is like a patient who has had practically all his organs injured by an explosive catastrophe. Such a patient cannot simply come to the physician and ask for a pill to make him well; rather, it is necessary to cure each organ through special methods . . . That would indeed be a work of years, but it comes down to the psychological effect [on entrepreneurs] that would ensue if this work were begun in earnest."[1]

When he wrote these words in 1922, Schumpeter was not an academic observer but one of those entrepreneurs himself. After departing from government service in 1919, he had returned to Graz only to find that he had little heart for teaching. Being a professor now seemed just a way to earn a living, and he did little to reinvigorate his academic career. He pursued but then rejected a tenured offer to teach in Berlin at the School for Trade and Business. And in 1921, having already taken several leaves of absence, he resigned from the University of Graz.[2]

He had relished the celebrity of being finance minister and, like many people who hold power, was loath to leave the stage. Determined to stay in Vienna and to keep living well, he decided to try to get rich. He had earned a small fortune years before in Cairo and saw no reason why he could not do it again. This time he would assume still another fresh identity, as banker and professional investor.

His adventures began during the winter of 1920–1921, when Austria's Parliament awarded him a license to operate a bank in Vienna. His friends in the government thought he had been mistreated as finance minister, and they fixed on this bank "concession" as appropriate recompense. The concession carried no specified value, but as a charter to run a bank it had high potential, since there were only twenty-odd banks of much importance in Vienna. Schumpeter might have sold the concession right away or held onto it until better economic times arrived. Instead, he decided to execute it quickly himself.[3]

That decision led to an alliance with a financier named Artur Klein, senior partner of the private Biedermann Bank, Vienna's oldest. The Biedermann family, Jewish natives of nearby Bratislava, had founded the bank in 1792. During the nineteenth century they had financed the first railroad in Austria and many other enterprises. Associating themselves with the Rothschilds, they had also opened a branch of the bank in London. In the meantime, the Biedermanns had become Catholics and joined Vienna's aristocratic "second society." The last male Biedermann died in battle during World War I.

After the war, the bank fell into trouble, like almost all banks in countries on the losing side. It still had high prestige but was bereft of funds. The capable Artur Klein, as head of the firm, decided that the best route to new resources would be a formal incorporation of the bank, which for 130 years had been run as a partnership. If he now offered shares to investors, he could bring in fresh money. The bank could then lend out this money, operating in the way investment banks do today. But for the privilege of incorporation, Klein needed a concession from Parliament.

Knowing Schumpeter to have such a concession, Klein offered the former finance minister a large number of shares in the Biedermann Bank, as well as its chairmanship and presidency. In return, Schumpeter would transfer his concession to the bank, enabling it to incorporate. The role he himself would take in the bank's management remained uncertain.[4]

From Schumpeter's perspective, this arrangement served several purposes. It would keep him in Vienna and would likely make him rich. His annual salary was set at a sum equivalent in the early twenty-first century to about $250,000. As an officer of the bank, he would also enjoy an automatic line of credit in the form of overdrafts. He could draw on this credit for his own investments, and he had some reason to be hopeful about the prospects of Austrian companies. As he said in 1921, with typical optimism, "The level of business is growing after all, and the financial and commercial infrastructure is still largely intact." Most importantly, he would receive bank stock of significant value. Within two years, he held 90,000 of the outstanding 780,000 shares, which made him the bank's second largest stockholder.[5]

Schumpeter now had an opportunity to put into action the principles he had emphasized in his academic writing: the importance of entrepreneurship for economic growth and the key role of banks in creating credit for funding new ventures. In the particular situation of 1921, however, there was plenty of poison in his new Eden. Austria's spiral of inflation continued, much as Schumpeter himself had predicted in "The Crisis of the Tax State." Between 1920 and the end of 1922, the national currency proceeded to inflate by a factor of 2,100. Among its many ill consequences, high inflation meant that a bank lending out funds without providing for interim adjustments could expect to be repaid in devalued currency, thereby losing a lot of money.

The management problems facing any bank in this context of significant inflation were very daunting. Customers trying to move their funds rapidly in and out of their accounts caused huge increases in the number of transactions. During Schumpeter's years at the Biedermann Bank, for example, inflationary pressures forced the Deutsche Bank, Germany's strongest financial services company, to double its staff even though the number of its accounts increased by less than 10 percent. The Deutsche Bank's staff grew to 37,000 employees, a very large number for a financial institution at that time.[6]

Once he took up his new position, Schumpeter left staffing and almost all other management decisions to Artur Klein, the real professional. Not for him the daily routine of entering debits and credits, or even the strategic planning necessary to ensure the bank's prosperity. Schumpeter oversaw meetings of the Board of Directors, but by mutual agreement with Klein he took no role in running the bank. Instead, he devoted his energies to personal investments, and for nearly three years he performed capably as a money manager. He did not become fabulously wealthy, but he did accumulate a significant fortune in an unfavorable economic climate.[7]

Meanwhile, he lived very well. He kept up two elaborate residences in addition to Johanna's original Kéler apartment. He dined at the city's most expensive restaurants. He bought both a racehorse and a riding horse. He continued his womanizing and seemed to enjoy mocking protocols of all kinds. Often he behaved more like a free-spirited artist in possession of inherited wealth than a conventional businessman, let alone a banker. Inevitably, his conduct attracted the attention of the press. In a long and critical piece, a reporter for Vienna's version of the *Wall Street Journal* described him this way: "A smart brain, a witty writer, a handsome chap, whose doctoral hat sits somewhat askew on his head—and over it, a pale blue cloud from playing the comedian—that is Schumpeter."[8]

Then, just as he was approaching his goal of great personal wealth, disaster struck Austria's already troubled economy. In 1924 Vienna's stock market crashed, losing three fourths of its value. This calamity took most investors, including Schumpeter, completely by surprise. He held shares in numerous firms, including several startups. When the market collapse killed these companies, he lost most of his money. He still had his position at the Biedermann Bank, but soon he was plunged into debt because of another bank's refusal to honor its commitments to companies in which he held big investments.[9]

At this point he resigned from the Biedermann Bank, under pressure from his fellow directors. He reimbursed the bank for his overdrafts, using loans from friends. Eventually, he paid off all his debts, but this took many years of hard work that "I would not wish on any one of my enemies." As a friend later put it, Schumpeter had "an almost feudal sense of honor."[10]

Even though he had done nothing unethical, his recent status in the Finance Ministry made him an inviting target for journalists. The most conspicuous new charge had to do with his business relationship with a former classmate at

Schumpeter in 1923 at forty years of age: private banker and man-about-town.

the Theresianum who in fact did cross the line into illegality. Schumpeter had personally guaranteed loans that this acquaintance had taken out for the completion of a new glass-making factory. The official investigations cleared Schumpeter, but his ill-advised loan guarantee bankrupted him.[11]

That single misjudgment, he later wrote, "meant for me complete financial ruin." Angry about charges of chicanery when the real reason for his downfall was misplaced loyalty, he went on to say that "whoever expresses moral qualms about my behavior should do this himself"—that is, go through the same ordeal—if he wished to be taken seriously. For more than a decade after 1925, Schumpeter committed almost all of the money he received from his writings and his many public lectures to paying off the balance he owed from this one incident.[12]

Because of the bad economic situation in postwar Austria, it is difficult to assess Schumpeter's performance as a businessman. On the one hand, he made a great deal of money during the early part of his new career, and that was an impressive achievement. On the other hand, he lacked the cold-blooded sense of timing that characterizes superior money managers. Reluctant to unload his stocks as their value fell, he remained loyal to failing firms—especially the entrepreneurial companies for which he had a personal affinity as well as a financial stake.[13]

In the end, the experience of making and then losing a large sum of money taught him more than books ever could about issues vital to his research. He later wrote that in capitalist economies, rewards and punishments for good and bad judgment come quickly and cruelly. "Prizes and penalties are measured in pecuniary terms. Going up and going down means making and losing money . . . The promises of wealth and the threats of destitution that [this system] holds out, it redeems with ruthless promptitude." Unlike most academics, he knew these things first-hand. Just as his time in the Finance Ministry exposed him to the dilemmas of politics, his years in business gave him a direct education in the nature of capitalism.[14]

The philosopher Alfred North Whitehead once observed that "intelligence is quickness to apprehend as distinct from ability, which is capacity to act wisely on the thing apprehended." The absent-minded Whitehead had even less ability in practical affairs than Schumpeter. But his comment captures the essence of Schumpeter's career in politics and business as distinct from his life as an academic economist. His performance as an investor, like his experience as state secretary for finance, ended in failure.[15]

The larger context is that most people in Central Europe who tried to succeed as investors or public servants during this period also suffered a *gran rifiuto* of some kind. The reason was simple enough: they were on the losing side of the Great War. None of the many finance ministers of either Austria or Germany had much success. Several fared better than Schumpeter, but others even worse (one was assassinated). Austria's political situation remained unstable, prices continued to rise, money to invest was scarce, and decent jobs even more so. Large numbers of people wandered the streets of Vienna, hollow-eyed and undernourished.[16]

Times were especially bad for the entrepreneurial firms of which Schumpeter was so fond. As he put it in 1921, the essence of the economy lay not in paper securities or even in production equipment "but in the psychological relations between people and in the mental state of the individual." The crucial element was capitalism's orientation toward the future; but when the future looked bleak, people were reluctant to take risks. "The spiritual community is an infinitely complex and sensitive organism," and it is "each individual industrialist or merchant who sets afloat his own little boat."[17]

He went on to emphasize still again the crucial role of credit. Austria had to modernize its business system, for "we are now standing before the most significant case of credit need in capitalistic society—the one case in which credit is indispensable." To survive and prosper, Austria desperately needed infusions of new money. But the postwar Treaty of St. Germain had paralyzed large sectors of the nation's economy, making it very hard to attract investments from abroad. And even when foreign credit did appear, the government managed it poorly.[18]

Austria "begs for foreign capital," Schumpeter wrote, "and then when it comes screams about being overwhelmed by foreigners." The country was behaving "like some towns dealing with tourism: they can't live without tourism, but when tourists arrive, they insult or hassle them, or try to exploit them in a petty-minded manner." Meanwhile, Austria was using both its own capital and foreign loans to finance consumption as well as investment. Even necessities such as food and clothing were being paid for through credit. "Of course, this state of things cannot last."[19]

Because Austria's return to economic health required a more favorable balance of trade, Schumpeter found the trend toward world protectionism especially disturbing. Speaking to the Austrian League of Nations Club in 1922, he said that the League must fight high tariffs not only for economic reasons but to minimize the chance of another war. "In a capitalistic world, free trade is the cement which holds together the idea of peace."[20]

In sum, Austria's industries lacked credit and modern technology; its tax system was wrongheaded; its wages were too high in comparison with labor productivity; and its exporters faced high tariff barriers in almost all countries, including those that had been part of the prewar Austrian Empire. Even the future of Vienna as an important financial center remained uncertain.[21]

It was especially exasperating to Schumpeter that the level of trade and finance had plummeted within the area of the old empire. After the war, ethnic hatreds had found fresh outlets, and the newly independent nations appeared to take perverse pleasure in thwarting one another's ambitions. They seemed bent on establishing distinct identities regardless of the cost to themselves. Austria found no support for its policies of economic reintegration. Nationalist passions in each of the new countries prevented cooperative measures that would have benefited all of them. And they reserved a special loathing for Vienna, the financial core of the old empire.[22]

Czechoslovakia, Yugoslavia, and Romania all rejected Vienna's proposals for free trade and monetary union. Hungary, the most nationalistic of all the Habsburg successor states, wanted to raise its tariffs across the board and rely entirely on its own resources. Politics and the quest for a national identity simply overrode economic self-interest, everywhere. The most advanced of the new countries was Czechoslovakia, Schumpeter's birthplace, which had contained a fourth of the old empire's population but well over half its industrial capacity. Czechoslovakia's fourteen million people now outnumbered Austria's by more than two to one, and its industrial output was nearly six times as large. The Czechs had long memories about the haughtiness of Habsburg Vienna and showed little sympathy for their now-enfeebled southern neighbor.[23]

This, then, was the backdrop of Schumpeter's five years as a Viennese banker and investor. Austria could find no way out of its economic dilemma, and it was in this context that Schumpeter failed in business, much as he had failed in the Finance Ministry. He made many mistakes, but the desperate circumstances of his country dragged him down at least as much. As he himself wrote in his diary many years later, "Really, I don't quite regret any of my efforts and failures—every one of them taught me something about myself and life that uniform success would have hidden."[24]

Fortunately, he was soon to find a double deliverance: in his return to academia and in the one truly romantic love of his life.

8

***

Annie

There is only one happiness in life, to love and be loved.

GEORGE SAND, letter to a friend, 1862

DURING HIS *GRAN RIFIUTO*, Schumpeter made one good invest-
ment that yielded significant returns: he fell in love with the beautiful young
Anna Josefina Reisinger. Annie was the daughter of Franz Reisinger, concierge
of the apartment building in Vienna where Schumpeter grew up. Annie and
her siblings, Willy and Emilie (Milly), shared their parents' modest quarters in
the building. The family also operated a small store there.[1]

Schumpeter was twenty years older than Annie and had known her since she
was a child. At the age of fifteen she had begun work as a bank clerk while continuing her high school studies. Annie had few intellectual pretensions but did
have an earnest drive for self-improvement. She took courses in shorthand,
business correspondence, and accounting, besides her academic subjects. At
the People's University in Vienna, she also studied English, French, Italian, and
Spanish. Apart from her exceptional good looks and glowing demeanor, she
was a typical young woman of her time and station.[2]

Annie kept a daily diary in which she recorded nearly all of her activities.
She often went to movies and plays, enjoyed music and dancing, and took regular hikes with family and friends in the Vienna Woods. Her diary shows little
evidence of reflection on serious topics, even though political tensions were

boiling over in Vienna. But in one entry, dated June 15, 1919, she writes about the communist street riots that were beginning to plague the city: "Demonstration, lots of gunfire, 12 people dead, 80 injured, horrible, lots of blood. Stayed at home." This was during Schumpeter's tenure as finance minister.[3]

Annie attracted boys and had numerous flings, all apparently innocent enough until she reached her twenties. When she was seventeen and Schumpeter thirty-seven, he began to notice that the girl next door was becoming a lovely young woman. Schumpeter had moved back to Graz after leaving the Finance Ministry, but he often visited Vienna and would run into Annie as he entered or left his mother's apartment. He and Annie began to exchange letters and occasionally go out together. At first her parents, to whom she was very close, forbade her to continue making dates with the much older Schumpeter. On the other hand, he was someone they had known and respected for many years, and he was hardly the only man in Annie's life. When she turned eighteen, they relented and permitted her to see him, within fairly strict limits. Her father, meanwhile, put a stop to her going out with one of her several other boyfriends on the grounds that he was too young.[4]

Annie seems to have recorded in her diary every contact she had with Schumpeter over the next few years. Hundreds of entries show how their relationship developed, starting when she was seventeen:

> *May 26, 1920:* [Schumpeter] called me by name for the first time.

> *June 7, 1920:* Schum [and I] beginning at 6 pm [attended a musical], after that we had dinner at Hupfer's in the extra room. Will I become his girlfriend? No.

> *June 18, 1920:* Letter from Schumy from Graz. Thank God Mother [didn't find it].[5]

She continued seeing Schumpeter and corresponding with him by mail. But during this same period she also went out with men her own age or younger.[6]

Recognizing Annie's beauty, her parents kept her on a tight leash. They allowed her to attend horse races with Schumpeter as part of a larger group but did not let her go to the theater alone with him. Once she stood him up on a restaurant date, then wrote him what she called "a rude letter." She told him she knew he was married (though he had not seen Gladys for seven years), was "a big egoist," and had relationships with many women. "Why can't I meet with you? In short: my good reputation will not permit it." But just after sending the letter, Annie began to worry about making Schumpeter angry, since he "is nice after all." Being so young, she was filled with whimsical feelings and not ready for any stable relationship. Nor, at this time, was Schumpeter.[7]

"Finally a response from Schumy," she wrote in her diary shortly after sending him the rude letter. "Isn't insulted. But sad. I am too. But there's nothing we can do about it . . . I'm always waiting for the opportunity to talk to Schump.—I feel so sorry for him. I don't know, but I feel as if he could play a role in my life. I also have this hollow feeling now, I wish it would be like that. But the different backgrounds—People would say it is only because of the money . . . But at the same time I feel so sorry for Schump, I almost could say I love him, no, I know that I do."[8]

She continued to correspond with him in Graz and to see him when he came to Vienna. After Annie was laid off from her job, he wrote recommendations for her to several banks. But she found no work, and economic times remained hard. Once "a colleague of Schumy asked me for a rendezvous," which she declined. "Cheeky rascal."[9]

During the early part of 1921, as Annie turned eighteen, her diary entries become less regular, saying little about Schumpeter or any other subject. Her main problem during this period was earning enough money to live on—a stark reality for many people in Vienna, and certainly for the Reisinger family. Annie's brother, Willy, worked intermittently in the family store. But her sister, Milly, had to move to Germany, where she took a servant's position in a wealthy household. Annie herself could find no satisfactory job. She worked briefly as a maid, then as a seamstress.[10]

As bad times worsened, she decided to follow her sister's example. Still only eighteen, she left Austria to work for a moneyed family in France. Her employers spent most of their time in Paris, but to Annie's chagrin sent her to their farm in nearby Pontagny. She worked long hours but got along well with others on the staff and managed to have at least some social life. She also tried hard to learn the language of her new country; her diary from this period is in a crude French.[11]

After eighteen months in Pontagny, she left to try her luck in Paris. Her first job there turned out badly: "Madame does not know how to deal with her domestic servants." Her fellow staff members were also rude, but at least she was able to send money home to her mother in Vienna. Soon she found a more pleasant job as an au pair, still in Paris. She enjoyed working with children, and in her new household became particularly fond of her employer's young son. "I would like a child like François," she wrote—a comment that came to haunt Schumpeter. Even so, during her time in Paris she was "unhappy almost all the time," having little money or leisure hours to enjoy the city's charms.[12]

In the fall of 1923, after nearly two and a half years in France, Annie returned to Vienna. She found a part-time job, but it lasted just four months. Not once during her long absence had she seen Schumpeter, and she had corresponded with him only during her early weeks in France. But on New Year's Eve of 1923 she paid a visit to Johanna's apartment and there encountered Schumpeter for the first time in more than three years. He was now a rich man, still handsome at forty, but seemingly less interested in her. During the next seventeen months, he saw Annie, spoke with her on the phone, and took her out from time to time. This was the period of the stock market crisis in Vienna, and Schumpeter's financial troubles had begun in earnest. Within a year he resigned his position at the Biedermann Bank.[13]

Meanwhile, as Austria's economic difficulties continued, Annie kept looking for work and finally got a decent job in a retail store. But, having at last settled her money problems, she allowed herself to get into serious trouble with her love life. Now twenty-one years old and exceedingly attractive, she warned herself in a diary entry of April 5, 1924: "Don't turn the heads of married men!!!"[14]

Ignoring her own advice, she soon became involved in a turbulent relationship with a man her diary calls "Gerhard L." or "G." A businessman with a wife and children, G. traveled frequently to Switzerland, Hungary, and Germany. He treated Annie with alternating cruelty and kindness, stealing her diary on one occasion ("What does he want with it, blackmail?") but bringing her gifts on others. Several months into their affair, Annie learned that she was pregnant. She became terrified that her family might find out and that she would lose her job. "What a horror!" she wrote. "He disgusts me."[15]

In October 1924, when G. "leaves for Switzerland with his wife," Annie reluctantly planned to have an abortion. She traveled to Linz, a small city northwest of Vienna, where a doctor performed the procedure.[16]

Annie then had a rough time:

> *October 30:* Slept at home . . . Everyone cried [because] I looked
> terrible.
>
> *November 4:* G. returns from Switzerland. I am happy to know he
> is near me and unhappy that it is he whom I love.
>
> *November 7:* Rendezvous [with G.] . . . Gave me candy. Was nice
> after a long time with me.
>
> *November 19:* I was again very disagreeable, at noon I growled at
> him—and what of it?

Over the next few months Annie tried to break off the affair but could not
seem to take the final step. Her infatuation, along with G.'s irresponsibility,
put her in an emotional quandary.[17]

In the meantime, she began to get reacquainted with Schumpeter. She visited his mother on Christmas Day in 1924, and went out with him occasionally. She was starting to think of him in a new light, his courtliness and respect
a vivid contrast with the boorish behavior of G. As for Schumpeter himself, he
was becoming enthralled with Annie. The young girl he had known as the
daughter of his concierge had now grown into a gorgeous twenty-two-year-
old woman—still full of her characteristic good cheer but now much more
poised and sophisticated. He began to think that this was someone he might
want to marry.

By the spring of 1925 they were seeing each other almost every day. Again
Annie's diary shows the course of their relationship, which now began to move
very fast:

> *May 13:* Letter with shamrock to Schumy.
>
> *May 15:* Talked to Schumy on the phone. He was delighted with
> the shamrock.
>
> *May 16:* At the photographer. Rendezvous with Schumy and Milly.
> Went for a walk . . . Had dinner, went dancing, then back with
> the car.

Annie, Schumpeter, and Annie's mother in mid-1925, as Schumpeter's courtship became serious.

May 17: Went to Baden [near Vienna] with Milly and Schumy. Ate at the "Green Tree," spa park.

May 18: Schumy at his mom's.

May 21: With Schumy (in a tux) at the opera, "The Bartered

Bride," then Hotel Imperial to dine, in the car to the summer-house. Marriage proposal.[18]

Annie had known Schumpeter for many years, but his proposal came unexpectedly, and she did not give him an immediate answer. In dozens of diary entries over the next two months she reports occasional contacts with G. but constant outings with Schumpeter—day trips, mornings at art museums, evenings at dinner. Under this barrage of attention, she began to make up her mind:

> *July 3, 1925:* Dining at the Kobenzl [in the Vienna Woods], then
> walked to Grinzing [a neighborhood in Vienna], [Schumpeter]
> talked to mother [about getting engaged to Annie].

> *August 6:* Tense atmosphere [likely involving a discussion with
> Schumpeter about G. and perhaps even her abortion].

The next day, she wrote him a letter about "how grateful I am for your behavior yesterday. You are so good—this question has always stood like a shadow between us and now I am so cheerful and happy that it has been cleared away. Thank you for helping me . . . You will not be disappointed in your great love for me—I have the best intentions and also believe now that we understand each other and can be happy together. I kiss you tenderly. Your Annie." On August 14, 1925, as Schumpeter later recalled, Annie told him "that I was the only one whom she ever really considered marrying and who would 'concern himself' with her." They then had a talk "about the little notebook," and Annie's anger at G. Having decided to marry Schumpeter, Annie saw G. on August 22 and broke up with him for good. In early September, still beset by problems of conscience, she again made sure that the details of her prior relationship with G. were clear to Schumpeter. For him it made no difference.[19]

Her diary for these months contains almost daily reports about Schumpeter and their activities—shopping, preparations for the wedding, and vacation trips:

> *September 4:* Met at noon. Trip to Puchberg hotel [a resort], then
> after that Sebastian waterfall return . . . the first night together
> alone. [They made love for the first time, as Schumpeter later con-

firmed. This seems remarkable in view of Annie's affair with G. and Schumpeter's reputation as a rake; they had been seeing each other off and on for six years and nearly every night for six months, without having sex.]

September 5: In the morning Schneebergbahn [train around the mountain]; to the Hotel Hoch Schneeberg . . . In the room pretty much until noon.[20]

Though bedazzled by Annie, Schumpeter had not lost his head regarding practical matters. During these months of intense courtship he had decided to resume his academic career and had begun to write articles and search for a professorship. He was too proud to approach the faculty at Graz, which might have spurned him anyway. As for his long ambition to teach at the University of Vienna, academic politics and his own reckless behavior had closed that door forever.

But his reputation as a creative scholar remained very high not only in Austria and Germany but throughout the world. Colleges in Tokyo and Kobe invited him to give a series of lectures and to stay in Japan for at least two years. He never forgot that timely compliment, but he had no wish to spend two years so far away. Meanwhile, he appealed to everyone he knew who might help him find a good job in Europe.[21]

Two influential friends took up his cause, and their efforts bore fruit in October 1925. Authorities in Berlin invited him for interviews with the Prussian Ministry of Art, Science and Public Education, which governed universities in most of Germany. Soon the prestigious University of Bonn made him an offer, which he accepted at once. Elated that they could now get married, he telegrammed Annie: "Bonn Erobert" [Bonn conquered].[22]

Annie received that message on October 5. "Joy!" she wrote in her diary, and events now moved quickly.

October 12: Met with J. around noon, [planned] non-denominational [wedding].

October 13: Got an engagement ring—very happy.

November 5: Wedding.[23]

Schumpeter's marriage to Annie seemed to defy every aspect of his carefully crafted identity. After decades of casual affairs and nonchalant dandyism, he became a devoted husband and a deliriously happy man. Despite his and his mother's aristocratic pretensions, Annie's working-class background never mattered to him in the least. Some loves break all the rules, and this one broke the persona of Joseph Schumpeter. But it did not spell the end of the new bridegroom's image-making. He soon set about inventing a fresh public identity for young Annie as the dignified wife of a great economist.

Not so happily, Annie's true background did matter a great deal to Schumpeter's mother. Annie was an extraordinarily appealing person, but class meant much to Johanna, and a monopoly of her son's affection even more. Years earlier, she had opposed his marriage to the upper-class Englishwoman Gladys Seaver, and she had not expended so much energy climbing Vienna's social ladder only to see her son now marry the daughter of her concierge. As for the twenty-year age difference, Johanna herself had wed a man thirty-three years her senior, but with a very different goal in mind: she had married up, not down, and certainly not for love. Her only consolation was that Schumpeter's philandering on the seedier side of Viennese life might now cease. At least Annie was respectable. Still, for Johanna the whole matter came as quite a shock, the more so because her son's departure to faraway Bonn would follow immediately after the wedding.

Nor were Annie's own parents delighted with the marriage. Schumpeter was nearly twice their daughter's age and had a raffish reputation. Then there was the issue of his relationship with Gladys, whom he had not seen for a decade but to whom he was still legally married. But the bride's parents took no steps to block the wedding.

By the spring of 1925, when Schumpeter became serious about Annie, he had lost his fortune in the market crash and been forced out of his position at the Biedermann Bank. His finances lay in shambles, and he had few prospects. In part because everything else in his life seemed so bleak, he tended to idealize Annie—her ebullience, beauty, and youth a welcome refuge from the chaos and gloom otherwise engulfing him. But all of that aside, there is no question of his complete love for her. For the first and only time in his life, he was totally smitten.

Annie herself may or may not have been aware of the full extent of

Schumpeter's business problems. But she certainly knew him to be in a financial slide. He had lost his money, he owed large sums to a variety of creditors, and he had no job. Whatever else she may have been, Annie was no gold-digger. Her diary shows without question that she was extremely fond of "Schumy."

Still, the stronger passion came from his side. In his infatuation, he was ready to throw over his prejudices about the importance of class, as well as the possibility of recouping his fortune by marrying an available heiress. At the age of forty-two he had fallen hopelessly in love with a twenty-two-year-old working-class woman. Reason had nothing to do with it. The opposition of Johanna and of Annie's parents mattered not a whit.

There did remain the nagging issue of his prior marriage to Gladys. The Church did not permit Catholics to divorce or to marry divorced persons. But in Vienna, the Socialist city government had recently enacted a civil measure to allow the termination of an unsatisfactory union, provided the original partner was willing to go along. The Church adamantly opposed this measure, and even its legality under civil law remained a bit cloudy. Schumpeter well knew that if Gladys had been aware of his intentions, she would have blocked his marriage to Annie or at least have exacted some recompense. But somehow he managed to secure the civil waiver without Gladys's knowledge.[24]

Meanwhile, in the weeks before their wedding he and Annie acted as if nothing stood in their way. Having borrowed still more money, Schumpeter bought expensive gifts for his fiancée in Vienna's elite stores. Anyone not aware of his financial situation would have thought that here was a wealthy middle-aged man lavishing gifts on his future bride and squiring her around European resorts during a joyous prenuptial tour. This is how Schumpeter behaved, and it may well have been how he felt. Having gone through such a long series of painful experiences since the outbreak of war in 1914, it was as if he were a new man.

ON NOVEMBER 5, 1925, eighteen years to the day after his first marriage, Joseph Schumpeter exchanged vows with Annie Reisinger at a Lutheran church in Vienna. They had not wanted to renounce Catholicism, but the rules had left them no choice. Neither Johanna nor Annie's parents attended the ceremony. Annie's brother gave her away, and her sister served as brides-maid. As best man, Schumpeter chose his former Graz colleague Hans Kelsen, a Jew and an eminent lawyer who had written Austria's republican constitution. After the wedding, the new couple took a week's honeymoon in northern Italy. Then they visited Cologne and other German cities, finally stopping in Bonn to find a place to live. After returning briefly to Vienna, they moved to their new home near the university, where the academic term had already begun.[25]

It was quite a bold gamble for Schumpeter to marry anybody while the obstacle of a previous marriage stared him in the face. When Gladys found out what had happened, she threatened to sue him, and she could even have had him prosecuted as a bigamist. On the other hand, her own refusal to return to Graz in 1914 did not reflect well on her, and it could have provided proof of desertion had the issue ever come to court. But no evidence exists that Schumpeter had made any serious effort at reconciliation. He had always seemed to regard Gladys as something of an ornament, a credential of his upper-class pretensions, a fashion accessory that he could dispose of once it had served its purpose. He had seen Johanna do just this in her marriage to Sigmund von Kéler.[26]

Then, too, during the decade after his separation from Gladys, he had pursued no serious relationships with women he might regard as his peers. Instead, he took mistresses and consorted with other amenable sex partners. Libertine behavior was not at all unusual for Viennese men at this time, but as Schumpeter had grown more prominent, his affairs had become more conspicuous. His behavior was unlikely to escape the attention of women belonging to the class to which he aspired, and of whom Johanna might have approved. Nor would it encourage his colleagues at Graz, or his former schoolmates from the Theresianum and the University of Vienna, to match him up with their sisters, cousins, or respectable friends.

Perhaps Johanna's own powerful influence over Schumpeter's life might have led him, either deliberately or unconsciously, to avoid close attachments with his peers—even men, but more particularly strong women. He had few male friends among his contemporaries; and with people of either sex he always seemed more comfortable with those a generation older or younger than he was. Nor did he have at close hand any model of a marriage based on long-term mutual love and support. His own father had died when he was four. Johanna had moved him far away from Triesch, where his aunts, uncles, and cousins continued to live. Neither he nor Johanna kept up with their relatives or visited their former home. Many details of this kind in his personal history make his unconditional love for Annie all the more remarkable and unexpected.

Of course, the relocations to Graz and Vienna had opened up priceless opportunities for Schumpeter. Starting with his years at the Theresianum, he had played many parts—boy genius, Austrian aristocrat, English gentleman, Cairo attorney, Viennese economist, university professor, minister of finance, investment banker, socialite, and free-spirited Casanova. Had he remained in Triesch, the family seat for four hundred years, the pursuit of these roles would have been impossible.

The same could almost be said of his creation of a new background for Annie Reisinger. To his colleagues at the University of Bonn, and later on to his friends at Harvard, he portrayed Annie less as the plebeian daughter of the Kélers' concierge than as a woman of distinction. Her years as a domestic servant metamorphosed into stays at elite academies in France and Switzerland—her tuition and living expenses paid for by Johanna and Schumpeter himself. White lies, but symptoms of deep psychological impulses: fierce ambition, protection of Annie, and the old question of his own identity.[27]

Whether he had worked out the details of Annie's new past before they left Austria is unknowable. But once they arrived in Bonn, he presented both himself and his bride as upper-class Viennese. He resumed his expensive lifestyle, and he and Annie began an active social schedule, entertaining in lavish new quarters and again relying on borrowed money.

At last, Schumpeter had settled on a stable identity. As Herr Professor Doktor Joseph Schumpeter of the University of Bonn, he held a splendid job with life-long tenure. He was married to a beautiful young wife whom he adored. With his obsessive work habits intact, he had reason to anticipate high academic honors still to come. He also had a sensible plan for paying off his creditors. Deeply in debt but more deeply in love, he was happier than he had ever been before. The future seemed abundant with promise.

Annie Reisinger, age twenty-two, at the time of her marriage to Schumpeter.

9

Heartbreak

I many times thought peace had come
When peace was far away.

EMILY DICKINSON, published in 1890

BONN, THE SCHUMPETERS' new home, lies in a pleasant spot
along the banks of the Rhine on the western edge of Germany, fifteen miles
south of the great metropolis of Cologne. Both cities are near Germany's borders with Belgium, Holland, Luxembourg, and France and are much closer to
Paris and London than to Vienna. Bonn had originated as a center of regional
government, and its founders had actively discouraged factories and other industrial developments. Its economy was organized around services and commerce, and during the nineteenth century it became a kind of millionaires' retreat. When Joseph and Annie Schumpeter moved to Bonn in 1925, it had a
population of about seventy thousand. As a quiet academic city in a peaceful
river valley, it appealed to wealthy retirees, much as Graz had done.

In the hierarchy of Germany's superb educational system, the University of
Bonn ranked in the top five, along with Berlin, Göttingen, Heidelberg, and
Munich. In 1925 it enrolled about four thousand students, most of whom had
grown up in the surrounding region. Long before, one such student had been
Karl Marx, who came from a prosperous family in the nearby town of Trier.
Marx stayed only briefly, enjoying his membership in a fraternity and cavort-

The University of Bonn at the time of Schumpeter's arrival. About one-half of the very wide main building is visible here, and a small corner of the large sunken lawn. Just behind this structure is downtown Bonn.

ing like a typical freshman, before leaving for the University of Berlin. Another short-term student had been Crown Prince Wilhelm, later the wartime kaiser of the German Empire.

In 1925 most of the university's facilities were housed, as they still are today, in a handsome three-story stucco building with an unusual shape—about 100 yards long and 40 yards deep, with a tower at each of its four corners. From one side of this building, 135 enormous windows—each four panes wide and seven panes tall—look out onto a huge sunken lawn bordered by long rows of trees. In the winter, groundskeepers flood the lawn, and the water freezes into a vast skating rink. On the other side of the university lies Bonn's downtown center, with its bustling public square and ornate city hall.

After the Schumpeters arrived in Bonn, they leased the villa that Crown Prince Wilhelm had occupied during his student days—a grand mansion atop a bluff, with a big glassed-in room overlooking the Rhine. It was typical of Schumpeter to choose such an elaborate residence, both as a gift to Annie and a way to maintain his pose as a wealthy aristocrat. How he might find enough money to make the lease payments did not concern him. His salary at Bonn was generous for an academic, but it amounted to no more than a quarter—at most—of his compensation at the Biedermann Bank. His financial misadventures in Vienna had in fact almost cost him his new professorship. He owed the appointment to his own academic achievements and the strenuous efforts of two prominent friends: Arthur Spiethoff, a professor at Bonn, and Gustav Stolper, a journalist in Vienna.[1]

Spiethoff, dignified and self-righteous, seemed a polar opposite of the playful Schumpeter, who was ten years his junior. He had trained at the University of Berlin with Gustav von Schmoller and other leaders of the German Historical School. But unlike his mentors in Berlin, Spiethoff had an affinity for economic theory. He never became a topflight theorist himself, but he did have a thorough understanding of business cycles, which was becoming a hot topic in economics.

As different as they seemed, Spiethoff and Schumpeter had much in common, and they developed a deep friendship. Fifteen years earlier, when the Law Faculty at Graz was deciding who should succeed the retiring Richard Hildebrand, the minority reports had mentioned Spiethoff as a superior candidate along with Schumpeter, who eventually got the job. Five years after that, in 1916, it had been Spiethoff who wrote Schumpeter to warn about the planned German tariff agreement with Austria. This was the issue that drew Schumpeter away from academics and into his public career.

At that time, in 1916, the German-born Spiethoff had been teaching at the University of Prague, where professors could conduct their classes in German. After the postwar creation of Czechoslovakia and the takeover of the university by Czechs, he moved west to Bonn. In 1921 he wrote Schumpeter about the possibility of joining him on the faculty at Bonn, but Schumpeter declined. He had also turned down a position at a university in Berlin. Schumpeter went on to say, however, that if he did decide to leave the Biedermann Bank and return to academic work, he would welcome an opportunity to come to Bonn.[2]

Three years later, in April 1924, as his financial situation continued to deteriorate, Schumpeter wrote Spiethoff, "I can't stop thinking of scholarship and the scholarly life as a distant and unreachable home." In subsequent letters he added that the relative quiet of Bonn was especially attractive and that, if an invitation came, he could probably join Spiethoff in Bonn during the fall of 1925. A clear opportunity then arose when one of the four economists at Bonn— Heinrich Dietzel, a capable but aging theorist—announced his retirement. This opened the way for Spiethoff to recruit his friend Schumpeter.[3]

But, as had happened at Graz in 1911, many obstacles blocked a smooth transition. The Bonn faculty had already sent the names of two nominees to the education ministry in Berlin, and Schumpeter's was not one of them. The ministry rejected both nominees as inferior and asked Bonn to propose other candidates. Lobbying hard, Spiethoff managed to get Schumpeter's name onto this second list. As he wrote to the Ministry of Science, Art and Public Education,

> Schumpeter is a genius and, with enormous precocity, published at the early age of 27 a book on the main content of theoretical economics, which was broadly accepted as an unusual demonstration of talent. Everything that he has published since has remained at a very high level and has always been seen as an event in the academic world . . . In the field of the history of economic thought, Schumpeter is by far the leading German scholar. In the field of sociology, judging from what we have seen, he need not fear any comparison. His qualification in the field of finance has been proven through his practical activity as a finance minister and a politician. As a lecturer and speaker Schumpeter has had the greatest success. The faculty would gain a shining addition in him.[4]

Schumpeter himself, still in the midst of his courtship of Annie, did everything he could to promote his own candidacy. He wrote Spiethoff several letters saying how much he would like to join him, and he sent along the names of a dozen personal references in Vienna. He also implied that if Bonn did not act quickly, he would go to Tokyo "for at least two years." There, he would succeed his old friend Emil Lederer, who was returning to a post at the University of Heidelberg.[5]

At top universities everywhere, then and now, a lot of gossip and devil's advocacy often goes on in the appointment of full professors. These positions carry high prestige and lifetime tenure and are hotly contested. Sometimes the supporters and opponents of particular candidates try to undercut one another's nominees, either openly or, more often, with hidden hands and backroom slander.

In 1925 Schumpeter's opponents had plenty of ammunition. His recent academic career had been erratic, and his private life provided ample material for juicy gossip. A case against him was easy to make. After a precocious start with his brilliant *Theory of Economic Development,* two other books, and several seminal articles, he had abandoned academia. He had resigned a tenured professorship at Graz and, after campaigning for a similar job at a second-tier university in Berlin, had rejected that offer when it came. He had published no important work in five years. Having taken up careers in politics and business, he had failed at both. He had behaved like a spendthrift and a rake. Worst of all, there were rumors of dark dealings in Austria's Finance Ministry and the Biedermann Bank.

These issues had already arisen once before, in 1923, when Spiethoff had seriously put forward Schumpeter's potential candidacy. In 1925 he wrote the ministry a confidential letter saying that in 1923 the rumors about "X" had been "so unfavorable that a submission of his name before the committee seemed impossible and I had to drop his candidacy." Since that time, however, Spiethoff had investigated the whole matter thoroughly and was continuing to do so.[6]

But there were still many questions he could not answer. He therefore appealed for advice to the economist and newspaperman Gustav Stolper, one of the dozen names Schumpeter had sent him as references. Five years younger than Schumpeter, Stolper was a fellow graduate of the University of Vienna. The descendant of four Jewish grandparents who had emigrated from the empire's "Polish East" (Galicia), Stolper had grown up in Vienna. He and Schumpeter knew and respected each other, though they often disagreed on matters of policy. In 1925 they were not the close friends they became later on.[7]

Stolper was in a unique position to help. As the leading economic journalist in Vienna, he had close contacts in business, government, and academia, and he could give full answers to all questions raised by Spiethoff's opponents. One of these questions dominated the others: Schumpeter's dealings at the Finance Ministry and the Biedermann Bank. Spiethoff asked Stolper to comment on these "rumors about Professor Schumpeter."[8]

Replying to Spiethoff, Stolper pulled no punches in his evaluation of Schumpeter. But he concluded that it would be inexcusable to disqualify him because of groundless gossip about his integrity. It was true, he wrote, that

> Schumpeter has always had many enemies. That problem is due
> not only to his meteoric rise but also to the fact that his whole life
> style is un-Austrian, if you wish, un-bourgeois. And Schumpeter
> was careless enough not to hide this but to stress it in a manner
> that can be explained only by inadequate knowledge of human na-
> ture or lack of experience of life. That a University Professor does
> not go to the local pub, or repeats unthinkingly current political
> slogans left or right, that a bourgeois Minister in a Government
> consisting of petty bourgeois wears silken handkerchiefs and
> shirts, or even keeps a riding horse—this cannot, given the hori-
> zon of these people, be quite above board.
>
> I know how all this has been held against him. Of course, this
> life style could not be financed with his professorial or ministerial
> salary. Hence [rumors arose that] it had to come from shady in-
> come sources. In reality Schumpeter probably lived off his capital.
> And as this was insufficient to pay for his needs at the time, he was
> after his Minister episode forced to accept a position [at the
> Biedermann Bank] which gave him a large income and the possi-
> bility of quickly accumulating a large fortune. As inexperienced as
> a politician who thought he could navigate between the parties
> and in reality made enemies of all of them, he proved to be equally
> so in the field of practical business which was even more foreign to
> him. Long before last year's [stock market] crash I told him to re-
> sign from the Bank and to return where alone he belonged: to sci-
> ence.[9]

It was appalling, Stolper went on to say, that Schumpeter should have any difficulty finding a top academic position. An old enemy had already blocked his chances for a professorship at the University of Vienna. This person, whose promotion Schumpeter himself had once prevented at the University of Graz, had taken his revenge from a high post he now held in the Austrian govern-ment. "I believe it simply to be a matter of honor of German [speaking] uni-

Right: Gustav Stolper, Viennese journalist and scholar—a patron whose help was crucial in 1925, and Schumpeter's lifelong friend thereafter.

Below: Schumpeter with his new colleagues in economics on the faculty at Bonn. From left: Arthur Spiethoff, his sponsor and close friend; then Herbert von Beckerath, Schumpeter, and Karl Friedrich Roessle, a junior instructor.

versities to right this wrong," Stolper wrote. "It would be a crime if German universities would let malicious gossip of malevolent people alienate such a person who has already to his credit so great scientific and pedagogical achievements and who can produce more such achievements in the future."[10]

In the end, Spiethoff and Stolper carried the day. After months of negotiation—extending several weeks beyond the start of the fall academic term—the ministry finally chose Schumpeter. He was not hired to teach economic theory, because Spiethoff wanted to keep that prestigious assignment for himself. Instead, he would become a professor of public finance. This title made sense, in view of his famous article "The Crisis of the Tax State" and his experience as Austria's finance minister. But it was not long before a substantial amount of theory crept into his courses at Bonn.

The year 1925 was a good time for a theorist like Schumpeter to make his mark, and not only in Bonn. Universities throughout Germany were still short of first-class theorists, even though the grip of the Historical School had begun to weaken. Before leaving Vienna for Bonn, Schumpeter had resumed writing articles on important theoretical subjects, and soon his old habit of copious publication was in full swing. Among many other projects, he planned to issue a revised edition of *The Theory of Economic Development,* which was then out of print. After his experience in government and business, he was also full of new ideas about capitalism as a social system. "My reception by my colleagues and the students was extremely friendly," he wrote a friend in Vienna, and "I hope to be drowning in research activities pretty soon."[11]

As one of his students later recalled, Schumpeter's arrival in Bonn "was a sensation for the academic world of [German] economics," because up-to-date theory would now get full exposure. In Schumpeter's classrooms, "Names like Cournot, Walras, Pareto, Wicksell, Böhm-Bawerk, Wieser, Edgeworth, and others, were daily fare. Use of the language of mathematics . . . became a matter of course in lectures and seminars." Bonn's program in economics began to attract students from all over Germany and from other countries as well. "What Göttingen was for mathematics and physics, Bonn became for economics—and this in spite of the fact that Schumpeter did not officially represent economic theory as a field." In his seminars Schumpeter did not hesitate to present his characteristic mixture of theory, statistics, and history. Here he had the tacit approval of his friend Spiethoff, who held the chair in theory and might have protested against a younger colleague's poaching. But Spiethoff knew the reach of his friend's talents. As he later wrote, "Schumpeter was never a beginner but, a precocious genius; he entered the scientific arena a full-fledged master."[12]

Schumpeter's experience at Graz had made him a much better teacher, and within the lecture halls at Bonn he gave memorable performances. As one student put it, everyone "sensed that an original mind—filled with new ideas—was creatively at work, letting the audience partake in the process of reasoning, offering known truths in a new light as well as developing new ideas while teaching. I cannot recall ever having listened to a more inspiring academic teacher."[13]

Two other students wrote in a similar vein about Schumpeter's classes. "At first he would give the impression of being amiable, but you immediately became aware of something searching and very firm about him. His eyes were calm, steady and often somewhat mischievous." If someone asked a challenging question, "he would quickly come alive when he answered; and he was full of fire when his counterattack led to victory." He always "spoke in a clear and amiable manner as the Viennese tend to do; he was a little playful, but also measured and emphatic." He gestured a great deal, his hands slashing the air as he brought his points home.[14]

Ever the showman, Schumpeter was once more in his element. But the readjustment was harder than it looked. "At the beginning," he wrote a friend, "it strikes one as strange, all the young chaps and the professors with the mentalities of the young chaps." He himself had "gotten older and more experienced and, how shall I say it, it is not so easy for me to take *seriously* what moves this [academic] world."[15]

Nor did Schumpeter confine his activities to teaching and writing. He went out of his way to get for the Bonn library more materials for students and for his own research. Only three months after his arrival, he was petitioning the ministry in Berlin for a huge new allotment. He successfully urged the purchase of more books and journals in economics and sociology, particularly those in English.[16]

MEANWHILE, he and Annie were quickly becoming the toast of Bonn society. Professor and Mrs. Spiethoff served as their sponsors, and the two couples went on regular outings together. The Schumpeters accepted numerous requests to dine at the homes of colleagues and new friends, and they entertained frequently themselves. Visitors from other universities often spent weekends in their opulent villa.[17]

The only serious problem during their early months in Bonn came from Gladys, who by now had learned of their marriage. As Schumpeter told a friend in January 1926, Gladys had written from England "a fire-breathing letter, in which she threatens me with a lawsuit and scandal." But with his knack for compartmentalizing his life, he went on as if nothing could threaten his new happiness. He pursued a frenetic schedule—teaching his classes, revising *The Theory of Economic Development,* writing articles, and speaking at other German universities.[18]

In April 1926 Annie went to Paris for a two-week vacation and took in all the city's charms. She had not had the time or the money to enjoy Paris when she lived there as a servant girl. Now feeling a bit torn between her working-class origins and her elevated station in Bonn, she did not look up her old friends, as she had expected to do.[19]

By this time it had become evident that Annie was pregnant. Her due date, August 1926, would be only nine months after her wedding the previous November. Schumpeter was elated at the prospect of fatherhood, but neither he nor Annie wrote of their news to Johanna or the Reisingers back in Vienna. They wanted the baby to be a surprise, and they began to make plans for both families to visit Bonn during the late summer. Schumpeter asked his mother to come at the end of the July academic term, and Annie invited her sister, Milly. But as the summer approached, there were signs that Annie's pregnancy was going to be problematic. One doctor told her that the birth was likely to be difficult, and another advised her to terminate the pregnancy. Whether the difficulties had to do with the abortion two years earlier could not be determined.[20]

Shortly into her third trimester, Annie began to have intermittent but apparently minor hemorrhages. Today, seeing such symptoms, any competent doctor would hospitalize her at once. But at that time, many medical people still believed that little could be done in the event of trouble, short of abortion. Annie did not want to take that step, and there is no evidence that she discussed her problems at any length with her husband. Schumpeter, for his part, did not so much ignore the warning signs (as he later blamed himself for doing) but rather just found it hard to imagine that anything bad could happen to Annie. He continued to idealize her as his vigorous, beautiful young wife, the picture of health.

What happened next was a series of nightmarish events, vividly recorded in Annie's diary entries:

> *June 18, 1926:* Bleedings. Received a telegram in the night.

This telegram, from Vienna, brought word that Johanna von Kéler, now sixty-five years old, had suffered a cardiovascular event that threatened her life. She wanted her son to come to her bedside at once. Again, Schumpeter found it hard to believe that the news could be as bad as it in fact was. For two days he exchanged messages with Vienna and struggled with the decision of when to go. Finally, as Annie wrote in her diary,

> *June 21:* J. departure for Vienna.

> *June 22:* Death of M[adame] Kéler, Dr. Spiethoff was here.[21]

Schumpeter had arrived just before Johanna died. The next day, Annie wrote to him in Vienna:

> My sweet little darling. Received your telegram in the afternoon and am so unhappy with you, that you couldn't talk more with your mom about our baby, that she would have been happy about it with us . . . I think about our baby all the time and I shouldn't excite myself now. I held out from four o'clock to now, eight o'clock, but I can't hold out any longer and it is really better when one cries oneself out, then it is easier for me.
>
> A little later. I have just eaten with Mrs. Spiethoff and the stupid crying is all over . . . Everything went very well and I feel no pain. The little one is very lively and now makes me so happy, and I hope that will continue to be so . . . You see, my sweet Go-Go, you really don't need to worry about me. I am really already completely healthy, and need only to be careful . . . I wait with longing for a letter from you and love you so much . . . I kiss you tenderly and can only repeat that I love you beyond all measure and think about you all the time. Your Annie."[22]

Then more diary entries:

> *June 25, 1926:* Funeral of M[adame] Kéler [Annie, still in Bonn, did not attend].

> *June 27:* (Sunday) Dölles [friends from Bonn] and Spiethoff here. In the evening arrival of Jozsi.

> *July 19:* Mrs. Spiethoff with me—in bed [with complications of the pregnancy].

> *July 20:* In the movies with Mrs. Spiethoff. Shopping . . . Mrs. Dölles at my place for dinner. Then at Spiethoffs.—fight.[23]

The fight was between Annie and her husband over the receipt of still another nasty letter from Gladys. This letter turned Schumpeter's mind toward the question of bigamy for himself and possible illegitimacy for the child Annie was about to deliver.

Still in a daze from his mother's funeral, he could not accept that Johanna—the light of his youth, the foundation of his life—was now gone, without warning and in the blink of an eye. The one connection with his boyhood in Triesch, Graz, and Vienna, the single constant in a turbulent life filled with conflicting identities, had suddenly disappeared. "It is as if the guardian angel leaves us as soon as the mother goes," he later wrote. He asked the Reisingers to tend to Johanna's grave in Vienna until he could return. He could think of nothing except her death.[24]

Unfortunately, there was much else to think about. And threats from Gladys, however annoying, were trivial compared to the real issue. Annie's diary:

> *July 23:* Very strong bleedings.

> *July 25:* (Sunday) Bleedings, in bed, on the porch, Mrs. Husserl [another friend] was here at noon—later also Dölles—in the evening also Mr. and Mrs. Spiethoff—very tired.

> *July 26:* Thank God bleeding better—[did not have to go] to the Johanniter Hospital. Very tired. Mrs. Schulz [another friend] always very nice. Dölles here. Didn't get anything from J., only from mom embroidery.

This was the feast day of Anna Christa, Annie's patron saint, and a traditional "name-day" occasion for gift-giving. Annie's feelings were hurt because her husband, distracted with grief, forgot to get her a present.

> *July 27:* Still very tired, but my condition is somewhat better. Still in bed, very careful. Very busy sewing, in the evening Spiethoffs at our place.

> *July 28:* In bed. J. gone almost the whole day.—Dölles here in the evening.

> *July 29:* If only Milly would come! In the evening Mrs. Schulz with a friend of hers. Mrs. Dölles and Mr. Spiethoff came by.

> *July 30:* My condition is not particularly good! Cold weather. [Will Milly] visit today?

Milly finally did come, but the words of July 30 are the last in Annie's diary. Two days later, Schumpeter wrote Gustav Stolper that, beset with worry about Annie's health, he found it impossible to perform his work and meet his writing deadlines. And two days after that, Annie went into labor and was rushed to the hospital, bleeding badly.[25]

She died in childbirth on August 3, 1926, not yet twenty-four years old.

Within moments, Schumpeter and Milly jumped into a taxi and took the baby, who was in critical condition, to a better hospital. But it was too late for him as well. He lived for a little less than four hours.

Stunned by the triple loss of his mother, his wife, and his newborn son, Schumpeter wrote that evening to his close friend and former secretary at the Biedermann Bank: "My beloved Annie is no more . . . Everything looks so grim now that I do not care what happens . . . I may have deserved much, but this, no."[26]

After Annie's funeral, he wrote other letters, describing the "tortured expression of her eyes" during her final agony, but "also in the last seconds her aesthetic beauty, and her quiet majesty in the coffin . . . with the child in her arms." Completely at sea, he thrashed about, dreading what lay ahead. "I suffer like a soul damned in hell . . . I loved Annie passionately, just as she deserved. I am now living silently in my grief over memories of the one big miracle of my life . . . I don't have what other people have to anesthetize themselves: resignation to destiny and to God—or its opposite, *quarreling* with destiny or God, which seems pointless to me . . . I am trying to understand the miracle and to live my grief . . . I am only leaving the house to go to her grave."[27]

He wrote that when he returned to Vienna to settle his mother's affairs, he would have to go back to her apartment. And there, "another shadow will be talking to me"—that of Johanna. "I do not want consolation, I rather would despise myself if I could find consolation." He would have welcomed some other way to ease his pain but could find no escape, just "infinite despair." The days went by in a dark cloud of numbness. "I am constantly thinking of Annie. I now understand how gods come into being. Today I wanted to start working at 7:00 in the morning—and ended up sitting in front of her pictures until 1:00 in the afternoon, in some sort of devotion." He had "once in my life truly and really loved . . . another human being [who] was everything to me and I to her." A few years later, after rereading the final entries in Annie's diary, he wrote on the anniversary of the "first day by myself in our house":

> I shudder at the years that will come
> I shudder at life without you.[28]

He buried her in a cemetery in Bonn, near the top of a hill. Thinking that he would lie beside her when he himself died, he leased a double lot. But today the grave of Annie and their son is not marked, although it is possible to locate the site. The cemetery in Bonn leases its lots for specified periods of time. Later, the same lot can be leased by someone else for another limited interval. So others are now buried at the gravesite.

In "Ode to Melancholy," Keats wrote, "Then glut thy sorrow on a morning rose." This is what Schumpeter did. Every morning for the rest of his time in Bonn, he walked a half-mile to the cemetery and laid a single rose on Annie's grave. He kept death masks of her and their child in a prominent place, preserving the rest of the house just as it was. For years he could not bring himself to remove her clothes from her closet.[29]

At the end of August 1926, four weeks after Annie's death, he wrote a long letter to his American friend Wesley Clair Mitchell, whom he had not seen in twelve years and who was now a famous economist. He wanted to tell about all that had happened to him, in business, government, and academia: "I entered upon my duties [at Bonn] in Nov. 1925, feeling extremely happy. And I should, I believe, have kept on feeling happy, trying to make up for lost time and to exploit my 'practical experience' as well as new ideas. Only I had married, about the same time, a wife twenty years my junior, whom I adored and who taught me the possibility of a paradise on earth. And four weeks ago, giving birth, before the time, to a boy she met a terrible death. This is one of the first letters I write. Of course, my days are falling slowly into their new order, but . . . all light has gone out of them."[30]

The deaths of Annie, Johanna, and his newborn son were the pivotal events of Schumpeter's life. They marked the belated onset of his adulthood. Now too old to be an *enfant terrible,* he was also too scarred to go back to his reckless existence as bachelor *bon vivant.* "Everything now hangs on my ability to work," he wrote to Stolper. "If so, the engine will keep running, even if my personal life is over."[31]

And as time passed, he was somehow able to right himself from the triple tragedies of 1926. He grew much more serious, tapping into reservoirs of character he had no idea he possessed. He drew heavily on his memories of Annie and Johanna and began to compose prayers asking their help with his labors— as someone of his Catholic upbringing would invoke the assistance of saints. Under a burden of almost unbearable grief, he again took up his mission of trying to unravel the enigmas of capitalism and human society. And over the next twenty-three years, often in the face of severe despondency, he produced a vast and incomparable body of work.

Dienstag, den 3. August, um ¹/₂5 Uhr nachmittags, verschied an den Folgen einer Frühgeburt meine Gattin, unsere Tochter und Schwester

Frau Annie Schumpeter
geb. Reisinger

im 24. Lebensjahr.

Joseph Schumpeter
Franz und **Anna Reisinger**
Emilie Reisinger
Willy Reisinger.

Bonn, den 4. August 1926.
Koblenzerstr. 39

Die Trauerfeier findet Freitag, den 6. August, nachmittags um 3 Uhr im Trauerhause, die Beisetzung anschließend auf dem Poppelsdorfer Friedhof statt.

Bonner Universitäts-Buchdruckerei, Gebr. Scheur

The notice sent to friends. It gives the day and hour of death, following "a premature childbirth, of my spouse, our daughter and sister, Mrs. Annie Schumpeter, born Reisinger, in the 24th year of her life." The words at the bottom tell the time and place of Annie's funeral and the name of the cemetery.

PART II

The Adult, 1926–1939:

Capitalism and Society

PROLOGUE

What He Had Learned

We would rather be ruined than changed.

W. H. AUDEN, "The Age of Anxiety," 1948

THE ONSET OF widespread entrepreneurial capitalism is very recent. There were early forerunners in Venice, Florence, and the Netherlands, but they did not develop into full-fledged market economies. These kinds of economies, measured backward from the twenty-first century, have a short history—the equivalent of four human lifetimes of seventy-five years each. Before about 1700, human beings had organized themselves almost everywhere according to traditional patterns.

The most striking fact about capitalism, therefore, aside from its economic efficiency, is its late appearance. Why did it take so long to arrive? Once it did emerge, why was it so widely resisted for so many years? And why do so many otherwise intelligent people in so many parts of the world still fight against its adoption? Why would they rather be ruined than changed? Obviously, these questions are as much cultural and social as they are economic. And in the period after the deaths of Johanna and Annie, Schumpeter deflected much of his attention away from economic theory and toward the exploration of cultural and social phenomena.[1]

He already knew, or was soon to discover, that the patterns of pre-capitalist society reflected some very deep-seated human values and traditions:

A conviction that spiritual life suffered grievous damage if people became immersed in materialism. In the sixth century B.C. the Athenian statesman Solon observed that "many evil men are rich, and good men poor." Most major religions also warn against the corruption that accompanies the pursuit of wealth. Confucius said, "The chase of gain is rich in hate." The Hebrew Bible asserts that "the love of money is the root of all evil." The Christian Gospel of Matthew declares that "it is easier for a camel to go through the eye of a needle than for a rich man to enter into the Kingdom of God."

The absence of belief in upward social and economic mobility. Before the Industrial Revolution, which began in about 1760 and hit full stride after 1840, most people believed that they should stay in their place and live according to their means. They were supposed to know and accept their lot in life. "There's place and means for every man alive," Shakespeare wrote in *All's Well That Ends Well* (1602). The notion of widespread social and economic mobility would have seemed incomprehensible. So would the idea of geographic mobility, unless one were a trader, seafarer, or member of a nomadic tribe. Schumpeter's own travels, coming after his ancestors' four-hundred-year residence in Triesch, exemplified a new sense of mobility, born in the eighteenth century and burgeoning in the nineteenth. Schumpeter's financial ups and downs also typified the quick changes in social and economic status characteristic of modern capitalism—but wholly different from prior human experience.

No widespread sense of personal freedom and individual autonomy. In 1772, four years before the American Declaration of Independence, only 4 percent of the earth's people were "free," according to estimates by the English economic writer Arthur Young. The remaining 96 percent labored as slaves, serfs, indentured servants, or vassals. They owed much or all of their work to their owners, kings, warlords, landlords, tribal chiefs, or other masters. Their incentives to work hard were very low, since people will generally toil and innovate more for their own benefit than for others'.

Prussia did not liberate its serfs until 1805, and Russia not until 1861. The United States did not outlaw slavery until 1865, Brazil until 1888, Saudi Arabia until 1962. And despite recent progress in many countries, opportunities for women and oppressed ethnic groups are still constrained almost everywhere. The potential economic energy never released because of all this subjugation, over such a very long time, is incalculable.[2]

The governance of most occupations and crafts by cartels (agreements to divide markets and keep prices high) and guilds (exclusive associations of craftspeople). These pervasive feudal conditions meant that the vast majority of workers, whether in agriculture or crafts, could not change jobs. Systems of apprenticeship typically lasted for seven years. Employers could hire few people from outside the guild or fire few from inside. What modern economists call "labor mobility" was almost nonexistent, and Schumpeter was about to analyze the reasons why.

Even today, the human impulse that lies behind this tendency has extraordinary power. Most people, consciously or not, regard their jobs as a type of personal property. In much of the contemporary world, even the capitalist world, it remains very difficult to fire employees. Owners or managers who undertake to lay people off do so at the risk of their own safety, or even their lives. (If this sounds like an exaggeration, ask someone from India, Mexico, or some other country where layoffs are difficult or impossible.) In a global context, the American tradition of freedom to fire people, which in law is called "employment at will," represents the exception, not the rule.

Entailed estates marked by primogeniture. Entailment (imposition of a specified succession of heirs) and primogeniture (inheritance solely by the family's eldest son) had numerous results, almost none of which promoted economic progress. For one thing, they discouraged innovation because they dampened risk-taking. Most owners behaved like stewards preserving property they already held rather than like entrepreneurs striving to gain more. Then, too, eldest sons were expected to make at least some provision for their siblings, and these subsidies drained capital that might have been put to better use elsewhere. Most seriously, entailment prevented the sale and therefore the widespread ownership of land. In Schumpeter's own Austria, some laws of entailment persisted until 1919. In most of the world, from the seventeenth century onward, the gradual dispersion of land ownership became a fundamental democratic movement that had powerful results for economic growth. People work harder and more intelligently on their own land than as hired hands on someone else's.

A primitive financial system that lacked paper money, stocks, bonds, or any other credit mechanism. This was a particularly telling reason for the late arrival of capitalism, and a key to why Schumpeter laid such heavy emphasis on the creation of credit. For well over a thousand years, long past the Middle Ages, most major religions forbade the lending of money at interest. These religions included both Christianity and Islam. In 1910 when Schumpeter was practicing law in Egypt, he barely escaped an ugly incident when he inadvertently insulted his creditor by offering to pay interest on a loan.

There were, of course, important exceptions: the Medici bankers, the Fuggers, and individual Jewish bankers, who faced no religious barriers to their profession. But largely as a consequence of Christian and Islamic taboos, banks did not become common in most parts of the world until the nineteenth century. As late as the 1790s there were only three in the United States; a hundred years later there were thirty thousand. Without funds from royal, aristocratic, or religious patronage—the sources of money not only for art and architecture but also for enterprises such as Galileo's experiments and Columbus's voyages of discovery—inventors and businesspeople could find no credit to finance their ventures. Almost by itself, this situation was enough to stifle the surges of technology and entrepreneurship that came to define modern capitalism.

The absence of the two pillars that support all successful business systems: a modern concept of private property and a framework for the rule of law. Without the institution of private property—the freedom of individuals to own, buy, and sell—no capitalist system can prosper. And in the absence of effective legal protection, the fruits of capitalism will be stolen by criminals, robber barons, and corrupt governments, thereby destroying people's incentives to work hard. In addition, capitalism is such a powerful engine that it can easily spin out of control. Capitalism is so innovative that it is forever advancing into gray legal areas, and business scandals—especially in finance—have been so frequent that they may be regarded as endemic to the system. As a result, capitalism requires repeated adjustments of the law, credible enforcement mechanisms, and constant vigilance. Public regulation through intricate legal frameworks—the law of contracts, competition, partnerships, corporations, and so on—is essential.

Schumpeter understood almost all of these things very well by 1925. He knew that capitalism could take quite different forms in different countries and that it carried strong but not necessarily decisive political implications. As a longtime subject of the Habsburg monarchy, he sensed that capitalism promoted democratic and representative government but did not require them. The distinction between varieties of capitalism became especially evident in

Germany during the 1930s, when the Nazi government kept the outward form of a market economy while burying individual rights under a totalitarian government. A similar lesson has reappeared in the twenty-first century, when China and other countries have partially converted to capitalism while retaining authoritarian political regimes.

In democratic nations, meanwhile, the "mixed economy" appeared during the 1930s and afterward, as governments took on stronger regulatory roles and began to erect welfare states. The possibility of *stable* mixed economies was one of the few aspects of modern capitalism that Schumpeter could not foresee. Only in the last half of the twentieth century did it become clear that the spectacular success of mixed economies in Europe, the United States, and Japan was going to continue for a long time. Their success showed that capitalism is a more flexible economic and social system than even Schumpeter had thought, with many possible blends between the public and private sectors.[3]

As early as 1911 Schumpeter had flatly asserted in *The Theory of Economic Development* that individual entrepreneurship held the key to economic growth in any country. And he recognized that the freer a system became—the more rights a government guaranteed to individuals—then the greater the opportunity for unfettered entrepreneurship and therefore the higher the potential for economic growth. In this sense he was an early messenger of the connection between capitalism and personal freedom.

As might have been predicted for a prophet of innovation, he developed a special fascination with the United States. In an article published in 1919 he wrote that in nineteenth-century America, unlike other countries, the best brains had flocked to business. But he might well have gone back further in time. In large measure, the United States achieved its position as the world's leading economy because it had a strong entrepreneurial spirit from the start. As the historian Carl Degler once put it, "Capitalism came in the first ships." The colonies that later made up the United States were settled mostly by entrepreneurial Europeans in the seventeenth and eighteenth centuries—the precise moment in history when modern capitalism was beginning to sweep aside traditional systems.[4]

Schumpeter argued that once a full-fledged capitalist system did arrive, it improved primarily not the lives of kings, warlords, and aristocrats but those of ordinary people. He went on to say that it helped some far more than others, because it distributed its fruits unequally, both within the same country and among different countries. In this assertion, he and many others who came to the same conclusion were correct, however unjust the result might be. Even in the twenty-first century, the so-called rich countries are getting richer, though they contain only 15 percent of the world's population. (Of the approximately 190 countries now in existence, only about 25 are classified by the World Bank and other agencies as rich.) The 15 percent of the earth's people who live in the rich countries enjoy incomes about six times those of the other 85 percent.[5]

The full list of reasons why these variations exist is long, and it begins with the characteristics of traditional systems listed above. It includes not only economic factors but also cultural, religious, and social mores. The number of sayings and proverbs warning against change has been legion, in many languages. As late as the nineteenth century, the Spanish adage, "Let no new thing arise" *(Que no haya novedad)* was used as an everyday valedictory between friends. Most people have been inherently fearful of uncertainty, and not quick to embrace the risks that accompany capitalism's creative destruction. Nor, generally, have those who benefit most from capitalism's bounties been notably eager to share their good fortune with the disadvantaged, either at home or abroad. Again, there are conspicuous exceptions: Andrew Carnegie, Henry Ford, Bill and Melinda Gates, and Warren Buffet. But the generalization still holds.[6]

Schumpeter spent the rest of his career explaining the elements necessary for a full understanding of capitalism—as an economic, social, political, and even psychological system. The remainder of this book shows how he did that, what the doing of it cost him, and how much the world has benefited from his having done it.

I O

New Intellectual Directions

I burned my life, that I might find
A passion only of the mind.

LOUISE BOGAN, "The Alchemist," 1922

AFTER THE DEATHS of Johanna and Annie, Schumpeter could hardly concentrate on anything except his grief. It seemed inconceivable to him that so many blows had hit in such quick succession. And in addition to his personal tragedies, he worried about his large financial debts in Vienna—envisioning subpoenas, indictment, and a scandal that would "damage me as a professor." This nightmare, though much exaggerated by his sorrows, was not entirely irrational, and he lived with it for many years afterward.[1]

In the meantime, he tried to bury his miseries through constant work. As he wrote Gustav Stolper, "I now know what it feels like within the unalterable, impregnable walls of the cells in which one keeps the raving mad. Only, when the raving lunatic has moments of clarity, perhaps he recognizes—I do at least—that he is best off in the cell with its padded walls. My padded walls are the notes, the open books, etc., of which I can take hold and to which I react."[2]

But even immersion in his work proved very difficult. In order to function at all, he looked for some way to keep drawing on the support of Johanna and Annie. In his diary he began to refer to them as his *Hasen,* a German pet name for dear ones (its literal meaning is "rabbits"). Week after week, he would write

"O Mother and Mistress, help me," and ask for the strength to do his research and writing. Sometimes his diary entries and lecture notes begin with the initials H s D (*Hasen sei Dank*—an expression thanking his *Hasen*). His salvation came from work and still more work, all sustained by these ritualistic appeals to his wife and mother.[3]

As he tried to submerge his emotions and live strictly within his intellect, he began to search for a new "scientific" home beyond the narrow strictures of his discipline. And he found it through a creative fusion of economics and social theory, which he laid out in a broad new stream of work. Soon his publications brought him more invitations to speak before academic and business groups in Germany, Britain, and other countries. Travel took him away from Bonn, the scene of his heartbreak, and also earned money to help pay his debts. He took these trips alone, trying to lose himself in his wanderings. He met new people, charmed new audiences, and spread his fame. He also visited dozens of cathedrals—sketching their stained-glass windows, stone adornments, and even entire buildings. He did this year after year, and kept the drawings as mementos.[4]

Without quite realizing it, he was looking for a new physical home as well as a new scientific one. More restless than ever, he traveled throughout Europe and in 1931 took a long cruise to Asia, where he spent three weeks lecturing in Japan. Most importantly, he began to teach at both Bonn and Harvard, making five transatlantic trips between 1927 and 1932.

But his immediate task was to prepare a new edition of *The Theory of Economic Development*, which he had started to revise before Annie died. The lessons of this seminal work had begun to fade during the upheavals of World War I, and by the 1920s the book was out of print. The publisher wanted to issue a new version as well as an English translation, and so did Schumpeter, who turned to the task with new fervor. The result was that *The Theory of Economic Development* became the only one of his major works on which he spent sufficient time and energy to rethink, revise, and condense. The second German edition appeared in 1926, a third in 1931, and the English translation in 1934. To underscore the book's breadth, he added a subtitle: *An Inquiry into Profits, Capital, Credit, Interest, and the Business Cycle.*[5]

The English version is only 235 pages long, less than half the length of the 548-page German original of 1911. Most translations from German into English result in a 15–20 percent decrease in length without any condensation. But

Schumpeter had already shortened *The Theory of Economic Development* to 369 pages for the revised German edition, and he cut it even more for the English version, trying to make the book more accessible to readers. The second German edition is less technical and easier to follow than the original, and at its appearance in 1926 received very favorable notices in numerous journals. *The American Economic Review* called it "one of the most stimulating and fascinating books that has been written on economic theory. It is, since it gives the first elaborate *dynamic economics* in the proper sense, very revolutionary."[6]

Schumpeter delegated almost all decisions about English-language publication to the venerable economist Frank Taussig, whom he had known for twenty years and who in 1927 recruited him as a visiting professor at Harvard. Taussig wrote one prospective translator that Schumpeter "has a bubbling mind, always ranging into new regions and new thoughts. His sentences are full of parenthetic matter, and they are usually too long . . . there will often be need of dividing one of his German sentences into two or three of an English version." In the end, Taussig found the perfect translator—his own son-in-law, Redvers Opie, a bright young English economist who knew Schumpeter and greatly admired his work. Taussig wrote Schumpeter that "there is no need of troubling you about the personality of the translator. Take my word for it that it is a competent person."[7]

Opie began the translation in early 1931. During the summer of that year, he traveled to Bonn and cloistered himself with Schumpeter for several weeks of intense discussion. He then returned to Harvard and worked until the middle of 1932, when he sent the manuscript to Schumpeter. In September, after still more revisions, Schumpeter mailed it back. An exuberant Opie then wrote to him, "My admiration for your English is now unbounded . . . I really do believe that you have expressed yourself more clearly in English than in German." And indeed the English version is much more readable than the German.[8]

Taussig then offered the now-finished English translation to Harvard University Press, which brought out the book in 1934. In his new preface, Schumpeter asserted that "some of the ideas submitted in this book go back as far as 1907; all of them had been worked out by 1909." In other words, he had done the basic analysis during his time in Czernowitz and the years leading up to it. He had benefited from his experiences in politics and business, but they

Schumpeter with Redvers Opie, 1931, crossing the street in downtown Bonn, about a block from the university.

had only reinforced his thinking about the essence of capitalism. More than ever, he believed entrepreneurship and credit creation to be the wellsprings of economic growth.[9]

Even as he revised *The Theory of Economic Development,* Schumpeter worked hard on another big manuscript, which he called his "money book." Money is one of the most difficult subjects in economics to understand and explain, but Schumpeter had already published a long and excellent article on it in 1917. In that essay, which—typically for Schumpeter—covers several centuries of history, he had emphasized the role of money and credit in economic progress, amplifying what he had written in *The Theory of Economic Development.*[10]

But the more he labored on his money book—"day after day like a mad buffalo," as he wrote Gustav Stolper in 1930—the more intractable the job seemed to become. He poured endless hours into the book, but he never published it. Finally, he judged the whole effort "a thoroughly bad performance." Although he never understood what had gone wrong, the answer was actually quite simple: he had tried to include far too much detail. Schumpeter believed that to study money or any other economic subject properly, one must give due attention to history, sociology, and other fields. Without insights from those quarters, one could never understand the institutions that affect economic growth, such as capital markets, legal systems, and political bodies, all of which relate directly to the phenomenon of money.[11]

In 1930 John Maynard Keynes brought out his own book on the subject, which he titled *A Treatise on Money.* Although this book has many shortcomings, Keynes said most of what Schumpeter had intended to say, and in more compact form. Schumpeter believed that Keynes had appropriated some of his own ideas without attribution, but he nevertheless wrote him profuse congratulations on a "splendid achievement."[12]

One of the hallmarks of first-rate economic theorists is their ability to present a stripped-down model of reality without losing its essence—and by this measure Keynes was Schumpeter's superior. As Einstein once put it, "Everything should be made as simple as possible, but no simpler." And with a different take on the same issue, T. S. Eliot observed that "Anyone can carve a goose if there are no bones." When Schumpeter took up a subject such as money, he insisted on working with the whole goose, bones and all. He knew so much about so many things that he sometimes lost sight of the "simple as possible" part of Einstein's dictum. Schumpeter wanted to create an "exact" economics for money and other complex subjects. But often there were just too many variables, and he was unwilling to give them up—no matter how hard he had to work to include them.[13]

His erudition was far more extensive than that of Keynes, who knew less about history, had scant interest in sociology, and could not read German well. On the other hand, Keynes had a real genius for persuasive simplification and did not hesitate to use it—on the subject of money or anything else. As Schumpeter later said of the kind of analysis at which Keynes excelled, "We always put, against the heavy sacrifices it entails, its one great virtue, Simplification." Implying, of course, the danger of *over*simplification. Schumpeter once wrote to a former student of his, "My model [of entrepreneurship] may seem fuzzy and difficult to handle mathematically but it is *real* and you can see it. The Keynesian determinants (so-called) are a paper screen interposed between the student and reality." Schumpeter's fascination with the growth of industrial society—and therefore with its history and sociology—greatly enriched his analysis. He knew that many "dilettantes," as he put it, took up the practice of sociology as a means of escaping the strictures of other fields. But he did not consider himself a dilettante, and he knew from his work with Max Weber that the discipline was indispensable to the analysis of capitalism and of social classes.[14]

In 1927, when he made a year-long trip to Harvard as a visiting professor, the university's sociologists had not yet split off from the Economics Department to form their own independent Social Relations group. For Schumpeter this was a fortunate circumstance, since his own approach to economics was becoming more sociological and he was able to converse with some of the brightest young people in the field. Economics would remain the center of this thinking—the living room of his intellect. But history, sociology, and psychology would claim their own spaces as well.[15]

In avoiding narrow specialization, Schumpeter was going against the prevailing academic tide. Instead, he was following a long European tradition aimed at constructing grand social theory. This custom was exemplified by writers such as Hegel, Comte, Nietzsche, Mill, Marx, Freud, and Weber, all of whom sought, in their own ways, to conceptualize the human condition as a unitary whole and to avoid undue simplification. Most of them freely crossed disciplinary lines—embracing philosophy, history, law, and economics as well as the newer disciplines of sociology, psychology, and political science. In particular, the writings of Marx and Weber directly influenced Schumpeter, as he reworked and absorbed their ideas into his own original syntheses. Meanwhile, he read everything of importance ever written on economics, from ancient times to the present.

His move toward a more historical and sociological approach is particularly evident in an article he published in 1926, titled "Gustav von Schmoller and the Problems of Today." Here he honored Schmoller for extending economics beyond pure theory. This was a change from Schumpeter's earlier views, which had not been as generous to the German Historical School. But he now believed that Schmoller, along with Weber, had pointed the way toward a new kind of historically grounded economic sociology—or social economics, as the German *Sozialökonomie* is perhaps better translated. Schumpeter had changed his mind because of his own study and his experience in politics and business, which strengthened his appreciation of the importance of institutions. His greatness as a thinker is nowhere better exemplified than at turns such as these: moments when his intellectual restlessness propelled him toward new ways of thinking, even when that meant changing the views he had carefully worked out at some previous time.[16]

As HE SHUTTLED between Bonn and Harvard—still trying to escape his grief through unremitting work—he brought out two more articles related to *Sozialökonomie*. Both were in the European tradition of grand theory, and both stand as benchmarks in Schumpeter's growth as a social thinker.

In the first article, "The Tendencies of Our Social Structure" (1928), he examines the relationships among a nation's political, social, and economic ways of organizing itself. He writes that in contemporary Germany, numerous problems derive from a mismatch between the country's economic order and its social structure. He says that Germany is now fully capitalist in its economic organization but that the new order had come so fast that the nation's social customs remained stuck in rural and even feudal ways of thinking. As recently as 1871, he points out, nearly two thirds of Germany's people lived on farms or in towns of fewer than two thousand inhabitants, and less than 5 percent in cities of over one hundred thousand. But by 1925, the proportion living in large cities had grown more than five-fold, while the percentage in rural areas had shrunk by half.[17]

Big leaps in agricultural productivity had caused this shift. Whereas only 4 percent of Germany's farms used machinery in 1882, over 66 percent did by 1925. Most farms did not grow in size during this period, but mechanization enabled their owners to produce much more output with fewer hired hands. Mechanization pushed workers off the land and into cities. The number of landless laborers thus shrank drastically, and the formerly divisive political issue of small farms versus big estates ceased to be a national controversy. Those who remained on the land became prosperous self-employed farmers, working mid-sized acreages with modern machinery. "As much as agrarian reformers still agitate," Schumpeter wrote, "*within the rural sphere* the farmer has got what he wanted." In the process, farmers changed from being the most radical segment of society to being the most conservative.[18]

For industrial workers, on the other hand, the social structure evolved quite differently. Traditional craftsmen, who regarded their trades as personal property, detested the new factory-based capitalist order. Exclusive craft guilds fought hard against industrialization, sometimes demanding that machinery itself be outlawed. But these backward-looking craftsmen were fighting an unwinnable battle. Capitalism was not only mechanizing industrial production but was also bringing an influx of farm laborers into cities to operate the new machines.[19]

Schumpeter goes on to say that in the early twentieth century, some segments of the old craft classes had made honest attempts to adapt by pursuing industrialization themselves. As examples he cites "the bakers in Danzig and Berlin in building a bread factory in which they are workers, 'capitalists,' and salesmen all at the same time." Many former craftsmen became owners of small businesses and then aligned themselves politically with the upper middle class. It was therefore easier to predict how their thinking might evolve than to forecast the ideology of urbanized former peasants.[20]

Meanwhile, very large businesses had also appeared, although they were not nearly as numerous in Germany as was commonly thought. "This is an interesting reflex of the petty bourgeois attitude . . . so characteristic of Germans. But if one defines a big business as employing more than 1,000 persons, then there are only 892 such firms, with about 2.1 million total employment"—a small fraction of the total work force. The trend toward bigger companies will continue, Schumpeter predicts. But in any modern economy, the class structure has no sharp divisions between labor and capital; it "is not even close to being as simple as Marxist theory."[21]

The real divisions, Schumpeter says, lie *within* the new industrial order. "The differences between a tycoon and a medium factory owner are so big that one might speak of two different classes." Nevertheless, though these two groups seldom recognize it, they have one important thing in common: their social position is more unstable than that of any other class. In the new economy, business families rise and fall so quickly that it becomes difficult to speak of them as social classes at all. In "the fast change in the position of families in the upper classes," Schumpeter says, "there is clearly taking place a very democratic and effective selection of brains." The economy had entered the realm of meritocracy, which is inherently hostile to hereditary class. Entrepreneurship had become a *function,* not a marker of class.[22]

In the case of workers, a similar division had evolved. "Maybe it is not even appropriate to speak, in the Marxist tradition, of contemporary social battles as between labor and capital; maybe it is more a battle between different categories of labor"—skilled versus unskilled. The number of industrial employees will continue to grow, but in the meantime it is simply inaccurate "to say that the worker is the exploited proletarian who is just a tool in someone else's hand, who can never gain his own living space. In fact, the worker today is the biggest stakeholder of the capitalist economy."[23]

In the new high-wage industrial system, skilled and even many unskilled workers can live a bourgeois life. "This is exactly what is despised by both socialists and intellectual visionaries," says Schumpeter. "It is utmost rubbish to argue that the worker is barred from any social advancement. One should never forget that today's entrepreneurs very often are themselves former workers and sons of workers." Thus, "the work force is no homogeneous mass. The united proletarian conscience of class is only a utopian idea, with little connection to reality." Skilled and unskilled workers think in very different ways, and skilled workers in particular have a real stake in the new social and economic order. It is the untrained laborer who is more likely to become politically radical and whose future attitude is least predictable.[24]

Schumpeter's unique approach to social theory, exemplified in this 1928 article, expressed an altogether novel vision of both capitalism and class structure. His insights stretched far beyond what most other economists and sociologists of the time were writing about. He was not "revolutionizing" either economics or sociology. Instead, he was integrating the two disciplines into a fresh and invaluable social economics that elucidated the fundamental nature of capitalism. Harnessing his personal grief, Schumpeter had thrown himself into an intransigent intellectual problem and broken through to something very near a solution.

Schumpeter published the 1928 essay in a journal sponsored by the German chemical industry, and for that reason he did not regard it as "science" in the academic sense. But at about the same time, he brought out a related article, "Social Classes in an Ethnically Homogeneous Environment," that soon took its place as a seminal contribution to the young discipline of sociology.

This piece ranges widely over European history, from medieval times to the present. In its opening pages, Schumpeter once more alludes to Marxist thinkers, who at that time were very influential in European social thought. He notes the temptation of the theorist "to stoke his sputtering engine with the potent fuel of the class struggle"—and then proceeds to demolish the premises on which the alleged struggle is based.[25]

In a remarkably simple formulation, he defines the "class phenomenon" by saying that members of a particular class behave toward one another differently from the way they do toward other classes. That is pretty much all there is to it: "They are in closer association with one another; they understand each other better; they work more readily in concert; they close ranks and erect barriers against the outside; they look out into the same segment of the world, with the same eyes, from the same viewpoint, in the same direction." The best single test of the existence of a class is "one that makes it outwardly recognizable and involves no class theory—in the fact that intermarriage prevails among its members."[26]

Even though Schumpeter explicitly abjures the word "elites" in this article, he is in fact writing about the rise and fall of capitalist elites. He says hardly anything about either middle or lower classes, except to note their potential rise to elite status themselves through entrepreneurship. Most strikingly, he argues that class status at any given moment is the result of prior events, and is therefore likely to be out of date. Thus, much of the existing social order at any particular time "can be explained only by the survival of elements that are actually alien to its own trends." The original unit of classes was the family, and the most common path into a higher class—for individuals or families—was "a single-minded marriage policy pursued over centuries." The industrial revolution made this kind of marriage policy more difficult but by no means put an end to it.[27]

"How does it happen," Schumpeter then asks, "that one family rises, while the other falls?" This was a real puzzle, but he believed he had the answer. He begins by pointing out that most of the wealthy families that led society at the midpoint of the nineteenth century were no longer on top three generations later. This situation wholly contradicted Marx's insistence that the rich would get richer and the poor poorer. "This [Marxist] view is a typical example of how bias in favor of a theory blinds the theorist to the simplest facts, grotesquely distorting their propositions."[28]

A truer diagnosis lies in the incessant dynamism and competitive innovations that occur within capitalist business. Marx himself saw this dynamism—better than any other economist of his time—but even he did not begin to grasp its full implications. For it is never enough, as Marx believed, simply to "plow back" profits into the family business. No company, Schumpeter countered, can ever retain a position at the top of its industry without doing very much more than this—"without blazing new trails, without being devoted, heart and soul, to the business alone."[29]

One might think that the sound practices of saving, living frugally, and maintaining the company on a solid foundation would suffice. But Schumpeter argues that any company following these routines—however admirable they seem at first glance—will soon be overtaken by aggressive, risk-taking, competitive entrepreneurs. He is very emphatic on this point: "The introduction of new production methods, the opening up of new markets—indeed, the successful carrying through of new business combinations in general—all these imply risk, trial and error, the overcoming of resistance, factors lacking in the treadmill of routine." He concludes by saying, "As to the question why this is so, it is answered by the theory of entrepreneurial profit." Newcomers to the industry will bring fresh ideas, earn much higher profits, and drive incumbents out of business—through the simple device of fixing on economic growth as their sole objective.[30]

This is very hard to do, Schumpeter concedes. Most successful people, especially once they become wealthy, do not want to continue obsessing over economic growth. They come to abhor the relentless demands of continuous innovation. They want to enjoy themselves and live a better-rounded life. For these reasons, great enterprises typically outgrow the abilities of founding families to sustain a position at the top of their industries. "Mere husbanding of already existing resources, no matter how painstaking, is always characteristic of a declining position."[31]

Under truly modern forms of capitalism, the task of maintaining a prime position becomes even more difficult. "Industrial leaders must shoulder an often unreasonable burden of current work, which takes up the greater part of each day." Entrepreneurs need "extraordinary physical and nervous energy." The best of them can sustain their efforts on a high level only if they have "that special kind of 'vision' . . . concentration on business to the exclusion of other interests, cool and hard-headed shrewdness—traits by no means irreconcilable with passion." And entrepreneurs working in very large corporations must have even more talents. They must know how to "woo support" among their colleagues, "handle men with consummate skill," and give others ample credit for the organization's achievements.[32]

But simply being born into a prominent family confers none of these abilities. In modern industrial society, therefore, "the persistence of class position is an illusion . . . Class barriers *must* be surmountable, at the bottom as well as at the top." The key to a higher class position is for an individual to strike out "along unconventional paths. This has always been the case, but never so much as in the world of capitalism." Most industrial families have risen from the ranks of workmen and craftsmen "because one of their members has *done something novel*," and this is "virtually the only method by which they can make the great leap out of their class." One reason why Schumpeter admired the British aristocracy was precisely its versatile and permeable character— quite different from the static society of snail-racing degenerates he had known in Vienna. In Britain, one could rise into a higher class much more quickly than in Austria.[33]

Schumpeter concludes by asserting that "class barriers are always, without exception, surmountable." How? Through superior "aptitude with respect to those functions which the environment makes 'socially necessary.'" And when economic progress became *the* socially necessary function, then high-aptitude entrepreneurs rose to the top. But the dynamic nature of capitalism made their position, and that of their families, inherently unstable, and this represented a momentous change: "The warlord was automatically the leader of his people in virtually every respect. The modern industrialist is anything but such a leader."[34]

Overall, Schumpeter's essay on social classes is full of pertinent history, shrewd observation, and counterintuitive truths. For these reasons, it has been a staple in the discipline of sociology since the time of its original publication and has enlivened graduate seminars in universities all over the world.[35]

A third important article Schumpeter wrote during his long trauma over the deaths of his *Hasen* was "The Instability of Capitalism." This 1928 piece appeared in the world's leading quarterly in the field at that time, the *Economic Journal,* edited by Keynes. Here, Schumpeter argues that capitalism's defining trait of constant change and innovation makes the whole idea of a capitalist "equilibrium" misleading.[36]

He also insists that economics cannot be confined to abstract theory but must incorporate the empirical realities of modern business. Conversely, realities alone are not sufficient without theory. As he puts it, "Mere 'recognition' of a fact means nothing unless the fact be welded into the rest of the argument and made to do theoretic work."[37]

The way to understand general economic expansions, Schumpeter goes on to say, is to break them down by looking closely at particular industries. The origins of broad expansions always come from innovations in specific industries, which then ramify into other parts of the economy—the suppliers of these industries, the distributors, and ultimately the customers. In the nineteenth and early twentieth centuries, economic growth came in clear sequences of leading-sector breakthroughs: first in textiles, then in steam engines and iron, then in electricity and chemicals. Overall, industry-specific innovation "does not *follow,* but *creates* expansion."[38]

None of this, Schumpeter adds, can be explained in the usual economists' terms of equilibrium. Instead, innovation requires continuous *dis*equilibrium—led by entrepreneurs obsessed with what they are doing. Innovation itself is primarily "a feat not of intellect, but of will . . . a special case of the social phenomenon of leadership." The barriers to innovation consist of "the resistances and uncertainties incident to doing what has not been done before." These difficulties are often immense, and to surmount them "is the function characteristic of the entrepreneur."[39]

Here, Schumpeter again emphasizes the crucial role of credit—not common credit for the purpose of running an existing business but large amounts of money placed on the table as bets on the success of a new venture—money that can be lost completely if the venture fails. "Innovation, being discontinuous and involving considerable change and being . . . typically embodied in new firms, requires large expenditure previous to the emergence of any revenue . . . 'Credit-creation' therefore, becomes an essential part both of the mechanism of the process and of the theory explaining it."[40]

All of these elements, Schumpeter writes, are endemic to the capitalist routine. Outside influences—wars, earthquakes, even many new technologies and inventions—are not the sources of the perpetual changes that characterize capitalism. Instead, change is part and parcel of capitalism itself, and it comes from entrepreneurial behavior within the system. This "one element in the capitalist process, embodied in the type and function of the entrepreneur," will "destroy any equilibrium." In other words, remorseless uproar is the natural state of capitalism, and the only real equilibrium is a constant state of disequilibrium.[41]

In 1928, when Schumpeter published this article, companies in certain industries in Germany, the United States, and elsewhere were becoming much larger. Addressing this subject, he argued that innovation often benefited from the rise of big business, because giant firms could afford to gamble on new techniques. They were willing to absorb losses in some of their new ventures because they could be confident of profits in others. "Failure in any particular case loses its dangers, and [innovation] tends to be carried out as a matter of course on the advice of specialists." Bank credit becomes less important, because large companies can retain substantial sums from their earnings and they have better access to the outside money market.[42]

He cites the United States as his best example. Early in the twentieth century, firms such as American Telephone and Telegraph, General Electric, Eastman Kodak, and DuPont set up research departments specifically for the purpose of developing new products and processes. They made innovation itself part of their business routine—and this was a profound change. Later in the twentieth century, most large firms in all countries added a research and development department to their corporate structures.

At the same time, as Schumpeter had foreseen, new companies continued to spring up and to operate alongside the giants. Contrary to the expectations of many other analysts, "trustified" capitalism neither stifled innovation nor prevented the ongoing creation of new startups. Once again, Schumpeter had gone against the grain in his analysis and predictions, and he lived to see his vision confirmed by the march of time.

The analysis of big business, together with Schumpeter's foray into the sociology of classes, required intense and concentrated work. Persisting in his quest to get to the bottom of the capitalist process, he labored extraordinarily long hours and brought all of his talents to bear. Sometimes, as in the futile effort to write his "money book," he failed. But much more often he succeeded brilliantly. His new editions of *The Theory of Economic Development,* his fusion of sociology and economics into *Sozialökonomie,* his pioneering articles on social classes and the instability of capitalism—all of these were conceptual breakthroughs that helped to shape the future of social science.

For the remainder of his life, Schumpeter labored under continuous emotional stress, unable to escape the tragedies of 1926 except through the oblivion of unremitting work. And during the high plateau of his torture, which lasted from 1926 until the middle 1930s, Johanna and especially Annie remained so real to him, so much a part of his daily existence, that he brought them into the act of work itself. Night after night, he composed prayers imploring his *Hasen* for help in getting through the tasks he set for himself. The number of these prayers in his diary runs into the thousands. And he compulsively copied Annie's own diary—day by day, year by year—often annotating it with his own recollections. Sometimes Annie's diary and his own were merged into one running commentary.

During this same period, he also kept up a correspondence with members of Annie's family and received regular consolation, particularly from Milly Reisinger, her sister. Four years after Annie's death, Milly responded to one of Schumpeter's letters, "You write that you are becoming older, sadder and grayer . . . You feel this way only because apart from all your work you have no diversion and are so much alone." And shortly afterward, out of the blue, Milly sent him a virtual marriage proposal:

> Annie was certainly happy with you, I saw that and she said it to me repeatedly, in those few days that I was in Bonn. Before that time when she was taken to the hospital, she said to me: I might look after you, so that you had everything and didn't feel alone. I have thought about these words again and again, then the idea awoke in me that I would gladly marry you and that I would love you. Anyway I don't actually want any other man so long as you are so alone and lonely.

When Schumpeter offered no encouragement, Milly married one of her several suitors. But for the rest of his life, Schumpeter sent money to the Reisinger family in Vienna.[43]

In his autobiographical novel fragment, composed a few years after Annie and Johanna died, he wrote:

> And for modern man his work is everything—all that is left. . .
> Doing efficient work without aim, without hope. . .
> No family.
> No real friends.
> No woman in whose womanhood to anchor.

Constant work is what he continued to do, and not only to suppress his grief. He still had his enormous debts in Vienna to pay, and that task required a different type of work from the "scientific" economics and sociology he was pursuing.[44]

II

Policy and Entrepreneurship

Turn him to any cause of policy,
The Gordian knot of it he will unloose.

SHAKESPEARE, *The Life of King Henry the Fifth,* 1599

As SCHUMPETER'S WORKLOAD grew heavier in Bonn, he decided to hire someone to run his household. Fortunately, a good candidate was at hand. In January 1926, three months after he and Annie arrived in Bonn, he had employed as his secretary Maria Stöckel, an intelligent young woman from the town of Jülich, forty miles northwest of Bonn. About a year after Annie's death, he asked Mia, as she was called, to move in and manage his large residence. Mia soon proved to be an exceptionally capable assistant. She continued her work as secretary, typing his manuscripts and organizing his correspondence. She also brought order to his haphazard household.[1]

Twenty-one years old in 1927, Mia was attractive and fashionable. Her impish face often expressed the kind of sparkle characteristic of Schumpeter himself in happier times. After the loss of Annie and Johanna, he was so despondent that he needed not only the help of someone like Mia but also the companionship. In the years after she began working with him, she became more and more devoted to his well-being. She was so efficient that she could type full drafts of his letters and articles almost as fast as he could dictate them.[2]

During his time in Bonn (1925–1932), the number of Schumpeter's publications exceeded that of any comparable period in his life—a measure of the fixation on work that he used to escape constant sorrow. The total was sixty-five articles, compared with only eight from 1920 through 1924. Much of this new work was "science," as he called his books and his essays in professional journals. But he also wrote dozens of policy-oriented pieces directed toward a wider audience. Taken together, these articles are the equivalent of two medium-sized books.[3]

He did this less technical work in part to earn money for the payment of his debts in Vienna. The articles spread his reputation as an economic expert, which in turn brought a flood of invitations to speak before civic and industrial groups. Showman that he was, Schumpeter sometimes enjoyed the lecture circuit. "After my address in front of the glass industrialists of Germany," he wrote from Berlin to Ottilie Jäckel, his former secretary at the Biedermann Bank, "I almost have a moment of ease. Odd, something radiates from me when I talk publicly that catches not only the others but also myself!" Fourteen years his junior, Ms. Jäckel was one of Schumpeter's closest confidantes, and he sent her many candid letters.[4]

But often he professed to hate the kind of work he was doing. In September 1928 he told Ms. Jäckel that "what led me here [to Munich]—to give a lecture at a conference for the Union of German 'Wholesale and Overseas Merchants'—and what I did on the 18th in Cologne—lecture in front of the 'German Cement Union'—is the most unbearable [part] of my existence." These activities took time from his "scientific" work and demeaned him in his own eyes. "This prostitution," he wrote. "This lecturing and writing for money!" But he felt that he had to keep speaking and writing if he were ever going to pay off his many creditors. His debts were still so large that he estimated that it would take him twenty years to settle them in full. In fact, it took him only seven more years, until 1935.[5]

In journals analogous to today's *Fortune, Financial Times,* and *Wall Street Journal,* he pitched his message primarily to business audiences. Many pieces appeared in periodicals edited by his Viennese friend Gustav Stolper, who had moved to Berlin shortly after his own departure for the University of Bonn. With Schumpeter's help, Stolper founded and edited *The German Economist,* modeled on *The Economist* of London, then the world's leading magazine on

economics and business, as it remains today. In 1926 Schumpeter promised
Stolper that he would write articles for the new journal himself and recruit
other talented contributors. After a shaky start, the magazine proved very successful.[6]

Even though Schumpeter was a first-rate policy analyst who went straight to
the heart of any economic problem, he disliked prescribing public remedies,
because he thought he might compromise his scientific objectivity. "I am not
running a drug store," he once told an American business group. "I have no
pills to hand out; no clear-cut solutions for any practical problems that may
arise." As a consequence of his restraint, economists and historians do not usually speak of activist "Schumpeterian" national regimes in the way they do of
Marxist and Keynesian ones. Nor is Schumpeter identified with strict free-
market approaches, as are Adam Smith, Friedrich von Hayek, and Milton
Friedman.[7]

Yet it is not difficult to identify a Schumpeterian program—at whatever
level of analysis one chooses: the individual entrepreneur, the business firm, the
industry, or even the country. At all levels, Schumpeter's litmus test is whether
the players are pursuing innovation and bringing about creative destruction. If
they are, then the program is Schumpeterian. If they are not, it isn't.

When he broke his own rule about not running a drugstore and recommended specific policies—as in many of his articles for Stolper's *German Economist* and similar magazines—he always pushed for vigorous measures to promote entrepreneurship. But during the late 1920s and early 1930s, neither
Germany nor any other major country was in an advantageous position to pursue a long-range Schumpeterian program. The convulsion of the Great Depression made it very difficult for entrepreneurs to contemplate new projects.

In 1925, when Schumpeter moved to Bonn, Germany was not in quite the
mess that Austria had been during his time as finance minister in 1919. Even
so, Germany was a long way from economic and political stability. "Truly,
many times when I look at its leading figures in politics and the economy,"
Schumpeter wrote in 1928, "I feel sorry for Germany." Speaking of the government's "incompetence" and "lack of principles," Schumpeter compared its
politicians and civil servants unfavorably to those of the Hohenzollern and
Habsburg monarchies that had formerly ruled Germany and Austria. By the
time of Schumpeter's arrival in Bonn, Germany had recovered from its period

of hyperinflation, but it still bore a crushing burden of war reparations to Britain and France. As an added insult, the French army had occupied the Rhineland—the western region of Germany that includes Bonn—since 1919, and would continue to do so until 1930.[8]

During the middle 1920s, crucial financial assistance had arrived in the form of large American loans to the German government and to firms engaged in rebuilding the nation's industry. Through wages and profits, these companies helped the national tax system generate money to resume reparations payments, which had been suspended in 1923. Britain and France then used much of this money to repay their own wartime debts to the United States. In this way a triangular flow of funds originating in the United States supported the economies of Britain, France, and Germany, laying the basis for whatever economic progress they were able to make during the 1920s. Germany went through a depression during Schumpeter's first two years in Bonn, and only in 1928 did the country's gross domestic product reach its prewar level.[9]

Schumpeter's stay in Bonn came during the period between the end of World War I and the accession to power of Adolf Hitler in 1933. Germany during these years is often referred to as the Weimar Republic. Weimar is the small town in which the postwar writers of the new constitution did their work, having fled the revolutionary uproar in Berlin. The constitution set up a democratic government, but one far too weak and fragmented to operate effectively. More than a dozen political parties vied for power. Many won seats through the system of proportional representation, and they often showed little inclination to compromise. Ranging from the far left to the far right or representing some particular interest or region of the country, they often canceled out one another's influence—not unlike the factions within the Austro-Hungarian Parliament during Schumpeter's youth.

Some parties openly opposed the Weimar constitution, and the German judiciary did not penalize them, as it was charged to do. The judiciary was far sterner toward communists than toward right-wing ideologues: Adolf Hitler served only a few months' jail time for openly trying to overthrow the government. Since no party ever held a majority, coalition governments became necessary, but none stayed in office for very long. Constant quarrels between the federal and state governments further paralyzed policy-making. The only political sentiments that united the German people were resistance to the harsh terms of the Versailles Treaty—reparations in particular—and a growing nationalism directed toward restoring the country's place among the Great Powers.[10]

During this period, Germany was home to some of the world's strongest Socialist and Communist parties. In the elections of 1928, the Social Democratic Party won 153 of the total 491 seats in Parliament, and the Communist Party 54. Hitler's National Socialist German Workers' Party (whose name belied its ideology), won only 12 seats in 1928, less than one-fortieth of the total. In the elections of 1930, no fewer than 16 different parties won seats. Again the Social Democrats led, with 143 of the 577 total seats. The Communist Party won 77, while the Nazis' percentage increased to almost one-fifth, with 107 seats—an ominous development too little noticed. On the basis of Schumpeter's own analysis of changes in Germany's social structure, he should have taken heed of the ripeness of displaced craftsmen and newly urbanized peasants to Hitler's appeal; but he did not.[11]

At this time, Germany's business institutions were far better organized than its government, and Schumpeter's seven years in Germany brought his first prolonged encounter with a truly modern business system. Sophisticated companies excelled in heavy industries such as steel (Krupp, Thyssen) and motor vehicles (Mercedes, BMW). German firms led the world in chemicals and were second only to the Americans in electrical equipment.

A major trend in German business during the 1920s was a movement toward industrial self-regulation through the setting of standards. Associations in the private sector led these efforts, which the government then endorsed, giving them the force of law. The German Standards Committee, established in 1926, became a model for similar organizations in other countries, which created their own national standards, many of which eventually became international. During Schumpeter's time in Bonn, the number of industrial standards in Germany grew from 1,100 in 1925 to 4,500 in 1932.[12]

To this day, the achievements of capitalist business owe much to the adoption of such standards as horsepower for engines, sizes for cuts of lumber, thicknesses for sheets of steel, and safety regulations for electrical equipment. The United States adopted two-by-fours in the construction industry, the label UL (Underwriters' Laboratories) in electrical appliances, and SAE (Society of Automotive Engineers) for grades of motor oil, to name just a few. In the absence of standards, many routine operations that everyone takes for granted—shifting gears in a car, tuning radios to AM and FM stations, operating a computer—would be almost impossible. Standards can be used to exclude new companies from an industry, but on the whole they have benefited producers and consumers across the board.

Scores of German companies restructured themselves during Schumpeter's years in Bonn, a phenomenon that provided him with more evidence of capitalism's constant transformations. Small and medium-sized businesses, most of them family-owned, upgraded their operations and earned worldwide reputations for high quality. Many of these *Mittelstand* companies still operate today, in both manufacturing and service industries. Most maintain close ties to their communities and in numerous ways remain the heart of the German economy. Some have been acquired by larger firms, but many of the original brands are still familiar all over the world (Stihl chain saws, Zeiss optics, Hohner harmonicas), as well as newer brands that sprang up during the last half of the twentieth century (Tetra tropical fish food, Krones labeling machines, Hugo Boss and Jil Sander clothing).[13]

Big business also changed in major ways between 1925 and 1932, most notably through a wave of large-scale mergers. When Schumpeter moved to Bonn, five of the country's ten largest firms manufactured steel. By the time he left, four of the five (all but Krupp) had combined to form the Vereinigte Stahlwerke (United Steelworks), the nation's largest company. In 1925 three of Germany's twelve biggest firms were in chemicals (BASF, Bayer, and Hoechst). By 1932 these three plus several others had merged to form IG Farbenindustrie, which became the nation's second largest company. Many big mergers also occurred in banking. Schumpeter became fascinated by this process, which he called "trustification," using the American term.[14]

From the viewpoint of business executives, the motives for mergers were primarily to reduce price competition and upgrade production and marketing. Often, as with the great steel merger, the reorganizations imitated the American model (United States Steel). Sometimes the strategy worked well, but often it did not. The overall verdict is clouded by the coming of the Great Depression, which hit Germany initially in the form of declining exports.[15]

The world economic downturn, first evident in Britain, spread quickly from one country to another. When it reached the United States in 1929, the export of American cash dried up, and the German economy began a steep dive into full-scale depression. Unemployment reached 10 percent in 1929, 25 percent in 1931, and a whopping 33 percent during the winter of 1932–1933. These were portentous events, and many of Schumpeter's articles on public policy addressed them directly.

As GERMANY GRADUALLY descended into economic crisis, Schumpeter stepped forward with analyses and proposals that he offered in more accessible form than his typical academic writings. Between 1925 and 1932 he wrote a major series of articles on the condition of the German economy and on the government's economic policies. These articles, for *The German Economist* and other nontechnical magazines, display Schumpeter at his rhetorical best as he tries to sway his new countrymen away from disaster and toward sound business judgment. He concentrates on four topics that, at the time, were intensely controversial in Germany's national debates: tax levels and public budgets in the face of the reparations question; wages and unemployment; business booms and busts; and the underlying nature of capitalist society.

He begins his first article by attacking the policy of public bailouts of old or low-growth industries—an issue still familiar in many countries today because of large voting blocs employed in these sectors. But he does support government intervention. The way back to prosperity in Germany, Schumpeter writes, is by selective lending to companies in industries with high growth potential. "The strong ones, or those that can become strong, are to be strengthened, but the weak ones are not to be nursed." As conditions for public assistance, he argues, the companies must be forced to adopt innovative practices. He acknowledges that it will be hard to implement this kind of program, because politicians need votes and voters tend to look backward. But he urges a forward, long-term perspective, and avoidance of any quick economic fix.[16]

He next takes up the subject of why Germany's tax and budget systems were not working well. He shows that under the Weimar constitution, the central government provided minimal basic services and left most public functions to be paid for by state and local taxes. He then specifies how reform should move toward the goal of "fiscal equilibrium," that is, coordination of the tax system at all levels of government.[17]

As sources of new funds, he advocates additional taxes on luxury goods, rental income, and especially alcohol. The level of taxes on beer and hard liquor is so low, he says, that an increase can be exploited by state, federal, and municipal governments all at the same time. Citizens will accept this kind of tax so long as most of the revenues stay in the regions where the taxation takes place.[18]

Schumpeter wrote many of his articles on tax policy before the German economy began its decline. By 1929 the country was headed for serious trouble, and the tenor of his writings became more probing and insistent. Why, he now asked, was Germany drifting into such dangerous waters? Poor tax and budget policies were partly to blame, but both could easily be improved. The magic words were "accumulation of capital" for public and private investment directed toward entrepreneurial growth sectors. To the objection that favoring one sector over another might seem unfair, he counters that targeted investment pays returns to the whole economy within a few years and therefore helps everybody.[19]

On the touchy issue of personal income taxes, Schumpeter argues that they are justified but have been set too high. In his view, income taxes are effective only if they stay low enough to be accepted by society as a whole. During hard times, if a tax takes away a quarter or a fifth of someone's income, then it becomes destructive—inhibiting investment, diminishing consumption, and encouraging tax evasion. This is exactly what had happened in Germany during the 1920s. By today's standards, of course, these tax rates appear low, but at the time they were extremely high. When Schumpeter moved from Germany to the United States, his own income tax rate dropped from 25 percent to about 4 percent, even though his new salary was much higher.[20]

He also warns against the excessive use of inheritance taxes, especially as a means of reducing government deficits. Aimed at anyone except the very wealthy, they discourage savings and promote consumption as a way to avoid future estate taxes. A low inheritance tax rate is acceptable, but the government must take consumer psychology into account. The tax rate must be held to a level that potential savers consider reasonable, so that people will want to build up family nest eggs.[21]

As the German economy worsened, Schumpeter's writings took on an increasingly urgent tone, particularly with regard to widespread consumer demands for lower prices. If prices are reduced for too long a time, he argues, investors will become discouraged. A better approach would be to implement the measures he has advocated all along: setting the sales tax at a minimum of 1.5 percent (up from about 1 percent); introducing higher taxes on tobacco and alcohol; promoting investment and savings by any means possible. Had these policies been adopted at an early date, he says, the economy would have been in much better shape by 1930. Through a concurrent cut in "capital-hostile" taxes, the nation might have achieved a higher level of investment. Germany's "destiny" now depended on adopting a sound budget and tax policy, and the nation stood at an economic crossroads.[22]

Schumpeter had begun to worry that voters and leaders of low-income groups were becoming desperate and therefore ripe for demagoguery from both the right and the left. In one article published in 1930 he actually uses the word *Führer,* a likely allusion to either Hitler or some communist leader. A demagogue of this kind might cause "the masses" to demand a socialist program directed against business. Schumpeter argues that if a mild form of socialism were installed and then failed to work, a more severe version would likely follow. And if that happened, then economic growth would stall and almost everyone's standard of living would plummet.[23]

Addressing the issue of wage and employment policy, Schumpeter argues that in Germany the power of labor unions has not caused high wages and unemployment, as many people believe. Instead, these problems derive mainly from obsolete industrial structures—businesses honeycombed with guilds, cartels, and other quasi-monopolies that restrict production and reduce employment. The ongoing merger movement, if not managed properly, could shrink the level of employment still further.[24]

In a speech to the German association of textile manufacturers, Schumpeter argued that wage increases must be tied to rising productivity (output per hour worked). Mere redistribution of entrepreneurial profits from employers to workers would not help employees very much and would damage overall economic prosperity. And if wages rose without equal gains in productivity—as was happening in Germany—then living standards would soon go down overall. Wage increases in themselves could never lead to faster development, especially if they came at the expense of investment. Additional redistribution of money from the rich to the poor would not be sustainable because it could not lead to increased output; and in any case there was not enough money being created for redistribution to make much difference.[25]

At this time Germany had the strongest labor movement and most generous employee benefits of any major country. Corporate executives, while accepting the idea of social welfare, protested that their firms could not compete under too heavy a burden. In 1924 the director of the Reich Economic Council, a leading business group, said, "We do not need to follow the 'like it or lump it' policy of the Americans in the area of social policy, which is simply 'work or you die.' In America there is no social welfare policy at all. We certainly don't want that." On the other hand, "We need foreign credit, and the outside world asks: what are you going to do with the credit? We cannot afford things they cannot afford."[26]

Schumpeter agreed only partly with this line of thinking, because he did not regard welfare expenditures as the chief problem. In an article published in 1928, he concedes that the *sum* of German companies' wage payments, taxes, and welfare contributions is too high. Over time, this would lead to economic decline and then to social decay. As a remedy for the problem of wage levels, he proposes that two new institutions be set up under public/private sponsorship—one representing employers, the other workers. The two would meet continuously to coordinate wage levels. The overriding question is not an ideological one of "labor versus capital," as in the Marxist model. Instead, it is a practical matter of cooperative management for the common good.[27]

Long-term unemployment, he writes, can be mitigated by fighting monopolistic tendencies, but the present situation in Germany was inopportune for such a policy. Instead, he says that large firms and some cartels are appropriate for the time being, especially for industries facing high-tech foreign competition. Employing the "infant industry" argument that startups need temporary protection within the domestic market, Schumpeter defends time-limited cartels as helpful to further development. But he insists that the practice must not artificially limit output, as cartels usually do.[28]

For both wages and other issues, Schumpeter acknowledges that government policies can smooth out the business cycle and prevent severe crises. But he warns against trying to eliminate cycles altogether. This, he says, will hinder the innovation necessary for future prosperity. He grants that much remains to be learned about business cycles, but he sees almost no possibility of eliminating cycles altogether, because they are endemic to capitalism and essential for innovation.[29]

For Schumpeter there were no limits to innovation and thus none to economic progress under capitalism. In a 1930 essay called "Change in the World Economy," he argues vehemently against a then-popular idea that the limits of technological progress were rapidly approaching. This notion, he asserts, is preposterous. Fresh opportunities abound, and new innovations will interact with old ones to produce even faster progress.[30]

He also questions another prevalent assertion: that the aftermath of the Great War gave Americans such pronounced economic advantages that Europeans could never again compete effectively. Pessimists, Schumpeter points out, always cite America's rich raw material endowments as the reason for its robust growth. But he says that it was the efficient *use* of these resources that thrust the United States ahead of Europe.[31]

In a 1932 article titled "Enduring Crisis," he asks whether there would be periods of prosperity and depression even if economies were not affected by external circumstances. He says that this is a false question because external changes always do occur. So too do internal changes deriving from entrepreneurial initiatives. By definition, innovation causes obsolescence, and Schumpeter warns against allowing the old to block the new. Novel ways of doing things have to be fitted into the "organism" of the existing economy by eliminating obsolete methods, and this is what happens in some phases of a depression.[32]

In an important piece called "The Function of Entrepreneurs and the Interest of the Worker," which he published in 1927 in a labor magazine, Schumpeter tries to show how the long-term interests of entrepreneurs and workers are almost identical. He begins with an overview of nineteenth-century industrialization in Britain and finds that even with the immense increase in wealth, the distribution of income remained almost constant. Therefore, the widespread notion that industrialization brings the impoverishment of the masses is mistaken.[33]

He then asks whether wealthy people in Britain received too large a share of the rewards of industrialization. He says the answer may well be yes, but that the question itself is flawed. The more appropriate issue is the way in which high earnings motivate entrepreneurs to translate innovations into actual production—and thereby raise the general standard of living. He underpins his argument with a simple calculation of how much money rich people in Britain actually possess—an amount which, if divided among the rest of the population, would hardly raise living standards at all.[34]

Schumpeter's key point here is one he hammered home many times: it is the insatiable pursuit of success, and of the towering premium it pays, that drives entrepreneurs and their investors to put so much of their time, effort, and money into some new project whose future is completely uncertain. High entrepreneurial returns are essential to generate gains not only for individuals but also for society, through the creation of new jobs. Financial "speculation," though it gets a very bad press, is an important part of this process. Speculators often turn out to be investment bankers funding the entrepreneurs who in turn push innovations through the economy.[35]

Also a myth, Schumpeter argues, is the notion that people become entrepreneurs only if they already have enough money to start a new enterprise. The record shows that new companies nearly always begin with a "normal" worker—one who has a vision and the fortitude to make that vision a reality. The sons and daughters of successful entrepreneurs maintain the founder's position only if the family firm continues to innovate, which it often does not. Echoing the argument in his article on social classes, Schumpeter writes that the history of entrepreneurship shows a continuous up-and-down pattern of families reaching and then losing top positions. Unlike hereditary aristocracies, the majority of wealthy people in any capitalist economy tend to rise and fall rapidly from one generation to the next. Here Schumpeter quotes a saying he heard in America: "Three generations from overalls to overalls."[36]

He concludes with the question of why workers and entrepreneurs often oppose each other even though they have the same social roots. He finds the answer in day-to-day contacts, where entrepreneurs must organize and administer work schedules. This in turn leads to disagreements and perceptions that the entrepreneur is not acting in the workers' interest. Thus, attention falls on the short-term negative consequences for individuals rather than on the long-term benefits of innovations for society as a whole, as new jobs are created. Opportunistic politicians and radical intellectuals invariably emphasize the short-term costs; and once the image of exploitation becomes fixed in people's minds, it is not easily excised.[37]

In a similar article he wrote as a chapter in a book called *Structural Changes in the German National Economy* (1929), Schumpeter points out that the entrepreneurial function changes when companies become too big for a single individual to manage. In giant firms, the key entrepreneur has therefore evolved from a person who simply creates new ideas to someone who also ratifies or rejects innovative suggestions coming from specialists within the firm. For big businesses, the entrepreneur needs some technical knowledge; but even more, the ability to visualize the good of the firm as a whole. Thus, the emergence of "trusts" has changed the inventory of abilities that entrepreneurs in big firms must have and has cut out family members in favor of real professionals.[38]

In summary, Schumpeter says, roles have now evolved for two different types of entrepreneurs. One type is in big business, as just described. But the concurrent emergence of entrepreneurs who start new firms continues unabated. Regulators should bear this in mind when they consider breaking up big firms through overly aggressive antitrust prosecutions. Schumpeter makes it very clear that he is not opposed to state economic intervention. He only wants to highlight the continuing importance of entrepreneurship. When the state intervenes in the economic "organism"—a living entity, not an abstraction—it must remember that without entrepreneurship no growth can occur.[39]

SCHUMPETER USUALLY refrained from prescribing economic programs for any country. Thus, the nontechnical articles he wrote from 1925 to 1932 represent a major exception to his usual approach. Throughout his career, he asserted that academic economists should stick to science lest they cloud their judgment and taint their analyses with political advocacy. Yet, at the same time, he always argued for policies that would promote innovation.

The test of a Schumpeterian innovation is easy to apply at the level of the entrepreneur, and only a little harder for the firm. Students of business history are familiar with a long list of great innovators: Josiah Wedgwood and Richard Arkwright in the eighteenth century; Andrew Carnegie, John D. Rockefeller, August Thyssen, and Alfred Nobel in the nineteenth; Henry Ford, Giovanni Agnelli, Estée Lauder, Akio Morita, and Sam Walton in the twentieth; Bill Gates, Oprah Winfrey, Richard Branson, and Toshifumi Suzuki in the late twentieth and early twenty-first. The same is true—for most of their histories—of innovative twenty-first-century companies such as Microsoft, IKEA, Nokia, and Google. But by Schumpeter's definition, *all* successful firms have

Schumpeter on a rare outing in the wooded hills around Bonn, 1931. He was writing at a furious pace at this time, preaching his gospel of innovation as the key to economic progress.

been entrepreneurial at some moment in their histories, though a given company is certain to be more entrepreneurial at one point and less so at another. When their innovations dwindle, firms begin to die.

For a whole industry, the litmus test of innovation becomes more complicated. Any industry more than a few years old contains powerful elements pulling in opposite directions. Some companies, often the incumbent market leaders, tend to be more conservative and risk-averse than startup firms. By contrast, in new industries with hundreds of companies—such as automobiles in 1900—the more Schumpeterian the particular firm's culture, the likelier its chances to win the race. Companies in "mature" industries, such as today's tires, textiles, steel, and automobiles, often do not appear to be Schumpeterian at all. Key innovations have long since worked their way into the routines of every company. But time and time again, as Schumpeter liked to point out, innovative firms have unexpectedly altered an industry's apparent maturity.

To take a modern example, when the French company Michelin started mass producing the radial tire in the 1940s, it began a sequence of creative destruction that by the 1980s had shattered America's long dominance of the industry. The shift to radials killed off all of the big five tire companies except Goodyear and ended the reign of Akron, Ohio, as the Rubber Capital of the World. An industry-wide culture of complacency, deriving from long success, simply prevented American firms from responding effectively.

During the twentieth century, innovative companies also transformed the "mature" textile industry by developing rayon, nylon, polyesters, spandex, and other synthetic fibers. In steel, the advent of basic oxygen furnaces and minimills ended the supremacy of United States Steel, British Steel, and other giant firms.

One of the best examples of all has been the revolutionary Toyota Production System. Toyota Motor, founded in the 1930s, produced only 42,000 cars in 1960—but 2.3 million in 1980, an increase of 5,240 percent. And its new production system not only transformed the making of cars—ending seven decades of supremacy by Detroit—but also changed the face of manufacturing in general. From the 1970s onward, Toyota's quality-control mechanisms, its lean manufacturing, and its empowerment of assembly-line workers spread to innumerable factories throughout the world.

What about entire countries? Is it possible to identify a coherent Schumpeterian program for national economic growth? Are there particular patterns of tax, fiscal, monetary, and employment policies? Did Schumpeter ever specify political measures for the systematic promotion of national economic health?

The answer is yes. He never became a policy-obsessed economist like Ricardo, Marx, or Keynes. Nor did he denounce governmental activism with the passion of his fellow Austrian Friedrich von Hayek or the American Milton Friedman. Nor did he serve as a frequent adviser to politicians, as thousands of other economists have done—including his own Nobel Prize–winning students Paul Samuelson and James Tobin. Nevertheless, there is plenty of evidence about the policies Schumpeter favored, and it comes mainly from two sources: his tenure as Austria's finance minister and the dozens of articles on public policy that he wrote during his years in Bonn.[40]

The evidence for the *results* of policies Schumpeter favored is circumstantial—but so many factors affect a nation's economic performance that the same is true for almost any set of policies. During the twentieth century, the line of evidence from Schumpeterian ideas to policies to outcomes is perhaps clearest in the high-performing East Asian economies of the late twentieth century, especially Japan, Korea, Taiwan, and Singapore. In Japan, during the period between the departure of the American occupation forces in 1952 and the oil shock of 1973, policy-makers adopted many of his suggestions quite closely. There was an extraordinary emphasis on saving and investment, a broad range of innovation across many industries, and a tremendous outburst of entrepreneurship in new companies such as Sony, Sanyo, and Honda. During those years Japan achieved the highest sustained economic growth of any major country in the history of the world.[41]

DESPITE SCHUMPETER's unusual attention to policy during the years 1925–1932, he did not spend all of them in Germany. Even before he took the position in Bonn, he had begun to field invitations from as far away as Tokyo and Kobe. And once he was in Bonn, he quickly became a hot academic commodity. In 1926 a technical university in Berlin invited him to join its faculty. In 1927 came an offer from the University of Prague and shortly afterward another from the University of Freiburg, this one at a much higher salary than

Bonn's. Soon he received still another solicitation, from the University of Kiel. He thought about moving but in the end turned down all of these invitations.[42]

In 1927 Harvard University came calling—his seventh offer in two years, but this one so attractive he could not dismiss it out of hand. Being Viennese to the core, Schumpeter had little love for Germany, but he had now made Bonn his home. His magazine articles were directed not toward an Austrian audience but a German one, and he did not really want to leave the country. His daily pilgrimage to the cemetery with a rose for Annie's grave had become an anchor of his emotional stability. His growing fame had attracted a group of first-rate students to whom he was becoming attached as a surrogate parent. And with Arthur Spiethoff and a few others, he had formed some of the warmest friendships of his life.[43]

But Harvard—with its large and elite economics department and its very high salaries—was different from other suitors. Schumpeter, still mired in debt, could put Harvard's money to good use and reduce his "prostitution" on the speaking circuit. Several of his old debts from Vienna were about to come due, and his absence from Germany might delay payment for another year; as he wrote a friend, "Isn't it a chance to flee with decency?" He therefore decided to accept a one-year visiting appointment, even though he would have to make still more speeches to pay for his transatlantic steamer ticket. He asked the German Ministry of Science, Art and Public Education to continue his salary during his sabbatical at Harvard, informing the authorities that Spiethoff would teach his courses while he was gone. In this way he could receive money from both Bonn and Harvard. Just as important, in the United States he might again feel the intellectual stimulation he had enjoyed at Columbia University fourteen years earlier.[44]

If the fit at Harvard seemed good and the offer of a tenured post came forth, he might even leave Bonn permanently. It was much too early to make this kind of life-changing decision, but there was little risk in going to Harvard as a visitor. Mia Stöckel, if she were willing, could maintain his house during his absence and look after his obligations in Germany. So, with her consent, Schumpeter agreed to spend the academic year 1927–1928 teaching at Harvard. His duties there would begin a little over thirteen months after Annie's death.

12

The Bonn-Harvard Shuttle

The world stands out on either side
No wider than the heart is wide.

EDNA ST. VINCENT MILLAY, "Renascence," 1912

LONG BEFORE SCHUMPETER revised his *Theory of Economic Development* or brought out the English-language edition, the book had piqued the interest of Harvard's Economics Department. One of its members published a favorable review of the original German version of the book, written in 1911. The university itself had also shown early interest in Schumpeter as a rising star of the profession. The longtime leader of the Economics Department, Frank W. Taussig, had corresponded with him in 1912 and had met him during his term as Austrian exchange professor at Columbia. In October 1913 Taussig wrote Harvard's president, A. Lawrence Lowell, that this "very well-known and highly respected scholar" should be invited to present his research at Harvard. "Schumpeter speaks excellent English and could certainly give an acceptable lecture." During the academic year, Schumpeter spoke at Harvard, met Taussig, and began one of the closest friendships of his life.[1]

Taussig had received his training at Harvard and at the age of twenty-four had joined its faculty. This was in 1883, the year Schumpeter was born. For the next half-century, Taussig made himself part of the heart and soul of the university. Like some of Schumpeter's professors in Vienna, he took periodic

Frank Taussig, the eminent economist who brought Schumpeter to Harvard and became his closest confidant.

leaves to work for the government—advising Woodrow Wilson on the Treaty of Versailles and serving as the first chairman of the U.S. Tariff Commission.[2]

Taussig was a big, sturdily-built man—a physically imposing figure in the classroom. He used a subtle Socratic style that made him, as Schumpeter later wrote, "one of the greatest teachers of economics who ever lived." He drew out the best from his students, and he also had a special gift for spotting new faculty talent. By 1927, when he persuaded Harvard to invite Schumpeter as a visiting professor, Taussig was sixty-eight years old and respected at the university almost to the point of reverence. Schumpeter could not have asked for a better patron.[3]

Nor a closer soul mate. Taussig's father, a Jewish immigrant from Prague, had prospered as an entrepreneur in St. Louis. His mother came from an immigrant family of Protestant Germans, and Taussig himself spoke fluent German. Like Schumpeter, he had been a boy wonder, having entered Harvard at the age of sixteen and graduated at twenty. Also like Schumpeter, he held a law degree in addition to his Ph.D. in economics. Both had studied briefly at the University of Berlin, and both had a keen interest in history and sociology. As professors, each spent prodigious amounts of time on the work of students and colleagues. Most important, the two men simply liked each other. Much as Arthur Spiethoff had been in Bonn, Taussig became a kind of substitute father for Schumpeter. Like other close friends and members of Taussig's family, the younger man called him "Pa."[4]

Taussig had gained international renown as an expert on foreign trade, especially for his many publications on tariffs. He also wrote a popular textbook, and he shared some of Schumpeter's fascination with entrepreneurs. Among his several books, he published in 1915 a volume called *Inventors and Money Makers,* and in 1932 another entitled *Origins of American Business Leaders.* Taussig's example of crossing disciplinary boundaries, Schumpeter later wrote, led toward a future "full of promise, in which theoretical illiteracy will no longer be a badge of honor for the economic historian to carry, nor historical illiteracy a badge of honor for the theorist." He might with equal accuracy have been describing himself.[5]

By the 1920s, Harvard's Economics Department badly needed fresh talent, its best professors having grown old together. Economics expected to enroll more students than any other department at Harvard for the school year 1927–1928, and the senior professors had fixed on Europe as the best hunting grounds for new faculty members. Early in 1927 they recommended that the university invite Schumpeter for a one-year visit, with the possibility of a permanent appointment. The department's proposal was then approved up the bureaucratic ladder: by Dean Clifford Moore, President Lowell, and Harvard's governing board (the Corporation). At this time there were only about one hundred full professors in the Faculty of Arts and Sciences, compared with almost five hundred today.[6]

Schumpeter had mixed feelings about leaving Bonn, even temporarily. Having lost Johanna and Annie just months earlier, and still in the throes of mourning, he dithered for weeks over Harvard's offer. "Anxiously awaiting reply," department chairman Allyn Young telegrammed Bonn on May 12, 1927. Schumpeter responded with waffling answers. May 31, 1927: "Still trying [to decide]. Answer within week." June 15: "Practically certain to accept. Writing [a letter]." He was not eager to move, but he did not want to lose the chance of joining so renowned a university. Finally he decided to go. After making several speeches in Europe to earn money for his ticket, he boarded the liner *Amsterdam* on October 20, 1927, and arrived in Boston ten days later. This was on a Saturday. On the following Monday, he taught his first Harvard class, in the course "Money and Banking."[7]

Once in Cambridge, Schumpeter moved into rooms adjacent to Harvard Yard at the Colonial Club, which at that time served as the university's faculty club. The building was the former home of Henry and William James, along with other members of the James family. Taussig nominated Schumpeter for a visiting resident membership at the club, which had a few upstairs suites. Schumpeter found his new surroundings not only convenient—mere steps away from his office and classrooms—but also inexpensive and sociable. Unlike his large house in Bonn, where he had daily contact only with Mia Stöckel, the faculty club bustled with activity, especially at mealtimes.[8]

What struck Schumpeter most about Harvard was the sheer size of the Economics Department and the attentiveness of his students and colleagues. "I lecture every day for an hour and the very intense audience devours me—and I like that!" Whereas at the University of Vienna, with all its emphasis on economics, only three full professors and four juniors comprised the economics staff, Harvard had eight full professors and thirty-two junior faculty members. The number of graduate students was approaching one hundred. "No comparison," he wrote his friend Ottilie Jäckel. "I would stay here if Bonn were not Bonn . . . I slowly settle into my psychic monastery, so that I often have a feeling of ease, if work goes quite all right. It happens that I really look forward to my lectures."[9]

In another letter to Ms. Jäckel, Schumpeter expressed his delight that "students and young faculty gather around me very nicely—it is a pleasure to work with these people." As always, in his personal contacts he felt more at ease with generations either younger or older than his own—people with whom he could be patriarchal or filial. Taussig provided the surrogate father, and Harvard's students and young instructors the children. The department was full of bright young scholars such as Edward Mason and Seymour Harris (both of whom became famous economists) and Talcott Parsons (later the most influential sociologist of his generation). They provided the intellectual excitement Schumpeter needed, and he reveled in their company.[10]

Meanwhile, however, the shadows of his *Hasen,* Johanna and Annie, remained in his mind every day. "We both know," he went on to tell Ms. Jäckel, "that this is not life but it is a substitute for life." Even in Cambridge he continued his restless activity. Only a month after his arrival, he took the train to New York to address the Academy of Political Science. A month after that, he went to Washington, D.C., for the annual meeting of the American Economic Association. Ten days later, in early January 1928, he embarked on a Caribbean cruise that lasted for two weeks.[11]

He returned from the Caribbean to teach during the spring semester and continued to enjoy his lively discussions with students and with Taussig and other colleagues. He worked extremely hard at both his teaching and writing. Once more he tried to bring order to his "money book," but again in vain. He had great success, however, with his articles on social classes and his piece on "The Instability of Capitalism" for Keynes's *Economic Journal.*

In April 1928 he asked the university's permission to leave early because he was committed to teach the summer term in Bonn. His Harvard appointment had been for a calendar year—September 1927 to September 1928—but the university reluctantly allowed him to depart in April. Few professors offered courses during the summer but instead did research, so Harvard in effect had hired him for nine months' teaching. Yet he spent a little less than six months in residence, from late October through mid-April.[12]

Overall, his initial visit to Harvard had turned out to be a great success for someone still in the depths of grief. His sojourn had been lucrative and intellectually stimulating. It had also been an escape, a diversion, a glimpse at a possible new life. As he wrote Gustav Stolper, Harvard offered attractions available "at no other university in the world." He felt tempted to stay permanently, as Harvard wished him to do. Yet he was still financially strapped and had committed to return to Bonn and teach for most of the summer. "I will rest in August," he told Stolper.[13]

But Schumpeter seldom rested for more than a few hours, even when he was on vacations. He worked constantly, losing himself in his speeches and writings. He was prolific during this period, with both his academic writing and his business journalism. Whether at Harvard or Bonn, he also spent more and more time in intellectual discourse with students, helping them think through their own projects. He had begun to do this after Annie's death, often meeting one-on-one with bright pupils. The habit grew during his time at Harvard, and it increased still more when he returned to Bonn in 1928.

He moved back into the grand house he had shared with Annie and now shared with Mia Stöckel. Mia had continued to live there, looking after both the house and Schumpeter's other European commitments. Soon the two drifted into a sexual affair. "Let me go over the details once again—they are so vivid to me," Mia later wrote, "kneeling before your bed."

> It was on a spring evening. I came home from the movies and, happy to still see a light in your room, went in to wish you a good night; and you, probably buried deep in your work said, without looking at me, in an almost unfriendly tone: "Good day." I turned to a pillar of salt . . . I staggered back to my room, threw myself on the bed and cried bitterly. The idea that you could be mad at me, that I had done anything at all that could make you angry with me, made me deathly unhappy. I couldn't comfort myself. Eventually I gathered up my courage and came to you to learn what I had done wrong. And you were so sweet and stroked me and assured me that nothing was wrong between us and then you kissed me with your warm soft lips . . . The feeling of belonging to you, which perhaps had lived in my unconscious for a long time, came to me fully now.[14]

Schumpeter's relationship with Mia had no apparent effect on his abiding worship of Annie. He continued to copy her diary and to appeal to her and Johanna for help with his work. He took Mia seriously but did not intend to marry her. She hoped he might, but in his affections she could never rival the *Hasen.* Schumpeter kept up his daily pilgrimage with the rose for Annie's grave, and he was at last able to afford a large and expensive headstone. During his absences from Bonn, Mia herself took care of the gravesite, which she knew represented a kind of shrine for him.[15]

Many economists visited Schumpeter in Bonn and often stayed at his home. He still enjoyed these visits, but his conversations turned more toward intellectual matters than social ones. The jollity that had filled the house before Annie's death never returned. Mia did not openly take the role of hostess, but Schumpeter's life in the enormous rooms would have been very difficult had

Mia Stöckel at age twenty-three.

she not been there. He had never been able to look after his daily needs without the help of family members or servants. Whether this convenient inability to cope came from his aristocratic pretensions or from real ineptitude did not matter. By this time he was forty-five years old and was not about to change his lifelong habits if he could avoid it.

He also resumed his longstanding custom of frequent train travel. He visited almost every important university in Germany, giving lectures and seminars. He delivered numerous speeches to business groups, still earning money to repay his debts. He took brief vacations in Switzerland, France, and Italy. Because he did not want to advertise his relationship with Mia, she stayed in Bonn during most of these trips.[16]

His teaching and writing so totally consumed his daily routine that he took little part not only in running his household but also in administrative and social affairs at the university. But he never neglected his students. Many exalted him as a model intellectual—the kind of scholar and teacher they themselves aspired to be.

One of the students Schumpeter liked best, the talented Cläre Tisch, wrote an influential thesis on socialism under his direction. A Jew, she remained in Germany after the ascent of Hitler in 1933 and was murdered by the Nazis in 1941. Another of his Jewish students, Hans Singer, escaped to Britain, then worked in the U.S. Development Agency, and finally taught at the University of Sussex. Singer recalled that as a teacher, "Schumpeter opened up a new world in economics and general thinking." The activity of the Bonn Seminar revolved around him. "He was our idol and mentor. The cliché that a good professor 'opens doors' in the minds of his students seems exactly right in this case."[17]

Several of Schumpeter's students went on to distinguished careers: August Lösch and Erich Schneider, who became important academic economists; Herbert Zassenhaus, who held a high post in the International Monetary Fund; Gustav Stolper's son Wolfgang, who followed Schumpeter to Harvard and then had a long career as an academic economist and adviser to developing nations; and E. F. Schumacher, who achieved nothing less than cult status after the publication of his best-selling book of 1973, *Small Is Beautiful*.[18]

The message of *Small Is Beautiful* is not necessarily one that Schumpeter would have endorsed. But unlike many teachers, he never pressed his own views on students. He loved to perform from the podium, and he enjoyed few things more than coffeehouse-style intellectual debates. But he always tried to educate and entertain, not to convert. It was often impossible to tell where he stood on an issue. In the classroom and out, he delivered eloquent arguments in favor of both sides of any controversy, much like a talented lawyer. Several aspects of his background contributed to this distinctive trait: his curriculum at the Theresianum, his legal training in Vienna, his brief experience as a lawyer, and his absorption of learning from different economic schools. Most important of all was his playful intellectual temperament. When Schumacher was still a student at Bonn, he wrote his family that Schumpeter was "a terrific fellow! I am already looking forward to his next lecture on Monday. He doesn't parade dry scholarliness but an incredibly lively knowledge. One feels the whole fellow behind each sentence."[19]

The devotion of his students infused Schumpeter with energy. Yet he often brooded that things could never be as they had been. "I feel that I do not enjoy life and feel happiness," he wrote in his diary late in 1931. "I want to play and speak and laugh and flirt whenever I have the strength and desire for it." But his obsession with work continued to dominate: "Again, again, work, for my bread and for God in my heart and for the *Hasen*."[20]

He wrote dozens of articles during the period of his Bonn-Harvard shuttle, but he remained frustrated over his lack of progress with the money book. As he told Ottilie Jäckel during September 1929, "I had a feeling of impotence, of failure . . . ergo depression and continuing struggle and agony." It surprised him that after the deaths of Annie and Johanna he had to expend so much more effort to turn out his work. He was achieving some of his aims, but "the former easiness of my creative power is gone." His lectures went well enough but not his writing. "Every day I throw out everything that I wrote the day before. It is really sad."[21]

SCHUMPETER STILL HAD not decided where to spend the rest of his career. When he left Harvard in April 1928, both parties assumed that he would likely return. The exchange of letters speaks of his departure as a leave of absence. Late in that same year, Harvard began another strong effort to lure him back. The campaign started with a long letter from the new department chairman, H. H. (Burbie) Burbank, a rotund and jovial economist who, unlike his more talented colleagues, was glad to assume administrative duties. In December 1928 he wrote Schumpeter: "As each month passes and our need for you becomes more pressing we are increasingly eager to know your plans."[22]

In a long handwritten letter, Schumpeter replied: "It is with more regret than I can well express, that I have now to return a negative answer to your letter . . . Things being as they are, and your invitation having arisen out of circumstances which I partly owe to the [education] Ministry, I have got to take No [from the Ministry] for an answer. Perhaps it would have been different if I could have delayed going away for a few years. But at present I have no choice but to stay."[23]

Schumpeter added that he had tried to resign from Bonn, but "a week ago, I was told by the Minister, that he had no means of *preventing* my resignation, but that he thought he would be failing to his duty if he *assented* to my leaving." Very likely, Schumpeter's having received pay from Bonn during his first visit to Harvard complicated his request for either a second leave or an outright resignation. In his correspondence he does not appear to be playing the two universities off against each other, as professors of high visibility sometimes do. Instead, he seems genuinely undecided about where he wanted to live.[24]

The next letter Schumpeter received from Harvard came directly from President Lowell: "Since I last heard from you Professor Allyn Young has died [suddenly, at age 53]. It is a sad loss to us, and leaves a severe gap in our Department of Economics . . . Will you not consider again the question of accepting a chair here?" Schumpeter replied that perhaps he could meet Harvard halfway. "The hope has opened up of an intermediate arrangement which might enable me to take some share in Harvard's great work whilst keeping up part of my duties here."[25]

Chairman Burbank then wrote once more and, after receiving a second negative reply from Schumpeter, teamed up with Frank Taussig in May 1929 to send a joint cable: "Regret profoundly but understand. Consider following plan. You to come for one term yearly, preferably first half year, for as many years as you can. Remainder of your work at Bonn as now. Cable at your convenience if any such arrangement possible and welcome to yourself and ministry."[26]

Schumpeter responded that the new proposal might be viable beginning with the academic year 1930–1931. He suggested offering two half-year courses. One would be on schools of economic thought, which he proposed to rename "Current Problems of Economic Theory." The second course would be called "Business Cycles," which was becoming one of the most conspicuous issues of the time because of the emerging Great Depression. "I welcome the opportunity of dealing fully with that subject," Schumpeter wrote, and his new course foreshadowed the huge book of the same name that he eventually published in 1939. Schumpeter asked that he teach one course every day rather than doubling up and having two or three days free. In addition, "As far as may be, I like to have [class]rooms, which are not booked for the hour following my lecture—for it is often both pleasant and useful to continue the discussion with those of the students who wish to."[27]

Harvard's new faculty club was not yet finished, and there remained the question of where Schumpeter would live. The university was then converting from dormitories to its "house" system, in which undergraduates, professors, and graduate tutors would gather together in large new brick buildings. Senior faculty members, many with their spouses, would preside as "masters," on the Oxford-Cambridge model. The new houses contained suites, bedrooms, public rooms, dining halls, and small libraries. To Harvard's administrators, Schumpeter seemed a perfect candidate for residence in the first new facility, Dunster House, a graceful structure on the banks of the Charles River. Its master wrote him of the "unequalled opportunity to get acquainted with undergraduates and to do them good by your presence among them."[28]

The invitation included free room and board, a big advantage since Schumpeter was still paying his debts. But then Frank Taussig's wife died, and Schumpeter accepted Taussig's offer of an apartment in his own elegant home, located just a few blocks from Harvard Yard. It was "very nice of him to invite me and again a great savings, although I, the hermit crab, would rather be completely by myself." Later on, Schumpeter had a long association with Dunster House, which gave him a suite and where his young colleague Edward Mason, a rising economist, served as head tutor. But he never lived there.[29]

Before Schumpeter left for the United States, he told the Ministry of Science, Art and Public Education in Berlin that he intended to spend most of his time at Harvard but would speak at other American universities as well. He again asked to be paid by the University of Bonn during his semester's absence.

Frank Taussig's home in Cambridge, where Schumpeter lived briefly in 1930–1931 on his second visit to Harvard, and then for five years beginning in the fall of 1932. The house is much larger than it appears here and is now divided into several apartments. This picture was taken after a light snowfall during the winter of 2003.

Meanwhile, he was becoming more and more pessimistic about Germany's future. On the day he sailed from Europe, he wrote Keynes that "I am glad to get away from our financial and political situation. Here indeed, if ever, personal shortcomings [within the government] have created what may easily develop into a national catastrophe."[30]

When he arrived in Boston in 1930 for his second visit to Harvard, he moved into the spacious house at 2 Scott Street that Taussig had built in the 1880s. Now the two widowers, one forty-seven years old, the other seventy-one, began to spend much of their free time together. "My life is so unromantic," Schumpeter wrote Ottilie Jäckel, adding that he found the United States an uncomfortable country. "But Cambridge with its mansions is still a quite civilized place, the colleagues are nice, the scientific interests are all round alive, and I don't think about anything else." Soon he reported having "fallen in love with my friend and host." Taussig "is such a charming human being, so kind and wise, kind in the sense of strong natures, who want to look after others and want to pamper them—he has done that very well for me in the last three months."[31]

Schumpeter enjoyed his second visit to Harvard a great deal and wrote a friend that at some point he intended to settle at Harvard permanently. Toward the end of the 1930 fall term he again asked permission to leave a bit early, skipping the Reading Period that covered the holidays in December and the first weeks of January. By giving his exam in the first part of December, he could save more than a month of time. During that period, he would attend the annual meeting of the American Economic Association and then begin his round-the-world cruise. Chairman Burbank, accommodating as always, arranged for him to do this, and Schumpeter told Burbank that he would definitely return to Harvard in 1932–1933.[32]

At the meeting of the American Economic Association in Cleveland in late December 1930, Schumpeter gave a paper on "The Present World Depression: A Tentative Diagnosis." More importantly, on December 29, 1930, he chaired a meeting of sixteen economists who established the new Econometric Society. The moving spirits were Schumpeter himself, the Norwegian economist Ragnar Frisch, and Irving Fisher of Yale. All three wanted to promote more precise mathematical and statistical methods. Even though Frisch had invented the term "econometrics," Schumpeter vetoed his proposal that the group be affiliated with the University of Oslo or with any other university. Schumpeter believed that the organization should be worldwide but headquartered in the United States.

At their initial meeting, the group elected Fisher president, with Schumpeter, Frisch, and seven others as members of the first council, which included representatives from seven countries. During the years since the Econometric Society's founding, it has grown to include several thousand members, living in scores of countries. Schumpeter wrote the lead article for the society's first issue of *Econometrica,* a prestigious journal which began publication in 1933 and is still prospering today.[33]

After leaving the American Economic Association meetings in January 1931, Schumpeter traveled from Cleveland to San Francisco to Japan. And, despite

Schumpeter with Yale's Irving Fisher at Fisher's home in New Haven, Connecticut. The two were prime movers in the founding of the Econometric Society.

success on every front, two thoughts occupied his attention—his growing concerns about events in Germany, and the morbid loneliness that followed him wherever he went. In a letter to Bonn, he asked Arthur Spiethoff to announce that he would resume his teaching there in April. The letter then turns toward Germany's escalating political conflict: socialism on the one hand versus fascism on the other. Schumpeter hoped (and believed) that each force would hold the other in check and that the expected world economic recovery might move voters away from extremists on both sides.[34]

Describing his crossing of the Pacific and his three weeks in Japan, Schumpeter wrote to Dean Moore of Harvard: "My trip has been a failure as far as the purpose of having a rest is concerned . . . Yet I have enjoyed it greatly and I carry away with me a very good impression not only of Japanese colleagues and students, but also business leaders and politicians. As to the latter, it is perhaps the aristocratic element in Japanese politics that makes them show up so very well as compared with what one meets in Europe. And now I have to work out half a dozen addresses for publication! That's the good of it."[35]

Schumpeter lectured to great acclaim all over Japan. His appearances attracted blanket coverage by the Japanese media (*Radiobombardement,* as he

Schumpeter during his triumphant visit to Japan in early 1931. For the rest of his life he was fascinated by the culture of Japan and by the country's extremely rapid industrialization.

called it), on a scale that is hard to imagine for any academic today. Japan itself fascinated him. "Here is a culture," he wrote Gustav and Toni Stolper, "that thinks of itself not only as an equal to ours, but superior, and is ready to adapt any technical devices, but nothing else." In particular, the Japanese aesthetic sense appealed to Schumpeter, and he told the Stolpers that he was sorry to have had so little time for sightseeing. Actually, he visited shrines in Tokyo, Hakone, Nara, Kobe, Nikko, and the ancient city of Kyoto, where he was taken with the serene architecture of Japanese temples—many of which, like his favorite European cathedrals, were hundreds of years old.[36]

Despite his triumphs in Japan and his other interesting stops in Asia, Schumpeter's tour gave him little inner peace. "There are no travels," he wrote from Singapore to Ottilie Jäckel; "One is always locked in oneself. And there is no real deliverance." Trying to analyze his own state of mind, he reflected that "it is psychologically not uninteresting that lapses, failures, distresses, etc. and the year 24 [1924, when he lost all his money] were never so clear to me, as they were when I traveled on a beautiful ship, apparently safe and comfortable, across the Indian Ocean. And the feeling of decline, mental and physical, often condensed into an immediate presentiment of death, is always with me."[37]

Back in Bonn, he resumed a heavy schedule of teaching, research, and "above all invitations to Copenhagen, Stockholm . . . Christiania [Oslo], and half a dozen Dutch universities that I postponed before my departure [and] can't be deferred any longer." As time passed, he became still more concerned about political unrest in Germany. Having just traveled all over the world, he believed that other countries were now willing to help Germany in its economic difficulties—but that this was the only important difference between the current situation and the one just after the Great War.[38]

During the spring of 1931, two months after his return to Bonn from Harvard and Japan, he became a candidate for a professorship at the University of Berlin. Its leading economist had just retired, and Schumpeter, one of the best-known scholars in Europe, was an obvious choice to replace him. A second position at Berlin was also open at this time.

Most of the university's economics professors, still in the grip of the Historical School, looked askance at Schumpeter, whom they regarded as a high-flying theorist. "The Berlin economists are not my friends," he wrote Stolper. He did not particularly want to go to Berlin, but he did covet the honor of an offer. In 1930 Stolper had been elected by a left-leaning party to a seat in Germany's Parliament and had begun lobbying the ministry on Schumpeter's behalf. The two men had been discussing the possibility of just such an appointment since 1929.[39]

Because of Schumpeter's credentials, the economists in Berlin who opposed him were in an awkward position. But, as often happens in academic politics, they managed to shift the grounds of discussion. First they argued that they needed an agricultural economist, not a theorist like Schumpeter. "This is the first time that I am in a position to admire my Berlin colleagues' genius," Schumpeter wrote Stolper. "For this is a way to sail by me without the need to make themselves ridiculous by offering some nonsense about my work."[40]

Failing in this ploy and facing strong support for Schumpeter in the ministry, his opponents now began to malign his integrity. They brought up old charges about his conduct at the Biedermann Bank and began a formal investigation into this seven-year-old issue. Schumpeter responded with great vigor, writing a long account of the affair. Yet he felt very frustrated. He wrote Stolper that in academic life, "I now understand that slander is an established practice" and that "every letter from me could be misinterpreted in malicious hands." Stolper urged Schumpeter to sue, and had he chosen a fight to the finish, he might well have won. But no matter what happened in a court of law, he was not going to get an offer from the University of Berlin; and in any case he had made up his mind to return to Harvard.[41]

"I have gotten over any desire for Berlin," he soon told Stolper. At Harvard he would have "immediate access to a wider circle, and this in a milieu in which scholarly competence and not party affiliations are imperative. Because of that and because of self-respect I cannot run after the Berlin [position]." But he also felt that he could not ignore the personal attacks. The whole matter infuriated him; and, ever conscious of his personal honor, he wanted the investigation to continue. In the end, the controversy became moot, and Schumpeter was pleased that one of the positions at Berlin went to Emil Lederer, his old friend and seminar mate from Vienna.[42]

EARLY IN 1932 Schumpeter wrote an article on war reparations, still a bitterly divisive subject a dozen years after the Treaty of Versailles. When the essay, published in *Lloyd's Monthly Review,* was attacked in a German newspaper, he told an administrator at the University of Bonn that the author of the critique was not sufficiently intelligent to understand his article. He compared the attacker's approach to Adolf Hitler's inarticulate way of addressing complex issues.[43]

None of Schumpeter's students became Nazis, even though he told them in his farewell speech to go their own way—that if they felt some affinity for the National Socialists, then they might use their expertise to do some economic good within the party. His former student Hans Singer later wrote that "in the days before Hitler our group [Schumpeter's Bonn seminar] dominated the economic faculty's Fachschaft, a student organization, certainly intellectually and to some extent also organizationally in a liberal and anti-Nazi direction." Schumpeter himself failed to take the Nazi movement seriously until it was too late. Six months before Hitler took power, he wrote his friend Gottfried Haberler, "I don't believe that anything serious is going to happen [in German politics]. Germany has the government that it has been used to for the last 500 years." But, as he correctly mused a decade afterward, "It is not much to my credit as a political analyst that I had no idea whatsoever of Hitler's impending rise."[44]

For a long time, the Nazis' anti-Semitism did not seem to Schumpeter markedly different from the scapegoating of Jews that he had witnessed in Vienna under Karl Lueger twenty years earlier—an abhorrent practice but nothing like the decades of bloody anti-Jewish pogroms and killings in Russia. Like most people at the time, Schumpeter had little understanding of the Nazis' plans, despite Hitler's diatribes in *Mein Kampf.* His real worry was that German voters, disaffected by bad economic conditions and still smarting from the open wound of Versailles, would listen to impossible promises from demagogues on all sides: communists, fascists, and extreme socialists. Schumpeter had scant faith in the ability of electorates anywhere to keep their heads during a real economic crisis. This feeling persisted even after he moved to the United States, where he quickly suspected Franklin D. Roosevelt of ambitions to become a dictator.

Taken as a whole, Schumpeter's public and private writings during the late 1920s and early 1930s show a complex mixture of attitudes toward the European political situation. He was convinced that Germany had been very badly mistreated at Versailles, but at the same time he was fed up with the country's own feckless government. Ever since 1919, Parliament and a succession of cabinets had consistently failed to follow constructive policies—as Schumpeter himself had documented in his many articles for the popular press. He did not regard Hitler as a competent thinker, especially on economic matters. But he was pleased that at least someone was strongly asserting Germany's rightful place in the community of nations. Schumpeter doubted that Hitler would actually come to power and had no inkling that if he did he could somehow gain the latitude to become a murderous dictator.

Before Hitler's accession to office, these views were probably shared by a majority of non-Jewish Germans, as well as by very large numbers of Britons, Americans, and Continental Europeans—especially those who had not taken the trouble to read *Mein Kampf.* (There is no evidence that Schumpeter read it himself.) Needless to say, all who failed to take the Nazis more seriously, including Schumpeter, were woefully naive and uncritical—in retrospect, appallingly so.[45]

In February 1932 Chairman Burbank at Harvard resumed the full-court press for Schumpeter to return to the United States. "I have hesitated to write you in the fear that we may appear to be urging your decision unduly." But the Economics Department needed to be sure that he was coming, in order to include him in its budget and schedule his classes. Burbank reassured Schumpeter that Harvard was making every effort to entice Wassily Leontief, a brilliant young Jewish economist from Russia who was then in Berlin and whose hiring Schumpeter had urged in vehement terms. The university would also try to keep Gottfried Haberler, another young friend of Schumpeter's, on leave from the University of Vienna. "These items are really more than interesting gossip," wrote Burbank. "It is conceivable that the policy of which they are a part may bear somewhat on your decision . . . All of us will be very happy when your acceptance is received."[46]

Schumpeter replied that although his resignation from Bonn had not yet been formally accepted, "I *can* now write to you just as if I were your colleague already, which I assure you gives me great pleasure indeed." From Harvard, Chairman Burbank wrote "Dear Joe: Professor Taussig's letter and the cables have told you that your appointment has passed the Governing Boards and is ready for release." The issue was now settled, after four years of uncertainty. "It was a tough decision, by God," Schumpeter wrote Stolper. "But maybe it is a good thing that this painful breakup has happened."[47]

Two difficult goodbyes still remained. The first was to his mistress Mia Stöckel, who had taken such good care of his household and correspondence for five years, including the periods of his absence at Harvard. He felt guilty about leaving Mia, who was now twenty-six years old and still hoping to marry him.

A month before his departure, he took her on a short vacation trip and afterward wrote in his diary, "I want to concentrate on work. And if I do not work, I want to rest, really." Mia, being so much younger, would interfere with this plan in a way that his silent *Hasen* would not. "You are my home, *Hasen*," he wrote. He had a frank talk with Mia, telling her that marriage was out of the question. He then pondered the matter again in his diary: "For more than a year, Mia has been dissatisfied and unhappy and moves away from me. If I marry her, disregarding the disturbances [that it might cause] at Harvard, she will be just as unhappy. It is good that we have spoken. It is good that I leave. There would always be more and more unrest." Schumpeter had by no means seen the last of Mia, and he assured her that he would spend the next summer in Europe. In the meantime, Mia promised to visit Annie's grave regularly, a vow she fulfilled for many years to come.[48]

His second goodbye was to his circle of colleagues and students at Bonn. He remained close to Arthur Spiethoff, who had brought him to the university seven years earlier and had helped him cope with the deaths of Johanna and Annie. And he was genuinely devoted to his students, who gave what turned out to be a memorable farewell party for him. At the request of the university, he delivered a long speech, and his remarks amount to a personal creed about the role of economics in science and politics:

> A man expressing his political will and the same man explaining a
> theory in the lecture hall are two different people . . . Especially in
> my case, ladies and gentlemen, because *I never wish to conclude.* If
> I have a function, then it is not to close, but rather to open doors,
> and I never felt the urge to create something like a Schumpeter
> school . . .
>
> Quite a few people are upset about this point of view, because
> in Germany itself there are a half dozen people who feel they are

the leaders of such schools, who feel like fighters for total light against total darkness. That gets expressed in the harsh criticisms that one school levies against the other. But it doesn't make any sense to fight about these things. One shouldn't fight about things that life is going to eliminate anyhow at some point. In science momentary success is not as important as it is in the economy and in politics. We can only say that if something prevails in science, it has proven its right to exist; and if it isn't worth anything, then it's going to die out anyway. I for myself completely accept the verdict of coming generations.[49]

After departing Germany and crossing the Atlantic, Schumpeter sent one final letter—a very emotional one—to Gustav and Toni Stolper. In it he expressed how hard it was for him to leave. He had come to feel at home in his house on the Rhine, and the Stolpers' long friendship was the kind of precious thing "that I don't want to miss anymore in my life. Do you hear me? You can't let this established contact vanish, which means practically that one of you has to write on a regular basis." He did intend to visit Europe every summer, but from now on his new home would be the United States.[50]

13

Harvard

Those new regions which we found and explored with the
fleet ... we may rightly call a New World.

AMERIGO VESPUCCI, letter to Lorenzo de' Medici, 1503

WHEN SCHUMPETER ARRIVED at Harvard in 1932, the focal point
of the campus was Harvard Yard, the shady grove where the university had
been founded in 1636. The Yard was framed with old brick structures, one
of which still survived from the seventeenth century. Harvard's many small
and medium-sized buildings contrasted strikingly with the models of Vienna,
Czernowitz, Graz, and Bonn, where a single imposing structure housed most
classrooms, libraries, and offices.

Today, Harvard Yard remains a living architectural museum, attracting hundreds of thousands of tourists each year. But Harvard in the twenty-first
century is a very different place from the quiet and parochial community
Schumpeter encountered in 1932. Periodic construction booms have created
dozens of new buildings outside the Yard, and Harvard's immense endowment
has made it by far the world's richest university.[1]

Harvard has nine professional schools, but its undergraduates and its Faculty of Arts and Sciences comprise the core of the university, as they did in
Schumpeter's time. Today, these academically well-qualified students come

from each of the fifty American states and from about seventy-five countries around the world. In the class of 2010, 52 percent of the students admitted were women, 18 percent Asian American, 11 percent African American, 10 percent Latino, and 1.4 percent Native American.[2]

When Schumpeter joined the faculty in 1932, the university accepted about 1,000 of every 1,200 applicants—83 percent of those who applied, as against today's 9 percent. And the applicants themselves were remarkably homogeneous in 1932: all male, almost all white, and overwhelmingly local. About 40 percent came from Massachusetts and most of the rest from other northeastern states. More than half of all students had attended expensive private prep schools, and between 30 and 40 percent did not have very good academic records when they arrived. The prevailing standard, both before and after enrollment, was the Gentleman's C—not just in stereotype but in fact. Whereas only 12 percent of American undergraduates' families earned more than $2,500 annually in 1932, 84 percent of Harvard's did.[3]

So Harvard was essentially a college for the scions of rich local Brahmin families. Generations of their sons—some bright, some mediocre, some dull-witted—had enrolled almost as a rite of passage. The politics of the university, and especially its alumni, was strongly Republican. A 1934 poll of students and faculty showed disapproval of Franklin D. Roosevelt's New Deal by a margin of two to one. Catholic students were rare, and Jews were limited to a quota of 12 percent. Anti-Semitism pervaded Harvard's culture, often in overt forms. Many student organizations were closed to Jews, and some of the university's official records contained an asterisk in front of the name of any student known to be Jewish. Few professors were Jews, and those who were often suppressed this part of their identity. On this point Schumpeter's friend and patron, Frank Taussig, was typical.[4]

Harvard treated Radcliffe College, the adjacent and affiliated women's school, with little respect. Radcliffe students could attend most Harvard classes but were barred from many university spaces—even including the Reading Room of Widener Library, then the nation's second largest book repository after the Library of Congress. The Medical School admitted a few women, but the Law and Business Schools refused all. When Gustav and Toni Stolper visited Schumpeter in 1937, he arranged a dinner party at the new Harvard Faculty

Club. But he was embarrassed to write his old friend that "it will only work if you come alone, since ladies are not allowed."[5]

Whatever else Harvard may have represented, it was not a fresh world of higher education open to hordes of middle-class students. That American ideal found better expression in the wide array of state and city colleges and universities scattered throughout the country, many of which then rivaled any private institution, and still do today. In a 1937 ranking of overall graduate programs at U.S. universities, three of the top ten were state schools, and one (Cornell) was a hybrid with substantial support from both state and private sources: (1) Harvard (2) Chicago (3) Columbia (4) Yale (5) California (6) Johns Hopkins (7) Cornell (8) Princeton (9) Michigan (10) Wisconsin.[6]

To a greater extent than most universities, Harvard operated under a federal system of governance, and it still does. The professional schools enjoy an unusual degree of independence, being mostly responsible for their own fundraising, hiring, and promotions. Both the professional schools and the Faculty of Arts and Sciences today contain a profusion of tenured prima donnas. In the 1930s, Harvard had plenty of academic stars but a smaller proportion of prima donnas. Faculty luminaries included Schumpeter himself (by far the most notable economist), the philosopher Alfred North Whitehead, the historians Samuel Eliot Morison and Arthur Schlesinger Sr., the political scientists Arthur Holcombe and Charles McIlwain, the literary critics George Lyman Kittredge and Ivor A. Richards, and the sociologists Pitirim Sorokin and his junior rival Talcott Parsons.[7]

Schumpeter had a special relationship with Parsons, who had been a graduate student in economics when Schumpeter was a visiting professor during the late 1920s. Parsons went on to become one of the most influential social scientists of his generation, and he often said that it was Schumpeter who taught him to think systemically. Since Parsons also translated much of Max Weber's work and brought it to wide attention in the United States, the rich line of intellectual influence from Weber to Schumpeter to Parsons was brought full circle.[8]

The natural sciences at Harvard during the 1930s boasted their share of eminent scholars as well. These included the astronomer Harlow Shapley and the chemist James Bryant Conant, who in 1933 succeeded the seventy-six-year-old

A. Lawrence Lowell as president of the university. Conant, only forty, was brilliant, sometimes fiery, and self-consciously middle-class. He quickly embarked on a campaign to replace Harvard's complacent Brahmin culture with something closer to a meritocracy. He overhauled the ingrown system of hiring and promotion and strove to recruit better-qualified students. During his twenty-year tenure as president, he did as much as any person in the university's history to enhance its intellectual stature.[9]

As a meritocrat himself, Schumpeter supported these efforts, having arrived at just the time when Conant was replacing Lowell. And even before that change, he knew he was entering a world very different from that of Bonn or Graz. He depended on his friend Taussig for advice about how to conduct himself. "I have never been good at dealing with faculties or councils of administration and that sort of thing generally, and it is to your teaching that I look for guidance . . . I hope, or shall I say I am afraid, that you understand but too well what I want to express."[10]

Barely a month after his arrival in the fall of 1932, Schumpeter accepted an invitation to address Harvard's Economics Seminar on the "Monetary Acts of the Republican Administration." Discovering that his remarks would come just a week before the Roosevelt-Hoover presidential election, he wrote President Lowell, "When I consented to take part in that discussion, I thought it would turn on an entirely non-political professional problem, and I did not expect that the announcement would pass in terms suggesting political connotation." When it did, "I felt I had no choice but to excuse myself from taking part." Lowell replied, "You have taken the course which I should have taken had I been placed in a similar position at a university in some other country, and I am very much obliged to you for writing to me about it."[11]

When Taussig, Lowell, and others had started the intense recruitment of Schumpeter, there had been much discussion about his pay. Taussig proposed that he receive the university maximum, a level equaled in the Economics Department only by Taussig himself. Since Schumpeter's first visit in 1927, Harvard had raised the top annual salary for full professors from $10,000 to $12,000.[12]

In October 1930 Dean Clifford Moore wrote to President Lowell: "I understand that if I have the conversation with [Schumpeter] I am authorized to of-

fer him $12,000 a year; but perhaps you will prefer to talk with him yourself."
Lowell replied in detail:

> Frank Taussig has been in to see me to say that Schumpeter's sal-
> ary, etc., and pension at Bonn and Harvard are as follows:
>
> Bonn Salary and lecture fees   36,000 marks
>
>   Less income tax 25%   9,000 marks
>
>   27,000 marks
>
> Pension 20,000 marks [per year]
>
> Harvard Salary $12,000
>
> Income tax U.S. and Mass. 500
>
> Harv. deduction (pension?) 600
>
> Retiring allowance about $2,800 [per year]
>
> In view of the different purchasing power of money in Germany
> and the United States, this is some sacrifice in salary, and very dis-
> tinctly so in the pension. Is there anything—and if so, what—that
> we ought to do about this?

Either Lowell or Taussig, who evidently supplied the president with these numbers, was misinformed. Schumpeter's pay at Harvard would be much higher than at Bonn, even before tax deductions. At then-current exchange rates, 36,000 Marks equaled about $8,600, compared with the Harvard offer of $12,000.[13]

For the pension allowance, on the other hand, the contrast was correct, 20,000 Marks being the equivalent of $4,761. Taussig therefore proposed that Schumpeter's Harvard pension be increased from $2,800 per year to $4,000. The dean balked at this suggestion, since Schumpeter was forty-seven years old and by retirement age would not have had enough money set aside to justify such a generous pension. But Taussig remained adamant and succeeded in getting his request approved by Harvard's governing board. As President Lowell wrote, "Without making any general ruling, the Corporation were of the opinion that it would be wise to guarantee Professor Schumpeter a retiring pension of not less than $4,000 provided he occupy his chair for fifteen years, that is, for a reasonably long period."[14]

These numbers are revealing in several ways. Obviously, the income tax rate in Germany for people in Schumpeter's bracket far exceeded that in the United States. Then, too, in the depression year 1932, the average per capita income in the United States stood at the very low figure of $394, about one-thirtieth of $12,000. In the Economics Department itself, the lowest-paid member earned $1,375. Schumpeter was single, with no unemployed family members to care for. In 1930 he had written a European friend that based on his time as a visitor at Harvard, he estimated living expenses at $150–200 per month, or $1,600–2,400 per year. So his salary of $12,000 was very lucrative.[15]

At the end of the negotiations—brokered almost entirely by Taussig—Schumpeter wrote Chairman Burbank, "I am not joining strangers, but if I may presume to say so, friends." Always gracious and flowery in his personal correspondence, he wrote President Lowell that "it will ever be my foremost wish to prove worthy of Harvard's great name in the realm of science, and to express a hope that you never may find any reason to be disappointed with the choice you have made."[16]

From the time of his appointment in 1932 until his death in 1950, Schumpeter received the maximum salary for Harvard professors. His new prosperity meant much to him. Not only did he enjoy living well, but he also sent money regularly to friends and former students in Europe who were hard pressed: the Reisingers, Mia Stöckel, Cläre Tisch, and others. In 1935 he paid the remaining balance of his debts from Vienna, which for ten years had plagued him with worry.[17]

AS A TEACHER at Harvard, Schumpeter soon became a campus "character"—not an eccentric but certainly no conventional professor. As Paul Samuelson put it, "The America of Mickey Rooney and Coca-Cola he knew almost nothing about." During his entire time at Harvard, he went to no football games. He had attended one in 1913, during his visit as an exchange professor at Columbia, and that was enough. He rode the subway that rumbles beneath Harvard Square exactly once. Incapable of driving a car, he traveled by taxi or with friends who drove. Even for very long trips, he preferred to go by rail. He did not board his first airplane until 1937, flying from an academic meeting in Chicago to Miami for a midwinter vacation. He wrote from Miami that he half-expected the plane to crash during his return to Boston.[18]

His fellow economist John Kenneth Galbraith, who arrived at Harvard two years after Schumpeter, remembered him as "a slightly swarthy man of solid frame and a little less than average height." At 5′8″ he was actually about average, but to the 6′8″ Galbraith almost everyone seemed short. Schumpeter had "an amused and expressive face and an unremitting love for company and conversation . . . Given the choice between being right and being memorable, Schumpeter never hesitated."[19]

Whatever the occasion, he was always "on." As Samuelson later wrote, "Clothes were important to him: he wore a variety of well-tailored tweeds with carefully matched shirt, tie, hose, and handkerchief. My wife [a fellow graduate student] used to keep track in that period of the cyclic reappearance of the seemingly infinite number of combinations in his wardrobe: the cycle was not simple, and it was far from random."[20]

Each morning, after the elaborate ritual of dressing himself, Schumpeter would walk the six blocks from Taussig's house to Harvard Yard. At precisely the appointed hour, he would make his entrance into the filled classroom, then remove his trademark topcoat, fedora, and gloves—"slowly, finger by finger, as everyone watched," a student recalled. "It was all very dramatic." Next, Schumpeter would write something on the blackboard, then whirl around and begin his lecture. Speaking in an aristocratic Viennese accent, he gave the impression of complete spontaneity, even though he prepared every class with meticulous care. Using no notes, he dazzled students with his erudition. "He never told jokes," Samuelson remembered, "but somehow made the class itself seem witty." Engaging in quick back-and-forth repartee, "He took you out of the flat dull textbook world and into the three dimensional world of living economics and economists."[21]

Without missing a beat in these discussions, Schumpeter often jotted some new thought onto a scrap of paper, which he then thrust into his pocket. Students noticed that he was their only teacher who came to class with no written materials at all but left with jacket and trousers stuffed with messages. Both in class and out, he scrawled these notes to himself compulsively. He even scissored incoming letters into small squares to feed his need for more scraps of paper. He once referred to his filing system as that of "a most disorderly person," and some of his records came to resemble boxes of confetti. But almost none of the notes went unused, either as one-shot mnemonics or as fodder for his upcoming work.[22]

Very few professors relish both teaching and writing, and only a tiny fraction excel in both arenas. But Schumpeter did. He published literally millions of words, all the while remaining an unforgettable performer at the podium—the most entertaining of teachers and also the most accessible. He required heavy reading assignments but dispensed abundant A's. In his official reports about graduate students, he found something favorable to say about almost everyone.[23]

Light-hearted and chipper in public, Schumpeter lived an altogether different life in private—a continuing, desperate internal struggle with melancholy. His weekly diary entries still began with thanks and appeals to the *Hasen*, then lapsed into something like self-flagellation over the slow progress of his research. During the early 1930s he poured his energies into his ill-fated money book and even more so into what he called his "crisis book"—the mammoth *Business Cycles*, which he finally completed in 1939. His diary expresses an amalgam of emotions, overlaid with frustration at being distracted by academic minutiae:

> *1933, Monday 9 October–Sunday 15 October.*
> I close this week on Sunday evening, the day of my engagement
> [to Annie]; with thanks to the Hasen that I was allowed to do my
> duties—and it was not unhappy—and cheerful and not painful,
> but nevertheless I am sad—my thoughts, lectures and so on float
> by and cannot be anchored and my current work holds back the
> progress on important matters and even in teaching![24]

During his first few years at Harvard he had lunch and dinner almost every day with students and other professors, ranging from teenagers at Dunster House to Taussig, now past seventy. One graduate student said that he had "never known a teacher who took a more personal and painstaking interest in his students . . . He was faculty adviser to the Graduate Economics Club and always helped to shape its program. He organized private seminars and discussion groups, and entertained them with good food and wine to bring the students, often of many nationalities, into intimate relationship with one another." In countless lunches with graduate students, Schumpeter always paid the check. He attended many of their parties as well, where he behaved "as one of the liveliest and, in spirit, youngest of the participants."[25]

He also organized numerous small discussion groups. These consisted mainly of himself and selected young colleagues, whom he called in his diary the "inner circle." One group named itself the Chance, Love, and Logic Society; another the Cournot Group, in honor of the nineteenth-century French mathematical economist. Still a third was the Schumpeter Group of Seven Wise Men, most of whom were rising young economists.[26]

Informal meetings of these groups occurred weekly, bi-weekly, or monthly—sometimes for lunch, more often for dinner. A member would present a research paper, which the others would then discuss for at least two hours. The dinner sessions met at good Boston restaurants, where the wine flowed freely and the talk often continued past midnight. Most of the discussion groups, and especially the Wise Men, included the cream of the Economics Department: Schumpeter, Edward Mason, Seymour Harris, Edward Chamberlin, Gottfried Haberler, D. V. Brown, O. H. Taylor, and Schumpeter's special favorite, Wassily Leontief, the emigré from Russia and a future Nobel Prize winner. Schumpeter, as the senior member present, enjoyed himself immensely, managing to reproduce something like the Viennese coffeehouse ambience of his own youth.[27]

He lavished attention on the efforts of junior colleagues, whether their work merited it or not. The concern of so famous a scholar flattered the recipients, but sometimes it could be daunting. Harris, a stalwart of the Economics faculty for decades thereafter, remembered that he often "dreaded" his lunches with Schumpeter. With the utmost courtesy, the older man would punch holes in whatever argument Harris was making—thereby casting a pall over the rest of his day.[28]

Schumpeter did everything he could to push his graduate students to do their best work and to safeguard their time for research. The Harvard system required that junior instructors spend many hours in one-on-one tutorials with undergraduates. This custom, a legacy of President Lowell's laudable emphasis on teaching, would have made better sense had Harvard been more meritocratic and its undergraduates more diligent. But Schumpeter hated the

Top left: Talcott Parsons, whom Schumpeter met during his first visit to Harvard. The two had many interests in common and developed great mutual admiration. Parsons went on to become the most prominent sociologist of his generation. This picture was taken in 1949, at the height of his influence.

Opposite top right: The young John Kenneth Galbraith, who arrived at Harvard in 1934 as an agricultural economist. He and Schumpeter were never close, but they did respect each other. Galbraith left Harvard on three occasions during Schumpeter's time: to study in England, to work in the government during World War II, and to write for *Fortune* over a period of several years. He returned in 1948 and became a tenured full professor in 1949. His many books—directed toward a mass audience and written with unrivaled wit—made him by the 1960s the university's most famous faculty member.

Opposite bottom left: Edward Mason, one of the half-dozen talented young economists in what Schumpeter liked to call his own "inner circle." Like others of the inner circle, Mason went on to a distinguished professional career. He specialized in the subfield of industrial organization, which includes antitrust.

Opposite bottom right: Seymour Harris, another member of the inner circle, and one of Harvard's most prolific economists—writing or editing more than forty books. Harris received tenure later than others in his cohort, perhaps because he was a Jew.

Above left: Wassily Leontief, a Jewish immigrant from Russia whom Schumpeter regarded as his most brilliant colleague. The possessor of first-rate mathematical skills, Leontief originated input-output analysis, a complicated method made easier by the advent of computers. He was one of three future Nobel Prize winners with whom Schumpeter was closely associated.

Above right: Wolfgang Stolper, still another member of the inner circle. The son of Gustav Stolper, he followed Schumpeter to Harvard from the University of Bonn, then had a long and productive career at the University of Michigan and as an adviser to developing nations.

system. As Harris wrote, he was "galled" to see that "young scholars should have to give their best energies to wearying conferences with students, most of whom should not become important citizens, instead of to scientific work."[29]

A scholar's most creative years, Schumpeter often said, came between the ages of twenty and thirty, the "sacred third decade." For this reason, he urged students and colleagues to avoid the distractions of marrying young. Instead, they should concentrate on their work—sifting their brains for fresh ideas. After persuading the brilliant twenty-six-year-old Leontief to submit an article to the *Economic Journal,* he wrote to Keynes, "I want to apologize for Leontief. He has indeed produced what I consider a most original and interesting piece of work but then instead of finishing the article he got married in spite of my disapproval of this step. This explains the delay. I am awfully sorry."[30]

Meanwhile, Schumpeter himself took on heavy teaching loads. One professor said that he "preached wine for others but drank water himself." Harris wrote that "it was a sheer waste of energies for him to teach three courses (and if he had his way, he would have taught almost every course)" and devote endless hours to student "consultations" during office visits. In these sessions, he dispensed advice not only on academic subjects but about life itself. In a letter to a former student who had completed law school and was now thinking of getting an MBA, Schumpeter wrote that he would be glad to write a recommendation to the Harvard Business School. "There is one point, however, on which I want to scold you, and that is the turn of phrase 'a bloated tool of the vested interests.' There is no worse policy in life than a running-down of one's own line of activity and working oneself up into a sort of hostility against what one has to do every day. Why should the activity of a corporation lawyer be worse than the activity of a trade-union official, for instance? Both stand in their own ways for human civilization."[31]

He made himself accessible to almost everyone who sought him out. After a strenuous meeting of economists in a faraway city, Harris and Schumpeter happened to run into a student of ordinary ability on the train back to Boston. "Schumpeter spent exactly seven hours going over the student's thesis outline with his characteristic vigor and enthusiasm (heard throughout the car). Generous? Yes. A wise use of his waning energy? No. Endearing? Yes."[32]

At the end of 1933 Schumpeter wrote a poetic diary entry expressing a rare peace of mind:

1933: Week of 25 December to end of year:
Mommy and Annie
Watch over the last week of the year!
Thank you for everything—I am not worth it
And save me from the consequences of my foolishness.
O thank you for this year.
You guided me wonderfully
And strewed beautiful things along my path.
What ever may come. . .
And let me feel you alive.
However things might turn out to be—
We, Hasen, we stay the same, eh!

In many letters written during his first years at Harvard, Schumpeter mentioned how hard he was working and how difficult it was for him to balance teaching with writing.[33]

IN HIS OWN APPROACH to research, Schumpeter remained open-minded almost to a fault. His fellow Austrian Fritz Machlup, who taught at Columbia, recalled that "when others reiterated their bigoted patter, Schumpeter could not help coming back with his own message, which urged methodological tolerance and was intolerant only of illiteracy and intolerance itself." His Norwegian friend Ragnar Frisch, co-winner of the first Nobel Prize in Economics, wrote that Schumpeter's salient qualities were "generosity and willingness to listen." Frisch added that "we must appreciate this attitude all the more when we think of how far it is from that which we encounter most frequently amongst economists, statisticians and mathematicians."[34]

Schumpeter's embrace of mathematics, in which he himself did not excel, demonstrates this attitude. His very first articles, published in 1905, took a mathematical approach, and he often advocated "exact" economics, by which he meant a science buttressed with mathematics and statistics—something more akin to physics than to sociology or history. He co-founded the Econometric Society and later served for two years as its vice-president and two more as president. He developed warm friendships with first-class mathematical economists: Frisch, Fisher, and his own student, Samuelson, the first American to win the Nobel Prize in Economics.[35]

Schumpeter's fullest and most representative statement about the role of math came in 1933. In his lead article for the first issue of *Econometrica,* he wrote:

> We do not impose any credo—scientific or otherwise—, and we
> *have* no common credo beyond holding: first, that economics is a
> science, and secondly, that this science has one very important
> quantitative aspect. We are no sect. Nor are we a "school." Noth-
> ing is farther from our minds than any acrimonious belief in
> the exclusive excellence of mathematical methods, or any wish to
> belittle the work of historians, ethnologists, sociologists, and so
> on. We do not want to fight anyone, or, beyond dilettantism,
> anything.[36]

This statement captures the mind of Schumpeter at its best. At the very same time that he is proselytizing for greater mathematical rigor and preci-sion—in the inaugural article of *Econometrica,* no less—he cautions that math is not the only game in town and that the contributions of other disciplines are no less valid. He is a zealot only in his opposition to zealotry. Schumpeter be-lieved in the necessity of math in economics, but he was too great a thinker to believe in numbers and equations alone. For him, algebra and calculus could never entirely capture the far-reaching complexity of life. Throughout his ca-reer, he advanced the cause of math while always also advancing the integration of history, sociology, and psychology into economics as well—without feeling any sense of contradiction.

His statement in *Econometrica* goes on to say that because economists re-quired so much quantitative data, they were going to have to learn more about business. He noted that as early as 1826 the German economist J. H. von Thünen had shown how "cost accounting, bookkeeping, and neighboring headings, cover a mass of material which economists have entirely neglected." Economists, on the one hand, and "the specialists of 'Business Administra-tion,'" on the other, had gone off in opposite directions, to the detriment of both. Schumpeter emphasized that economics had to be a cooperative en-deavor. "Our aims are first and last scientific, [to help] build up the economic theory of the future."[37]

Schumpeter made every effort to keep up with mathematical economics as a way to achieve more exactitude, principally in his own work but also in his teaching. Much as he had done at Bonn, he inaugurated a seminar that he called "Introduction to the Mathematical Treatment of Economic Theory." He confessed to "a humble aim." He wanted "to provide beginners in economics with so much of mathematical tools as to enable them not to do anything in that line themselves" but to be able to understand the writings of Cournot, Walras, Marshall, Edgeworth, Pigou, Pareto, and Fisher. "Of course," he wrote in 1934, the seminar had been intended for undergraduates, but "it was mainly all the members of the staff who came to it last year."[38]

Because he thought himself poorly qualified in math, he looked for another faculty member who could do a better job. He found him in Professor Edward B. Wilson, a distinguished statistician four years his senior. Wilson taught at the School of Public Health and was president of the American Academy of Arts and Sciences. "I want to say again how intensely grateful I feel to you for giving yourself to the subject and to the cause," Schumpeter wrote Wilson. "You are the first eminent scientist to do so to this extent and if we shall be able to show results at Harvard and establish ourselves as one of the nurseries of economic thought in this field it will be your merit." He attended Wilson's seminars himself, as if he were still a student. The four members of one class were the twenty-year-old Samuelson, two other math whizzes aged nineteen and twenty-one—and Professor Schumpeter, who at fifty-two was still giving it his best shot.[39]

In his own course on advanced economic theory, he never took offense when the bold Samuelson would correct some mathematical error he was making in class. Instead, as another student recalled, "He would applaud. He admired brilliance." In 1937 Schumpeter wrote to a Harvard dean, "I am positive that [Samuelson] is the most gifted graduate we have had these many years." Schumpeter nonetheless worried that "owing to the mathematical turn of [Samuelson's] mind, he will not be very acceptable to the common run of economists," whose conventional methods were threatened by econometrics. But during the next epoch in the history of economics, Paul Samuelson did as much as anyone to move math to the core of the discipline—and with the full support of his mentor.[40]

Schumpeter evangelized about the need to teach more mathematics and asked advice from many quarters. In 1933 he wrote to Theodore Schultz, an economist at the University of Chicago: "As long as I was in Germany I took it as a matter of course that exact methods had really no room in the curriculum of the average student and I was quite content to give occasionally a course on mathematical economics to a small group." By contrast, at the best universities in the United States, where economics is taught at a higher level, "I really feel it a duty to do whatever is in my power in order to help the teaching of our science."[41]

At about the same time, he urged his young friend and future colleague Gottfried Haberler, then teaching at the University of Vienna, to accord more importance to math:

> I sometimes feel like Moses must have felt when he beheld the Promised Land and knew that he himself would not be allowed to enter it but you do not see that Promised Land which you, being young, could certainly enter but always insist on denying its existence. Forgive my preaching. It was your remarks about measuring utility which prompted it . . . if we confine ourselves to telling each other that it is impossible, we shall never get beyond what is a rather uncomfortable transition stage. It is supreme courage which is wanted just now.[42]

One of Schumpeter's greatest admirers was Paul Sweezy, a young Marxist economist who served as his assistant in the course on economic theory. Sweezy found it exceptional that in all of Schumpeter's teaching, he completely omitted any reference to his own work. "I tried to convince him that students often came to Harvard to study under him and that he owed it to them to give an exposition and elaboration of his own theories. He listened sympathetically but never did anything about it." When people argued that Schumpeter did not try to establish a Schumpeterian school analogous to the German Historical School or the Austrian School, Samuelson responded that "he did leave behind him the only kind of school appropriate to a scientific discipline—a generation of economic theorists who caught fire from his teaching."[43]

Schumpeter had that "rarest of all qualities in a teacher," Sweezy wrote. "He never showed the slightest inclination to judge students or colleagues by the extent to which they agreed with him. Keynesians (regularly in a substantial majority after 1936) and Marxists (often in a minority of one as long as I was in Cambridge) were equally welcome in his circle. He didn't care *what* we thought as long as we *did* think." On the other hand, for those who did not think, Schumpeter could be derisive—often ridiculing the intellectual flabbiness of his fellow conservatives. "When I see those who espouse my cause, I begin to wonder about the validity of my position."[44]

In grading his daily performances, he gave himself numerical credit for writing and research—including his endless effort to master mathematics—but seldom for teaching, counseling students, or any other duty. He enjoyed reading Latin and Greek texts, as well as European novels and biographies—Tolstoy's *Anna Karenina,* Morley's multivolume *Gladstone,* Lytton Strachey's *Eminent Victorians.* Sometimes he indulged himself with Ellery Queen and other detective novelists. He loved to dine out and to attend art exhibitions and classical music concerts. But he regarded most of these activities as unseemly distractions. The only thing that really counted was work. On that dimension Schumpeter held himself to unattainable standards and wrestled constantly with his conscience. He was still trying to work out an "exact economics"; and in so doing he was setting a real intellectual trap for himself.

14

Suffering and Solace

The problems of the human heart in conflict with itself.

WILLIAM FAULKNER, Nobel Prize Acceptance Speech, 1950

DURING HIS EARLY years at Harvard, Schumpeter tried to write two big books at the same time—one on money, the other on business cycles. He had begun both projects before coming to the United States, and in each he sought to achieve an unprecedented level of scientific exactitude. He aspired to this imposing goal by trying to fuse statistics, mathematics, economics, history, and other social sciences into a grand, all-encompassing synthesis of each of his two subjects. The money book ate up years of effort. And despite Schumpeter's frequent assertions that he was almost finished, his chapter drafts never saw the light of day—by his own wise choice, given their flaws. The book on business cycles finally appeared in 1939.[1]

During this period of superhuman effort, Schumpeter obviously should have dedicated his time and energy to only one of his big books. And to write even one of them well, he would have had to reduce his other responsibilities to their absolute minimum. Yet some of his own propensities led in the opposite direction. As the undisputed star of the Economics Department, he organized faculty discussion groups, spent endless hours with graduate students, and counseled scores of undergraduates. As an inveterate showman who needed an audience, he took on heavy teaching loads. Being Joseph Schumpeter was just as important to him as being a great economist.

He also lavished time on the many economists who visited Harvard from Europe and Japan. As always, he especially liked the company of junior scholars. He enjoyed his discussions with a stream of young Rockefeller Fellows and British Commonwealth Fellows, many of whom later became well-known professors: Fritz Machlup and Oskar Morgenstern of Austria; Nicholas Kaldor and Abba Lerner of England; Oscar Lange of Poland; Nicholas Georgescu-Roegen of Romania; and Arthur Smithies of Australia. (Smithies became Schumpeter's Ph.D. student, joined the Harvard faculty, and was a close friend.) He hosted numerous lunches and dinners for these guests from abroad, and often conversed with them late into the night. So, like many other famous academics, then and now, Schumpeter allowed his daily choices to divert him from long-term research.[2]

The inevitable results were frustration with the slow progress of his book projects and the beginnings of self-doubt about his abilities. This was something new to Schumpeter. As a young man, he had been phenomenally productive—able to keep many intellectual balls in the air and to turn out first-rate work at almost unbelievable speed. He wrote his 626-page first book in eighteen months, while practicing law full time in Cairo. He completed *The Theory of Economic Development* in less than two years, while teaching at Czernowitz and publishing numerous articles and reviews. And all of this while he was still in his twenties.

But very few creative people, no matter how gifted, can work during their fifties at the pace of "the sacred third decade," as Schumpeter called it. He was still blessed with immense drive and energy, but he now bore the scars of time and tragedy. "My work is my only interest in life," he wrote his friend Irving Fisher at Yale, and he seemed incapable of adjusting his goals to a realistic level. As a result, he suffered increasing discontent, hypochondria, and bouts of despondency bordering on clinical depression.[3]

On many occasions he believed himself to be physically sick. "How weak and old I feel," he wrote in his diary. "Am I dying?" And yet, as he told Fisher, whenever he would "consult some doctor, the result has been so far invariably that there is nothing organically the matter with me and that hence nothing ought to be done. This is precisely the reverse of the truth. It is before a definite breakdown has occurred that investigation ought to show the weak points in order to take them in hand while there is time." But the doctors were right. His problems were not primarily physical. His lingering grief, his research ambitions, his need for an audience, and his sense of duty were constantly colliding, and his inability to reconcile these feelings was the source of his psychological distress.[4]

Schumpeter seldom allowed his darker emotions to surface in public, where he maintained his veneer of effervescence. But in private, and especially at night, he went through more or less continual suffering. He poured out his soul to his *Hasen,* beseeching them for help:

> *1934: 21–27 May*
> O mother and mistress—whatever you want—
> Only stay close to me!
> No trace of comfort! Only torture and pretty fruitless work [on
> the money book, and] nothing on mathematics.

> *1935: 11–17 February*
> O mother and Hase—thank you for lots of beautiful things,
> But please, please help me further with my work!
> Again a week full of mostly cheerful and nice activities and a few
> broad insights, but I didn't get further with my work! [Dinners,
> concert,] not one quiet evening! New plan, but Sunday I couldn't
> work; Thursday and Friday tired and paralyzed.

> *1935: 6–12 May*
> Was not as I hoped it would be—still too much distraction, talk
> to Boston Economic Club, 1 [one] morning dictated letters, con-
> sultations [with students] . . . Sunday was also nothing, but in the
> evening I did four hours of [work]. But I didn't get far enough—
> thwarted and it becomes clear, I can only get further if I'm alone
> and if I have nothing else to do.

> *1936: Monday 19 October–Sunday 25 October*
> O mother and mistress—thank you for everything
> O for all the help, every day!
> Again a week vanished in exertion and without a doubt sometimes
> desperation. This week ended with a disconcertingly small result
> and the scary question, if my brain really can't do it anymore—
> just moves in circles—but not entirely without success. After com-

plete breakdown for two days (even my will refused to work) the
few things seemed still like a kind of success.

0, 4/6, 0, 0, 1/3, 5/6, 1 [daily grades]

1/2 [overall grade for the week]

The longer Schumpeter taught at Harvard, the more he came to resent the
bureaucratic routines of academic life that impinged on his research and writing. He especially disliked departmental meetings, and after several years he
began to refer to his colleagues as the "fools" (full professors, a play on the German pronunciation of "full") and "asses" (associate and assistant professors).
"These committees!" he wrote a friend, "This mentality, that believes that the
core of the world is that one committee dines and makes a report for another
committee, which in turn dines." Though maintaining his polite demeanor, he
began to take less care in muffling his feelings. As Seymour Harris recalled,
"His occasional lack of tact, a tendency toward exhibitionism, a desire to be
the center of attention, a low evaluation of some of his colleagues which he did
not conceal too well, his popularity with students and young colleagues—all of
these alienated some of his contemporaries and reduced his influence."[5]

In a part of Schumpeter's mind, he began to blame Harvard itself for his
problems. In 1934 he wrote to Abraham Flexner, director of the Institute for
Advanced Study in Princeton, hinting that he would welcome an invitation to
join. The institute had recently been established as a gathering place for eminent scholars from around the world. Unburdened by teaching duties, they
would devote time exclusively to their own work, amply supported by research
grants. Albert Einstein became the institute's best-known member.

Schumpeter told Flexner of the "uncomfortable stage of transition" that economics was going through, "from inexact philosophies to exact methods." He
mentioned a few lively centers of inquiry, such as the London School of Economics. "I could not adequately describe the sense of frustration I feel at my
inability to create another one as I hoped I would, first at Bonn and later at
Harvard." The bureaucrats whose support was essential did not understand the
importance of the goals. "I really believe that you, being the only man I know
of who commands both the understanding and the means, have a fair chance
of creating what may in the end turn out the foremost centre of the study of
exact economics." Flexner was about to go to England, and Schumpeter listed

seven top British economists whom Flexner might consider. But the invitation Schumpeter likely had in mind for himself never materialized.[6]

A year later, in 1935, he wrote his friend Ragnar Frisch in Oslo, "I have a very pleasant term behind me. It almost looked at times as if an intellectual milieu of some intensity would form here after all." Several brilliant visitors from Europe had enlivened the atmosphere of economics at Harvard. "But to carry as it were all the discussion and the work round me takes a lot out of me and my own progress was slowed down correspondingly." Hence his goal of quickly finishing a draft of *Business Cycles* turned out to be impossible.[7]

In 1936 Schumpeter composed a long letter to President Conant on the state of economics at Harvard. He recommended that the university hire several new faculty members, and named six outstanding candidates, all from overseas: Oscar Lange of Poland, Nicholas Georgescu-Roegen of Romania, Arthur Smithies of Australia, Ragnar Frisch of Norway, and two economists from Britain: John Hicks, and his wife, Ursula Webb Hicks. In suggesting five men and only one woman, Schumpeter told Conant that he had "submitted to the apparently invincible Harvard prejudice against women." He then added another recommendation: "Mrs. Joan Robinson of Cambridge, England, an economist of international fame, would be an extremely good acquisition and could probably be had for $4000 or a little more. I may add that if there were any wish to break that anti-feminist tradition, which to me seems, frankly, to be somewhat reactionary, her appointment would afford an excellent opportunity."[8]

Schumpeter went on to say that in Harvard's internal policies, "promotion is almost as rigidly regulated as it was in the old Prussian army." If a candidate managed to stay around long enough, promotion seemed almost certain. But the process took so long that "really able men" often departed. Meanwhile, "other universities are not systematically combed for rising talent."[9]

Harvard's own teaching requirements, he told Conant, were so heavy that professors are "hardly ever able to concentrate on a more ambitious task, [and] in many cases not even able to keep in step with the general march of science. In the various discussion groups which I am in the habit of running, I have observed again and again that I have before me (and this applies to the higher ranks as well) a set of tired teachers, thoroughly averse to engaging in a breathless hunt for new truths . . . what is the good of insisting on achievement while at the same time insisting on a load of current work which makes that achievement impossible?" Schumpeter added that many of his senior colleagues in the

Economics Department, "having accepted the situation and given up the hope of fulfilling themselves the measure of their intellectual ambitions, would not agree with me." But even without reference to research projects, "in order to teach better we must teach less, and teach less without on that account reducing the number of appointments."[10]

During these struggles over his situation at Harvard, Schumpeter showed no inclination to cut his ties with the Old World. As early as 1933 he made inquiries about becoming an American citizen but did not actually take this step until 1939. Meanwhile, he wrote frequent letters to Mia Stöckel and to former students and colleagues, and he thought about Europe a great deal. He regarded most Americans as hopelessly uninformed about the world situation, noting in his diary that the love affair between the Prince of Wales and the American divorcée Wallis Simpson got more press attention in the United States than Italy's conquest of Ethiopia.[11]

Yet Schumpeter continued to criticize academics who mixed scholarship with politics. Even if they were personal friends, he was hesitant to recommend professors who were strong partisans. As early as December 1932, for example, writing to Keynes about who should take his own place as German correspondent for the *Economic Journal,* Schumpeter expressed doubts about Emil Lederer. Although a superior economist, Lederer was also an ardent Socialist— "a party man of the type which obeys orders without asking a question. And in all matters which can be brought into any relation at all with politics he is absolutely unable to see them except through party glasses." The issue was not Lederer's socialism but his partisanship. If Keynes wanted to appoint Lederer anyway, Schumpeter would be happy to see the honor "conferred on an acquaintance of mine of very old standing whom I always looked upon with sympathy."[12]

Schumpeter's friend Gustav Stolper wrote him a letter from Berlin on January 31, 1933, which happened to be "the day on which the German people have experienced the shame of the [appointment to the] chancellorship of Adolf Hitler." But the purpose of his letter was to send Schumpeter a birthday greeting:

> What should we wish for you, the fifty-year-old? You have in your
> youth, as very few persons selected by fate, enjoyed fame and
> power, the love of women and all marvels of this earth, you have

experienced the good fortune of inscribing yourself through unforgettable achievements with golden letters in the history of our science, and now you, the fifty-year-old, are free to begin a second youth, or as a wise man to pluck the lavish fruits which begin to ripen in your garden. In your place I would opt for both at the same time.

Regarding the ominous appointment of Hitler, Stolper concluded, "When one has experienced the years 1914, 1918, and 1923, one already has a little experience in the fatalistic acceptance of catastrophes. Perhaps even this time it will not be so absolutely bad as it looks at this moment." But Stolper, a Jew, was too wise not to know better.[13]

At the time of Hitler's ascendance in January 1933, the full impact of the Great Depression had hit the world economy. Prices were declining almost everywhere (even though some signs of Germany's recovery had begun to appear a few months before). Discussions arose in many countries about public inflationary measures as a way to stop price slides. Having witnessed Austrian hyperinflation a decade earlier, Schumpeter believed policies of "reflation" to be a bad idea. He was no laissez-faire economist, and he thought that public works and a one-time burst of massive deficit spending by governments were the best ways to get out of the depression. But he was suspicious of broad public intervention.[14]

In February 1933 he wrote Irving Fisher that "the accession of the Hitler government meant, of course, somewhat of a shock to business confidence in Germany for at the moment when that government came in, recovery was fully under way. Very great progress had been made on the way to normal circumstances and this progress had been made without any reflationary measure." Schumpeter added that "I am unable to look upon all the [international] sufferings of the last two years as an unmixed evil." Like most other economists, he regarded the depression—then in only the third year of what, in the United States, would turn out to be twelve—as a severe but normal downturn in the business cycle. Thus, it did not seem appreciably different from what had happened during the 1870s and 1890s. All who thought this way, including Schumpeter, were mistaken. They should have known better when the unemployment rate in 1933 reached 25 percent.[15]

The following month, he wrote to Gottfried Haberler, then at the University of Vienna and later his Harvard colleague, "I was very glad to hear that the times do not affect the scientific activity of the Viennese circle . . . As to Germany, I find it very difficult to form an opinion. Recent events may mean a catastrophe but they also may mean salvation."[16]

But in that same month, March 1933, the Hitler government moved to suspend Jews, socialists, communists, and assorted others from academic positions. A few weeks later, the Nazis dismissed about three thousand teachers in these categories from Germany's educational system. Among the victims were several hundred economists, including some of Schumpeter's closest friends.

This drastic measure got his immediate attention. In cooperation with Wesley Clair Mitchell of Columbia, he tried his best to launch a rescue campaign. He proposed a committee of "six to ten economists of standing" who should

1. Act as an employment agency . . . for the victims of the Hitlerian ardours . . .

2. Take up the matter of temporary stipends, research fellowships, etc., with the great Foundations and also with such members of the Hebrew communities in America as can be expected to have sympathy for their kin . . .

3. Stand ready to help if it should happen that any of those Germans should one day land [in the United States] without any means . . . I can take care of Harvard and [its] neighborhood but know less than nothing about such places as Baltimore, Washington, St. Louis, Denver, or the Pacific coast, or of the state universities of the middle west.

Schumpeter added that the situation in Germany might be worse than most people believed. A former Bonn colleague had just written him asking "how much longer it would be possible to serve at the same time Science and Germany honourably. Now this proves very much because the man is not a Jew. On the contrary, he is even a very strong anti-Semite. He comes from an old industrial Rhenish family and is as conservative and national as anyone could wish. Now if he begins to feel uncomfortable, things must indeed be a bit thick."[17]

Believing that the rescue committee should be chaired by an American, Schumpeter asked the eminent pastor of Riverside Church in New York, Harry Emerson Fosdick, to preside. Fosdick declined, but Schumpeter continued his campaign. He sent Wesley Clair Mitchell a list of nine stranded Jewish economists whom he knew well and whose achievements made them outstanding candidates for jobs anywhere. "Of course all of them want to get out and besides it is an open question how long their salaries will be paid to them. I have had a letter from [Emil] Lederer which, although perfectly dignified, displays pathetic anxiety and despair."[18]

To Alvin Hansen, an economist then at the University of Minnesota, he recommended the sociologist Karl Mannheim of the University of Frankfurt, whom he had once tried to recruit to Bonn. "Of course, he is a Jew," one of many "who are now being removed from their chairs by the German government." In May 1933 Schumpeter recommended two economists to Edmund Day of the Rockefeller Foundation, which provided short-term funds for emigrant scholars. Schumpeter wanted Day to understand that his own efforts were on behalf of "exceptional men" and should not be construed as "an unfriendly act towards the German government." He added that "you probably will have heard of Alvin Johnson's comprehensive plan."[19]

Johnson was a fifty-nine-year-old American economist at the New School for Social Research in New York, which he had founded in 1918 as an experiment in adult education. Johnson's plan in 1933, developed in collaboration with E. R. A. Seligman of Columbia, was to set up a "University in Exile" for refugee scholars, housed within the New School. Schumpeter wrote to Johnson in May 1933, saying that he himself had been working to relieve the situation for German economists. Frank Taussig had "brought your excellent plan to my attention and, of course, now I feel that I must not get in your way as long as there is any chance of realizing your plan." Schumpeter enclosed with this letter the same list of nine scholars he had sent to Mitchell.[20]

On the same day, he wrote Mitchell that the Johnson-Seligman plan, which contemplated paying fifteen economists $3,000–$4,000 annually for two years and therefore required up to $120,000 in funding, might actually work. But "if they fail and we have to start again not only much time will be lost but some people who would have cooperated with us will be more difficult [to] approach after refusing someone else." In the end, Johnson did succeed in getting funds for his University in Exile, which proved to be a great boon for several dozen refugee scholars.[21]

Early in April 1933 Schumpeter heard once more from Stolper about the situation in Berlin. With characteristic insight, Stolper—whose magazine, *The German Economist,* was far too liberal for the Nazis—made plans to leave the country as soon as he could. Schumpeter recommended him to Mitchell as number one in his list of nine scholars. He also wrote on Stolper's behalf to Johnson at the New School, to Day at the Rockefeller Foundation, and to Thomas Lamont, a prominent Harvard alumnus and partner in the J. P. Morgan bank. Schumpeter told Lamont that for several years Stolper "had been fighting the Hitler movement with all the ardours of his democratic soul. And the Hitler government, as soon as established, avenged itself" by shutting down *The German Economist.* Stolper did manage to escape, emigrating to the United States before the end of 1933.[22]

Schumpeter's efforts to help "displaced colleagues" yielded some good results, he wrote to Haberler. Meanwhile, he continued his letter-writing effort and his attempts to get funding at Harvard. He wrote to Smith College and Bryn Mawr recommending Professor Frieda Wunderlich, a Jew whose "case is still more difficult than that of the other economists who have been dismissed because she is a woman, which fact very much restricts the range of possible employment." Wunderlich secured a post at the New School. In 1934 Schumpeter recommended to the Catholic University of America Karl Bode, a "fervent Catholic" who had been "one of my best pupils" in Bonn. "When the present German government came in, he was of course not at all affected by the fact as he is neither a Socialist nor a Jew. But he found the spirits of the new political era so repulsive to his convictions that he went to Vienna to go on with his studies."[23]

In 1935 Schumpeter wrote to the Social Science Research Council urging help for still another member of his Bonn circle, Herbert Zassenhaus. "In the ordinary course of things he would have with the greatest ease been awarded a Rockefeller Fellowship. This he did not get, on the ground that he could not show reasonable chance of academic appointment in Germany—which of course he could not owing to the fact that his attitude to the existing regime is entirely negative. But the various organizations which help displaced German scholars would not lend their help to him either because he is in no sense 'persecuted', being neither a Jew nor a Socialist and having only his convictions to thank for the fact that he is ineligible for academic office in Germany."[24]

Schumpeter sent many letters, but academic jobs were scarce during the Great Depression, and without an independent source of funds he could not do much more. He and Mitchell redirected their efforts to the Rockefeller program, which helped numerous scholars get exit visas, and to Johnson's University in Exile at the New School, which Schumpeter supported throughout the 1930s. His friends Emil Lederer (who became Johnson's key European ally), Adolph Löwe of the University of Frankfurt, and several other economists found employment at the New School. So did a variety of scholars from other disciplines—political science, psychology, musicology. Toward the close of the decade, as war was approaching, Harvard itself finally moved to set up a small fellowship program.[25]

By one careful count, some 221 economists successfully emigrated from Germany, Austria, or occupied countries: 151 to the United States, 35 to Britain, and the rest to other countries. Of the 221, 131 found jobs at universities. A substantial number did not escape. Many perished at the hands of the Nazis, and a few committed suicide.[26]

Schumpeter's emotional attachment to Europe never died, and his attitude toward his old home remained complicated for the rest of his life. Sometimes he seems to have felt not like an expatriate, nor even an exile, but something worse: a man without any country at all, doomed to endless wandering. He had no particular affection for Germany, and the beloved Austria of his youth was gone forever. Most of his friends had departed Vienna, and the university's once splendid economics faculty had declined markedly, its elite professors replaced by mediocrities. By the 1930s he did not even want to visit Vienna.[27]

YET SCHUMPETER REMAINED a European at heart, and he spent almost a third of the time during his first three Harvard years in Europe—the maximum possible interval, given his academic duties. Each June from 1933 through 1935, as soon as he had graded his students' exams, he would depart on "my yearly summer sojourn." He would not return until late September, just before fall classes started. He thus kept one foot in the Old World without quite making the leap into the New.[28]

After crossing the Atlantic by ship, Schumpeter usually stayed for a week or

Schumpeter and Mia Stöckel on a cool June day in 1933, standing at the University of Bonn. After it became clear how vicious the Nazi regime was going to be, Schumpeter ventured into Germany less often during his summer sojourns with Mia.

two in Britain. He would visit economists in London, Oxford, and Cambridge, his outward ebullience always on display. Lionel Robbins, a prominent scholar at the London School of Economics, recalled that in 1934 Schumpeter "turned up unexpectedly from the United States on the day of our annual seminar outing . . . It was a lovely day in June; and, as we glided down the Thames between Twickenham and Datchet, I can still see him, cheerily ensconced in the prow of our ship, surrounded by the eager spirits of the day, Nicky Kaldor, Abba Lerner, Victor Edelberg, Ursula Hicks"—all of them first-rate economists. Schumpeter took charge as "the master organizer of the party—[his] four fingers and thumb of each hand pressed against those of the other, discoursing with urbanity and wit on theorems and personalities."[29]

From England he would cross the Channel to Ostend in Belgium. There he would rendezvous with Mia Stöckel, who was then in her late twenties and still unmarried. With Mia at the wheel of a rented car, the two would criss-cross France, Italy, and Switzerland, reveling in the freedom of the open road. Occasionally they drove a few miles into Germany, for a stop in Bonn or in Mia's home town of Jülich. Then they would spend two or three weeks in some resort city—Vlissingen on the southern shore of Holland, Biarritz on the French Atlantic Coast, or Spa in Belgium, fifty miles southwest of Bonn. Schumpeter did not like Spa but believed that his health required that he take the waters there.[30]

During these trips, Mia served as Schumpeter's companion, frequent bed partner, and, as she liked to put it, "chauffeur." As in the old days, she also took his dictation and typed his letters and short manuscripts. Schumpeter usually kept up his unstinting work patterns in the summer—drafting articles and catching up on his reading. He was seldom able to do significant work on either his money book or the business cycles book, but he did think hard about these two big projects and discussed them with British and European economists.

On his sojourns in Europe, he graded himself even more harshly than usual. For one period, he recorded zeroes for fourteen consecutive weeks. In the summer of 1934, he visited a half-dozen countries and more than thirty towns and cities—most of them home to an interesting cathedral, which he would sketch in numerous pencil drawings. He also kept up his diary entries, thanking his *Hasen* and recounting details of his travels:

1934: 18–24 June, in England
O mother and mistress—O thank you for everything
In this beautiful week!
Anniversary of mommy's death . . . Monday still [aboard the
ocean liner] Laconia. Tuesday and Wednesday London (school
and gallery). Thursday Oxford. From there Friday and Saturday:
Winchester, Salisbury, Wilts[hire] and Malmesbury.

1934: 9–15 July
O mother and mistress—O thank you for everything.
I am indeed not worth it.
Amiens, Beauvais, Mantes, Chartres—Paris, Seux, Auxerre, where
Annic was [during her time as a servant in France], Vezelay . . .
Lots of beautiful things . . . Thank you, you Hasen. It was worth
the trouble, without a doubt. But how much more complete and
more fruitful would it be not to be alone! [though in fact he was
with Mia].

1934: 23 July–5 August [a 2-week report]
Journey through Alsace, Sauerland, Moseltal, in Bonn, then . . .
Vlissingen. And on Saturday the 4th I started with my work on
the money book.

1934: 27 Aug–2 Sep [still in Vlissingen, trying to work]
Spa, some tennis, but also Baccarat, a concert; literature . . . but
whole week dominated by money book. 4 times full [grade of 1],
but tormented myself also the other three days—with little result.

After 1934 Schumpeter took one more summer trip with Mia. By that
time their relationship had grown less physical and more companionable, and
throughout the 1930s they kept up a close correspondence. Mia and the Stöckel
family remained extremely important to Schumpeter, as a continuing lifeline
to Europe. But in the meantime he had met another woman who was to play a
major role in his life.

When Schumpeter first encountered Romaine Elizabeth Boody Firuski in
1933, she was a thirty-five-year-old graduate student in economics at Harvard.
Lizzie, as her friends called her, had grown up in Lawrence, Massachusetts,

thirty miles north of Cambridge, the daughter of a Swedish immigrant mother and a father who came from a prosperous old New England family. She attended the Lawrence public schools (where she was known as Romaine Boody), then went on to Radcliffe College. There, she earned Phi Beta Kappa honors, played on the varsity hockey team, served as class historian and editor-in-chief of the Radcliffe *News,* and was elected president of the Socialist Club. In 1920 she received the first *summa cum laude* degree Radcliffe had ever given in economics.[31]

After a year away from school and a three-month tour of Britain, France, and her mother's native Scandinavia, Elizabeth returned to Cambridge to begin work on a master's degree. To help support herself, she found employment at the Harvard Economic Service, a data-gathering institute affiliated with the Economics Department. She received her M.A. in 1925 and then spent almost two years in England on a Whitley Traveling Fellowship from Radcliffe. She attended lectures at the London School of Economics and put in very long hours doing research at the British Museum and the Public Record Office. Working with reams of official eighteenth-century documents, she compiled a statistical record of English overseas trade during an era of great expansion by the British Empire. She then returned to the United States, intending to write her dissertation on this topic. Meanwhile, she accepted an assistant professorship at Vassar College. From January 1927 through June 1928 she taught economic history, theory, and labor problems, at a salary of $2,500 per year.[32]

Indecisive about her academic future, Elizabeth then resigned her job at Vassar and, now thirty years old, married Maurice Firuski, a Cambridge bookseller, four years her senior. A native of Brooklyn, Firuski operated a shop in Harvard Square and soon bought a second bookstore in Salisbury, Connecticut, near the western border of Massachusetts. Sometimes he also taught in the Salisbury public schools. He owned an estate in the Berkshire Mountains near Taconic, a tiny Connecticut town not far from Salisbury. The main house, Windy Hill, was an uncommonly pleasant rural retreat. On the property surrounding the house, Elizabeth began what would become a lifelong project of landscape design and development. As she later put it: "From earlier 1929 until late 1933 I was simply a housewife living in the country in Connecticut."[33]

Before long, however, she began to miss the intellectual stimulation of Cambridge and to grow unhappy with her marriage to Firuski. The two separated, and from March through June 1933 she vacationed in Greece and Italy. She then moved back to Cambridge and divorced Firuski. In the settlement, she received the Taconic estate.[34]

Elizabeth returned to Radcliffe, where she was already well known to the other economists at Harvard. She participated in their seminars, served as a faculty research assistant (with Schumpeter, among others), and resumed writing her dissertation on English foreign trade. Her thesis director was Abbott Payton Usher, a distinguished economic historian the same age as Schumpeter. Because of Schumpeter's own interest in this subject, he became co-director. Elizabeth received her Ph.D. in 1934.[35]

Schumpeter was fifty years old in 1933, fifteen years Elizabeth's senior. He carried about 160 pounds on his 5'8" frame—fifteen pounds more than in his early adulthood. He was no longer dashingly handsome, but his sophistication and warm attentiveness still appealed to many women. Elizabeth was 5'4" and weighed about 125 pounds. Emotionally well-grounded and very attractive (her photographs resemble Annie as she might have looked in her thirties), she combined quiet poise with a tough and formidable intellect. As a close friend recalled, Elizabeth "was a scholar all her life, but very much a woman as well. Her professional interests never diminished her essential femininity . . . She was a woman of character: forthright, honest, a staunch and loyal friend."[36]

Elizabeth came closer to being Schumpeter's intellectual peer than any other woman in his romantic life, ever. She had a superb analytical mind, a graceful writing style, and mathematical skills in some ways superior to his own. She was determined to pursue her work as a scholar, and preferably at Harvard, despite its blatant sexism. From 1934 to 1937 she worked as a research associate at Radcliffe and for Harvard's Bureau of International Research, starting at $2,400 per year and receiving raises to $3,000. This was more than some instructors were making, and quite good pay during the Depression. She served on the staff of the *Review of Economic Statistics* and later edited it herself. She was not wealthy, but she had in addition to her salary some money from her family, as well as her divorce settlement from Firuski.[37]

She lived most of the time in a house near Radcliffe and the rest at Windy Hill, 115 miles west of Cambridge. She worked on her dissertation in both places, and in August 1934 returned to London to do six months' research on topics beyond her dissertation. Soon she became fascinated by the rapid indus-

ROMAINE ELIZABETH BOODY

142 South Broadway, Lawrence, Mass.
Born August 16, 1898, Lawrence, Mass.
School and year of graduation: Lawrence High School, 1916.

College Concentration: Economics.

Junior Welcoming Committee. Guild 1916-1920. Idler 1916-1920. Business Manager Freshman Play. Lunch Room Committee 1916-1917. Civics Club Debate (Negative) 1916-1917. Socialist Club 1916-1920. Class Treasurer 1917-1918. Chairman Budget Committee. History Club 1917-1920. Christmas Supper Committee 1917. Reporter for *News* 1917-1918. Socialist Club 1918-1920; President 1919. Phi Beta Kappa 1918. Civics Club Treasurer 1918-1919. Associate Editor of *News* 1918-1919. Science Club 1918-1919. Vice-President Civics Club 1919-1920. Speaker Debating Club. Vassar-Radcliffe, Radcliffe-Emerson Debates 1920. Editor-in-Chief of *News* 1919-1920. Chairman Committee of Five for Halls of Residence 1919-1920. Class Historian. Varsity Hockey Team 1919-1920. Class Hockey Team 1919-1920. Undergraduate Secretary Phi Beta Kappa 1919-1920. Wild Worm in ''Rivesby Sword Play.'' Third Division Club 1919-1920. Guild Constitutional Committee.

''What I says is no: frank and honest, I says no.''

Elizabeth Boody's senior yearbook picture at the time of her graduation from Radcliffe in 1920. The list of her activities is one of the longest for any student.

trial development of Japan, an interest that was to cause her more than a little grief in the coming years, as American-Japanese relations deteriorated.

Elizabeth dined with Schumpeter occasionally after receiving her Ph.D. in 1934. Then they began to see each other more often, and by 1935 they had become a regular twosome in the Harvard social circuit. Schumpeter found Windy Hill immensely appealing—the ideal setting for quiet concentration. He was very troubled about his two book projects, and increasingly vulnerable to sudden mood swings. In the spring of 1936 he decided not to take a fourth summer trip to Europe, despite Mia's strong protests. By this time he was seeing a great deal of "E.B.F.", as he called her in his diary, and spending many days and nights at Windy Hill.[38]

Elizabeth was no free-spirited divorcée but a mature, modest, and circumspect woman whose chief interest was scholarship. Despite her beauty and her previous marriage, she had much less experience with men than Schumpeter had with women. She was a bit dazzled by him but, unlike most of his male associates, was seldom misled by his outward gaiety. Instead, she quickly perceived his melancholy side. She knew that he had a great soul and believed that she could provide the emotional support he so obviously needed.

Elizabeth concluded that because of all that had happened to Schumpeter, he was in danger of losing his balance altogether. His diary entries denouncing himself show that she was correct:

> You are an ineffective fool
> They laugh at you
> And they are right
> And you can't defend yourselves [sic]
> And nobody cares.[39]

By the time he wrote these lines in 1937, Elizabeth had become irresistibly attracted to him. "You are the only man (besides my former husband) whom I have really loved and known with any degree of intimacy." And in another letter, "Although I succumb very infrequently I seem to fall very hard."[40]

She had decided without any question that she wanted to marry Schumpeter, but he was not ready. He knew that he would never marry Mia Stöckel, but he was still in such thrall to Annie's memory that he found it hard to imagine making a commitment to any other woman. At the same time, he was very fond of Elizabeth. To the extent that he could think about the matter rationally, he saw that it would be hard to imagine a better partner. As a professional economist, Elizabeth could talk knowledgeably with him about his work. She had lived in Cambridge on and off for twenty years and was no stranger to the local society of either town or gown. Having endured one failed marriage, she had no illusions about the stresses of domestic life. And as someone who not only loved him deeply but also understood his greatness as a scholar, she made it clear that she would do everything possible to facilitate his work.[41]

The only real obstacle was her health. Elizabeth was a diabetic, and she did not know whether it was wise to try to have children. Since the death of his newborn son in 1926, Schumpeter had not given up his hopes of fatherhood, even though by now he was past fifty. Elizabeth made it clear that if he would marry her, she was willing to risk her own well-being to accommodate his wishes. The problem was that he could not discern what his wishes were. His

Elizabeth Boody Firuski in 1936, by which time she was very much in love with Schumpeter.

waffling, which dragged on for many months, put her in an extremely awkward position.[42]

In the summer of 1937 matters finally came to a head. "Darling," she wrote to him, "Please remember that you have hopelessly compromised me, and that all decisions are automatic as a consequence. It is feeling some responsibility about decisions which is *so* difficult. E.B.F." In another letter:

> Am I an unmitigated nuisance? If I am—and I suspect you think so just now—this is the one thing for which I can put responsibility absolutely on you. It was you who told me again and again that one should fight for the things (or people) one really cares about. I had been inclined to the view that in personal relations, pride and dignity required that one retire without a struggle in the face of difficulty or reluctance. You mustn't be too annoyed at me for following your advice—and struggling . . .
>
> It is true that your pendulum-like movements make life somewhat uncertain and difficult at times—but these difficulties are the results of your life and your temperament and I accept them as such . . .
>
> It is important that we love one another and that you are fighting against it—but that you haven't fought against it consistently. You know it is no light thing with me.[43]

Seeing that she was going to have to force the issue, Elizabeth then presented him with a series of near-ultimatums. Writing from Windy Hill:

> You must have realized in the last three years that I was not a very happy person. I was pretty much sustained by pride and self-respect—and now that these have vanished—a little slump is quite natural . . .
>
> This is really to say "goodbye" unless you should come to feel yourself that you are prepared to follow out the implications of some of your conduct and some of your conversation. Please do not bother to telephone or to write unless you really want to give me a little time and a little consideration. I do not expect any very large amount—you have made it quite clear that this would be

useless—but no real friendship can exist with one person making all of the adjustments.

You have my love and all my good wishes. Elizabeth.[44]

As Schumpeter continued to vacillate, she decided to give him one last chance. In a final letter she openly criticized his indecisiveness, his mood swings, his despondency, and his hypochondria. And this time there was no "Darling" in the salutation:

Dear J.A.S.

I am not cross, but I am puzzled and discouraged and unhappy. I am frightfully tired of uncertainty about everything. There are two immediate problems. One of them is you and the other is the house in Taconic. [Two houses were on the property, and she intended to sell one of them].

Almost the most difficult thing about you is the way you swing back and forth like a pendulum. You advance a little—then you get by yourself and become distrustful—and swing back to your original position. In the process of doing it, you are likely to be a little cruel as you were last night. This is not said in any spirit of criticism or disapproval, but merely as a statement of fact.

It is more important than you realize for you not to disappoint me at the last minute under present conditions. It is you who make all the decisions as to where and when we shall meet. I cannot do any of the natural normal things like calling you up on the telephone to "chat" a little or stopping in to see you for a minute in your study. I have to wait for the king's command.

You mellow in my society and then you go away and think dark thoughts. I have been willing to try to draw you back again and again because I love you and because it seemed to me that almost any life would be preferable to the one you are now leading with its concomitant state of mind. It is, of course, your mind much more than your body which makes you feel so ill and weak.

I cannot go on doing this. You must see that this uncertainty added to the rest of the uncertainty (as to work, finances, Taconic,

etc.) and insecurity of the last five years might be too much even
for a stable and serene person.

If you go to the Big Horn Mountains [where he was planning a
summer vacation in connection with a speaking engagement], you
will go back again into your lonely gloom and distrust about the
future. And this time, I shall not be on hand when you return,
and I shall not be able to draw you out of it. Much as I love you, I
shall not try again.[45]

At this point Schumpeter surrendered. He agreed to the wedding, leaving all
remaining details to Elizabeth, including the selection of an engagement ring.
She learned that they could be most easily married in New York, where the
waiting period was less, at least for a while: "I gleaned from yesterday's N.Y.
Times that it will be possible to be impulsive in New York State for another
two months." She went to Manhattan for a few days to make the arrangements
and then wrote him again that "You can call me here when you return from
dinner. If you think I go soundly to sleep at an early hour, you are insufficiently aware of your own charms."[46]

In New York she also saw a physician about her diabetes and informed
Schumpeter of a negative recommendation about trying to have children. This
was a reversal of what other doctors had told her. ("I find that it takes a long
time to learn all about the facts of life.") Schumpeter was disappointed but did
not waver, no doubt recalling Annie's death in childbirth. Elizabeth then re-
joined him in Boston. About ten days later, on the morning of August 15, 1937,
the two traveled by train to Manhattan and got a room at the Waldorf Astoria.
They were married the next day in a small private ceremony at the non-
denominational Community Church. Given Schumpeter's emotional state—
his diaries suggest that he was very close to a breakdown—marrying for a third
time was one of the hardest things he ever did. But it would prove to be one of
the wisest.[47]

PART III

The Sage, 1939–1950:

Innovation, Capitalism, and History

PROLOGUE

How and Why He Embraced History

History hath triumphed over time, which besides it nothing
but eternity hath triumphed over.

SIR WALTER RALEIGH, *History of the World,* 1614

BY THE MID-1930S Schumpeter had already marked the way for-
ward for his new approach to economics by integrating the discipline of sociology into it. Now, on the eve of World War II, history took center stage both in
the world at large and in Schumpeter's work. The new emphasis on history in
his thinking was neither radical nor abrupt, nor did he forsake his earlier preoccupations. He had turned to other disciplines in order to extend the power
of economics to comprehend the vast complexity of life. He now pushed that
expansiveness even further by grounding the study of capitalism in the rich soil
of history.

Schumpeter had lived through a great deal of tumultuous history himself,
and he was about to be caught in still more cross-currents. As a native Austrian
who had emigrated to the United States from Germany, he developed very
conflicted feelings about the events of the 1930s and about American foreign
policy. He soon found himself out of step with his new countrymen, whose
apathy toward world affairs disheartened him. Then, after the United States
entered the war, he faced the opposite problem of jingoism, perhaps best
expressed in the nation's insistence on its enemies' "unconditional surrender."

This idea, though familiar to Americans from their own Civil War, struck many people in other parts of the world as a novel and potentially brutal doctrine.

Elizabeth Schumpeter shared her husband's doubts about the wisdom of certain policies. Both Schumpeters accepted that the Nazis could be defeated only with help from the Soviet Union, yet they both regarded the Soviets as a more formidable long-term threat to world stability than either the Germans or Japanese. Elizabeth, as one of very few Americans not of Asian descent who had a deep knowledge of Japan's economy, foresaw with great clarity what would happen in the event of a war in the Pacific. During the late 1930s and right up to the moment of the attack on Pearl Harbor, she warned of Japan's growing industrial strength. She coauthored a book on Japan, and in numerous articles she predicted that a Pacific war was likely to be long, ruthless, and ultimately advantageous to the Soviet Union. But most Americans still regarded Japan as weak and remote, and her forecasts were dismissed—until December 7, 1941.

After the Japanese attack, first Elizabeth and then Joseph were investigated by the FBI on suspicion of disloyalty—she because of her writings on Japan, he because of his former German citizenship. They were only two of several thousand "suspects," many of whom had fled Europe precisely because of Nazi or Soviet persecution. Meanwhile, the government also interned over a hundred thousand Americans of Japanese descent. Both Schumpeters regarded these policies as uncivilized. And they viewed the massive bombing of civilians in Japan and Germany—a campaign that killed nearly a million people—as little short of barbaric. They believed that the extremely brutal tactics of the Japanese and especially the Germans had led the United States to retaliate in a way unworthy of the country's traditions. Their views on these subjects made them unpopular even with some of their friends. But rather than fight against what they believed were misguided American policies, they retreated into the world of scholarship.

As Schumpeter became ever more absorbed in his work, he paid increasing attention to history as the key to understanding not only capitalism but economic life in general. This shift is clear in the three big books he wrote during the 1930s and 1940s: *Business Cycles,* which appeared in 1939; *Capitalism, Socialism and Democracy,* in 1942; and *History of Economic Analysis,* issued posthumously in 1954. All together, the three total about two million words. A typical book of 300 pages contains about 100,000 words. So beginning in the 1930s until his death in 1950, Schumpeter produced the equivalent of twenty books of conventional length. During this same period he also wrote some three dozen articles, public lectures, and memorial tributes.

In almost all of this work, whether in books or other forms, he took a fundamentally historical approach. He never abandoned his fascination with social theory, nor with mathematics, law, or political science. But he now consolidated them under the umbrella of history and economic theory. The result was an interdisciplinary mix that deployed all of his interests, learning, and literary skill.

Sometimes, as in *Business Cycles,* the combination did not work well. Here Schumpeter tried to embed his central message about the dynamics of capitalism within a plausible but dubious framework he borrowed from other theorists. In his other two books, however, the result was never less than cogent and persuasive. As the Dutch scholar Henrik Wilm Lambers wrote of *Capitalism, Socialism and Democracy,* Schumpeter accomplished "the feat of moving five layers of thought—the firm, the markets, the institutions, the cultural values, the leaders of society—as one interwoven dynamic process. With incomparable skill he made history go through time as one stream."[1]

Schumpeter's final book is also primarily a work of history, as its title suggests. In this mammoth volume, he covers the intellectual history of his discipline over the space of more than two thousand years, and in the process he delves deeply into the sociology of knowledge in general. The Chicago economist Jacob Viner described Schumpeter's *History of Economic Analysis* as "by a wide margin, the most constructive, the most original, the most learned, and the most brilliant contribution to the history of the analytical phases of our discipline which has ever been made." It remains so to this day.[2]

Toward the end of his life, Schumpeter issued a remarkable credo about the primacy of history. Of the three basic building blocks of economics—theory, statistics, and history—he wrote that the last "is by far the most important."

> I wish to state right now that if, starting my work in economics
> afresh, I were told that I could study only one of the three but
> could have my choice, it would be economic history that I should

choose. And this on three grounds. First, the subject matter of economics is essentially a unique process in historic time. Nobody can hope to understand the economic phenomena of any, including the present, epoch who has not an adequate command of historical *facts* and an adequate amount of historical *sense* or of what may be described as *historical experience.* Second, the historical report cannot be purely economic but must inevitably reflect also "institutional" facts that are not purely economic: therefore it affords the best method for understanding how economic and non-economic facts *are* related to one another and how the various social sciences *should* be related to one another. Third, it is, I believe, the fact that most of the fundamental errors currently committed in economic analysis are due to lack of historical experience more often than to any other shortcoming of the economist's equipment.[3]

Schumpeter's belief in the indispensability of history expanded as he wrote his three big books, but his disenchantment with his fellow man continued to grow as well. While maintaining his outward good cheer, he sometimes drifted into a world-weariness that bordered on despair. The closer he looked at politics and diplomacy, the more folly he found. He believed that the catastrophes of the First World War and its awful aftermath, which had destroyed the culture of his youth, were now about to be replayed in the Second World War. He especially dreaded the triumph of Stalinism in Europe, and he all but predicted the Cold War and what it would mean for the permanent militarization of the United States.

During the early 1940s he wrote in his diary hundreds of biting "aphorisms," as he labeled them—about everything from economics and politics to academic life and the nature of humanity. Almost self-consciously, he took on the role of sage. He often thought that no one was listening, but here he was wrong. Some of his writings were indeed ignored. But his *Capitalism, Socialism and Democracy* was destined to be one of the seminal works of the twentieth century, in any field. And his final book, *History of Economic Analysis,* was still another towering achievement, a *tour de force* not only of economics but also of intellectual history and biography.

15

Business Cycles, Business History

History abhors determinism but cannot tolerate chance.

BERNARD DE VOTO, *The Course of Empire*, 1952

THROUGHOUT THE FIVE-YEAR period before his marriage to Elizabeth, and for two years afterward, Schumpeter spent more time researching and writing *Business Cycles* than working on all his other duties combined. The job took twice as long as he had anticipated, and Elizabeth helped enormously in keeping him sane. In 1939 the huge treatise at last appeared—in two volumes totaling 1,095 pages.[1]

Measured by its professed aims and several other yardsticks as well, *Business Cycles* was one of the least successful works of Schumpeter's career. Yet this first foray of his historical period changed the way he thought about capitalism. The prodigious research that went into the book curtailed, though it did not end, his quixotic pursuit of "exact economics." And in its powerful narrative sections, *Business Cycles* presaged the emergence of modern, rigorous business history—a new academic subdiscipline. The book also laid an extraordinarily solid foundation for Schumpeter's next major work, the brilliant *Capitalism, Socialism and Democracy*.

Today, research efforts on the scale of *Business Cycles* employ teams of half a dozen statisticians, economists, and other social scientists. But in the 1920s and 1930s this method of organizing big projects was just getting started, and

Schumpeter undertook the job almost entirely on his own. To Harvard's Committee on Research in the Social Sciences, which provided some minimal assistance, he reported in 1937 that the effort had "proved much more laborious and time-consuming than I had expected." Early in 1938 he wrote Harold Burbank, chairman of the Economics Department, that "I am half dead and certainly entirely dazed from the long hours I must spend on rereading and touching up my manuscript."[2]

The design of *Business Cycles*—a three-country study covering the whole capitalist epoch—was simply too formidable for Schumpeter to handle alone while he pursued his other academic duties. As he told Wesley Clair Mitchell in 1937, he had committed himself to "an immensely laborious analysis of every historical pattern within the reach of our material." The project loomed so large that "in order to carry out so detailed an investigation as would be necessary I would have to have a whole research staff working for me." To another friend he wrote, "I am still a slave to my manuscript and for instance . . . worried last night till 2 a.m., on such questions as whether potatoes were important enough in Germany in 1790 to count in the business cycle."[3]

Schumpeter chose the title *Business Cycles* not only because the topic was then fashionable (it was *the* economic puzzle of the time, and had been so even before the Great Depression) but also because he wanted to emphasize the economic ebb and flow that defines capitalism. "Cycles," he writes in his preface, "are not, like tonsils, separable things that might be treated by themselves, but are, like the beat of the heart, of the essence of the organism that displays them."[4]

This is true enough. But Schumpeter's approach to cycles veers perilously close to historical determinism. In his pursuit of a more exact economics, he attempts the hopeless task of fitting historical patterns of business booms and busts into predictable wave periods of standard lengths. "Barring very few cases in which difficulties arise," he writes, "it is possible to count off, historically as well as statistically, six Juglars [8–10 year cycles] to a Kondratieff [50–60 years] and three Kitchins [40 months] to a Juglar—not as an average but in every individual case."[5]

Clément Juglar, Joseph Kitchin, and Nikolai Kondratieff were prominent business cycle theorists. References to their work appear hundreds of times in Schumpeter's text and make it extremely difficult to read. Here is a representative sentence: "Both crises [the downturns of 1826 and 1836] occurred when, taking the Juglar and the Kondratieff phase together, we should be prepared to find major dips in prices and values: a Juglar recession on a Kondratieff depression forms the background of the one, and a Juglar depression on a Kondratieff revival, the background of the other." Paul Samuelson later commented that the book's arguments "began to smack of Pythagorean moonshine."[6]

Schumpeter had ambivalent feelings about his own framework. As he told Mitchell, "I must repeat again, lest misunderstanding shall arise, that I file no theoretical claims for the three-cycle schema. It is primarily a descriptive device which I have found useful." In the text of *Business Cycles* he admits that it "is indeed difficult to see" why boom-and-bust patterns might occur at such determinate intervals. Indeed it is, and Schumpeter's own stance is guarded and empirically informed: "Any such diagnosis stands and falls with the historical evidence on which it rests." Theory is indispensable to understanding business cycles and capitalism itself. But detailed historical analysis is no less so.[7]

One perceptive reviewer assessed *Business Cycles* as "Schumpeter's interpretation of the history of capitalism. That and nothing else is the actual goal of the book." Schumpeter himself notes that his subtitle, *A Theoretical, Historical, and Statistical Analysis of the Capitalist Process*, "really renders what I have tried to do." His preoccupation with the evolution of business and his mention of numerous companies by name confirm that *Business Cycles* is as much a work of history as of economics.[8]

Oddly enough, references to actual companies were not common in the professional writings of economists at the time and are almost nonexistent today. Rigorous historical analysis of firms and industries has become the purview of business history. Before the appearance of *Business Cycles,* business history had been in existence for only a few years, and much of its practice was confined to case studies done for classes at Harvard Business School.[9]

This is not to say, of course, that nobody was writing in the popular press about business or the history of companies. In the United States, Britain, Germany, and a few other countries, there were plenty of works on individual firms and entrepreneurs; but many were so laudatory as to be devoid of intellectual value. At the opposite extreme, the muckraking movement in America and the socialist tradition in Europe had yielded a rich series of polemics attacking firms, industries, and capitalism itself. American writers often denounced specific companies (Ida Tarbell's *History of the Standard Oil Company,* 1904), individual businessmen (Matthew Josephson's *The Robber Barons,* 1934), and entire industries (Upton Sinclair's *The Jungle,* 1906, on meatpacking; Louis D. Brandeis's *Other People's Money,* 1914, on banking). Books and articles on business, both pro and con, had some merit, especially literary merit, since they were narratives complete with plots and memorable characters. But most portraits were painted in stark hues of good versus evil and, at least in the United States, were largely bereft of theory.[10]

Schumpeter's *Business Cycles,* by contrast, is full of economic and sociological theory. And it has the additional virtue of strong historical passages, complete with actual characters and a central plot. Not long after completing *Business Cycles,* Schumpeter wrote that "I have been primarily a theorist almost all my life and feel quite uncomfortable in having to preach the historian's faith. Yet I have arrived at the conclusion that theoretical equipment, if uncomplemented by a thorough grounding in the history of the economic process, is worse than no theory at all."[11]

The core of *Business Cycles* is its copious detail about the flowering of business systems in Britain, Germany, and especially the United States. Schumpeter focuses on companies in five industries that led economic development: cotton textiles, railroads, steel, automobiles, and electric power. He also emphasizes three institutional innovations crucial to the rise of capitalism: the factory, the corporation, and the modern financial system.

He begins by setting forth a general theory of capitalist evolution that comes near to being an allegory. In his model, recurring "Innovation" propels the economy, which exists in a state of constant tumult. "New Men" or "Entrepreneurs," operating within "New Firms," drive innovation. (Like many other writers of the time, Schumpeter capitalizes some of his key terms.) All companies react "adaptively" to change, but creative "responses" come only from innovative acts by entrepreneurs. Their innovations can take many forms: for example, "the case of a new commodity," "a new form of organization such as a merger," and "the opening up of new markets." Innovating firms do not arise evenly throughout the economy. Instead, groups of these firms emerge just after an organizational or technological breakthrough in a particular industry— either in that same industry or in others allied to it.[12]

Meanwhile, powerful elements of society resist major innovations, because they tend to wreak havoc on existing arrangements. As a result, "the history of capitalism is studded with violent bursts and catastrophes." It is no gentle process of adjustment but something "more like a series of explosions." The building of a railroad where none had existed, for example, "upsets all conditions of location, all cost calculations, all production functions within its radius of influence." Innovation, then, is very much a double-bladed sword.[13]

Schumpeter next turns his attention to the main protagonist of the system, the entrepreneur (or "New Man") and to the entrepreneur's necessary companion, "Profit." He concedes that in some situations it is hard to identify the entrepreneur. In the real world of business, "nobody ever is an entrepreneur all the time, and nobody can ever be only an entrepreneur." Particularly in large firms, the entrepreneur often not only innovates but also carries out day-to-day management.[14]

For any given innovation, the entrepreneur "may, but need not, be the person who furnishes the capital." Of all economic systems, capitalism alone enables people to become entrepreneurs before they possess the necessary funds to found an enterprise. In the end, "it is leadership rather than ownership that matters." The failure of both the classical economists and Karl Marx "to visualize clearly entrepreneurial activity as a distinct function *sui generis*"—a distinction Schumpeter himself always underscored—was a crucial flaw in their analysis of capitalism.[15]

The prior possession of money makes it easier to become an entrepreneur, of course, and successful ones usually become wealthy. But the historical record shows unmistakably that, in the countries Schumpeter is discussing, entrepreneurs come from all income groups and social classes. "Risk bearing is no part of the entrepreneurial function. It is the capitalist who bears the risk. The entrepreneur does so only to the extent to which . . . he is also capitalist, but qua entrepreneur he loses other people's money."[16]

Having staked out the distinctive role of the entrepreneur, Schumpeter identifies entrepreneurial profit as the prime motivator—"the premium put upon successful innovation." When other participants in the same industry see the new level of high profit, they quickly try to imitate the innovation. The entrepreneur tries to preserve his high profit for as long as possible, through patents, further innovation, secret processes, and advertising—each move an act of "aggression directed against actual and would-be competitors." These are forms of what Schumpeter would famously call "creative destruction" in *Capitalism, Socialism and Democracy.*[17]

Thus, a new firm's intrusion into an existing industry always entails "warring with an 'old' sphere," which tries to prohibit, discredit, or otherwise restrict the advantage afforded to the new firm by its innovation. But whatever may happen in a particular case, *every* entrepreneur's high profit is temporary, because competitors will copy the innovation, causing market prices to fall. This sequence of cutting prices, which Schumpeter calls "competing down," is observable in all industries except those protected by government monopoly. Competing down may take several years and is often hard for contemporaries to see. But one way or another, competing down always happens, and it is why Schumpeter seldom worried about price-fixing by monopolies, other than those sponsored or propped up by governments (as many firms had been in the Austro-Hungarian Empire).[18]

Having laid out his basic model of capitalist behavior, Schumpeter proceeds to deluge the reader with historical examples. He begins with the origins of the factory system in Britain, the first major nation to industrialize. In the late 1500s, he writes, a few British entrepreneurs systematically cut their production costs so that they could reduce their selling prices. Lower prices stimulated demand and enabled producers to manufacture in larger volume and to distribute their products more widely. Over the long term, the new factory system flourished beyond the dreams of its proponents. It gathered large numbers of workers into one place, set uniform standards for quality, and divided production into separate steps performed by specialists—all under the discipline of the clock.[19]

Schumpeter was careful to point out that the factory system introduced more efficient production even into "old industries" such as textiles. The shift from home spinning and weaving to mechanized production of cloth was so profound that it launched the first industrial revolution (1760–1840). Consumers' demand for affordable factory-made cloth turned out to be almost unlimited. Men could now have not just one or two shirts and pairs of pants but six or seven; women, not just a few dresses and blouses but many. And—very significantly—the new cotton clothing could be washed frequently, unlike woolens.[20]

The factory system modernized many other existing industries. In iron and steel, bigger furnaces facilitated "production on a large scale of standardized intermediate goods, such as ingots, sheets, rods, and wire." Factories increased the output of a wide range of products: metalwork made of copper and brass, paper made in mills "driven by water wheels . . . potteries, sugar refineries . . . glass, soap, and gunpowder factories, and salt-boiling establishments." Factories triggered a new era in British economic life, raising the overall standard of living and bringing fortunes for entrepreneurs.[21]

But the shift did not come easily. A major theme of *Business Cycles* is the extreme difficulty of changing traditional ways of doing things. More than most analysts, Schumpeter emphasized that the destructive part of creative destruction has always been quite real, and he stressed that those whose interests are being destroyed will fight hard to preserve their culture and status. In Britain and elsewhere, small-scale craftsmen and their guilds had esteemed artistry, community, and tradition over low prices, increased output, and expanded exports. These predilections went back for centuries, and the only way to change them was through overwhelming economic defeat.[22]

Entrenched interests fought tenaciously against mechanization and the factory system. Unlike the Prussian inventor of a ribbon-weaving loom, who was put to death in 1579 by order of the Danzig municipal authority, "Entrepreneurs were not necessarily strangled," but "they were not infrequently in danger of their lives." Craft guilds in Britain invoked medieval laws to prevent both outsiders and their own members from using innovative methods. They petitioned for regulations outlawing factories and particular mechanical devices. Schumpeter cites the Weaver's Act of 1555 and a "royal proclamation which in 1624 directed that a new machine for the manufacture of needles be destroyed." And regardless of what the law might allow at a particular time, craftsmen themselves continually smashed the new machines.[23]

In response, British entrepreneurs often moved their factories out of guild-dominated towns. Operating in the countryside, they could proceed without the fetters of official repression and with the advantage of cheaper labor— although even here, in the new outposts, innovators had to "fix things" with local authorities. Yet, whatever the obstacles, in certain industries they were almost sure to win in the long term. Large-scale factory production offered more jobs for workers, cheaper goods for consumers, a richer tax base for governments, and a dominant foreign-trade position for Britain. In London, "the political world wavered in its attitude and motivation," but soon business interests became a major force in politics; and by the eighteenth century, Parliament had largely submitted.[24]

Besides innovating in production, entrepreneurs often had to change habits of consumption. Industrialists had to convince reluctant customers that they actually *needed* the new goods. Here Schumpeter places heavy emphasis on the role of marketing in mass consumption and in economic growth itself. "It was not enough to produce satisfactory soap," he writes, "it was also necessary to induce people to wash—a social function of advertisement that is often inadequately appreciated."[25]

From the perspective of producers and investors, it did not matter whether new wants were real necessities. "Needs," says Schumpeter, "whatever they may be, are never more than conditioning factors, and in many cases mere products of entrepreneurial action." Undeniable needs such as food, clothing, and shelter do not, by themselves, "set the capitalist engine into motion." This is why "economic development (capital consumption included) has *never* been conspicuous in the countries which to the observer seem to be most lavishly supplied with needs." In order to understand capitalism, analysts are therefore best advised to study industries in economically advanced countries, not in the underdeveloped world. And in *Business Cycles* Schumpeter does exactly that: he grounds his narrative of capitalist evolution in the actual industrial histories of Britain, Germany, and the United States.[26]

THE FIRST OF HIS CASES, that of cotton textiles, begins in medieval Germany and Switzerland, but the story of cotton is a story not of farmers but of entrepreneurs. And so the main events in Schumpeter's narrative occur in Britain, thanks to the East India Company's cotton imports. That one step helped to set off the first industrial revolution. And, as usual, the change met fierce resistance. In 1721, old firms in woolens and silks "secured, with due reference to the interest of the English workman, a prohibition of the sale as well as the wearing of printed, painted, or dyed [Indian] calicoes."[27]

At that time, a small British cotton industry provided thread as weft for linen warp in blended fabric. In 1736 the government granted the industry an exemption from the ban on cotton, and in so doing it created a new demand for yarn. It then repealed anti-cotton laws altogether in 1774, and thereafter

British producers could make fabrics from cotton alone. By the 1780s, abundant innovations had set the stage for a giant leap in production. The use of cotton fabrics spread quickly, inducing "improvement, dislocation and absorption, copying, following, and competing." As prices fell, "the real avalanche of products came."[28]

Again, traditional craftsmen reacted violently. In the early years, weavers wrecked John Kay's new loom with its so-called flying shuttle (invented in 1733) and drove Kay himself to France. Other protestors smashed many of James Hargreaves's new spinning engines ("jennies," patented in 1770). In 1792 still others destroyed the factory that manufactured Edmund Cartwright's power looms. And from 1811 to 1816 the notorious Luddites hammered textile machinery to bits.[29]

In describing the industrial revolution—and in probing the nature of change, which is the heart of his thesis—Schumpeter draws sharp distinctions between inventors and entrepreneurs, and between inventions and innovations: "The making of the invention and the carrying out of the corresponding innovation are, economically and sociologically, two entirely different things." Often the two interact, but they are never the same, and innovations are usually more important than inventions.[30]

The career of Richard Arkwright (1732–1792) exemplifies these distinctions especially well. Arkwright was an inventor, but—much more critically—an innovating entrepreneur. Before he developed his machines, which spun cotton faster and produced stronger thread, weavers had problems in blending cotton thread with linen fibers, which come from flax. But Arkwright's innovations, including his own emergent factory system, soon began to revolutionize the industry. Other industrialists paid him handsome fees for the use of his patented machines, and he operated several factories himself. Before long, he became very rich and received a knighthood. In Schumpeter's terms, Arkwright was a New Man organizing a New Firm and reaping a high entrepreneurial Profit.[31]

Arkwright's multiple innovations and skills in organizing the whole system far surpassed the significance of his inventions alone. "Doing the thing," as Schumpeter puts it—"the actual setting up of new production functions—is a distinct phenomenon." The falling domino of one innovation topples the next domino, in an endless series radiating in all directions. "We readily see how every step conditions other steps—yarn and cloth, for instance, alternating in offering new demand to each other and in running up against bottlenecks, the removal of which then makes the next achievement."[32]

Necessity may be the mother of invention, but it does not automatically produce innovation. New men operating new firms—such as Richard Arkwright in textiles, Josiah Wedgwood in pottery, James Watt and Matthew Boulton in steam engines, and many others—had to "do the thing." In silks and woolens, which had previously dominated the British textile market, the necessary action was not taken. Both industries should have been reorganized during the 1700s. Yet as Schumpeter points out, "The rich and well-established woolen industry lagged behind, right into the thirties of the nineteenth century. It accepted progress under pressure [from cotton] and was drawn along by the more active younger sister." The silk industry held its own but did not expand. Meanwhile, production of cotton textiles simply exploded, yielding billions of yards of fabric for export to Britain's markets all over the world.[33]

Eventually, after many decades of prosperity, the cotton industry itself drifted into torpor. British firms prospered so handsomely that they had little incentive to innovate further. They held to traditional mule-spinning, turning their backs on the vastly superior ring-spinning technique. And they recoiled from the commonsense idea of having the same company spin thread and weave cloth. For about 150 years after the breakthroughs of Hargreaves, Cartwright, and Arkwright, thousands of family-owned companies specialized in only one or two steps in the long process of production and were very slow to innovate. The industry declined because of "the presence of many small or medium-sized firms which were inefficient but unencumbered [with debt] and could muddle on indefinitely." Schumpeter notes that "the hand jenny and the hand loom persisted for the greater part of the period and even toward the end of it there seem to have been firms which used not only antiquated power machinery, but no power machinery at all."[34]

Meanwhile, the Americans had innovated as early as the 1830s, integrating spinning with weaving under one roof, in giant factories. Toward the end of the nineteenth century, the British began to lose ground to more efficient firms in the United States and Europe, and by the time they finally modernized their factories, it was too late. Both the rise and decline of the British cotton textile industry demonstrated Schumpeter's argument almost perfectly. Britain's most important industry had neglected the *organizational* innovations so important in Schumpeter's scheme. For this entrepreneurial negligence, the cotton textile industry paid a grievous price, particularly in the twentieth century.[35]

In Germany, the cotton textile industry benefited from the pioneering efforts of both Britain and the United States. Germany was not unified as a nation until 1871, a century after the key innovations in Britain. The Germans did not become world leaders in textiles, as they would be later in chemicals and electrical equipment. Instead, German textile entrepreneurs contented themselves with "introducing methods that had already been successful abroad, mechanizing by means of partly imported machinery, setting up new factories, [and] especially solving the problems of the large-scale factory." The Germans were better than the British at organizing their textile industry, even though they contributed little to its mechanical technology.[36]

Schumpeter concludes his analysis of textile manufacturing by describing the rise of rayon, the world's first synthetic fiber. This story epitomizes the way in which innovation can revolutionize industries already thought to be "mature." In rayon, the dominant figure was the French Count Chardonnet, "a very characteristic type of entrepreneur." In the late nineteenth century, Chardonnet worked out the necessary chemical processes and then set up new factories in France and Switzerland. "He became the founder of the industry—the New Man in whose wake the host was soon to follow."[37]

Other innovators in France, Britain, and the United States quickly developed their own ways of making rayon. Eventually, what had started as a modest effort to manufacture cheap artificial silk grew to a major industry that by 1924 was producing 29 million pounds of fabric annually.[38]

Rayon brought a new type of competition to textiles—not among thousands of small firms but among several big chemical companies. Demand grew very fast. Entrepreneurial profits soared in the beginning, and a few firms with deep pockets emerged as the leaders. In the United States, after a shakeout of numerous companies, three came to dominate the industry: American Viscose, Celanese, and Industrial Rayon. Each was affiliated with a European firm that had pioneered in rayon but was handicapped in selling to the American market by U.S. tariff protection.[39]

SCHUMPETER'S FAVORITE EXAMPLE of innovation by new men and new firms was the American railroad industry. In the 1830s, entrepreneurs started a few rail lines as a means of moving raw materials from inland producers to seaports. A little later, as steam engines became more efficient and coal mines better developed, railroads almost entirely displaced canal and turnpike systems.[40]

The "railroadization" of the United States, beginning in the 1840s, was a monumental engineering achievement and a milestone in the development of both American business and the nation itself. Over the next few decades, millions of immigrants from Europe poured into the country, enticed by free or cheap land along the new rail lines. Large land grants from the government to both railroad companies and pioneering homesteaders subsidized a frenzied westward migration across the continent.[41]

By the 1890s an immense railway network linked every region of the United States with every other region. With such cheap and fast transportation, a unified domestic market arose for an unprecedented variety of industrial products and consumer goods. Manufacturers, wholesalers, and retailers could now ship and receive goods very quickly. Assisted by the telegraph, they could communicate with one another in seconds and minutes.[42]

Meanwhile, the multitude of construction programs undertaken by railroads stimulated a host of other industries. "Everything else," Schumpeter writes, "turned on the roads and was either created or conditioned by them." Railroads vastly increased the use of coal, iron, steel, machinery, and petroleum-based lubricants and fuel. Across the continent, railroads created new communities of all sizes, from small junctions to vast new industrial centers. Chicago was a child of the railroads, as were Omaha, Fort Worth, Denver, and thousands of smaller towns. Even established manufacturing cities such as Pittsburgh once more mushroomed.[43]

Soon the competing-down element hit the railroad industry itself, from within. Under intense pressure from new railways, established companies slashed their freight and passenger rates, sometimes to levels below their own costs. Construction slowed, few new firms appeared, and the industry went through a violent shakeout—with mergers, refinancings, and the loss of individual fortunes.

At that point, railroading became part of the general business "organism," as Schumpeter calls it, with "mutual dependence" all around. This was typical of capitalist evolution. "The more an innovation becomes established, the more it loses the character of an innovation and the more it begins to follow impulses, instead of giving them." Railroad mergers and refinancings occurred "by way of spectacular struggles between controlling groups." The shakeout appeared to the general public in the form of "freight wars, cutthroat competition, discrimination, and the evils of unregulated enterprise." But the real story was one of "consolidation, efficient administration, and sound finance, thus ushering in the last step of America's railroadization."[44]

Because railroads cost colossal sums and took months or years to build, entrepreneurs needed more capital than their own funds and revenues from the business could supply. Thus, construction was "mainly financed by credit creation." Huge amounts of money flowed into the United States from Britain and Europe, through the purchase of railroad bonds and the use of overdrafts on banks (lines of credit). Some of these British overdrafts were granted "with almost unbelievable freedom and carelessness." In the United States itself, credit creation was often even more reckless—but it was also extremely innovative.[45]

The pattern of railroad finance exemplified for investors the tumultuous business cycles typical of capitalist economies. By the time of the worldwide depression of 1873, the ups and downs of railroading had made it clear that the process of "liquidation, absorption, adaptation"—the frequent companion of innovation—was going to be "an unusually long and painful affair." Railroads had brought about an entirely new level of financing, particularly through stocks and bonds. In America, this movement gave birth to modern Wall Street during the 1850s. By 1897 "'net capital' of the railroads stood at $9,168,072,000," an almost unimaginable sum for that time.[46]

"Railroadization," then, was Schumpeter's "standard example by which to illustrate the working of our model." Hundreds of innovations emerged, both large and small. Great sums of money changed hands, the speed of commerce leapt forward, and a vast array of new products reached national markets. All of these characteristics "combine to make the essential features of our evolutionary process more obvious in this than they are in any other case."[47]

In addition to propelling new instruments of finance, railroads fostered the growth of corporations. The corporate form represented a vital organizational innovation, but its development took a long time. The first corporations were devised mostly in the sixteenth and seventeenth centuries in England and Holland. They served as legal frameworks for the discharge of a particular public purpose, such as the formation of municipalities, universities, guilds, and overseas trading companies.[48]

But from the seventeenth century to the nineteenth, the function of the corporation gradually changed. "It implied raising 'capital,'" Schumpeter writes, "which was first done (even in the case of the East India Company) for each individual venture." From this practice emerged "the independent and impersonal capital of the company," not just that of its shareholders as individuals.[49]

As long as businesses financed ventures of limited duration, the old partnership form of commerce functioned well. Every participant shared all the burdens and profits. Each was assessed for his contribution, and each could be held liable to pay the debts of the partnership as a whole out of his own personal assets. This arrangement worked so long as the funding of ventures did not exceed the sum of the personal fortunes of the individual partners.

But industrial enterprises such as mining and a few early factories required permanent financing beyond the means of even a large group of wealthy partners. Governments, in order to support the new economic reality of industrialization, then created, through law, a new arrangement known as a joint stock company, which laid the basis for the modern corporation. In this type of company, shares could be bought and sold among a potentially unlimited number of investors. For this to happen, says Schumpeter, "both legal and financial devices had to be invented in quite the same sense as the steam engine had to be invented." In most nations where corporations became common, monarchs or legislatures created them one at a time, through specific acts. Corporate charters typically went to investors in state-sponsored enterprises such as canal companies and banks, some of which operated as monopolies. By the nineteenth century, corporations spread to other kinds of business.[50]

Still today, the most important advantages of the corporate form over the partnership are its permanence (it does not die when its founders die) and its limited liability (shareowners risk only their investments in that corporation, not their entire personal wealth). A big refinement came with the privilege of free incorporation, instead of the earlier system requiring royal or legislative acts. By the second half of the nineteenth century, entrepreneurs in Britain, the United States, and a few other countries could launch their new corporations by simply registering them in the jurisdictions where they did business.[51]

The corporation turned out to be a crucial innovation. Its permanency prevented forced liquidation of the business when one or more of the old-style partners wished to dissolve the partnership or died. Limited liability enabled people to participate more freely in the economy as investors, without unlimited personal risk. The separation of ownership from control created opportunities for talented managers to climb the corporate ladder and lead great enterprises. At the same time, the secondary market for corporate shares, run by stock exchanges, allowed holders of stocks and bonds to convert their investments into cash at a time of their own choosing.[52]

In Schumpeter's mind, railroadization was the best single example of entrepreneurship facilitated by the corporate form. "New types of men took hold of [the railroads], very different from the type of earlier railroad entrepreneurs." Although this trend had begun as early as the 1850s, the need for a new managerial class peaked in the 1890s. By that time, Schumpeter writes, the new managers served as "organizers and financiers," carrying out complex tasks of "liquidation and reconstruction . . . combination, amalgamation, and merger." Out of hundreds of independent railroad companies formed during the nineteenth century, consolidations climaxed in the early twentieth with ten principal systems, each of them many thousands of miles long.[53]

Railroads were the first examples of truly big businesses, but hardly the only ones. The consolidation of the railroad system foreshadowed hundreds of other mergers in manufacturing, distribution, and retailing, plus the internal expansion of many other firms. From 1897 through 1904, 4,227 American companies merged into 257 large entities. Many of their names, along with those of companies expanding internally, are still familiar today: Goodyear, Pepsico, General Dynamics, Kellogg, Gillette, Monsanto, 3M, Texaco. This movement would not have occurred without the completed railroad network, which created the first truly national markets. Through mergers, acquisitions, and internal growth, entrepreneurs sought to stabilize prices and reduce what contemporaries called "cutthroat competition."[54]

Schumpeter saw the rise of big business, including the merger movement, as a major innovation in finance and management—carried out by new men and new firms. Unlike social critics who fretted over the giant size of the new companies, he believed they brought great advantages: "new units of control, new principles of management, new possibilities of industrial research, and, at least eventually, new types of plant and equipment." They facilitated the "absolute optimum" way to commercialize new technology.[55]

While acknowledging some destructive abuses associated with big business, Schumpeter argues in *Business Cycles* that the movement was a logical phase in the growth of industrial economies. But entrepreneurial startups always emerge and grow uninterrupted alongside big businesses. He writes, for example, of the "traveling salesman who turned into a promoter of combinations [mergers and acquisitions]." This phenomenon seemed obvious to Schumpeter, as it had been even before he moved to the United States. He always rejected the idea that opportunities for entrepreneurs to succeed in new firms had suddenly dried up.[56]

As usual, Schumpeter approached this issue by taking the long view. He understood why many politicians and social critics protested against damages to incumbent craftsmen, small businesspeople, and unskilled workers. But to him it remained clear that innovations drove entire national economies forward and that long-term progress far outweighed short-term pain. Regarding the great political power of large corporations, he believed that the function of regulation belonged primarily to governments, not to the private sector. But, as he wrote in many of his works, this required intelligent civil servants, tuning the engine of capitalism with a careful hand, lest they stifle entrepreneurship.

IN ADDITION TO railroads, another of Schumpeter's favorite examples of capitalist growth was the automobile. Car manufacturing combined many innovations: interchangeable parts, modern machine tools, the internal combustion engine, and new ways to make steel. The whole process was "a purely entrepreneurial achievement turning to new uses not only existing resources but also existing technology." Schumpeter notes that most of the technological problems were worked out in France and Germany during the 1890s and early 1900s. But the real automotive innovations occurred in the United States, where no fewer than 322 firms entered the business during the five years after 1902. By 1907, sales totaled 8,423 units and about $5.5 million, of which perhaps $1 million was profit. Then, in 1908 came the Model T Ford—a "great new thing," as Schumpeter describes it—designed not for the rich but for the masses. By 1925, after only twenty-two years in business, Ford had sold twelve million Model T's—at ever-declining prices to consumers.[57]

In the invention of new financial techniques, Schumpeter writes, the automotive industry was "almost in a class by itself." General Motors' introduction of installment buying created an immense amount of credit by turning consumers into significant borrowers. Installment buying increased the number of first-time car owners, encouraged buyers to trade up to more prestigious models, and provided an additional stream of income from interest on the loans. And customers who did not want to buy "on time" could still purchase a car with cash obtained through bank loans. With so many customers borrowing and repaying money to own a car, automotive manufacturers were able to minimize their own debt. "No better instance," writes Schumpeter, "could be found to show how credit creation for the purpose of innovation can *hide*"— that is, how it can be introduced invisibly and subtly. General Motors' innovations in financing—as well as in styling, marketing, and organization—were as significant to the industry as Ford's assembly line had been in production, and they enabled GM to overtake Ford during the late 1920s.[58]

By that time, motor vehicles, which had barely existed in 1900, ranked first among American industries in cost of materials purchased, wages paid, and value of products. Hundreds of firms had entered the industry initially, but from the 1920s onward it was dominated by a tiny handful. As Schumpeter puts it, there was "absolutely no other reason for this than the one embodied in our theory of entrepreneurial activity. Coincidence of high mortality and high profits ideally expresses this situation." The automobile story shows "how realistic the fundamental distinction is between the behavior of the mere economic man and the entrepreneur."[59]

Entrepreneurs built their auto empires in significant part on the foundation of steel, which has its own history of technological and organizational breakthroughs. As Schumpeter emphasizes, the key development for both cars and steel was sharply declining prices. The change in steel began in Britain with the introduction of Henry Bessemer's mass-production process in the 1850s. Schumpeter lauds Bessemer as one of the purest examples of the entrepreneur in action.[60]

In the beginning, Bessemer's contemporaries regarded him as an inventor. But he was much more than that. "Real genius, but of the typically entrepreneurial kind, was in the vision of the vast possibilities for *cheap* steel." Pursuing this goal, Bessemer combined existing methods with new ones. He then patented his system and waited for an onrush of licensees.[61]

When few applicants appeared, Bessemer entered the steelmaking field himself. He went directly to Sheffield, then the leading steel city, with the intention of underselling the top firms. His steel was of excellent quality, though not yet as inexpensive as Bessemer knew it would become. Soon he and his imitators were making rails for the booming railroad industry, steel plates for ships, and steel wire for weaving bridge cables. Even so, traditional resistance to innovations during the 1860s, along with Bessemer's relatively high prices, restricted the wide use of steel that was to come.[62]

At this point, competition between the Bessemer process and the even newer open-hearth method pioneered by William Siemens began to drive production up and prices down. British firms produced 77,500 tons of open-hearth steel in 1873, a figure that shot up to 436,000 tons in 1882. By 1896 they were turning out 2.4 million tons, in addition to 1.8 million tons manufactured by the Bessemer process.[63]

Innovations spawned by cheap steel had now spread to many industries. Steam engines became stronger and more efficient, as did machine tools. Manufacturers could now afford to use steel in "practically all parts of the economic organism": for making better rails, bridge trusses and cables, pumps, bicycles, cranes, and structural frames for buildings. They could improve ships by using stronger plates, keels, and propellers. By adding a small amount of tin to steel, they could retard rust and develop new markets in tin roofs for buildings and tin cans for food. And they could revolutionize many industries (sewing machines, weapons) through the use of interchangeable steel parts.[64]

In the United States, steel production at first lagged behind British output, then very rapidly overtook it in the closing decades of the nineteenth century. Near Pittsburgh, Andrew Carnegie's iron firm built the Edgar Thomson Steel Works. This was Carnegie's first Bessemer plant, and—with typical marketing insight—he named it in honor of his best customer, the head of the Pennsylvania Railroad. Carnegie then expanded by building or acquiring ever more modern steel mills at nearby Homestead and Duquesne. Illinois Steel, Colorado Fuel and Steel, and a few other companies quickly followed Carnegie's example.[65]

Even more important than cheap steel was the development of electricity, which Schumpeter regarded as a "New Industrial Revolution." Business applications of electricity had begun as early as the 1840s, with the telegraph. Yet, as with most new things, it took much time and hundreds of steps, large and small, to achieve the full impact of electrification. The key innovations were Thomas Edison's incandescent lamp and the triumph of alternating current over direct current, which made long-distance transmission of electric power possible.[66]

Gigantic turbines at Niagara Falls (manufactured by German firms, as Schumpeter neglects to mention) went into operation in 1895. Hydroelectric companies in other regions, led mostly by local entrepreneurs, followed in quick succession: "In New England (Holyoke Water Power Company), on the Mississippi (Keokuk), in Montana (Great Falls), on the St. Mary's River (Consolidated Lake Superior Company)." Many companies prospered on the Pacific Coast and in the South, in addition to large firms such as the Southern Power Company, the Alabama Power Company, and the hydroelectric plants of Alcoa in Tennessee. As these firms began to buy and sell current among themselves, the nation's electrical system expanded in the same way its railroad networks had done earlier.[67]

Schumpeter pointed out that "one essential peculiarity of the working of the capitalist system is that it imposes sequences and rules of timing." Nearly every company that could benefit from electric power now *had* to innovate, whether it wished to or not. Schumpeter emphasized this point repeatedly, and for many industries. Electricity provided the heat necessary to refine copper and aluminum ores. Electric motors spun and wove textiles, pumped water from mines, milled lumber with high-speed saws, and shaped metal with power drills and stamping machines. "For success in capitalist society," Schumpeter argues, "it is not sufficient to be right *in abstracto;* one must be right at given dates." Much of the success enjoyed by individual entrepreneurs came down to their talent for seizing the opportunities of the moment.[68]

Although he wrote *Business Cycles* in the middle of the Great Depression, Schumpeter sums up the story of electrification with an optimistic message. New uses for electricity were everywhere: radios, refrigerators, dial telephones, and so on. No single industry, he pointed out, had yet been fully electrified, let alone all households. And the electrification of farms had hardly begun.[69]

As was his habit, Schumpeter took pains to name the leading firms in the industry. "Electrical equipment was produced by the General Electric and the Westinghouse concerns and also by many other firms, some dating from the [eighteen] eighties (as, for instance, the Electric Storage Battery Company). Some of the most important ones were highly specialized (Electric Boat Company, National Carbon Company)." The industry also developed a healthy export market: "The equipment of the London Underground Railway was supplied by American firms (1897)." Meanwhile, of course, not every attempt succeeded: "It should not be forgotten that in 1914 there were still above 40 firms fighting the losing fight of the electric automobile."[70]

"Capitalist evolution spells disturbance," Schumpeter emphasizes again and again. "Capitalism is essentially a process of (endogenous) [sic] economic change." In the absence of change, "capitalist society cannot exist." If the capitalist engine stalls, the economic system will disintegrate. And the key that starts the engine and keeps it running is innovation: "Without innovations, no entrepreneurs; without entrepreneurial achievement, no capitalist returns and no capitalist propulsion. The atmosphere of industrial revolutions—of 'progress'—is the only one in which capitalism can survive." Hence there must be constant change, generated from within. "In this sense," Schumpeter concludes, "stabilized capitalism is a contradiction in terms."[71]

BUSINESS CYCLES, in both of its two volumes, has outstanding merits as economic and business history. But judged by Schumpeter's aim of explaining complex cyclical patterns, the book was not a success, and its tepid reception disappointed him bitterly. Most reviews were favorable but also tinged with complaint. Hans Neisser of the University of Pennsylvania noted several problems with Schumpeter's argument but was amazed by his vast erudition: "It will always be a marvel that such a book could be written by one man." Oscar Lange judged that in its "intention and horizon Professor Schumpeter's book can be compared with *Das Kapital* of Karl Marx," adding that "this comparison is intended by the reviewer as highest praise." In the *American Historical Review*, Hans Rosenberg of Brooklyn College wrote that "this work cannot be merely read; it must be studied."[72]

Simon Kuznets, a business cycle theorist and pioneering macroeconomist based at the University of Pennsylvania's Wharton School, wrote the most important critique, in the *American Economic Review*. Kuznets took a sympathetic tone but offered a long and skeptical analysis. He praised Schumpeter for having written a "monumental treatise" that raised all the right questions. But Kuznets argued that Schumpeter had strayed too far from the kinds of robust quantitative tests that the subject of business cycles required. The book contained plenty of numbers, but Schumpeter's treatment of them, along with his many historical examples, resembled "an intellectual diary." He told of his "journey through the realm of business cycles and capitalist evolution," disclosing "his encounters there with numerous hypotheses, diverse historical facts, and statistical experiments." These efforts were praiseworthy, but they could not substitute for tight mathematical analysis.[73]

At a Harvard seminar that Schumpeter's students organized in 1939 to discuss *Business Cycles,* it became evident that almost nobody had read the text. Afterward, several students said that they had never before seen Schumpeter genuinely furious, as he was on that occasion. One of them recalled that "in the discussion everyone talked about Keynes [whose *General Theory of Employment, Interest and Money* had recently appeared] and not about [Schumpeter's] work. So at the end he said 'whether you agree or disagree is up to you, but I wish you would at least have read it.' We felt ashamed after that, and we wrote a letter to Schumpeter about it." A few years afterward, Schumpeter told his friend Gottfried Haberler that his arguments had been misunderstood because "few if any people have read my ponderous volumes really through."[74]

Although the excessive length of *Business Cycles* was indeed a problem, a more serious one was the futility of Schumpeter's quest for exact economics. He took many liberties in constructing his cycles, such as adjusting his numerical data to reflect outside events. If a war or a natural calamity had interrupted a period's prosperity, he had still counted that period as part of a prosperous cycle. This alteration, while logical, was a slippery slope leading away from exactitude. Schumpeter and other analysts could select their relevant outside events arbitrarily, make whatever adjustments they wished, and thereby cause the resulting data to fit their preconceived framework.[75]

The whole idea of exact economics, in the sense that it could match the precision of physics or chemistry, had been a pipedream all along. The failure of *Business Cycles* thus represented something of a turning point in Schumpeter's decades-long intellectual wrestling match with himself. He did not give up his quest, but his preoccupation with exact economics diminished after the appearance of *Business Cycles.*

Above: Schumpeter at his desk at Harvard, not long after the appearance of *Business Cycles.*

Left: John Maynard Keynes, whose *General Theory of Employment, Interest and Money* thoroughly upstaged Schumpeter's *Business Cycles.*

Still another reason for the disappointing reception of his book was its inopportune timing. Schumpeter had been through this experience before, when the approach of World War I diverted attention from his brilliant *Theory of Economic Development*. And now *Business Cycles* happened to appear soon after Keynes's landmark *General Theory,* published in 1936.

From 1936 until the end of his life, a specter haunted Joseph Schumpeter, and that specter was John Maynard Keynes. In contrast to *Business Cycles,* Keynes's *General Theory* offered a new explanation for the Great Depression and outlined a way in which the world economy might be rescued. Using a method the world came to call macroeconomics, Keynes's approach dwelt on "aggregates"—the total amount of resources that national economies devote to consumption on the one hand and investment on the other. In Keynesian and other macroeconomic models, individual entrepreneurs, companies, and industries simply vanish from the scene. Very tellingly, no mention of a single business firm can be found in the entire 403 pages of *The General Theory.*

Keynes names dozens of economists, most of them British, and describes their ideas in detail—often devastating detail. But he takes no note of Schumpeter, and little of other European business cycle theorists. Sufficient homage is not paid to the giants of the great German and Austrian economic traditions: to Gustav von Schmoller, Werner Sombart, Max Weber, Arthur Spiethoff, and Adolph Löwe; to Carl Menger, Friedrich von Wieser, Eugen von Böhm-Bawerk, Ludwig von Mises, and Friedrich von Hayek.

When Keynes's book appeared in 1936, many distinguished reviewers gave it a negative assessment. In addition to Schumpeter himself, these included the British scholars Dennis Robertson and A .C. Pigou and the Americans Frank Knight and Alvin Hansen. The eminent Jacob Viner of the University of Chicago, reviewing *The General Theory* for the *Quarterly Journal of Economics,* praised some parts of the book but complained that "no old term for an old concept is used when a new one can be coined, and if old terms are used new meanings are generally assigned to them."[76]

Schumpeter begins his own review with a deft and generous touch: "Those who had the opportunity to witness the expectations of the best of our students, the impatience they displayed at the delay in getting hold of their copies [of *The General Theory*], the eagerness with which they devoured them, and the interest manifested by all sectors of Anglo-American communities that are up to this kind of reading (and some that are not) must first of all congratulate the author on a signal personal success." He goes on to exalt Keynes as "one of the most brilliant men who ever bent their energies to economic problems."[77]

There the politeness ends and the attack begins—rooted about as much in simple jealousy as in intellectual disagreement. Schumpeter reproaches Keynes for calling his theory "general" when it actually applies to a very narrow situation: a particular kind of capitalist economy in depression. Worse, under the guise of a "purely theoretical discussion," Keynes's logic moves from the policy he favors to a theory that will support it. This, says Schumpeter, is simply unacceptable: an "unholy alliance" that does not "have anything to do with science." Throughout *The General Theory*, Keynes "pleads for a definite policy, and on every page the ghost of that policy looks over the shoulder of the analyst, frames his assumptions, guides his pen." The policy itself—deficit expenditures by government over a long period—may well be the correct remedy for the current situation in Britain. But, says Schumpeter, this kind of argument confuses practical issues with scientific ones and divides economists along lines of political preference rather than analytical ability.[78]

These were justifiable criticisms, but neither Schumpeter nor most other reviewers gave Keynes sufficient credit for a series of ideas destined to become part of the everyday vocabulary of economics: the multiplier effect, the propensity to consume, the liquidity preference, and many others. All of these lend themselves to useful mathematization and have the appearance (if not quite the reality) of what Schumpeter regarded as exact economics. He dismisses each of them as a *deus ex machina*, of which "there is a whole Olympus."[79]

On the other hand, his criticism of Keynes's distortion of the essence of capitalism is squarely on point. For one thing, Keynes's way of explaining the reluctance of businesses to invest forces him to underplay the role of innovation. Schumpeter protests that Keynes thereby dismisses "the outstanding feature of capitalism," in which both technology and methods of doing business "are being incessantly revolutionized." In sum, "the capitalist process is essentially a process of change of the type which is being assumed away in this book." Keynes's insights may "still be of some use to the theorist. But it is the theory of another world and out of all contact with modern industrial fact."[80]

As critical as he was in his published review, Schumpeter took an even harsher tone in his private correspondence. "There is no question in my mind about the merits of Keynes's vital personality," he wrote to Lange in Chicago. "But what I find so difficult to understand is that so obviously bad workmanship is so readily condoned by people who know what good workmanship is." *The General Theory,* though it seemed to represent itself as exact economics, fell about as far short of that standard as *Business Cycles* did; and Schumpeter especially resented Keynes's popularity with young economists. At a student-faculty discussion of *The General Theory* at Harvard, he reported to Lange, "I did not take any part, precisely because I did not wish to give myself the opportunity of displaying what may look like and perhaps is ungenerosity and bad temper."[81]

What appealed to readers of *The General Theory* was the very aspect that offended Schumpeter: its prescription of a cure for the Great Depression. However legitimate Schumpeter's protests about the book's insults to science may have been—and a flood of scholarship over the next four decades did in fact wash away substantial parts of Keynes's argument—most people at the time naturally cared more about ending the Depression than anything else. Keynes may not have been precisely right *in abstracto,* but he was close enough to being right at this particular moment to make a difference. He provided a good roadmap out of the Depression, and that was a contribution of incalculable value.

Conversely, Schumpeter's own refusal to prescribe any remedy at all vastly reduced the appeal of *Business Cycles.* As an exercise in value-neutral "science," the book could hardly have appeared at a worse moment than at the dawn of the Keynesian age. "I recommend no policy and propose no plan," Schumpeter says in his preface. "But I do not admit that this convicts me of indifference to the social duty of science." The pressing need is not for polemics but for understanding, which is "the only service the scientific worker is, as such, qualified to render." Thus, *Business Cycles* can "be used to derive practical conclusions of the most conservative as well as the most radical complexion." But most readers wanted detailed remedies, and here the contrast between Schumpeter and Keynes was stark. Keynes had little interest in Schumpeter's cherished neutrality. Instead, he almost always had a specific policy goal in mind when he sat down to write.[82]

Keynes's approach takes a path directly opposite from Schumpeter's. It proceeds not from a bottom-up perspective based on entrepreneurs, firms, and industries but a top-down view based on government policies. Two reviewers of *Business Cycles* noted this difference, and one took care to mention Schumpeter's "vigorous stand against 'the curse of aggregative thinking.'"[83]

During the seven years he spent writing *Business Cycles,* Schumpeter had likely hoped that it would confirm his standing as the greatest economist of his time. The subtitle of the book, *A Theoretical, Historical, and Statistical Analysis of the Capitalist Process,* expresses the grandeur of his ambitions. But in addition to being upstaged by Keynes's book and failing to achieve the exactitude Schumpeter sought, *Business Cycles* has numerous internal defects. Read cover to cover, the two volumes convey the impression of an author trying desperately to squeeze a profusion of diverse and ill-coordinated topics into a single work.

Schumpeter had grown up reading ponderous German treatises containing sentences hundreds of words long, and his verbosity in *Business Cycles* contrasts with Keynes's tight prose. The book that had made Keynes famous, *The Economic Consequences of the Peace* (1920), is a model of concision, very easy to read. *The General Theory* is much more technical and difficult but no less a rhetorical triumph. In neither book does Keynes stray from his main subject. He writes with total self-assurance. He derides opposing arguments, conceding nothing to the opposition. With consummate skill, he sweeps readers along to the conclusions he wants them to reach, even though his evidence is often weak.[84]

None of this was accidental. During the years when Keynes was writing *The General Theory,* he tried out his ideas again and again within his elite circle of young economists at Cambridge University. He incorporated their many insights, particularly those of Richard Kahn, who practically invented the idea of the multiplier effect, so crucial to Keynes's argument. Meanwhile, Keynes discarded some of his own wrong-headed arguments and excess verbiage.

Schumpeter, working almost alone, never exposed his work-in-progress to anyone. He badly needed what Keynes had—a peer group who would tell him, "No, this won't quite do." But he did nothing to assemble such a group. Any number of his colleagues and students—Wassily Leontief, Paul Samuelson, James Tobin (all three future Nobel Prize winners), Gottfried Haberler, Paul Sweezy—could have helped. But Schumpeter never asked them. He did not even ask his wife, Elizabeth. Instead, he plunged ahead, putting far too many words to paper and publishing reams of untested ideas and unedited copy.[85]

As James Tobin recalled, "He wrote *Business Cycles* pretty much on his own. He didn't recruit students to help him; he didn't suggest topics arising in his own research to students for papers or dissertations; he didn't try out the ideas or findings of his draft chapters in seminars. That so enormous an achievement was the product of lonely research tells what a great scholar Schumpeter was." Because of his well-known generosity in evaluating the work of his own friends and students, his method here represents still another personal paradox. But whatever its source, the prolix and chaotic character of *Business Cycles* greatly diminished its influence with the general public and other economists.[86]

In effect, Schumpeter behaved as if authors have no need for editors, and scientists have no need for pre-publication criticism. Whereas Keynes in *The General Theory* maintains a sharp focus and brooks no disagreement, Schumpeter strays onto whatever tangents interest him. With his typical intellectual playfulness, he gives ample space to dissenting opinions. If this made his book more difficult, then so be it. Striking an almost defiant tone, he says in the preface to *Business Cycles* that "the reader will find the structure of the argument complex. To his justifiable groan I have nothing to oppose but the question whether he expected to find it easy." However much an author's reach should exceed his grasp, it is not by this much.[87]

His approach resembled that of the American novelist Thomas Wolfe, another untamed genius who was writing huge and unwieldy manuscripts at about the same time. Wolfe's fertile brain, like Schumpeter's, teemed with stream-of-consciousness associations that he scribbled down with a pencil in the heat of composition. But unlike Schumpeter, Wolfe had a brilliant editor—Maxwell Perkins of Scribner's. Perkins reorganized Wolfe's great novel *Look Homeward, Angel* and cut its length by almost one third.[88]

Had an editor of Perkins's quality applied his skills to *Business Cycles,* the book might well have fulfilled Schumpeter's ambitions. It would likely have appeared not as one long work of two volumes but as three totally separate books. The first editorial step would have been to strip the difficult three-cycle scheme from the text and publish it as a provocative hypothesis of business booms and busts. A second book would have drawn off about 250 of the 309 pages in *Business Cycles* that summarize events of the 1920s and 1930s.[89]

The third book would have brought together the splendid passages on the long-term evolution of business in Britain, Germany, and the United States, in more or less the way I have delineated in this chapter. In that form the book might well have been a masterpiece—a grand marriage of history and theory. Among other contributions, it would have signaled the birth of a rigorous new subdiscipline—business history.[90]

But because of the flaws of *Business Cycles* as it was actually published, together with Schumpeter's great success with his next work, *Capitalism, Socialism and Democracy* (1942), the contributions of the earlier book have gone underappreciated. Its insights for business history are still there, however, in rich abundance—a cornucopia for the patient and discriminating reader. Then, too, it is very clear that Schumpeter could never have written such a marvelous sequel as *Capitalism, Socialism and Democracy* without having done so much first-hand research for *Business Cycles*. His years of intense labor on that book added immensely to his empirical knowledge, and he absorbed reams of information about the inner workings of business. His immersion in the histories of firms and industries led him toward a uniquely powerful understanding of modern capitalism.

16

Letters from Europe

We work in the dark—we do what we can—we give what
we have.

HENRY JAMES, *The Middle Years,* 1893

EVEN BEFORE SCHUMPETER wrote *Business Cycles,* he had begun to
worry more and more about the deteriorating political situation in Germany.
There was plenty to worry about, as his copious letters from Mia Stöckel show.
Nor were the problems confined to Germany. Many of the other new democratic republics so hopefully established in the wake of World War I had begun
to weaken and crumble. What had seemed to the planners at Versailles a universal blueprint for democratic pluralism became, in practice, a pattern of parliaments unable to govern.[1]

During the twenty years between the Treaty of Versailles in 1919 and the
publication of *Business Cycles* in 1939, political systems in more than a dozen
European countries experienced two sea changes: first into parliamentary de-
mocracy, then into authoritarianism that often slid into outright dictatorship.
Before World War I only three republics existed in Europe—Switzerland,
France, and Portugal—as compared with seventeen monarchies, which in-
cluded the empires of the Habsburgs in Austria-Hungary, the Romanovs in
Russia, the Hohenzollerns in Germany, and the Ottoman regime in Turkey.
Each of these dynasties had ruled immense territories, in some regions for cen-

turies. But by 1919, in the brief span of five years, all had vanished—becoming mere relics of history.

The postwar shift from imperial to republican government, in which Schumpeter himself took part as Austria's finance minister, occurred in numerous other countries as well. By the early 1920s, Europe contained thirteen republics and thirteen kingdoms, most of the latter now operating as constitutional monarchies with broad-based suffrage, elected parliaments, and expanded rights for citizens. Overall, this change was a giant leap forward for democracy.

But in one enormous country—the Soviet Union—Bolshevik revolutionaries had installed a totalitarian and self-styled leftist regime that no European nation, large or small, could ignore. Many a statesman looked toward the East with a sense of dread, and many a left-leaning intellectual gazed with exhilaration. Active Communist parties prospered in Germany, Poland, France, Italy, and other countries, and a long-term contest seemed to be emerging between capitalism and communism. This situation appalled Schumpeter, who regarded communism of the Soviet variety—and Russia itself, regardless of its form of government—as a dire threat to world stability.[2]

During the 1920s, fascism had also entered the picture, fed by fears of communism and by the apparent ineffectuality of parliamentary systems. Under many national constitutions of the post-Versailles period, proportional representation had multiplied the number of political parties involved in government, and almost never did any one party hold a working majority of seats. In this fragmented condition, some parliaments began to resemble the Austro-Hungarian legislature described by Mark Twain in 1897, rather than the stable two- or three-party systems of Britain, Canada, and the United States. This was true not only in Weimar Germany, where sixteen parties won seats in 1930 (including one called the Party for Spiritual Renewal) but also in the parliaments of Czechoslovakia, Yugoslavia, Poland, Latvia, and Estonia, some of which had twenty or more parties. The result was unstable coalitions and electoral gridlock. In Germany and Austria, the average cabinet lasted eight months; in Italy, five months; in Spain, four.[3]

Under such circumstances, it became very hard for governments to get anything done. Populations grew restive, and control began to gravitate toward nationalist strongmen. In a portent of what was to come, Benito Mussolini became prime minister of Italy in 1922 and expanded his powers to the point of dictatorship by 1925. Mussolini proclaimed the need for strict discipline, declaring that "Fascism rejects in Democracy the conventional lie of political equality . . . The present century is the century of authority, a century of the Right, a Fascist century." Mussolini soon "made the trains run on time," a phrase that became an international cliché. For his apparent efficiency he won tributes from prominent public figures all over the world, including Britain and the United States.[4]

More than a dozen countries took a turn toward the authoritarian right. In 1922, Italy. In 1923, Spain, Bulgaria, and Turkey. In 1925, Albania. In 1926, Portugal, Poland, and Lithuania. In 1929, Yugoslavia. In 1930, Germany, where Parliament drifted into paralysis and a new right-leaning chancellor had to rely on emergency decrees under Article 48 of the Weimar constitution. In 1933, Austria. In 1934, Latvia and Estonia. Only Switzerland, Scandinavia, and the Benelux countries seemed immune.[5]

By 1937 dictators ruled openly in many countries, with varying degrees of brutality: Stalin in the USSR, Hitler in Germany, Mussolini in Italy, Franco in Spain, Salazar in Portugal, Horthy in Hungary, Metaxas in Greece, and so on. During this same period, much of Latin America was also ruled by dictators: Batista in Cuba, Vargas in Brazil, Somoza in Nicaragua, Trujillo in the Dominican Republic, Ubico in Guatemala, Hernández in El Salvador, Carias in Honduras, Contreras in Venezuela. In Argentina, the Fascist Juan Perón took power in 1943.

Even the great parliamentary democracies showed signs of unsteadiness during the 1930s and blindness toward the new reality. British statesmen, fearing another European war, dithered in their attitude toward both Germany and the Soviet Union. In France, the tenure of the average cabinet, never very long under the 1870s constitution of the Third Republic, now shrank to only four months. Between 1931 and 1939, twenty-odd French cabinets held power. Meanwhile, the Great Depression lingered like a stationary weather front of constant rain and gloom. In their economic policies, nearly all countries turned inward—rearming, tinkering with their currencies, and enacting "beggar thy neighbor" tariff barriers. International trade sank to its lowest peacetime level in generations.[6]

To the chagrin of the capitalist democracies, the new dictatorships—of both the right and left—seemed to be doing a much better job than they themselves were in putting people back to work. When Hitler assumed power in January 1933, more than six million Germans were out of work—about a third of the national labor force. Within two years, that number had dipped under three million; and within six years, to only 300,000—one-eighteenth of the 1933 figure. Germany's economic resurgence owed something to a business recovery that began before Hitler's appointment. It owed much more to vast public works sponsored by the Nazi regime. And still more to war mobilization.[7]

During the second half of the 1930s, Schumpeter became so immersed in writing *Business Cycles* and in his shifting relationship with Elizabeth that his usual attention to world affairs began to stray. After 1935 he ceased taking his annual summer vacations in Europe, in part because of the political chaos. He seldom listened to the radio, but he did read "a lot of disquieting news." Much of what he knew came via first-hand reports from his European friends.[8]

Among these, by far the most important was Mia Stöckel, who wrote him a long letter every week for almost a decade after he left Bonn in 1932. Before his departure, Mia had lived with Schumpeter for a total of about three years, not counting his stints as a visiting professor at Harvard. After he moved to the United States for good, she spent three additional summers traveling with him through Western Europe, with ever-fewer stops in Germany as the Nazi regime tightened its grip. Among Mia's many roles—secretary, chauffeur, confidante, lover, and caretaker of Annie's grave—she also managed the big house overlooking the Rhine and attended to Schumpeter's affairs in Europe. Following his permanent departure in 1932, she sublet the house to a Berlin lawyer.

Mia had a brother, Otto, and two sisters, Toni and Treschen. One of the three sisters or their father, who was also named Otto, placed flowers on Annie's grave several times each year for twenty-two years and made lease payments to the cemetery. Members of the family corresponded with Schumpeter right up until the time of his death. The Stöckels represented his lifeline to Europe—and, together with the Taussigs in Cambridge, his most important family relationship of any kind until his marriage to Elizabeth in 1937.[9]

From 1927 until 1949 Schumpeter sent innumerable gifts to the Stöckels—usually money, and sometimes in large amounts. He did the same for members of the Reisinger family in Vienna. In the 1920s he gave them most of the furniture from Johanna's apartment, and during part of the 1930s he sent 200 Marks each month to Annie's mother. The equivalent amount today would be between $7,000 and $8,000 per year.[10]

For Mia Stöckel, he financed several terms of education in France, as she studied French literature in Grenoble. He also supplied her with a generous monthly stipend that she liked to call "pocket money." He bought new furniture for the Stöckels and gave them his own from the house in Bonn. Year after year, he sent them clothing and paid most of their medical bills—for Mia's appendicitis, Toni's tonsillitis, Treschen's various illnesses, and their mother's radiation therapy during her battle with cancer. When Mrs. Stöckel lost that fight, he paid for her gravestone. He sent lavish sums as wedding presents when Treschen was married in 1934, Mia in 1936, and Toni in 1939. In today's currency, his wedding gift to Mia would be over $6,000. During and after World War II he sent funds and CARE packages to the surviving Stöckels.[11]

In a sense Schumpeter became a member of the Stöckel family. Apart from his *Hasen,* he had never had relationships with a real family of his own, and he behaved toward the Stöckels like a thoughtful and generous in-law. He wrote hundreds of letters to Mia, telling her things he apparently told no one else. He received even more letters from her, and some from her sisters. At Harvard he cut up most of his incoming correspondence into the squares of paper on which he wrote notes to himself. But he preserved the letters he received from all the Stöckels. His own letters to them did not survive the war— nor did his library, his private papers from Europe, or his mementoes of Annie and Johanna, which were stored at the Stöckels' home in Jülich. In November 1944, bombers of the U.S. Army Air Forces leveled the town, which lay only ten miles from the Belgian border.

The vicissitudes of the Stöckel family provide in miniature a portrait of the upheavals that wracked millions of civilians throughout Europe during the 1930s and 1940s. Like many other Germans, Mia and some members of her family (not all) initially welcomed Hitler's ascent to power. They hoped that their country might somehow throw off the yoke of Versailles and recover its dignity and prosperity. The world's quick condemnation not only of Hitler but also of the German people angered Mia and increased her prejudice against Jews. In one letter to Schumpeter she described a social occasion that "could have converted you to anti-Semitism forever."[12]

But before long Mia began to see the repressive realities of life under Nazi rule. In 1934 she noticed that Schumpeter's letters from the United States had been opened and presumably read by government agents. She worried that the articles he had published in German magazines could cause trouble if he returned and might even result in his detention. During her third and fourth terms as a student in Grenoble, she grew reluctant to leave France and return to Germany. As the decade wore on, it became clear to her that the future was full of peril. The anti-Semitic comments that had once appeared in her letters gave way to complaints and forebodings about Hitler's regime.

The relationship between Mia and Schumpeter was not a simple one. Having begun as his academic secretary, she might have turned out to be just one of the scores of women with whom he had affairs. But their connection went much deeper. When they met, he was twice her age, and her letters address him in a German diminutive of *Vater* (Father), best translated as "Daddy." She calls herself his *Mädi,* an untranslatable diminutive of *Mädchen* (girl). She was passionately in love with him, star-struck by his academic prominence, and, as the years passed, reliant on his financial support.

For Schumpeter himself, Mia gradually came to represent less a bed partner than a continuing link with Bonn, Europe, and—strangely enough—the memory of Annie. From time to time, in his Hamlet-like fashion, he would refer vaguely to some future that he and Mia might share in Europe. In the early 1930s he hinted that he would leave Harvard after a few years, or in any case after the fifteen years necessary to qualify for his pension. But by 1936 Mia realized that Schumpeter might never come back to live in Europe and that he was not likely to marry her and take her to the United States. So, in December of that year, she wed a young Serbian economist named Stojan Bicanski, whom she had met in Grenoble. Stojan worked for the Yugoslav government, and after their wedding the two moved to Novi Sad, a medium-sized Yugoslav city on the Danube, fifty miles south of the Hungarian border.

Schumpeter's relationship with Mia and her family becomes vivid in her long and often very intimate letters to him, both before and after her marriage. Mia's letters narrate in microcosm, and at poignant first-hand, the epic tragedy of Europe during the 1930s and early 1940s. They have never before been translated and published, and they provide details about Schumpeter's life and temperament available from no other source. For these reasons, they are worth quoting in short excerpts over their entire ten-year span.[13]

Nov. 9, 1932, Jülich: What a spring means to the thirsty traveler, that's what a letter from you means to me . . . Your words about our future home make me infinitely happy.

Dec. 3, 1932, Jülich: Today [General] Schleicher has been commissioned [chancellor], the situation becomes daily more colorful and the end is going to be Hitler or Heil Moscow. [Schleicher lasted two months. Hitler became chancellor on January 31, 1933.][14]

Dec. 8, 1932, Jülich: Your zeal for work is greater than I would like and I worry. The American squeezes you like a lemon and you should put a stop to it. So many lectures . . . have you not yet learned to say no?

March 13, 1933, La Trouche [in southern France, where Mia has begun her study of French at Grenoble]: Just yesterday evening I got your last letter, in which the troubling sentence is to be found: "I hope that there will not be a war between France and Germany before we meet again." Do you seriously believe that something like that is possible, dear Jozsi?

April 4, 1933, Zurs, Austria: Hitler seems already to have achieved great things. Mother writes of jobs with the railway and the setting up of great factories.

April 9, 1933, Zurs: So that Jews don't fly abroad in order to live there in peace on their assets, their passports have been taken away. Everyone—even non-Jews—needs a visa, if he wants to go abroad.

April 14, 1933, Jülich: Peace and order are everywhere, finally an iron discipline among the young. Things are being controlled purposefully and strongly. 90,000 people have been employed with the railway already.

April 29, 1933, Jülich: I didn't know that [Gustav Stolper's magazine] the Volkswirt had been outlawed. I'm sorry . . . By the way I am not a little astonished to hear some things from you, so I want to give you all the news . . . Jozsi please don't take these Jewish people on your back [in Schumpeter's campaign to rescue professors dismissed by the Nazis]. Shrug your shoulders with regret, what does it have to do with you . . . Jozsi I don't know, actually I am happy, that you haven't been here for this transformation. I'd almost like to call it anxiety, you could even be blacklisted for some article that those people didn't understand. Think about the L— article![15]

September 27, 1933, Oxford: I am really in my heart not for Hitler, never was and will, as I see things now, never be. But, I can't help myself, if I am abroad and hear things, how disparagingly they are discussed, I have to defend G[ermany].—I can do no other. [This sentence is an allusion to Martin Luther's famous statement at the Diet of Worms in 1521, which became a common saying.] . . . I want the road to Germany to stay open for you.

Mia wrote this last letter just after having spent the summer with Schumpeter, who had returned to Europe as promised. At that time he was still uncertain in his own mind about how long he would remain at Harvard. Would it be for five years, as he sometimes speculated with Mia? For the fifteen necessary to qualify for his pension? He too wanted the road to Germany to stay open, both for the long summer visits he intended to make and perhaps eventually for a permanent return. This was true whether his decision not to marry Mia was irrevocable or not. He was now past fifty, their sex life had begun to cool off, and—as soon became clear—he had fewer reservations about her seeing other men than she herself did.

November 26, 1933, Jülich: [In response to a question from Schumpeter, Mia says that she is reading art history so as to build a bond between them.] Another bond joined us up to now. I don't want to say a bond of love, because that will always exist—but the bond of passion I feel has fallen apart.

March 28, 1934, Jülich: Your letter made a strong impression on me that you are sick, depressed, and worn down by work to the limit. I sit here totally powerless . . . I wrack my brains. Good advice flies away in the wind like dust. I have the feeling that you can scarcely hold out for five years in America, still less fifteen.

April 5, 1934, Jülich: [Mia's sister Treschen has been ill, and Schumpeter has sent 200 Marks for her treatment] a happy donation for us, [her family having] used up the last savings. My parents are on the mat like never before.

April 12, 1934, Jülich: From your Mädi there is also a bit of news . . . a young Yugoslavian economist proposed to Mädi a little while ago and entertains the greatest hopes about it . . . The answer is still open, because Mädi will not make a step without Father. I would like you to meet him because he is an extremely nice person. He calls himself: Stojan Bicanski.

April 16, 1934, Jülich: [Goes back to the subject of Stojan] How carefree, peaceful and happy my life was up until now. Certainly there were also storms, particularly at the time, dear Father, when it became clear to me, that my young well-rested body was more of a burden than a blessing to your tired and overworked organism. But a peaceful fate understood how to transform this temperamental love for the beloved into a peaceful love, like a child honoring her father. And I was so happy over this solution which seemed to have overcome all difficulties. But it was probably meant to be that a second man should enter my life . . . The thought of being able to have children—to be able to be a mother some day becomes so vivid . . . Do not forget that I belong to you and that I will never follow another man, if it is not your will.

April 29, 1934, Jülich: [In letters dated 15 and 20 April, Schumpeter had expressed no objection to Stojan. Mia responds] As I already wrote you he is Yugoslavian, studied law and political science in Vienna, got his doctorate at 22 and then on his own studied international law in order, as the government probably was happy to see, to go into the diplomatic service. Naturally he must in that case marry according to the wishes of the government; so he dropped this plan at the moment he met me. [Stojan faces military service and won't be able to marry until 1936.]

May 23, 1934, Jülich: [Mia says she is looking forward to] our working together this summer [but worries that Schumpeter needs] to rest the whole time [because he's so exhausted]. I am glad that Bicanski's letter has made a good impression on you . . . I said to him that . . . even when married I want to spend at least three months of the year with you. And not a word of contradiction, no curious questions, only this answer: "It will certainly be hard for me to be without you for so long, but your wishes are holy to me. You can always travel when you want." He doesn't dream of thinking anything if I am with you for the summer—he is happy, he says, to know that I am in such eminent company.

May 29, 1934, Jülich: Spiethoff seems to be very much in the good books with the SDAP [Nazi Party], holds lectures, writes articles and the papers are full of praise for him. With all that the man can look on calmly, as really valuable people are persecuted. I am murderously angry with him.

At this time, Mia was twenty-nine. The situation in Germany had continued to deteriorate under the heel of Nazi oppression, and she was inevitably concerned for the future of her country and the course of her own life. She wanted to have children, was inclined to marry Stojan Bicanski, but did not want to lose Schumpeter's counsel—or his continued financial support for her schooling in Grenoble. And she was surprised at the ardor of her own sex drive. At the end of the second summer she spent touring Europe with Schumpeter, she writes him about all of these issues.

September 27, 1934, Jülich: Actually I am very unsatisfied with the end of the novel *[Lady Chatterley's Lover]*. I have the impression that she runs after him much too much—he just has no desire at all to marry her. God, women are lustful creatures—you can certainly also sing a song about that.

October 27, 1934, Jülich: [Thanks Schumpeter for his letter.] So without exception all letters seem to have been opened. God, what does it matter; in the end one gets used to anything.

November 30, 1934, La Trouche, back at Grenoble: Even political events don't make much impression in this pleasant and calm milieu—while at home one lives constantly in nervous agitation—daily a catastrophe before one's eyes. So you too have fallen victim to pessimism . . . I in no way overlook the moment of danger that we are in and yet I think less than ever about a war.

December 10, 1934, La Trouche: I am so unhappy to know that you work through half the night. No horse can endure that! . . . You don't know how to be moderate with your strength and it seems you will never learn.

December 18, 1934, La Trouche: [Thanks him for all he has done.] There is first the lovely pocket money that makes life for me so beautiful and easy and pleasant. And the countless gifts on the side, and not least the summer trips with all their attractions, joys and driving pleasures. How I will think back on these times full of yearning when I am on the breadline with my twelve children.

January 14, 1935, La Trouche: If I had seen things in Bonn as clearly as I do now, I would have been able to profit very differently from our living together.—I like it so much when you philosophize a bit in your letters, then I see today's world with totally different eyes . . . Yes, that is even clear for everyone: seen from an economic standpoint it really appears that politics is carried out by idiots.

March 17, 1935, La Trouche: Your letter of the 19th sounds depressed [about his inability to get work done] . . . That probably also explains why you see the political situation as being so black. If you knew with what stoic calm the rearmament of Germany has been accepted here [in France], you would worry yourself less about the future.

May 5, 1935, La Trouche: [Has bought some books, including] *Les Liasons dangereuses* by Laclos. Your degenerate Olle [a pet name for herself] has an adult taste for that kind of reading. What can it hurt at my age, in a few months I will reach my thirtieth year.

Mia and Schumpeter then spent their third consecutive summer together, touring through Europe and spending much of their time in Italy. At the end of the summer Mia submitted an article on their travels, along with many photographs, to a magazine sponsored by the German Automobile Club. Her article was rejected on a sheet of club stationery whose letterhead was decorated with a swastika. The message ended with "Heil Hitler!" Mia wrote on the back of this rejection, "The pigs! I almost cried."

Over the next several months, Mia's letters dwelled on Schumpeter's persistent melancholy, the life they might have had together, the resolution of her relationship with Stojan Bicanski, and the ever-worsening situation in Europe.

October 12, 1935, Jülich: I have your sweet letter from 9/27 . . . You complain about something worth living for; haven't you long since created that; haven't you already made your name immortal in science? What more do you want. Who will ask if you have written a book more or less. Why trouble yourself in the evening of your life with unattainable goals.

October 17, 1935, Jülich: Yes, 10 years have gone by already since [Annie's death]. Just a few days ago while tidying up the little secretary your engagement notice fell into my hands, and in my thoughts your short happy marriage, so far as I could see it, passed before my eyes. Then I reach for the next sheet. It is the notice of Annie's death. Then warm tears come to my eyes. I quickly fold up the piece of paper again and stick both in the big envelope in which years ago I wrote: "cher souvenirs."

November 13, 1935, Jülich: Father [Otto] was in Bonn on your marriage day in order to take a cross of roses to [Annie's] grave. The wreath from All Souls' was still totally fresh and besides that there was a crowd of flowers put there by strange hands so that the dear hill was a sea of [blossoms].

January 10, 1936, La Trouche: When you receive this little letter the 10th anniversary of our acquaintance will already have gone by . . . Why didn't you marry me, Daddy? You will answer me—it was good that you didn't; your nervous way, and my loss of strength . . . And yet I think you did wrong! It's true, the last while in Bonn I was unbearable—nervous, irritating, unfair. But only our relationship had brought me to that. I believed that I possessed you and yet I didn't. Before the world there was a great barrier between us. I understand now more than ever that you had to consider the society [and] the intellectual milieu in which you live. And yet there were moments that hurt me endlessly . . . The satisfaction of being your wife would have fully balanced out the limited intimate relations, and even the wish for motherhood . . . It isn't the tie of sensuality that binds the tightest, it is the mutual friendship and trust. My life would be poor in spite of Stojan, bare and senseless if I could not turn to you with my thoughts and feelings. And could you ever deny me that, even if you had a dozen other women by your side?

February 2, 1936, Grenoble: Adolf [Hitler] is gravely ill. If he wants to be guarded by his people in eternal memory he must die quickly!

March 25, 1936, La Trouche: You believe that a Mussolini-Hitler game will emerge—never in life. The first certainly amuses himself in this affair but his downfall won't be long in coming . . . Not for a minute have I thought of war. France, after all its pacifist declarations, cannot start it. And Germany would not trust itself to fire the first shot; that would be the end of everything. Besides, they are at the end of their strength . . . One can count on food rationing and an aggravation of the social situation. The elections bring nothing new—overseen by the state, there cannot be a defeat. By a

show of force—in my opinion—[Hitler] expects to regain the love
of his people, which is always ready to soak up [fill itself with]
vanity. And when he succeeds, the next step will be the Anschluss.
He only waits for Mussolini to weaken in order to get hold of Austria . . . One can read on the frightened faces of mothers and
grandmothers the fear of war.

April 2, 1936, La Trouche: Your letter of the 23rd plunged me into a
deep depression [Schumpeter told her that he would not be coming for the summer as he had for the last three years] . . . You separate us—little by little and charitably, but surely. I have the impression that you are going to remarry an old American broad
[une vielle carne americaine; for most of 1936 and all of 1937, Mia's
letters to Schumpeter are in French] who will call you Jooo and
will take off your shoes in the evening and tie your cravat in the
morning.

On April 18, 1936, Mia wrote from Beočin, Yugoslavia, Stojan's home town,
that Stojan and his family had welcomed her warmly. The trains ran well despite the political situation. Stojan, she said, is sweet, gentle, devoted; they are
going to Belgrade to meet his friends and the rest of his family.

May 1, 1936, Beočin: [Mia comments that Anschluss, the Nazis'
move into Austria, is imminent] to reestablish once more Hitler's
prestige and position at the head of his people. Italy is at the end
of its strength—France alone will not budge and England will be
too happy to know that the Italian influence won't respond regarding Eth[iopia] . . . Everyone [in Austria]—except the Jews—are
national socialists and Hitler will be received with open arms . . .
God preserve us, this will be a terrible war . . . In case of war, I will
be more secure here [in Yugoslavia] than at home.

May 18, 1936, Beočin: [Mia describes Mussolini as menacing Europe.] Germany is Paradise in comparison [with Italy]. France has
received what she deserves. On bad terms with England and then
with Italy, she remains only with Russia. The prophecy of Hitler is

even realized since several [French] ministers on the left propose a Soviet Republic. Goodbye liberty!

June 25, 1936, Jülich: [She hasn't heard from Stojan, his letters presumably lost in the mail.] I suppose they have been opened by the police and as our letters are written in French, they didn't bother to decipher them.

August 3, 1936, Bonn: [Mia has accepted Stojan's proposal of marriage, after] long nights of tears, worries, a clenched heart, a tormented head . . . You were always too good for me . . . I have betrayed you.

This last comment, more than any other she ever wrote, captures the psychological dilemma into which Mia's relationship with Schumpeter had trapped her. She was turning thirty, she wanted to have children, but she felt an inexplicable and wholly baseless guilt. Of course she had not betrayed Schumpeter. If anything, he had betrayed her. He had allowed their affair to continue for nearly a decade, thereby causing Mia to throw away her twenties in the forlorn hope that he might some day marry her. On the other hand, Mia had revealed herself to be a needy person, often given to the same kinds of mood swings that afflicted Schumpeter himself. But however doomed their relationship, they would not have maintained such an intimate and long-term attachment had they not cared a great deal for each other. Over the course of his life, Schumpeter wrote more letters to Mia Stöckel than to any other person.

AFTER HE STOPPED spending his summers in Europe, Mia's letters to him focused even more on the political situation than before, as well as on her new life with Stojan Bicanski.

September 8, 1936, St. Hilaire: I have the impression that the anti-German movement grows day by day. And the events in Spain [civil war] don't appear to help the European situation. All nations declare themselves neutral, and all send arms such as they can. For the moment, I have a pessimistic view. A world war seems more and more certain.

December 14, 1936, Jülich: [Mia and Stojan will be married within two weeks. She thanks Schumpeter for all he's done for her over the years.] And finally for your paternal love and all your generosity.

January 9, 1937, Beočin, Yugoslavia: [Describes her wedding night] He was tender, sweet. He hopped around me like a little flea . . . He was absolutely inexperienced [un debutant]. I was in a better humor about my dear Fatherland when I stepped foot in this ill-run, badly organized country. [They had settled in Yugoslavia after honeymooning in Vienna.] But a glance at the paper this morning apprised me of the German occupation of Spanish Morocco. What does this mean? Hitler has put all in the hands of Goering. I see black . . . Many things are no longer to be had—cooking oil, eggs, etc., how you want—they're going into the war.

February 17, 1937, Novi Sad: [Is happy to hear from Schumpeter that he's feeling better and has regained some of his old vitality.] Pardon me this foolish jealousy that I entertain the idea that you will be able to have a liaison with any woman.

March 19, 1937, Jülich: [Mia's mother is dying, and Mia has been summoned from Novi Sad by her sister Toni.] My God what is life anyway—is it worth living at all. Nothing but unhappiness and misery wherever one looks.

April 2, 1937, Jülich: I almost wanted to cry, thick, hot, tears, because I have heard nothing, but absolutely nothing, from you. Especially now, when I need so much comfort and strength, because Daddy, I have to hold myself together like everyone here, inside I am exhausted and churned up from all the suffering I see here . . . [But while she was writing this letter, one came from Schumpeter, dated March 11 and "discreetly unopened by Stojan," together with letters for Toni and their father, Otto, the latter including a check for 300 Marks] the greatest good Samaritan deed that you have ever done and [we] never never will be in a position to make it up to you.

May 18, 1937, Novi Sad: My husband takes great pains to make me savor our sweetest moments. Nevertheless it is rare, very rare, for me to be fully excited. It is not his fault, I am sure; an inexplicable coldness on my part; nevertheless I love him.

September 10, 1937, Novi Sad: We are thinking of sending food packages to Jülich. It's frightful how everything is rationed there. A 1/4 pound of lard per week for a family—without bacon—little butter, no oil. Did you know that the priests are expelled from the schools. There is no longer religious education. In place of this, children will henceforth go to shooting lessons.

October 6, 1937, Novi Sad: When there is no weekly letter for the sixth week I can only say with a frown: there is a woman behind this! I really would be happy if in the meantime you were sailing around somewhere in quiet oceans but with a girl on your tail— God keep me from wild jealousy. Or are you sick. But Taussig would have informed me, wouldn't he? [Schumpeter went through the fall without telling Mia of his marriage to Elizabeth Boody on August 16, 1937.][16]

November 20, 1937, Novi Sad: Do you know that the other day I dreamed that you had remarried with a young and beautiful girl and that I collapsed in grief. A thousand feelings—a thousand foolish ideas pass through my head to explain your silence . . . I regularly send provisions to Jülich because it appears that Germany is full of misery. The people who go back recount unreal things—almost unbelievable.

November 30, 1937, Novi Sad: [Schumpeter had finally written with news of his August marriage.] After a difficult effort of several days to calm myself from the feelings that came from your letter, today I am up to being able to congratulate you, chasing away all selfish feelings . . . May it be that your perfect and apt good fortune will restore to the autumn of your life a blooming and sunny bent. You deserve it!

December 1, 1937, from Toni in Jülich: [Answers questions about photographs of Annie's grave, which Toni encloses.] I had already taken the pictures of the grave on All Saints' Day & did not get around to having them developed . . . I found the grave very beautiful, it was a sea of flowers of white chrysanthemums . . . Because of you dear Herr Professor, father was in the position to give mother this relief [radiation treatments]. We thank you from the bottom of our hearts.

February 22, 1938, Novi Sad: [Mia's first child, a daughter she named Zora, has been born.] The newly minted Mama announces that she is healthy and has returned to everyday life. [Thanks him again for the money he sent her parents.] You wouldn't believe how they are often in need.

March 15, 1938, Novi Sad: [Hitler has moved into Austria.] This act of violence has taken away my milk—not just my breath—and my child is suffering hunger. No joke—one gradually becomes ashamed of being German.

April 4, 1938, Novi Sad: [Caring for her baby has improved Mia's morale.] And you know Daddy: only now have I reconciled myself to my existence. Now I know where my place is—where I belong. I must confess that even in the happiest moments of my marriage, my last thought was always of how and when I could sometime return to you. You then set an end and still I could not reconcile myself with it until I stood at the cradle of my child.

July 8, 1938, Jülich: [Stojan has tried to get a Rockefeller fellowship, and Mia implies that Schumpeter has recommended his own students more than he has Stojan, which was not in fact the case.] Perhaps you would rather he didn't come and above all myself. But I had already let go of all plans [to go to America] for myself and would have stayed modestly in Jülich.[17]

From this point forward, Mia's letters become sadder and less frequent. Events are beating her down, and there is no more lively talk of books and travel, as in her early letters. She is having to deal with the press of multiple problems: her mother's slow death from cancer, Stojan's bout with typhus, persistent financial hardship, loneliness, and the ominous political situation in Europe.

On the night of November 9–10, 1938, mobs in Germany—incited by the government—went on an anti-Semitic rampage. They murdered dozens of Jews, brutally beat others, and looted Jewish-owned stores. They smashed the glass fronts of these stores, thereby giving rise to the term *Kristallnacht* (night of [broken] glass), which became symbolic of the start of this even more violent phase of anti-Semitism. Mia writes:

> *December 5, 1938, Novi Sad:* How good that Mother didn't see the last coup against the Jews. She always protected them and greatly condemned the government's line . . . I could fill pages with all these inhuman atrocities.

> *March 1, 1939, Novi Sad:* I have not received such a long sweet letter for such a long time. Just a few days ago I could not keep away the fear that our correspondence and with it our close connection had slacked off or even sustained a breach. And now the sun smiles again. [She approves of his reports of stays in Taconic and his more peaceful life and work.] How much I would like to look in on you some day. Do you still hold your finger to your mouth when you are thinking deeply and do you still always close your left eye when you read? [To the end of his life, Schumpeter never wore glasses. But he read so much that he suffered from persistent eyestrain.]

> *May 18, 1939, Novi Sad:* I thank you especially for the precise handling of the most delicate question of all questions. [Mia had asked for advice about her sex life with the inexperienced Stojan, and Schumpeter had provided detailed counsel about how to guide him toward greater skill as a lover.]

> *June 1, 1939, Novi Sad:* God preserved you from a great evil when he separated us, even I have to see that now. I pray and hope that this [European political] situation will soon change otherwise it threatens me and my family with a great misfortune. I speak in all seriousness!

In August 1939 Mia wrote from Jülich that after a visit with her family on the occasion of Toni's wedding, she was returning home to Novi Sad. She would go by way of Berlin, where Toni had been honeymooning with her husband, Hermann, a soldier in the German army. She would try to console Toni because, only two weeks after the marriage, Hermann had been called up to the Polish border. Before Schumpeter received Mia's letter, Hitler invaded Poland, thereby initiating World War II.

October 30, 1939, Novi Sad: You said once that a new war would be the end of Europe and all too often it seems that you didn't exaggerate. [Stojan is doing better professionally.] A rise on his part would comfort me a lot. And another thing: our intimate connections have also improved.

January 28, 1940, Novi Sad: All the best for the rest [of the year]; new great fruits of your labor, health, well-being. You live in a country in which such wishes do not need to be dismissed with an ironic laugh. In this country the new year's wishes for this year have been left unsaid. It sounds really too comic in view of the given circumstances. [Toni is unable to visit Mia in Yugoslavia because the German government forbids foreign travel except in cases of family death.] So I have little prospect of seeing my family again soon, because I have sworn to myself not to go to Germany again until Hitler is gone from there.

July 1, 1940, Novi Sad: I hope you are healthy and at work at full tempo, which can be the only excuse for your silence . . . I will not forget the grave on August 3 [the day Annie died] . . . The sad fate of our beloved France [which fell to the German army in June] has gone very much to my heart—but it is not over yet. Please write just a line—you don't know how much comfort and aid it would bring me just at the moment.

December 6, 1940, Novi Sad: [Mia is pregnant again, the child due in the spring of 1941.] Zora [now almost three years old] has already outgrown me, a rascal of the first rank.

February 8, 1941, Novi Sad: Today is your birthday and I will not fail to wish you all the best on this day: inner peace, the strength to work, joy of life. [Wishes] just once more [to] look in your dear good eyes, just once more to be near you . . . I see you in spirit creating, restlessly researching, working, and it will stay like that so long as the strength lasts. And so will your Mädi fill up her life in her way, even if it is only spanking children and washing diapers. I am round again like a ton. In three months the child will be here—it should only be a son say the brave Serbs, everything else is unimportant. [Toni is visiting Mia in Novi Sad but is very sick.] They will all end with consumption before the war is over. It is wretched to see it. You know I am poor myself but I must [grieve for her]. No coat, no shoes, and with it all the great cold. In 10 days she must go again [back to Germany]—hope she will be out of bed. I had so looked forward to her coming but I am now so disappointed, it is so sad and one can't help. [Asks for $200 from her own account Schumpeter has set up in America] if from there you believe that a transfer will become impossible later, send me the money before the birth, before it is too late . . . I will arrange things for [Annie's] grave on March 22. Also the cemetery bill that was due in January has been taken care of.[18]

March 20, 1941, Novi Sad: The anxiety for the difficult and unde-fined future, my circumstances, and the many terrible rumors cause me to hasten to you, partly for comfort, partly to vent my complaints and not least in order to ask for your opinion and help . . . it looks very bad for us here, everyone is under arms although any resistance in my eyes is pointless bloodshed . . . The grave has not been forgotten for Annie's birthday! We will leave our little ac-count [for the flowers] for later. Did you receive the Christmas packet and the birthday letter? Write, even if it's only a couple of lines. We hug and kiss you warmly. Many heartfelt greetings. Mia and Zora and Stojan.

This was the last communication Schumpeter received, apart from a post-card from Stojan with the news that Mia had given birth to a son, whom they named Vlado. Five days after Mia's letter of March 20, Yugoslavia allied itself with Nazi Germany. A week later the Yugoslav government was overthrown in a coup, and Hitler decided to invade. The German attack began on April 6, 1941, with the bombing of Belgrade, fifty miles southeast of Mia's home in Novi Sad. The Yugoslavs surrendered on April 17. Control of the country was then divided among the Germans' allies, Novi Sad going to Hungary. Fierce partisan resistance to the Nazis in the former Yugoslav territories brought vicious reprisals.

After the war, Schumpeter received the following letter from Mia's father Otto:

> Dear Professor,
>
> Permit me to inform you that I, along with Treschen, her husband, my son-in-law Hermann, Toni's husband, and my son Otto, am among the survivors. Mia, her husband, and Toni are dead. On the orders of the former Hungarian Reichsverweser von Horthy [provisional ruler of Hungary] a state of siege was declared in the period from 21 to 23 January 1942 in Novi Sad. With no further ado countless inhabitants, among them lawyers, doctors, clergymen, government officials, Jews, business people and landowners were shot. As I have learned, the shootings supposedly were carried out because these people were opposed to the Nazi government or belonged to the English Club. Mia and Stojan belonged for years to the English Club. Both were shot in their apartment, other people below by the Danube. We were informed by telegram by some acquaintances. Treschen and I went there immediately and brought back the two children. Zora was four and Vlado a half-year old . . .
>
> We were all great opponents of the Nazi government. The suffering, the want and the misery that have come to Germany are a punishment from God. Unfortunately the innocent have to suffer too, but I can count myself among them and have always said to my children, we Germans alone are responsible for all the misery in the world.[19]

At the time of her murder in 1942, Mia Stöckel Bicanski was thirty-six years old.

Mia not long before her death.

17

To Leave Harvard?

Tempt not a desperate man.

SHAKESPEARE, *Romeo and Juliet,* 1596

IN AUGUST 1937, eight months after Mia had married Stojan but was still devoted to Schumpeter, he himself married Elizabeth Boody. At that time he was lodged in his modest rooms at Frank Taussig's house six blocks from Harvard Yard, where he had taken up residence five years earlier. Elizabeth, meanwhile, had lived in a cottage on the opposite side of Harvard. For a few months after their marriage, the two rented a small house not far from Elizabeth's former cottage. They then purchased a large shingled house at 7 Acacia Street, only a five-minute walk to Harvard Yard. Acacia Street is only one block long, a quiet island of repose hidden in the midst of apartment buildings and heavy traffic. Its tiny, maze-like neighborhood of one-way streets is so secluded that even today it can hardly be discovered by chance.[1]

For the rest of Schumpeter's life, he and Elizabeth divided their time between the Acacia Street house and Windy Hill, Elizabeth's rural retreat near Taconic, Connecticut. Noise of any kind distracted Schumpeter from his work, and both of his new addresses offered the quiet he craved. In Taconic, he benefited from almost total calm, which Elizabeth fiercely protected. Even their mail was delivered to a nearby store. In the late 1930s, when a neighbor wanted to install a driveway next to Windy Hill, Elizabeth contested his plans, writing a lawyer that the issue "is directly concerned with the problem of my husband's nerves and health."

> He has had many heavy responsibilities and many difficult situa-
> tions to face in the past. As a consequence his nervous system has
> become more or less disorganized. He is able to carry on his work
> at Harvard only if he has fairly long periods of complete quiet and
> rest. He is, of course, being subjected to careful medical treatment.
> He is extremely sensitive to noise of all kinds and especially to the
> noise made by automobiles stopping, starting, turning, and pass-
> ing. Our present house in Cambridge was selected because it lies
> well back from the road on a quiet side street. The telephone in
> our house rings only in the kitchen. If an attempt is made [at
> Windy Hill] to drive cars in the restricted space around the large
> trees in the corner near our house, he will, of course, be disturbed
> every time a car drives in. He will be awakened every time some-
> one leaves in the evening and has to start up a car.[2]

Occasionally the Schumpeters entertained weekend guests at Windy Hill—
her friends, his graduate students and young colleagues, and economists visiting from abroad. Sometimes Schumpeter ventured onto the estate's modest
tennis court. Never athletic, he wielded a feeble racket, but he did enjoy himself. With Peter, their Irish setter, he often took long walks by the shores of the
nearby Twin Lakes, and he liked to climb the wooded hills around the Taconic
property. For the great majority of the time, though, both he and Elizabeth
worked on their academic writings. Over the next few years they began to
spend more of their days at Windy Hill and fewer in Cambridge.[3]

After his disappointment with *Business Cycles,* Schumpeter began a project
he called in his diary "the book of essays" and sometimes "the book on socialism." This became *Capitalism, Socialism and Democracy,* the most widely read
of all his works. As he wrote it, he felt himself under increasing stress from several different sources: the failure of *Business Cycles,* the success of Keynesianism,
the prospect of war in Europe, and the anxiety about aging that often plagues
former boy wonders. He turned fifty-five in 1938, and his diary records frequent complaints about his health.

At Harvard, Schumpeter continued to teach well and to draw intellectual

Top: The big house at 7 Acacia Street in Cambridge. Today it is divided into several apartments.

Bottom: Windy Hill, the rural retreat near Taconic, Connecticut. This house, even in Schumpeter's time, was larger than it appears here, a substantial addition and patio having been built at the rear. The grounds are very spacious, and they still bear the charm of Elizabeth's landscaping talents.

sustenance from his faculty discussion groups. In 1939 he and the sociologist Talcott Parsons inaugurated a seminar on problems of "rationality." This group flourished, stimulated by an initial paper from Schumpeter. Even so, as he wrote to Parsons, "I feel stale and oppressed by a feeling of futility." His dissatisfaction with Harvard was now growing worse.[4]

One policy that especially bothered him was Harvard's insistence on individual tutoring for undergraduates. He believed that this practice derived in part from the early exposure of American academics to poor teaching methods in Europe, and particularly in Germany—where "the professor read from a manuscript that was often yellow with age, or presided languidly over seminar meetings." Schumpeter believed that visitors from elite American universities saw this kind of thing and became hostile to the lecture method, at which he excelled.[5]

Then, too, he had come to have less patience with affairs in the Economics Department. In October 1938 he wrote President Conant asking to be excused from a university-wide conference on Harvard's policies, where a long report by the faculty was to be discussed. The conference, he noted, conflicted with his teaching schedule.

> This would not, of course, prevent me from fulfilling a duty to the university if I thought that my presence would be of service. Allow me to explain why I doubt whether it would. When I came to Harvard I had great admiration for the efficiency of her teaching in general and for the tutoring system in particular. Observation, however, has somewhat modified my views [because intensive tutoring required a much larger staff than Harvard was willing to provide].
>
> But in this as in other points of university policy my views are hopelessly at variance with those of the majority of my colleagues. Now departments are living organisms with corporative interests and views of their own and have a tendency to claim that deviating views should not be pressed, especially in discussions with offices of the administration. To some extent I admit the justice of this claim, and that is one of the reasons that I have never intruded upon you with any views of mine. Although originally I

did hope that long experience with university affairs in other countries would qualify me to serve Harvard by my advice, I soon discovered that the attempt to do so would seem offensive to colleagues whom I respect and with whom I sincerely wish to cooperate smoothly. For similar reasons I refrain from giving you my reaction on the report which you have transmitted to all of us.

Schumpeter then proceeded to do just the opposite. He analyzed the report in detail, telling Conant that some of Harvard's recent hires were unimpressive, and not just in economics. The new professors quickly became discontented because they were required to do both their research and individual tutorials, for which they were poorly qualified. The solution was not in hiring still more faculty, nor in any "democratization of appointments." In a revealing comment, Schumpeter wrote that "happiness and contentment in academic life can only come from intellectual achievement, and stressing this (if necessary by instituting formal proof of scientific performance as a condition to promotion) and reducing the number of appointments to the number of the people that are up to the standard seem to me the only way out of present difficulties."[6]

Conant responded the next day. "May I suggest that perhaps you tend to overemphasize the divergence between your views and those of other members of your department . . . In any event I am very glad to have your letter and to know how you feel. I wish you would write me at any time or come to see me in regard to the many problems with which we are all confronted." But Schumpeter was not to be mollified. He remained close friends with the young stars of his department—Gottfried Haberler, Edward Mason, and especially Wassily Leontief, who lived just across the street from the Schumpeters. But he had little respect for the intellects of most of the senior economics professors, all of whom were roughly his own age: Harold Burbank, Eli Monroe, J. H. Williams, and John D. Black. (He had much higher regard for Alvin Hansen, A. P. Usher, and Sumner Slichter.)[7]

Schumpeter had few confidants of his own generation, and the retirement of his beloved Frank Taussig, who by 1940 was eighty-one years old and in failing health, left him without the kind of father figure he had relied on in the past. In departmental meetings with his senior colleagues, he wrote in his diary, "the atmosphere is languid and has no go. Not once has it happened within the writer's observation that at a meeting of the 'full professors' a scientific question has forced itself into conversation, let alone being passionately canvassed. [Their] work lacks intellectual ardor." He was extremely displeased when, early in 1940, the department's old guard refused to offer Paul Samuelson an assistant professorship.[8]

By the late 1930s Schumpeter had begun to take a few liberties with his position, as many tenured professors do at one time or another. He spent as many days as possible in Taconic. He often frustrated the departmental secretaries by being late in turning in a syllabus for his upcoming courses and in specifying what his office hours were to be. And, although he still handed out heavy reading assignments, he had earned a reputation for giving too many A's.

Issues like these are routine in university life and are best settled through a quiet word from the department chair, one on one. Instead, in January 1940 the full professors of the Economics Department chose to raise them in a general meeting. Schumpeter, easily the most distinguished person in attendance and the envy of those who now saw a chance to needle him, deeply resented the episode. He wrote in his diary of having "worked for a lifetime in order to have that Department to decide what I may or may not do." He complained of the "unpleasantness and mortification and humiliation" and of "eating humble pie in my old age" (he was about to turn fifty-seven).[9]

This incident, along with Schumpeter's general disenchantment, almost cost Harvard dearly. Within any organization, the management of geniuses is not an easy task, and the Economics Department was about to make a real botch of things. (Aristotle once wrote that "the business of household management is more concerned with human beings than it is with inanimate property.") As Schumpeter's discontent became more widely known, Harvard's competitors sensed a ripe opportunity.[10]

In the spring of 1940 Yale launched a strong effort to recruit him. On May 1, Provost E. S. Furniss, who ranked just below the president of the university, wrote Schumpeter with the offer of a Sterling Professorship, Yale's highest faculty position. Not knowing of his $12,000 salary at Harvard, Furniss suggested $10,000 plus "a small sum for secretarial assistance," a perquisite Schumpeter did not have at Harvard. He went on to say that "as regards duties, you would be virtually in position to write your own program." He proposed that Schumpeter might offer a course on business cycles, but "with regard to other subjects to be taught, as well as the total amount of teaching to be undertaken, we should expect to be guided by your own desires." This kind of freedom was extremely rare in academic life. Schumpeter reacted with immediate interest, underlining the words "to write your own program."[11]

He then invited Provost Furniss to visit Taconic, which is only 65 miles from New Haven, compared with 115 miles from Cambridge. Because he and Elizabeth were spending more time at Windy Hill, this proximity in itself was part of Yale's attraction. Taconic lies near the highest peak in Connecticut, and mountain driving in the snowy winter months sometimes became impossible. And even year-round, Taconic was far more accessible from New Haven, because at that time passenger trains directly connected the two areas, as was not the case with Cambridge or Boston.

After receiving Schumpeter's response, Furniss went to Taconic and began serious negotiations. Yale increased its offer to $12,000, along with a retirement allowance of $4,000, matching Schumpeter's Harvard compensation. After returning to New Haven, Furniss wrote to thank the Schumpeters for their hospitality "in your altogether charming country home." He pointed out that New Haven's housing situation was superior, and not only because of lower prices. "The University owns a few homes and if one of these appeals to you there should be no difficulty in arranging terms." Furniss emphasized that Yale's Economics Department "supports this invitation unanimously and enthusiastically, as do the University officers. If you come to Yale we shall look to you for leadership in the development of our graduate work and rely upon your counsel in selecting personnel to carry out the program." This too was a very unusual prospect—the opportunity to rebuild Yale's department according to his own vision.[12]

Schumpeter again sent an encouraging answer. "Taken together with what you said about my duties, your letter seems to settle all that can be settled at the moment." He wanted to inform Harvard of the situation before proceeding further, because it was already late May and he was scheduled to teach there in the fall term. If he did leave, he wished it to be done "in the most amiable manner possible." He therefore asked Furniss whether he might teach at both schools during the academic year 1940–1941. He had done this ten years earlier at Bonn and Harvard. He would offer his course on business cycles at Yale beginning in January and do much else "concerning the general direction of graduate studies in economics." Furniss's response made it clear that Yale expected Schumpeter to come permanently but was willing to settle for half of his time during the first year.[13]

Schumpeter really did want to move to New Haven. Harvard's dismissive attitude toward *Business Cycles* had hurt him badly, and now Yale was inviting him to focus on the very subject of that book. In addition, New Haven was the home of the now-retired economist Irving Fisher, one of his best friends. Schumpeter wrote Provost Furniss that it would take him some time to work out the payment of research grants he was receiving through Harvard from the Rockefeller Foundation. "But I assure you at the same time that, if I do see my way to accepting, I shall do so with enthusiasm." Meanwhile, in Cambridge, he gave strong hints that he intended to leave.[14]

In academic life, moves of high-profile professors are sometimes greeted with studied nonchalance, the jilted lover being too proud to protest. But this case was different, and Harvard's usually laconic Economics Department swung into quick action. All seventeen of its members signed a letter urging Schumpeter to stay, while leaving no doubt—in true Harvard fashion—that they viewed themselves as superior to Yale's economists and even knew what was best for Schumpeter himself:

> We, the undersigned members of the Economics Department,
> wish you to know our deep concern at your projected departure
> from Harvard in favor of Yale University. We feel that here you
> play a vital part in a department diverse in interests and capacities,
> so that your loss would be even greater *because* of our very size and
> the obligations which lie upon us. By contrast, the greater scope
> for the exercise of your gifts within the department at Yale is more
> than offset by the restricted obligations and possibilities of the de-
> partment itself. We value you as a colleague, we need you and we
> want you to stay. We believe, furthermore, that your departure
> would be detrimental to your own interests as well as to those of
> economic science which you have so much at heart. We urge upon
> you that these factors be given their due importance in reaching
> your final decision, and hope and trust that this decision will be to
> remain with us.[15]

Schumpeter received an even warmer letter from twenty-six of his graduate students. This group included two future Nobel Prize winners (Samuelson and Tobin) and at least a dozen other future leaders of the profession:

> We have heard that you are considering leaving Harvard. To us who have been closely associated with you as students for many years this news is most disturbing.
>
> Each one of us has been stimulated by the breadth and vision of your thought. As no one else, you have always shown intense interest in our problems regardless of the field; and we have always had reason to be extremely grateful for your willingness to give us your time and energy. Our research has been greatly aided by your helpful criticism and generous encouragement. You have implanted in us a belief in the importance of a more exact and objective economic science and a desire to contribute to its development. Above all, you have been more than a teacher to us; we have always been proud to think of you as a true friend. We feel that your departure would be an irreplaceable loss to us and to future Harvard students.
>
> Rightly Harvard has been regarded as a world center of research and teaching in the fields of theory and business cycles, and in large measure this has been your own achievement. We know that these branches would suffer without you. You have been a nucleus around which economic discussion and personal fellowship have taken form. We fear that this esprit de corps would not survive your departure.
>
> We may not have conveyed well the loss to us and to the University which your leaving would mean, but we trust that you will sense the sincerity of our spontaneous expression. We beg you to consider these views in forming your decisions.[16]

Schumpeter spoke to some of his students and responded to his fellow professors in a letter he sent to each of them: "I only wish I could convince myself that you are right. I am attached to Harvard and to the Economics Department and fully realize the value of the privilege of being a member of so excellent a group. But my departure appeared to me in the light of a relief of the departmental structure that might prove beneficial to the department as well as to myself. However, I am glad to know that you do not agree with me in this and sincerely hope that I am wrong."[17]

Edward Mason, one of Schumpeter's most capable young colleagues, then made an appointment for him to see President James Conant. Harvard's president did his best to placate Schumpeter—praising his work and emphasizing his stature as the jewel of the Economics Department. On June 21, 1940, seven weeks after receiving the original letter from Yale, Schumpeter told Elizabeth—in words perhaps showing a Freudian slip—"I am resigning myself to declining the Yale offer."[18]

After hearing from Schumpeter, Provost Furniss wrote from Yale, "I shall not try to conceal the fact that I am grievously disappointed by your decision. We had quite set our hearts upon having you here." He would not "embarrass you by any attempt to dissuade you from it." Furniss added that he was "delighted that you are willing to come down next year on some part-time arrangement." President Charles Seymour of Yale later wrote that "I need not say how pleased I am that you find it possible to give us this service."[19]

Schumpeter waited until the fall of 1940 to make his final arrangements for staying at Harvard while teaching at Yale one day per week during the next academic term. E. H. Chamberlin, who was chairing the department at Harvard and knew of Schumpeter's recent essay on rationality, wrote him that "this has all appearances of being a 'rational' decision." Harvard's dean William Scott Ferguson expressed his own "congratulations on your decision . . . My only concern is lest we and Yale jointly are going to work you too hard."[20]

The letters from his colleagues and particularly his students likely had much to do with his decision to stay at Harvard. So did the feelings of Elizabeth, who was not anxious to start over in a new city. For twenty-five years, since she was a freshman at Radcliffe, she had lived mostly in Cambridge, near her friends, professional contacts, and prospects for employment.

Yet Yale's offer pleased Schumpeter greatly, and he came very close to taking it. Like the business entrepreneurs he wrote about, he was always sanguine about a fresh start and had made many himself: at the Theresianum, the University of Vienna, the University of Czernowitz, the University of Graz, the Austrian Ministry of Finance, the Biedermann Bank, the University of Bonn, and finally at Harvard. Yale represented a chance to reinvent himself one more time. Had he been just a bit younger, or still single, he likely would have gone.

And had that happened, the harm to Harvard would have been severe. Not only would the move have cost the university one of its brightest stars. It also would have meant that two years later, the man who published *Capitalism, Socialism and Democracy*—one of the great books of the twentieth century—would have been a professor not at Harvard but at Yale.

18

Against the Grain

Do I contradict myself?
Very well then I contradict myself,
(I am large, I contain multitudes.)

WALT WHITMAN, "Song of Myself," 1851

AT THE TIME when Schumpeter was mulling over his decision about Harvard versus Yale, international affairs dominated the world's attention. Here, as elsewhere, Schumpeter's foresight and independence as a thinker set him apart from most of his American friends and colleagues. And he himself realized that his own thoughts about the looming crisis were sometimes paradoxical, inconsistent, or simply incorrect.

As a Viennese, he had little affection for Germany, but he still chafed over the injustices wrought by the victors of 1918. As a close student of history, he tended to think in the very long term, within a framework of Great Power politics and changing spheres of influence. The power that worried him most was not Germany but the Soviet Union, a much larger country whose government openly called for an end to capitalism and democracy.[1]

During the 1930s he regarded both Germany and Japan as vital long-term barriers against Russian expansion, and for that reason he measured the faults of their governments in relative rather than absolute terms. He did not believe that the hideous excesses of Nazism would last beyond a few years. This was extremely wishful thinking, and one of the biggest mistakes of his life. After all, he had seen dozens of his Jewish and socialist friends in Germany dismissed from their academic posts, and he was receiving from Mia Stöckel a steady stream of reports on the Nazis' cruelty. But he never believed Germany to be as formidable a threat as the Soviet Union—nor Hitler, as a long-term leader, to be nearly as dangerous as Joseph Stalin.[2]

As the 1930s wore on, Schumpeter became dejected and often cynical about the likelihood of another world conflict. In 1937, he wrote a French economist, "Yes, the invasion of politics into everything is of course mildew to all cultural values and aims . . . Every issue, every bond, every value and every intellectual ambition is being swallowed up by that struggle alone and it makes very little difference that what threatens to swallow what we understand by civilization is not one rising phase but two"—communism and fascism.[3]

By the end of the 1930s, communist and fascist movements in Europe were squaring off against each other either as nation versus nation or, more often, as factions within the same country. Occasionally, they fought by proxy: in the Spanish Civil War of 1936–1939, the communist Soviets assisted one side while the fascist Nazis helped the other. Democratic parliamentary governments were caught in the middle, trying desperately to avoid another general European war even as they themselves also began to spend huge sums on armaments.

Much more clearly than most analysts, Schumpeter intuited that no single one of the three contending systems—fascism, communism, and democratic capitalism—would be able to defeat the other two militarily. Before war came, he anticipated that there would be a victorious alliance of strange bedfellows—capitalist with communist, democrat with autocrat, socialist with fascist. But who would ally with whom? And with what results?

An alliance of fascism with communism came first, expressed in the Nazi-Soviet Nonaggression Pact of August 1939. Publicly, it promised neutrality in the event that either country went to war with other nations. But in a secret protocol, the two powers agreed to invade and divide their neighbor, Poland. The signing of this momentous document triggered Germany's lightning attack on western Poland of September 1 (the *Blitzkrieg*). The Soviets invaded eastern Poland three weeks later to claim their piece of the territory. Britain and France declared war on Germany, and World War II was under way.

After Hitler and Stalin dismembered Poland, the Soviets, acting on another secret agreement with Germany, moved to take over Estonia, Latvia, and Lithuania. They then launched an invasion of Finland. A few months later, Germany rapidly conquered Holland, Belgium, and France. Stalin now commanded Eastern Europe, and Hitler dominated the West. Only Great Britain lay outside Germany's grasp. After the Luftwaffe failed to win the Battle of Britain during the fall of 1940, Hitler turned eastward in June 1941 and attacked his communist conspirator. Shocking the world, he launched a massive invasion of the Soviet Union, directly breaching the pact of 1939. That step drove the Soviets into a new alliance of convenience with Britain. Since British survival was at stake, the enemy of its enemy became its friend, regardless of ideology.

Schumpeter, like many other Americans, feared that Britain would now draw the United States into the war. His adopted country was, he wrote in his diary, "at the mercy of groups which are not oriented on its interest—nobody cares for its interest—except of course the majority of Americans—but those don't matter: bewildered and cowed they obediently mumble: 'We've got to be prepared' and they will, in silent disgust, soon mumble: 'We can't stay out.'" He felt about the United States much as he had felt about Austria in 1915 and 1916, when he was marooned in Graz. As he wrote during the period before the United States became involved, in a kind of poem of self-examination,

> To see this country rush to unknown futures
> Spoiling all chances to the right or left
> And have to sit here and not be able to warn, to help . . .

But, having experienced so much frustration when he did get into public affairs in 1916, he warned himself in 1940: "Think before you let yourself be drawn into 'political strife' . . . Remember: if you do you must do so with a will." In the end, he did not do so at all.[4]

Schumpeter's first reaction to the outbreak of war in Europe had been numb disbelief. "Sorrow of course," he wrote in his diary, "but for the rest it's as always in the great catastrophes I have experienced and lived through—there is *no* reaction, my secret garden is dumb, birds are still; *that old stunned feeling* . . . funny I don't even feel that [it] is world war."[5]

He thought of the European war as a fight between Britain and Germany that perhaps need not have begun in the first place. "There are wars not because people want to fight for something, but because people want to fight." His diary entries show a confusion of inconsistent emotions. Three weeks after the war began, and ten months before Hitler's invasion of the Soviet Union, Schumpeter wrote:

> As soon as, quite foolishly, Germany was driven [by British and French policy] into the arms of Russia, the chance for Germany to succeed became considerable.
>
> Yes there may be mistakes, mismanagement on West Front etc; attack on neutrals and so a world war (which it is not *yet*); also Italy and Japan may possibly be won over—but in the normal course of things the war is really decided in Germany's favor and even U.S. [participation] would not necessarily change the result.
>
> But the comfort is: if Germany wins in the sense of warding off the attack and securing what she can get in the East, there will be . . . a much more stable state of things—the structure of Europe better balanced and strains removed and more hope for peace than for a long time past.
>
> But what about Hitlerism? Well history should have taught us that it is no good fighting religion—that's why nobody would think of fighting bolshevism—: if it is to stay, it will stay. But even so it is not unlikely that it will settle down—precisely after success—whereas I don't see what is to be done if Germany is *beaten:* I see nothing but another unstable structure.

Here, Schumpeter radically underestimated the Nazis' strength and capacity for evil; but at the same time he anticipated with great insight the situation that led to the Soviet-American Cold War of 1945–1989.[6]

He was hardly the only confused person in the United States. A large proportion of Americans, convinced that in 1917 their country had been duped into entering World War I, responded to events of the 1920s and 1930s by trying not to think about foreign affairs at all. In 1920 Congress rejected the Treaty of Versailles and refused membership in the League of Nations. In 1932, when the Japanese took over Manchuria and set up the puppet state of Manchukuo, the United States (and the League of Nations) did almost nothing. And in 1935, when Mussolini invaded Ethiopia, Congress passed the first of a series of ever-stronger Neutrality Acts, forbidding any assistance to foreign combatants.

"Isolationist" may be too broad a term for Americans' attitudes, but during the mid-1930s their consensus view of foreign affairs was as ostrich-like as at any time in the nation's history. Opinion polls throughout the decade showed a strong and consistent distaste for overseas conflict and a determination to stay out of war. Even President Roosevelt, a confirmed internationalist, felt it necessary to say during his third-term election campaign of 1940 that "your boys are not going to be sent into any foreign wars." As late as October 1941, a full year after the Battle of Britain and just a few weeks before the Japanese attack on Pearl Harbor, opinion polls continued to show that a majority of Americans opposed the nation's military involvement in war.[7]

The same was true of Harvard University, a sometime bastion of internationalism. One member of the class of 1940, Thornton Bradshaw—later a respected business statesman, CEO of Atlantic Richfield and RCA—believed that the Spanish Civil War was "not our affair. If fascist Germany and Italy and communist Russia were involved, then 'a pox on both your houses' reflected my view." Another student, Arthur M. Schlesinger, Jr., recalled that "Harvard was a cocoon" and his cohort of students "an innocent generation."[8]

Schumpeter wanted to stay out of war as well, but he could not claim innocence as an excuse for his partially blind eye toward Nazi cruelties. Although he shared his fellow citizens' distaste for war, he was aware that in many of his other opinions he stood against the majority. Schumpeter especially disliked Franklin D. Roosevelt, whom he misunderstood and undervalued. Today, Roosevelt is widely regarded as the greatest American president of the twentieth century. He entered office in 1933, when the United States faced economic catastrophe. His New Deal program, enacted during the first five years of his administration, dealt almost entirely with domestic affairs arising from the Great Depression.[9]

Wealthy Americans turned bitterly against the New Deal because of Roosevelt's innovative economic measures. They included a complex series of securities laws, which were absolutely essential in bringing Wall Street and the capital markets under effective public regulation; the Wealth Tax Act of 1935, which increased income taxes on corporations and high individual earners; and a significant inheritance tax, the first in the nation's history. While the rich fumed against "that man" in the White House, the canny Roosevelt found a way to exploit their hostility. In his brilliant and successful campaign for re-election in 1936, he denounced them as "economic royalists." And in an election-eve speech at Madison Square Garden in New York, he told his frenzied audience that the rich "are unanimous in their hate for me, and I welcome their hatred." (Roosevelt was capable of demagoguery, although he seldom used it. The Madison Square Garden speech upset even Eleanor Roosevelt, the First Lady.)

Given his background and conservative leanings, Schumpeter perhaps inevitably regarded Roosevelt as a dangerous politician. He observed the New Deal from the viewpoint of a European intellectual who had personally witnessed the collapse of numerous democratic governments. He had seen the subsequent rise of strongmen, and he feared that this same pattern might emerge in the United States. He distrusted all politicians, writing in his diary that "more lies enter into governing than in the selling of any hair restorer."[10]

But Schumpeter misunderstood President Roosevelt's willingness to enact all kinds of measures to speed recovery, mistaking it for an unprincipled drive toward authoritarianism. It was true enough that the New Deal's economic philosophy was not very coherent. But Schumpeter missed the powerful psychological effects of Roosevelt's activist program—and his bringing into the national mainstream millions of marginalized Americans. The New Deal did not solve any of the nation's leading problems: the economy, the structural unfairness to working people, the racism, or the severe poverty in particular regions of the country. But it ameliorated all of these problems. Both Franklin and Eleanor Roosevelt, though born into wealth and social prominence, seemed to a majority of Americans to be humane friends who cared about them personally.

Schumpeter was not part of that majority. The New Deal struck him as still another prelude to authoritarianism. He became convinced that Roosevelt's program represented a step toward either fascism or socialism, and in either case potential dictatorship. He wrote a friend that Roosevelt was like a child, mindlessly breaking a machine because he did not understand its design. The president "is going to turn me into a fan of [Ludwig von] Mises," his classmate at the University of Vienna who had become a free-market fundamentalist and an opponent of almost all government intervention. In the spring of 1937, when the president tried to pack the Supreme Court with new appointees, suspicion of his intentions crossed the minds of many other Americans as well. As Schumpeter wrote in his diary, "Roosevelt can't—won't—take an apple without upsetting the whole applecart."[11]

In the late 1930s, as war loomed in Europe, Schumpeter believed that the president would try to maneuver the United States into the conflict, on the side of Britain. Here he was far more accurate than in his assessment of the New Deal. Yet he still found the policies of Washington hard to understand. As the administration began to spend more on both domestic projects and military preparations, Schumpeter complained in his diary: "*Roosevelt's new spending*—good sign? If he got his war, [domestic spending] would not be necessary and since he tries to dissolve opposition, honor and duty in a torrent of money—must he not think that he can't have the war? Is it the last card of the New Deal?" Despite everything the American government could do—and it tried almost all reasonable remedies—economic recovery remained elusive. In 1933 unemployment had stood at 25 percent. Under New Deal policies, it initially declined, only to go back up. In 1939 it still stood at a depression-level 17.6 percent of the work force.[12]

One of the few measures Roosevelt did not attempt was a radical step that Schumpeter himself suggested during the early 1930s: a single $9 billion burst of emergency public spending. This sum, immense for that time, far exceeded anything tried by the New Deal or suggested by other major economists. It was three times the size of the annual federal budget when Roosevelt took office. As a rule, Schumpeter opposed the kind of fiscal manipulation recommended by Keynes, with its chronic deficit spending and disincentives for saving. But he did think that, as an emergency measure, the American economy needed one enormous infusion of public investment.[13]

ALTHOUGH HE HAD no role in shaping his adopted country's policies, Schumpeter found various ways to make his opinions known. In 1940, just after deciding to decline Yale's offer and remain at Harvard, he began working on a project that led him to organize and refine his views. The Lowell Institute, a prestigious society headquartered in Boston, invited him to deliver eight public lectures, beginning in March 1941, entitled "An Economic Interpretation of Our Times." For the Lowell Institute, it would be the 102nd season of a tradition begun in 1839 that had included as prior speakers Oliver Wendell Holmes ("The Path of the Law"), William James ("Pragmatism"), Alfred North Whitehead ("Science and the Modern World"), and Bertrand Russell ("Our Knowledge of the External World").

Schumpeter accepted the invitation, even though both he and Elizabeth were extraordinarily busy at the time. During parts of the academic year 1940–1941 he taught one day a week at Yale in addition to his regular duties at Harvard. Also, as president of the Econometric Society, he had charge of planning the program for its annual meeting—a time-consuming task involving communication with dozens of prospective presenters and commentators. And he had begun to work hard on the book that became *Capitalism, Socialism and Democracy.*

In the Lowell Lectures, he foreshadowed many ideas he developed more fully in the book. For four weeks during March 1941, he spoke each Monday and Friday, beginning at 5:00 in the afternoon. Some of the lectures show flashes of Schumpeter's trademark turns of phrase and memorable showmanship. Overall, however, they take a gloomy tone. He was heartsick about the carnage in both Europe and Asia, and ruefully convinced that the United States would soon take part in both wars.[14]

He began his first lecture by contrasting current popular sentiments with those of the Western world seventy years earlier. During the decades before the outbreak of war in 1914, Schumpeter observed, "practically all civilized nations professed allegiance to the democratic ideal," and there was ample basis for optimism. "Popular education and steady extension of the franchise were generally accepted policies. The freedom of the individual to say, think, and do what he pleased was also, within very wide limits, generally accepted."[15]

Pre-1914 civilization "was essentially rationalist and utilitarian. It was not favorable to cults of national glory, victory, and so on." It tended to regard war as a wasteful sideshow. In all, its outlook reflected "the beliefs and attitudes of the business class." Over time, however, people had begun to take economic success for granted and to lose sight of core business principles. By the 1930s the world had "grown out of humor with the capitalist system." As a result, "we now frequently find that the most obvious facts about it are being made light of or even flatly denied." The Great Depression had exacerbated anti-capitalist and anti-democratic feelings that had been on the rise even before the stock market crash of 1929.[16]

For that matter, intellectual trends had begun to undermine bourgeois values even before the guns of August boomed in 1914. "There had been Nietzsche, there was Bergson, and there were Sorel and Pareto. None of these was a socialist, yet none of these was a friend of either capitalism or the ethics which were congenial to capitalism." It was therefore "an essentially unstable world on which the first world war impinged."[17]

Then, instead of settling disputes as most wars do, "the 1914 hurricane" greatly multiplied the world's problems. The peace treaties thrust impossible economic burdens on the losers. Attempts to install democratic governments foundered in many countries. Most seriously of all, the Soviet Union began to threaten both capitalism and democracy by successfully combining state socialism with the obliteration of civil liberties.

Schumpeter believed that most Western intellectuals had lost their heads over the Soviet Union and were wildly romanticizing its practices. The respected American journalist Lincoln Steffens, returning from a visit to Russia, said "I have seen the future, and it works." Intellectuals seemed blind to the brutality of the Stalinist regime. But by 1940 the ruthless collectivization of agriculture and forcible diversion of food to the cities had brought death by starvation to between 5 and 8 million people. As with the Holocaust, these incredible totals did not become fully known until after World War II. But it was clear even before the war that many thousands of Soviet citizens had died or disappeared in the political trials and forced relocations of 1933–1939. Russian communism, said Schumpeter, showed "much more affinity with Ivan the Terrible than with Karl Marx."[18]

Meanwhile, in capitalist countries, the market crash of 1929 had hit disproportionately hard because of the legacy of 1919. By its very nature, "capitalism is not gentle to the capitalist," and the 1929 downturn had struck a weakened world economy with malignant force. The ensuing crisis "was an unprecedented catastrophe spelling complete breakdown of the capitalist system which, though it might be now patched up by government action, stood discredited forever."[19]

Conceding that his analysis was likely to be unpopular with his audience, he went on to say that the Great Depression had begun as a normal downturn—a routine capitalist stock market crash "which I personally have never been able to waste any tears over. It was for moral reasons a most sanitary thing." During the 1920s "certain pathological processes" had beset the stock exchanges—corners had been cut, laws broken, and prices inflated in the quest for quick profits. This, Schumpeter said, was a normal, if very unattractive, capitalist reaction to a boom period. So too was the plunge in the market once the bubble burst. American stocks lost about 90 percent of their value between 1929 and 1933, but much of the loss came after 1931, the year that U.S. banking began to collapse.[20]

The banking crisis, Schumpeter argued, was the real calamity, and government policy had made it much worse. The American banking system, because of its extreme decentralization, was "by far the weakest in the world." Most countries counted their banks by the scores or the hundreds and encouraged multiple branches. By contrast, America's historic suspicion of centralized power had prevented financial concentration; and interstate banking and branch banking were still illegal in most states. At the time of the 1929 crash, there were about thirty thousand independent American banks, the great majority of them small and bereft of sufficient reserves.[21]

About seven thousand of these banks failed during the short period from 1931 to 1933, bringing financial ruin to millions of citizens. The result for public opinion, said Schumpeter, was a mass indictment of the whole economic system: "Capitalism stood condemned to a point where it was hardly possible to present to any audience in 1933 a dispassionate view of events . . . anything that did not end in a condemnation of the system was out of court when the New Deal came. I am not criticizing this frame of mind of the American people and many other people; I am only drawing your attention to it."[22]

In this situation, and given the conspicuous and indefensible scandals on Wall Street, large numbers of businessmen lost their nerve. "They all acted as if they had something terrible to hide. As a matter of fact, there wasn't anything very bad to be hidden." Meanwhile, "the intellectuals went around to what they believed to be the rising sun [of socialism]" and proceeded to propagandize against capitalism. "Bewildered by events they could not understand and dreaded, even sensible people believed the wildest schemes." Although he mentioned no names, Schumpeter assumed that his audience knew of the radical programs proposed by the populist Huey Long and the anti-Semitic "radio priest" Father Charles Coughlin.[23]

Schumpeter went on in his lectures to analyze economic policies enacted during the 1930s in various countries. In many, including the United States, governments installed some form of planning. What, he asked, does "planning" mean in a market economy? "It is the replacement of the entrepreneurial decisions of how, what, and how much to produce by the decision of some other social organism." The New Deal experiments followed no definite pattern and showed no coherence. Even so, some agencies—particularly the National Recovery Administration, which cartelized numerous industries—represented the kind of system found in Mussolini's Italy. As a European who had witnessed in one country after another the gravitation of power toward strongmen, Schumpeter saw no reason to believe that the same thing could not happen in the United States. He knew Roosevelt to be as charismatic as any European autocrat, and a much more adroit politician than most leaders anywhere.[24]

He next turned to international diplomacy. Taking aim at the policy of economic sanctions against aggressive countries, Schumpeter said, "Never was there a more unfortunate idea." For one thing, sanctions compelled nations to pursue autarchy (economic self-sufficiency). In so doing, they reduced international trade, which in itself was a powerful force for peace and continuous diplomatic engagement. Severe sanctions against the Japanese, for example, had led them to develop their own supplies of raw materials and to seek new sources through further aggression. "This almost childish belief that so many people hold . . . that by means of managing raw materials you can force foreign nations to their knees, has been a boon to autarchists, militarists, and dictators all over the world."[25]

Sanctions also moved the world economy farther from the ideal of free trade. Schumpeter speculated that after the wars in Europe and Asia ended, internal trading blocs might develop, led by four groups: the Americans, the Europeans, the Russians, and the Japanese. If each of the four blocs became a relatively independent sphere of influence, complete with economic integration, then the need for further wars might diminish. This was hardly the ideal situation that free trade represented, but it was better than other alternatives.

Let me give you an analogy. Not all of us are enthusiastic about the practices of modern labor leaders, yet we do not on that account advocate shooting them down. We may think them unreasonable and unethical, yet we accept them. Likewise, in our homes we accept the recalcitrant child. Similarly, if the great parts [of the world] in which the group divides are left to themselves, that is the best chance to avoid war; or else there will be war, and to war, in a war without end, there can be only one victor, Russia and bolshevism.[26]

In his final lecture, "Possible Consequences for the United States," Schumpeter told his audience even more things they likely did not want to hear. He asserted that in many parts of the world, a widespread hostility prevailed against the perceived arrogance of Anglo-American power. This resentment went back to the imperial "Rule, Britannia" era of the nineteenth century and had been aggravated considerably by the Great War and the harsh treaties of 1919. "But quite independently of that, the mere sense of being thwarted, of not being as good as other people, acts more on domestic and foreign policies of European powers and Japan than you are prone to admit."[27]

The United States, meanwhile, was seen by many as a tool of British interests. America enjoyed automatic security because of its self-sufficiency and huge ocean barriers. It could not be directly threatened by either Germany or Japan. Even so, it "will presently enter the war and keep on with the English standpoint about the European problem and add to the English standpoint only its determined hostility to Japan. This unfolds the picture of what I call ethical imperialism, an imperialism whose ethos it is to put the world into order according to American ideas." Here Schumpeter clearly anticipated the enthusiastic marketing abroad of American products and culture that to this day is offensive to citizens of many countries.[28]

The most serious danger would come, said Schumpeter—again quite presciently—"if America embarks on a military career" over the long term. This could be fatal to the nation's democracy. "The American who sees these possibilities and expects to avoid them in case the country embarks on a prolonged war is an optimist. The American who sees them but says from moral considerations that nevertheless he is going to enter upon the course he thinks is right is a saint. The American who does not see these dangers is a fool."[29]

Despite his pessimistic tone, Schumpeter stopped short of predicting disaster for the United States. "The flu need not develop into pneumonia," he said in his last lecture. Even so, his suspicions about President Roosevelt had become extreme; and shortly after delivering the Lowell Lectures, he wrote a friend that "a ten-year's war and a ten-year's Roosevelt dictatorship would completely upset the social structure." And he was even beginning to doubt his own ability to judge contemporary events. "Well I did not foresee either the lasting of Bolshevism or fascism or Hitlerism," he wrote in his diary. "Not much to my credit and now, after having believed that this won't happen here . . . I see the nation rushing into Fascism and Imperialism [under the] Freudian camouflage of Defense." And in still another entry, again puzzled by his own strong feelings, "Why am I *always* so out of sympathy with my milieu"?[30]

19

The Courage of Her Convictions

Nothing is more damaging to a new truth than an old error.

GOETHE, *Proverbs in Prose*, 1819

JOSEPH SCHUMPETER FELT anxious and isolated in his views about Europe and Germany. Elizabeth Schumpeter faced a similar predicament in her opinions about Asia and Japan. As the 1930s drew to a close, Elizabeth, like her husband, was extremely busy. For the academic year 1938–1939 she taught economics as a visiting professor at Wheaton College, a small school forty miles south of Boston. But her major intellectual effort of the decade was a book on Japan's modern industrial history, a collaboration with three established experts on Japan that she had begun in 1934.

By 1940, when the book appeared, Japanese–American relations had all but collapsed, and her topic had become very timely—and very controversial. Elizabeth herself had become more directly involved than she would have preferred, writing articles and making speeches in an attempt to convey some complex and uncomfortable truths to the American people. In doing so, she too began to feel out of sympathy with her milieu.[1]

During the 1930s Japan had grown increasingly militaristic, and the army had gained much more leverage within the government. In the midst of this nationalist upsurge, several prominent cabinet ministers and businessmen had been assassinated. By the end of the decade, the country was divided between what Elizabeth called the "liberal element—democratically inclined politicians, journalists, and others—and "mad extremists" who advocated aggressive moves of territorial expansion.

Japan was already a major power in East Asia. Taiwan had been a Japanese colony since 1895. Korea was made a protectorate in 1905 and was annexed in 1910. But Japanese militarists wanted far more and were determined to get it. Soon their eyes turned to Manchuria, a large three-province area of China north of the Great Wall and adjacent to Mongolia and Siberia. For several decades, Chinese, Russian, and Japanese interests had clashed in Manchuria, often violently. The Japanese had retained commercial establishments and small garrisons there since their victory in the Russo-Japanese War of 1904–1905. In 1931 the Japanese engineered a takeover of Manchuria, and in 1932 they set up a puppet state called Manchukuo (which means Manchu country). They installed as its titular ruler the last Manchu emperor of China, Pu Yi, who had been deposed in Beijing twenty years earlier, when he was five years old.[2]

The Japanese continued to skirmish with the Russians in Manchuria, but they did not disturb nearby Vladivostok. Besides being the major Russian city closest to Japan, Vladivostok was the eastern terminus of the eight-thousand-mile trans-Siberian railway, part of which ran through a corridor of Manchuria. Russia and Japan had been wary of each other since before their war of 1904–1905. In the Treaty of Portsmouth, mediated by President Theodore Roosevelt, Russia conceded most of southern Manchuria to Japan, the victor.

Despite its two millennia of empire, China was then a very poor and overwhelmingly rural country, governed largely by regional warlords. The Qing (Manchu) dynasty, its rulers for three centuries, fell in 1911 to revolutionaries led by Dr. Sun Yat-sen. He had become a hero in Western countries, including the United States, as the founder of the Kuomindang, a party that espoused nationalism and a form of democracy.

In the years after World War I, the Kuomindang modeled some of its economic policies on those of the Soviet Union. Beginning in 1923 it absorbed Communists into its ranks. Then, as it tried to unite the vast regions of China, many of which were still ruled by warlords, the Kuomindang grew increasingly corrupt. Eventually it evolved into a military dictatorship led by Sun Yat-sen's son-in-law, General Chiang Kai-shek. In 1927 the forty-year-old Chiang expelled the Communists from the Kuomindang and consolidated the country in 1928 under his Nationalist government. But soon afterward, Mao Zedong and Zhou Enlai launched a Communist revolution against Chiang's regime. Both Mao (then only thirty-four years old) and Zhou (just thirty) were true believers in Marxism-Leninism.

Civil war between the Chinese Communists and Nationalists had been raging when in 1937, under the pretext of a series of "incidents," Japanese troops from Manchukuo invaded additional parts of China. In response to Japan's action, the clashing Chinese armies declared a truce and forged a temporary alliance with each other—another marriage of strange bedfellows, somewhat similar to what was about to happen in Europe. Mao Zedong ceded overall leadership to Chiang Kai-shek, and their sometimes poorly equipped armies fought gallantly against the Japanese invaders. The war became extremely brutal, and atrocities by the Japanese army—most conspicuously the "rape of Nanking"—were reported throughout the world.

In the United States, public opinion strongly favored the Chinese. Private campaigns of assistance were led by former Christian missionaries and by a well-organized "China lobby" that included several members of Congress. Many Americans had a romanticized notion of the democratic and capitalist convictions of Chiang Kai-shek and his Nationalist government. Madame Chiang, Sun Yat-sen's daughter, spoke English fluently and was an exceptionally appealing symbol. But on the whole, very few non-Asian people in the United States knew much about either China or Japan.

Elizabeth Schumpeter stepped into this tangled and passionate debate almost inadvertently. Her primary academic interest was not the contemporary Far East but seventeenth-century England. Yet, having been asked in 1934 to lead a major research project on the Japanese economy, she was not about to abandon that work. Between 1937 and the appearance of her book in 1940, Elizabeth published seven articles, in journals such as *Pacific Affairs, Far Eastern Survey, The Oriental Economist,* and *Annals of the American Academy of Political and Social Science.* She spoke before numerous groups and kept up a lively correspondence with public figures who shared some of her views about Japan: the journalists Walter Lippmann and David Lawrence; the scholars A. Whitney Griswold and Charles A. Beard; and the philanthropists David and John D. Rockefeller, Jr. The Rockefeller Foundation funded her book project through Harvard and Radcliffe's Bureau of International Research.[3]

Like her husband, who had been struck by Japan's economic progress during his three-week visit in 1931, Elizabeth was more interested in the country's rapid industrialization than in questions of war and diplomacy. She had taken note of the unparalleled speed of the country's economic modernization during the years since the Meiji Restoration of 1868. More recently, Japan's quick recovery from the Great Depression had piqued her interest and that of other economists as well.

In 1936 the American business magazine *Fortune*—then a thick, lavish, and very expensive monthly—devoted its entire September issue to Japan. (Today this issue is a collector's item.) The articles in *Fortune* included long and sophisticated analyses with titles such as "The Rising Sun of Japan" and "The Proof of the Pudding." The issue appeared several months before Japan's invasion of China and took a generally sympathetic and admiring tone. Most of the articles said little about Japan's politics and foreign policy.[4]

But attitudes toward Japan changed quickly after its invasion of China in 1937. In one of her own articles, "Japanese Economic Policy and the Standard of Living" (1938), Elizabeth Schumpeter wrote that "the most serious threat at the moment is the ambitions of the Japanese army. If they can be kept in check, further progress in raising living standards in Japan may be hoped for." In another, she argued that additional economic sanctions against Japan by the United States and other countries—such as prohibiting exports of steel and oil—were not likely to work. Japan could carry on its war with China by getting these materials from other sources (oil from the Dutch East Indies, for example), a prospect that in itself held many dangers.

Anticipating an unpopular theme her husband was to strike three years later in his Lowell Lectures, Elizabeth wrote in 1938: "Economic sanctions have not yet proved themselves an effective method 'short of war.' Partial sanctions will not stop a nation prepared to make every sacrifice for what it looks upon as its national existence. Strong sanctions applied after a nation is deeply involved will, in all probability, lead to war."[5]

In her effort to inform public opinion about Japan's strength, Elizabeth faced an uphill fight against the China lobby, which was calling for more and more sanctions. In a letter to Frederick V. Field of the San Francisco-based Institute of Pacific Relations (publishers of *Far Eastern Survey* and *Amerasia*), she wrote, "I think that your contributors have been far too pessimistic about economic conditions in Japan" and therefore too optimistic about the success of additional sanctions. "On the political side I agree that it is a hopeless business for Japan to go on fighting China, but I think she is much better equipped to do so than the current publications indicate." The articles so far published in Field's magazines had "bitterly antagonized the Japanese. Perhaps this was inevitable and perhaps you don't care." But the Institute of Pacific Relations would be more effective "if it could refrain from what seems like extremely pro-Chinese propaganda. I know of no one who wishes the Japanese to be successful in their present campaign against China. It is, of course, all a hideous mistake. I have encountered no Japanese who is really whole-hearted about this war." She later wrote Field that she herself was willing to extend the economic embargo on moral grounds, but "I do not agree with you at all that a war against Japan now would be an easy war, and I have met almost no military or naval experts who feel that it would be an easy war."[6]

In an article published in 1940 and titled "The Policy of the United States in the Far East," Elizabeth delivered a scorching indictment. She accused the United States of moralizing to other countries without any cost to itself; of keeping its markets closed while Japan and other exporting nations suffered; and of having no clue as to why otherwise civilized countries would "turn to such leaders as Mussolini and Hitler." Most Americans emphatically did not want to fight, but many seemed to be encouraging everyone else to fight. In her own view, the United States could not do much in Europe (she was writing in April 1940, before the fall of France and the Battle of Britain), but it could exert effective pressure in the Far East. There, the Chinese were trying to get help from the Soviet Union in their war against Japan, and the whole situation was far more convoluted than American policymakers seemed able to grasp:

> If, to avoid this growing influence of Stalin in China, the United
> States should extend active assistance to China on a large scale,
> there is the same reason for a Russian-Japanese pact as there was
> for the Russian-German pact [the one signed in 1939]. In the long
> run the interests of Japan and Russia are conflicting, but in the
> immediate future they are both interested in weakening the position of the "democracies" of "capitalistic imperialism." This possibility cannot be ignored at a time when France and England are

engaged in a life-and-death struggle in Europe and when India is
so discontented that she offers fruitful soil for Communist propaganda. The menace of a great Communist belt from the Baltic and
the Black Sea to the Pacific Ocean may be a matter of much more
concern than the aspirations of the Japanese military. Russia may
be the real winner of the present war, not only in Europe but also
in the Far East, with her strength left unimpaired because other
nations have fought her battles.

As Elizabeth predicted, Japan and the Soviet Union did sign a nonaggression
pact in April 1941—each country protecting its flank against contingencies
elsewhere.[7]

Elizabeth went on to argue that economic sanctions against Japan and non-
recognition of its influence in Manchukuo could not bring the war in China to
an end. "Japan has behaved abominably toward China, but we must share the
responsibility." The Western powers had moralized against Japan's aggressive
territorial expansion but at the same time had blocked any peaceful economic
expansion. "Japanese exports were limited at first by high tariffs and exchange
regulations and eventually by discriminatory tariffs and quotas." Moreover, because of racial prejudice, "Japanese immigration was prohibited or virtually
prohibited in the United States, the British Dominions, Siberia, and Africa."[8]

Thus, Elizabeth argued, whatever one might think of Japan's aggression, the
country had some legitimate grievances. There was a special irony here, since
the vast Asian possessions of Britain, France, the Netherlands, and the United
States "were acquired by exploration, trade, and conquest. But such methods
are no longer permitted. Under these circumstances it would seem that the
powers should at least open their colonies under reasonable conditions as markets and sources of raw materials. If they wish to prevent territorial expansion,
they must afford opportunities for industrial and commercial expansion." But
instead the Western nations had done the exact opposite. They had closed to
Japanese commerce their colonial markets in Malaya, India, French Indo-
China, the Dutch East Indies, and the Philippines—markets formerly crucial
to Japan, as were the raw materials they supplied.[9]

The Western powers were absolutely correct, Elizabeth continued, to insist
that Japanese troops depart from China. But it would be well to recall that, for

a century, Western gunboats had plied up and down the rivers of China, in addition to patrolling the country's ports. It was true that some dangerous extremists in Japan had grandiose visions of conquest. But, Elizabeth believed, they were a minority in a deeply divided government. Most Japanese wanted a more democratic political system at home and an end to aggression abroad. Even the Japanese army, she argued, contained officers "who want to withdraw from China to be ready for the real enemy—Soviet Russia." But instead of helping these sympathetic interests, the United States and other Western powers were humiliating them by expressing moral indignation and shutting Japan off from its natural trade patterns.[10]

The position of Japanese who opposed the militarist government "has been made much more difficult by immigration and trade restrictions and by racial discrimination on the part of the Western powers." Elizabeth was correct in her feeling about racial prejudice, as the government's wartime "internment" of more than one hundred thousand Americans of Japanese descent would prove. Meanwhile, federal officials turned down Elizabeth's offer to employ and house internees at her horticultural nursery in Taconic. And in 1943, after sixteen months of war against Germany and Japan, a sample of the American people were asked: "Which country do you think we can get along with better after the war?" The response was 67 percent Germany, 8 percent Japan, and 25 percent no opinion.[11]

Much of what Elizabeth wrote was colored by her wariness of the Soviet Union: the continuing presence of Soviet troops in parts of Manchuria, Soviet assistance to Mao Zedong's Communist Revolution in China, and the long-standing rivalry between Russia and Japan. Ever since the Bolshevik Revolution, Japan had stood as a barrier to Soviet expansion in the Far East. So, just as her husband feared the Soviet Union as the most serious long-term threat to Europe, Elizabeth Schumpeter regarded it as a menace to Asia as well.

Elizabeth's articles brought vehement objections from pro-Chinese interests, but she never flinched. In one long reply to a hostile letter published in *Pacific Affairs,* she repeated that economic sanctions had no chance of turning the Japanese people against their nation's army. "Human nature does not react in that way unless on the point of exhaustion." Instead, a policy of further sanctions would "unite the whole [Japanese] nation and make even the moderates feel that there is nothing left to do but to support the army to the bitter end, and, if necessary, enter into an unholy alliance with Russia." She went on to say—again with notable foresight—that "if Japan is confronted with a choice between complete submission (which would reduce her to a third-rate power) or a final desperate attack in the South Seas, I believe it probable that the militarist party would choose to attack." She wrote these lines in July 1940, well over a year before the actual attack on Pearl Harbor in December 1941.[12]

ELIZABETH CONTINUED TO publish a stream of articles, but her principal statement came in her book of 1940, *The Industrialization of Japan and Manchukuo, 1930–1940: Population, Raw Materials and Industry.* In addition to organizing this project and editing the book, she wrote six of its twenty-eight chapters, including the introduction and conclusion. The book as a whole is an earnest and scholarly 944-page effort to understand Japan's capabilities and problems. Crammed with numbers and tables, it almost surely contained the most comprehensive set of statistics on the rise of the Japanese economy that existed in any single book available in English.[13]

But in the context of Japan's war with China, the book's subject was almost too hot for academics to handle. As Elizabeth stated in her preface, "It is difficult today for a scholar to be honest about political and economic conditions in the so-called totalitarian states. Anyone who concludes that a country such as Japan had certain legitimate economic grievances, that some of its economic policies and practices have been successful and that it is stronger economically than is commonly supposed, is widely suspected of being a sympathizer with aggression and a member of the 'fifth column.' This tendency seems rather unfortunate because to overcome aggression, we need to know what helped to bring it about and how strongly it is entrenched."[14]

At the very end of the book, Elizabeth concludes that Japan has serious but not insuperable problems. These are mostly political, and they derive not only from deranged militarists inside the country but also from the exclusionary policies of the Western powers. If these nations, including the United States, would open their colonies to trade, then "the potential markets for the output of Japanese industries would be tremendous." But if the war with China should continue, Japan's people "will be called upon to make heavier and heavier sacrifices because it is so easy to start a war and so difficult to negotiate a wise and generous peace."[15]

By the time the book appeared in 1940, Japan's war with China had been going on for three years, and Hitler's war in Europe had begun the year before. In this situation, as might have been expected, reviewers of the book expressed a variety of opinions. Nearly all of them noted the general ignorance of most people concerning Japan, and they praised the volume as a valuable reference work. While almost all reviewers admired the authors' diligent collection of statistics, some questioned the accuracy of figures supplied by the Japanese government, and several argued that the book should have been published in separate pieces. But for the most part, reviews were favorable.[16]

Unfavorable reviewers took particular aim at Elizabeth's apparent tilt in favor of Japan at the expense of China. Some were also annoyed by her observation that Japan's recovery from the Great Depression had been the most impressive of any industrialized nation—and very much stronger than those of the United States and France. She wrote that the Western democracies might have something to learn from this superior performance, even though it unfortunately coincided with the rise of authoritarianism.[17]

One of the clearest-minded reviews came from C. R. Fay of Cambridge University, who praised the research of the four authors and concluded that "the moral of this book for the West is twofold: (1) Economic sanctions recoil on those who impose them long before they hurt those on whom they are imposed; (2) Japan's war effort is not dependent on anything which America and Europe supply." Fay added that if sanctions were tightened, Japan "would miss oil, but if it is not sent from the United States or Mexico, it might be seized from Netherlands Indies [sic]. The authors of this book might perhaps have made it more clear that they are writing throughout of a State at war (actual or intended). In Japan, when finance ministers fail to please, the army assassinates them. This is barbarism, and it is a pity that the authors do not at some point say so."[18]

Elizabeth well knew that her attitude toward Japan did not accord with popular views in the United States. The American Council of the Institute of Pacific Relations, which favored very strong measures against Japan, stopped inviting her to participate in its programs. As she wrote David Lawrence, a prominent journalist and the editor of *United States News,* "In general the American public has been very badly informed as to the situation in Japan by missionaries, fellow-travelers [intellectuals who admired communism], and incompetent journalists." All were vastly underestimating Japan's industrial strength.[19]

Meanwhile, Japan's government was fast slipping into the hands of the army, which advocated aggressive expansion in East Asia and was known for its brutality. In October 1941 the besieged Prime Minister Fumimaro Konoye resigned because the army would not compromise. He was replaced by the authoritarian General Hideki Tojo, one of Japan's leading imperialists. Konoye had long sought some kind of accommodation with the United States, but the reckless Tojo and his cabinet had no such goal.

Convinced by her own research that Japan was a very powerful adversary, Elizabeth Schumpeter saw no reason to change her mind as the war clouds gathered. And she was growing frustrated by the deaf response to her warnings. As she wrote to David Rockefeller in 1940, "You mustn't feel that you have to be so polite about acknowledging the literature I send out. It is becoming a bad habit with me because I just don't like to be suppressed." Before the collapse of the Konoye government, she had continued to write articles warning of the consequences of heavy-handed pressure against Japan. In the fall of 1941 she wrote to members of Congress that during the previous March, the Post Office had stopped the entry of Japanese periodicals into the United States. That step deprived researchers of current information and was, Elizabeth wrote, "a wholesale and indiscriminate censorship of foreign newspapers and periodicals without any notification to American subscribers or to the general public." By November 1941 she had concluded that the chances of an American war against Japan were fifty-fifty.[20]

On December 7 the Japanese launched their surprise attack on the naval base at Pearl Harbor. The United States declared war on Japan the following day. Three days after that, Adolf Hitler declared war on the United States.

On December 15, 1941, Elizabeth wrote to Frederick Lewis Allen, editor of *Harper's Magazine,* offering to contribute an analysis of the strength of the Japanese economy and to warn the American people of the likelihood of a long war.

> If we are to defeat the Japanese and the Germans we must become
> a great deal more realistic and we must stop underestimating
> them. If, for example, Japan should take Singapore it would prob-
> ably solve her raw material problems. She would have access to all
> the iron ore, bauxite and petroleum she needs and would also be
> able to see that Germany got ample supplies of rubber, tin and
> tungsten.

Allen did not accept Elizabeth's proposal for an article. Just two months later, again to the world's amazement, thirty thousand Japanese troops seized Singapore. They captured eighty-five thousand defenders, in what Winston Churchill called "the worst disaster and largest capitulation in British history."[21]

Around the time of Singapore's fall, the journalist William H. Chamberlin wrote a review for the *New York Times* of two new books on Japan. He made a special point of the naive view of Japan held by most Americans before the attack on Pearl Harbor. "In that faraway period the optimist was the man who believed that Japan could be blotted off the map within six weeks, the pessimist the man who suggested that the Island Empire might hold out for six months." In the end the war consumed almost four years. Because the two books under review were so brief, aggregating only 247 pages between them, Chamberlin advised readers "to turn to a massive piece of research that attracted less attention than it deserved when it appeared: *The Industrialization of Japan and Manchukuo, 1930–1940* by E. B. Schumpeter and associates."[22]

Meanwhile, Elizabeth had been asked to interview for a job at the Office of Production Management in Washington, a mobilization agency heavily staffed with economists. "I talked it over with Joe and we decided that I should go if I could really be useful." Her departure would have entailed a substantial sacrifice for Elizabeth herself and a radical upheaval in her husband's life. But soon Elizabeth was dropped from consideration—blackballed because of her appraisals of Japan's power. As she wrote a friend, "Since you managed to live down being right about Germany perhaps you can advise as to how I can return to favor in spite of having been reasonably accurate in my predictions about Japanese strength." But she did not return to favor; and soon both she and her husband began to pay further penalties for their unpopular views.[23]

20

Alienation

Gossip is mischievous, light and easy to raise,
but grievous to bear and hard to get rid of.

HESIOD, *Works and Days,* c. 700 B.C.

THE SCHUMPETERS' VIEWS of America's potential adversaries got
them both in hot water as the nation moved closer to war. In April 1941 the
FBI began an investigation of Elizabeth Schumpeter because of her writings
on Japan. Later in the same year the inquiry expanded to include Joseph
Schumpeter. Their cumulative FBI dossier grew to a thickness of about two
inches, containing 330 pages. It is available under the Freedom of Information
Act, but many passages—and a few entire pages, apparently containing the
names of agents, informers, and others—are blacked out (in legal terminology,
"redacted"). Many of the passages that do survive are full of misinformation
and bumbling errors. In the quotations that follow, I have included corrections
in square brackets.[1]

The first FBI letter in the file, dated April 18, 1941, identifies Elizabeth as a
Cambridge resident living at 7 Arcadia [Acacia] Street, and as editor of *The Industrialization of Japan and Manchuko* [Manchukuo], *1930 to 1940.* It reports
that "the above individual may be engaged in activities detrimental to the national defense of this country," in addition to other "possible un-American activities." The letter cautions against interviewing "the suspect."

Joseph Schumpeter first appears as a target of investigation in an FBI report dated July 1, 1941. This document identifies him as "former Austrian Finance Minister, reported escaped to the United States with considerable sum of money." Schumpeter's salaries at Harvard and Yale for the academic year 1940–1941 are accurately recorded in the file. An FBI directive instructs the New Haven office to "locate the present whereabouts" of Elizabeth and "conduct an investigation as to her present activities." A similar probe of Joseph is to be managed from the Boston office. Thus, the two Schumpeters became part of the same investigation, and their activities treated as part of a single case.

A report of July 22, 1942, discloses that Joseph Schumpeter married Elizabeth D. [Romaine Elizabeth] Boody in 1935 [1937]. Joseph is "considered sympathetic towards Germans by one informant but otherwise a loyal American. No evidence of espionage. Elizabeth B. Schumpeter has written books praising Japan and previous to Pearl Harbor in favor of Japanese over Chinese." Later in 1942, FBI Director J. Edgar Hoover ordered the Boston SAC (Special Agent in Charge) to inquire as to Elizabeth's connection with "Harvard University and Radcliff[e] University [College]." He instructed the agent to interview "Japanese informants" and try "to secure evidence that she has acted as a paid propagandist." Hoover advised in a memo of January 1943 that there is "a fairly strong possibility of a violation" of the Espionage Act. He ordered that the investigation be stepped up.

In a communication dated three months later, Hoover identified Elizabeth as "a member of the Bureau of National [International] Research at Howard [Harvard] University and Radcliffe College." The FBI chief directed the Boston SAC to question former employees of the Japanese Consulate, the Japanese Chamber of Commerce, and the Japanese Institute "regarding their knowledge of Mrs. Schumpeter's propaganda dissemination for the Japanese." On April 15 the SAC reported that in the FBI's weekly conference with ONI (the Office of Naval Intelligence) and G-2 (the army's intelligence unit), the ONI agent "advised that he knows the Subject of this case well; that his wife is particularly friendly with Schumpeter's wife; that Schumpeter is a former banker from Vienna; that he is strictly anti-Nazi" but that the FBI should question him.[2]

The following month, Hoover urged a more detailed inquiry into Elizabeth's book, giving as the title *The Industrialization of Japan and Manchukuo—1930–1931* [1930–1940], including "an examination of the records of the McMillan

[Macmillan] Publishing Company." He directed that "consideration should be given to the possibility that this book was deliberately published as a Japanese propaganda item and that Mrs. Schumpeter sought the collaboration of other recognized writers in order to remove any suspicion that the book contained propaganda." In a second directive, Hoover instructed the Boston office to determine the source of large bank deposits made by Elizabeth Schumpeter.

In May 1943 an agent from Boston forwarded to Washington his own evaluation of Elizabeth's book. All four of its authors appear on the title page with only their initials; thus, Elizabeth is E. B. Schumpeter, "with aliases, Elizabeth Romaine Boody [Romaine Elizabeth], and Elizabeth Romaine Furski [Firuski]." The agent's nine-page summary speculates, but does not conclude, that "ten per cent of the material written by the Subject, ELIZABETH SCHUMPETER, is propaganda, which expresses her's or other's [sic] views on the Japanese question, and is pro-Japanese. The rest of the book is considered basically sound economically."

The report goes on to say that "Mrs. Schumpeter's material might reflect the views and attitudes of a loyal American, anxious to secure an American policy toward Japan which would be more acceptable to the latter, and less likely to lead to international friction. In any case, information is not available to this unit which shows clearly any intention either to aid or to oppose the Japanese, in writing this material. There is no information available, moreover, which indicates that pro-Japanese propagandists made any effort to use this material." The report adds that a search of materials "at the Widner [Widener] Library at Harvard" yielded no further information. The agent concludes by summarizing "Undeveloped Leads," such as: "It should be noted that Mrs. Schumpeter was at one time married to a man by the name of Romaine Furski [Maurice Firuski] and lived in the vicinity of Hartford" [actually 55 miles from Hartford].

In a memo dated two weeks later (May 27, 1943) J. Edgar Hoover reported to his field agents that "this case presents fairly good possibilities for eventually reaching prosecution." Accordingly, he ordered "continuous investigative attention." In response, the Boston office advised that in October 1939 Joseph Schumpeter had given a speech to the Cambridge Club about the war in Europe. He had said, according to the FBI report, that even if the Allies won, Germany would likely end up under tyrannical rule, either by the Nazis or the

Bolsheviks, and that the best way to halt the war would be to make concessions to Germany.

In the same document, the FBI described at some length Schumpeter's Lowell Lectures of March 1941. Schumpeter had said, according to the reporting agent, that even those Germans not friendly to Hitler would fight hard to preserve the country's borders and avert another Versailles-type humiliation. Schumpeter had indicated that the likeliest possibility was that "come what may Russia will be the victor and things will be done in the East as Russia wants and not as the allies wish." Schumpeter further "declared himself to be Champion of Democracies—and therefore against Nazi Doctrines, pointed out that he is a realist not given to wishful thinking and feels obliged to face facts and accept them as means of minimizing the sad state of the world." The FBI agent acknowledged that in his own analysis of the Lowell Lectures he had relied on newspaper accounts. "I guess the only way you can get the subject matter and substance of this birds [bird's] lectures is to ask him if he ever had them published or ask him if he retained his notes from which he lectured."

The FBI then turned its attention to Elizabeth's articles. The bureau's report quoted at great length from her essay, "The Policy of the United States in the Far East," published in July 1940. When Elizabeth wrote this piece in April of that year, the war had been going on in Europe for eight months and in China for three years. America's entry was still twenty months in the future.

In the article, Elizabeth judged U.S. policy to be ineffectual—the product of "obviously wishful thinking" that vastly underestimated the industrial might of Japan. "Countries in the position of Italy, Germany, and Japan cannot be coerced by means of economic sanctions with the ease we once thought possible." Attempts to do so "may even seem to give a kind of moral justification to what would otherwise be a campaign of pure aggression."

An FBI agent reported in August 1943 that "the Bureau has advised that prosecution is probable in this case," that is, the consolidated case against both Schumpeters. In his Lowell Lectures, the report continued, Schumpeter had "advised that Germany had the war won and the only sensible thing to do would be to give Germany her gains and to make peace." This was not an accurate characterization. Nor was a statement in the same report that Elizabeth had married Joseph after her "two previous unsuccessful marriages." Nor was still another statement in a supplementary memo that Elizabeth had "traveled in Japan." She never did, either before or after the war.

After several months of relative quiet, FBI Director Hoover upbraided the special agent in charge of the Schumpeter investigation, in a memo dated March 17, 1944. "This case is extremely delinquent in your office and it is desired that the outstanding leads be covered and that the case be brought to a conclusion in the near future." Hoover instructed the Boston office to interview Elizabeth, and he went on to provide two sets of guidelines for about twenty-five questions to be asked, such as: Why did she choose to study the economic conditions of Japan? Did she believe any of the book she edited and coauthored was propaganda? Prior to 1941 who did she wish to see victorious, China or Japan? Does she feel Japan has been treated unfairly by the United States? Did she know that the Japanese would buy her book before she wrote it? Did they help her with suggestions or proofread it before it was published?

Agents interviewed Elizabeth in July 1944. She told them that in approximately 1934, [name blacked out] had asked her to supervise research on Japan. At that time, very little was known about the Japanese economy, and "the United States and especially various economists in this country were interested in Japan as a competitor in commerce. She advised at this time there was no thought of war and that she, like most Americans, had no idea that a conflict was to follow."

The sources for her work were mainly Japanese publications. Also, the majority of her correspondents in Japan were scholars who themselves were "opposed to the military group of Japan . . . [and] were by and large anti-Tojo and believed that a catastrophe in the Far East could be avoided. She stated that this group did not favor war and believed until the last moment that difficulties would be settled through negotiations."

Her book was on general economic conditions and "did not take up to any extent strategic materials." She never solicited or received any money from the Japanese government for her work. "She stated she had pointed out that Japan was ready to go to war and that economic sanctions imposed upon Japan by any nation would probably have to be backed up by force. She stated her opinions stated at that time were later borne out by the present conflict . . . most of the research done on the book was finished by 1938 which was before the Far

Eastern situation became tense . . . All logical leads in this investigation having been concluded, this case is being closed."

J. Edgar Hoover had other ideas, however. Deeming the agents' interview with Elizabeth unsatisfactory, he did not accept the closing of the case. He noted that her book was published at the expense of the Bureau of International Research at Harvard, with no provision for royalties. This led him to surmise that some sort of subsidy might have been funneled from Japanese sources to the book's publisher. Also, bank records showed that Mrs. Schumpeter had deposited a substantial sum of money during the late 1930s. The FBI, Hoover ordered, should ascertain where these funds came from. He ended with the admonition that "the Bureau is forced to the conclusion that a very cursory review of the file must have been made prior to interviewing the subject. She should be reinterviewed by an agent who has adequately prepared himself in advance for the undertaking. You should see to it that this is done and that Mrs. Schumpeter is reinterviewed at an early date."

The reinterview occurred in three sessions during late October and early November 1944, at the Schumpeters' country home in Taconic. The interviewer learned that "large bank deposits made in 1938 [$12,000 in several installments] came from proceeds of sale of house in Taconic." (This was the old house that Elizabeth and Joseph never occupied.) Elizabeth "denies that she received any proceeds from the sale of the book whatever. Admits, however, she was paid a total of $55 for two articles written on Japan, one for 'Oriental Economist' and other for 'Living Age.' States that article written for 'Living Age' never published." She "called attention to the fact that all books published by the Bureau of International Research were published by the McMillan Company" under an ongoing contract. The agent who conducted the reinterview concluded that because "it appears there are no further logical leads to be covered in this case, it is being closed, subject to being reopened upon request for further investigation by the Bureau."

Three weeks later, on December 1, 1944, Assistant Attorney General (and future Supreme Court Justice) Tom C. Clark advised J. Edgar Hoover "that prosecution of either of the above subjects [Joseph and Elizabeth] is not contemplated by the Criminal Division." With that, the investigation of the Schumpeters ended, at least for the time being. Nowhere in the thick FBI dossier is there any mention of Schumpeter's landmark book of 1942, *Capitalism, Socialism and Democracy,* which evidently escaped the bureau's attention.

After the war, in a memo of April 19, 1948, the FBI reported that Joseph Schumpeter's name had come up in a series of articles in *The Chicago Tribune* "relating to reported Communist infiltration and activity at Harvard University." And in 1950 and 1951 Elizabeth was questioned still again.[3]

The main investigation of the Schumpeters went on for three years and eight months, from April 1941 to December 1944. During that period, the managers of Elizabeth's bank provided statements of her accounts. Both Harvard and Yale divulged Joseph Schumpeter's salary. FBI agents interviewed not only the two "suspects" but also their friends, associates, and neighbors. Word quickly got around in Cambridge, Taconic, New Haven, and elsewhere that the Schumpeters' loyalty was in question, at a time when the United States was engaged in a deadly two-theater war. Inevitably, many of their acquaintances began to view them in a different light, and they suffered some cold shoulders and rejection. In this sense, they were simply unlucky, like large numbers of other citizens with prewar ties to Germany and Japan.[4]

Throughout the war years, both Schumpeters dropped most of their usual social intercourse. Hundreds of their friends, students, and colleagues had joined the army or navy. Others had left for Washington to work in mobilization agencies, as Elizabeth herself would have done had she not been blackballed. Wartime Harvard took on some of the tenor of a military academy. The enrollment of regular students diminished, and large parts of the university were given over to the training of officers.

Meanwhile, Joseph Schumpeter's contacts with Europe also shrank, as war engulfed the continent. A professor at the University of Kiel wrote him in 1940 that "as far as your work goes, it seems up to now to have been insufficiently disseminated in Central Europe." The professor himself had finally received his copy of *Business Cycles* but only after long delays. "In Germany I hear again and again from colleagues that they haven't seen it," as mail connections with the United States grew ever less dependable. Then, too, Schumpeter's weekly letters from Mia Stöckel unaccountably ceased in March 1941. "How the world turns fascist!" he wrote in his diary later that year. "Nobody *wills* it & it comes like a geological age."[5]

As the academic year ended in June 1941, the Schumpeters retreated to Taconic and began to live a cloistered life. Schumpeter wrote his friend Redvers Opie that "I want to bury myself in my work, mainly of a purely theoretical character, and to do my best to live through that most irritating of all situations, which is to have to look on events without being able to help."[6]

Their one great comfort was scholarship. Elizabeth continued writing about the Far East. Joseph, toiling obsessively in both Taconic and Cambridge, turned out an immense amount of work. He wrote his Lowell Lectures and labored very hard on *Capitalism, Socialism and Democracy*. In addition, he launched what was to become a monumental history of economic analysis. During the academic year, from September to June, he taught his classes on economic theory, business cycles, and the history of economic thought. He usually held one class session per day, six days a week. (Saturdays were not yet holidays at American universities.) Even though he often taught the same courses in successive years, he never gave the same lecture twice, either then or at any other time during his career. This kind of fresh attention to teaching is rare in academic life. Many professors speak from old dog-eared drafts year after year, with minimal changes.[7]

Schumpeter also continued to give talks and seminars at other schools, though less often than before. "I love to establish contact with groups of graduate students," he wrote his faculty host at Johns Hopkins in 1940, "and I hope you will allow me to have consultation hours for any who may care to have a personal chat with me." But the Keynesian craze was still on the rise, and he complained in his diary that "I am *vexed* in my inability to convey my message to youngsters."[8]

As Schumpeter worked on the manuscript of *Capitalism, Socialism and Democracy*, he grew more depressed about the state of the world. His diary entries during this period contain few references to his friends and colleagues, or to Elizabeth. Nor do the *Hasen* make their customary appearance. He even says little about the specifics of his own work. He does refer occasionally to a huge new project on the history of economic analysis, and he makes one telling reference to his continuing labors on *Capitalism, Socialism and Democracy*: "I have pushed hard on that socialism book and the situation simply teaches me once again that any achievement, however small, requires desperate concentration and neglect of all other plans . . . God what suffering 'writing' means!"[9]

In his self-imposed isolation and rigorous work routine, his correspondence dwindled to practically nothing. For several months he even stopped opening his mail. Just before the Japanese attack on Pearl Harbor, he wrote an extraordinary confession of how he was living his life and mailed it to a professor at the University of Florida whom he barely knew. He apologized for not responding to repeated invitations to speak there:

> I am ashamed about my behavior . . . your letters, though they
> didn't elicit any answer, have set me thinking and this is what I
> discovered. I do not work less but rather more than I used to in
> former years and I am even not aware myself (though other people
> may [be]) that my work declines in quality. I can even discuss with
> students into the small hours of the morning occasionally and I
> have as yet no difficulty in learning new techniques. But the secret
> of this is that all the rest of my life has almost completely ceased. I
> have discontinued my various interests in art, never go out if I can
> help it, and severely disregard all social obligations. There are, for
> instance, friends of mine here in Cambridge who are quite inti-
> mate but whom I never see. Well, and this explains the almost
> pathological attitude I have in my correspondence. It accumulates
> in heaps and most of it I do not even open except what immedi-
> ately asserts itself as part of professional duty as the correspon-
> dence of and for the Econometric Society. I have been so prolix
> because I really do not want any misunderstanding and only per-
> fect explicitness and frankness avail to avoid it. Having done so,
> however, I do wish to express a hope that I shall mend my ways at
> least with respect to you and a few others.[10]

During this time of isolation and self-doubt, Schumpeter continued to work tirelessly on *Capitalism, Socialism and Democracy*. In this effort, his emotional agonies did not diminish his genius at all, and may even have fueled his creativity.

Certainly he seems to have had little idea that he was composing a book destined to become a classic. In April 1942 he wrote to the prominent New York publisher Cass Canfield of Harper & Brothers:

> Thanks for your letter. With apologies for the delay, I am now sending the manuscript to you. Knowing nothing of the organization of your House, I have to address it to you personally.
>
> There exists only the copy which I am sending. For this and other reasons I should feel much obliged if, in case you should see objections to acceptance, you would be good enough to have the manuscript returned to me as soon as convenient.[11]

Harper made a fortune on *Capitalism, Socialism and Democracy* and is still earning handsome revenues on the book to this day. Luckily for all concerned—author, publisher, and the world at large—mail service between Cambridge and New York was in those days very reliable, and a masterpiece reached the hands of generations of readers.

2 1

Capitalism, Socialism and Democracy

The inherent vice of capitalism is the unequal sharing of
blessings; the inherent virtue of socialism is the equal sharing of miseries.

WINSTON CHURCHILL, at a White House luncheon, 1954

ONLY THREE YEARS after the relative failure of *Business Cycles,*
Schumpeter made a spectacular recovery, publishing in 1942 the most popular
of all his works, *Capitalism, Socialism and Democracy.* He wrote most of this
book in thirty months, during which he faced many other demands on his
time. He composed it more or less from his personal intellectual storehouse,
fusing all the learning and passion of forty years of scholarship into one brilliant synthesis. At 381 pages, *Capitalism, Socialism and Democracy* is only one
third the length of *Business Cycles* and unencumbered by the academic minutiae of the earlier work. Even so, it radiates profound erudition. It is an eloquent book, bursting with apt metaphors and telling asides. It ranges through
world history and literature all the way from ancient Greece and Rome to the
time of its publication.[1]

Translated into at least sixteen languages, *Capitalism, Socialism and Democracy* is still purchased widely in paperback editions throughout the world.
Although the author liked to disparage it as a potboiler and to compare it
unfavorably with his more scholarly books, it spawned many thousands of fu-

ture citations by journalists, political scientists, sociologists, economists, and historians.

Schumpeter began writing the book as a series of essays, partly in response to the rising popularity of Marxist thinking during the 1930s. In his diary he referred to it as "that socialism book." But the most compelling argument in *Capitalism, Socialism and Democracy* is about capitalism—appropriately, the first word in its title. Schumpeter shows how capitalism shapes not only the economic life of communities in which it operates but also their intellectual, social, and political cultures. The book contains one of the most perceptive analyses of capitalism ever written.

It is especially strong in its treatment of big business, and Schumpeter could not have written it without having done so much research for *Business Cycles*. Given the disappointing reception of that book and its unfavorable comparison to Keynes's *General Theory*, the content and ironic tone of *Capitalism, Socialism and Democracy* take on a different light. It is as if Schumpeter decided to spurn all caution and unburden himself on a wide array of subjects in addition to economics, narrowly construed. Hence the book's uncommon breadth and stealthy wit. Parts of it are written in a deadpan satirical style worthy of Jonathan Swift or Mark Twain. Schumpeter does not want to hit the reader over the head with a paean to capitalism, and much of what he writes—particularly in the sections where he seems to be supporting socialist ideas—cannot be taken at face value.[2]

Although it draws on almost all of Schumpeter's earlier works, *Capitalism, Socialism and Democracy* is framed against the particular backgrounds of the Great Depression and World War II. He poses three momentous questions:

> First, is capitalism, by its own nature and process, doomed to failure?
> Second, if socialism replaces capitalism, can it produce comparable economic success?
> Third, is democracy likely to accompany either system?

The book begins with a penetrating and wholly serious fifty-eight-page analysis of Karl Marx's work, presented in four chapters: Marx as prophet, as sociologist, as economist, and as teacher. It is hard to avoid the thought that Schumpeter regarded himself in these same roles. Certainly he credited Marx with a dynamic vision of capitalism much like his own: "Now Marx saw this process of industrial change more clearly and he realized its pivotal importance more fully than any other economist of his time." Marx "was the first economist of top rank to see and to teach systematically how economic theory may be turned into historical analysis and how the historical narrative may be turned into *histoire raisonée*." He accomplished a blend of history and theory whose result represented something different from either one alone.[3]

Nevertheless, Schumpeter rejects Marx's version of the story. Marx the sociologist was wrong because of his oversimplified view of social classes. In the Marxian system, capitalist society contains only two classes: capitalists, who own and control the means of production, and proletarians, who do not. Schumpeter's response is that workers are not all alike, and that in the modern era "supernormal intelligence and energy" have enabled large numbers of proletarians to found businesses and become capitalists themselves.[4]

Still more mistaken was Marx the economist. Among his many errors, Marx insisted that as capitalism matured, workers' share of society's total income would steadily fall. Their misery would increase, and finally they would revolt and seize the means of production from the capitalists. After this action, in which "the expropriators are expropriated," workers would control the economy for the benefit of all.[5]

Schumpeter's rebuttal was two-fold. First, he pointed out that in historical fact, workers' share of total income had not diminished during the rise of industrialism. Measured by percentages, their share had either held steady or increased. And in absolute terms, workers' incomes had grown dramatically, and their standard of living had risen, because capitalism both raises incomes and reduces the cost of goods.[6]

Marx had also argued that the mechanization of production would create a "reserve army" of the unemployed—a growing mass of workers ripe for still more exploitation. That too had simply not occurred. Marx had "swallowed hook, line and sinker" David Ricardo's argument about the deleterious effects of mechanization on employment, while paying scant attention to Ricardo's careful qualifications. These were not Marx's only serious errors, and Schumpeter recites a litany of other mistakes and omissions. Marx had "no adequate theory of enterprise." He failed to "distinguish the entrepreneur from the capitalist." He had no tenable conception of big business. His system did not deal effectively with business cycles. And, like the classical economists, he usually thought in terms of what came to be called "perfect competition."[7]

Regardless of the faults Schumpeter found with Marx, he fully appreciated the breadth and depth of his influence in setting the agenda of public discourse. And it was especially easy to see why Marx the prophet and Marx the teacher had become so fashionable during the 1930s. People embraced his "message of the terrestrial paradise of socialism" not only because it seemed such an improvement on current conditions but also because it addressed "that feeling of being thwarted and ill treated which is the auto-therapeutic attitude of the unsuccessful many." Marxism promised that "socialistic deliverance from those ills was a certainty amenable to rational proof." By creating a system that explained not only economics but also historical events, Marx enabled common people to "no longer feel out of it in the great affairs of life—all at once they see through the pompous marionettes of politics and business."[8]

During the Great Depression of the 1930s, masses of jobless workers undeniably bore some resemblance to Marx's reserve army of the unemployed. As Schumpeter observed, "Disheartened bourgeois and elated intellectuals" interpreted the Depression and the subsequent tepid recovery as "symptoms of a structural change in the capitalist process such as Marx expected to occur." But, Schumpeter argued, equally severe depressions had come and gone, and the elusiveness of strong recovery in the 1930s could be explained in ways Marx had never considered. Keynes had provided one plausible explanation: consumers' insufficient purchasing power. And in Schumpeter's own analysis, "difficulties incident to the adaptation to a new fiscal policy, new labor legislation, and a general change in the attitude of government to private enterprise" had made the Depression worse. Most serious of all—particularly in the United States—there had been a wholly unnecessary epidemic of bank failures.[9]

TURNING FROM THE simplicity and purported certainty of Marx's economic utopia, Schumpeter poses his own deceptively guileless question and answer: "Can capitalism survive? No. I do not think that it can."[10]

The argument that follows this memorable beginning to the second part of *Capitalism, Socialism and Democracy* is complex, closely reasoned, and filled with historical detail. The assertion itself is very carefully hedged, in numerous passages. Schumpeter's real purpose is not to prophesy capitalism's downfall but to explain how it works. He is at pains to demonstrate why capitalism has been a very good thing—and then to underscore its fragility.[11]

He acknowledges that many readers will lack the patience to give his discussion sufficiently close attention. He goes so far as to say that "the public mind has by now so thoroughly grown out of humor with it as to make condemnation of capitalism and all its works a foregone conclusion." Writers and speakers of almost all political persuasions believe in "the inadequacies of capitalist achievement." Many have come to regard capitalism itself as antisocial and even immoral. Therefore, the path of refutation Schumpeter has marked out for himself will not be easy.[12]

He begins his argument by demonstrating that modern industrial capitalism has produced the greatest per capita output of goods ever recorded. And, in direct contravention of the Marxian forecast that workers' share of income will steadily fall, Schumpeter repeats that "relative shares have substantially changed in favor of the lower income groups." Regardless of subjective assessments by popular writers and literary intellectuals, statistics show that the average worker, under "an avalanche of consumers' goods," has a better material existence than ever before. In other words, "the capitalist process, not by coincidence but by virtue of its mechanism, progressively raises the standard of life of the masses."[13]

As James Tobin, one of Schumpeter's best Harvard students and himself a Nobel laureate, later wrote, "I have always thought that Schumpeter's ambition was to develop a theory of history of the same sweep and scope as Marx's, while at the same time turning Marxism upside down." And one major way in which Schumpeter upended Marx was in his treatment of the controversial question of monopoly. Writing in the 1930s and early 1940s—a time of mounting public anger over industrial concentration—Schumpeter emphasized that enormous improvements in the lives of common people had "evolved during the period of relatively unfettered 'big business.'" Far from diminishing the benefits consumers derived from the workings of the capitalist engine, businesses of grand size had increased them.[14]

In explaining how this happened, Schumpeter introduces his famous term "creative destruction": "The opening up of new markets, foreign or domestic, and the organizational development from the craft shop and factory to such concerns as U.S. Steel illustrate the same process of industrial mutation—if I may use that biological term—that incessantly revolutionizes the economic structure *from within,* incessantly destroying the old one, incessantly creating a new one. This process of Creative Destruction is the essential fact about capitalism. It is what capitalism consists in and what every capitalist concern has got to live in."[15]

Since creative destruction is an evolutionary process, the performance of capitalism must be judged "over time, as it unfolds through decades or centuries." Here, Schumpeter criticizes the approach of his fellow economists to the study of big business. It is useless, he says, to analyze a large company's behavior at a single point in time—that is, to "accept the data of the momentary situation as if there were no past or future to it." Yet this is the customary method. The typical economic theorist or government commission does not see the behavior of a major firm, "on the one hand, as a result of a piece of past history, and, on the other hand, as an attempt to deal with a situation that is sure to change presently—as an attempt by those firms to keep on their feet, on ground that is slipping away from under them. In other words, the problem that is usually being visualized is how capitalism administers existing structures, whereas the relevant problem is how it creates and destroys them."[16]

Creative destruction constantly sweeps out old products, old enterprises, and old organizational forms, replacing them with new ones. "Every piece of business strategy acquires its true significance only against the background of that process and within the situation created by it." Strategy, he goes on to say, "must be seen in its role in the perennial gale of creative destruction; it cannot be understood irrespective of it or, in fact, on the hypothesis that there is a perennial lull." Any investigator who does not recognize these essential characteristics, Schumpeter concludes, "does a meaningless job."[17]

In using the term "business strategy" and likening corporate initiatives to military behavior, Schumpeter helped to set off a revolution in the analysis of business that is still thriving today. "Business strategy" and "corporate strategy" have gained extremely wide currency not only in the business press but in popular media as well. Numerous consulting firms specialize in strategy, and all business schools teach courses in it. Most of these schools have an entire department with the word "strategy" or "strategic" in its name. Hundreds of business books and thousands of articles published over the last six decades include "strategy" in their titles. It has been one of the most significant new ideas in business thinking since the 1940s.[18]

In *Capitalism, Socialism and Democracy,* Schumpeter next mounts a spirited assault on the idea of "perfect competition," a key theoretical tool used by academic economists in his own time and in ours as well. Models of perfect competition cannot take business strategy into consideration because they assume that every industry contains innumerable firms, each of which is by definition too weak to affect the economic landscape through strategic behavior. Perfect competition assumes unlimited numbers of both buyers and sellers, all of whom possess complete information about all products and services being bought and sold. Such models contemplate frictionless transactions, with no need for lawyers, accountants, brokers, partnerships, corporations, contracts, or other essential accoutrements of actual business.

Perfect competition lends itself very well to mathematical modeling, however, and that advantage has been almost irresistible to economists. But because it neglects the dynamics of creative destruction, Schumpeter finds perfect competition wholly unsuitable for understanding a modern capitalist economy. When, for example, a new product or process is introduced, all buyers and sellers cannot possibly have complete information about potential markets. "As a matter of fact," Schumpeter writes, "perfect competition is and always has been temporarily suspended whenever anything new is being introduced." And the continual emergence of new products and new ways of doing things is "the fundamental impulse that sets and keeps the capitalist engine in motion."[19]

Despite its irrelevance to perfect competition, he continues, big-business capitalism has proved its superiority, in the long run, at expanding total output and raising living standards: "The actual efficiency of the capitalist engine of production in the era of the largest-scale units has been much greater than in the preceding era of small or medium-sized ones. This is a matter of statistical record . . . the technological and organizational possibilities [of firms in the perfect competition model] could never have produced similar results. How modern capitalism would work under perfect competition is hence a meaningless question."[20]

Schumpeter underscores the deficiencies of any conceptual system that proceeds from perfect competition and static assumptions. In so doing, he compares the universe of Adam Smith and other classical economists with the reality of modern industrial capitalism. Neither Smith nor most other classical and neoclassical economists "saw that perfect competition is the exception and that even if it were the rule there would be much less reason for congratulation than one might think." In real life, anything approaching perfect competition is extremely rare.[21]

Instead, much of modern business in advanced industrial countries has evolved into a form of organization known as "oligopoly." This word was introduced by Sir Thomas More in *Utopia* (1516), then revived 410 years later by Schumpeter's Harvard colleague E. H. Chamberlin. It now refers to industries in which a small number of large and powerful firms compete with one another in the same line of business: oil, steel, automobiles, chemicals, and a few others. Most of these companies are engaged in mass production, mass distribution, or both; and they often require very large capital investments. In oligopolies, Schumpeter writes, "there is in fact no determinate equilibrium at all and the possibility presents itself that there may be an endless sequence of moves and countermoves, an indefinite state of warfare between firms." Hence the analogy with military strategy. But these new situations—like other aspects of Schumpeter's theories, such as the pivotal importance of entrepreneurship—do not easily lend themselves to equilibrium analysis and to mathematical modeling.[22]

One result of the alternative approach Schumpeter proposes would be a sharper focus on product quality and marketing as elements of competition. This new perspective would reduce what had been an overwhelming emphasis on the analysis of price. "In capitalist reality as distinguished from its textbook picture, it is not [that kind of] competition which counts but the competition from the new commodity, the new technology, the new source of supply, the new type of organization." This kind of competition "strikes not at the margins of the profits and the outputs of the existing firms but at their foundations and their very lives." It is effective even "when it is merely an ever-present threat. It disciplines before it attacks." A theoretical analysis that "neglects this essential element of the case neglects all that is most typically capitalist about it; even if correct in logic as well as in fact, it is like *Hamlet* without the Danish prince."[23]

The reader of these passages should make no mistake about the radical nature of what Schumpeter is asserting. He is indicting his own economics profession for what amounts to a capital crime: failing to acknowledge that continuous innovation is "endogenous to" (inherent in) capitalism. If this one conceptual alteration were adopted in orthodox economics, then a whole series of methodological shifts would ensue. To the extent that economists become more focused on change, they would pay more attention to the *record* of change. They would have to pursue a much more thorough investigation of economic and business history, as Schumpeter himself had done in *Business Cycles.* And against that historical background, they would recognize that large-scale units of control were not merely to be tolerated as necessary evils. Instead, they would see big businesses as part and parcel of "the most powerful engine of [economic] progress and in particular of the long-run expansion of total output" that the world had ever witnessed.[24]

Schumpeter then returns to the question of monopoly, mounting an attack on many Americans' mistaken idea that monopoly and big business are the same thing. The word monopoly itself, he says, is a label "sure to rouse the public's hostility" because of its association with privileges bestowed by British kings during America's colonial period. Then, too, the evils of monopoly had been invoked by scores of American statesmen, from Andrew Jackson to Theodore Roosevelt and Woodrow Wilson and now by Franklin D. Roosevelt. But under modern capitalism, *long-run* cases of monopoly are almost nonexistent—even rarer than instances of perfect competition. Hence, high entrepreneurial profits are always temporary. And on balance, big business is unquestionably a positive force for innovation and growth.[25]

It was perverse, Schumpeter believed, that so many people in the United States had confused monopoly with big business and made the latter into a whipping boy. The country was, after all, the seedbed of giant firms. Because of its huge internal market and its entrepreneurial culture, it was the home of about half of the world's largest companies. Schumpeter felt very strongly about this issue, even more so than he reveals in *Capitalism, Socialism and Democracy.* And he believed that he had found a psychological reason for it. As he wrote in his diary: "American opinion is so anti big business precisely because big business has made the country what it now is and in doing so it has set the secret standard of the American soul: who is not part of big bus., feels he does not meet the standard and by compensation turns against it."[26]

It seemed plain to Schumpeter that continuous technical innovation and organizational remodeling, not monopolistic profits, accounted for the prosperity of most great companies. "These units," he says in *Capitalism, Socialism and Democracy,* "not only arise in the process of creative destruction and function in a way entirely different from the static schema" but often actually make their own markets: "They largely create what they exploit." Monopoly profits might flow for a while, but only briefly, in the form of big but single-pay-off "prizes offered by capitalist society to the successful innovator." Pushing his analysis to its limits, Schumpeter identifies capitalist entrepreneurship with technological progress itself. As a matter of historical record, they were "essentially one and the same thing," the first being "the propelling force" of the second.[27]

Schumpeter ends this part of his discussion of capitalism with a remarkable statement that foreshadows the ironic style he uses later in the book:

> I am not going to sum up as the reader presumably expects me to.
> That is to say, I am not going to invite him, before he decides to
> put his trust in an untried alternative advocated by untried men,
> to look once more at the impressive economic and the still more
> impressive cultural achievement of the capitalist order and at the
> immense promise held out by both. I am not going to argue that
> that achievement and that promise are in themselves sufficient to
> support an argument for allowing the capitalist process to work
> on and, as it might easily be put, to lift poverty from the shoulders
> of mankind . . . I am not going to argue, that on the strength of
> that performance, that the capitalist intermezzo is going to be
> prolonged. In fact, I am now going to draw the exactly opposite
> inference.[28]

He next lays the foundations for his much-quoted argument that capitalism has developed the seeds of its own destruction —not for economic reasons but for social ones. To show how this happened, he forthrightly traces the evolution of capitalism from its origins down to the present.[29]

In pre-capitalist times, he writes, no economic achievement, by itself, could advance anyone into the living standards of the ruling class. But when capitalism began to spread, persons of "supernormal ability and ambition" could now reach a much higher standard of living, provided they would pursue business careers. Yet business success did not confer the charisma that had attached to feudal lords and other leaders of earlier times: "no flourishing of swords about it, not much physical prowess, no chance to gallop the armored horse into the enemy."[30]

As time passed, however, the economic juggernaut of capitalism began to subvert most of the underpinnings of feudal society—knightly service, the craft guild, the village, the manor. In place of the old webs of reciprocal personal responsibilities—lord and knight, landowner and peasant, patron and artisan—capitalism substituted impersonal efficiency and opportunity. People were no longer part of an organic social system. They could achieve material gains, but they also became "free to make a mess of their lives." They now had sufficient "individualist rope" to hang themselves.[31]

Meanwhile, the talents necessary for business success did not translate well into other realms of life. "A genius in the business office may be, and often is, utterly unable outside of it to say boo to a goose—both in the drawing room and on the [political] platform." So, without protection from some other source, "the bourgeoisie is politically helpless and unable not only to lead its nation but even to take care of its particular class interest."[32]

That protection, Schumpeter says, had been provided—and still was—by those whom the capitalists had partially bested. As merchants and manufacturers began to dominate economic life, the groups who had led pre-capitalist society largely retained their old political and social positions. They lived more and more on their invested capital, which was expanded by the new business classes. And in return they played their traditional governing roles for the benefit of business.[33]

Even so, the rise of capitalism, and particularly of big business, undercut not only lords and kings but also many small producers and merchants. This was not a trivial consequence. Because of their large numbers, the owner-managers of small and medium-sized firms had great political and social clout. Nor did the big firms that sometimes superseded them embody quite the same proprietary spirit—the right and ability "to do as one pleases with one's own." In modern capitalism, the substitution of a share of stock for tangible assets "takes the life out of the idea of property." And if this trend goes on long enough, "there will be *nobody* left" to defend bourgeois values with vigor and determination. Also, large businesses do not command the same degree of loyalty from their workers as proprietorships and partnerships. Employees take economic progress for granted, but they have little emotional attachment to the success of their companies, or of the capitalist system as a whole. As replaceable cogs in a large wheel of enterprise, they feel personally insecure.[34]

Still other social and psychological effects can plague capitalist success, says Schumpeter. Because people have come to expect a continual flow of new products and methods, "innovation itself is being reduced to routine . . . economic progress tends to become depersonalized and automatized." Bureaucratic procedures and tiresome committee projects displace flashes of genius. Innovation does not cease (it may actually increase), but individual entrepreneurship becomes less salient.[35]

In addition, capitalism works gradual changes within the minds of individuals. By reducing everything to a calculus of costs and benefits, it "rationalizes" people's habits of thought. It "creates a critical frame of mind which, after having destroyed the moral authority of so many other institutions, in the end turns against its own." And unfortunately, the philosophical justification for capitalism is too detailed and complicated for the intellectual capacity of average citizens.[36]

The case for capitalism, says Schumpeter, "must rest on long-run considerations." In the short run, it is impossible for people generally, and even intellectuals, to ignore what seem to be unreasonable "profits and inefficiencies." They therefore have difficulty in seeing long-range trends in which capitalism is benefiting society as a whole. Uniquely among economic systems, therefore, capitalism "creates, educates and subsidizes a vested interest in social unrest." With its bountiful production, it underwrites the education of a class of hostile intellectuals who have no "direct responsibility for practical affairs" and little experience in managing anything.[37]

In the larger sense, the emotional feelings of human beings are so complicated that there can be no assurance that people in general are "happier" or "better off" under industrial capitalism than they had been in medieval manors or villages. Economic efficiency is only one of many human goals, and not necessarily the most important to every individual. Thus the future of capitalism cannot be assured on the basis of its superior economic performance alone.[38]

Much of Schumpeter's argument about the social decline of capitalism might be interpreted as a cry from the heart of a brilliant but chronically depressed European elitist who had witnessed one catastrophe after another during the bloody first half of the twentieth century. But from Schumpeter's viewpoint, even in the America of his own time, a unique opportunity for the development of an advanced capitalist society seemed to be tottering on the edge of disaster—because of the Great Depression, the ascendance of fascism and communism in Europe, and the onset of World War II. And irrespective of Schumpeter's own state of mind, the intellectual climate of the 1930s was almost surely more hostile to capitalism than during any other decade in American history.

No serious threat to capitalism had appeared earlier in the United States, Schumpeter explains, because "the scheme of values that arose from the national task of developing the economic possibilities of [the U.S.] drew nearly all the brains into business and impressed the businessman's attitudes upon the soul of the nation." The lackluster quality of American presidents in the late nineteenth century corroborates his point. Between 1865 and 1901, forgettable men such as Rutherford B. Hayes and Chester A. Arthur occupied the White House, while the entrepreneurial leadership of Andrew Carnegie, John D. Rockefeller, and many others left its mark on American history. But by the 1940s the era of "drawing all the brains into business" had long since passed.[39]

SCHUMPETER COVERED ALL that—his critique of Marx and his deep dissection of capitalism—in just the first two parts of *Capitalism, Socialism and Democracy.* Part III, "Can Socialism Work?" is perhaps his greatest achievement as a prose writer. Here he moves from a style of straightforward exposition to a mode of irony largely unknown in the discipline of economics. His method is to defend socialism by arguments of seemingly airtight logic, which nevertheless lead to very dubious conclusions. The challenge to the reader is to untangle the two and thereby discover the truth about socialism's shortcomings.

In answer to the question that opens Part III, "Can socialism work?" Schumpeter responds with the provocative statement, "Of course it can." But a close reading of the subsequent text reveals that he actually means, "Of course it can't," at least in comparison with capitalism. He is now writing in full ironic mode, like the satirist Jonathan Swift. "A Modest Proposal"—Swift's famous pamphlet of 1729—had suggested that problems of famine and overpopulation could be met by one simple step: feeding children from poor families to the rich. His proposal, Swift argued, was "innocent, cheap, easy and effectual."[40]

Schumpeter's Swiftian approach to socialism recalls to mind the delight he took as a young man in Vienna's coffeehouses, where political and artistic discussion often continued well into the night. In this kind of setting, no proposition was too absurd or too subtly hedged with conditions and exceptions. Speakers won admiration for their sarcasm and wit, no less than for the cogency of their arguments. To puncture a point of view while seeming to recommend it was especially delicious.[41]

When Schumpeter's fellow Austrian Fritz Machlup wrote a review of *Capitalism, Socialism and Democracy,* he recognized its "humorous-ironic rococo" style. Machlup knew Schumpeter well, and he had few doubts about his friend's high esteem for capitalism. In addition, "I have the firm impression that Schumpeter dislikes socialism, nay, despises it." Yet on the basis of the text alone, Machlup concedes that the book's argument is so subtle that "I read this between the lines only."[42]

Early in his treatment of socialism, Schumpeter asserts (contrary to almost everything else he had ever written) that he himself does not attribute "more than secondary importance" to the economic sphere of life. He then declares that "there is a strong case for believing in [socialism's] economic superiority." But it soon becomes clear that his supposedly affirmative view depends on a long series of far-fetched, though not wholly implausible, conditions. In what appears to be a closely reasoned argument, he describes these conditions and professes to foresee socialism's likely triumph.[43]

He begins by saying that to be successful, a socialist system must replace an economy based on mature, big-business capitalism. It must come into being through routine governmental action rather than violent revolution. And the process is likely to take fifty to a hundred years to complete. Schumpeter's approach here is mostly abstract, in contrast to his analysis of capitalism earlier in the book. There, he draws heavily on his detailed knowledge of Britain, the United States, and Germany—all of whose economic histories he knew intimately from his exhaustive research for *Business Cycles*. The only socialist nation in 1942 was the Union of Soviet Socialist Republics, which had been established by bloody revolution and civil war in an essentially preindustrial country. But a genuine socialist system, Schumpeter says, "as yet is but a mental image—no socialist will accept the Russian experience as a full-weight realization."[44]

Both capitalism and socialism, he writes, are more than mere economic phenomena. For many socialists (as for many capitalists), noneconomic attributes and aspirations may be not only important but even *the* primary motives for loyalty. Thus, psychic rewards to adherents of socialism are worth the price of potentially reduced economic efficiency. "Socialist bread may well taste sweeter to them than capitalist bread simply because it is socialist bread, and it would do so even if they found mice in it."[45]

Then, too, socialism can be quite flexible. There is, says Schumpeter—using capital letters—a "Cultural Indeterminateness of Socialism." It can be aristocratic or proletarian; authoritarian or democratic; theocratic or atheistic; peaceful or warlike; energetic or lazy. It can even *permit some people to pursue individual creativity.* In an ingenious rhetorical feint, Schumpeter then pauses to wonder, on the other hand, whether socialism will release the innovative impulses that capitalism does, in its distinct way of providing "the ladders for talent to climb." Here he is making what appears to be a harmless concession to the opposition, when in fact he is setting up a fatal thrust *by* the opposition (himself).[46]

Delaying that thrust for a moment, he blandly asserts that nothing is "wrong with the pure logic of a socialist economy." Indeed, "there is a strong case" for believing that a socialist system could produce, over a given period, a larger volume of consumers' goods than the big-business, regulated capitalist economy of the United States. Like a clever defense lawyer arguing what he knows to be a weak case, Schumpeter coyly adduces as evidence five benefits that would accrue to productivity under socialist control.[47]

First, managers would not have to contend with the uncertainties that competitors pose for capitalist businessmen. The socialist central authority could "act as a clearing house of information and as a coordinator of decisions" in much the same way that a capitalist cartel does. Energies expended in the "endless moves and countermoves" of competitive strategy could be turned to more productive purposes, and "much less intelligence would be necessary to run such a system" than is required in modern capitalist business.[48]

Second, technological and organizational improvements, rather than spreading gradually from one capitalist firm to others, could be disseminated forcibly by a central authority. This would overcome stubborn resistance along the way.[49]

Third, a central authority under socialism could eliminate the business cycle. Central planning "would be incomparably more effective in preventing bursts at some times and depressive reactions at others." Through careful coordination, a socialist regime "would eliminate the cause of the cyclical ups and downs whereas in the capitalist order it is only possible to mitigate them."[50]

Fourth, unemployment would be a less serious problem. Workers whose jobs disappeared because of advancing technology could be redeployed to other positions prepared for them by the central planning authority. Again, severe downturns in the business cycle would be minimized—in effect, outlawed altogether.[51]

Fifth, and most important, the disappearance of the private sphere from the economy would eliminate the friction and antagonisms between business and government that now "hamper and paralyze the private engine of production." Among the vanishing costs would be those of "incessant inquiries and prosecutions," including "a considerable part of the total work done by lawyers." Taxes, which under capitalism have been seized "by political force," would simply disappear. In a socialist economy, the central authority could simply set lower pay levels, rather than "run after the recipients in order to recover part of them."[52]

Schumpeter has now drawn what he calls the "blueprint" of a socialist economy. From this overview of purported advantages, he turns to the practical conditions and exceptions to his argument. Here he subtly shifts from defense counsel to prosecutor—and, like a good ironist, seldom tips his hand.

He begins with another apparently bland concession: "There never can be a general case for socialism, but only a case with reference to given social conditions and given historical stages." The conditions and stages are those of the "capitalism of our own epoch, that is to say, big-business capitalism *in fetters*." In this situation, government has long since assumed a larger and more active role in economic affairs. And within business itself, corporate bureaucracies, managerial committees, and faceless stockholders have come to outnumber individual entrepreneurs. Under these conditions, the transition to socialism can begin through the simple step of nationalizing the big-business parts of the economy. Meanwhile, government will look with benign neglect on farmers, small craftsmen, small retailers, laborers, and clerks. They can continue "indefinitely" to function with no essential change in their attitudes or patterns of work.[53]

The crucial test will arise with the group most symbolic of capitalism: the bourgeoisie. The giving or withholding of their cooperation "may make all the difference between success and failure of the socialist order." Far from liquidating this group, Schumpeter suggests, a successful socialist economy should encourage it to continue performing vital managerial functions. Otherwise, the economy cannot prosper.[54]

But how will the socialist regime motivate its managers without according them high incomes? How will it deliver to them "that most subtle of all economic goods, Social Distance"? In the Soviet Union, Schumpeter notes, the government has addressed this issue by developing a class of managers "compensated not only by honors but also by official residences staffed at public expense, allowances for 'official' hospitality, the use of admiralty and other yachts, special provisions for service on international commissions," and further emoluments. Another kind of socialist regime could achieve social distance in some alternative way. For example, it might employ the device of authorizing high performers "to stick a penny stamp on their trousers." Society would recognize the stamp as a mark of superior achievement. (Here the satirist, delighting in his own wit, betrays himself.)[55]

Continuing his apparently random references to the Soviet Union, Schumpeter then says that the function of saving—so essential for providing investment funds—can be decreed rather than merely encouraged. Soviet Russia has done this by the uncomplicated method of minimizing people's disposable income while conserving pools of money for investment. "Hardships and 'abstinence' have been imposed such as no capitalist society could ever have enforced." Under the banner of socialism, however, this kind of discipline "presumably will command that moral allegiance which is being increasingly refused to capitalism." The individual motive of economic survival, so necessary under capitalism, will disappear. The state will take care of the "subnormal" 25 percent of the population that is unable to fend for itself.[56]

Having ostensibly dealt with issues of motivation and saving, Schumpeter next considers how a socialist system might discipline its workers. Under capitalism, obedience in the workplace had been "inculcated by the feudal predecessor," whose capitalist heirs had somehow preserved it for three centuries. But in more recent times, "by accepting equality in the political sphere, by teaching laborers that they were just as valuable citizens as anyone else, the bourgeoisie forfeited that advantage." Then, too, the protective stratum of the old aristocracy no longer helped very much in mediating between managers and workers.[57]

But under socialism, Schumpeter says, industrial managers could use the tools of authoritarian discipline much more freely, and "intellectuals as a group will no longer be hostile." To oppose the employer "will amount to attacking the government," and the public would regard workers' resistance as a "semi-criminal practice. A strike would be mutiny."[58]

Again citing the Soviet Union, Schumpeter argues that by 1932, toward the end of the first Five-Year Plan, "the industrial proletariat was more in hand than it had been under the last Tsar." While purporting to champion trade unions, the government had actually used them for its own disciplinary purposes. Factory managers had installed policies of longer hours, dismissals at their own discretion, and premiums for high-performing or favored workers. And they accomplished all of this with few objections from the work force. Thus, whatever its shortcomings and "sinister connotations," the Bolsheviks' system had been effective.

> The fact that the Russian state, unlike the capitalist state, is in a position to enforce, in the teaching and guiding of the young, conformity with its ends and structural ideas immeasurably increases its ability to create an atmosphere favorable to factory discipline. Intellectuals are evidently not at liberty to tamper with it. And there is no public opinion to encourage infractions . . . "visits" by shock brigades and occasionally also by comrades of the Red Army are, whatever their legal construction, practically independent means in the hands of the government by which to safeguard performance. There is motive to use them and, as a matter of universally admitted fact, they have been unflinchingly used.[59]

Even this kind of brutality, Schumpeter observes—still writing in the ironic mode—does not necessarily undercut a theoretical case for socialism. In Soviet

Russia, the "unripeness" of the industrial situation encouraged the viciousness of the regime. Any objections must therefore be lodged not against "socialism *per se*" but only a certain type. "Whether such a socialism is compatible with what we usually mean by democracy is another question."[60]

It soon becomes clear that Schumpeter believes that something similar to the Russian experience is likely to happen with other socialist regimes. It is only under what he calls an "idyllic type" of socialism that "comparison with fettered capitalism does not turn out unfavorably for the socialist alternative." And his own long list of conditions and assumptions yields up only a single potential site for his "idyllic type": Britain during the mid-twentieth century. Elsewhere, socialists could not gain control of the government without a bloody revolution, in which they would "use force not against isolated individuals but against groups and classes."[61]

Why Britain? In the first place, it already had a strong tradition of trade unionism. Then, too, in the years since World War I, the British people had become "state-broken"—that is, accustomed to a strong governmental hand. Combined with the nation's industrial maturity, these conditions had now made Britain readier than any other country for the start of a transition to socialism.[62]

As part of the overall program for achieving "socialization in a state of maturity," executives in important firms could be co-opted through perquisites and honors. It would not be economically necessary to expropriate holders of stocks, bonds, mortgages, and insurance. Instead, their claims could be turned into temporary annuities, or be gradually taxed away. Of course, no more founding of new firms would occur. But the changeover, if done with care and without revolutionary fervor, could happen smoothly, perhaps through a few small changes in the national constitution.[63]

In a setting less hospitable than Britain's, a socialist movement might seize a political opportunity to govern even before the country's economy had reached capitalist maturity. There, Schumpeter admits with seeming reluctance, the outlook is clouded. "Drastic assertion of equalitarian ideals of course might spoil everything." It was unfortunate that this kind of assertion was so tempting to committed socialists. Most of them "would be unable to put up with anything less fascinating than the spectacular slaying of the capitalist dragon by the proletarian St. George."[64]

Theoretically, however, the socialist leadership could prevent its supporters' demands for a forcible dispossession of the capitalists and instead accomplish its aims through a strategy of monetary inflation. "For, as Lenin has pointed out, nothing disorganizes like inflation: 'in order to destroy bourgeois society you must debauch its money.'" Property holders could ostensibly be paid "any amount of indemnities," but they would have no recourse if the state determined that the currency in which they were paid would soon be valueless. "Inflation expropriates the holder of claims in terms of money in a delightfully simple way," Schumpeter seems pleased to observe.[65]

In that situation, of course, retaining the expertise of incumbent capitalist managers would be impossible and replacing them with people of similar talent very problematical. Even so, the transition to socialism might still be accomplished, as the Russian Bolsheviks proved after 1917. If socialist leaders were sufficiently brutal, with "a red army strong enough to quell open resistance . . . by firing impartially to right and left, and sense enough to leave peasants and farmers alone," then the deed could still be done. Regrettably, the socialist leaders "will hardly be able to help behaving with criminal ferocity."[66]

Schumpeter's abhorrence of that prospect is clear, as he pauses—this time without irony—to comment on the function of the analyst as opposed to that of the agitator:

> It should be obvious that socialization in any situation immature
> enough to require revolution not only in the sense of a break in le-
> gal continuity but also in the sense of a subsequent reign of terror
> cannot benefit, either in the short or in the long run, anyone ex-
> cept those who engineer it. To work up enthusiasm about it and
> to glorify the courage of risking all that it might entail may be one
> of the less edifying duties of the professional agitator. But as re-
> gards the academic intellectual, the only courage that can possibly
> reflect any credit on him is the courage to criticize, to caution and
> to restrain.[67]

As a whole, the organization of Schumpeter's discussion of socialism has elements of a shell game. At first his argument seems designed to establish the viability of socialism and its likely replacement of capitalism. But there follows such a lengthy series of convoluted qualifications and assumptions as to raise doubts about his candor. Although he has adopted the outward form of an inquiry rather than a polemic, a careful reading leaves little question that his purpose has been to praise capitalism and condemn socialism.

Even so, Schumpeter's irony escaped many readers. At least one reviewer concluded that the book showed its author to be "a socialist." And certainly it was small wonder that admirers of socialism were likely to read *Capitalism, Socialism and Democracy* with great interest—as they would not have bothered to read a frontal attack. As Swift wrote, "Satire is a sort of glass wherein beholders do generally discover everybody's face but their own, which is the chief reason for that kind of reception it meets in the world, and that so very few are offended by it."[68]

SCHUMPETER TITLED THE next part of his book "Socialism and Democracy." But like the rest of his text, the analysis has as much to do with capitalism as with socialism or democracy. It is here that he provides answers to one of the animating questions of the book: Can democracy survive—under either capitalism or socialism? He begins by rehearsing the socialist critique of capitalism: ownership of the means of production gives the capitalist class power to exploit labor and to dominate politics. Even if a capitalist government has the outward form of democracy, that form is but a sham—or so says the standard socialist argument.[69]

Now dropping the ironic mode altogether, Schumpeter points out that the historical record of socialists themselves in bringing true democracy to any country is dismal. As an economic system, socialism "does not imply anything about political procedure. As far as that goes the only question is whether and in what sense it *can* be democratic." Socialists in Germany, for example, both before and after World War I, spoke the language of democracy to keep themselves politically palatable. But they neither achieved actual democracy nor governed effectively. They even remained complacent as Hitler's Fascism began its rise to power. Then, too, both in Russia under the Bolsheviks and in Hungary during the months of Bela Kun's Communist rule, the world observed "cases both of which represent the crucial combination of a possibility of the conquest of power with the impossibility of doing so by democratic means."[70]

Having cast doubt on the ability of socialists to implement democracy, Schumpeter turns to problems inherent in democracy itself. At bottom, he says, "democracy is a political *method*" for arriving at legislative and administrative decisions. Hence democracy is "incapable of being an end in itself . . . and this must be the starting point of any attempt at defining it." The literal meaning of the word, derived from the Greek *demos,* means government by the people. Yet throughout history, definitions of "the people" have often excluded women, slaves, foreigners, and others.[71]

Here the book becomes deadly serious, as the author invites the reader to perform a "mental experiment." Imagine a democratic society, by definition governed by majority rule, which reaches "the decision to persecute religious dissent." The Republic of Geneva, for example, had burned witches during the sixteenth century. And in many modern countries, "anti-Semitism has been one of the most deep-seated of all popular attitudes," easily exploited by opportunistic office-seekers. During Schumpeter's own youth, Vienna's most celebrated politician, Karl Lueger, capitalized on anti-Semitism in winning numerous mayoralty elections.[72]

> Now for our experiment. Let us transport ourselves into a hypothetical country that, in a democratic way, practices the persecution of Christians, the burning of witches and the slaughtering of Jews. We should certainly not approve of these practices on the ground that they have been decided on according to the rules of democratic procedure. But the crucial question is: would we approve of the democratic constitution itself that produced such results in preference to a non-democratic one that would avoid them? If we do not, we are behaving exactly as fervent socialists behave to whom capitalism is worse than witch hunting and who are therefore prepared to accept non-democratic methods for the purpose of suppressing it.[73]

How, then, "is it technically possible for 'people' to rule?" The answer is that true democracy is feasible only where every adult votes on every issue, as in a town meeting. In larger venues, "we are prepared to drop government by the people and to substitute for it government approved by the people." But this characteristic is hardly unique to democracy. Numerous non-democratic regimes—Napoleon's France, for one—have had popular approval in abundance.[74]

Schumpeter next explores whether governance in the interest of the common good (as opposed to the tastes of the majority) is not a sufficient criterion for democracy. It is certainly desirable, he says, but there are two problems. The common good means different things to different people; and agreement often cannot be reached by rational argument. He goes on to raise doubts about "the definiteness and independence of the voter's will, his powers of observation and interpretation of facts, and his ability to draw . . . rational inferences from both." Here Schumpeter makes an analogy with the economic behavior of consumers. Under modern capitalism, consumers' wants are "nothing like as rational" as they appear in economics textbooks. Among other reasons, consumers have proved to be easy targets for clever advertisers.[75]

So it is with voters and politicians. Voters are often "bad judges of their own long-run interest, for it is only the short-run promise that tells politically and only short-run rationality that asserts itself effectively." The farther removed an issue is from voters' daily lives, the more remote its rationality becomes to them. And the greater the distance from rationality, "the greater are the opportunities for groups with an ax to grind" to affect electoral outcomes through "psycho-technics." Ultimately, the voters' will is "largely not a genuine but a manufactured will . . . exactly analogous to the ways of commercial advertising."[76]

Nevertheless, Schumpeter argues, socialism poses more problems for democracy than capitalism does. Capitalism has the advantage because bourgeois life restricts "the sphere of politics by limiting the sphere of public authority." Once the requisite legal framework is in place, capitalist business is largely self-regulating. It does not require constant political interference, because its laws adroitly guard individual freedom and autonomy. "Modern democracy rose along with capitalism, and in causal connection with it."[77]

Therefore, when socialists argue that bourgeois democracy is fraudulent, they are being "absurd." This was true even during crises such as the Great Depression, when authoritarian regimes actually did a better job of combatting unemployment and restoring prosperity. But that record was a mere historical detail. Even under the handicap of economic stress, bourgeois democracy was remarkable in "how wide and *equal* the opportunities it offered . . . how large the personal freedom it granted to those who passed its tests . . . and how well it functioned, when faced by demands that were outside of and hostile to the bourgeois interests." As a matter of logic, bourgeois democracy is preferable to socialism, because "it is easier for a class whose interests are best served by being left alone to practice democratic self-restraint than it is for classes that naturally try to live on the state."[78]

Can there even *be* a democratic socialism? Yes, Schumpeter answers, but only with great difficulty. Historical instances of democratic socialism are virtually zero, and here Schumpeter cites his personal experience as a case in point. In the deliberations of the German Coal Socialization Commission of 1919, there was little suggestion that socialism should proceed under democratic principles. "The idea that managers of plants should be elected by the workmen of the same plants was frankly and unanimously condemned." The workmen's councils that had already arisen "were objects of dislike and suspicion."[79]

Even so, if capitalism should happen to evolve into socialism in the manner described earlier, modern democracy theoretically *could* be preserved. But socialist democracy will not function "unless the vast majority of people in all classes are resolved to abide by the rules of the democratic game." And that condition will not hold at the present time—because so many people have been so harsh in their indictment of capitalism. Perhaps future socialists might "reestablish agreement as to the tectonic principles of the social fabric." But in the practical circumstances of most countries, "effective management of the socialist economy means dictatorship not *of* but *over* the proletariat."[80]

Overall, Schumpeter's discussion of democracy in *Capitalism, Socialism and Democracy* is as fertile with ideas, and as original, as are other parts of the book. But it is not nearly as well informed. Although he was a first-rate economic theorist and a keen student of history, he was not as well-read in political theory. The great students of democracy—from Plato to John Locke to Thomas Jefferson—make scant appearance in his pages. His argument shows a preoccupation with one of the great tragedies of the twentieth century—the failed democratic experiments in Europe between the wars. Had democracy succeeded in Germany and Italy, there would have likely have been no fascism and no World War II.

Schumpeter's relatively skeptical stance toward democracy forms an odd counterpoint to his more favorable view of capitalism. It is as if he were discussing capitalism in America but democracy in Europe. The historian Eric

Hobsbawm described *Capitalism, Socialism and Democracy* as "a notable and very central European work." One of Schumpeter's former students remarked that he wrote on democracy as simply a mechanism, while ignoring its powerful ethical dimension; and that he had likely never read such American classics of democratic theory as *The Federalist Papers.*[81]

WHEN *CAPITALISM, SOCIALISM AND DEMOCRACY* was first published in 1942, it received a good deal of favorable attention but did not become an immediate best-seller. World War II was dominating all aspects of life, including economic and political discourse. So, for the third time, a big book by Schumpeter appeared at an inopportune moment.

But the second edition of *Capitalism, Socialism and Democracy* (1947) attracted more notice, and the third (1950) a very great deal more. By that time the messages of the book could hardly have been more relevant to contemporary events. Communism and capitalism—each side equipped with nuclear weapons—were engaged in a lethal worldwide struggle for supremacy. The Soviet Union had exploded its first atomic bomb by 1949, and Mao Zedong's Communist Revolution in China had triumphed during that same year. A large number of former colonies—most notably India—were following socialist plans for economic development, often assisted by the Soviet Union. Forty percent of the world's people were living under Communist regimes, and about 25 percent more in partly socialized economies.

Reviewing the first edition of *Capitalism, Socialism and Democracy,* the Cambridge economist Joan Robinson judged that "this book is worth the whole parrot-house of contemporary orthodoxies, right, left, or centre." As Schumpeter's "many tart phrases reveal," he himself "has little love for socialism, and none at all for socialists. His natural sympathy is all with the heroic age of expanding capitalism." Robinson, herself a leading theorist of *im*perfect competition, found Schumpeter's analysis of that subject the "most brilliant" part of the book: "His argument blows like a gale through the dreary pedantry of static analysis." Although Schumpeter had little to say about evidence contrary to his ironic prediction about the possible fadeout of capitalism and its replacement by socialism, "The reader is swept along by the freshness, the dash, the impetuosity of Professor Schumpeter's stream of argument."[82]

Another admiring reviewer, A. B. Wolfe of Ohio State, found *Capitalism, Socialism and Democracy* "a 'must' book," that "could hardly have been written by an American-born and American-educated scholar." Wolfe judged that "Professor Schumpeter is a capitalistic Jeremiah. Unlike Marx, he likes capitalism; he believes it good; if it is not the most efficient and productive of all possible systems, at least it is the best that has yet been devised." And after thinking hard about Schumpeter's style of argument in his treatment of socialism—and even of capitalism—Wolfe adds that "one begins to wonder whether the whole book is not a deep satire."[83]

Some of the most gratifying comments came to Schumpeter in letters from friends and former students. In a letter from wartime London in 1943, Schumpeter's acquaintance Barbara Wootton, a writer and a pioneer in adult education, told him that "when publication over here was first proposed, Allen and Unwin sent it [to] me to read. They were in a hurry, but I didn't need to read many pages before saying YES, PUBLISH QUICK as loud as I could." Wootton went on to say that the moment she picked it up, "I said: this is going to be a swell book. And isn't it just? It is such a joy to read something fresh and real and to be stimulated to think on topics which have been made such clichés. I was immensely stimulated, did a lot of thinking, a certain amount of quarrelling and a great deal of agreeing. I am just starting myself on a little book (alas! not the result of forty years thinking) on *Freedom Under Planning*, and I was therefore particularly interested and delighted with much of your section on democracy. I don't know when I have got so much from anything that I have read."[84]

David McCord Wright, an economist at the University of Virginia who had studied under Schumpeter, sent him a warm letter of congratulations and received this revealing reply:

> Concerning the "tremendous" stock of actual knowledge with
> which you are good enough to credit me, I can give a very simple
> piece of advice: never miss an opportunity to add to it, and fur-
> thermore choose your leisure-hour reading so as to add to the his-
> torical part of it, and the stock will automatically grow beyond
> your own expectations . . .
>
> This is, indeed, the one thing in my theoretical (so far as it is
> not purely technical) writing on which I pride myself; it is all seen,

and in this sense there is nothing in my structures that has not a living piece of reality behind it. This is not an advantage in every respect. It makes, for instance, my theories so refractory to mathematical formulations. They can never be so cut and dried as Keynes' schema is; but there are compensating advantages, and one of them is that so many people have told me, as you have done, "Yes, that is so. I know that from my own experience and observation."[85]

In a review of the 1947 edition, Arthur M. Schlesinger, Jr., wrote that the book "burst into the generally sterile atmosphere of political discussion like a collection of firecrackers and skyrockets." Schumpeter's analysis made it pointless for Americans to keep repeating mindless slogans about the evils of monopoly. Even if Schumpeter were wrong, "there is no percentage in dodging the uncomfortable points he raises. The intellectual rigor of his analysis sets a standard that liberal writers should try to meet." The book "is the performance of an intellectual virtuoso, brilliant, complex, perfectly controlled."[86]

A retrospective analysis appeared in 1981, titled *Schumpeter's Vision: Capitalism, Socialism, and Democracy after 40 Years.* Here, several of Schumpeter's former students and associates joined with prominent European scholars in evaluating the book's legacy. In one of the most telling comments, the Dutch scholar Henrik Wilm Lambers recalled Schumpeter's influence on him as a youth and the continued attraction that *Capitalism, Socialism and Democracy* held for his own students. "After many an oral graduate examination, I have often heard remarks like: 'to be honest, the one stimulating book was Schumpeter.'" Radical and conservative students alike "say, each in their own way, 'he keeps me puzzled: is it my fault or did he intend to?'"[87]

The ongoing appeal of Schumpeter's book has something to do with its ironic style—but even more to do with the author's insistence on the indivisibility of intellectual inquiry. He knew, of course, that specialization is essential to academic progress. He understood that multidisciplinary work runs a constant risk of dilettantism. But if the scholar does his or her homework, as Schumpeter always did, this danger can be transcended. His own insistence on a multidisciplinary analysis of capitalism and socialism, rather than one by economists alone, is akin to Talleyrand's maxim that "war is much too serious to be left to the generals."[88]

Above all, Schumpeter knew that at some point partial and general syntheses of the insights from all relevant disciplines become essential if people are going to make mature sense of the world. From the beginning of his career in 1905, he had castigated scholars who hid behind disciplinary shields. By contrast, he himself would take his insights wherever he could find them. From multiple sources he would create something new—like a chemical compound altogether different from the elements that went into its molecular structure. How can one understand H_2O, a liquid, by knowing only hydrogen and oxygen, the gases that make it up?[89]

In the end, *Capitalism, Socialism and Democracy* exemplifies the best kind of synthetic analysis. It continues to puzzle and provoke readers—to make them think, to measure their perceptions against their ideologies, and even to wonder about the author's intentions. Only the greatest books do this and age so well.

2 2

War and Perplexity

It takes your enemy and your friend, working together, to
hurt you to the heart.

MARK TWAIN, *Following the Equator*, 1897

SCHUMPETER HAD BEEN out of step with American opinion in the
run-up to World War II. During the war, when he wrote most of *Capitalism,
Socialism and Democracy,* he found himself perplexed by the conduct of combatants on both sides and extremely conflicted in his thoughts. The war years
were torturous for Schumpeter emotionally, and he had great difficulty in deciding what to wish for. In many of his diary entries he would argue first one
position, then its opposite. No coffeehouse cleverness here but rather an earnest effort to work through a chaotic mixture of feelings.

During the seven years that Schumpeter lived in Germany, Hitlerism had
been little more than a lunatic fringe. He knew, from Mia Stöckel's letters and
from his own involvement in finding jobs for Jewish intellectuals fleeing
official persecution, that the Nazi regime's anti-Semitic actions were vicious,
systematic, and far-reaching. But like many other Europeans—including, for a
time, a substantial number of Jews themselves, who were integral to the social
fabric of Germany—Schumpeter seems to have regarded Nazi oppression as a
dreadful but temporary phase through which Germany would pass before
long. This widespread feeling, of course, was a tragic miscalculation by all
concerned.

During Schumpeter's youth, tens of thousands of Jews had poured into Vi-enna, fleeing persecution and murderous pogroms—not in Germany but in Russia. So, like most people on the Continent, he was accustomed to thinking of Russia as the most anti-Semitic country. Indeed, many of the Jews who left Russian shtetls had gone to Germany, as had political exiles such as commu-nists and social democrats during the tsarist government, and anti-Bolshevik émigrés after 1917.

Schumpeter's ideas about both Russia and Germany reflected the picture he had formed during his life in Europe, before coming to the United States in 1932. This put him at odds with the views of most Americans during the late 1930s and early 1940s. To them, Russia was so remote that they could hardly conceive of it as a threat. And whatever the flaws of the Soviet regime, had it not brought down a divine-right monarchy and aristocracy and replaced them with a system in which workers were the equals of all? Numerous Ameri-can intellectuals—Van Wyck Brooks, Louis Fischer, Dashiell Hammett, Lillian Hellman, Granville Hicks, Max Lerner, Lincoln Steffens, Richard Wright, and many others—praised the Soviet system in newspaper and magazine articles. Most of these writers, but not all, would temper their praise after the Nazi-Soviet Pact of 1939.[1]

The distinction in Schumpeter's mind between what Hitler was doing and what the war might mean for Germans and German culture proved impossible for some of his American friends to understand. "Nor," his former student Sey-mour Harris recalled, "did courageous attacks on American foreign policy dur-ing the forties endear him to his colleagues. These pronouncements reflected a peculiar trait in Schumpeter: his unwillingness to stand with the majority." He was often his own worst enemy and tended to be stubborn on any subject if he thought that modifying his views would please the crowd.[2]

As his Harvard colleague and fellow European Gottfried Haberler later wrote, "Needless to say he had no sympathies with the Nazi regime. He knew and said repeatedly, that if he had remained in Germany he would have been one of the first candidates for the concentration camp." He was, in fact, "vio-lently attacked by National Socialist writers on the ground that his economic theories were not German in spirit." Even so, "he felt that Germany had genu-ine grievances, that she had been treated badly after World War I, and that ex-cessive nationalism was the unfortunate reaction." For that reason, and because

Above: Schumpeter at lunch with a colleague at the Faculty Club, about 1942. At this time, after the publication of *Capitalism, Socialism and Democracy*, the strain of the war years almost caused Schumpeter to lose his emotional balance altogether.

Left: A formal portrait in 1945. Age and the war have visibly taken their toll.

he foresaw a grave long-term threat from the Soviet Union to both Europe and the United States, he "reacted strongly against anti-German (as distinguished from anti-Nazi) propaganda and policies. Thus the war years must have been among the most somber and depressing of his life."[3]

In September 1941 Schumpeter wrote in his diary: "Why am I so pro-German? . . . I look fearfully at the headlines, where in Russia disaster [from the Nazi invasion] is growing . . . and this hate against Russia, where is it coming from?" In diary entries during the spring and summer of 1943, he wrote such things as "Why, why do I *grieve* so much about this war and its obvious outcome? Why not embrace the possibilities that open up?" People seemed to be fighting less for principle than "because they love it."[4]

Even in the early phases of the war, Schumpeter was appalled by the number of civilian casualties. In no other conflict in human history had a willingness to kill masses of noncombatants been so commonplace. And the grisly toll was soon to become much worse—whether perpetrated by the Japanese in Asia, the Russians in Eastern Europe, or the Nazis in their death camps. In November 1944, less than six months before Germany's surrender, Gallup pollsters asked a sample of Americans, "Do you believe the stories that the Germans have murdered many people in concentration camps?" Although 76 percent answered yes, their estimates of the number of deaths varied widely—27 percent speculating 100,000 or less and 25 percent unwilling to make any guess at all. Each of the other choices, which ranged from 100,000 victims to over six million, was selected by fewer than 9 percent of those polled. But in fact a large percentage of Hitler's extermination of Jews had come in 1942 and 1943. And in 1944, as was later revealed, he took the almost inconceivable step of diverting military resources from battle fronts in order to arrest and kill as many Jews as quickly as possible.[5]

Schumpeter had long believed the American people to be idealistic and principled. Writing in 1919, he had attributed America's role in the First World War not to its national interests but instead to "moral forces," which "have real power there." But now he began to regard certain aspects of American policy as merciless. One of these was the official doctrine of unconditional surrender, first set forth in a casual remark by President Roosevelt at the Casablanca Conference early in 1943. "Why must we insist on Knock out?" Schumpeter asked in his diary; "because people love to Knock out." Although the idea was familiar to Americans because of their own Civil War (in which General U. S. Grant had been nicknamed General "Unconditional Surrender" Grant), it was less well-known to Europeans, who from long experience were accustomed to negotiated settlements.[6]

The question of "Germany's guilt" also haunted Schumpeter. In 1919 the Allies' insistence on the "war guilt" clause had formed the basis for the disastrous Treaty of Versailles. Its imposition on Germany of extravagant reparations and other punishments, along with a weak parliamentary government, had sowed the seeds of World War II. "All mistakes made over again," he wrote; "a sad subject." Once more, in the eyes of the world, Germany was a "wicked nation." Schumpeter objected to the idea of "'guilt' applied to a nation" instead of to the Hitler regime. Most Americans agreed with this view, especially during the early years of the war. In a 1942 poll, about 80 percent of respondents said that the "chief enemy" was the German government, as opposed to 6 percent identifying the German people. As was his habit, Schumpeter thought in a context of historical parallels: France wrongly regarded as a wicked nation after Napoleon's defeats in 1814 and 1815, and blame against whole countries in the aftermath of the Thirty Years' War in the seventeenth century.[7]

Like many other native Europeans, Schumpeter feared that the experience of 1919 was about to be repeated, and made even worse by Soviet domination. Only by a narrow margin, he believed, had Soviet-style communism not triumphed in the earlier period. "It is true," he had written in *Capitalism, Socialism and Democracy*, "that communist republics [in 1919] were actually established only in Bavaria and Hungary. But in Germany, Austria, and Italy the social structure was perilously near toppling and there is no saying what would have happened in those countries and possibly farther west if Trotsky's war machine had been in working order at that time and not engaged in the civil and Polish wars."[8]

In 1945 he believed that there was no need to "whip" the Germans further. "They have been whipped." Their country lay in ruins. Seventeen million German-speakers, expelled from other nations, were pouring into the mother country, raising the prospect of mass starvation. And no effective governing structure was in place. In this situation, what would be the point in punishing "a corpse"? He was disturbed about the gratuitous cruelties to German civilians carried out by Soviet troops, who were raping and pillaging as badly as the German army had done in its invasion of Russia four years earlier. Beyond these immediate atrocities, Schumpeter was even more concerned about the powerful new geopolitical status of the Soviet Union. His one happy note was an entry of April 14, 1945: "Austria liberated!" But even here, the Red Army had done much of the liberating, and the Soviets would not remove their heavy hand from conquered Austrian territory until 1955.[9]

"Finis Germaniae," Schumpeter recorded in May 1945, when the war in Europe ended. He added—very naively, in view of the 1938 Munich episode—that Germany "could have got what it really needs if it had humbly begged of the great Democracies." Above all he wondered what was now going to happen in Europe, destabilized as it was after the Red Army had overrun vast territories. "For once I feel that I should like to contact those of 500 years hence" to see how things turned out.[10]

Meanwhile, Schumpeter believed that the American people were "shutting our ears to [a] muffled cry of anguish." The United States "can defend herself against a world of enemies but who is going to protect her from her allies?" Britain's aims were a bother, but Soviet ones were horrifying: "The world and civilization is at the mercy of a giant—in terrible armor—without a brain."[11]

In the closing pages of *Capitalism, Socialism and Democracy* Schumpeter had predicted not only Soviet domination of Eastern Europe but also what he called "Ethical Imperialism" by the British and Americans. In the theaters of war where they were victorious, he expected them to impose "a world order of this kind in which the interests and ambitions of other nations would count only as far as understood and approved by England and the United States." He also foresaw that the maintenance of this order would require "permanent readiness to use military force"—which would be something new in American history but which actually occurred after World War II.[12]

In a series of diary entries from 1943 through 1945, Schumpeter wrote that an "Anglo-American Alliance" to preserve the domination of the "white man in Asia" would be a very sad development. He referred to Churchill's "genius" in using the United States to help preserve the British Empire, a policy based partly on Churchill's own "racialism." And in Europe, "Oh insolent question: What shall we do with Germany? Roosevelt . . . is but a catspaw for Churchill and Stalin." Then a little later, "While this country is fighting England's battles, it allows itself to be snubbed and lectured so soon as its government modestly and casually tries to assert its interest." (By contrast, many British officials accurately suspected that Roosevelt was much more inclined to bring their empire to an end.) Then, in a series of telegraphic entries on both Britain and the Soviet Union, Schumpeter wrote such short phrases as "sprawling Empire," "source of war," "the rest of the world in conquest too," "and by God this is what they are trying to do!" He felt very strongly that during the postwar period "a dissatisfied Germany and a dissatisfied Japan" would play into both British and Soviet plans for world domination.[13]

In another wartime diary entry he remarked, "How the English sit quietly and let other people fight . . . husbanding their resources." And again, "Oh these English, they fought with American soldiers and now they will rule with American money!" He noted that Bertrand Russell had once said, "What England's feeling towards [the] US was: 'hate'. This is not however all: the feeling is contempt whipped into hate by envy for what is considered to be Uncle Sam's unmerited good fortune."[14]

Much more ominously, Schumpeter believed that American policy was playing into the hands of the Soviet Union. "After having pulled down our two natural bulwarks: Germany and Japan," President Roosevelt, who had "thought to open the Amer. century," was actually "ushering in the Russian . . . buckling to Stalin." It was all a "horrible thing!" Conscious of the rich cultural history of Central Europe, Schumpeter hoped for America that "whatever you do in Germany after having conquered do not forget to learn from her. Have respect for great achievement. You who have only just emerged from the squalor of boss rule in your cities." In May 1945, as the Red Army rolled over Eastern and Central Europe, capturing one country after another, Schumpeter wrote of the Americans and British "handing over populations to most villainous tyranny . . . and standing by to shoot them if they defend themselves—Liberation— Oh infamous lie on top of infamous crime."[15]

Schumpeter expected wartime atrocities from the troops of Germany and the Soviet Union, and he knew about the Japanese army's monstrous proclivities from Elizabeth's many writings. But having held the United States to such a high moral standard for so long, he was shocked by the bombing of civilians in Germany and Japan. The Germans and Japanese themselves conducted air raids over populous cities. But the British and Americans (the British much more than the Americans) raised the practice to unimagined levels over Germany. This was a controversial policy, opposed in Europe by many Allied military planners because it diverted air power from the battlefields. But during the early years of the war, Churchill and Roosevelt could strike Germany only from the air. And they needed to placate their Soviet ally through dramatic action that would at the same time delay the opening of a "second front" in Western Europe. From 1942 onward, Stalin had demanded that the Allies launch a ground war in the West so as to relieve the intense German pressure on his Soviet army along the Eastern Front.[16]

The Allies did fight the Germans and Italians in North Africa, and they invaded Italy itself in 1943. But because the likely numbers of infantry casualties were unacceptable to the British and Americans, the major second front, in France, did not come until June 6, 1944—D-Day. By that time, the German army had been much weakened by the Soviets. And meanwhile, Britain's Bomber Command and, to a much lesser extent, the U.S. Army Air Forces had concentrated their military efforts in Europe on what came to be called the "area bombing" of cities. This practice, which continued long after D-Day, engendered in Schumpeter a sense of righteous anger and almost unbearable shame.

In marked contrast to what would be their policy in Japan, American planners tried in Germany for "precision" daylight bombing of military or munitions targets. Britain's Bomber Command, having suffered heavy losses in its early campaigns, came to prefer flying at night, when air defenses were much less effective—but also when their bombing was much less accurate. As horrible as Germany's air assault on London, Liverpool, and other British cities had been, things were much worse when the tables were turned. Allied bombs fell on both of Schumpeter's former hometowns, Bonn and Vienna. And late in 1944 huge fleets of British and American planes commenced virtual carpet-bombing of urban Germany. For every ton of explosives dropped on Britain during the war, seventeen tons fell on Germany—sometimes on cities of scant military importance, such as Dresden. By the spring of 1945, nearly every large and medium-sized city lay in ruins. The books and private papers Schumpeter had left in the care of the Stöckel family in Jülich were mostly destroyed, along with 97 percent of the town's buildings.[17]

In 1945, American B-29s started fire-bombing Tokyo and other Japanese cities day after day, week after week. Now on the brink of despair, Schumpeter could hardly believe what was happening: "Headline: 'Every Jap City to be wiped out.' Another headline: 'Miles of Ruin.' And no voice even of decent regret—they gloat over it and . . . feel elated at being so above sentimentality!" After the atomic bombs in August 1945, "It is a stupid bestiality or a bestial stupidity"; "Violence approved—no hatred like the hatred of the murderer against the victims."[18]

General Curtis LeMay, the principal architect of this campaign in Japan once the policy decision had been made, acknowledged that if the United States had lost the war, he and his staff would have been tried as war criminals. But Schumpeter did not need an Allied defeat to know that his adopted country, though fighting for right, was wrong in bringing death to so many civilians. In still another diary entry he expressed "doubts about the possibility of universal peace and democracy under American bombers." In all, American bombs killed about 400,000 civilians in Japan—roughly the same as the total number of American military deaths on all fronts during the war.[19]

Military deaths among the major combatants over the course of the war included 11 million Soviets, 2.5 million Nationalist Chinese, 5 million Germans, 2 million Japanese, and fewer than a half-million each of British and American. Throughout the war, both Britain and the United States emphasized naval and air combat, as an indirect means of holding their infantry casualties to a minimum. Even more important, they *had* to win the naval Battle of the Atlantic in order for Britain to survive. And in the Pacific, both naval and air superiority were essential to the amphibious island-hopping campaign that took the war to the edge of Japan. There were heavy infantry tolls in the Normandy landings, the Battle of the Bulge, and the fighting on Pacific islands. But nothing on the Western Front or in the Pacific came close to matching the carnage on the Eastern Front. In the Battle of Stalingrad alone, immense Soviet and Axis armies hurled themselves at each other in a prolonged orgy of slaughter that killed 486,000 Soviet and 270,000 Axis troops.[20]

While the Americans and British tried to avoid large ground-war casualties, the Soviet Union had no such hesitation. The huge and powerful Red Army, after recovering from its early defeats at the hands of the Nazis, marched in 1944 and 1945 across the entirety of Eastern Europe and into the heart of Central Europe. And for four decades after the war ended, Soviet troops remained in the territories they conquered at such tremendous cost in 1944 and 1945. The Kremlin installed totalitarian puppet regimes in Poland, East Germany, Hungary, Czechoslovakia, and several other countries.

Despite its horrendous casualties, the Soviet Union appeared to Schumpeter to be the war's single biggest winner in both territory and influence. He had written in the last pages of *Capitalism, Socialism and Democracy* that "even now [July 1942], many observers seem to expect that Russia will emerge from the war with a great access of power and prestige, in fact that Stalin will emerge as the true victor." This, he believed, would spell the end not only of capitalism in countries overrun by the Soviets, but also the death of the social democratic parties that had governed much of Europe before the war. In the Soviet Union itself, said Schumpeter, "the really terrible point about the Stalinist regime is not what it did to millions of victims but the fact *that it had to do it if it wished to survive.* In other words, those principles [of Stalinism] and that practice are inseparable."[21]

By the end of the war, every nation in Eastern Europe and most in Central Europe had fallen under the control of the Soviets. They stripped industrial machinery, works of art, gold, and other movable assets from many of these countries and shipped them all to Russia. The total amount stolen equaled in value the aid to Western Europe under the American-sponsored Marshall Plan, the largest foreign aid program in history. In China, meanwhile, the long civil war resumed, ending in 1949 with the victory of Communist armies under Mao Zedong and the escape to Taiwan of the remnants of Chiang Kai-shek's Nationalist forces.[22]

Like his wife, Elizabeth, Schumpeter was appalled by the USSR's influence in China. "Oh America!" he wrote early in 1945. "Bullying China into submission to Stalin: the English are at least strong beasts of prey and have the esthetics of such a beast—but U.S. bullying China into submission to Stalin just because a group without which Roosevelt cannot do wants it—and the rest just bleating approval." As both Elizabeth and Joseph Schumpeter had feared, Soviet Russia and Communist China ended the 1940s conflict with control over about 40 percent of the earth's population.[23]

THE CONSEQUENCES OF World War II are so profound as almost to defy analysis. The war reshaped national boundaries, brought longstanding colonial regimes to an end, and created dozens of independent new countries. It introduced effective democracy for the first time into Germany, Italy, and Japan. It gave a tremendous push to some of the most important industries of the future. In the United States and in other countries, from South Africa to India, it accelerated a series of social revolutions in human rights, civil rights, the women's movement, the welfare state, and the economic responsibilities of governments.

But whatever kinds of progress might be laid at the door of the war, it was the most lethal episode in human history since the Black Death of 1346–1353, on the basis of fatalities as a percentage of world population. In the final reckoning, between 60 and 70 million people lost their lives. Of these, over 21 million were military, and at least twice that number innocent civilians—who died from starvation or bombing or, in the case of six million Jews and another six million non-Jews, in Nazi death and forced-labor camps. Civilian deaths were particularly astronomical for Russians, Chinese, and Poles. The ratio of civilians killed by the Axis powers compared with the Allies was approximately nine to one.[24]

Schumpeter saw the war through his own particular lens, parts of which were very clear, other parts badly distorted. Like many other people who lived through the war years, he badly underestimated the staying power of Hitler and overestimated the durability of the British Empire. Only in his evaluation of the Soviet Union—its drive for new territory during the war, its likely patience after the war before trying to expand further, its brutality—did he hit the mark squarely.

John Maynard Keynes's biographer Robert Skidelsky later wrote that "Roosevelt was never concerned about who should liberate whom, because he dreamed of a post-territorial condominium with 'Uncle Joe' [Stalin] . . . This can be counted as the most spectacular misjudgment in American history, aided and abetted by a network of Soviet spies in the Treasury and State Departments." This indictment overstates the case, but it also suggests that Schumpeter's feelings during the 1940s were shared by others and were not wholly without foundation. He had no suspicions of pervasive spying, but he did believe that Stalin had outmaneuvered Roosevelt, and badly.[25]

Schumpeter understood America's economy well, but his grasp of its government was rudimentary. He had a far better knowledge of the politics and traditions of Austria, Germany, Britain, and even the Soviet Union. Like other transplanted Europeans during the 1940s, he allowed himself to be guided by what he saw as parallels between World War I and World War II. Consequently, he believed Roosevelt to be as innocent of world affairs as his onetime patron Woodrow Wilson had been at Versailles in 1919. Schumpeter knew Roosevelt to be a master of domestic politics, a genius Machiavelli would have admired. But isolationism in the United States during the 1930s had reinforced Schumpeter's conviction that Americans were simple-minded neophytes when it came to international affairs. And by the 1940s, Roosevelt's close personal relationship with Churchill clinched Schumpeter's belief that the U.S. government was unable to think independently about world politics.

He did not appreciate the extraordinary achievements of the United States in constructing new policies for war diplomacy and mobilization. He knew about the FBI's bumbling investigations of himself and Elizabeth and about the Office of Production Management's rejection of her services. But he had almost no familiarity with the cadre of first-rate talent working in Washington and abroad, on a wide range of issues: the grand strategy of defeating Germany before Japan; the Lend-Lease aid to the British and Soviets to help crush the Nazis; the plans for postwar stabilization through a complex web of international agencies.

Schumpeter knew little about the great public servants in the military who were his own approximate contemporaries (Admirals Chester Nimitz, William Leahy, Ernest King, and William Halsey; Generals George Marshall, Dwight Eisenhower, Omar Bradley, and George Patton); nor of the superb diplomats from the foreign service or on loan from private law firms (Henry Stimson, Averell Harriman, George Kennan, Dean Acheson, John McCloy); nor even of the lawyers and business executives who went to Washington to manage American war mobilization (Robert Patterson of the federal judiciary; James Forrestal and Ferdinand Eberstadt of Wall Street; Donald Nelson of Sears, Roebuck; Edward Stettinius of United States Steel; William Knudsen of General Motors). These gifted public servants of the 1940s did for the United States what the Austrian civil service had done for Emperor Francis Joseph over many decades; or what the British civil service, which a younger Schumpeter so admired, had done for 150 years.

Despite having taught at an elite university for more than a decade, Schumpeter had almost no direct exposure to this element of American society. He knew a few people at Harvard who distinguished themselves as public servants during the war, such as James B. Conant and John Kenneth Galbraith. He had no idea, however, that his own former students and colleagues Abram Bergson, Edward Mason, Paul Sweezy, and Wassily Leontief worked in secret for the Office of Strategic Services, the forerunner of the Central Intelligence Agency. He thought they were simply army officers. He never had any significant contact with Washington, D.C., which he viewed as a backwater by comparison to the much larger and more cultured cities of London, Paris, Vienna, Rome, Berlin, Tokyo, and Moscow. His experience of politics in Boston and most of Massachusetts was restricted to the corrupt boss rule of Mayor James Michael Curley and to the state's mostly undistinguished congressional representatives.[26]

Not until after the war did Schumpeter begin to change his mind about America's lack of sophistication. He had not foreseen its leadership in vital postwar initiatives such as the United Nations, the World Bank, the International Monetary Fund, the Marshall Plan, the North Atlantic Treaty Organization, or the General Agreement on Tariffs and Trade (now the World Trade Organization). Nor would he have predicted the wisdom and restraint shown by American Occupation authorities in Germany, Japan, Italy, and Austria from 1945 until the 1950s.[27]

On the other hand, Schumpeter was far more optimistic than most economists—or the American people as a whole—about the prospects for postwar prosperity. On Easter Sunday 1942 he wrote Gustav Stolper that Washington was already preparing for a "postwar slump," a development which in fact was "completely out of the question, unless one manufactures it." Yet very large numbers of people expected a return of some form of depression. Asked in a national poll during December 1944, "After the war, do you think that everyone who wants a job will be able to get one?" 68 percent of the respondents said no, and only 25 percent yes. Few economists other than Schumpeter predicted that consumer demand would help to create a golden age of American business. Yet that is what happened. An era of unprecedented affluence began during the war and was not seriously interrupted until the 1970s.[28]

In 1939 unemployment in the United States had stood at 17.2 percent. By 1944 it was only 1.2 percent, the lowest in the nation's history up to that time or since. The U.S. Army, with 190,000 troops, had ranked eighteenth in the world in 1939, just behind Bulgaria, and total American military forces numbered only 334,000. By 1944 this figure had multiplied thirty-four fold, and 11.5 million men and women were in uniform.[29]

American industry, fully mobilized by that time, was turning in one of the greatest economic performances in the world's history, for both consumer goods and military equipment. From 1940 to 1945 the United States built the almost incredible totals of 300,000 warplanes and 813,000 engines to power them. By comparison, during the entire twenty-year period preceding 1939, the nation had produced a total of only 13,500 military aircraft. During 1944 alone the United States built 96,000 such planes, including a large percentage of heavy bombers and large transports. In that same year, Germany and Japan produced a combined total of only 68,000, almost all of which were small fighter planes designed to defend against bombers.[30]

The miracle of American war mobilization confirmed numerous propositions about the dynamics of capitalism that Schumpeter had been proclaiming for thirty years. Of equal significance, the organization of war production in the United States lent support to Schumpeter's arguments about the importance and efficiency of large-scale business. His detailed research for *Business Cycles* had moved him toward this conviction; and in *Capitalism, Socialism and Democracy,* he had made no bones of his belief that big companies lay near the heart of advanced capitalist success.

Under the life-and-death pressure of war mobilization, the U.S. government concluded that established firms offered the most reliable source of arms, munitions, and equipment of all types. The Roosevelt administration, which had been hostile toward alleged monopolies, now decided that big businesses must lead in the job that had to be done. In 1942 a Senate subcommittee criticized this decision, pointing out that three fourths of all contracts for munitions and other military goods had gone to only fifty-six of the nation's 184,000 manufacturing firms. Of the prime defense contracts made during the first four years of mobilization, 30 percent (by value) went to only ten companies, ranked as follows: General Motors, Curtiss-Wright (aircraft and engines), Ford, Consolidated Vultee (aircraft), Douglas Aircraft, United Aircraft, Bethlehem Steel, Chrysler, General Electric, and Lockheed.[31]

These major firms, and about two hundred more like them, led the way in producing the immense amounts of matériel needed to fight the war. In the first two years, the organization of war production was chaotic. Numerous agencies overlapped one another's jurisdictions, and the military services competed among themselves (and even *with* themselves, as bureaus inside both the army and navy bid against each other for the same materials). But by 1943 the government had simplified procurement by focusing on three major items—steel, aluminum, and copper—and by rationing these three "controlled materials" to prime contractors, who in turn parceled them out to hundreds of thousands of subcontractors.[32]

In addition, the War Production Board prohibited the manufacture of a whole series of items that competed with military goods. The board forbade the making of civilian radio sets, electric washing machines, irons, toasters, stoves, waffle irons, heating pads, and electric shavers. The production of home refrigerators dropped by 99.7 percent between 1941 and 1943. Federal agencies rationed rubber, fuel oil, gasoline, meat, nylon, coffee, sugar, fats, and oils. Most important of all, the government forbade the production of automobiles—the last models left Detroit in March 1942, three months after Pearl Harbor. No new Chevrolets, Fords, Plymouths, or any other models reappeared on the market until 1946.[33]

Meanwhile, the Office of Price Administration, led by John Kenneth Galbraith, ably managed the crucial problem of war-induced inflation—the issue that had bedeviled Schumpeter as Austria's finance minister in 1919. Some of his former Harvard students and colleagues joined other economists in working at the Office of Price Administration, and by all accounts the group did a superb job.[34]

One of Schumpeter's many complaints about Roosevelt's New Deal was what he regarded as its "soak the rich" tax policies. He opposed this pattern of taxation not out of sympathy for the rich but because he believed that it deprived business of investment capital. Schumpeter regarded such measures as the Wealth Tax Act of 1935—which increased levies on both corporations and wealthy individuals—as counterproductive to economic recovery. World War II caused another sea change in the American tax system, but this time in the opposite direction, toward broadening its base.[35]

In 1932, when Schumpeter came to Harvard, less than 3 percent of the American people—taxpayers and their dependents—were even covered by an income tax return. His own generous salary of $12,000 placed him among the top 2 percent of earners, and he did file a return. But in 1942 the government added a "Victory Tax" of 5 percent of all annual gross incomes over $625, and this measure alone almost quadrupled the number of taxpayers. By 1943, because of the need to finance the war, the 3 percent of the 1933 population covered by a tax return had grown to 69 percent. Overall, the number of individual taxpayers soared from 4 million in 1939 to 43 million in 1945.[36]

Early in the war Congress had insisted on taxing the middle classes more than the Roosevelt administration wished, overriding a presidential veto. In 1943, to help implement this measure, the government enacted the modern system of the payroll withholding tax. This law, now familiar to almost everyone who has a job, largely replaced the old practice of voluntary annual or quarterly payments by individuals. Henceforth, employers would subtract taxes from workers' paychecks and forward the funds to the Internal Revenue Service. Overall, the government financed a little less than half of all war expenditures through current taxation. It borrowed the rest, issuing bonds ranging from very small to very large denominations.[37]

The war wrought numerous other economic and social changes: the entry of masses of women and minorities into the military services and into jobs from which they had long been excluded; the movement of huge new populations to the Sunbelt, as training bases and military production gravitated toward Florida, Texas, and California; an enormous jump in research and development, which created or boosted entire new industries (antibiotics, synthetic chemicals, advanced telecommunications, commercial aviation, and medical technology); and the smoothing out of the business cycle, as federal and state governments took more responsibility for overall prosperity. Many of these trends gave additional evidence of the flexibility and immense productivity of capitalism as an economic system.[38]

In addition to aircraft production, the American business system produced during the war years 86,000 tanks, 193,000 artillery pieces, 17 million handguns and rifles, 41 billion rounds of ammunition, 12,000 warships and merchant ships, 65,000 smaller vessels for coastal patrols and amphibious landings, 2 million army trucks, and an even larger number of "Jeeps." Nearly all of this colossal production was done by private companies, as the government negotiated 350,000 contracts with 40,000 prime contractors. "In addition," as a Commerce Department document reported after the war, "many times that number of contracts were made between these prime contractors and their suppliers or subcontractors." The civilian work week in manufacturing grew from 38 hours to 45. Defense-related employment rose from 9 percent of the total in 1941 to 40 percent by 1943.[39]

War profiteering by private firms was held to a minimum by the threat of severe penalties for violations. Because the evils of the Nazi regime were so abhorrent, because the country had been attacked by Japan, and because the message of patriotism was so effectively put forth by the Office of War Information (which did not hesitate to use racism to demonize Japan), the American people were united as never before or since.[40]

Viewed in long retrospect, it is clear that the economic performance of the American economy during World War II validated the theories of both Schumpeter and Keynes. The Keynesian prescription for ending the Great Depression through deficit financing for public investment found expression in the expenditure of vast amounts of borrowed money to help pay for the war. Schumpeter's argument that ample credit creation and private-sector innovation would lead to immense economic production came true well beyond even his own expectations. Because the U.S. economy performed such miracles during the war—the instances of innovation and entrepreneurship being so numerous as almost to defy calculation—Schumpeter had every reason to believe that his ideas about the nature of capitalism had been confirmed in grand style.

He might also have taken pleasure from a very unusual personal honor he received during the war. In celebration of his sixtieth birthday, fourteen of his friends and students contributed articles that make up the February 1943 issue of the *Review of Economic Statistics,* an elite quarterly published at Harvard. As the contributors say in their introduction, "May this number of the *Review* be regarded by Professor Schumpeter as an expression of friendship and as a token of gratitude and appreciation of his contributions to economic science and for the stimulating influence of his written and spoken word."[41]

This homage to Schumpeter suggests that his unpopular views of American foreign policy did not significantly affect the esteem in which he was held by the people who meant most to him. About half of the fourteen contributors were Jews, and five had emigrated to the United States from Europe during the 1930s. Most of the articles in the special issue address some aspect of Schumpeter's work, directly or indirectly. All but two contain the kind of mathematical notation he encouraged though seldom used himself. None is primarily concerned with wartime economics, but several do refer to the war. Each is a thoughtful engagement of an important economic question, and the quality of the essays is very high.[42]

Despite this exceptional tribute, and despite the success of *Capitalism, Socialism and Democracy,* Schumpeter was not a happy man during this period. He was dissatisfied with the Harvard milieu, and the war had plunged him into a hopeless confusion of emotions. He felt generally alienated from American society, which he still did not understand. For example, in a poll conducted in November 1944—six months before the end of World War II in Europe—the Gallup organization asked Americans about their views of the postwar world. To the question, "Do you think Russia can be trusted to cooperate with us when the war is over?" 47 percent of the respondents answered yes, 18 percent had no opinion, and 35 percent said no. Schumpeter believed this kind of thinking to be still another example of Americans' almost willful ignorance of history and foreign affairs.[43]

By contrast, as he looked at Europe and Asia through his customary lens of well-informed analysis, he grasped the long-term instability of the international situation far better than most of his contemporaries. He all but predicted the Cold War, which was to last for forty-five years after the end of World War II. When Franklin D. Roosevelt died on April 14, 1945, Schumpeter again went to his diary to record his thoughts:

> I can say this for me that I did not feel anything improper but I want to set down two first impressions
> 1.) lucky man: to die in fullness of power and what to the man in the street seems success—4 years later he would have died discredited and defeated
> 2.) His death makes no difference *now*—the harm is done . . . to swing the country into the new position dictated by the Russian tiger.
> Know nothing about Truman, but my guess is that he will nail his colors to the Rooseveltian mast . . .
> We have produced what we feared—the military world power [the Soviet Union] that rules Europe and Asia; much more, too, than

in their wildest dreams the Germanophobes can ever have believed Germany would. We have set up the very thing we went out to fight.[44]

In the 1990s, after the Czechs threw off the Soviet yoke, the street on which Schumpeter was born was renamed for Roosevelt, whom he had never trusted—another irony in a saga replete with ironies.

HARPER & BROTHERS, the publisher of *Capitalism, Socialism and Democracy,* asked Schumpeter to prepare a second edition for publication in 1947. Without changing the text, he added a long chapter entitled "The Consequences of the Second World War," which he wrote in 1946. Much of the new material dealt with the threat to world peace posed by the Soviet Union, which Schumpeter outlined in a lengthy section called "Russian Imperialism and Communism." As was his custom, he related it to long-run historical forces as well as to the current situation. There, he focused on another of his favorite themes—the role of individual leadership—in this case, the dominant figure of Joseph Stalin.

He begins with a provocative statement: "If the reader recalls the aims by which the United States Government motivated its policy since 1939—democracy, freedom from fear and want, small nations, etc.—he will have to realize that what has occurred amounts to a surrender." This defeat derived not from any triumph by Germany or Japan but "from a military victory of Russia over her two chief allies." The United States and Britain could not possibly have wished for the kind of Soviet takeover of Eastern and Central Europe that actually evolved. And the manner in which the conquest was being administered—through captive states with allegedly independent voices—augmented Soviet power more than outright annexation would have. It increased by about ten the number of countries speaking the Kremlin's party line in forums such as the United Nations.[45]

Joseph Stalin, Schumpeter believed, had displayed a "master's handiwork" in his conduct of the war:

> The impersonal or objective factors were all against Russia. Even her huge army was not simply the product of a numerous popula-

tion and a rich economy, but the work of one man who was strong
enough to keep that population in abject poverty and submission
and to concentrate all the forces of an undeveloped and defective
industrial apparatus on the one military purpose. But this would
not have been enough . . . Political genius consists precisely in the
ability to exploit favorable possibilities and to neutralize unfavorable ones so completely that, after the fact, the superficial observer
sees nothing but the former.[46]

Schumpeter was harsh in his indictment of the United States for allowing Soviet domination to occur, and he believed he knew why it happened.
"In Stalinist Russia, foreign policy is foreign policy as it was under the tsars.
In the United States foreign policy is domestic politics." Because of the country's longstanding aversion to overseas alliances, "there is no tradition and
there are no organs for playing the complex game of any other foreign policy."
(The anti-Soviet North Atlantic Treaty Organization did not come into existence until 1949.) The American national resolve aroused by Pearl Harbor,
Schumpeter argued, was being overcome by a longing to return to familiar
peacetime life. This was an accurate diagnosis of majoritarian feelings in the
United States in 1946.[47]

No significant American interest group was inclined to challenge the Soviets, Schumpeter argued. Labor was even more antiwar in 1946 than it had been
in 1940. And, whether they realized it or not, the views of businesspeople
amounted to giving Russia a free hand. Schumpeter presented a pastiche of
comments he had heard Americans express: "Soviet Russia may become a very
big customer. She has never yet failed to pay promptly . . . Let Russia swallow
one or two more countries, what of it? Let her be well supplied with everything
she needs and she will cease to frown. After twenty years Russians will be just
as democratic and pacific as we are—and think and feel just as do we. Besides,
Stalin will be dead by then."[48]

But Schumpeter feared that the problem of Soviet Russia would persist long
after the disappearance of Stalin. While never espousing a "great man" theory
of history, Schumpeter believed that "in a given situation, brains and nerves of
the man at the helm are just as objective facts as are iron content of the country's ore and presence or absence of molybdenum or vanadium." Although Sta-

lin's ability might have been necessary to create the leviathan of Soviet power, "it does not require genius to run it once it has been built up. The Russian century once started may run its course almost of itself."[49]

From the tendencies he had observed, Schumpeter was prepared to predict that Stalin would avoid provoking a war for whatever period was necessary to permit the Soviet Union to restore its economy and develop overwhelming military strength. "Perception of this fact is, of course, the essence of Churchillian warnings [such as the Iron Curtain speech] and the rationale of the armament race that has already started."[50]

Schumpeter identified the driving force of Soviet expansion as simple imperialism, not a desire to convert the world to some Marxist paradise of classless equality. "The trouble with Russia is not that she is socialist but that she is Russia. As a matter of fact, the Stalinist regime is essentially a militarist autocracy." If a new war did come, it would be so brutal that contending ideologies would be mere details.[51]

As he wrote his new chapter for *Capitalism, Socialism and Democracy,* Schumpeter was also working on his huge new book, *History of Economic Analysis.* A brief but significant section of that book is devoted to what he calls "Economics in the 'Totalitarian' Countries"—Germany under Hitler, Italy under Mussolini, and the Soviet Union under Stalin. The patterns of economic governance in these three countries, he argues, were more different than one might expect.[52]

In Germany, the fundamental Nazi doctrines, based on racial superiority, had little to do with economics per se. They were therefore "compatible not only with all kinds of technical economics but also with the advocacy of widely differing policies." Within German universities, the politicization of economics had begun during the Weimar Republic of 1919–1933, on the assumption that the subject more closely resembled philosophy than a pure science such as physics. Universities themselves resisted this pressure, but the precedent had been set; and the Nazi regime proceeded to take full advantage of it, appointing Nazi party members and removing Jews and socialists. Administrators in some universities took a harder position than their counterparts elsewhere in Germany, and in many cases teachers of economics felt strong pressure to conform to the Nazi line.[53]

Oddly enough, however, professional research was allowed to continue, though less in economics than in the physical sciences. "Nobody would have got into trouble in consequence of having worked out new theoretical or statistical tools. A work like Keynes's *General Theory* could have appeared unmolested—and did." This was true. Many Nazis argued that Keynes's blueprint for recovery through deficit financing by government closely resembled what the Hitler government had been doing since 1933. (Indeed, the Weimar chancellors who preceded Hitler had already begun programs of Keynesian-style demand management in 1932.) One of Schumpeter's major points about Nazi economics was that Hitler himself had little interest in the subject and tended to leave individual decisions to his subordinates.[54]

In Italy, by contrast, Benito Mussolini held much stronger and more definite views about economics than Hitler did. The details of Fascist economics in Italy were embodied in a type of syndicated capitalism, in which private interest groups would organize and police themselves under public authority. Transcending competitive individualism, they would unite for the greater glory of the nation. Mussolini, an intellectual and former journalist, wrote about these issues himself; and the economic measures of his government, even in their details, were widely considered to be his own personal policies. Yet, as in Germany, strictly scientific research was allowed to continue without much harassment.[55]

Not so in the Soviet Union. There, the very *basis* of the totalitarian state was economic, and no one could deviate in the slightest from official doctrines. This was especially true after Stalin gained complete ascendancy in 1927. At that time, most elite Russian economists were either exiled or liquidated or both. Nikolai Kondratieff, on whose work Schumpeter had relied in *Business Cycles,* was banished to Siberia in 1930 and executed in the purges of 1938. As Schumpeter wrote, "Scientific research itself, not only discussion of policies, was regimented in a manner unheard of in Germany or Italy, not only because of the nature and methods of the bolshevist administration but also because of two other reasons that contradicted and, nevertheless, reinforced each other."[56]

The first of these reasons was that the fundamental ideological dogmas underlying the Soviet state were not racial, as in Germany, but economic. Thus, as with German racism, no departure from sacred doctrinal truth, however trivial or hypothetical, could be tolerated. The other reason, somewhat paradoxically, was that "the bolshevist government very naturally exploited to the full the naive emotionality of 'the revolutionary people,' who necessarily believed that, the millennium having arrived, there were no longer such things as 'economic laws' and hence no need for any economic analysis at all." In this bizarre setting, economic discussions deteriorated into attempts to please officials in the Kremlin. Censure of alleged dissenters began to displace reasoned scientific disagreement.[57]

The Bolsheviks' appeal to their own versions of Marxist purity met scant resistance. In part this was because many Russian economists had been Marxists even before the revolution of 1917. Even so, until Stalinist absolutism triumphed in 1927, disagreements among theorists were not prohibited. In this pre-1927 milieu, serious thinkers such as Kondratieff and Nikolai Bukharin were able to contribute original economic insights. "This work," Schumpeter wrote, "in spite of the sinister implications of the fact that some of the authors have not been heard of since, may be taken as proof that serious economics survived until the rigors of the Stalinist regime fully asserted themselves."[58]

After Stalin gained complete control, matters often took ludicrous turns. In 1937 the Census Board reported a Soviet population of 162 million. Since state demographers had told Stalin to expect the total to be 177 million, he had the Census Board arrested and shot for the crime of "treasonably exerting themselves to diminish the population of the USSR" (the government's own words). The Communist Party economist S. G. Strumilin announced that "our task is not to study economics but to change it. We are bound by no laws."[59]

Even in the Soviet Union, however, the abandonment of common sense had practical limits. Soviet planners continued to use techniques inherited from the pre-Stalinist period, especially in statistical and mathematical methods too subtle for easy political assault. Some Soviet contributions in these subfields even received international recognition. Writing in the 1940s, Schumpeter pointed out that the current trend in Russian economics was to "smuggle" basic principles such as "actuarial norms and the concepts of value, marginal productivity, and interest" into the Soviet system by disguising their "capitalist" origins. Although progress along these lines remained slow and was hostage to potential denunciation, Schumpeter predicted that it would continue. The reason was that economics itself has a logic that transcends capitalism. Any regime, if it is to administer a government at all, needs the tools of modern budgeting techniques and national income accounting—even the USSR.[60]

Yet Schumpeter went on to underscore a particular problem of scientific economics within the Soviet Union. The Bolshevik leaders—Trotsky, Stalin, and especially Lenin—had themselves produced reams of writing on issues better left to professional economists. According to Schumpeter, he did not take up their arguments in more detail because the book he was working on was a history of serious *analysis,* not just of economic thought—however politically powerful the thinkers may have been.[61]

As things turned out, Schumpeter was proved partly right and partly wrong. Soviet bureaucrats did adopt sophisticated macroeconomic methods. But the party line sometimes required that they distort their data so as to indicate progress when in fact none had occurred. In an Orwellian pattern, Soviet ideology led to a system in which different sections of the government routinely lied to one another, and this was an important element in the ultimate collapse of Soviet Communism in 1991.

All of this notwithstanding, certain aspects of the Soviet record in the twentieth century remain remarkable—and indisputable. During the seventy-four years in which it held power (1917–1991), the Communist regime managed to industrialize the country beyond the most far-fetched dreams of the tsars; to defeat the Nazis in the Great Patriotic War of 1941–1945; to build not only the world's most powerful army but also an immense navy, air force, and nuclear arsenal; to govern the largest country on earth, plus more than a dozen others as well through puppet regimes; to launch into space the first satellite *(Sputnik),* and then the first cosmonaut (Yuri Gagarin); and, for seven decades, to threaten the capitalist West in a deadly contest for global supremacy.

Exactly how the Soviets were able to achieve these goals under such a dysfunctional economic system remains something of a puzzle. Certainly a radical indifference to the production of consumer goods played an overwhelmingly important role. And the command-economy nature of Soviet management was often effective in pursuing large projects such as the nuclear weapons and space programs. The mass murder or imprisonment of all real and imagined internal opponents may have been necessary to keep the system running, or it may not have been. But the tyranny of fear proved effective in perpetuating one of the most brutal regimes in human history.[62]

23

Introspection

I, a stranger and afraid
In a world I never made.

A. E. HOUSMAN, "The Laws of God," 1922

THE YEARS OF WORLD WAR II were a time of intense personal reflection for Schumpeter. When he submitted the manuscript of *Capitalism, Socialism and Democracy* in 1942, he had fewer hopes for the book than for any of his other major works. He had learned, as all authors do, that books have unpredictable lives of their own. So he took little joy in its publication. His overall mood continued as it had been while he was writing the book: anxiety about his health, nostalgia for happier times, and despondency about the war.

In his copious diary entries of 1939–1945, he wrote a great deal about the war but even more about himself. At no other period had he been so introspective, so obsessed with his successes and failures, his mortality and legacy. His comments about his environment, and about Harvard in particular, are almost all negative. "The serious thing about it is my reaction," he wrote in 1942. "Instead of being amused by the cunning antics in the professorial monkey cage I was so irritated that I could not work at all and I felt so defeated, so defeated! So frustrated and weak and old—so lost in this stifling atmosphere of Harvard which is more like a brewery." And in 1945: "Harvard—despicable playground of despicable little tyrants self-ruining of splendid possibilities."[1]

In most of his diary entries he scrawled out disjointed comments on the state of humanity, the war, the Soviet Union, the condition of his health, and the course of his career. Now and then, he expressed a kind of muted joy at the blooming of spring and other seasonal changes—but very seldom. His diary also contains occasional negative remarks about blacks, Jews, "sub-normals," and the English—his former Anglophilia now a casualty of his anti-imperialism. But in frequency and feeling these entries do not approach his censures of President Roosevelt, the Soviet Union, and Harvard—a curious trio of villains.

His most absorbing concern was a growing sense of his own mortality. He gained about twenty pounds during the early 1940s and began to suffer from high blood pressure. He got little exercise except for his walks beside the lakes near Taconic, and even these were often impossible because of bad winter weather.

He usually felt physically unwell, and he expressed his forebodings in crude poems jotted down in haste, as in this entry of September 6, 1941, written in Taconic:

> My death comes like the servant
> Who walks about the room
> To blow out the candles
> After the feast
> Wouldn't do to blow them earlier
> While life and joy goes on
> Wouldn't do to leave them burning
> After the feast
> So it's all right.
> It would have been a pity to blow them before
> But neither should they go on burning after the feast.
> To live the lives which are our own
> To manage our affairs
> That's what the people wanted
> Who founded this recourse
> Those lives are gone forever
> So is our management

Lives and affairs alike are now managed for us
So what?

But, as always, salvation through work, as expressed in January 1942:

I have no time for growing old
Nor for lament
I have
my work to do.

Occasional self-dramatization, in early 1942:

And if I worthless was and frivolous
in many junctures of my life
. . . vain & snob. . .
it is still time now that the day
draws to the end
and darkness & dreary invest me
that the last day of my force
I am at least
doing my duty
Putting up a brave fight
in the last ditch
in the valley of death.

And a persistent sense of being apart, a pilgrim in an alien land, penned on January 6, 1942:

This is no longer my world
I am a stranger to the mortals and their doings
to the shadows and their marionette drama.

Yet, in an entry on the same day: "I took a stride toward old age or more directly toward death. Heart & brains & limbs all go . . . I don't know that I can do much about it or that I want to. This should color my plans but it does not—thank God! For they are my life & joy & my heart I must play with them as long as I can . . . This should color my attitude—for this is the worst, I worry just as much as if I had children and a life before me!"

All of these diary entries were made before he submitted the manuscript of *Capitalism, Socialism and Democracy* in the summer of 1942. Afterward, in October and November, he continued along the same introspective vein: "I think the most interesting fact about life is death. God has the kindness to show me that I don't lose much in dying. It is some comfort! What is that world to me from which all the little futilities will have vanished which are civilization to me?"

In contemplating the irrational forces that seemed to be moving the wartime world, he wrote:

> Preference and prejudice play a greater role . . .
> I have given my life to analysis and reason
> I believe in the value of reason . . .
> And in applying reason to human affairs . . .
> What then remains—[2]

And he speculated on the distractions that prevented his accomplishing more work. (The words in brackets are his own):

1. Women
2. Art [and architecture]
3. Sport [and horses]
4. Science [and Philosophy]
5. Politics [Public Career]
6. Travel
7. Money [Business]

But he then concludes that "I did not do so badly."[3]

These thoughts were set down in the early years of the war. They appear randomly, mixed with other diary entries dealing with foreign policy, his impatience with bureaucrats at Harvard, and the prospect of Soviet domination of the postwar world. Only when the passages about himself are consolidated does it become evident that these were the most sustained series of self-revelatory thoughts Schumpeter ever recorded.

"I singularly lack the quality of leadership—with a fraction of my ideas a new economics could have been founded," he wrote, and then continued:

> Funny when I survey my life and my present situation—I see that
> I was favored in many respects and I also see a mosaic of many
> successes. Yet, as a whole and in a worldly sense, and quite apart
> (tho perhaps not so "apart" after all) from the fact that subjectively
> I was unhappy most of the time, it was a failure. And the reason is
> quite clear—even in my scientific activity and in spite of an
> "oeuvre" a fraction of which would have been enough for "fame", I
> do not carry weight: For I am typically "unleaderly"—in fact I am
> a man without an aura (and without antennae)—and since I am
> subordinating everything to "analysis", I will use even this in order
> to better understand how history is created . . . What is that
> "aura"? It is not the sense of the humors of the people, it is not
> simply tactical . . . judgment, it is not simply "quiet attitude of
> strength" nor "efficiency"—all these are but necessary outworks of
> a force (electrical perhaps) that I have not yet discovered.

In the purely intellectual sense, Schumpeter was a good deal more leaderly than he thought. But he seems to have meant a type of leadership (and the fame that went with it) exemplified by economists such as Gustav von Schmoller, Alfred Marshall, and John Maynard Keynes.[4]

In the very perceptive sketches he would later write about each of these men, Schumpeter emphasized their personal magnetism and the energy they infused into the schools of economics they came to represent. Yet he continued to scorn all such schools—just as he rejected schools of mathematics, physics, and other hard sciences. He insisted that there were only good and bad economists, not superior or inferior schools. Being the leader of a distinct school of economics therefore would have violated one of his own tenets.

In any case, he was far too much the showman, the solo performer, to be leaderly in the sense he meant. The number of first-rate theorists and artists who are also topflight stage performers is very small. It includes practically nobody who could be characterized as leaderly in Schumpeter's sense. Mozart was not leaderly. Nor were Charles Dickens, Mark Twain, or, more recently, Orson Welles, John Lennon, or even the American physicist Richard Feynman, a Nobel Prize winner. None was willing to give up his role as performer in favor of gathering acolytes and founding a school of artistry or thought.

Schumpeter's own streak of showmanship ran much deeper than he realized. He needed the applause of audiences, in all its immediacy, far more than he needed discipleship. Even during his acute introspection of the 1940s, when he was past sixty, he was still performing his dramatic routines not only in the classroom but also at professional meetings. Paul Samuelson once estimated that no economist ever addressed more of his peers than Schumpeter, who always turned in a stellar performance. And in the classroom, where he really let himself go—roaming through economics, history, and sociology in stream-of-consciousness monologues—students still found him as fascinating as ever. In 1944 Harvard's student newspaper reported that "Schumpy is just wonderful." As always, his public persona remained ebullient regardless of his inner turmoil.[5]

Beyond disliking "schools" and being a showman, a third reason for his alleged unleaderliness was his fondness for "aphorisms," as he called them in his diary. These comments, which peppered his conversation as well, seem to reflect his growing sense of himself as a detached and skeptical sage:

10/9/42: Mankind is prepared to believe anything except the truth.

4/25/43: The doctor who in dying puts down the symptoms—that is man at his best.

5/29/43: Humanity does not care for freedom. The mass of the people realize that they are not up to it: what they want is being fed, led, amused, and above everything, drilled. But they do care for the phrase [freedom].

11/11/43: The Roman Empire did not fall when its administration was brutal, inefficient, corrupt, but after it had reason to be the cultural center of the world.

11/19/43: To hunt for food and women and to kill enemies—that is and always was what man wanted and was fitted for, and this is the greatest happiness for the greatest number.

12/12/43: Hatred is all right and even a poisoned dagger; but it should not be hidden in a prayer book.

12/21/43: Two kinds of people I distrust: architects who profess to build cheaply and economists who profess to give simple answers.

12/21/43: There are two values in life: the first is victory the second is vengeance.

1/2/44: What is a day and what is life? A block of marble that God gives to you to make a work of art.

1/3/44: And humanity is but marble in hands that as little care about its joys and sufferings as the sculptor cares about the feelings of the marble.

2/28/44:
To live is to love
But also to hate
To live is to fight
But also to lie.

6/?/44: Politicians are like bad horsemen who are so preoccupied with keeping in the saddle that they can't bother about where they go.

?/1944: This country [the United States] never sees facts. Nothing exists for it but the slogan.

5/27/44: That rara avis—an honest idealist.

8/?/44: The more I know about modern humanity the more I am impressed by the comparative gentleness of Jinghis Khan.

11/?44: Victory—revenge—love—hate: the four pivots of life.

2/?/45: A statesman is the criminal who works with phrases instead of with the burglar's jimmy.[6]

The dark humor of his aphorisms may be worthy of Oscar Wilde, Ambrose Bierce, Noel Coward, or the Viennese Karl Kraus, but not of someone who aspires to be leaderly.

As quick as he could be with the *bon mot* in conversation or on the podium, Schumpeter refused to simplify his writing. By comparison with other major theorists, stretching from Adam Smith to Keynes, he insisted on giving opposing arguments not only their due but far more—elaborating on them at length. This is one of the traits that make *Capitalism, Socialism and Democracy* such a compelling book, so provocative and puzzling to readers of many political persuasions. In the end, the book delivers solid conclusions—but not until the full panoply of reasoning from several perspectives has been put on display. No significant question, Schumpeter implies, has an easy answer. He preferred to give briefs for all sides, not a polemic for only one.

More generally, in both his own work and his artistic tastes he disdained any message that could be quickly grasped by masses of people. At just the time when the student newspaper was waxing eloquent about his being a wonderful teacher, he wrote in his diary that a course in economics offered by one of his colleagues pandered to the simple-minded. Its popularity "was partly due to its didactics—accessible—pedestrian nature. [Maybe like certain] successes in Art. Yes! Only look—Venus de Milo, Laocoon, Rafael's Madonnas!"[7]

In the book that became *History of Economic Analysis,* which he was composing at this same time, he writes something similar about Adam Smith: that Smith's appeal derived from a simple presentation of obvious thoughts. "Had he been more brilliant, he would not have been taken so seriously. Had he dug more deeply, had he unearthed more recondite truth, had he used difficult and ingenious methods, he would not have been understood. But he had no such ambitions; in fact he disliked whatever went beyond plain common sense. He never moved above the heads of even the dullest readers. He led them on gently, encouraging them by trivialities and homely observations, making them feel comfortable all along." Most importantly, Adam Smith's appeal was "enlivened by advocacy which is after all what attracts a wider public."[8]

Had Schumpeter truly wished to be leaderly, he would have embraced advocacy—as did Smith, Ricardo, Schmoller, Keynes, and many younger economists such as Hayek, Friedman, Galbraith, and Samuelson. Schumpeter rejected not only advocacy but any form of sustained controversy. He insisted on using all contributions that seemed relevant. From the time of his very first book, in which he tried to reconcile warring factions in the German and Austrian schools of economics, he was convinced that polemics were hostile to scientific progress.[9]

In this he was badly mistaken. The annals of science are full of advocacy and polemics, which are often the only ways to break out of stalemates and false paradigms. Sometimes intellectual infighting *has* been wasted over useless political turmoil. But much more frequently, controversy has fueled the progress of knowledge—from the time of Plato's *Dialogues,* to Galileo's heretical theories about the cosmos, and down to contemporary disputes about how best to study a field such as biology. Academic fights between molecular and evolutionary biologists have caused many a bitter split, but they have moved the life sciences forward. Often the same has been true of economics, as in the post-World War II clash between Keynesians and Monetarists.[10]

But Schumpeter tried to remain above it all. In neither his undergraduate lectures nor his graduate seminars did he ever make the slightest mention of his own enormous body of work. He separated his writing from his teaching, just as he separated his upbeat public persona from the despair of his private diary. As the Chicago economist George J. Stigler put it, he "had an almost otherworldly detachment with respect to theories and policies, and it was reinforced by the mischievous pleasure he got from keeping out of step with the crowd." From the onset of Schumpeter's life as a scholar, he insisted on striking a value-neutral stance. This is one of the qualities that made him unleaderly, not only in his own eyes but also in those of some contemporaries. Had he wanted to be leaderly, he would have embraced the rough and tumble of controversy. (Samuelson coined a memorable phrase, "revealed preference," to gauge by a person's behavior what that person really wanted.)[11]

Schumpeter, at heart, was a scholar in the purest sense—a contemplative—but one who also happened to be a magnificent showman. This extremely rare blend of temperaments, almost by itself, precludes leaderliness. Schumpeter resorted to showmanship not so much to persuade his audiences as to entertain them with his erudition and wit, and to bask in their response. These were supreme values in the Vienna of his youth, and they were still essential to his sense of self.

In the closing years of World War II he again went through a period of introspection similar to that of the war's early period. From 1944 to 1946 he wrote in his diary dozens of thoughts that might have been expressed by a refugee, a displaced person, a stranger in a world he never made. As he told his friend Irving Fisher in February 1946, "I feel ill in mind and body (and not only because of what happened in the war), always tired and downcast and am dragging myself through work which nevertheless *is all I do not hate.* This is of course for you alone."[12]

In the spring of 1946 he decided not to attend the annual meeting of the American Economic Association, as he had done regularly for many years. "All right, then," he told himself in his diary, "but don't be sort of nettled at being left 'out of it' so far as [the Association] is concerned, in the future. There is no doubt [much] to be said for keeping to myself, going my way, retiring from the world—but it must then be accepted that I don't count." For the moment, Schumpeter was content not to count on the world stage—so long as the world did not look behind the stage curtain. But he was being much too pessimistic. Some of the best work of his life lay just ahead, and he was about to receive unprecedented recognition by his peers.[13]

24

Honors and Crises

So teach us to number our days, that we may apply our
hearts unto wisdom.

PSALM 90:12

THE POSTWAR YEARS proved Schumpeter wrong: his influence and
prestige on the world stage far surpassed his own estimation. But his newfound
acclaim did not come without pains elsewhere in his life. The two relationships
that structured his existence—his marriage to Elizabeth and his position at
Harvard—both underwent dramatic changes.

In 1947 the second edition of *Capitalism, Socialism and Democracy* made a
splash, and by then Schumpeter had hit another stride of high productivity in
his writing. In addition to almost constant work on his *History of Economic
Analysis,* he had begun to compose important articles on a variety of topics: entrepreneurship, inflation, history, and the sociology of knowledge. He did not
attend as many professional meetings as before, but he had been to so many
over the years that the slight reduction meant little. As always, he was his affa-
ble self on any public occasion—joking with others, introducing himself as
"Joe Schumpeter," and giving memorable performances from the platform.[1]

In December 1947 his peers elected him president of the American Economic Association, the most prestigious office in the country for an economist,
and the first time in the association's seventy-five-year history that a foreign-

born scholar had been chosen. Nor was it merely an honorary post, because the president had to plan and organize the program for the next annual meeting. This task required hundreds of letters and telephone calls, careful diplomacy with fragile egos (most proposals for papers had to be rejected), and interim sessions with the program committee. Schumpeter worked throughout 1948, organizing such a superb program that, as one colleague recalled, he "effectively dissipated the impression of casualness and helplessness in practical matters that he strove so sedulously to cultivate." And he could do the necessary correspondence and telephoning as easily from Taconic as from Cambridge.[2]

He was living his life within the two havens of scholarship Elizabeth had constructed for him, like fortresses against intrusions from the outside world. Throughout the 1940s, both Schumpeters devoted themselves almost wholly to their scholarly work. His own main effort was on the book that became *History of Economic Analysis.* Another project that took up much of his time was a "General Theory" book "aiming at doing from my standpoint, what Keynes aimed at doing under that title from *his* standpoint." But his heart was really in his history of economic analysis, and Elizabeth helped a great deal with the research. She accompanied him on hundreds of trips to Harvard Business School, helping to dig out obscure tracts from the Kress Library's treasury of rare books and pamphlets.[3]

In addition to assisting her husband's research, Elizabeth continued her own work on the economy of Japan. She studied the Japanese language and looked forward to publishing more articles and another book. But the war and its aftermath had made some of the essential new materials inaccessible. At the same time, Americans' continuing prejudice against Japan increased the kinds of problems she had experienced before Pearl Harbor—an aversion of the reading public to thinking about life in Japan at all, even in the economic way Elizabeth emphasized.

This kind of popular distaste does not necessarily deter scholars, and for a long time it did not shake Elizabeth's commitment. But it did affect the potential market for the book she wanted to write. Harvard's subventions to Macmillan, the house that had published her first book, had ceased when the Rockefeller Foundation's grants to Harvard itself expired. McGraw-Hill, which had brought out *Business Cycles,* turned her down, and other publishers were no more receptive.

Confronted with this situation, Elizabeth reluctantly dropped work on Japan and returned to her history of British overseas trade, the topic of her dissertation. As she helped her husband with his history of economic analysis, she resumed the compilation of British trade statistics from the seventeenth and eighteenth centuries. In 1960 this work was published by Oxford University Press in a slim but oversized volume that looks like a hardcover magazine. The book has a short text, followed by dozens of pages of statistics elegantly transcribed in Elizabeth's own hand. But she did not live to see it in print.[4]

Ever since her marriage to Schumpeter in 1937, Elizabeth had taken care of the family finances, done all the shopping, and arranged every aspect of their daily lives. During the academic year, she drove Schumpeter back and forth between Cambridge and Taconic. In the late 1940s he began to commute the 115-mile distance to teach his courses, which usually met on Mondays and Wednesdays. Dividing the week into halves, he and Elizabeth would arrive at their Cambridge house on Sunday, and then depart for Taconic on another 115-mile trip late Wednesday or early Thursday, after his classes and office hours.

Elizabeth's efforts enormously increased her husband's productivity. His career was now fully resurrected, and both his teaching and writing were going very well. In Cambridge, she made no objection when he stashed his books and manuscripts haphazardly in a half-dozen rooms and closets. At Windy Hill in Taconic, she adapted a bedroom upstairs to be his main office—an ideal place to write, silent except for the pleasant sizzle of logs burning in the fireplace during wintertime. She also converted a downstairs pantry into an additional study. As in Cambridge, she made no complaint when he scattered his notes, research materials, and work-in-progress all over the house. Nor did she object to his keeping a picture of Annie on his bedside table—an inconsiderate reminder of her husband's great love, which she could never dislodge.[5]

Early in 1948 Schumpeter began to consider retiring from Harvard to devote all his time to writing. He had just turned sixty-five and had completed the fifteen years of faculty service required for his pension. In 1931 he had negotiated with President Lowell a retirement allowance of $4,000. But because of inflation, $4,000 in 1948 had less than a third of its purchasing power in 1932, and it was also less than a third of Schumpeter's salary of $14,000—the university's maximum at the time.

As he wrote in his diary, "I brought [up] topic of retirement and asked E.

whether she still considered it possible. But hesitatingly she said retirement is possible only if Taconic is sold. But that amounts pretty much to No." Elizabeth knew how much her husband loved their idyllic retreat. In June 1948 he acknowledged "how impossible retirement is. Even when no further inflation is threatening, I even could not keep up sending checks"—to the Reisingers in Vienna, the Stöckels in Jülich (where Treschen was bringing up Mia's two children), and to about a dozen other European friends in desperate straits. Nor was Schumpeter particularly anxious to retire. He needed an audience and was still a star classroom performer. And his recent routine of commuting to Cambridge from Taconic had made his life more peaceful and stable than it had ever been before.[6]

Then disaster hit. Just before her fiftieth birthday in August 1948, Elizabeth learned that she had breast cancer. Schumpeter assumed the worst, having never forgotten that he had done the opposite when Annie fell ill twenty-two years earlier. In his diary, he wrote "Despair"—in huge letters covering much of a page. For two weeks he seemed unable to bring himself out of a tailspin, as he tried to put his thoughts into some kind of rational order:

> The lightning from blue skies has struck me. Note that 1.) the sky was clear. 2.) I completely depend upon Elizabeth. And that my feelings were not felt [sic] and even those expressed were but a sham and a deception. That she gave me more than I her, and that I actually did not know it. 3.) Still beneath this there is a deep attachment, the product of 11 years together. 4.) I could not go on without her. All that is only half whining. Now suddenly everything becomes serious. Since the end approaches anyhow and nothing enjoyable will happen between now and then, it is irrational to continue to live.

On the night before Elizabeth's mastectomy at a hospital near Taconic, he wrote out another long entry. Again the thought of suicide seemed to cross his mind:

> Tomorrow is the operation. In this book [his diary] there is little about the whole matter and the bravery with which the courageous woman faces her ordeal. And this is the beginning of the

end. I have no desire to philosophize and to write about it. It is
just too serious. One does not philosophize on a sinking ship. And
also there is not much to plan any more. Just the little papers and
the necessary correspondence. And now what do you have? What
do you want? What is so unbelievable is the emptiness and eeri-
ness. Is death avoidable? If it is not, then it is clear that there is
nothing. Why not go yourself? I will not feel sorry for Elizabeth
when she has to depart. All good is done and past for her and
for me.

But to Schumpeter's great surprise and relief, Elizabeth's surgery and follow-up
radiation therapy were successful, and her prognosis good. She would never
again be quite as strong or vigorous, but she did not seem to be terminally ill.
Even so, like other cancer patients, she had to worry that the threat was not over.[7]

Meanwhile, Schumpeter became much more attentive to her needs and to
her own disappointments. He wrote in his diary of "this poor child" who had
endured a long series of ordeals: her failed marriage to Maurice Firuski, her extreme frustration about the work on Japan, her inability to win more attention
from him, and now this life-threatening illness. He even appealed to his *Hasen*
for the strength to cope—and also to God, to whom he was now speaking with
some regularity—"Let me help her and not to fall and be a burden." In the
coming months, he would occasionally refer to the possibility of his own "voluntary death" as a step that might follow Elizabeth's possible death.[8]

By the spring of 1949, and with unprecedented help from her husband, Elizabeth had recovered sufficiently to teach again at Wheaton College. She also
enjoyed once more working in her nursery at Taconic, although she had to be
careful about becoming overtired.

Elizabeth's illness was not all that went awry in Schumpeter's world. Throughout the 1940s he often complained in his diary about the situation at Harvard.
In June 1947, a year before Elizabeth's diagnosis, he wrote "Why am I so disgusted? Why am I so sad? Why do I feel that these people and I have nothing
in common . . . It is not my world anymore." A little later in the same year,
"You may cry over the ruins of civilization, but Harvard is but a laugh." Even
in his correspondence he occasionally criticized the university. To Shigeto
Tsuru, a leading Japanese economist who had been his student before the war

and who wrote him about possibly visiting Harvard, he replied: "Of course, distance always beautifies but I who am near enough to Harvard cannot say that I experience very much stimulus from my surroundings. Scientifically, [Wassily] Leontief is the only man who is really alive and even he is now so much buried in administrative work . . . that not so very much remains of him either. The fundamental ideas, methods and approaches you know [already], and original achievement can be built upon this in Tokyo as well as in Boston."[9]

Harvard had undergone a transformation during the postwar years, as returning veterans enrolled in large numbers. Like the rest of the university, the Economics Department was not well prepared for this new situation. Nor was Schumpeter himself. The spurt in enrollment meant more student papers and exams to read, more office hours for consultations, and more administrative demands. In addition, as one of his students recalled, many of the new arrivals "were married and most were intensely career oriented, in a hurry to get started. With only a practical interest in theory, they viewed economics as a means to play a role in the country's life, a view that Schumpeter abominated. For Schumpeter there were no Samuelsons, Margets, Smithies[es], Hoovers, Metzlers, Masons, Harris[es], Chamberlins, Sweezys, Stolpers, or others of their caliber . . . Everybody, including faculty and students, worked in their own little niches, with less togetherness than when the department was smaller."[10]

One memorable break in this new routine came in a public debate between Schumpeter and Paul Sweezy, his close friend and former student. The son of an executive at the J. P. Morgan Bank in New York, Sweezy was a confirmed Marxist and a first-rate economist. In 1947 the Socialist Club of Boston asked the Department of Economics to stage a debate on the comparative virtues of capitalism and socialism. Because of Schumpeter's great success with *Capitalism, Socialism and Democracy*, the department requested that he respond. He told the Socialist Club that he would ask Harvard's Graduate Economic Club to sponsor the debate. When the club resisted, he agreed to an unsponsored public forum at Harvard's Littauer Center.

There, he and Sweezy packed the auditorium. Samuelson later described the event:

Great debaters deserve great moderators, and that night [Wassily] Leontief was in fine form. "The patient is capitalism. What is to be his fate? Our speakers are in fact agreed that the patient is inevitably dying. But the bases of their diagnosis could not be more different. On the one hand there is Sweezy who utilizes the analysis of Marx and of Lenin to deduce that the patient is dying of a malignant cancer . . . On the other hand, there is Schumpeter. He, too, and rather cheerfully, admits that the patient is dying . . . but to Schumpeter, the patient is dying of a psychosomatic ailment. Not cancer but neurosis is his complaint. Filled with self-hate, he has lost his will to live. In this view, capitalism is an unlovable system, and what is unlovable will not be loved. Paul Sweezy himself is a talisman and omen of that alienation which will seal the patient's doom."

After the opening remarks by Sweezy and Schumpeter, moderator Leontief invited discussion from the audience. When Elizabeth Schumpeter rose to offer some comments, Sweezy joked that his opponent's reliance on the family's "big guns" violated the spirit of the proceedings. In the end, Schumpeter permitted his young friend to win the debate, and everyone went home happy.[11]

Despite Schumpeter's general disenchantment with Harvard, there was no drop-off in his attention to teaching. Undergraduates continued to feel that he was the kind of professor they had come to Harvard to hear. Graduate students as well held him in very high esteem. In the 1930s they would have ranked him number one among their professors, by a wide margin. And in a confidential survey done in 1948, they graded him second only to Alvin Hansen, a very personable Midwesterner and the department's most avid Keynesian. Since many bright young professors had risen by that time—Mason, Haberler, Leontief, Chamberlin—this was lofty praise. Asked to list their favorite courses and justify their choices, graduate students wrote the following comments:

> Schumpeter's advanced theory of economics. The stimulation.

> History of Economic Thought. Scope of Professor: Emphasis of salient points. Most especially the man himself, a rounded gentleman who could never be accused of knowing only economics.

> Technical mastery of field of econ. and profound insights into general social context within which the econ. problems lie.

Schumpeter's History of Ec. Thought. Schumpeter's ability to lecture.

Schumpeter's History of Ec. Theory. Careful organization of material, so that each lecture was a development of those previous, and each lecture was interesting and informative from end to end. Humor, personal insights, etc. sprinkled throughout added a good deal.

Prof. Schumpeter in all his courses. He is the best economist of the World.[12]

After decades of experience in academic life—he had taught at five universities, counting his exchange professorship at Columbia—Schumpeter well understood how faculties function. As he wrote in 1946,

> The layman thinks he knows what a professor is. However, this term denotes a group of people who differ widely in type, function, and mentality. There is the academic administrator; the university politician; the teacher in the sense of a man who imparts current knowledge; the teacher in the sense of a man who imparts distinctive doctrines or methods; the scholar in the sense implied by "learnedness"; the organizer of research; the research worker whose strong point is ideas; the research worker whose strong point is skillful technique, experimentation and its counterparts in the social sciences. And all these—and others—are very different chaps and hardly ever fully understand and appreciate one another. Yet it takes all of them to make a modern university and it takes recognition of all these types and the way they cooperate or fail to cooperate in order to understand what a university is and how it works. And he who insists on merging them into a unitary professorial type and leaves it at that will obliterate not only secondary details but essentials.[13]

Schumpeter himself fulfilled more of these roles than most of his colleagues did. Even at this stage of his career, when he was working almost constantly on his research and writing, he continued to put arduous efforts into his teaching and to demand hard work from his students. He not only gave heavy reading assignments. He also spoke at such a level of sophistication in classes and seminars that students had to do additional work in order to understand the breadth of what he was saying. During classes, one of them recalled, "He was most gracious in answering student queries, even the stupid ones. His consultation hours had become famous, and few were the students who did not avail themselves of his help." Schumpeter directed fewer dissertations during this period than he had done in the 1930s, because not many students wrote on his favored topics: economic theory, business cycles, and the history of economic thought. He continued to speak to the Graduate Economic Students' Club at least once annually, more than any other professor.[14]

He also counseled numerous Ph.D. candidates even when he was not a formal member of their committees. In 1947 he learned that the young Harry Johnson had discovered a mathematical error (an inverted ratio) in David Ricardo's *Principles of Political Economy and Taxation.* Thousands of economists had read Ricardo's famous book, which was first published in 1817; but apparently none except Johnson had noted the error. Schumpeter immediately advised him to write an article about it and then helped him place the piece in a 1948 issue of the *Quarterly Journal of Economics,* published at Harvard. Johnson, a Canadian who also studied at Cambridge University, later said that nobody at that English institution would have been so generous or supportive. He went on to become one of the most insightful and prolific economists of his generation.[15]

On the whole, however, trends in Harvard's Economics Department deeply vexed Schumpeter. The demographics were changing drastically, evidenced by a report the department prepared in 1947 as background for a long-range plan. The report began with a twenty-year review, and the period coincided with Schumpeter's own time at Harvard (he had first arrived as a visitor in 1927). The effects of the Depression, the war, and postwar growth are strikingly evident. The planning document noted that the balance between undergraduate and graduate instruction, "always a delicate adjustment," had gone askew. Professors were now spending most of their teaching hours with graduate students and only a third with undergraduates.[16]

Opposite top: Paul Sweezy, one of Schumpeter's favorite students. A first-class scholar and a war veteran, he was also a Marxist. He was not promoted at Harvard, almost surely because of his politics. Here he appears about a decade after the debate, in front of covers of *Monthly Review,* a radical magazine he edited.

Opposite bottom: Littauer Center, the scene of the Schumpeter-Sweezy debate. This building, which opened in 1937, is wholly out of character with what had been the traditional Harvard architectural styles of colonial and Georgian brick. Schumpeter's office included two rooms in the building.

Above: Schumpeter after teaching a seminar in 1947, his emotional balance now restored.

Academic year	Permanent faculty positions	Undergraduate concentrators	Graduate students
1925–1926	10	324	75
1935–1936	13	376	47
1947–1948	17	726	264

The report then recommended that the department's earlier decision to abolish its undergraduate tutorial system—a decision long urged by Schumpeter and enacted during the late 1930s—must now be reversed, which it was. The additional staff required to conduct tutorials would be raised by "rebuilding a strong group of younger teachers in the assistant professor and annual instructor rank." Since the number of undergraduates had mushroomed, the number of new faculty recruits would have to be very large.[17]

For Schumpeter, at his stage of life, the renewed emphasis on undergraduate tutorials was not good news. It meant that a multitude of junior faculty members would now be added to the hordes of new graduate students. With neither group would he be able to develop the kinds of relationships he was accustomed to having. Nor would either group likely embrace his own brand of economics. The field was becoming much more narrow, specialized, and policy-oriented—all to Schumpeter's dismay. Topics congenial to him seemed less relevant to immediate problems of public policy and therefore less attractive to graduate students. Economic theory, which he had taught since coming to Harvard, had become increasingly Keynesian. And so the attractions of solitary scholarship at Windy Hill, and his withdrawal from departmental and university affairs, increased year by year.

He still hosted the usual flow of distinguished scholars who visited Harvard, and sometimes he invited them to stay overnight at Taconic. In the summer, they could accompany him and Elizabeth to the Boston Symphony's concerts at nearby Tanglewood. On one occasion, Erich Schneider, a former student of Schumpeter's at Bonn, came for a visit. As one graduate student later recalled, "Dr. Schneider, a leading German economist of the day, followed Schumpeter around like a little puppydog, in the fashion of European assistants to the master professor."[18]

Meanwhile, outside the gates of Harvard, Schumpeter's standing continued to rise. Throughout 1948 and 1949 he resumed his old habit of accepting frequent invitations to speak at other universities and before professional groups. He also gave two series of five lectures each in Mexico City, as well as his presidential address to the American Economic Association. In none of these many appearances did Schumpeter repeat the same prepared talk, as academics and other public speakers usually do. Lecturing spontaneously from brief outlines prepared beforehand, he gave his usual star turn—offering provocative opinions on a range of topics such as "The Decay of Capitalism," "Old Ideas and New Facts," and "The Inadequacy of Economics." In these talks, he himself was trying to reach a better understanding of the new kinds of mixed public/private economies evolving in Britain, Continental Europe, and the United States.[19]

In 1949, just after his year as president of the American Economic Association, Schumpeter was chosen president of the new 5,300-member International Economic Association, headquartered in Paris. These tributes—the highest possible recognition by his peers in both the United States and abroad—meant a very great deal to him. Despite the dissatisfactions of postwar Harvard and the dread aroused by Elizabeth's cancer, Schumpeter finally had the satisfaction of scaling the professional heights in ways that had long eluded him. Now in his mid-sixties, he had without question achieved one of the goals he had set as a teenager in Vienna—*celebrity*—not as a short-term finance minister but as the world's most famous living economist (Keynes having died in 1946). As yet no Nobel Prize was given in economics, but if it had been, there is no question that he would have received that honor as well.[20]

25

Toward the Mixed Economy

The mixed economy is *mixed*. That is its strength: to mobi-
lize for human ends the mechanisms of the market and to
police those mechanisms to see that they do not wander too
far away from the desired common goals.

PAUL SAMUELSON,
"The Public Role in the Modern American Economy," 1980

IN 1943, SHORTLY after the appearance of *Capitalism, Socialism and Democracy,* Schumpeter wrote a brief essay for a book entitled *Postwar Economic Problems,* edited by Seymour Harris. He began his essay with a historical survey, then speculated about the future. He noted that even during periods of presumed laissez-faire, "law, custom, public opinion and public administration enforced a certain amount of public planning . . . our question concerning the immediate future should not be couched in terms of 'capitalism or socialism': there is a great variety of intermediate possibilities."[1]

Here, in his typically pioneering way, Schumpeter almost perfectly anticipated what later became known as the mixed economy. That kind of system—private enterprise leavened by the public sector's assumption of responsibility for prosperity—became the norm in advanced industrialized countries during the years after World War II. It remains so to this day. But despite Schumpeter's comment in 1943, neither he nor most other analysts believed that the mixed economy would have long-term staying power. They tended to assume that all systems would gravitate toward either traditional capitalism or pure socialism. Somewhat like Marx's division of society into only two warring classes, Schumpeter (and many others) found it hard to imagine that there could be a long-term compromise between the two systems.

This conceptual difficulty is clear in other comments he made in the 1943 article: "However much we may approve of some or all of the policies of the New Deal, we cannot fail to be struck by the absence of any serious resistance to them . . . The all but general opinion seems to be that capitalist methods will be unequal to the task of [postwar] reconstruction . . . This opinion in itself will be a political factor of first-rate importance." Schumpeter feared that the ad hoc economic adaptations of wartime might warp the nation's commitment to capitalism—at the very moment of its most triumphant performance—and set the country on the road to socialism.[2]

This would be an extremely ironic result, given the record of the American economy during the war. In 1944, at full mobilization, gross national product stood at double its figure for 1939. And despite the rationing of numerous everyday items, Schumpeter believed that even the consumer economy was actually growing rapidly, along with military production. Here he was right. Statistics compiled later on showed that from 1938 to 1944 per capita consumer spending increased by 22 percent in the United States. This was an almost unbelievable achievement by the American economy, never matched by any other country fighting a major war. (In Britain during the same period it *dropped* by 20 percent.) These gains came at a time when about 40 percent of American economic output was going not into consumer products but into war materials.[3]

As early as 1943 Schumpeter saw that what came to be called "pent-up demand" could thrust the American economy forward even after a radical drop in military production. People had saved a lot of money during the war, and despite the increase in consumer spending, they had not been able to buy new cars, refrigerators, or many other items. The returning GIs wanted to settle down, buy these goods and new houses, and start families. So the solution to the economic problem was going to be much easier than most experts believed.[4]

For Schumpeter, the troubling issue was not economic at all but ideological: widespread prejudice against business, held over from the New Deal. "The public mind has renounced allegiance to the capitalist scheme of values. Private wealth is under a moral ban." Thus, entrepreneurs would have to do their work "in the face of public antagonism, under burdens which eliminate capitalist motivation and make it impossible to accumulate venture capital." (In these last two words Schumpeter made early use of a term that became commonplace four decades later. He did not invent the phrase—its origin is obscure—but was one of the first economists to use it.) He feared that the profusion of new federal mobilization agencies policing the economy would not quickly disappear, as had happened in 1919. Instead, they would become permanent institutions because of support from farmers and workers. Hence, the country would take further steps on the road to socialism—not for economic reasons but out of political expediency by elected officials. The resulting set of policies, he surmised, would prevent large-scale businesses from ever again becoming sufficiently free of government interference. Working conditions and pay levels would become perennial political issues. Although people might still call their system capitalism, it would be "capitalism in the oxygen tent."[5]

Schumpeter went on to argue that both in the United States and in capitalist countries abroad, a high rate of public spending during the postwar period would likely evolve into total government control of investment. Some industries might be nationalized, and if the government "should try to run the nationalized industries according to the principles of business rationality, Guided Capitalism would shade off into State Capitalism, a system that may be characterized by the following features: government ownership and management of selected industrial positions; complete control of government in the labor and capital market, government initiative in domestic and foreign enterprise."[6]

Governments would be likely to nationalize only big businesses, because farmers and small businesspeople would resist nationalization, and in any case there was no particular reason to bring small enterprises under public control. The overall result would likely be "an amphibial state for the calculable future." The amphibial state might well generate frictions among business, labor, and government and would not benefit from the "motive power" of either capitalism or socialism. "On the other hand, amphibial states conserve many human values that would perish in others. Thus there may be as little reason for the fears of some as there is for the hopes of others."[7]

Here Schumpeter was practically acknowledging that much New Deal legislation—the Social Security Act, the National Labor Relations Act—had made American capitalism a good deal more humane and that those measures were not going to be repealed. Other vital measures from the 1930s, such as the Securities Act and Securities Exchange Act, had rescued the nation's capital markets from their own habitual corruption and were also here to stay. But for Schumpeter the much bigger question for 1943–1945 was whether the government's detailed management of production and distribution would continue after the war had been won.

In writing of amphibial states and capitalism in the oxygen tent, he vividly described many aspects of the emerging mixed economy. In turning to these metaphors, he was signaling his own sense that no one really knew what to expect, and that the future would bring novel conditions requiring imaginative thought. But in fearing the permanence of wartime agencies—let alone a significant degree of nationalization—he erred badly. In the end, virtually no nationalization took place. The Republican Congress elected in 1946 even tried to roll back parts of the New Deal, but with little success. And except for the Selective Service System (the draft), almost all important U.S. wartime agencies were quickly dismantled beginning in late 1945. (A few would be reinstituted in 1947–1949, as the Cold War started to heat up.) Much of what Schumpeter wrote in the 1943 article applied more aptly to Britain and Continental Europe than to the United States. Given his background, this kind of emphasis might have been expected. He was sixty years old when his 1943 essay appeared, and he had lived only twelve of those years in the United States.

Whereas widespread nationalizations did take place in Britain and Europe during the postwar period, the American-style mixed economy fixed on demand-side macroeconomic management. In line with the Keynesian orthodoxy that prevailed in Washington from the 1940s through the mid-1970s, emphasis fell on public support of consumer purchasing power. This "fiscal revolution," as it has been called, included very steeply graduated income taxes and other measures Schumpeter opposed. But in saying, as he did in 1943, that "amphibial states conserve many human values that would perish in others," he put his finger on the appeal of the mixed economy and on the way in which—despite his fears—it preserved and strengthened American capitalism.

In a long article entitled "Capitalism" that he wrote in 1945 for the *Encyclopaedia Britannica,* Schumpeter took stock of the present situation and speculated about what might happen next. He correctly sensed that the world economy stood at a unique historical moment and that either very good or very bad things might happen. Here again, much of what he said applied more to Britain and Europe than to the United States. And he was still feeling his way toward a firmer grasp of the emerging mixed economies:

> Much light may be shed on the *immediate* future by visualizing how far the process of transformation has advanced already. Government control of the capital and labour markets, of price policies and, by means of taxation, of income distribution is already established and needs only to be complemented systematically by government initiative in indicating the general lines of production (housing programs, foreign investment) in order to transform, even without extensive nationalization of industries, *regulated*, or *fettered*, capitalism into a *guided* capitalism that might, with almost equal justice, be called socialism. Thus, prediction of whether or not the capitalist order will survive is, in part, a matter of terminology.

Schumpeter had made these kinds of comments before in times of crisis: in articles written during World War I and the Great Depression, and during World War II in *Capitalism, Socialism and Democracy*. At those times, as in 1945, his greatest concern was the preservation of capitalism.[8]

Approaching the same question from still another angle, Schumpeter in November 1945 delivered a lecture entitled "The Future of Private Enterprise in the Face of Modern Socialistic Tendencies." He was speaking to an association of Catholic industrialists in Montreal, at the invitation of Emile Bouvier, a Jesuit priest who had been one of his graduate students at Harvard. Schumpeter was very pleased that he could make the speech in French.

He began by saying that arguments in favor of socialism all seemed to rest on economic criteria such as capitalism's exploitation of workers; but that the facts belied these arguments. As he had pointed out many times, real wages for workers in capitalist countries had been rising for decades, interrupted only by depressions. They had held steady as a percentage of national income except in down cycles, and their percentage had increased in Western democracies with progressive income tax systems. It was natural enough that socialist thinking had thrived during the Great Depression. But it no longer made sense "when we can look forward to prodigious industrial development." Arguments based on the class struggle were particularly inappropriate because modern businessmen do not usually own their own capital—as both Adam Smith and Karl Marx had believed, in "a profound error." Instead, the businessman's role "is comparable to the role of a military commander; the businessman is essentially a worker who is the leader of other workers." He has as much conflict with his own banker as with his workers.[9]

Schumpeter emphasized that no answers to the economic problems of the postwar era were to be found in bolshevism, nor even democratic socialism. Instead, and especially in Catholic countries where the Vatican's influence might carry weight, Schumpeter recommended "corporate organization in the sense advocated by *Quadragesimo Anno*," an encyclical issued in 1931 by Pope Pius XI. The economic part of the encyclical "recognizes all the facts of the modern economy. And, while bringing a remedy to the present disorganization, it shows us the functions of private initiative in a new framework. The corporate principle organizes but it does not regiment. It is opposed to all social systems with a centralizing tendency and to all bureaucratic regimentation; it is, in fact, the only means of rendering the latter impossible."[10]

The doctrine of *Quadragesimo Anno* is what political theorists call "corporatism." Under this kind of system, voluntary associations in agriculture, industry, mining, construction, and labor organize to govern themselves and promote harmony within and among different groups—all in the broader interest of society. Historically, corporatism had been advocated most notably by Catholic theorists in the nineteenth century as an alternative to both socialism and laissez-faire capitalism. Corporatism is much more consistent with capitalism than with socialism. But it imposes some limits on competition in order to soften the impact of creative destruction on human values, especially those of the family.

Pope Leo XIII's famous encyclical of 1891, *Rerum Novarum,* had supported capitalism (with qualifications), while opposing socialism outright. It had advocated many corporatist principles: the legitimacy of private property, labor's right to bargain collectively, cooperation between labor and capital, and government intervention when necessary to secure a living wage. Pius XI's *Quadragesimo Anno* of 1931 (so named because it came on the fortieth anniversary of *Rerum Novarum*) reaffirmed these principles and went on to acknowledge that wage levels must be set so as not to bankrupt firms and promote inflation. Both documents were written with extraordinary care and precision, and to this day they remain the cornerstones of Catholic economic doctrine.[11]

Schumpeter had advocated some corporatist measures in his magazine articles in Germany during the late 1920s, mainly in response to the emerging crisis over wage levels. At that time, he had proposed a system of cooperative organizations of industrialists on the one hand and workers on the other. These organizations would meet periodically to work out wage, price, and employment settlements that were fair to all sides. During the 1930s, when both Germany and Italy had claimed to be following corporatist principles, corporatism became associated with fascism. But Schumpeter's suggestions of 1945 were no more fascist than the two popes' had been in 1891 and 1931, because they all opposed the fierce nationalism and authoritarianism that defined fascist regimes. Rather, Schumpeter was seeking some middle ground between unfettered capitalism, whose perceived inequity was costing it popular support in precarious times, and socialism, which he believed to be the dysfunctional (and almost surely authoritarian) wave of the future.[12]

The economic and political problems to be solved in the postwar world, Schumpeter acknowledged, could not be met solely through laissez-faire capitalism. They required government intervention to enforce the cooperative private agreements reached by participants within an industry and between industries and their workers:

> To give only one example, let us ask ourselves what happens in a
> depression. Business firm A cannot work because firm B is not
> working; B can't because C finds itself incapable of producing, and
> so on. No single firm can, by its own action, break the "vicious
> circle." Whence the closing down of an entire industry, a closing
> down that ends only too easily in the ruin which menaces all en-
> terprises and of which the workers are the victims. But the corpo-
> rate action of professional associations . . . is the most natural rem-
> edy for the situation. It follows that the corporatism of association
> would eliminate the most serious of the obstacles to peaceable co-
> operation between worker and owner.

These kinds of arrangements were going to be difficult to achieve, in part because of the growing power of communism throughout the world. But the usefulness of corporatism was not merely economic and social. It also "implies a moral reform."[13]

Corporatist solutions, by their nature, assumed that harmony could be achieved between industries and workers. Schumpeter, unlike Karl Marx, did not believe that antagonism between workers and their employers was inevitable. And historically, corporatist arrangements had worked fairly well in several settings. Germany had promoted industrial self-government *(Selbstverwaltung)* both before and after the First World War. The aims were to achieve industry-wide standards, maintain price and wage levels, and promote labor peace. One key to the German system was cartelization, in which all members of an industry group would be allotted a share of the existing market and no member would cut prices or raise wages beyond agreed limits. Japan, under the American Occupation, was about to adopt similar arrangements.

The trouble with these practices—especially when transplanted to countries with powerful traditions of dog-eat-dog competition, such as the United States—was that businesses in the same industry would sign agreements with one another and then promptly break them. And because American common law frowned on "restraint of trade," the agreements could not be enforced in court. Even when businesses did comply with their mutual agreements, consumers often suffered from higher prices and reduced outputs. By and large, this had been the experience of the United States during the period 1933–1935, when many industries operated under corporatist agreements sponsored by the National Industrial Recovery Act of 1933. In Congress's effort to help working people as well as industries, that legislation also gave a great boost to the labor movement. In 1935 the U.S. Supreme Court invalidated the National Industrial Recovery Act on the grounds of unlawful delegation of legislative power to the executive branch. Congress then re-enacted, in strengthened form, the provisions of the law that applied to workers, and the Court upheld this new legislation.[14]

Since Schumpeter almost never advocated any kind of specific program, his Montreal speech represented a radical departure from his practice of scientific objectivity. It also signaled, once more, that he did not believe that creative destruction injured masses of people. Rather, it primarily injured capitalists themselves, who were overtaken by more innovative businesses. Corporatism might soften creative destruction but would certainly not bring it to a halt. The reason for Schumpeter's praise of *Quadragesimo Anno*—which he brought up again a few years later in his presidential address to the American Economic Association—was that it represented one escape route from what he saw as the world's postwar political turn toward socialism. He was looking, almost desperately, for *any* non-authoritarian alternative to the bolshevism and socialism he had described so vividly in *Capitalism, Socialism and Democracy*.[15]

SCHUMPETER'S POSTWAR anxieties carried over into the new chapter he wrote in the summer of 1946 for the second edition of *Capitalism, Socialism and Democracy*. Here, he argued that capitalism's greatest hope for survival might lie not in compromise with other systems but in American prosperity itself. Using italics for emphasis, he stressed that "*in the United States alone there need not lurk, behind modern programs of social betterment, that fundamental dilemma . . . between economic progress and immediate increase of the real income of the masses.*" He speculated that during the postwar years American affluence and example could ramify throughout the world. At a sufficiently high level of national income, a country could afford to be hospitable to business and at the same time pay for social welfare programs. If that country's economy were as large as America's, it could even lead the entire capitalist world back to full prosperity, like a powerful locomotive pulling a long train. To be sure, he saw several potential problems: high taxation in the United States, which had continued as a necessary means of paying for the war; the powerful inflationary forces that plague all countries after major wars; and what he regarded as the bureaucratic immaturity of America's federal government.[16]

On the whole, however, "the colossal industrial success we are witnessing" gave cause for real optimism. It had the potential for supporting very high wage levels, "to an extent that may annihilate the whole case for socialism so far as it is of a purely economic nature." The astonishing wartime growth of the American economy, if it continued for just a few more years, "promises a level of satisfaction of economic needs even of the poorest members of society including the aged, unemployed and sick, that would (with a forty hour work week) eliminate anything that could possibly be described as suffering or want." Of course, as Schumpeter had said in the first edition of *Capitalism, Socialism and Democracy,* the appeal of socialism was not solely economic; but postwar America's performance was so dramatic as to cast any rival system onto the ideological defensive. The U.S. economy had become so affluent that it could absorb a tax burden of about 20 percent without harming industrial production. This was a strong statement, coming from the tax-averse Schumpeter.[17]

But several homegrown obstacles threatened America's prosperity. The first was simple mismanagement. Hosts of overlapping boards, agencies, and other authorities—federal, state, and local—all got in one another's way and prevented rational coordination. The American government was fragmented and underdeveloped, lacking the integrated and experienced ministries typical of seasoned European and British civil services. A second problem was a honeycomb of politically imposed wage and prices controls, left over from wartime necessity. Schumpeter believed that these controls would hinder entrepreneurship and impede economic advance. And finally, "the bureaucracy's persistent hostility, strongly supported as it is by public opinion, to industrial self-government—self-organization, self-regulation, co-operation—is a third obstacle to orderly progress."[18]

That progress might include, among other things, management of the business cycle and an indirect discouragement of socialist tendencies. Here Schumpeter was again endorsing the kind of corporatist self-government he had praised in his Montreal speech. But instead of moving toward that goal, American policy was weakening entrepreneurship in a way that many analysts did not even recognize. As he noted in an angry aside directed toward leftist extremists, "Injury to the economic process of capitalism is for some people precisely the feature of reform they like best. Reform without such injury would be all but unattractive to them. And reform paralleled by a policy that insures capitalist success would be the worst that could befall them." By contrast, Schumpeter's answer to America's postwar institutional problems was the kind of program he had always advocated in the past: more encouragement of entrepreneurship. The fiscal system he outlined was designed to promote savings that could finance new ventures and ensure the American prosperity far into the future.[19]

The Keynesians' opposite emphasis on consumption rather than investment drew Schumpeter's pointed criticism. The Keynesian doctrine held that only public promotion of consumption would reliably induce business executives to build more plant and equipment. Investment, in other words, would not occur without government's artificial stimulus of consumption. Schumpeter regarded this idea as wrong. He was convinced that except during temporary downturns in the business cycle, savings would automatically flow into investment. Keynes believed that it might not—that there could be prolonged equilibrium at low levels of investment and employment (he once invoked the pre-capitalist Dark Ages as an example). But Schumpeter's entire vision of capitalism rejected the possibility of long-term stagnation; and he could find only one reason "for the astounding fact that the theory in question is not simply laughed out of court."[20]

That reason was the Great Depression and the widespread fear of its postwar return. The stagnationist thesis and its oversaving, underinvestment corollary was a holdover from the 1930s. The experience of the Great Depression had been so profoundly unsettling that people had wrongly generalized from it and also from the views of Keynes, its chief interpreter. Schumpeter saw this phenomenon as analogous to the good Marx/bad Marx problem: a conclusion from a brilliant analyst is popularly accepted, even though it is based on a faulty initial vision and is therefore wrongheaded. In this case, Keynes's faulty vision was of a sluggish and outworn capitalism—the opposite not only of Schumpeter's own view but also of what was actually happening in the booming American economy.[21]

In 1948 Schumpeter delivered a series of lectures in Mexico City—two sets of five lectures each—at the invitation of the leading universities of the country. He and Elizabeth spent three very pleasant weeks in Mexico, basking in the culture of the capital city, touring museums and churches, and even visiting Mayan sites in the Yucatan. In Schumpeter's lectures, which he called "Wage and Tax Policy in Transitional States of Society," he again took up the question of postwar economic problems. In both the United States and Britain, he said, "we have neither laissez-faire liberalism nor socialism but a combination of the two that is perhaps inevitable but nevertheless illogical." Tax policy in both countries continued to follow Keynesian patterns of deficit financing—even apart from measures necessary to pay for the war—and also redistribution of wealth through inheritance taxes and steeply graduated income taxes. Although the key political battle might appear to be between social classes—as in fights over wage levels—Schumpeter thought the real struggle was "between two interests in society, the interest in present enjoyment, and the interest in the nation's economic future."[22]

This was still another area in which Schumpeter disagreed with Keynes. Whereas Schumpeter almost always looked to the long run, Keynes famously said that "in the long run we are all dead." He later tried to retract this remark, but he never meant it as a mere witticism. As many of his writings suggest, one of his fondest wishes was to reach a minimal threshold of economic prosperity and get material issues settled once and for all. When that end-of-economic-history goal had been reached, then people could focus on the finer things of life and conduct themselves on a higher cultural plane.

Schumpeter had no such illusions. He believed, as is evident from hundreds of comments he made throughout his life, that capitalism is a continuous evolutionary process without an end-point. Neither entrepreneurs nor consumers will ever be satisfied with their material lot. They will forever want more. Aspiration and desire are hard-wired into human beings, and the reasons for their striving are not based on what Schumpeter often called "hedonistic" motives alone. Entrepreneurs wish to excel for the sake of excelling; to fulfill their own expectations of themselves; to achieve "social distance" for the sake of recognition. And under capitalism, comparative wealth and income are the chief means of keeping score. Capitalist societies would never evolve into the cultural paradise of Keynes's imagination.

On the issue of present enjoyment versus long-term economic growth, it was obvious to Schumpeter (as well as to Keynes and all other competent economists) that growth requires investment, and therefore some degree of deferred gratification. In his Mexico lectures, Schumpeter pointed out that laissez-faire economies solved this tradeoff in one way, socialism in another. But for in-between systems such as amphibial states, explicit policies were essential to discourage conspicuous consumption and steer resources toward investment. The potential returns here were almost utopian, compared with anything that had gone before. Modern capitalism had become so productive that it was even possible to guarantee all citizens "a certain minimum annual income." This statement was a very bold assertion, and an indicator of just how confident Schumpeter was, in 1948, about the potential of capitalism.[23]

Later that year, after his return from Mexico, the editors of *Nation's Business* asked him to prepare an article on inflation, which was proving to be a difficult problem in the postwar period. During World War II the federal government had taken very strong and effective steps to limit inflation but had removed most of these measures after the war. Now, some form of control seemed necessary once again, and a national debate had arisen over just how far the government should go.

Since leaving Germany in 1932, Schumpeter had almost never embraced invitations such as this one to speak directly to the public. He made an exception in this case because he believed inflation to be the most immediate threat to the American economy. He began by noting that he himself had observed episodes of extremely high inflation after the First World War in Austria, France, Germany, and Italy. At that time, ruinous hyperinflation was traceable to the war and could have been easily corrected within a couple of years. But the political cost of doing so was too high for public officials in most countries. The exception was Italy: "Mussolini wanted to stop inflation. So he stopped it." In the early and mid-1920s, before he became an international villain, Mussolini was admired by many influential people in Western countries, for this success and others. In France, on the other hand, politicians were typically reluctant to take the steps necessary to limit inflation.[24]

The United States, Schumpeter argued, was now behaving like France. Politicians and important interest groups were avoiding the issue because of the short-term pain caused by price controls. The immense Marshall Plan expenditures to aid European recovery had added a major new demand on the federal budget and, despite its obvious merits, would make the control of inflation all the more difficult. The impending U.S. congressional elections of November 1948 would complicate the issue still further. Schumpeter concluded his article with a warning that stopping inflation altogether would likely bring on a depression. So it should only be *controlled*—through the restriction of credit, reduced public spending, and the encouragement of savings. These measures, of course, could not be implemented by the private sector but would require governmental action.[25]

In his persistent search to find a way to characterize the evolving mixed economy, Schumpeter hit upon the term "laborism." In the summer of 1949, at a presentation he gave at a public seminar, Schumpeter disputed the orthodox Marxist doctrine that imperialism was the final phase of capitalism, and suggested a substitute: "I advance the proposition that not imperialism, but *laborism* is the last stage of capitalism. Laborism signifies here . . . capitalist society at that stage in which the labor interest is predominant. Marx would have thought this impossible." But Britain had already traveled far toward laborism, and so had Sweden. The Soviet Union, Schumpeter added, was not a laborist state at all, but an outright dictatorship.[26]

Again, rapid changes in the world economy were pushing Schumpeter to be more imaginative about what might lie ahead. He pursued his theme of laborism further in a long review article on contemporary books by six British economists. At the end of World War II, he wrote, British voters had turned out the Conservative government of Winston Churchill and elected a Labour majority in the House of Commons. During the years since, "practically everything that has been sponsored, done or proposed by the Labour party qualifies, in fact, much better for the title of 'laborism' than it does for 'socialism.'" Laborism "implies not only the possible maximum of public expenditure for the benefit of labor but also the reduction to a minimum of incomes other than wages." And the Labour government in Britain was doing just this: it had enacted tax laws designed to separate wealthy people from their fortunes, step by step. Meanwhile, the British civil service, which Schumpeter had admired ever since his youth in Vienna, had become enamored of their new role in economic planning, encouraged by the Labour government. Civil servants had drifted into "downright bureau-sadism" in their attitude toward business.[27]

For the annual meeting of the American Economic Association on December 30, 1949, Schumpeter prepared still another article about recent changes in Western economic policies. Entitled "The March into Socialism," this brief essay was published as a new chapter for the third edition of *Capitalism, Socialism and Democracy*, which appeared in 1950. In it, Schumpeter reviewed the long list of what he regarded as laborite policies enacted during the last twenty years in Britain, the United States, and other industrialized countries. Then— once more the showman, and partly the ironist—he said:

> It would spell complete misunderstanding of my argument if you thought that I "disapprove" or wish to criticise any of these policies. Nor am I one of those who label all or some of them "socialist." Some were espoused, even in the eighteenth century, by conservative or even autocratic rulers; others have been on the

programs of conservative parties and have been carried by them
long before New Deal days. All I wish to emphasize is the fact that
we have traveled far indeed from the principles of laissez-faire capitalism and the further fact that it is possible so to develop and
regulate capitalist institutions as to condition the working of private enterprise in a manner that differs but little from genuinely
socialist planning. The economists I have in mind no doubt emphasize the differences they think likely to persist. They are not all
agreed as to the precise location of their movable halfway house.[28]

Schumpeter asserted that many economists were now arguing that laborist
arrangements might have real staying power. But he stressed again that capitalism is much more than an economic system:

> Capitalism does not merely mean that the housewife may influ-
> ence production by her choice between peas and beans; or that the
> youngster may choose whether he wants to work in a factory or on
> a farm; or that plant managers have some voice in deciding what
> and how to produce: it means a scheme of values, an attitude to-
> ward life, a civilization—the civilization of inequality and of the
> family fortune. This civilization is rapidly passing away, however.
> Let us rejoice or else lament the fact as much as everyone of us
> likes; but do not let us shut our eyes to it.[29]

He acknowledged "the present spectacular development of society's productive powers" and noted that optimists believed that it could continue forever.
But he went on to argue, as he had done many times before, that capitalism
was not an easy system to sustain. There was constant temptation to lay even
more straws on the camel's back, and real danger that the camel might collapse
altogether. If this happened, then the socialist alternative would appear attractive even to those who had opposed it in the past.[30]

IN HIS MEXICO lectures of 1948, Schumpeter had spoken of transitional states of societies moving from capitalism to laborism. But as it turned
out, "transitional" was not an apt adjective. Throughout the two generations

following Schumpeter's Mexico lectures, the capitalist system not only survived—in the form of the mixed economy that reigned even as he spoke—but also swept through much of the world, prospering beyond his own expectations. Modern capitalism did sometimes live partially in an oxygen tent. During downward turns in the business cycle and periods of high unemployment, it had to be supported by public welfare payments. It was indeed an amphibial capitalism. But in the animal world, amphibians prosper as robustly as creatures living only in water or on land, and so it was with modern mixed economies.

In 1952 Schumpeter's Harvard colleague John Kenneth Galbraith would publish a book called *American Capitalism: The Concept of Countervailing Power*. In it he would argue that the former domination of American society by business had now been balanced by the increased potency of both the government and of labor unions. (Union membership had been rising steadily since the 1930s and continued to do so until the 1960s.) Without using the term, Galbraith was describing the mixed economy. When Schumpeter said in his 1948 Mexico lectures that such an arrangement was "illogical," he revealed his conviction (and that of most economists of his generation) that one or the other system must triumph. This thinking—irrefutable on its own terms—was conditioned on the obvious incompatibility between pure socialism on the one hand and pure capitalism on the other. During the 1940s, neither Schumpeter nor most other serious theorists had anticipated a viable blend that might remain in equipoise over the long term, and bring unprecedented economic prosperity.

Yet, by the early twenty-first century, all major democratic countries had enjoyed success with mixed economies for at least four decades, and some for as many as seven. In these countries, the total tax burden at all levels of government combined—local, state, and national—had ranged from about 25 percent to about 60 percent. The different percentages depended on the particular array of social services (retirement, health care, housing, child care) paid from public funds. Sweden and Holland typically had the highest rates, while Japan, Switzerland, and the United States recorded the lowest. This broad hybrid, then, appears to be the long-run outcome of what Schumpeter saw as the struggle in democratic countries between capitalism and socialism.

Schumpeter's thinking during the 1940s was conditioned by two extremely powerful overseas trends of that time. The first was the growing size and strength of the totalitarian "Communist bloc"—the USSR, Eastern Europe, and also China, Mao's revolution having triumphed in 1949. The other trend was the frequent election of Socialist governments (many at the local level and some at the national) in numerous areas: Britain, the Scandinavian countries, Western Europe, and newly independent former colonies, most notably India. Each of these trends seemed even more solidly entrenched because of the continued electoral potency of pro-Soviet Communist parties in France, Italy, and other Western democracies. As late as the 1970s, Communist candidates for the Italian Parliament received one third of the votes cast, and many local officials in Western Europe were Communists.

For more than three decades after Schumpeter's 1948 Mexico lectures, there were few signs of an effective rollback of these trends, either abroad or at home. In the United States, the elections of the Republican Presidents Eisenhower (1952, 1956) and Nixon (1968, 1972) were not followed by any significant dismantling of the New Deal–based welfare state. Proposals to cut back on Social Security, unemployment insurance, and collective bargaining rights for labor made little or no progress. During the Nixon administration, government officials such as Daniel Patrick Moynihan and even very conservative economists such as Milton Friedman called for guaranteed annual incomes as a substitute for traditional welfare measures. Meanwhile, in most of Northern Europe, the welfare state had become ever more pervasive. Analysts began to speak of Sweden's thoroughgoing system of social supports in particular as a "middle way" or "third way" (between capitalism and socialism) that likely held the key to the future.

Not until the onset of Reaganism and Thatcherism in the 1980s did right-wing "free market" movements return with real force, in both rhetoric and substance. And even then, in most countries the fraction of national incomes allocated to taxation did not substantially diminish (in the United States, this was in part because of increased military spending). What did happen was a combination of deregulation in numerous industries, outsourcing of public services, and privatization in those countries (including Britain) that had folded into the public sector such industries as electric power, rail transportation, telecommunications, coal mining, and automobile manufacture. During the 1980s and 1990s, few economic topics were more written about than deregulation

Left: Schumpeter did not fully accept the mixed economy, but several of his best students became ardent advocates of it. All were Keynesians, but none ever lost his respect and high esteem for Schumpeter. The most prominent was the intense Paul Samuelson, in this picture teaching at MIT during the 1950s.

A second student, James Tobin, home for Christmas after the end of World War II in 1945, just before he was released from active duty. One of Tobin's fellow officers, the novelist Herman Wouk, wrote him into *The Caine Mutiny* as a character named Tobit. Tobin taught at Yale for most of his career, served on the Council of Economic Advisers under President Kennedy, and, like Samuelson, won the Nobel Prize.

A third prominent Schumpeter student interested in the mixed economy was Arthur Smithies, who first came to Harvard as a Commonwealth Fellow from Australia during the 1930s. Smithies, who received tenure at Harvard in 1949, was especially close to both Joseph and Elizabeth Schumpeter. Together with his wife, Katherine, he often visited Windy Hill.

and privatization. They became mantras for what was hailed as a revival of unfettered capitalism—but which in reality was a measured retreat from laborism and a predictable readjustment of the mixed economy. The biggest single loser was organized labor.

Despite Schumpeter's keen powers of imagination, reflected in the brilliant metaphors and other terms he used to describe what he saw (amphibial systems, capitalism in the oxygen tent, laborism, movable halfway house, bureau-sadism), he remained dubious about the long-term viability of a mixed economy. In this he was hardly alone. Both professional economists and ordinary citizens had grown so accustomed to thinking in black and white—Adam Smith's capitalism versus Karl Marx's socialism—that shades of gray eluded them. One such shade of gray was Keynesianism; but to some self-styled conservatives, it soon became symbolic (inappropriately so, and certainly not in the way Keynes himself had intended) of left-wing political extremism.

These habits of mind, nurtured during the ideological battles of the Great Depression and the propaganda-soaked environment of World War II, hardened even further during the Cold War's death struggle. In the United States, the fight pitted "the American Way of Life" against "Godless Communism." Slogans, as Schumpeter had often complained, again became substitutes for clear thinking and hard analysis. Too few people took the time to understand that the preservation of the American way of life (and of the British, French, German, Japanese, and all others operating under mixed economies) depended as heavily on government as on business. But by the twenty-first century, after sixty years of ascendancy in dozens of countries—the precise blend varying from one nation to the next—mixed economies seem as durable as any capitalist arrangements have ever been or are likely to be.[31]

26

History of Economic Analysis

To produce a mighty book, you must choose a mighty theme.

HERMAN MELVILLE, *Moby Dick,* 1851

THROUGHOUT THE 1940S Schumpeter was hard at work on his longest and most ambitious book, *History of Economic Analysis.* More than any other project he ever started, this one depended for its success on the selflessness and support of Elizabeth, in both sickness and health. For an entire decade, the Schumpeters were to spend most of their days together holed up in Taconic or secluded at Harvard Business School's Kress Library. Elizabeth very much wanted to work with her husband: "Since we cannot have a child, let's have this book together," he quotes her in his diary. "Why can't we have a child—many children?"—that is, many books.[1]

This, of course, is an extremely poignant and revealing comment. For Elizabeth, the prospect of working with her eminent spouse meant more than just assisting his scholarship. It filled a deep emotional need created by the circumstances of her professional and married life. Had she been a tenured professor at Harvard or another major university, she likely would have continued her work on Japan. But the severe strictures against women typical of the times had all but foreclosed that option. Since she could neither study Japan nor have children, helping with her husband's work served as a substitute for these opportunities—and for others precluded by her decision to marry a famous man fifteen years her senior and to elevate his needs above her own.

When Schumpeter began this new research program in 1940, he had thought he might produce a short book every year and an article each semester. This plan echoed his aspirations of 1916, when he had outlined a similar proposal to his publisher. Although the idea of bringing out a book each year sounds far too ambitious, Schumpeter actually did achieve a comparable goal. When his landmark *History of Economic Analysis* finally appeared, it had reached the gargantuan length of 800,000 words, the equivalent of eight medium-sized books.[2]

Throughout the 1940s Schumpeter castigated himself for making meager progress, and even for choosing the wrong topic. Early in 1943 he wrote in his diary, "Should I not rather take as deep a draft of theory as I can?" He upbraided himself again a few months later, as he and Elizabeth worked in Taconic. "I have relaxed very much these days . . . [the history book] practically at standstill." But in fact he was making good headway. Then still again, in February 1945, "How *did* I get into this mess with this History? Which never can repay the trouble and which was so much nicer in the short sketch . . . But the question is what I am to do *now*? Only answer I see—finish as quickly as possible with reasonable care!" To a Harvard colleague he wrote, "I am working my head off at this cursed history of econ. analysis (which will be my death I am sure)." Meanwhile, the years continued to pass, and in 1949 he wrote another colleague that the book was "like an illness and yet I cannot get myself to make short work of it."[3]

Schumpeter knew that he was a master of the brief sketch, a gifted critic of other economists' theories and student of their lives. He very much enjoyed doing this kind of work, and in the end his *History of Economic Analysis* became a very long series of mostly short critiques, covering well over a thousand writers. But the book is far more than this. It captures, in close detail, the gradual evolution of economic thinking. Like all great intellectual histories, it portrays successive generations of analysts building on the work of their predecessors or failing to do so. It tracks important thinkers down both productive and nonproductive paths. It shows how potentially seminal ideas often get lost, only to be rediscovered decades or even centuries later.

Schumpeter spent much of the last nine years of his life working on this book, and he had not quite finished it when he died. In the face of her own illness, Elizabeth performed the heroic feat of assembling its disparate parts and preparing it for publication. Brought out by Oxford University Press in 1954, the book contains 1,260 closely printed pages of about 700 words each. It is the longest of all Schumpeter's works, and in some ways the most impressive. One of its many remarkable aspects is the author's complete omission of the formidable body of theoretical work he had written himself. His name appears in the text only in a few parenthetical comments added by Elizabeth. A reader who did not know better would conclude that Schumpeter had contributed nothing at all to analytical economics.

In her long introduction and appendix to the book, Elizabeth describes its composition and her own task of bringing it to publication. She writes that the project began as an effort to "translate, revise, and bring up to date the 'little sketch of doctrines and methods'" that Schumpeter had published in 1914. It was the first volume in a famous series (Foundations of Social Science) edited by Max Weber and published only in German.[4]

Schumpeter's book of 1914 had long been out of print, and for years many scholars had urged that it be translated into English. Meanwhile, as Elizabeth put it, "J.A.S. had finished his monumental *Business Cycles* in 1938 and sought relaxation in *Capitalism, Socialism and Democracy*, which he regarded as distinctly a 'popular' offering that he expected to finish in a few months." From 1939 to 1948, Schumpeter taught a course on the history of economic thought, and Elizabeth speculates that this course stimulated him to begin work on his *History of Economic Analysis*.[5]

He centered his research at the small L-shaped Kress Library, tucked into a separate room of the Business School's main library. The Kress was one of the most beautiful enclaves at Harvard—and, to the Schumpeters' delight, one of the least visited. Its walls were lined with priceless original editions in many languages, dating from ancient times to 1850. Working in this room engendered a feeling of academic sanctity—of participating in a liturgy of the intellect. Elizabeth later described the Kress as "a kind of scholar's Paradise."[6]

Digging ever deeper into his project, Schumpeter found it a congenial way both to combine his own diverse approaches to economics and to escape the horrors of World War II. "It is simply the subject, among all those at hand, that is furthest removed from current events," he wrote a former student in 1943. As Elizabeth recalled, "He could weave together the threads of all of his interests—philosophy, sociology, history, theory, and such applied fields in economics as money, cycles, public finance, socialism. I believe also that the war had something to do with it . . . It removed him temporarily from a grim reality which grieved him beyond measure because he was convinced it would destroy the civilization he loved."[7]

But in a sense, Schumpeter had been working on this book "all his life," as Elizabeth put it. "Even his reading for pleasure and recreation—he loved to read biographies, preferably those in many volumes—contributed to that fascinating knowledge of men, events, and backgrounds which is apparent throughout the *History*." The research became an avocation in addition to a scholarly task.[8]

Writing to his publisher, he said, "This book will describe the development and the fortunes of scientific analysis in the field of economics, from Greco-Roman times to the present." Throughout the text he drew a distinction in economic writing between "what is and what ought to be" and tried to minimize the space he devoted to the latter.[9]

As always in his scientific work, Schumpeter wrote the entire book in longhand. Having almost no secretarial assistance, he would send off his handwritten drafts to typists whom he trusted. His filing system remained chaotic, and after his death Elizabeth found portions of the manuscript in many different places: "some of it in file boxes, some of it piled on shelves—in the Cambridge study on Acacia Street, in the Taconic study, and a little of it in his office at Littauer Center." For several months, she kept coming across still more fragments. Many pages were not numbered, and those that were appeared only in short batches.[10]

The immense length of the book raised formidable problems of organization and sequence. "Even though I am an economist with some editorial experience," Elizabeth wrote, "it was not easy to put together so long a work dealing with so many economists, writing in so many languages over so long a period." Her own repeated edits, carried out with help from Schumpeter's friends and the staff of Oxford University Press, finally produced a coherent book.[11]

SCHUMPETER HAD SET for himself a task of colossal scope. Early in the book he writes, "The economics profession reminds the outsider of nothing so much as the Tower of Babel," and he applies a kind of creative destruction to that towering edifice—that is, to the discipline of economics. His purpose is to describe "the process by which men's efforts to understand economic phenomena produce, improve, and pull down analytic structures in an unending sequence."[12]

The best approach, he says, is a close study of "doctrinal history." In economics, unlike a hard science such as physics, "modern problems, methods, and results cannot be fully understood without some knowledge of how economists have come to reason as they do." One of the book's many virtues is its memorable sketches of major (and numerous minor) figures in the context of their times.[13]

> On Plato (427–347 B.C.)
> Plato's aim was not analysis at all but extra-empirical visions of an ideal *polis* or, if we prefer, the artistic creation of one. The picture he painted of the Perfect State in his *Politeia* (The *Republic*) is no more analysis than a painter's rendering of a Venus is scientific anatomy. It goes without saying that on this plane the contrast between what is and what ought to be loses its meaning.[14]

> On Thomas Aquinas (1225–1274)
> [His] *Summa Theologica* is in the history of thought what the southwestern spire of the Cathedral of Chartres is in the history of architecture . . .
>
> The individualist and utilitarian streak and the emphasis upon a rationally perceived Public Good run through the whole sociology of St. Thomas. One example will suffice: the theory of property. Having disposed of the theological aspects of the matter, St. Thomas simply argues that property is not against natural law but an invention of the human reason, which is justifiable because . . . the social order will be better preserved if possessions are distinct, so that there is no occasion for quarreling about the use of things possessed in common.[15]

> On Adam Smith
> Few facts and no details are needed about the man and his sheltered and uneventful life (1723–90). It will suffice to note: first, that he was a Scotsman to the core, pure and unadulterated; sec-

ond, that his immediate family background was the Scottish civil service . . . [with its] critical attitude to business activity . . . third, that he was a professor born and bred . . . fourth—a fact which I cannot help considering relevant, not for his pure economics of course, but all the more for his understanding of human nature— that no woman, excepting his mother, ever played a role in his existence: in this as in other respects the glamours and passions of life were just literature to him.[16]

Schumpeter praises Adam Smith's dedication to his work (lavishly so) but says that "the *Wealth of Nations* does not contain a single *analytic* idea, principle, or method that was entirely new in 1776. Those who extolled A. Smith's work as an epoch-making, original achievement were, of course, thinking primarily of the *policies* he advocated—free trade, laissez faire, colonial policy, and so on." Smith's arguments struck very strong chords of harmony with what large numbers of people already believed. But no one, Schumpeter notes, had yet been able to articulate these beliefs with the eloquence that Smith—a former professor of rhetoric and one of the most persuasive writers of the entire eighteenth century—brought to the task:

> Where would the *Wealth of Nations* be without free trade and laissez faire? Also, the "unfeeling" or "slothful" landlords who reap where they have not sown, the employers whose every meeting issues in conspiracy, the merchants who enjoy themselves and let their clerks and accountants do the work, and the poor laborers who support the rest of society in luxury—these are all important parts of the show. It has been held that A. Smith, far ahead of his time, braved unpopularity by giving expression to his social sympathies. This is not so. His sincerity I do not for a moment call into question. But those views were not unpopular.[17]

In Adam Smith, Schumpeter found a perfect foil for some of his own convictions. To Smith, human beings seemed "to be much alike by nature, all reacting in the same simple ways to very simple stimuli." Most important, Smith "was thoroughly in sympathy with the humors of his time," and his "argument and material were enlivened by advocacy which is after all what attracts a wider public." By contrast, Schumpeter believed people to be quite dissimilar—individualized characters very different in their desires and especially in their endowments of talent. As a scholar, he was reluctant to write "down" to his readers in order to enhance his popular appeal. He was usually out of sympathy with the tempers of his time, and thoroughly averse to advocacy, irrespective of what that meant for the size of his audience.[18]

Schumpeter discovered many shortcomings in *The Wealth of Nations*. At times he seemed, inappropriately, to equate Smith's strength as a rhetorician with some weakness as a thinker. But in the end, he argued that *The Wealth of Nations* deserved all of its success. "We have a masterpiece before us, a masterpiece not only of pleading but also of analysis." Adam Smith was far and away the most influential writer on economics who ever lived.[19]

> Before the [18th] century was out the *Wealth of Nations* had run to
> nine English editions, not counting the ones that appeared in Ireland and the United States, and had been translated (so far as I
> know) into Danish, Dutch, *French, German,* Italian, and Spanish
> (italics indicate more than one translation; the first Russian translation appeared 1802–6). This may be taken to measure the extent
> of its success in the first stage of its career . . . But this was as nothing compared with the really significant success that is not so easy
> to measure: from about 1790 on, Smith became the teacher not of
> the beginner or the public but of the professionals, especially the
> professors . . . he was invested with the insignia of "founder"—
> which none of his contemporaries would have thought of bestowing on him.[20]

Having dealt at length with Adam Smith and his precursors, Schumpeter pauses to applaud some "consultant administrators and pamphleteers," most of whom turn out to be Americans. He especially praises Alexander Hamilton, the first secretary of the treasury, whose "*Report on Manufactures* (1791), though no doubt intended as a description with a program, is really 'applied economics' at its best." In passing, Schumpeter also cites Benjamin Franklin's excellent writings on economic subjects, "though there is little to commend for purely analytic virtues."[21]

In a chapter on the French Physiocrats, from whom Adam Smith learned so much, Schumpeter writes that the strength of the group derived from the labors of one man: François Quesnay, a figure still admired today as one of the greatest of all economists. In the Physiocrats' total devotion to Quesnay's teachings, "there are but two analogues in the whole history of economics: the fidelity of the orthodox Marxists to the message of Marx and the fidelity of the orthodox Keynesians to the message of Keynes." Each of the three groups constituted a "school" held together by personal relationships and doctrinal agreement. Their members "always acted as a group, praising one another, fighting one another's fights, each member taking his share in group propaganda."[22]

Here again, Schumpeter's analysis reveals much about his own attitudes. Throughout his career, he abjured the idea of doctrinal schools. Yet in his *History of Economic Analysis* he lays great importance on the role of personal leadership—not only in the cases of Quesnay, Marx, and Keynes but also David Ricardo, Gustav von Schmoller, Carl Menger, and Alfred Marshall. In each instance, he credits much of the success of the economic message to the style and personality of its progenitor. Although he does not use the word, he obviously regarded these figures as entrepreneurs of their discipline.[23]

Schumpeter is quite emphatic on this point. In assessing the reasons for the influence of Ricardo (1772–1823), he writes:

> By far the most important one was, I think, the priceless gift of
> leadership. He refreshed and irritated. In either case, he shook up
> . . . His teaching, in its middle and higher layers, established itself
> as the new thing, compared with which everything else was infe-
> rior, obsolete, stale. Very quickly his circle developed the atti-
> tude—so amusing but also, alas!, so melancholy to behold—of
> children who have been presented with a new toy. They thought
> the world of it. To them it was of incalculable value that only he
> could fail to appreciate who was too stupid to rise to Ricardian
> heights. And all this meant controversy, impulse, new zest,
> new life.[24]

As for the substance of Ricardo's contributions, Schumpeter goes into detail about not only their intrinsic merit but also the setting in which Ricardo wrote. And again the contrast with Schumpeter's own career and his own sense of being "unleaderly" is vivid. Ricardo made his reputation through ardent engagement of the most prominent political issues of his time—monetary policy and free trade. And he was always on the side likely to win the policy debate: "People took to his theory because they agreed with his recommendations. He became the center of a circle that looked to him for guidance and in turn defended his opinions. It is neither his advocacy of winning policies per se, nor his theory per se, that, to this day, makes of him, in the eyes of some, the first economist of all times, but a felicitous combination of both." Schumpeter invites the reader to note the similarities between Ricardo and Keynes. "Every word in the paragraph above might have been written with reference to the latter." Also like Keynes, Ricardo had a very full life outside academic economics. He was so busy with other matters that "we have before us the record of a wrestler who fought his matches with his right hand tied behind his back."[25]

In Schumpeter's judgment, this was one reason for the serious flaws in Ricardo's (and Keynes's) methods of analysis. Neither plumbed the full depths of his discipline. Neither accorded due credit to opposing arguments. Both used a few basic principles in their approach to any issue, whether or not those principles sufficed, or even applied. The principles themselves constituted an "engine," which "grinds out results, within wide limits, no matter . . . whether the problem is the effect of a tax or of a wage policy, or of a piece of regulation, or of protection and what not. Hence the engine, within those limits, may be constructed once and for all to stand ready for use whenever needed for an indefinite variety of purposes . . . But, of course, if a defective engine meets with success, that advance may easily prove to be a detour. And let me state at once: *a detour Ricardian analysis was.*" (Keynes agreed with this assessment: "If only [Thomas] Malthus rather than Ricardo had been the parent stem from which nineteenth century economics proceeded, what a much richer and wiser place the world would be today.")[26]

THERE WAS NO denying that the classical economists, inspired chiefly by Smith and Ricardo, led in the establishment of economics as an independent discipline. That process went forward slowly during the nineteenth century but without interruption. New societies were formed, new journals founded. In the United States, Columbia University established a chair in moral philosophy and political economy in 1818. In 1824 South Carolina College assigned a professor of chemistry to give lectures on economics. In Britain,

Oxford instituted a lectureship in 1825; University College, London, in 1828; Dublin in 1832. And before any of these, in 1805, the East India College at Haileybury had established a position in history, commerce, and finance, to which it appointed Thomas Malthus.[27]

During the Victorian period, British economists led all others, despite their erroneous view of capitalist economies as "stationary." Partly, Britain's leadership derived from the economic primacy of the country itself, which, ironically enough, was dynamic and not at all stationary. But mainly it reflected the high intellectual abilities of a large number of British analysts.[28]

The doctrine of free trade, for example, reached its zenith in Britain during the Victorian period. Its advocates "claimed perfect generality for their argument. For them, it was absolute and eternal wisdom for all times and places; he who refused to accept it was a fool or a crook or both." But free trade, Schumpeter notes, is a policy that gives the advantage to the lowest-cost manufacturer, which for many products at that time was Britain. And this circumstance accounted for free trade's triumph in Britain more than did the general validity of the doctrine. In most European countries, few people believed in free trade. And in the United States the policy was seldom practiced, though often preached by professional economists.[29]

In Schumpeter's view, the intellectual progress of economics during these years was not matched by Western culture generally:

> The business and professional classes lived, as a rule, uninspired
> lives in ugly homes that dishonored the elements of past styles
> they combined; bought ugly furniture of similar type and nonde-
> script pictures; supported a theatrical and a musical tradition of
> which the glories were inherited from the past; and read a litera-
> ture that was largely commonplace in all varieties except the pro-
> fessionally scientific one. This style of life in all its manifesta-
> tions—in England it came to be called Victorian—is now a
> byword of stodginess or dreariness and in fact testifies to the bour-
> geoisie's lack of capacity for cultural leadership, which is as pro-
> nounced as is its lack of capacity for political leadership. [30]

But, Schumpeter adds, undistinguished bourgeois culture produced its own backlash, in still another type of creative destruction. In late-nineteenth-century Europe, cultural and artistic Modernism arose in music, painting, architecture, and literature. And this renaissance emerged mostly from the same bourgeois background that had produced its dull predecessors. Capitalist society was thus in the process of creating a new type of culture "when it was overtaken by the meaningless catastrophe of 1914–18 that put its world out of gear."[31]

A major trend that Schumpeter documents for the fifty years before the First World War is what he calls the "professionalization and professorialization" of economic analysis. Before about 1870, most economists had little or no academic affiliation, and very few were professors. But in the next generation, all of that changed. Harvard created its first professorship of political economy in 1871, Yale in 1872, and a dramatic expansion followed in the United States. Meanwhile, "Germany, Italy, Spain, and the northern [European] countries developed their economic professions on old-established lines, but France took a big step by establishing in 1878 professorships of economics at all the faculties of law in the country." In many places, notably Germany, universities had on staff only two full professors of economics, and in England and Scotland often only one. The natural result was questionable competence, which led to a series of uninformed quarrels over methods. Nor did professionalization do much to end economists' preoccupation with social reform.[32]

Politically, professors could be found all across the ideological spectrum. Most, however, especially in the United States and France, espoused classical laissez faire economics. But in Britain, the birthplace of this doctrine, Cambridge's Alfred Marshall "professed himself in sympathy with the aims of socialism and spoke without explanation and qualification of the 'evils of inequality.'" In Germany, most economists were more in tune with Marshall than with his classical British predecessors. The Germans "were pillars of *Sozialpolitik* and thoroughly averse to 'Smithianism' or 'Manchesterism,'" which they regarded as almost criminally oblivious to social welfare. Schmoller "once asserted publicly that a 'Smithian' was unfit to occupy a professorial chair. Even American 'New Dealers' did not go quite so far as this."[33]

Schumpeter believed that, during the period from 1870 to 1914, Britain had the best-qualified practitioners of economics (or, as he expresses it, the fewest unqualified). In the United States, some economists sympathized with the populist movement—an agrarian-based egalitarian program of the 1880s and 1890s, strongest in the South and Midwest. Others supported the reformer

Henry George, whose single-tax idea held that the appreciation of real estate values properly belonged to the people at large and should be directed toward the public treasury. Views truly hostile to capitalism were weakly expressed by professionals, with the conspicuous exception of Thorstein Veblen. "No economist whom anyone would care to call 'leading,' in any sense whatsoever, identified himself with any radical scheme of social reform." In Schumpeter's judgment, the best American economists at the start of the twentieth century were John Bates Clark of Columbia, Frank Taussig of Harvard, and Irving Fisher of Yale.[34]

Earlier, the comparative poverty of professional economic analysis in America had derived from the bounteous business opportunities that drew most good economic brains into commerce and industry. During the mid-nineteenth century, universities were beginning to teach economics, but "the demand for courses and textbooks produced courses and textbooks and not much else. Does this not show that there is something to one of the theses of this book, namely, that need is not the necessary and sufficient condition of analytic advance and that demand for teaching produces teaching and not necessarily scientific achievement?"[35]

Many American economists who became leading professors were much influenced by the Historical School, having trained in Germany during the 1880s and 1890s. And Schumpeter's *History* provides one of the best short analyses of that school ever written. Its central tenet "may be summed up precisely in the proposition that the economist, considered as a research worker, should be primarily an economic historian." Under the leadership of Schmoller, the Historical School achieved enormous progress in economists' understanding of social processes. Schumpeter mentions the school's analyses of social classes, craft and merchant guilds, the growth of cities, fiscal policy, bank credit, particular industries, and the division of functions between government and the private sector.[36]

Generalizing from the battle over methods between Schmoller's Historical School and Menger's Austrian School (the *Methodenstreit*), Schumpeter speculates that scientific controversies often stem from mutual misunderstanding based on temperamental differences and intellectual prejudices. Workers in any field prefer their own approaches, and this tendency alone implies a kind of irrational distaste for others' methods. But in academics the phenomenon

may be inescapable, because intellectual schools of thought "are sociological realities—living beings," with "their flags, their battle cries, their moods, their
all-too-human interests."[37]

After considering the inevitable duels between proponents of various schools,
Schumpeter returns to his series of critical sketches, giving pride of place to
Léon Walras: "So far as pure theory is concerned, Walras is in my opinion the
greatest of all economists. His system of economic equilibrium, uniting, as it
does, the quality of 'revolutionary' creativeness with the quality of classic synthesis, is the only work by an economist that will stand comparison with the
achievements of theoretical physics."[38]

Conversely, Schumpeter was devastating in his critique of incompetent analysts. He described Herbert Spencer (1820–1903), a popular and influential
British writer, as

> A man of representative eminence who, to an amazing degree, was
> at the same time profound, clever, and silly . . . no other word but
> "silly" will fit the man who failed to see that, by carrying laissez-
> faire liberalism to the extent of disapproving sanitary regulations,
> public education, public postal service, and the like, he made his
> ideal ridiculous and that in fact he wrote what would have served
> very well as a satire on the policy he advocated. Neither his eco-
> nomics nor his ethics (normative as well as analytic) are worth our
> while.[39]

Throughout his *History,* Schumpeter is at pains not only to lampoon bad
work but also to credit good work, regardless of its source. The test is analytical
validity, not motive. "The most stubborn class interest may induce true and
valuable analysis, the most disinterested motive may lead to nothing but error
and triviality." Motives make no difference, and it is dangerous even to raise
the question. "The only mind accessible to us is our own. In talking about motives of individuals we may be revealing nothing but our own propensities."[40]

At its core, says Schumpeter, economic theory is not a political philosophy
but rather, in the "unsurpassably felicitous phrase" of the Cambridge economist Joan Robinson, "a box of tools." While acknowledging that economic
theory has yet to fulfill its potential, he notes that criticism of it often had political roots—in large part because "economists indulged their strong propen-

sity to dabble in politics, to peddle political recipes, to offer themselves as philosophers of economic life, and in doing so neglected the duty of stating explicitly the value judgments that they introduced into their reasoning." An unfortunate result of all this had been the discrediting of economic theory itself through the discrediting of the political stances of many theorists.[41]

One of the real bases of all social science, Schumpeter thought, should be psychology, which analyzes the human feelings "in terms of which all fundamental explanation must run." Schumpeter knew that Menger and others of the Austrian School, in their emphasis on individuals' choices, had implicitly moved psychology toward the center of economic thinking. Yet, he noted with regret, economists generally did not consult or work with professional psychologists. Instead, they preferred to invent their own assumptions about the mental processes of producers, consumers, and people in general.[42]

A unifying theme of *History of Economic Analysis* builds on a psychological point Schumpeter had made in his earlier writings: all human beings grow up having subconsciously developed a sense of how the world works. Everyone who writes on any subject, he says, has experienced "a preanalytic cognitive act that supplies the raw material for the analytic effort. In this book, this preanalytic cognitive act will be called Vision . . . vision of this kind not only must precede historically the emergence of analytic effort in any field but also may re-enter the history of every established science each time somebody teaches us to *see* things in a light of which the source is not to be found in the facts, methods, and results of the pre-existing state of the science." Schumpeter uses Keynes's *General Theory* as an example of the latter phenomenon. Keynes's vision was based on his conception that British capitalism was growing old and feeble. And whether right or wrong, this vision of a bleak economic future preceded Keynes's development of his own formal system of economic analysis.[43]

Schumpeter says that *all* analysis begins with a distinct intuition that is almost inherently ideological. "It embodies the picture of things as we see them," and usually our way of seeing them "can hardly be distinguished from the way in which we wish to see them." This is a dangerous situation for researchers, because it tends to limit the generality of their conclusions.[44]

On the other hand, the rules of scholarship typically correct almost all errors deriving from ideology. Different researchers begin with different visions and ideologies, and conflicting conclusions tend to cancel each other out. The canons of scholarship achieve this result "automatically and irrespective of the desires of the research worker." Even so, no set of rules—especially in economics, where few results can be proved beyond any doubt—will drive out ideology altogether, or even prevent deliberate dishonesty. A researcher may suppress troublesome evidence without thinking that any duplicity is involved. "The first thing a man will do for his ideals is lie."[45]

Later in the book, Schumpeter applies his idea of "Vision" to the methods of economic analysis that prevailed for much of the nineteenth century. He notes that starting with Adam Smith, the classical economists made use of the term "stationary state" to describe both an existing situation and some condition they thought would materialize in the future. Here, their vision became a real obstacle to progress, because it offered no explanation at all of the *process* of change, which Schumpeter regarded as the essence of capitalism. And the problem had persisted down to the present time in the form of the stagnationist thesis—the notion that the age of innovation had passed and "mature" capitalism was at hand. Schumpeter considered this idea ridiculous.[46]

In order to explain how economists had followed such a mistaken road, he retraced the early years of systematic economic analysis—roughly from 1790 to 1870. During that period, he said, there were three major visions of future economic development. The first was that of "pessimists" such as Thomas Malthus, David Ricardo, and James Mill, father of John Stuart Mill. The pessimists dwelled on limits to growth imposed by the pressures of increasing population and decreasing returns to agriculture. From these premises they inferred "falling net returns to industry, more or less constant real wages, and ever increasing (absolutely and relatively) rents of land."[47]

For Schumpeter, the pessimists' vision revealed a startling absence of imagination. They were writing even as the industrial revolution was transforming economic life, yet they saw only scarcity and want. For them the stationary state became not merely a tool of analysis (Schumpeter himself used it for this purpose) but a "future reality." Among other problems, this vision took no account whatever of "the element of personal initiative"—the touchstone of Schumpeter's own theories of entrepreneurship and creative destruction.[48]

A second early-nineteenth-century vision took an optimistic tone, and here Schumpeter's best examples were the American economist Henry C. Carey and the German Friedrich List. Carey and List, like the great French economist Jean-Baptiste Say, realized that the facts belied the future envisioned by Ricardo and other pessimists. Most of the optimists were not very good at technical analysis (Say was an exception), but their vision accorded with reality much better than did that of the pessimists. Schumpeter derived a pair of general principles from the example of the optimists. First, the accuracy of an economic vision is not always commensurate with the analytical ability of those who hold it. Second, pessimistic visions about almost anything usually strike the public as more erudite than optimistic ones.[49]

The other major vision of this period came from the imposing figure of Karl Marx. Despite his numerous errors, Marx saw more clearly than anyone else the dynamism of the capitalist engine. Had he not been so obsessed with the class struggle and the exploitation of the masses, his influence on other analysts would have been much stronger, in Schumpeter's view.[50]

Conventional economists' unwillingness to modify their vision so as to see the critical and legitimate roles of constant change, entrepreneurship, and the evolution of big business was a grievous flaw that persisted down to Schumpeter's own time, he believed. And in some respects it remains a flaw in mainstream economic theory even to this day.[51]

The extensive discussion of entrepreneurship in *History of Economic Analysis* represents Schumpeter's final statement on a subject that had fascinated him since the beginning of his career. So far as he could determine, the first analyst to use the term *entrepreneur* was the French economist Richard Cantillon (1680–1734), writing in a tract on the way business actually works. But Cantillon did not pursue his insight very thoroughly. Adam Smith, writing two generations later, "speaks occasionally of the undertaker, the master, the merchant—and, if pressed, would not have denied that no business runs by itself. Nevertheless this is exactly the over-all impression his readers get." Jean-Baptiste Say moved the argument forward "in the pithy statement that the entrepreneur's function is to *combine* the factors of production into a producing organism." But Say did not seem to realize that even this definition described little beyond the normal routine of everyday business.[52]

Neither Ricardo nor Marx followed up on the insights of Cantillon and Say. That step was taken by John Stuart Mill, who brought the term entrepreneur into general use among English economists and, in analyzing the entrepreneurial function, went from "superintendence" to "control" and even to "direction," which, he admitted, required "often no ordinary skill." But even Mill's definition did not progress much beyond administration. And Mill's ill-advised identification of the entrepreneur with the risk-bearer "only served to push the car still further on the wrong track. And there it stuck."[53]

Today, in the twenty-first century, many economists add entrepreneurship to the three factors of production as traditionally conceived: land, labor, and capital. That addition owes a very great deal to Schumpeter's own work. But large numbers of analysts still downplay the idea. Entrepreneurship is very difficult to measure, and virtually impossible to express mathematically. It therefore does not easily fit into formal models. As Schumpeter noted, entrepreneurial gains do not tend "toward equalization" because they "are not permanent returns at all." Instead, they emerge whenever an individual entrepreneur innovates in some important way—and then disappear as the innovation spreads. Meanwhile, they have contributed to general economic growth.[54]

They have also made the entrepreneur rich, because "entrepreneurs' gains will practically always bear some relation to monopolistic pricing. Whatever it is that produces these gains, it must of necessity be something that, for the moment at least, competitors cannot parallel." The best example is the offering of a new product or a new brand. And temporarily, at least, "there are means available to the successful entrepreneur—patents, 'strategy,' and so on for prolonging the life of his monopolistic or quasi-monopolistic position and for rendering it more difficult for competitors to close up on him."[55]

By connecting strategy so specifically to entrepreneurship in his *History*, Schumpeter shows that he has come to understand the connection far better than he did when he wrote *The Theory of Economic Development* (1911). There, he made much of entrepreneurship but said nothing about strategy. The key to this shift was his research into the history of corporations for his book *Business Cycles* (1939).

The idea of strategy came relatively late in economic thinking about capitalism because the business unit hypothesized by most theorists was of small or medium size. Such firms are unable to affect the behavior of other firms or even their own industry—which is the essence of strategy—so the concept could have no place in the thinking of these theorists. As Schumpeter puts it, "The facts and problems of large-scale production and, in connection with them, those of joint stock companies were recognized by economists after everybody else had recognized them." Most theorists preferred to work with models of perfect competition rather than with the complex reality of large firms behaving strategically toward one another. Schumpeter proposes that "we may call this the Principle of Excluded Strategy."[56]

The principle of excluded strategy certainly characterized the work of John Maynard Keynes. In the last chapter of *History of Economic Analysis,* titled "Keynes and Modern Macroeconomics," Schumpeter analyzes the sources and influence of Keynes's ideas and in so doing finally exorcizes the specter that had haunted him since 1936.

Schumpeter argues that the central problem with Keynes's work derived from a pre-analytic "vision of England's aging capitalism and his intuitive diagnosis of it (which he followed up without the slightest consideration of other possible diagnoses): the arteriosclerotic economy whose opportunities for rejuvenating venture[s] decline while the old habits of saving formed in times of plentiful opportunity persist." The result of this process, as Keynes saw it, was stagnation of the precise kind that had plagued that world during the Great Depression.[57]

Keynes's fundamental vision, Schumpeter continues, is evident in the early pages of *The Economic Consequences of the Peace* (written in 1919) and becomes steadily more obvious in the *Tract on Monetary Reform* (1923) and *A Treatise on Money* (1930), which was "Keynes's most ambitious purely scholarly venture. This *Treatise,* though no failure in the ordinary sense of the term, met respectful but damaging criticism and, above all, failed to express Keynes's vision adequately."[58]

When that happened, Keynes apparently decided to expunge from his future work all evidence and qualifying statements that might weaken his arguments. He "bent to the task of framing an analytic system that would express his fundamental idea *and nothing else.*" The crowning achievement of this work, *The General Theory of Employment, Interest and Money,* "seems to have satisfied him completely, so much so that he felt himself to have led economics out of 150 years of error into the land of definitive truth." (Keynes in fact says as much in *The General Theory,* as well as in his private correspondence.) His many disciples shared this view, while his critics—including Schumpeter—regarded the book as a discredit to Keynes's prior work.[59]

In the years after its publication in 1936, *The General Theory* was often enlisted in the service of radical egalitarianism. Schumpeter found this result ironic, because Keynes himself "was rather conservative in many respects, especially in matters touching freedom of enterprise." The impact of Keynes's message, often distorted by ardent disciples of big government from what Keynes had actually written, "seemed to reveal a novel view of the capitalist process not only, as we saw before, to the public and 'writers on the fringes' but also to many of the best minds in the sphere of professional analysis." The greatest appeal of Keynesianism was "to young theorists," whereas most veterans of the profession took an anti-Keynesian stance.[60]

In Schumpeter's view, *The General Theory* created such a jolt because of its electrifying analysis and also its timely arrival while the world was thrashing around in depression. "As in the case of Ricardo, it was the intellectual performance spiced by the—real or putative—relevance to burning questions of the time which achieved what, in our field, neither could have achieved by itself."[61]

Schumpeter both admired and envied Keynes and saw him as much more than an academic economist. "He was a forceful and dauntless leader of public opinion, a wise adviser to his country." He "would have conquered a place in history even if he had never done a stroke of specifically scientific work: he would still have been the man who wrote *The Economic Consequences of the Peace* (1919), bursting into international fame when men of equal insight but less courage and men of equal courage but less insight kept silent."[62]

Again, Schumpeter compared Keynes to David Ricardo: "His work is a striking example of what we have called above the Ricardian Vice, namely, the habit of piling a heavy load of practical conclusions upon a tenuous groundwork, which was unequal to it yet seemed in its simplicity not only attractive but also convincing. All this goes a long way though not the whole way toward answering the questions that always interest us, namely the questions *what* it is in a man's message that makes people listen to him, and *why* and *how.*" This last comment reveals part of the kind of motivation that led Schumpeter to write such a huge work. One reviewer conceded that the plan of the book "is unprecedented in its ambition. Yet it is not clear, to me at least, why Schumpeter or anyone else should want to write on such a scale."[63]

The answer to that interesting question is that *History of Economic Analysis,* as Elizabeth said in her introduction, wove together "the threads of all of his interests—philosophy, sociology, history, theory"; and then applied them to an exceedingly broad range of economic issues. Schumpeter was a pure scholar, and in that sense he wrote the book to satisfy his own curiosity. That was its foremost instrumental function.

Even so, the book is full of Schumpeterian *argument,* much of which is implicit in its structure. He discusses, for example, the economic ideas of the greatest philosophers—Aristotle, Plato, Aquinas, and many others—thereby demonstrating once more his belief that the proper study of economics must draw on all relevant disciplines. He makes much of Joan Robinson's famous definition of economic theory as a "box of tools." But what are such tools but forms of intellectual capital? Schumpeter portrays many of the great economists as entrepreneurs of the discipline, using and misusing its capital—its box of tools—as that capital accumulates over time.

Throughout the book, Schumpeter represents advances in economic reasoning as nonlinear. Most steps are forward, some are backward. Many pregnant insights come to nothing and are forgotten. The most successful advances are like industrial revolutions of the mind. Here they parallel Schumpeter's narrative account in *Business Cycles* of the revolutions wrought by the steam engine, the railroad, electricity, the corporation, and credit creation. And like that earlier book, *History of Economic Analysis* puts a human face on what in other hands becomes an austere, sterile chronicle of abstract ideas. Who can forget Schumpeter's description of Herbert Spencer as "silly"? Or his comment that to Adam Smith "the glamours and passions of life were just literature" because of the absence of women? Or his observation that Plato's portrayal of the perfect state "is no more analysis than a painter's rendering of a Venus is scientific anatomy"?

History of Economic Analysis succeeds where much economic writing of our own time fails, having sacrificed the messy humanity of its subject on the altar of mathematical rigor. Above all else, Schumpeter's *History* is an epic analytical narrative. It is about real human beings, moored in their own time, struggling like characters in a novel to resolve difficult problems. Sometimes the problems

Opposite top: Near Taconic on Mount Riga, one of the highest peaks in Connecticut, in 1947, as he worked on *History of Economic Analysis.* Schumpeter's diary during this period frequently mentions the new sense of peace he felt—though sometimes, as he put it, "peace without joy."

Opposite bottom: With a guest in 1948 at Windy Hill, where Schumpeter wrote most of *History of Economic Analysis.* Elizabeth is at the left. Both she and her husband were exceedingly fond of their pet Irish setter. When the dog was a puppy, Joseph had inaccurately identified her as a male and named her Peter. The name stuck.

Above: Baker Library at Harvard Business School, where both Schumpeters spent prodigal amounts of time throughout the 1940s doing research for *History of Economic Analysis,* in the small Kress Library hidden away on the second floor of this building.

are purely intellectual. Sometimes they are issues of public policy. Often they are both. But what Schumpeter was trying to do—and in fact did—was answer the deceptively simple question he posed in the early pages of his book: to discover "how economists have come to reason as they do."

His HISTORY OF ECONOMIC ANALYSIS was the most widely and thoroughly reviewed of all Schumpeter's works. Several long essays on this posthumous book amounted to eulogies, though none omitted critical comments. The typical tone was set by Frank Knight of the University of Chicago, one of the few great contemporaries of Schumpeter who shared his interest in entrepreneurship: "This volume suggests the expletive *c'est formidable!* . . . truly stupendous." And like Knight, nearly all of the reviewers were themselves at the top of their profession.[64]

In a seventeen-page notice in the *American Economic Review,* Jacob Viner wrote with a sense of wonder:

> Greek, classical Latin, mediaeval Latin, Italian, Spanish, Swedish,
> and Dutch contributions, as well as, of course, German, French,
> and English literature, are reported on from their original texts.
> Most important of all, this is a history of theory written on the
> grand scale by an economist who was an original, a powerful, and
> a versatile theorist on his own account . . . Nowhere else, I think,
> in the literature of our discipline, can one find, within comparable
> limitations of space, as brilliant, and as self-effacing, [an] exposi-
> tion by one economist, himself a master, of the analytical achieve-
> ments of other economists.[65]

Three future Nobel Laureates expressed their own kinds of praise. Simon Kuznets: "This is a grand and grandiose book." George J. Stigler: "There is splendor in Schumpeter's contempt for those who explain and appraise theories by the venal motives that their authors conceivably nurtured. There is intellectual chivalry in his attempts to divorce the quality of the analyses from the policies to which they were married." Friedrich von Hayek: "Nobody should profit more from [the book] than the economists of the younger generation . . . no work is better suited to show what they ought to know if they are to be not merely economists but cultivated persons competent to use their technical knowledge in a complex world."[66]

Two of the most insightful reviews were by G. B. Richardson of Oxford and Lionel Robbins of the London School of Economics, both of whom went out of their way to compare Schumpeter with Keynes. Richardson concluded that *History of Economic Analysis* is "one of the most important books on economics to be published in the last half-century." Schumpeter displays "all the bewildering contradictions of genius," and his personality "enlivens every page."

> One is obviously tempted to make comparisons with Keynes. Clear brilliance, authority, quickness and flexibility of mind, and a sense of fun seem common to both. Both seemed in reaction against the bourgeois virtues and had a strong personal aversion to utilitarianism . . . But in other ways they differed fundamentally. Schumpeter was, I should imagine, Keynes's superior as a scholar, at least within the field of economics . . . To some, Schumpeter's vision of life will seem less space- and time-bounded, deeper if more pessimistic than that of Keynes, his work more systematic and thorough. Largely it is a difference in nationality; Keynes was surely exceedingly English and in direct descent from the English empirical philosophers.[67]

The review by Lionel Robbins, appearing as the lead article in the *Quarterly Journal of Economics,* reached twenty-three pages in length and surveyed Schumpeter's entire career. "He was born and brought up in one of the most brilliant and cultivated societies of Europe . . . one of the chief centres of speculation in theoretical economics. As a young man he had travelled widely and studied in many other places; he had personal contact with many of the founders of modern economic analysis elsewhere." Thus, Schumpeter knew theory "from the inside; he spoke with the authority of a high practitioner. He was, moreover, an excellent expositor and showman; in our profession, with the single exception of Keynes, he was probably the best talker of his generation." Echoing what G. B. Richardson had said in his own review, Robbins implies that Schumpeter's dissatisfaction with many British economists derived from what he regarded as their assumption of regularity and smooth progression in economic life. Schumpeter's own view of the world "involved much more of discontinuity and seismic convulsions." Nowhere did this difference show up as vividly as in his analysis of the work of Keynes. "It is clear," wrote Robbins, "that the spectacle of much contemporary Keynesianism inspired in Schumpeter a distaste that must have been almost physical. It is clear too that he was profoundly shocked by Keynes's occasional indifference to scholarly considerations, his eccentric, and frequently unjust judgments of his predecessors, and his obvious ignorance of much earlier work."[68]

When Keynes died in 1946, Schumpeter wrote two perceptive pieces on his British rival, one of them a long obituary for the *American Economic Review.* But even amidst all the praise, as Schumpeter's friend and colleague Arthur Smithies later noted, he "does not credit Keynes with a single major improvement in the technique of economic analysis . . . There was no compromise, no hint of a concession that Keynes might have prepared the way toward an enlightened conservatism."[69]

Schumpeter's primary objection to Keynes's theories, Smithies continued, was that "in his opinion, Keynes, next to Marx, cultivated the intellectual soil in which anti-capitalist attitudes flourished." Keynes's worst flaw, in Schumpeter's view, was that "he made it intellectually respectable for other non-socialists to go further in an anti-capitalist direction than he had any inclination to go himself." During the 1930s Keynes's writings seemed to encourage any policy, no matter how ridiculous, that increased public spending—an extremely dangerous idea to plant in the minds of politicians. And the Keynesians' preoccupation with the short run seemed to assume that the long run would look after itself. "No wonder Schumpeter protested. Even if short-run policies were based on some notion of the common good rather than on the flow of the political tides, they would be anti-capitalistic in his view . . . Short-run inequity is the price that must be paid by the masses for the rising living standards that capitalism can achieve."[70]

Smithies was right; this was the crux of the matter. Schumpeter regretted that capitalism distributed its fruits so disproportionately—but in much the same way that he regretted that everyone has to die. He simply thought it an inevitable concurrent of capitalism's efficiency over the long run. As he wrote in his *Encyclopaedia Britannica* article of 1946, one of the commonest errors of economic thinking by masses of people "is the belief that the majority of people is poor *because* a minority is rich." This belief derived almost entirely from short-run observations. It overlooked enormous shifts up and down in individuals' prosperity over the medium term, let alone the long run; and it ignored the broad-based gains from entrepreneurial innovation that partly depended on investment by the rich.[71]

As Smithies went on to say, "Keynes's influence not only encouraged governments to take a short-run point of view, but it helped to free them from the major traditional restraints on short-run action." Keynes inadvertently provided spurious rationales for reckless deficit spending, huge national debts, and low savings rates. Keynes seemed to assume that governments would always be capable of acting rationally and for the good of the whole people. "Schumpeter must have felt all this to be exceedingly naive. He must also have thought it naive to regard Keynesianism as a reversible process. Mechanically the *General Theory* provided the cure for inflation as well as deflation. But whether it provided the political remedy is more doubtful." That is to say, governments can easily cut taxes and promote spending in order to combat downward dips in the business cycle. These steps are invariably popular with voters. But for this very reason, politicians find it nearly impossible to do the reverse: raise taxes and cut spending in order to cool an overheated economy or reduce fiscal deficits. In this sense, one of Schumpeter's contributions to political economy "was not to prove that Keynes was wrong in his conception of the functions of the state, but to show that the way to effective state action was more tortuous and difficult than Keynes was wont to assume."[72]

There was a good deal more to Schumpeter's commentaries on Keynes than academic analysis alone. The two were exact contemporaries, both having been born in 1883. But the contrast in their subsequent lives was as striking as their differing visions of capitalism—and could hardly have been more relevant to the formation of those visions.[73]

Keynes grew up in the cocoon of the English upper middle class. Domestic continuity was one of the keynotes of his life, and he seldom had reason to feel insecure about anything. His father, John Neville Keynes, had long been a respected economist and official at Cambridge University. His mother served as mayor of Cambridge. His brother achieved fame as one of England's finest surgeons. As a matter of course, he attended Eton and then Cambridge. At both schools, his homosexuality was generally accepted as ordinary. And in the Bloomsbury Group, Keynes's other intellectual home—which included

Virginia Woolf and her husband Leonard, the historian Lytton Strachey, the painters Duncan Grant and Vanessa Bell, and the art critics Roger Fry and Clive Bell, among others—homosexuality was practically celebrated. This would not have been the case in Austria, Germany, or the United States.

Compared to Keynes, Schumpeter had no reason to think that life was something a person could expect to enjoy automatically. It was one thing to grow up in Britain—stable, prosperous, and ever-victorious in its many wars—and quite another to be a child of the vanquished, and now vanished, Austria of Schumpeter's youth. His own vision of life resembled his vision of capitalism as a perennial gale of creative destruction. From the age of four, when his father died, it had become ever clearer to him that he could rely on nothing except his mother's love and his own wits. Throughout his life, one rock after another had crumbled under his feet. By the time he married Elizabeth Boody, he had lived in nine cities and five countries (seven countries by today's boundaries). He had relocated his household twenty-three times. No wonder his vision differed so thoroughly from that of the sedentary Keynes, as well as those of Smith, Ricardo, Mill, and other British economists. And no wonder he had such mixed feelings about Britain itself. While he admired its political system and yearned for the comfort and security it represented (his first wife had been an upper-class Englishwoman, after all), he came to feel something close to contempt for what he regarded as the stagnationist provincial vision of his British counterparts.

Unlike any of them, Schumpeter had to reinvent himself multiple times, and he did the same in his work. For every episode of destruction that he endured, he tried to convert his experience into a recreation or reinvention of some aspect of economics. Over the years, the long arc of his work describes the very same restless ambition that drove it. Schumpeter was one of the greatest intellectual innovators in the history of social science.

History of Economic Analysis, by itself, is such a spectacular performance that it invites comparison with Samuel Johnson's *Dictionary*—a titanic, almost unbelievably learned work born from a single mind. And Schumpeter can only be viewed as uniquely lucky that Elizabeth, his devoted wife, had the means, the determination, and the fortitude to bring the book to fruition.

27

A Principle of Indeterminateness

The race is not to the swift, nor the battle to the strong, neither yet bread to the wise, nor yet riches to men of understanding, nor yet favor to men of skill; but time and chance
happeneth to them all.

ECCLESIASTES 9:11

DESPITE ALL HIS pioneering work of integrating other disciplines
into economics, Schumpeter in the mid-1940s was still looking for a key to
"exact economics" in the sense of a determinate and predictive science. His diary makes frequent mention of "PV"—his preliminary volume on theory and
the overture to a full-length book. But he made little progress. He spent the
majority of his time on *History of Economic Analysis,* and he strove to use that
project, along with mathematics, as a springboard to more rigorous theory.
  As Elizabeth recalled,

> He envisaged a theory which might some day synthesize dynamic
> economics in the same way that the Walrasian system had
> summed up static economics. Eventually he modified this pro-
> gram to the extent that he would first write a little Introduction to
> Theory which would be for this kind of theory what the *General
> Theory of Employment, Interest and Money* was for Keynesian the-

ory. He read the current theoretical literature (largely in periodicals), worked at his mathematics, and assembled voluminous notes. The results of this work are reflected in some of the later parts of the *History [of Economic Analysis]*, especially in those parts which sum up modern developments.[1]

After his failure to achieve exact economics in *Business Cycles,* Schumpeter might have been expected to abandon his quest altogether. But he was not ready to give up. Nor did he divorce his own pursuit from his teaching of graduate students. In 1946 he published a brief text called *Rudimentary Mathematics for Economists and Statisticians,* coauthored with his Harvard colleague W. L. Crum. This book, which embodied the efforts he had been promoting since his years in Bonn, would take students "from the creeping to the crawling stage," Schumpeter told a friend.[2]

On his own, he performed daily exercises in calculus and tried to master advanced techniques such as matrix algebra. He even raised the question of a new type of math that would capture the dynamic changes that he saw as the heart of capitalism. One diary entry of 1948 mentions, with a question mark, "Evolutionary math?"—a tool that could do for his own system what conventional math had done for Walras's static equilibrium. But there was no evolutionary math at that time in the sense that Schumpeter meant, and there is still not enough today to "operationalize" his system thoroughly. Schumpeter knew that he had little talent in mathematics, but he continued to challenge himself and to enjoy the chase. "Whatever other advantages math may have," he wrote in his diary, "it is certainly the purest of human pleasures."[3]

Meanwhile, he kept working on his *History of Economic Analysis.* Because that task followed closely on *Business Cycles* and *Capitalism, Socialism and Democracy* (both of which are full of unpredictable historical twists), he arrived—at first without realizing it—at a new intellectual phase. Still unwilling to abandon his hunt for an exact economics with determinate predictive power, he began more and more to embrace sociology, political science, and, most importantly, history, in all its indeterminacy. Where he was headed now, mathematics was unlikely to follow.[4]

From 1945 through 1949, he displayed his new approach in a rich series of speeches and articles. This was the same period during which he was feeling his way toward a practical understanding of the mixed economy, with his metaphors about amphibial states, halfway houses, and capitalism in the oxygen tent. But in his other new work, he wrote more as a scholar—pursuing, in particular, questions of how and why people come to think as they do. These questions, he believed, were the provinces of history and "economic sociology" more than of economics itself.

In an essay marking the 1948 centennial of *The Communist Manifesto,* Schumpeter argued that the document's economic sociology "is far more important than its economics proper." In the *Manifesto,* Marx and Engels had pointed to economic issues as the sole source of changes in social structure and culture. But at the time Marx was writing, "he was hardly an economist at all: it was during the 1850's that he became one." The "social vision" that Marx would implement in *Capital* (1859) and his many later works "was quite set when he wrote the *Communist Manifesto.*" In other words, Marx's belief in economic determinism had preceded his study of economics. His many subsequent errors derived from his faulty original "vision"; and the whole sequence represented a good example of economic sociology, which includes the habits of mind that shape economic analysis.[5]

Of course, there was also a sociology of knowledge in the work of historians. Schumpeter had come to see that the contents of written history, like that of economics, depend not only on the facts but also on the pre-analytic vision of the individual historian: "Every investigator will distribute emphasis as he pleases and there are, in this as in other respects, irreducible personal equations—irreducible differences of visions: people will always differ as to whether the battle of Austerlitz was won by Napoleon, or by a social system, or by the French nation, or by a military apparatus and a technique inherited from the Revolution." But the obvious subjectivism of historians "does not preclude scientific analysis of that campaign" or of other historical topics.[6]

Schumpeter titled the paper in which this passage appears "Comments on a Plan for the Study of Entrepreneurship." He wrote it in 1946 at the request of his friend Arthur Cole, an economic historian who was proposing to establish a center at Harvard for the study of this subject. Cole naturally wished to involve Schumpeter, the world's leading scholar of entrepreneurship. And Schumpeter in turn helped Cole persuade the Rockefeller Foundation to fund what became the Center for Research in Entrepreneurial History, which had a

Left: Arthur Cole, economic historian and academic entrepreneur, pictured here in the 1930s. Cole taught in the Economics Department, then moved to the Business School, where as both librarian and professor he built Baker Library into the world's best repository for the study of business. Lobbying relentlessly, he then established the Center for Research in Entrepreneurial History.

Below: Schumpeter presenting one of his papers on economic history to fellow members of the Center for Research in Entrepreneurial History.

productive run at Harvard from 1948 until 1958. Immersed in his own work, Schumpeter never took the lead in the center's activities. But "without his zeal and support," Cole later wrote, "the Center might readily have 'died a-borning.'" Schumpeter attended its early meetings and presented very provocative papers.[7]

In his "Comments" paper, he made two striking assertions: first, that the investigative work of historians could serve as a counterpoint to the influence of ideology in economics; and second, that this kind of historical work should precede the development of econometric models and broad economic theory. He suggested that a team of scholars prepare a series of "carefully analyzed historical cases," each of which would address a list of standard questions. The collected answers to those questions would then "supply the theorist with strategic assumptions" and permit the theorist to "banish slogans"—the bane of economic analysis. In this way, investigators could create a substitute for their own ideologies as a guide to their choices of problems to analyze. They might thereby elucidate the balance between impersonal historical forces on the one hand and human agency on the other.[8]

The list of standard questions, Schumpeter wrote, all came down to "the one question that is to be repeated with reference to every country, time, industry, and possibly leading concern: *who* was it that acted *how* and *why* and what were the effects that may be traced to such action?" With enough comparative data at hand, theorists could then "arrive at scientifically reliable propositions about economic change and, therefore, about entrepreneurship."[9]

Comparative work of the kind Schumpeter described was exactly what the most gifted young scholars at Harvard's new Center for Research in Entrepreneurial History proceeded to do. The best individual example is Alfred D. Chandler, Jr., who, in a series of pathbreaking books and articles, pioneered the subdiscipline of modern business history in the way Schumpeter himself had foreshadowed in *Business Cycles*. In Schumpeter's essay of 1946 he wrote that if the kind of historical work he had in mind could proceed successfully, "it may result in a new wing being added to the economist's house." And that is what Chandler and his fellow business historians eventually accomplished.[10]

In the same "Comments" essay, Schumpeter also developed more fully a crucial distinction he had mentioned in *Business Cycles*: between what he called "adaptive" and "creative" responses in business behavior. He wrote that if an economy, an industry, or a firm reacts to a significant change in its environment by merely adjusting its existing practice, "we shall speak of *adaptive response*. And whenever the economy or an industry or some firms in an industry do something . . . outside of the range of existing practice, we shall speak of *creative response*."[11]

A creative response, which can never be predicted and is therefore indeterminate, shapes long-run outcomes in a country, industry, or firm. It often depends on the leadership of specific individuals, and, Schumpeter argued, it "changes social and economic situations for good." It creates new conditions that would never have developed without it. "This is why creative response is an essential element in the historical process: no deterministic credo avails against this."[12]

Schumpeter closed by saying that much of his essay was mere deduction and speculation: "We do not know enough in order to form valid generalizations or even enough to be sure whether there are any generalizations to form. As it is, most of us economists have some opinions on these matters. But these opinions have more to do with our preconceived ideas or ideals than with solid fact, and our habit of illustrating them by stray instances that have come under our notice is obviously but a poor substitute for serious research." Fortunately, there was an abundance of material for such research, and "a great and profitable task awaits the man or group to undertake it." The academic profession as a whole, Schumpeter believed, had nothing less than a civic obligation to bring more precision to the many "slogans which form an important part of the public's economics."[13]

In his papers for the Center for Research in Entrepreneurial History, Schumpeter argued strenuously that history might be instrumental in effecting a kind of intellectual reconciliation: between exact economics—as expressed in both theory and statistics—and other aspects of life that lent themselves neither to determinate theory nor statistical measurement. "Personally," he wrote, "I believe that there is an incessant give and take between historical and theoretical analysis and that, though for the investigation of individual questions it may be necessary to sail for a time on one tack only, yet on principle the two should never lose sight of each other." The combination of narrative, numbers, and theory could exercise a power that none of the three could do alone. Theories are stylized stories; but without real stories and statistics to back them up, they lose much of their force. Schumpeter concluded one of his papers with a sentence that has often been quoted and still resonates in academic life to this day: "Economic historians and economic theorists can make an important and socially valuable journey together, if they will."[14]

Schumpeter saw in the study of history not only great potential for revising economic theory but also a second salient element that he called a "principle of indeterminateness." He contrasted this principle with both the economic determinism of Marx and also with the one-size-fits-all fiscal prescriptions he found in Keynes's *General Theory*. Schumpeter had concluded that time and chance made most economic predictions risky and all determinisms futile. In capitalist economies, time yielded up an unending flow of endogenous economic innovations. And in the world at large, wars and natural disasters disrupted even the most sophisticated forecasts. So did many other events, such as the historic inflows of gold and silver into Spain from the New World, which brought unprecedented monetary inflations throughout Europe. Because of time and chance, no "deterministic credo," as Schumpeter called it, could ever be correct.[15]

Equally important for the principle of indeterminateness was the human element of leadership, a factor vital in Schumpeter's ideas about entrepreneurial innovation. In *The Theory of Economic Development*, he had written of the "Carusos" of economic life—whose outstanding abilities wrought strategic changes in industries and even in countries. Over the years, he had emphasized the pivotal significance of business and political leaders such as Rockefeller, Ford, Hamilton, and Gladstone.

In notes he prepared in 1949 for the prestigious Walgreen Lectures, Schumpeter headed one entire section "The Personal Element and the Element of Chance: A Principle of Indeterminateness." Here, he wrote that the time had come for economists to face a problem they had long tried to dodge:

> the problem of the influence that may be exerted by exceptional
> individuals, a problem that has hardly ever been treated without
> the most blatant preconceptions. Without committing ourselves
> either to hero worship or to its hardly less absurd opposite, we
> have got to realize that, since the emergence of exceptional indi-

viduals does not lend itself to scientific generalization, there is here
an element that, together with the element of random occurrences
with which it may be amalgamated, seriously limits our ability to
forecast the future. That is what is meant here by "a principle of
indeterminateness." To put it somewhat differently: social determinism, where it is nonoperational, is a creed like any other and
entirely unscientific.[16]

Schumpeter's quest for exact economics had finally ended. The long battle
he had waged with himself and with other economists—especially Marx and
Keynes—was settled at last, at least in his own mind. Exact economics on a
broad scale could *never* be achieved. But with the assistance of other disciplines—and history in particular—there could be constant progress. Like a
pebble pitched halfway to a wall in an endless series of tosses, economics could
not possibly reach the wall of exactitude. It could never achieve total certainty.
But it could come ever closer.

SCHUMPETER ANNOUNCED THE verdict of his intellectual wrestling match in his presidential address at the annual meeting of the American
Economic Association on December 30, 1948, in Cleveland. There, he put on
one of his finest shows, in a life filled with virtuoso performances—and it was
greater still because of the riskiness of his message. Speaking on "Science and
Ideology," he proceeded to accuse his fellow professionals of blindness to their
own subjective prejudices. Few people want to hear such indictments, and often their impulse is to shoot the messenger.

But in this case the audience recognized both the wisdom of the message
and the distinction of the speaker. And over the next generation, "Science and
Ideology" became a famous statement of a fundamental truth that characterizes all social sciences, including economics, no matter how "scientific" its pretensions. The speech was published in English, German, Spanish, Italian, Japanese, Norwegian, and several other languages.

Schumpeter began with Karl Marx—the first important scholar to note that
in economic analysis the outcome of "science" depended in large part on the
social situation of the individual thinker. Marx believed, said Schumpeter, that

"the social location of scientific workers . . . determines their outlook upon reality and hence what they see of it and how they see it." And here the social sciences differ fundamentally from the hard sciences:

> Logic, mathematics, physics and so on deal with experience that is
> largely invariant to the observer's social location and practically in-
> variant to historical change: for capitalist and proletarian, a falling
> stone looks alike. The social sciences do not share this advantage.
> It is possible, or so it seems, to challenge their findings not only on
> all the grounds on which the propositions of all sciences may be
> challenged but also on the additional one that they cannot convey
> more than a writer's class affiliations and that, without reference to
> such class affiliations, there is no room for the categories of true
> or false.

Most economists vehemently deny their own "ideological bias." They "do not admit that it is an inescapable curse and that it vitiates economics to its core." Given that ingrained conviction, how can members of the profession be made to see themselves as they really are and to take remedial action? At this point Schumpeter's audience was paying very close attention indeed.[17]

Anticipating a key passage in *History of Economic Analysis,* Schumpeter then said that the first step is to recognize that "perception of a set of related phenomena is a prescientific act. It must be performed in order to give to our minds something to do scientific work on—to indicate an object of research—but it is not scientific in itself . . . This mixture of perceptions and prescientific analysis we shall call the research worker's Vision or Intuition." And vision "*is* ideology by nature and may contain any amount of delusions traceable to a man's social location."[18]

The second step is a little more complicated. Schumpeter noted that economists love to speak of "model building," and justifiably so. He himself believed the term to be very useful. But, he added, the term "model" can be problematical unless it is defined very precisely. Model building "consists in picking out certain facts rather than others," then working to refine the chosen facts, to adjust them in light of opposing evidence, and to place them all in a theoretical framework. In this way, "factual" and "theoretical" research should "go on in an endless chain of give and take."[19]

The division between the factual and the theoretical is not, however, a matter of setting up contests between inductive thinking versus deductive reasoning. "Schoolmasters" often portray it this way, but the essence for science is the constant movement back and forth between the two. This reciprocal motion goes far toward eliminating ideological bias. Facts and theoretical hypotheses can be shown to be "provable, refutable, or neither." These tests, by themselves, go far toward bringing the researcher's prior ideology under control. But the problem of ideology cannot end there, because "the original vision, on the other hand, is under no such control."[20]

The question then arises: how much of the ideological vision of truly seminal thinkers remains undetected and uncorrected in their work? "And how far does it vitiate our analytic procedure itself so that, in the result, we are still left with knowledge that is impaired by it?" Schumpeter approached the answer by searching for ideological bias in the visions of three extraordinarily influential thinkers: Adam Smith, Karl Marx, and John Maynard Keynes. By this time, the attention of the audience in the Cleveland ballroom was riveted to his every word.[21]

Of the three great economists, Adam Smith's ideology has been the least harmful, said Schumpeter. Smith came from a civil service family and was himself a professor and a civil servant, with the prejudices common to both groups: "His attitude to the land-owning and to the capitalist classes was the attitude of the observer from outside and he made it pretty clear that he considered the landlord (the 'slothful' landlord who reaps where he has not sown) as an unnecessary, and the capitalist (who hires 'industrious people' . . .) as a necessary evil." Even so, Smith's analysis was factual, sound, and not seriously affected by his ideology.[22]

The case of Marx was altogether different, in both good ways and bad. First the good: "Marx was the economist who discovered ideology for us and who understood its nature." Then the bad: "Strange to relate, he was entirely blind to its dangers so far as he himself was concerned. Only other people, the bourgeois economists and the utopian socialists, were victims of ideology." Marx came from a prosperous bourgeois family in Trier, an old German city located not far from the French border. A person of very strong feelings, "he was a bourgeois radical who had broken away from bourgeois radicalism. He was formed by German philosophy but did not feel himself to be a professional economist until the end of the 1840's," at which time he was thirty-one years old. By then, says Schumpeter, "*before* his serious analytic work had begun, his vision of the capitalist process had become set and his scientific work was to implement, not to correct it."[23]

Marx's particular vision did not originate with him. "It pervaded the radical circles of Paris and may be traced back to a number of 18th century writers." It was an exceedingly powerful vision of life, "conceived as the struggle between classes that are defined as *haves* and *havenots,* with exploitation of the one by the other." There would be "ever increasing misery and degradation among the *havenots,* moving with inexorable necessity toward spectacular explosion."[24]

Certain elements of this vision, particularly the growing misery of the proletariat, were proved wrong by the simple unfolding of history, even during Marx's own lifetime. Nevertheless, "they were too closely linked to the innermost meaning of his message, too deeply rooted in the very meaning of his life, to be ever discarded. Moreover, they were what appealed to followers and what called forth their fervent allegiance." In the end, therefore, Marx's writings represent "the victory of ideology over analysis: all the consequences of a vision that turns into a social creed and thereby renders analysis sterile." Most members of the Cleveland audience, not being Marxists, agreed wholeheartedly with these statements.[25]

Not so when Schumpeter took up his third example, Keynes. He knew he was in danger of offending his listeners, most of whom were themselves Keynesians. But he marched fearlessly on. He said that Keynes's ideological vision, like Marx's, had been formed quite early. It did not emerge clearly in print until Keynes was thirty-seven years old, at which time the outlines of what became Keynesianism appeared "in a few thoughtful paragraphs in the introduction to the *Consequences of the Peace.*" Schumpeter asserted that "these paragraphs created *modern* stagnationism." They outlined Keynes's unshakable conviction that the business system was headed toward a state of permanent inanition. In the near future, companies would no longer be able to offer good investment opportunities. Funds accumulated by moneyed interests would go unspent. Wages would be insufficient to support increased consumption. Without government stimulus, capitalism itself would stagnate. "This vision," said Schumpeter, "never vanished." It reappeared in many of Keynes's other works but "was not implemented analytically" until the publication of *The General Theory* in 1936.[26]

Here, Schumpeter ratcheted up his language even more, delineating what he

In characteristic posture, delivering his presidential address to the American Economic Association. Because of what he said and how he said it, this speech marked both an intellectual and a professional climax to Schumpeter's career.

believed to be serious damage done to economic science by a uniquely clever theorist: "Again it was the ideology . . . which appealed and won the day, and not the analytic implementation by the book of 1936 which, by itself and without the protection it found in the wide appeal of the ideology, would have suffered much more from the criticisms that were directed against it almost at once . . . [Keynes] continued to become what he had become by 1914, a master of the theorist's craft, and he was thus able to provide his vision with an armour that prevented many of his followers from seeing the ideological element at all."[27]

The result of all this, Schumpeter continued, was that economics as a discipline had reached an almost bizarre state. "There are really no new principles to absorb. The [Keynesian] ideology of underemployment equilibrium . . . is readily seen to be embodied in a few restrictive assumptions that emphasize certain (real or supposed) facts. With these everyone can deal as he thinks fit and for the rest he can continue [on] his way. This reduces Keynesian controversies to the level of technical science." Keynes's message was so powerful, his gifts of persuasion so irresistible, and his vision of stagnation so resonant with people's experience of the Great Depression that almost all economists had become Keynesians to some degree.[28]

But their focus on the techniques of Keynesian macroeconomics—which are amenable to mathematical modeling and very useful in the new methods of national income accounting—had diverted attention from the vision that underlay the whole apparatus. Even though the Keynesian creed of stagnationism "has petered out with the situation that had made it convincing"—the Great Depression having given way to unprecedented prosperity—most economists had remained so enthralled with Keynesian technique that they seemed "bound to drift into one of those positions of which it is hard to say whether they involve renunciation, reinterpretation, or misunderstanding of the original message." And in taking this tack, as Schumpeter had said many times before, most economists had lost sight of the heart of the capitalist process, which in its endless dynamism was the opposite of Keynesian stagnationism.[29]

These were very strong words for the audience Schumpeter was addressing. Yet he plunged into even more hazardous waters. He accused his listeners of allowing their own ideologies to shape their thinking on the subjects of monopoly, oligopoly, and big business in general.

Negative attitudes toward genuine monopoly are entirely justified, of course, and date back at least to the time of Aristotle. But the current problem, said Schumpeter, is not opposition to monopoly. Instead, it is economists' simple distaste for big business, which they justify through the fallacious device of equating it with monopoly. "It is not this value judgment which is relevant to my argument—one may dislike modern largest-scale business exactly as one may dislike many other features of modern civilization—but the analysis that leads up to it and the ideological influence that this analysis displays" are something else again. The facts show that broadly negative generalizations about big business never hold up to close scrutiny. Yet, in the face of contrary evidence, numerous economists still support "*indiscriminate* 'trust busting,' and the interesting point is that enthusiastic supporters of the private-enterprise system are particularly prominent among them."[30]

Schumpeter confessed that he hardly knew what to make of these attitudes on the part of purported social *scientists*. They should know better. Yet, "no argument avails about the performance of largest-scale business, about the inevitability of its emergence, about the social costs involved in destroying existing structures, about the futility of the hallowed ideal of pure competition—or in fact ever elicits any response other than most obviously sincere indignation."[31]

Nearing the end of his long speech, Schumpeter turned to the subject of economic history. There, he argued, ideological bias shows up more vividly than in any other subfield of economics. In books and articles on economic development, scholars who believe in the efficacy of activist government emphasize the role of public policies in achieving healthy growth. Conversely, those who think governments to be less competent always minimize their contributions. As a group, said Schumpeter, "economic historians have systematically over- or understated the importance of this [governmental] initiative in a manner that points unequivocally to prescientific conditions."[32]

But economic historians are distinctive only by the conspicuousness of their ideologies; instances of prescientific visions hardening into credos occur in all branches of economics. Although he made no direct reference to himself in his speech, Schumpeter had come to realize that, like all other analysts, he had his own vision and accompanying ideology. Certainly it is evident in his writings, which show a need not only to explain but also to protect the capitalist engine.[33]

What, then, was to be done? Schumpeter's answer was: nothing. The passage of time—history itself—will take care of ideological biases, eventually correcting all errors. So long as intellectual freedom reigns, one economist's skewed vision will be balanced by another's. In this way, history will save the day despite historians' singular vulnerability to ideology. It will be still another form of creative destruction:

> This follows not only from the fact that social patterns change and
> that hence every economic ideology is bound to wither but also
> from the relation that ideology bears to that prescientific cognitive
> act which we have called vision. Since this act induces fact finding
> and analysis and since these tend to destroy whatever will not
> stand their tests, no economic ideology could survive indefinitely
> even in a stationary social world . . . But this still leaves us with

the result that some ideology will always be with us and so, I feel convinced, it will.[34]

Ironically, Schumpeter concluded, the persistence of ideological vision is not a bad thing but a good thing—because no new departure in any science would be possible without the vision that motivates scholars to do their work. "Through it we acquire new material for our scientific endeavors and something to formulate, to defend, to attack. Our stock of facts and tools grows and rejuvenates itself in the process. And so—though we proceed slowly because of our ideologies, we might not proceed at all without them."[35]

At these closing words, the audience rose as one and gave Schumpeter a thunderous and prolonged standing ovation. It was a spontaneous expression of respect and gratitude, from a group of highly intelligent people seldom given to unanimous endorsement of anything. But they sensed that the most erudite member of their discipline had just defined for them a characteristic of the sea in which they all swam in their day-to-day work. Contrary to what they might have expected, their feelings, ideologies, and individual visions of the world were not barriers to reaching some mythical ultimate truth. Instead, these characteristics were legitimate and useful elements of their own human nature. Few members of the audience could have avoided—on the spot—looking into their own souls and asking why they had chosen to study particular subjects, and what kinds of preconceptions they had brought to their scientific inquiries.[36]

As he stood before them, Schumpeter was stunned by his peers' enthusiastic response. He had received scores of standing ovations over his long career but never one quite so satisfying as this. The high risk in speaking so candidly, and so personally, had brought a commensurate return. And why not take the risk, at a moment in his life when fears for Elizabeth's health, and his own, loomed so large?

After this speech of December 30, 1948—as always during times of deep emotional feeling—he turned in his diary to his bonds with Johanna and Annie:

> The might of the Hasen stood out gloriously. Thank you, Hasen,
> for supporting me and for one of the richest presents. Everyone
> rose for my presidential address. The whole of the Cleveland ball-

room audience rose and gave me applause. That was not poor and that was not small. And yet so undeserved. Thank you, Hasen. O give me the strength O Gott and Hasen. And let me slowly get accustomed to the idea of a voluntary death. Should I say, help me to a voluntary death? O Gott and Hasen, thank you. Bless 1949 if you want to. Not much more than a year can I expect.[37]

2 8

L'Envoi

Here was a rarity: an economist with a tragic sense of life.

DANIEL BELL ON SCHUMPETER,
The Cultural Contradictions of Capitalism, 1976

BY VOLUNTARY DEATH, Schumpeter probably did not mean an act of suicide. Nothing in his usual way of thinking pointed in that direction, not even the sobering prospect of life without Elizabeth. He seems instead to have meant a spirit of resignation, concurrence, acquiescence. When the time came, he would not rage against the dying of the light. He seldom felt well, and in January 1949 he wrote a friend who had urged him to vacation abroad that "I have simply not the moral courage to go to Europe because everything . . . would keep me in a transport of indignation that would be very harmful to my blood pressure." His prediction that he had not much more than a year to live proved to be exactly on the mark.[1]

Meanwhile, he worked as hard as ever on his research and writing and was still brimming with projects for the future. After his great speech in Cleveland, he returned to his work with gusto—teaching his classes, making good progress with his *History of Economic Analysis,* and drafting several essays. He recorded "a real surprise for my [66th] birthday—without misery, tiredness, or hopelessness . . . Do your duty. What is the duty? The necessity of the day. Strange, Goethe said that." As always, the necessity of Schumpeter's day was to write his books and articles and teach his classes. He did both with undiminished energy and distinction.[2]

During the calendar year 1949 and the first week of 1950, he published or composed twelve articles—the most in any comparable period since the 1920s. The first was "Science and Ideology," his presidential address to the American Economic Association, published early in 1949; and the last a series of notes for the distinguished Walgreen Lectures he was scheduled to give in Chicago during the second week of 1950. Of the ten others, the most important was "The March into Socialism," the paper he delivered on December 28, 1949, at the annual meeting of the American Economic Association and included as a chapter in the third edition of *Capitalism, Socialism and Democracy* (1950). Along with a new preface, this chapter represented his final statement about his alleged prediction of capitalism's collapse.[3]

On some occasions, Schumpeter did explicitly predict socialism's triumph over capitalism. More often he did not. Despite the contradictions, he always meant the same thing; and he was at pains to clarify that meaning in this final statement. He repeated that he saw Western democracies drifting toward more state-managed economies, but he denied that the drift would necessarily end in socialism. Neither he nor most other economists had yet reached a clear idea of the mixed economy, which was still evolving in the late 1940s. It was like trying to extrapolate in 1800 the ultimate outcome of the Napoleonic Wars. Schumpeter himself gave another example: no competent observer of Russia before World War I could have predicted the triumph of Leninism and Stalinism. "It was a war and the consequent military and administrative breakdown which produced the Bolshevist regime," he wrote, "and no amount of unscientific determinism avails against this fact."[4]

Regarding his own fear of the triumph of socialism, Schumpeter stated emphatically in 1949 "that I do not 'prophesy' or predict it. Any prediction is extrascientific prophecy that attempts to do no more than to diagnose observable tendencies" and then extend them to logical conclusions. His immediate concerns were the threat of inflation in the United States and the persistence of government interventions in Britain. These included the nationalization of the Bank of England, the socialization of Britain's steel industry, and "a torrent of detailed regulations about the admissible circumference of green onions and similar matters." Bank nationalization and standardized green onions might lead to socialism, but they might not. Nothing was inevitable.[5]

Throughout the last year of his life, Schumpeter was more fully engaged in affairs of the day, and more productive in his own writing and speaking, than he had been since before World War II. After the Harvard spring term of 1949, he wrote in his diary, "Professorship the second semester was terrific. It is true that teaching gives me joy. As some Greek students remarked 'you are enjoying yourself.'" On the other hand, he went on to write in this same entry, "It is not the less true that in the last years it has become different . . . My belief in the world's values and sense of things dies." For inner consolation, especially after Elizabeth's surgery, he had turned a bit toward religion. "What about this program," he wrote, "to conclude every day with a prayer and a request for concentration." He had done this before, but now he directed his appeals not only to the *Hasen* but to God as well.[6]

He and Elizabeth spent the summer of 1949 in Taconic, forgoing the kind of travel that had taken them to Mexico the previous year. Schumpeter planned to visit Paris in August 1950 for his presidential address to the new International Economic Association. He had not been to Europe since his last tour with Mia Stöckel in 1935. But it was too early to make specific arrangements. For the most part, he spent his time reading and toiling away on his *History.* As the summer ended, he wrote in his diary, "Tired. I have had a free and cheerful day . . . It is true that Elizabeth is sick and after the operation everything has become different." Even so, he had a "Polly Anna feeling . . . In September I am happy that again the new acad. year begins and I hope to use it well. H.s.D. [Thanks be to the *Hasen*]."[7]

In the fall months he had still another successful term of teaching, and his writing also went well. But he was now facing a very tight and heavy schedule. On December 28, 1949, he had to deliver his paper on "The March into Socialism" at the annual meeting of the American Economic Association in New York. Then, from January 9 through 20, he was scheduled to present in Chicago the distinguished series of lectures sponsored annually by the Walgreen Foundation. He had written most of his New York paper but had made only sketchy notes for the Chicago lectures. The spring term at Harvard would begin right after his stay in Chicago, and he had again volunteered for a heavy teaching load. In addition, he had agreed to write a piece for *Foreign Affairs,* and he still had quite a bit of final work for *History of Economic Analysis.* So he was under a great deal of pressure.

Just after Christmas he and Elizabeth took the train to New York. His paper on "The March into Socialism" was well received, and both Schumpeters enjoyed seeing many of their old friends. On New Year's Eve they boarded the train for the 140-mile trip to Taconic. After their arrival, Schumpeter went into one of his crash programs of composition. Laboring feverishly in his upstairs study, he completed most of the text and revisions for the published version of "The March into Socialism." He also worked on a fuller outline of the six Walgreen Lectures. They were to be called "American Institutions and Economic Progress," and he had sent a brief summary to Chicago on December 22.[8]

He showed no signs that anything was seriously wrong with his health. He had booked a ticket for the Chicago train, scheduled to depart on Sunday evening, January 8th. He was busy at his desk during most of Saturday, the 7th. After dinner, he worked a bit more before going to bed. He read for a while from Euripides' plays, in the original Greek. As was his custom, he left the book open on a bedside table next to Annie's picture. Then he went to sleep.

Shortly before midnight, he suffered a cerebral hemorrhage. Elizabeth discovered him comatose. He lived for a few more hours, then died in the early morning of January 8th—one month before his 67th birthday. He had never regained consciousness nor felt any pain. The death certificate notes that he had had arteriosclerosis for at least a year.[9]

It was the kind of death most people hope for—no distress, no physical or mental deterioration, no pity from others. One of the few lucky events of Joseph Schumpeter's life was the manner of his leaving it. As he had written at the time of Franklin Roosevelt's death, which also came suddenly from a cerebral hemorrhage, "lucky man: to die in fullness of power."

His funeral was held at the Episcopal church in Salisbury, Connecticut. A heavy snowstorm made the roads almost impassable, frustrating many of his Cambridge friends and colleagues who wanted to attend. He was buried in the Salisbury cemetery, three miles from Taconic. Long obituaries and his picture appeared in *The New York Times, The Boston Globe,* and other papers throughout the country. The European and especially the Japanese press gave heavy coverage, with front-page articles in several Tokyo papers. In 1950 Schumpeter was the most illustrious economist in the world—more famous at the time of his death than at any other period in his life, and at a moment when he probably cared least about his own celebrity.

The many tributes at Harvard were especially touching for Elizabeth and his close friends. A month after he died, the university held a service at Memorial Church in Harvard Yard, just a few steps away from his old office in Littauer Center. A committee of colleagues and former students wrote a long "Memorial Minute" for the service. Its authors were Wassily Leontief, Gottfried Haberler, Seymour Harris, and Edward Mason, who chaired the committee. Famous economists themselves, the first two were Europeans whom he had helped bring to Harvard, the last two were former members of what had been his "inner circle of youthful economists." After paying homage to "one of the great figures of this university," the memorial minute went on to describe their mentor and friend in what was—for Harvard—surprisingly personal terms:

> Although he became one of the most cosmopolitan of men, the experience of those early years in Vienna never really left him. He remained to the end the cultivated Austrian gentleman of the old school . . . Gifted with apparently boundless energy, Schumpeter expended it lavishly. He was always available for consultation by students and devoted a great amount of time to advising and guiding young scholars in all parts of the world. His intemperance in the giving of himself to others may well have contributed to his death . . . But neither he nor his friends would have wished him to live differently. Vitality was part of him and the lavish expenditure of it his characteristic way of life.[10]

In a very unusual step, Schumpeter's students and colleagues decided to dedicate a future issue of the *Review of Economics and Statistics* to him. They commissioned articles from prominent scholars, and the fifteen essays appeared in the issue of May 1951. These essays and five other memorial articles were then brought out together—at Elizabeth's urging—in a volume called *Schumpeter, Social Scientist*. Some of the essays were on substantive or methodological issues in economics. But most were personal reminiscences; and, page for page, no more revealing portrait of Schumpeter has ever appeared in print. Of the twenty essays, the most intimate are by Harris, Haberler, and Arthur Smithies.[11]

In his introductory remarks, Harris wrote, "Few will insist that Schumpeter was a perfect man. He had many faults. Yet with all of this, Schumpeter was a great and fine man. Below the superficialities, there was a man of the highest character, the most loyal and devoted of friends, a penetrating and creative mind, a great teacher, and an advisor to any member of the profession who needed his help." Schumpeter was a marvelous economist, Harris wrote, but "historians and sociologists can include him as one of their stars" too. Equally remarkable,

> It is significant that economists of all shades of views and opin-
> ions—extreme 19th century liberals, semi-Keynesians, Keynesians,
> and Marxists—would join in an enthusiastic tribute to
> Schumpeter . . . Surely no other great figure has received a similar
> tribute from economists of all schools . . . His appraisal of men
> was largely in terms of the quality of the job done, given the ideo-
> logical predispositions. In his personal relations he much preferred
> the bright Marxist or the Keynesian to the dull conservative. He
> once made this witticism: "When I see those who espouse my
> [often conservative] cause, I begin to wonder about the validity
> of my position."

Many people at Harvard, Harris continued, did not know Schumpeter as well as they seemed to think. They mistakenly regarded him as a contrarian who never wanted to go along with the majority opinion, "whether it be on matters of foreign policy or an appraisal of the merits of a dry martini."[12]

Gottfried Haberler echoed this theme. He wrote that those who knew Schumpeter only slightly often assumed that his independence of mind "was nothing more than a passion to contradict, to take the opposite view . . . He was a good laugher and could enjoy exuberantly a stimulating conversation, a good story, a brilliant joke, but he was fundamentally not a happy man." There was an "unbridgeable gulf" between his "high and austere ideals on the one hand and his human feelings and impulses on the other." Schumpeter himself had known this. He had envied economists who felt no reluctance to adapt what their principles told them to say to what their listeners wanted to hear.[13]

Arthur Smithies—Schumpeter's close friend, former student, and frequent guest at Windy Hill—composed the most personal and insightful of all the tributes. This was partly because Elizabeth gave him access to her husband's di-aries and private papers. Smithies wrote that Schumpeter had come to Harvard in 1932 "in a mood of resignation rather than enthusiasm." But he energized himself through a "ruthless program of incessant work." And he had found unequaled support in his marriage to Elizabeth. "Without her companionship and single-minded devotion he might well have sunk into a state of intolerable melancholy and loneliness. In Cambridge, but especially at her beautiful place in Taconic, Connecticut, she provided him with what he had never really had before—a home."[14]

Smithies considered that Schumpeter's early childhood, spent mostly alone with his widowed mother, colored his future relationships. Typical of his friends at Harvard were Frank Taussig, twenty-four years his senior, and Paul Sweezy, who could have been his son. Smithies felt that when Schumpeter was in the company of certain people—and especially his own contemporaries—he "found it difficult to persuade. He could win every point but fail to win the argument. He could fail in persuasion where others far less brilliant could succeed . . . In fact, time and again he seemed to stack the cards against himself so that he could be sure to lose with honor." These characteristics might account for his abortive political career in Austria and "the paradoxes in his later writing. *Capitalism, Socialism and Democracy* in particular is full of ironic twists that provide cold comfort for anyone who agrees with him. Capitalists, socialists, and intellectuals are all provided with strong emotional grounds for rejecting the argument."[15]

Even before captive audiences of students, Smithies added, Schumpeter avoided any mention of his own writings. Also, "one of the many ironies in his life is that his ardent support of mathematics in economics drove his students away from the fields of intellectual endeavor that made his own work so significant, and produced many results that he considered sterile."[16]

The world of politics and policy was a milieu where he might have exerted influence. But after his emigration from Germany to the United States, he never sought it. This was unfortunate, Smithies noted, because Schumpeter's writings are rich in practical value. In 1943, for example, he had forecast the post-war prosperity on the basis of pent-up demand; he also predicted great growth in per capita income, and said that all the social reforms called for would automatically ensue from this process, or at least be paid for by it.[17]

Perhaps the most significant way in which Schumpeter had set himself apart professionally was his refusal to learn anything important from Keynes.

Keynesianism had become the center of professional debates during the 1940s, but Schumpeter's attitude made it impossible for him to adapt Keynes's ideas to refine his own theories. The two eminent economists' distaste for each other's work was a very great pity, Smithies believed. Schumpeter's writings provided an ideal corrective to Keynes's fatal omission of innovation's important role in capitalist evolution. Conversely, Schumpeter's own shortcomings lay exactly in the areas that Keynes's theories illuminated—where consumption and investment could be considered as aggregates; where analysts could think in macroeconomic terms about the *total* output of national economies. This was especially ironic because Schumpeter himself had been one of the precursors of modern macroeconomic analysis, as Alvin Hansen wrote in another essay published in *Schumpeter, Social Scientist.* Hansen was both Schumpeter's friend and Keynes's chief American proponent.[18]

Schumpeter's personal streak of otherwise-mindedness affected his friendships as well as his professional relations with faculty and students (although his friends were almost all fellow scholars). At no time was this truer than during World War II, Smithies noted, when Schumpeter was unhappy and depressed. "Not only was he overcome, as always, by the futility of war, and the destruction of his values that it would bring, but he alienated many of his friends by taking extreme positions when he felt that they were carried away by the emotions of the moment. Needless to say, his opinions in 1940 would have evoked a different response in 1950." The need for strong buffers against Soviet expansion—including Germany and Japan—had become much clearer during the intervening ten years. Still, the isolation that he experienced in Cambridge during the war was a lasting injury, however much his blunt speaking had provoked it.[19]

Then, too, his own uncertain conception of himself contributed to Schumpeter's frustration. The confusion of identity that had begun in his boyhood had never been fully resolved. He was "neither aristocrat nor bourgeois," Smithies observed. He did not hew to bourgeois values, because he saw them as lacking—as Schumpeter put it—"glamour or passion." Here, Smithies surmised, "we have found fertile ground in which his vision of the innovating entrepreneur, who did have glamour and was not dominated by middle-class values, could grow." Among economists, Schumpeter was almost alone in having this kind of vision—and that said a great deal about both him and his profession.[20]

"There are few people who inspired as much loyalty as he did," wrote the German economist Oskar Morgenstern. Despite his quirks and flaws, and the loneliness he hid so desperately from view, Schumpeter's wit and force of intellect attracted hordes of students, colleagues, and strangers to the pleasure of his company.[21]

Of all the tributes, the one by Wassily Leontief—his brilliant protégé, fellow émigré, and Acacia Street neighbor—best evokes what that company was like:

> The strongest single impression with which one was left after having spent an hour with him in the classroom or at a scientific meeting, or even better on a leisurely walk along the wooded shores of the lake near his Taconic, Connecticut, country home, was that of the astounding width of Schumpeter's intellectual horizon. He was equally at home in early Greek philosophy, English parliamentary history, Italian literature, and French romanesque architecture . . .
>
> By conviction, as well as by temperament, he was a thinker rather than a doer . . . But what an unusual ivory tower it was! Set up in the very middle of the intellectual traffic of our time, it was ever full of visitors. Everyone was invited to enter its wide-open doors, everyone, that is, who had an idea to discuss, be it in economics or sociology, in history or art . . . A pessimist and a skeptic in his view on the future of our western civilization which he cherished so much, Schumpeter was an optimist in his belief in the boundless progress of the inquiring mind.[22]

Taken as a whole, the story of Joseph Schumpeter—"this very complicated person," as a good friend once described him—could hardly be richer or more nuanced. A reviewer of *History of Economic Analysis* wrote that "no simple account of Schumpeter could be true." The story is one of restless adventure, almost unbelievably hard work, and ultimate triumph in the face of persistently bad luck. It is a European story as much as an American one. Perhaps most strikingly, it is a tale of both the glory and the horror of the twentieth century—at once the wealthiest, most scientifically advanced, and bloodiest in human history.[23]

It is also the story of a boy and a man rescued time and again by the women who loved him and put his welfare above their own: Johanna, Mia, Elizabeth, and in some ways Gladys and Annie as well. Without them, he would likely have destroyed himself, so ferocious were the internal struggles between his reason and his emotions—the extraordinary potency of the one, the overwhelming intensity of the other.

The noblest person in the story may well be Elizabeth Boody. Had she not sheltered her husband, through a plan she conceived and then flawlessly executed, he might have fallen into hopeless depression or ruined himself in some other way. And had that occurred, the world might never have seen *Capitalism, Socialism and Democracy* or the great articles on history, science, and ideology. It certainly would never have seen *History of Economic Analysis* in anything like the coherent form of 1954. Elizabeth devoted the last three years of her life to assembling and editing this book. She sold the Acacia Street house in Cambridge and devoted a substantial part of the proceeds to shaping the huge manuscript into publishable form. As her own health declined, she poured all of her dwindling energy into the project.

When she gave her husband's personal papers to Harvard, she seems to have culled nothing: not the few photographs of Annie nor the dozens of Mia; not the love letters from herself and from Annie, nor the voluminous and sexually charged series from Mia; not Annie's diaries, nor Schumpeter's own, which record his depression, his prejudices, his frequent unhappiness with Harvard, and above all his unshakable obsession with his *Hasen*. Elizabeth's appearances in his diary remained sparse even after she became ill. Seven years before she met him in 1933, Schumpeter had formed a club with three members: Johanna, Annie, and himself. Elizabeth knew that she could never gain full admission. But she believed so devoutly in his greatness, and loved him so deeply, that she was willing to settle for auxiliary membership.

She died in July 1953 of the cancer that had first struck her five years earlier. Her death came one year before *History of Economic Analysis* appeared, and one month before what would have been her 55th birthday. "Since we cannot have a child, let's have this book together," she had said in 1943. "Why can't we have a child—many children?"—many books. In the end, they did. *History of Economic Analysis* by Joseph Schumpeter *is* many books, and Elizabeth, his wife, brought them into the world.

Epilogue

The Legacy

The independent scientist who is worth the slightest consideration as a scientist has a consecration which comes entirely from within himself: a vocation which demands the possibility of supreme self-sacrifice.

NORBERT WIENER, *The Human Use of Human Beings,* 1950

WHEN SCHUMPETER DIED in 1950, many of his friends believed that he had worked himself to death. Certainly there was no question of his compulsive devotion to the labor of learning. For almost five decades, never letting up, he had pursued every aspect of capitalism—its strengths and weaknesses, its social, cultural, economic, and personal aspects. And despite his deep commitment to scientific objectivity, he had wished to ensure that people would understand how to keep its "engine" running well. To do that, he believed, they would have to look beyond what they saw immediately in front of them—venality, inequality, corruption—and imagine the long-term rise in living standards that capitalism alone could deliver, throughout the world.

Schumpeter's signature legacy is his insight that innovation in the form of creative destruction is *the* driving force not only of capitalism but of material progress in general. Almost all businesses, no matter how strong they seem to be at a given moment, ultimately fail—and almost always because they failed to innovate. Competitors are relentlessly striving to overtake the leader, no matter how big the lead. Responsible businesspeople know that they ignore this lesson at their peril. Every day they feel themselves, as Schumpeter put it in *Capitalism, Socialism and Democracy,* "in a situation that is sure to change presently." They are "standing on ground that is crumbling beneath their feet."

Today, in an age of accelerating innovation and global industry, business-people feel more vulnerable than ever. This era is still in its infancy, and further seismic changes are certain to come, as the whole body of Schumpeter's work would predict. No country, regardless of how long it has been prosperous, can take permanent affluence for granted. Nor can any company assume its continued existence—as names such as Digital Equipment, Pan American Airways, Pullman, Douglas Aircraft, and the Pennsylvania Railroad remind us. Each of these companies once epitomized the cutting edge not only of its own industry but of American business as a whole. And all are now in the dustbin of history, along with hundreds of thousands of other businesses of all sizes— once as strong as dinosaurs but now just as extinct.

Only through innovation and entrepreneurship can any business except a government-sponsored monopoly survive over the long term. Schumpeter, of course, is the chief proponent and popularizer of the word "entrepreneur," which appeared in the 1934 English edition of his *Theory of Economic Development.* (In the original German edition of 1911, he had used the German *unternehmer,* which never caught on, partly because its literal meaning is "undertaker.") Because of the importance of entrepreneurship, and because Schumpeter wrote about it with such insight and verve, his name will be forever linked to the idea.

Beginning in the late 1920s Schumpeter made it clear that entrepreneurship could occur within large and medium-sized firms as well as in small ones, despite bureaucratic obstacles. By the mid-twentieth century, he was arguing that innovation "within the shell of existing corporations offers a much more convenient access to the entrepreneurial functions than existed in the world of owner-managed firms. Many a would-be entrepreneur of today does not found a firm, not because he could not do so but simply because he prefers the other method."[1]

Thus, "new men" founding "new firms" were still vital, but they were no longer the only agents of innovation. The same economic role could be accomplished within older and larger companies. Entrepreneurs were still recognizable personal types, but innovation could also be—and, given the large size of some companies, sometimes had to be—performed by teams of people. Meanwhile, the continual infusion of energy by the kinds of startup companies Schumpeter himself preferred remained vital sources of economic creativity.

The history of the information technology industry confirms his thinking especially well—both the scrappy young firms in Silicon Valley that either perished or remained small-to-medium-sized and others that grew to be giants (Hewlett-Packard, Intel, Oracle, Cisco Systems, Amazon, Google, Yahoo). Outside Silicon Valley, the same pattern obviously holds for Microsoft and Dell Computer, founded by the teenagers Bill Gates in 1975 and Michael Dell in 1984.[2]

Schumpeter's thinking has had an incalculable influence on business during the late twentieth century and the early twenty-first. His phrase "creative destruction" has become a byword. In addition, all kinds of companies, along with consulting firms and the business press, have so often used the term "business strategy" (or some variant such as "corporate strategy") that it has almost reached a par with such topics as finance and marketing. Especially since the advent of globalization, companies of every description have developed explicit "strategies" for themselves. Schumpeter's central preoccupations—innovation, entrepreneurship, and credit creation—have played prominent roles in the formulation of these strategies, regardless of whether a given firm is large or small.[3]

Within universities, Schumpeter's strongest influence has appeared not in economics departments but in departments of sociology, political science, and history, where his writings are frequently assigned. And far more than in any of these four traditional disciplines, his ideas have thoroughly pervaded the curricula of post-graduate business schools all over the world. These schools are much more numerous today (by a factor of about seven) than they were when he died, and research within their environs has grown far more rigorous. By the twenty-first century, every reputable business school offered numerous courses devoted to entrepreneurship, innovation, and business strategy, and many housed full-blown departments devoted to these subjects.[4]

Schumpeter often defended capitalism, and big business as well, at least as he had known it. But he would never have condoned the behavior brought into the public consciousness by the scandals of the 1990s and the early twenty-first century: accounting frauds, outrageous executive pay schemes, back-dating of stock options, and other looting of corporate treasuries by the very executives who were supposed to be their stewards. He would have considered these kinds of practices a betrayal of capitalism. All of them embodied the negation of the system Schumpeter had supported. They also represented reminders of the need for eternal vigilance and timely action by government regulators—factors that Schumpeter, along with a large majority of his fellow citizens, persistently underestimated.

Nor, despite his low-tax philosophy, would Schumpeter have countenanced the reckless deficits of America's federal government during the 1980s and especially during the first decade of the twenty-first century. Nor the encouragement of short-term consumerism, replete with billions of credit cards aggregating colossal personal debts. In 2005 the United States recorded a negative savings rate for the first time since the Great Depression. Given Schumpeter's insistence on savings and investment as fuel for the capitalist engine of innovation, he could hardly have regarded such developments with anything short of incredulity and disgust. With all his emphasis on credit creation, he did not have in mind the borrowing of titanic sums from the central banks of China and Japan for the purpose of funding government deficits and consumer excesses. One must hope that these aberrations will be transitory, as most comparable episodes in the history of capitalism have been.

Because of capitalism's constant transitions, the nature of the issues that interested Schumpeter has shifted since 1950. As the prophet of incessant change, he would have been the first to predict this eventuality. A few of the problems he worked on (money, the business cycle) are now less pressing; others (innovation, entrepreneurship, credit creation) are more so. The most difficult questions, such as the core nature of capitalism and the uneven distribution of its lavish fruits, will always deserve the attention of any thinking person.

During much of Schumpeter's life, two topics loomed especially large: the "money question" and the business cycle. Today, both are better understood and, with some important exceptions, under fuller control. Money management has undergone big changes that began during Schumpeter's lifetime. The cumulative effects of these changes, coupled with the rise of globalization and computer technology, have been little short of spectacular. Immense sums now move instantaneously from one country to another as a matter of routine.

Daily transactions totaling trillions of dollars are driven by intracorporate repositionings from one major currency to another (mainly, movements among the dollar, the euro, and the yen); by trading in stocks and bonds; and by hedge-fund management. Neither Schumpeter, Keynes, nor any other economist of their generation anticipated currency movements of such speed and magnitude. Central banks in all major countries have large and sophisticated staffs working to bring the system under better control, since much of it is almost impossible to regulate. But this pattern of continuous change fits perfectly into Schumpeter's general theory of innovation and credit creation as the touchstones of capitalism.[5]

The second issue—the business cycle—is still important but has become less conspicuous than it was during Schumpeter's time. The rise of mixed economies has propped up purchasing power throughout the industrialized world. All developed countries now use counter-cyclical policies such as the raising and lowering of interest rates by central banks and built-in stabilizers such as social security, health and unemployment insurance, and other measures. This modern mixed economy is perhaps the major legacy of Keynesianism. Whether or not it represents "capitalism in the oxygen tent" or a natural outgrowth of higher affluence does not really matter—Schumpeter said in 1943 that it meant both. The point is that the mixed economy has tended to flatten the business cycle.[6]

With the business cycle of less concern, economists have turned their attention to other subjects: the development of emerging markets, problems of globalization and unemployment, and an almost endless series of narrow but significant topics amenable to precise expression through algebra and calculus. The concise journal article with one or two penetrating insights has replaced the book as the stock-in-trade of academic economists. The overall path of economics since 1950 has been a fascinating chapter in what Schumpeter liked to call "economic sociology." By the early 1960s, economists had become by far the most self-confident of all academic social scientists but also—to their great credit—the most self-critical.[7]

In economics departments today, extremely smart people ply their trade using highly sophisticated mathematical theory and statistical techniques. They test intriguing hypotheses about relatively modest but important questions through clever research designs and computer analysis of large data sets. At the best-regarded graduate programs, no economics student can function without having been trained in advanced mathematics. Late in the twentieth century, a survey of graduate students at Harvard, Yale, MIT, Chicago, Stanford, and Columbia produced the following results, in answer to the question, "What abilities likely place students on a fast track?" Excellence in mathematics: 57 percent said very important; 2 percent said unimportant. Having a broad knowledge of the economics literature: 10 percent, very important; 43 percent, unimportant. Having a thorough knowledge of the economy: 3 percent, very important; 68 percent, unimportant. This is probably not what Schumpeter had in mind when he crusaded for more use of math in economics.[8]

In the new world of academic economics, neither the Schumpeterian entrepreneur as an individual nor entrepreneurship as a phenomenon attracts much attention. For professors in economics departments at most major universities, particularly in the United States and Britain, a focus on these favorite issues of Schumpeter's has become a quick ticket out of a job. This development arose from a self-generated isolation of academic economics from history, sociology, and the other social sciences. It represented a trend that Schumpeter himself had glimpsed and lamented but that accelerated rapidly during the two generations after his death.[9]

At the same time, however, a contrasting trend emerged. A few economists began broad inquiries into the nature of innovation, the phenomenon Schumpeter emphasized over all others. Economists studying this issue joined like-minded sociologists, political scientists, psychologists, historians, and professors of business administration in searching for answers to questions that Schumpeter had asked before them.

What is it, for example, that drives innovation? Is it just the prospect of making money? Or, as Schumpeter had argued early in his career, is it something more than "motivation of the hedonist kind"? Schumpeter believed that the innovator-entrepreneur also had a "will to conquer . . . Our type [a revealing choice of words that seems to include himself] seeks out difficulties, changes in order to change, delights in ventures." Several hundred case studies of innovation completed in the late twentieth century and early twenty-first confirmed Schumpeter's thesis. Just as forces besides money had motivated Carnegie, Thyssen, and Ford, the same was true of later entrepreneurs such as Akio Morita, Estée Lauder, Andy Grove, Richard Branson, Steve Jobs, and Oprah Winfrey.[10]

A second series of questions implicit in Schumpeter's writings was this: Do capitalist economies tend to promote democratic political systems, or vice versa? Should economic development precede political liberalization, as has recently occurred in China, or follow it, as in India? Most seriously of all, can countries with no strong tradition of either capitalism or democracy—such as Russia, Ukraine, Egypt, Congo, and Saudi Arabia—*ever* succeed in competing with capitalist democracies? If there is to be a "clash of civilizations," will it be between widespread modernization on the one hand (best represented by global capitalism) and backward-looking radicalism on the other (best exemplified by Islamist terrorism)? Or by some even broader type of conflict?

The answers to these questions are not to be found in Schumpeter's writings, of course. But rich meditations on the underlying issues *are* there, and in abundance—especially in *Business Cycles* and in *Capitalism, Socialism and Democracy*. As one of his students put it, Schumpeter shared a historic vision about capitalist dynamism with Karl Marx, but his real intellectual ancestors were even deeper thinkers such as Plato, St. Augustine, and Thomas Aquinas.[11]

Schumpeter recognized that ideological "vision" guided all analysts' choices of topics and sometimes shaped particular kinds of conclusions. At an early age, he chose capitalism as his central subject because he intuitively grasped its unique possibilities for promoting economic growth. And the more he worked on the topic—the more he probed its empirical and comparative dimensions—the more convinced he became that capitalism's creative elements outweigh its destructive ones. Destruction, however painful, is the necessary price of creative progress toward a better material life. But the correct sequence is vital: creative innovation first, then the destruction of obstacles that lie in its way.

The profundity of Schumpeter's insight becomes evident when misguided leaders attempt to reverse this sequence. At the beginning of China's Cultural Revolution of the 1960s, for example, Mao Zedong's guiding slogan was, "Destroy first, and construction will look after itself." This was the precise opposite of Schumpeterian creative destruction, and the result was catastrophic: the deaths of at least a million people, the uprooting of even more, and a long list of other calamities, including the devastation of the nation's educational system. For an entire decade, the mindless destruction of almost everything precluded the creation of almost anything. Only when the creative impulses of Deng Xiopeng and other successors of Mao destroyed the Cultural Revolution itself did it become possible to release China's huge human potential. And it is hardly accidental that the chosen path was a Schumpeterian market economy that encouraged innovation, entrepreneurship, and the creation of credit. Whether this path can persist over the long term in an environment of severe political repression and pervasive state intervention remains to be seen.

In the article on capitalism that Schumpeter wrote for the *Encyclopaedia Britannica,* he devoted three of his essay's nine sections to topics he labeled "The Class Structure of Capitalist Society," "Exploitation and Inequality," and "Unemployment and Waste." He took it for granted that serious abuses are as inescapable in capitalist systems as they are in all others. For many centuries the public mind had "reacted to the phenomena of capitalism in much the same way as it does in our time; it cried out against usury, speculation, commercial and industrial monopolies, cornering of commodities and other abuses, and the arguments used were, both in their common-sense content and in their one-sidedness, neither much worse nor much better than are the popular arguments of the 20th century. Governments reacted in sympathy, through regulation." This pattern was natural, predictable, and defensible. Government interference was entirely in order so long as the capitalist engine remained intact. Schumpeter never was as reflexively conservative an economist as many of his contemporaries believed. His colleague John Kenneth Galbraith described him in 1986 as "the most sophisticated conservative of this century."[12]

Schumpeter regarded inequality of opportunity as unacceptable, but he also held that the results produced by inequality of effort were deserved. On the whole, he found disparity of incomes not only inevitable in capitalist society but effective in stimulating innovation. Money was not the sole motivation for entrepreneurs, but it was a big one, and was also a way of keeping score among extremely successful people. "The importance of inequality *within* the highest income brackets should be particularly noticed. A single spectacular success may draw far more brains and means into an industry than would be attracted to it by the same sum if more equally divided. To this extent current views about unnecessarily or even absurdly high rewards and about the total cost to society of entrepreneurial performance should be modified."[13]

Here, Schumpeter was making a very subtle point: that the benefits to society of important innovations, and the lavish profits accruing to winning entrepreneurs, must be measured against the total costs of time and money invested in the same industry by *un*successful entrepreneurs as well. They receive no return for their efforts, but their competitive pressure spurs the winners to victory—to the great benefit of society. That the winners receive all the rewards is a mere detail—and a temporary one at that, since the "competing-down" element eventually diminishes that profit, as imitators copy the innovation.[13]

Not until the late twentieth century, long after Schumpeter's death, did the significance of his emphasis on innovation, entrepreneurship, business strategy, creative destruction, and ample credit as the wellsprings of economic growth become fully clear. No Schumpeter School existed during his lifetime, as he professed to wish. But one does exist today. It has no single location and is confined to no single discipline. Many economists, sociologists, historians, political scientists, professors of business administration, and other academics are self-conscious Schumpeterians. And all capitalist innovators are Schumpeterians, whether they realize it or not.

During the 1980s, as innovation and entrepreneurship became more conspicuous, Schumpeter's writings began to find a wider audience—and, in succeeding decades, a much wider one. The collapse of command economies in Eastern and Central Europe and the remarkable economic performance of China, India, and other Asian countries raised acute practical issues about the nature of innovation and entrepreneurship and the relationship between business and government.

Meanwhile, in the United States, the phenomenal run-up of securities markets during the late 1980s and throughout the 1990s piqued a sharp new interest in the anatomy of capitalism. During the 1980s the Dow Jones Industrial Average topped 1,000 for the first time in its history and then skyrocketed to 11,000 by 1999. Terms of art once restricted to businesspeople—IPO, venture capital, startup, emerging markets—entered the dinner conversation of ordinary citizens.[14]

In this setting, Schumpeter's pioneering work on innovation and entrepreneurship acquired a compelling new interest. Journalists and scholars began to find in his writings either answers to their own questions or priceless maps for new avenues of research. In 1983, the one hundredth anniversary of the birth of both Schumpeter and Keynes, *Forbes* proclaimed that it was Schumpeter, not Keynes, who provided the best guide to the rapid economic changes engulfing the world.[15]

In 1984 a German professor writing in the *American Economic Review* made the same point, arguing that the Age of Schumpeter was replacing the Age of Keynes. Soon, scores of articles began to appear in professional journals, and the popular press followed suit. In December 2000 *Business Week* ran a two-page spread on Schumpeter under the title "America's Hottest Economist Died 50 Years Ago." In the twenty-first century, computerized databases began to turn up more references to Schumpeter's works than to Keynes's—a situation that would have been inconceivable only a few years before.[16]

In 1986 a group of scholars formed the International Schumpeter Society. By the first decade of the twenty-first century, it had four hundred members from more than thirty countries and at least a half-dozen academic disciplines. The society meets biennially, and its proceedings are typically published as a book of essays by established scholars. It also awards a prize for the best publication in the Schumpeterian tradition.[17]

Still another regular outlet is the quarterly *Journal of Evolutionary Economics*, which explicitly specializes in Schumpeterian topics. Articles influenced by Schumpeter's writings also appear often in the *Journal of Institutional Economics, Economic Development and Cultural Change*, the *Journal of Economic History*, the *Business History Review*, and other academic quarterlies. Schumpeter's creative destruction is perhaps the most widely used metaphor in contemporary economic writing. ("Googling" it yields an astronomical number of references.) The phrase has also turned up in the titles of books outside of business and economics, including history and literature.[18]

After Schumpeter's death, Harvard's Economics Department awarded an annual prize in his memory to an outstanding student, endowed by money that Elizabeth Schumpeter and her husband's friends had donated. Since the 1990s the University of Graz has sponsored an annual series of Schumpeter Lectures, given by a distinguished scholar, and the speakers have come from many different countries. The Graz Schumpeter Society oversees this program and maintains a website on its activities.[19]

Perhaps more than any other top economic theorist, Schumpeter *humanized* his discipline. After a lifelong struggle, he concluded that exact economics can no more be achieved than exact history, because no human story with a foreordained plot can be anything but fiction. Because of the infinite mixture of influences on human behavior, no two real economic situations are ever exactly alike. Thus, economics does not lend itself to deterministic laws or experiments, as the physical sciences do. The best mathematics in the world cannot produce a satisfactory economic proof wholly comparable to those in physics or pure mathematics. There are too many variables, because indeterminate human behavior is always involved. As the Nobel Laureate in Economics Douglass North remarked in 1994, "The price you pay for precision is inability to deal with real-world questions."[20]

Often the best alternative for expressing what one knows about the world is not an equation but a narrative—a story with real characters facing some kind of dilemma. Curricula in business schools, unlike those in most economics departments, contain many classes based on stories—usually real-life case studies—designed to illustrate particular points about innovation, finance, marketing, strategy, entrepreneurship, ethics, and general management. By the end of a typical MBA education, whatever its other shortcomings, students have encountered hundreds of these cases; and the cumulative effect is of having lived through the dilemmas and choices facing businesspeople every day. Here again Schumpeter spoke directly to the human experience of economic life. In his description of the feeling among businesspeople that they are standing on crumbling ground, and in his portraits of specific entrepreneurs (and of specific economists as well), he put unforgettable human faces on the phenomenon of capitalism.[21]

Just after his death, one of Schumpeter's Harvard colleagues commented that he had engaged the hardest economic questions of his time, "in what we may legitimately describe as the grand manner." Thirty years later, in 1981, Paul Samuelson wrote that "a century after Schumpeter's birth, we take his writings seriously and treat them as living contributions to contemporary debate." In 1984, a third economist remarked that "today, as on any day in living memory, it is easy to admire Schumpeter's taste in problems." And still later, a fourth economist, Robert Heilbroner, in his best-selling *The Worldly Philosophers,* wrote that more than any other great economist delineated in his book, Schumpeter "speaks to us with a voice that is unmistakably contemporary."[22]

Schumpeter was never narrow, and always more than an economist. Three of his books—*The Theory of Economic Development, Capitalism, Socialism and Democracy,* and *History of Economic Analysis*—are still available in many languages, in inexpensive paperback editions. All, and especially *Capitalism, So-*

cialism and Democracy, are books for the ages. Since Schumpeter sometimes wrote in the ironic mode or contradicted himself, it is impossible to agree or disagree with everything he says. The experience of reading his books is like listening to Beethoven's symphonies or contemplating Picasso's paintings—forever challenging, sometimes irritating, and never dull. No matter how many times the experience is repeated, there always seems to be something new to discover.

NOTES

The abbreviation HUA denotes Harvard University Archives.

PREFACE

1. Comparative income figures quoted for the United States since 1800 are in inflation-adjusted pre-tax dollars. Income multiples for the last 200 years are derived from Angus Maddison, *Dynamic Forces in Capitalist Development* (New York: Oxford University Press, 1991), pp. 6–7, updated in later work by Maddison. For further elaboration, see Thomas K. McCraw, ed., *Creating Modern Capitalism: How Entrepreneurs, Companies, and Countries Triumphed in Three Industrial Revolutions* (Cambridge, Mass.: Harvard University Press, 1997), chs. 1 and 13. Per capita income comparisons for Germany, Austria, and the Czech Republic (and about 120 other countries) may be found in the World Bank's annual *World Development Report* (New York: Oxford University Press). The fractions I have cited for the Czech Republic, Austria, and Germany are for differences in Purchasing Power Parity, not comparisons of nominal incomes, where the differences appear very much larger.

   Statistics quoted for periods before the nineteenth century are imputed from scattered data, but they represent the best estimates the many scholars who have studied this subject have compiled. In addition to the works by Angus Maddison cited above, see, for example, William J. Baumol, Sue Anne Batey Blackman, and Edward N. Wolff, *Productivity and American Leadership: The Long View* (Cambridge, Mass.: MIT Press, 1989), p. 12; and Paul Bairoch, "Was There a Large Income Differential before Modern Development?" in Bairoch, *Economics and World History: Myths and Paradoxes* (Chicago: University of Chicago Press, 1993), pp. 101–110.

2. The quotation from Marx and Engels is from *The Manifesto of the Communist Party,* printed in Eugene Kamenka, ed., *The Portable Karl Marx* (New York: Penguin [Viking Portable Library], 1983), p. 209. As Schumpeter later wrote, "The

first thing about the 'economics proper' of the [*Manifesto* is that] Marx launched out on a panegyric upon bourgeois achievement that has no equal in economic literature." See Schumpeter, "*The Communist Manifesto* in Sociology and Economics," *Journal of Political Economy* 57 (June 1949), pp. 199–212, reprinted in Richard V. Clemence, ed., *Joseph A. Schumpeter: Essays on Entrepreneurs, Innovations, Business Cycles, and the Evolution of Capitalism* (Cambridge, Mass.: Addison-Wesley, 1951); the quotation is on p. 301.

3. Jacob Viner, "Schumpeter's *History of Economic Analysis:* A Review Article," *American Economic Review* 44 (December 1954), p. 894.

PART I PROLOGUE: WHO HE WAS AND WHAT HE DID

1. Schumpeter, *Capitalism, Socialism and Democracy* (New York: Harper & Brothers, 1942), p. 83; Schumpeter, *Business Cycles: A Theoretical, Historical, and Statistical Analysis of the Capitalist Process,* two vols. (New York: McGraw-Hill, 1939), II, p. 1033.

2. Fitzgerald, *The Crack-up* (New York: Scribner, 1936). The "techno-romantic" characterization was made by the Viennese writer Karl Kraus, and is quoted in Edward Timms, "Images of the City: Vienna, Prague and the Intellectual Avant Garde," in Robert B. Pysent, ed., *Decadence and Innovation: Austro-Hungarian Life and Art at the Turn of the Century* (London: Weidenfeld and Nicolson, 1989), p. 3.

3. Peter Cain, in *Economic Journal* 102 (1992), p. 1543, reviewing Richard Swedberg, *Joseph A. Schumpeter: His Life and Work* (Oxford: Polity Press, 1992; published in the United States by Princeton University Press in 1991 as *Schumpeter: A Biography*).

4. A physical description of Schumpeter appears in John Kenneth Galbraith, *A Life in Our Times: Memoirs* (Boston: Houghton Mifflin, 1981), pp. 48–49. Schumpeter's remark about taking an hour to dress is recorded by Frank Whitson Fetter, son of the Princeton economist Frank Fetter, in "An Early Memory of Joseph Schumpeter," *History of Political Economy* 6 (Spring 1974), pp. 92–94. For the other quotations, see Schumpeter's Diary, n.d. (1932), loose sheet, Schumpeter Papers, HUG(FP)—4.1, Brief Daily Records, notes and diaries, ca. 1931–1948, box 7, folder Ca. 32–33, HUA, hereinafter cited as Schumpeter's Diary; Robert Loring Allen, *Opening Doors: The Life & Work of Joseph Schumpeter,* two vols. (New Brunswick, N.J.: Transaction, 1991), I, p. 294; and Schumpeter to E. R. A. Seligman, November 23, 1913, in Ulrich Hedtke and Richard Swedberg, eds., *Joseph Alois Schumpeter, Briefe/Letters* (Tübingen: J. C. B. Mohr, Paul Siebeck, 2000), p. 53.

5. The development of Schumpeter's vision is one of the themes of this book. See also Enrico Santarelli and Enzo Pesciarelli, "The Emergence of a Vision: The Development of Schumpeter's Theory of Entrepreneurship," *History of Political*

Economy 22 (Winter 1990), pp. 677–696; and David Reisman, *Schumpeter's Market: Enterprise and Evolution* (Cheltenham, U.K.: Edward Elgar, 2004), ch. 2.

6. Schumpeter to Galbraith, October 28, 1948, in Hedtke and Swedberg, eds., *Briefe*, p. 366.

7. Schumpeter, *Capitalism, Socialism and Democracy,* p. 137.

8. Schumpeter, "Capitalism," *Encyclopaedia Britannica* (New York: Encylopaedia Britannica, 1946), VI, p. 801.

9. The quotation is from Schumpeter, *History of Economic Analysis* (New York: Oxford University Press, 1954), p. 555. A brief discussion of entrepreneurship, with useful definitions, may be found in Howard H. Stevenson, "A Perspective on Entrepreneurship," in H. H. Stevenson, Michael J. Roberts, and H. Irving Grousbeck, eds., *New Business Ventures and the Entrepreneur* (Homewood, Ill.: Irwin, 1985), pp. 2–15.

10. Schumpeter's Diary, June 30, 1944, notebook entry, box 4, folder 1944, June 30, 1944.

11. Here I don't wish to distort the positions of either Smith or Marx, about both of whom more will be said later in this book. In Marx's view, as Schumpeter himself makes clear in the first four chapters of *Capitalism, Socialism and Democracy,* the bourgeois entrepreneur was a person of almost miraculous achievements who was revolutionizing the world. But in Marx's mistaken prophecy, the entrepreneur was certain to be dethroned by the common man through the "dictatorship of the proletariat," and the destruction of capitalism was a historical inevitability. Schumpeter believed that Marx failed to distinguish between true entrepreneurs on the one hand and capitalist "expropriators" on the other.

12. Schumpeter, *History of Economic Analysis,* p. 1171. A classic analysis of the social implications of western societies' shifts to market economies is Karl Polanyi, *The Great Transformation: The Political and Economic Origins of Our Time* (New York: Rinehart, 1944). Like Schumpeter, who was three years his senior, Polanyi was a Viennese who left Austria during the 1930s. He became a British citizen, teaching at Oxford and the University of London.

13. As one might expect, there is a very large and diverse literature on this subject. One of the fullest and best arguments is Benjamin M. Friedman, *The Moral Consequences of Economic Growth* (New York: Knopf, 2005). Like many other proponents of growth, Friedman warns against the maldistribution of wealth and income.

14. Schumpeter, *Capitalism, Socialism and Democracy,* pp. 67–68.

1: LEAVING HOME

1. After the formation of the new state of Czechoslovakia in 1921, the town's name was changed from the German form Triesch to the Czech Třešť, pronounced "Tzesht" or, more easily for English speakers, "Chesht."

2. Richard Swedberg, *Schumpeter: A Biography* (Princeton, N.J.: Princeton University Press, 1991), p. 8.

3. Robert A. Kann, *The Multinational Empire: Nationalism and National Reform in the Habsburg Monarchy,* two vols. (New York: Columbia University Press, 1950), II, p. 302; and Robert Loring Allen, *Opening Doors: The Life & Work of Joseph Schumpeter,* two vols. (New Brunswick, N.J.: Transaction, 1991), I, pp. 7–14.

4. Iglau, now known by its Czech name Jihlava, was also the birthplace of Gustav Mahler. Born just a year before Johanna into an impoverished Jewish family, Mahler went on to become a celebrated composer and director of the Imperial Opera in Vienna, one of the highest positions to which any musician in the world could aspire.

5. The apartment on Mozartgasse was their second residence, to which they moved after a few months in a smaller building.

6. Swedberg, *Schumpeter: A Biography,* pp. 6–8; Allen, *Opening Doors,* I, pp. 7–14. One's nationality was seldom a clear issue in the vast and motley Austro-Hungarian Empire. Schumpeter's contemporary, Odon von Horvath, author of the famous *Tales from the Vienna Woods,* once said that "I have a Hungarian passport; but I have no fatherland. I am a very typical mix of old Austria-Hungary: at once Magyar, Croatian, German and Czech; my country is Hungary, my mother tongue is German." Schumpeter might have offered the same type of description for himself. See Horvath, quoted in Jacques Rupnik, "Central Europe or Mitteleuropa?" *Daedalus* 119 (Winter 1990), p. 251.

   The Habsburg family's Austro-Hungarian Empire contained no geographical entity named "Austria" that matches the boundaries of the present-day country. For the convenience of the reader I will use "Austria" to denote that part of the Empire that before World War I included all Habsburg domains except Hungary; and after the war to denote the small Republic of Austria. I will also use the term "empire" freely, although scholars properly differ on whether the Habsburg lands as a whole should be called an empire as opposed to a kingdom or monarchy.

7. Allen, *Opening Doors,* I, pp. 15–18; Richard Swedberg, ed., *Joseph A. Schumpeter: The Economics and Sociology of Capitalism* (Princeton, N.J.: Princeton University Press, 1991), pp. 4, 78n3.

8. Allen, *Opening Doors,* I, pp. 17–18.

9. Gottfried Haberler, "Joseph Alois Schumpeter, 1883–1950," in Seymour E. Harris, ed., *Schumpeter, Social Scientist* (Cambridge, Mass.: Harvard University Press, 1951), p. 25. This was a memorial volume of 20 articles published under the auspices of the *Review of Economics and Statistics,* where 15 of the 20 first appeared in the issue of May 1951.

10. Allen, *Opening Doors,* I, pp. 20–23; II, p. 229.

11. William M. Johnston, *The Austrian Mind: An Intellectual and Social History, 1848–1938* (Berkeley: University of California Press, 1972), pp. 66–69.

12. Some writers have asserted that Schumpeter himself was anti-Semitic, and a prima-facie case can be made through his occasional remarks and diary entries, plus the extensive anti-Semitism of the Viennese environment in which he grew up and of the Harvard milieu he encountered when he came to the United States. See, for example, Bernard Semmel, "Schumpeter's Curious Politics," *The Public Interest* 106 (Winter 1992), pp. 3–16; Melvin W. Reder, "The Anti-Semitism of Some Eminent Economists," *History of Political Economy* 32 (2000), pp. 834–856, which makes a fairly strong case against John Maynard Keynes, a much weaker one against Schumpeter, and no case at all against Friedrich von Hayek, the three economists he accuses of anti-Semitism; and John Medearis, *Joseph Schumpeter's Two Theories of Democracy* (Cambridge, Mass.: Harvard University Press, 2001). Each of these authors draws very heavily on *Opening Doors,* Robert Loring Allen's biography of Schumpeter, which is more balanced in its judgments but still concludes that Schumpeter sometimes tended toward anti-Semitism. Allen's own evidence comes primarily from Schumpeter's diaries.

These critics may be correct. But anti-Semitism is such a serious charge that confirmation would seem to require something approaching the "beyond a reasonable doubt" test. None of the four authors, including Allen, comes anywhere near to meeting this standard. None is sufficiently thorough or imaginative in thinking about the issue, and each neglects a substantial body of evidence pointing to the opposite conclusion. That evidence may be summarized as follows:

Many of Schumpeter's contemporaries in Vienna thought him a *Judenfreund,* or philo-Semite. In Viennese politics, he was regarded as insufficiently anti-Semitic by influential members of the Christian Social Party and other conservative groups. Most important of all, throughout his life a large number of Jewish friends provided indispensable support for Schumpeter at crucial phases of his career; or, as students and colleagues, expressed gratitude for his support of their own careers. These included Gustav Stolper, Rudolf Hilferding, Emil Lederer, Otto Bauer, Hans Kelsen, Frank Taussig, Wassily Leontief, Wolfgang Stolper, Hans Singer, August Lösch, Paul Samuelson, Seymour Harris, Abram Bergson, and many others. Most of these supporters and beneficiaries had two Jewish parents, some only one. Some practiced their inherited faith, others were agnostics, and a few chose to become Christians. The same is true for numerous Jewish scholars for whom Schumpeter helped to find employment after they fled Europe during the 1930s.

Of course, it is well documented that anti-Semitism is not incompatible with friendship with individual Jews. But a pervasive and long-term pattern of active *sponsorship,* in both directions, is something very different. For a well-informed (and angry) argument that he was not anti-Semitic, see Wolfgang F. Stolper, *Joseph Alois Schumpeter: The Public Life of a Private Man* (Princeton, N.J.: Princeton University Press, 1994), pp. 10–12, 217.

In this book, I present the evidence I have encountered on this issue, and invite readers to make their own judgments. To me the evidence indicates that Schumpeter did have his prejudices—he was an elitist with an excessive regard for aristocrats, for example—but that anti-Semitism was not one of these prejudices. For his time, he was remarkably tolerant and open-minded, respecting sheer talent and achievement far more than any other factors.

13. Johnston, *The Austrian Mind,* pp. 68–69.

14. Schumpeter, "Ships in the Fog," Schumpeter Papers, HUG(FP)—4.3, Misc. personal writings and notes, box 1, Material for Ships in the Fog, HUA. This important document is uncommonly difficult to read. It was written in tiny, penciled, and sometimes illegible script on small sheets of yellow paper. Schumpeter composed it intermittently during the middle and late 1930s, and although most of it is in English, portions are in French, German, and the now obsolete Gabelsberger form of shorthand. Parts of the manuscript (which total 32 pages in length) contain dialogues between lovers; other parts pertain to jobs in business or government the protagonist had taken or was considering; and a few list outlines of scenes that were apparently planned for later completion.

15. Ibid.

16. Paul A. Samuelson, "Schumpeter as a Teacher and Economic Theorist," in Harris, ed., *Schumpeter, Social Scientist,* pp. 48–49; Samuelson, "Joseph A. Schumpeter," *Dictionary of American Biography* (New York: Scribner, 1977, Supplement Four), p. 722. For an accessible introduction to the question of identity and some novel views of the difficulty in attaining accurate self-knowledge, see Timothy Wilson, *Strangers to Ourselves: Discovering the Adaptive Unconscious* (Cambridge, Mass.: Harvard University Press, 2002).

2: SHAPING HIS CHARACTER

1. In the large academic literature on Vienna and the Austro-Hungarian Empire, I have found the following works especially useful: William M. Johnston, *The Austrian Mind: An Intellectual and Social History, 1848–1938* (Berkeley: University of California Press, 1972); Hilde Spiel, *Vienna's Golden Autumn, 1866–1938* (New York: Weidenfeld and Nicolson, 1987); Carl E. Schorske, *Fin de Siècle Vienna: Politics and Culture* (New York: Knopf, 1979); Allan Janik and Stephen Toulmin, *Wittgenstein's Vienna* (New York: Simon & Schuster, 1973); Jacques Le Rider, trans. Ralph Manheim, "Between Modernism and Postmodernism: The Viennese Identity Crisis," in Edward Timms and Ritchie Robertson, eds., *Vienna 1900: From Altenburg to Wittgenstein* (Edinburgh: Edinburgh University Press, 1990), pp. 1–10; Arthur J. May, *Vienna in the Age of Franz Josef* (Norman: University of Oklahoma Press, 1966); Robert A. Kann, *A History of the Habsburg Empire, 1526–1918* (Berkeley: University of California Press, 1977); C. A. Macartney, *The Habsburg Empire, 1790–1918* (London: Macmillan, 1969); Arthur J. May, *The*

Habsburg Monarchy, 1867–1914 (Cambridge, Mass.: Harvard University Press, 1951); A. J. P. Taylor, *The Habsburg Monarchy, 1809–1918: A History of the Austrian Empire & Austria-Hungary* (New York: Harper & Row, 1965); F. R. Bridge, *The Habsburg Monarchy among the Great Powers, 1815–1918* (New York: St. Martin's Press, 1991); Alan Sked, *The Decline and Fall of the Habsburgs, 1815–1918* (London: Longman, 1989); and Samuel R. Williamson, Jr., *Austria-Hungary and the Origins of the First World War* (New York: St. Martin's Press, 1991).

   Informative but less academic books include *Danube,* by Claudio Magris, trans. Patrick Creagh (London: Collins Harvill, 1989), which nicely evokes the situation in formerly Habsburg regions during the late twentieth century; and two books by Frederic Morton, *A Nervous Splendor: Vienna 1888/1889* (Boston: Little, Brown, 1979), and *Thunder at Twilight: Vienna, 1913/1914* (New York: Scribner, 1989). The milieu of upper-class Vienna during this period is well captured by the novelist Sarah Gainham in her book of nonfiction essays, *The Habsburg Twilight: Tales From Vienna* (New York: Atheneum, 1979). See also the account by Schumpeter's friend Felix Somary, trans. A. J. Sherman, *The Raven of Zürich: The Memoirs of Felix Somary* (New York: St. Martin's Press, 1986), chs. 1–10.

2. This reconstruction was done "to proclaim," as Carl E. Schorske puts it, "the historical affiliation between modern, rational culture and the revival of secular learning after the long night of medieval superstition." Schorske, *Fin de Siècle Vienna,* pp. 8, 26, 38–40, 46. See also Herbert Muschamp, *New York Times,* Sunday, June 2, 2002, p. 30 of the Art and Architecture section, who uses Schumpeter's term "creative destruction."

3. Edward Timms, "Images of the City: Vienna, Prague, and the Intellectual Avant-Garde," in Robert B. Pysent, ed., *Decadence and Innovation: Austro-Hungarian Life and Art at the Turn of the Century* (London: Weidenfeld and Nicolson, 1989), p. 3. Here Timms is referring not only to Austria but also to Germany.

4. This Ferris wheel was made familiar to international audiences by the classic film of 1949, "The Third Man," which is set in post-World War II Vienna.

5. Mahler and Johanna were born at about the same time in the same place (Jihlava), but evidently they did not know each other.

6. Stefan Zweig, *The World of Yesterday: An Autobiography* (London: Cassell, 1943), pp. 21–22.

7. Edward Timms has written that some of the traditions of the Empire seemed "like a grandiose attempt to stop the clock." Timms, "Images of the City: Vienna, Prague, and the Intellectual Avant-Garde," p. 3. Karl Wittgenstein, father of the philosopher Ludwig, provided principal financing for the Secessionist museum, whose walls are still adorned with murals by the great Viennese painter Gustav Klimt.

8. Spiel, *Vienna's Golden Autumn, 1866–1938,* p. 56. See also Harold B. Segel, *The*

Vienna Coffeehouse Wits, 1890–1938 (West Lafayette, Ind.: Purdue University Press, 1993).

9. "By the 1890s the heroes of the upper middle class were no longer political leaders, but actors, artists, and critics." See Schorske, *Fin de Siècle Vienna*, pp. xviii, 8.

Given the recurring anti-Semitism of Viennese politics, it was a special irony that much of the cultural renaissance was led by Jews: in music, Arnold Schönberg and Gustav Mahler; in politics, Viktor Adler and Otto Bauer; in literature, Stefan Zweig and Karl Kraus; in psychoanalysis, Sigmund Freud.

10. Mark Twain, "Stirring Times in Austria," *Harper's New Monthly Magazine* 96 (March 1898), p. 530.

11. The Emperor usually preferred the Anglicized Francis Joseph, even though many of his contemporaries called him Franz Josef or, sometimes, Franz Joseph.

At 261,000 square miles, the Austro-Hungarian Empire was nearly as big as the German Empire, which at its founding in 1871 was almost exactly the same size as the American state of Texas: 267,000 square miles. Present-day Germany is considerably smaller: about 138,000 square miles.

The preamble to decrees issued from Emperor Francis Joseph's palace in Vienna read as follows: "We, by the Grace of God Emperor of Austria; King of Hungary, of Bohemia, Dalmatia, Croatia, Slavonia, Galicia, Lodomeria and Illyria; King of Jerusalem, Archduke of Austria; Grand-duke of Tuscany and Cracow; Duke of Lorraine, of Salzburg, Styria, Carinthia, Carniola and Bukovina, Grand-Duke of Transylvania, Margrave of Moravia; Duke of Upper and Lower Silesia, of Modena, Parma, Piacenza and Guastella, of Ausschwitz [sic] and Sator, of Teschen, Friaul, Ragusa and Zara; Royal Count of Habsburg and Tyrol, of Kyburg, Gorz and Gradisca; Duke of Trient and Brixen; Margrave of Upper and Lower Lausitz and in Istria; Count of Hohenembs, Feldkirch, Bregenz, Sonnenberg, etc.; Lord of Trieste, of Cattaro, and above the country of Windisch; Grand Voivode of the Voivodina Serbia, etc., etc."

On the theme of identity in some of these domains, see Ernst Bruckmüller, trans. Nicholas T. Parsons, "The National Identity of the Austrians," ch. 8 of Mikuláš Teich and Roy Porter, eds., *The National Question in Europe in Historical Context* (Cambridge: Cambridge University Press, 1993), esp. pp. 202–204 and 218–219. In this same book, chs. 9 (on the Czechs, by Arnošt Klíma, trans. Milan Hauner), 10 (on Hungary, by Emil Niederhauser, trans. Mari Markus Gömöri), and 11 (on Dalmatia and Croatia, by Mirjana Gross), also provide relevant commentary on the conundrum of nationalities in the Habsburg Empire.

12. Mark Twain, "Stirring Times in Austria," pp. 532–533.

13. István Deák, *Beyond Nationalism: A Social and Political History of the Habsburg Officer Corps, 1848–1918* (New York: Oxford University Press, 1990). Deák argues that the army was much more effective in this unifying role than in fighting ac-

tual wars; that it accomplished a "near miracle" of preservation with "a minimum of force" (p. 8). Joseph Roth, trans. Joachim Neugroschel, gives vivid evocations of provincial military life in the classic novel *The Radetzky March* (New York: Knopf, 1996, first published in the 1930s).

14. Edward Crankshaw, *The Fall of the House of Habsburg* (London: Longmans, Green, 1963), pp. 4, 82.

15. "Members of the lower nobility were not admitted to Franz Joseph's court. According to ancient heraldic practice, to be eligible for court (hoffähig) one must possess sixteen quarters of nobility, that is, one must have had sixteen great-great grandparents all of whom were noble . . . The aristocracy was concentrated in eighty families who had intermarried so often that they constituted one large family." See Johnston, *The Austrian Mind* pp. 39–40. See also Henry Wickham Steed, *The Hapsburg Monarchy* (London: Constable and Company, 1913), p. 133; and May, *The Hapsburg Monarchy,* p. 162.

16. Of the many biographies of Francis Joseph, the classic English-language work is Joseph Redlich, *Emperor Francis Joseph of Austria: A Biography* (New York: Macmillan, 1929). See also the brief and unusually readable Steven Beller, *Francis Joseph* (London and New York: Longman, 1996), whose first chapter provides a good historiographical overview of the Habsburg literature. On Francis Joseph's role in Austrian society, see also Johnston, *The Austrian Mind.*

17. Alan Bullock, *Hitler and Stalin: Parallel Lives* (London: HarperCollins, 1991), p. 22; Alan Palmer, *Twilight of the Habsburgs: The Life and Times of Emperor Francis Joseph* (New York: Grove Press, 1995), p. 270. See also Janik and Toulmin, *Wittgenstein's Vienna,* ch. 2. Of the many useful books on Austrian anti-Semitism, see particularly Bruce F. Pauley, *From Prejudice to Persecution: A History of Austrian Anti-Semitism* (Chapel Hill: University of North Carolina Press, 1992); Peter Pulzer, *The Rise of Political Anti-Semitism in Germany and Austria* (London: Peter Halban, 1988); Robert S. Wistrich, *The Jews of Vienna in the Age of Franz Joseph* (Oxford: Oxford University Press, 1989); and the collection of essays edited by Wistrich, *Austrians and Jews in the Twentieth Century: From Franz Joseph to Waldheim* (New York: St. Martin's Press, 1992).

18. On Lueger, see John W. Boyer, *Political Radicalism in Later Imperial Vienna: Origins of the Christian Social Movement, 1848–1897* (Chicago: University of Chicago Press, 1981), especially pp. 318, 319, 367, 379, 411; and, after Lueger's ascent to power, John W. Boyer, *Cultural and Political Crisis in Vienna: Christian Socialism in Power, 1897–1918* (Chicago: University of Chicago Press, 1995), chs. 1–4. Some critics have accepted Boyer's attempts to contextualize the anti-Semitism of Lueger's politics, while others have judged him too lenient toward Lueger.

19. Ibid. (both sources). See also Brigitte Hamann, trans. Thomas Thornton, *Hitler's Vienna: A Dictator's Apprenticeship* (New York: Oxford University Press, 1999), pp. 273–303, quotation from *Mein Kampf* on p. 399.

20. One of the most strongly argued interpretations of healthy economic progress

under Habsburg rule is David F. Good, *The Economic Rise of the Habsburg Empire, 1750–1914* (Berkeley: University of California Press, 1984).

21. Johnston, *The Austrian Mind*, pp. 64–66; Boyer, *Political Radicalism in Later Imperial Vienna*, pp. 318–319, 367, 379, 411; and Boyer, *Cultural and Political Crisis in Vienna*, chs. 1–4. For the petroleum industry, see Alison Fleig Frank, *Oil Empire: Visions of Prosperity in Austrian Galicia* (Cambridge, Mass.: Harvard University Press, 2005), which brilliantly analyzes the social and cultural aspects of the industry's evolution as well as the economic.

22. Steven Beller, *Francis Joseph*, p. 151. At the time of Mark Twain's visit in 1897, two big issues lay before Parliament. The first was the *Ausgleich* (the arrangement that united Austria and Hungary in the Dual Monarchy), which was up for its regular ten-year renewal. The second grew out of the perennial problem of nationalist pride within and among provinces. The Germans in particular chafed at a new regulation that made Czech as well as German an official language in Moravia and Bohemia for use in public documents. Even though Czechs far outnumbered German-speaking citizens in these areas, German-speakers protested vehemently, and the new law was later rescinded. Most Czechs knew the German language, but many fewer Germans knew Czech. So if Czech became one of the official languages of governmental affairs, numerous public jobs would likely gravitate toward the Czech majority. In the Habsburg lands, the civil service was growing very fast, from about 100,000 in 1870 to 400,000 by 1910. So the stakes were high. See Steed, *The Habsburg Monarchy*, p. 88; and Boyer, *Political Radicalism in Later Imperial Vienna*, p. 383. After the extremely controversial resolution of this question, riots broke out in Prague and other cities. Nor were riots uncommon in Vienna itself.

   The Berlin visitor is quoted in Hamann, *Hitler's Vienna: A Dictator's Apprenticeship*, p. 119. Hamann goes on to say (p. 132) that Hitler himself frequently attended Parliament in 1908 and 1909, and later wrote in *Mein Kampf* that the idea of parliamentary government "which at first sight seemed seductive to so many . . . none the less must be counted among the symptoms of human degeneration," parliamentarians being "a band of mentally dependent nonentities and dilettantes as limited as they are conceited and inflated."

23. Watching from the gallery above, Mark Twain was less surprised that the delegates would deliver such insults than that they would receive them without resorting to violence. "These men are not professional blackguards; they are mainly gentlemen, and educated; yet they use the terms, and take them, too. They really seem to attach no consequence to them . . . Apparently they may call each other what they please, and go home unmutilated." That, surmised Mark Twain, would never happen in America, or even in an English schoolyard. See "Stirring Times in Austria," pp. 533–537.

24. Boyer, *Political Radicalism in Later Imperial Vienna*, p. 363; on university fistfights, see also Somary, *The Raven of Zürich*, pp. 7–8.

25. The comment by Schumpeter's professor, the famous Eugen Böhm-Bawerk, was made in 1913, and is quoted in Richard Swedberg, *Schumpeter: A Biography* (Princeton, N.J.: Princeton University Press, 1991), p. 199; Somary, *The Raven of Zürich,* pp. 14–15.

26. Edmund Burke, *Reflections on the Revolution in France* (1790), ed. Thomas Mahoney (New York: Bobbs-Merrill, 1955), pp. 57–59.

27. The Irish were the only real exception. The Habsburgs had not tried to unite their domains forcibly into one nation, as had the rulers of Britain in the 11th century and afterwards (annexing Wales in 1536, Scotland in 1707, and Ireland in 1800). The French kings had done something similar in the 15th century, the Russian tsars in the 17th and 18th, and the Prussian kings in the 19th. But the Habsburg lands were even more ethnically diverse, and a very heavy-handed approach might have been necessary to meld them into a single nation. This point is discussed in Karl R. Stadler, *Austria* (London: Ernest Benn, 1971), pp. 56–70, but contested in Dominic Lieven, *Empire: The Russian Empire and Its Rivals* (New Haven, Conn.: Yale University Press, 2001), p. 193. Lieven's Chapter 5 examines the Austro-Hungarian Empire, and argues that by 1900 it "was moving in the direction of a democratic multi-national federation, able to offer its people the economic benefits of a huge market, legally protected equality in status, and the security that was empire's traditional boon."

28. Somary, *The Raven of Zürich,* p. 120.

29. Samuelson, "Joseph A. Schumpeter," in *Dictionary of American Biography,* Supplement Four, 1946–1950 (New York: Scribner, 1974), pp. 720–723.

3: LEARNING ECONOMICS

1. A complete list of the courses Schumpeter took, and the instructors who taught them, is reproduced in the introduction to Ulrich Hedtke and Richard Swedberg, eds., *Joseph Alois Schumpeter, Briefe/Letters* (Tübingen: J. C. B. Mohr, Paul Siebeck, 2000), pp. 3–5.

2. William M. Johnston, *The Austrian Mind: An Intellectual and Social History, 1848–1938* (Berkeley: University of California Press, 1972), pp. 69–73 contains a good description of the university's routine.

3. Schumpeter, "Eugen von Böhm-Bawerk," in *Ten Great Economists: From Marx to Keynes* (New York: Oxford University Press, 1951), p. 148, trans. Herbert K. Zassenhaus of the original article published in 1914.

In *History of Economic Analysis* (New York: Oxford University Press, 1954), Schumpeter notes that at Cambridge University, where the famous Alfred Marshall had taught for many years, "a Tripos in Economics and associated branches of political science was not organized until 1903. Before that economics was indeed taught but not recognized as a full-time professional study. After that, teaching expanded but throughout the period there was nothing like the 'economic faculty' [sic] of today" (p. 755n3). He goes on to say that in Germany and other countries, the bent for using economics as an instrument of reform was even stronger; but not so much in the emerging Austrian School.

4. There are many excellent histories of economic thought. The most readable text is Robert L. Heilbroner, *The Worldly Philosophers: The Lives, Times and Ideas of the Great Economic Thinkers* (New York: Simon & Schuster, 1953); from at least its sixth edition (1992), this book has contained a chapter on Schumpeter, one of only five individual economists to whom Heilbroner devotes an entire chapter. Other standard works include Mark Blaug, *Economic History and the History of Economics* (New York: New York University Press, 1986); Mark Blaug, *Economic Theory in Retrospect,* 5th ed. (Cambridge: Cambridge University Press, 1997); and Alessandro Roncaglia, *The Wealth of Ideas: A History of Economic Thought* (Cambridge: Cambridge University Press, 2005), all of which contain discussions of Schumpeter. David Warsh, *Knowledge and the Wealth of Nations: A Story of Economic Discovery* (New York: Norton, 2006), well captures the spirit and culture of academic economics since the mathematical revolution of the 1940s. Schumpeter's own *History of Economic Analysis* remains one of the best texts for the years up to 1949, and, in the opinion of many experts, *the* best.

5. Schumpeter, *History of Economic Analysis,* p. 181. Adam Smith, *An Inquiry into the Nature and Causes of the Wealth of Nations* (Chicago: University of Chicago Press, [1776], 1976). Smith had used the "invisible hand" metaphor at least twice in his earlier writings, in non-economic contexts. The phrase is not emphasized in *The Wealth of Nations,* but rather comes in the midst of a discussion of foreign trade on pp. 487–490 of the 1976 edition.

6. The eminent American economist John Bates Clark, who became one of Schumpeter's admirers and sponsors, made a related point in 1890, in a statement pertaining more to labor than to land. Clark's argument contained a quotation that grew famous among economists: "Put one man only on a square mile of prairie, and he will get a rich return [Clark seemed to assume that he could till the whole expanse alone, a questionable premise]. Two laborers on the same ground will get less per man; and, if you enlarge the force to ten, the last man will perhaps get wages only." Clark is regarded by many scholars as the most important pioneer of marginal productivity theory, of which this comment is a good example. See Clark, "Distribution as Determined by a Law of Rent," *Quarterly Journal of Economics* 5 (1891), p. 304. The example is still relevant in developing countries such as Mexico, where land has been subdivided into very small plots.

7. Schumpeter had more respect for Ricardo himself, who usually qualified his arguments with care, than for the Ricardians who followed the master's precepts without due revision. See, for example, Schumpeter, *History of Economic Analysis,* pp. 472–475, where he gives ample credit to Ricardo's rigor and leadership, while still rendering an overall critical verdict on his influence.

Increasing returns are harder to model mathematically than are decreasing returns, and the price theory of increasing returns much harder. Because of this, it took mainstream academic economists many years to cope effectively with the problem, and with its implications for public policies toward economic growth and other issues. Professional economists' persistent efforts to understand increasing returns began to bear fruit with their analysis of the railroad industry, as in the work of Arthur Hadley and Henry C. Adams during the 1880s. Pierro Sraffa introduced the problem to modern economic analysis early in the twentieth century. Among the many later pioneers writing from the 1960s onward were F. M. Scherer and Richard Nelson, who emphasized technological progress and what might be called dynamic increasing returns.

On the importance of the question of increasing returns to the "New Growth Theory" of the 1980s and 1990s, see Warsh, *Knowledge and the Wealth of Nations,* a journalistic treatment. Some significant works in this pursuit are Elhanan Helpman and Paul Krugman, *Market Structure and Foreign Trade: Imperfect Competition, Increasing Returns, and the International Economy* (Cambridge, Mass.: MIT Press, 1985); Paul Romer, "Increasing Returns and Long-Run Growth," *Journal of Political Economy* 94 (October 1986), pp. 1002–1037; and Paul Romer, "Endogenous Technological Change," *Journal of Political Economy* 98, part 2 (October 1990), pp. 71–102. Schumpeter's own work is very much a part of this story, even though he was never able to mathematize his argument.

8. Schumpeter, *History of Economic Analysis,* p. 571.

9. The journal was *Schmollers Jahrbuch* (yearbook), widely read throughout Germany and Austria. Schumpeter's comments appear in *History of Economic Analysis,* p. 809n4.

10. In the large literature of the subject, scholars have usefully identified both "Old" and "New" German Historical Schools. See, for example, the thorough analysis in Geoffrey M. Hodgson, *How Economics Forgot History: The Problem of Historical Specificity in Social Science* (London: Routledge, 2001), pp. 41–134. For a provocative view arguing that the German Historical School was neither German, nor Historical, nor a School, see Heath Pearson, "Was There Really a German Historical School of Economics?" *History of Political Economy* 31 (1999), pp. 547–562.

11. Schumpeter published in Weber's *Archiv für Sozialwissenschaft,* but he rarely cited Weber's work; and Weber, as far as I know, never cited Schumpeter's. Yet there *was* mutual influence. See Riccardo Faucci and Veronica Rodenzo, "Did Schumpeter Change His Mind? Notes on Max Weber's influence on Schumpeter," *History of Economic Ideas* 6 (1998), pp. 27–54; and Yuichi Shionoya, *The Soul of the German Historical School: Methodological Essays on Schmoller, Weber, and Schumpeter* (New York: Springer Science & Business Media, 2005).

During the mid-1920s, Schumpeter began to reconsider his own approach to economics, and concluded that both sociology and history mattered even more than he had thought. He then wrote a long article titled "Gustav von Schmoller and the Problems of Today," praising Schmoller's work for its contributions in broadening the discipline of economics beyond sterile theory and toward what Schumpeter calls a "universal social science." He connects Schmoller's work in systematizing history and social science with his own and others' efforts at economic theorizing. See Schumpeter, *"Gustav v. Schmoller und die Probleme von heute,"* Schmollers Jahrbuch für Gesetzgebung, Verwaltung und Volkswirtschaft im Deustchen Reich 50 (June 1926), I, pp. 337–388.

12. Richard S. Howey, "The Origins of Marginalism," in R. D. Collison Black, A. W. Coats, and Craufurd D. W. Goodwin, eds., *The Marginalist Revolution in Economics: Interpretation and Evaluation* (Durham, N.C.: Duke University Press, 1973), pp. 15–36.

The Austrian School by no means ignored public affairs. Schumpeter's teachers Friedrich von Wieser and Eugen von Böhm-Bawerk served in the imperial cabinet. And Carl Menger, a tutor of Crown Prince Rudolf, often stressed the responsibility of the aristocracy to set examples of good agricultural and other practices. See Erich W. Streissler and Monika Streissler, eds., *Carl Menger's Lectures to Crown Prince Rudolf of Austria,* trans. Monika Streissler with the assistance of David F. Good (Aldershot, U.K.: Edward Elgar, 1994), p. 183.

13. Léon Walras, *Elements of Pure Economics, or The Theory of Social Wealth,* trans. William Jaffé of *Éléments d'économie politique pure; ou, Theorie de la richesse sociale* (Homewood, Ill.: Irwin [1874], 1954); W. Stanley Jevons, *The Theory of Political Economy* (London: Macmillan, 1871); Carl Menger, *Principles of Economics,* trans. James Dingwall and Bert F. Hoselitz of *Grundsätze der Volkswirtschaftslehre* (New York: New York University Press, [1871] 1981); John B. Clark, *The Philosophy of Wealth: Economic Principles Newly Formulated* (Boston: Ginn and Co., 1887); Schumpeter, *History of Economic Analysis,* pp. 868–870, 909–919. See also William M. Johnston, *The Austrian Mind,* ch. 4.

In *History of Economic Analysis,* pp. 463–465, Schumpeter credits several other economists of the earlier part of the nineteenth century with anticipating certain aspects of marginal utility theory—Jules Dupuit, Hermann Gossen, William F. Lloyd—and of marginal productivity theory—Mountifort Longfield and Johann von Thünen.

14. Meanwhile, Jevons and Walras, like many innovators, never received their intellectual due until after their deaths. Jevons was a quiet and unassuming person whom Schumpeter admired because of his bold assertion about the indispensability of mathematics to economics.

On Walras and the importance of equilibrium, see Schumpeter, preface to the Japanese edition of *The Theory of Economic Development* (Tokyo: Iwanami Shoten, 1937), printed in Schumpeter, *Essays on Entrepreneurs, Innovation, Business Cycles, and the Evolution of Capitalism,* Richard V. Clemence, ed. (first published by Addison-Wesley, 1951, new edition by Transaction, New Brunswick,

N.J., 1989, with an introduction by Richard Swedberg), p. 165. The analogy with the Magna Carta is in Schumpeter, *History of Economic Analysis,* p. 242. Schumpeter went on to acknowledge that "It remains true, however, that both Walras himself and his followers greatly underestimated what had and has still to be done before Walras' theory can be confronted with the facts of common business experience." Ibid., p. 1015.

Several authors have explored the relationship between marginalism and equilibrium; for example, G. L. S. Shackle, "The Harvest," in Black, Coats, and Goodwin, eds., *The Marginalist Revolution,* pp. 321–336. Schumpeter himself wrote that "Most modern theorists, though not all, will agree that the historical importance of the utility and marginal utility theory rests mainly upon the fact that it served as the ladder by which these economists climbed up to the conception of general economic equilibrium, although this conception was much more clearly perceived and more fully developed by Walras than it was by either the Austrians or Jevons." See Schumpeter, "Vilfredo Pareto," in *Ten Great Economists,* p. 126, essay originally published in 1949.

15. Schumpeter's own sketch of Menger appears in ch. 3 of his book *Ten Great Economists,* and of the early Austrian School in his *History of Economic Analysis,* pp. 844–855. A very large literature treats the *Methodenstreit* (struggle over methods). For a brief overview from the Austrian perspective, see Samuel Bostaph, "The Methodenstreit," in Peter J. Boettke, ed., *The Elgar Companion to Austrian Economics* (Brookfield, Vt.: Edward Elgar, 1994), pp. 459–464.

16. Wieser, the son of a nobleman, had a distinctive combination of wisdom and artistic gravity that Schumpeter found hard to describe. He recalled that at Wieser's seventieth birthday celebration in 1921, three different speakers, including Schumpeter himself, "compared him, independently of each other, to Goethe." See Schumpeter, *Ten Great Economists,* p. 299.

17. Schumpeter's memorial essay on Böhm-Bawerk is reprinted in ch. 6 of *Ten Great Economists,* trans. Herbert K. Zassenhaus from the original 1914 version; the quotation is on p. 145. See also Schumpeter, *History of Economic Analysis,* p. 844: Böhm-Bawerk's public service "must be kept in mind in appraising his scientific work, exactly as Ricardo's business avocations must be kept in mind if we are to do justice to his. *What is before us to read is not the finished work that Böhm-Bawerk had in mind*—parts of the published performance were written in a hurry, the consequences of which Böhm-Bawerk never had the opportunity to remedy." In addition to Wieser and Böhm-Bawerk, Schumpeter's other most influential teacher at Vienna was Eugen von Philippovich, a distinguished economic historian. On the Austrian School in its Vienna context, see, generally, ch. 4 of Johnston, *The Austrian Mind.*

18. Schumpeter's definition, from a lecture he delivered in 1941, is quoted in Wolfgang F. Stolper, *Joseph Alois Schumpeter: The Public Life of a Private Man* (Princeton, N.J.: Princeton University Press, 1994), p. 35. Lederer, Mises, and

Schumpeter had careers in academic economics; Bauer and Hilferding in politics and public finance (both later sponsored Schumpeter's own participation in Austrian politics). Some writers have added Felix Somary's name to this list of students. Somary was a friend of Schumpeter's, and he later became one of the leading bankers of Europe. But his participation in Böhm-Bawerk's seminar came just a bit later.

For Böhm-Bawerk's critique of Marx, see *Karl Marx and the Close of His System* and Rudolf Hilferding's comments on Böhm-Bawerk's analysis, titled *Böhm-Bawerk's Criticism of Marx*. Both were re-published under the same titles in a volume edited by Paul M. Sweezy, himself a Marxist economist and one of Schumpeter's Ph.D. students at Harvard. Sweezy provides a useful 25-page introduction to the book (New York: Augustus M. Kelley, 1949).

19. Paul A. Samuelson, "Schumpeter's *Capitalism, Socialism and Democracy*," in Arnold Heertje, ed., *Schumpeter's Vision: Capitalism, Socialism and Democracy after 40 Years* (New York: Praeger, 1981), pp. 1, 13, and *passim*.

20. The Austrian School's reputation for vehement opposition to governmental interference with market forces—an ideology Schumpeter did not share—began mainly in the work of Schumpeter's classmate Ludwig von Mises and of Mises' brilliant student Friedrich von Hayek. Some writers have argued that Schumpeter should not be considered a member of the Austrian School. This is an interesting question, though not an especially important one. For an argument that places him squarely in the Austrian tradition, see D. Simpson, "Joseph Schumpeter and the Austrian School of Economics," *Journal of Economic Studies* 4 (1983), pp. 15–28. On one particular aspect of the German and Austrian intellectual legacies for Schumpeter's theory of economic development, see Guido Frison, "Some German and Austrian Ideas on *Technologie* and *Teknik* between the End of the Eighteenth Century and the Beginning of the Twentieth," *History of Economic Ideas* 6 (1998), pp. 108–133. On the mixture of influences, see Erich W. Streissler, "The Influence of German and Austrian Economics on Joseph A. Schumpeter," in Yuichi Shionoya and Mark Perlman, eds., *Innovation in Technology, Industries, and Institutions: Studies in Schumpeterian Perspectives* (Ann Arbor: University of Michigan Press, 1994), pp. 13–38.

21. Schumpeter, "Eugen von Böhm-Bawerk," p. 165.

22. Menger, *Principles of Economics,* pp. 45, 92–94; see also F. A. Hayek's comment on this issue in his introduction to the book, p. 16. In Schumpeter's view, Menger, for all his insights, did not use math nearly as much as he should have done, and certainly not as much as Walras.

23. Schumpeter, "The Common Sense of Econometrics," *Econometrica* 1 (January 1933), p. 9. Later on, Schumpeter wrote something like the opposite regarding theoretical changes during the marginalist revolution: that the new way of thinking came as "a purely analytic affair without reference to practical questions." But here he seems to be referring to questions of public policy, not of business prac-

tice. See *History of Economic Analysis,* p. 888. On the contemporary environment as it relates to marginalism, see R. W. Coats, "The Economic and Social Context of the Marginal Revolution of the 1870s," in Black, Coats, and Goodwin, eds., *The Marginalist Revolution,* pp. 37–58.

24. On this point and many others connected with marginalism, see, generally, Black, Coats, and Goodwin, eds., *The Marginalist Revolution.* Herbert Hovenkamp provides a survey of marginalism as a way of thinking about numerous issues relating to law in "The Marginalist Revolution in Legal Thought," *Vanderbilt Law Review* 46 (March 1993), pp. 305–359.

25. The thinking behind the idea of a just price was adumbrated by the Greek philosophers of antiquity, then articulated during the late Middle Ages in Aquinas's *Summa Theologica* and later texts by the Scholastics. A brief and learned exposition of both the question itself and of Schumpeter's treatment of it in *History of Economic Analysis* may be found in Raymond de Roover, "Joseph Schumpeter and Scholastic Economics," *Kyklos* 10 (1957), pp. 115–143. From the writings of the Scholastics, de Roover concludes that "according to the majority, the just price was either the market or the legal price. The textual evidence leaves little if any doubt." As a practical matter, enforcement of the just price (or of any other method of price control, throughout history) has been problematical because of black markets and other evasions.

Examples of the persistence of the just price idea into the early capitalist era appear in numerous works, such as Mack Walker, *German Home Towns: Community, State, and General Estate, 1648–1871* (Ithaca, N.Y.: Cornell University Press, 1998), and Bernard Bailyn, *The New England Merchants in the Seventeenth Century* (Cambridge, Mass.: Harvard University Press, 1955).

26. This may have been truer for Menger and Jevons than for Walras. See William Jaffé, "Léon Walras' Role in the 'Marginal Revolution' of the 1870s," in Black, Coats, and Goodwin, eds., *The Marginalist Revolution,* pp. 118–119.

27. Menger, *Principles of Economics,* p. 127. Chapter 3 of this seminal work is titled "The Theory of Value," and includes the following definition: "Value is therefore nothing inherent in goods, no property of them, but merely the importance that we first attribute to the satisfaction of our needs" (p. 116).

28. On the invention of the term "marginal utility," see Richard S. Howey, "The Origins of Marginalism," in Black, Coats, and Goodwin, eds., *The Marginalist Revolution,* pp. 30–32, which seems to credit Philip Wicksteed rather than Schumpeter's teacher Friedrich von Wieser with the first use of the term. The issue turns on the translation of German words, and is not of great significance because the idea was obviously present in Wieser's work. For a brief overview of the concept itself, see Jack High, "Marginal Utility," in Boettke, ed., *The Elgar Companion to Austrian Economics,* pp. 87–91.

29. Schumpeter, "On the Concept of Social Value," *Quarterly Journal of Economics* 23 (February 1909), p. 214. For a thorough treatment, see George J. Stigler, "The

Development of Utility Theory," a two-part analysis in the *Journal of Political Economy* 58 (August 1950), pp. 307–327, and 58 (October 1950), pp. 372–396.

For Schumpeter's own final statement on the importance of utility in economics, see *History of Economic Analysis,* pp. 912–913: "The concepts of marginal and total utility refer to consumers' wants. Hence they carry direct meaning only with reference to goods or services the use of which yields satisfaction of consumers' wants. But Menger went on to say that means of production—or, as he called them, 'goods of higher order'—come within the concept of economic goods by virtue of the fact that they also yield consumers' satisfaction, though only indirectly, through helping to produce things that do satisfy consumers' wants directly. Let us pause for a moment to consider the meaning of this analytic device that looks so simple or even trite and was nevertheless a genuine stroke of genius"—because it makes possible the extension of "marginal utility over the whole area of production and 'distribution.'" In this way, "The whole of the organon of pure economics thus finds itself unified in the light of a single principle—in a sense in which it never had been before."

30. Schumpeter, "On the Concept of Social Value," p. 231. See also Wolfgang F. Stolper, *Joseph Alois Schumpeter: The Public Life of a Private Man* (Princeton, N.J.: Princeton University Press, 1994), p. 38; and Arnold Heertje, "Schumpeter and Methodological Individualism," *Journal of Evolutionary Economics* 14 (2004), pp. 153–156.

31. More precisely, industries with a high ratio of fixed costs to variable ones. Marginal productivity theory provided a superior method for calculating optimal volumes of outputs and mixtures of inputs (labor, capital, raw materials). The theory of marginal productivity was worked out most notably by three economists born within a few years of each other: the British scholars Alfred Marshall (born in 1842) and Philip Wicksteed (1844), and the American John Bates Clark (1847).

32. As the output of a given industrial plant—whether it is producing steel or almost anything else—nears 100 percent capacity, marginal cost curves begin to arc upward, because less efficient equipment must be used to reach 100 percent. Optimal capacity utilization in most industries is usually between about 85 and 92 percent.

33. I have simplified this example in two ways. First, average cost does not fall in a linear pattern, as in the illustration. Nor is the spreading of fixed costs necessarily a true economy of scale, as the economist Henry Carter Adams showed as early as 1887.

34. Economists came to relate this phenomenon to the "price elasticity of demand." Like equilibrium theory, the mathematics of marginalism in its early years was most easily applied to static systems. Some of the early marginalists did, however, touch on aspects of dynamic economies, although they used mathematics sparingly if at all. To Carl Menger, for example, as F. A. Hayek puts it, "economic activity is essentially planning for the future, and his discussion of the period, or

rather different periods, to which human forethought extends as regards different wants has a definitely modern ring." See Hayek's introduction to Menger, *Principles of Economics,* p. 18. But the real leap into dynamic thinking came from the next generation of theorists, particularly Schumpeter and Ludwig von Mises, who was Hayek's most important teacher.

Marginalism in general is too encompassing and complex to discuss beyond the essentials I have presented in this chapter. It involves a host of consumer and producer variables such as current possessions, budget sets, substitutes, complements, plus the whole concept of monopolistic competition. Nor is my parallel in the text between economies of scale and marginal-cost pricing strictly precise, although the two obviously have a close relationship.

35. Carnegie's achievement derived from many circumstances: large plants, very significant technological progress (first the Bessemer process, then the open-hearth system), more efficient plant design so as to accelerate flows of the product from one phase to another (minimizing the loss of heat, for example, before steel was rolled into bars and sheets), "hard-driving," (intensive use of equipment, then its rapid replacement by facilities of equal or better quality), and rigorous cost-cutting at every opportunity. Schumpeter himself later wrote about some of these measures in the section on steel in his book *Business Cycles* (New York: McGraw-Hill, 1939). A brief but vivid description of Carnegie's method is in Harold C. Livesay, *Andrew Carnegie and the Rise of Big Business* (Boston: Little Brown, 1975). An important general lesson of Carnegie's experience (also Rockefeller's in oil, Ford's in automobiles, and so on) is that increases in scale almost always require advances in technology, which often reduce marginal costs still further.

36. Of course, marginal costs can, and sometimes do, go up as well as down. During the 1960s, for example, the marginal cost of producing electricity, after having declined steadily for eighty years, suddenly began a long curve upward, because of increasing fuel costs, environmental regulations, a slowdown in the pace of technological innovation in the industry, and much higher cost for new generating plants.

At that time, the prices for kilowatt-hours charged by most utility companies to their consumers were designed in "declining-block rate structures." The more electricity a consumer used, the lower the price of each new block of kilowatt-hours. This method, by encouraging ever-increasing usage of electricity, now sent exactly the wrong message to consumers. A revolution in pricing became necessary, involving differential time-of-day pricing (to combat the peak-load problem, which was especially severe during hot summer days when businesses and householders made wide use of air conditioners), and many other adaptations.

In this new situation, the most conspicuous pioneer in promoting marginal-cost pricing of electricity was Chairman Alfred E. Kahn of the New York Public Service Commission, an academic economist (he taught at Cornell) much influenced by Schumpeter. After an intense struggle involving the education and ca-

joling of both producers and consumers of electricity, Kahn succeeded in installing a brilliantly successful new rate structure based on marginal costs. Such
structures can never be precise, but Kahn habitually asked his dubious staff
members, "Do you want to be precisely wrong or approximately right?" In the
end, Kahn's commission succeeded in radically reforming rate structures—to the
extent that the price spread for electricity in New York ranged from 30 cents per
kilowatt-hour on a hot summer day to two and one-half cents on a winter night:
a *twelve-fold* difference. Kahn argued that consumers (especially industrial and
commercial users) would respond to these price signals by employing more
energy-efficient equipment, shifting from peak to off-peak usage, and lowering
their total consumption. And that in fact is what happened. Kahn later applied
similar marginalist principles to the telecommunications industry in New York
and to the airline industry when he became chairman of the Civil Aeronautics
Board in 1977. See Thomas K. McCraw, *Prophets of Regulation: Charles Francis
Adams, Louis D. Brandeis, James M. Landis, Alfred E. Kahn* (Cambridge, Mass.:
Harvard University Press, 1984), ch. 7.

37. As Carl Menger put it, "the quantity of consumption goods at human disposal
are [sic] limited only by the extent of human knowledge," and there is "a capacity
of human needs for *infinite* growth." Quoted by Erich Streissler, "To What Extent Was the Austrian School Marginalist?" in Black, Coats, and Goodwin, eds.,
The Marginalist Revolution, p. 165.

38. In English, the titles of the articles Schumpeter wrote as a student are "International Pricing," "The Method of Index Numbers," and "The Method of Standard Population." They originated as seminar papers in courses in statistics and
economic history. Both teachers of these courses, like Schumpeter's other professors Wieser and Böhm-Bawerk, also served in the government—in their case as
successive heads of the Austrian Central Statistical Office. Each of the three papers was brief, the longest being seven pages. All appeared in *Statistische
Monatschrift,* the Austrian statistical bulletin published in Vienna. Schumpeter's
article on mathematics is *"Über die mathematische Methode der theoretischen
Ökonomie," Zeitschrift für Volkswirtschaft, Sozialpolitik und Verwaltung* 15 (1906),
pp. 30–49.

39. Wolfgang F. Stolper, "Joseph Alois Schumpeter," *Challenge* 21 (1979), p. 65.

4: MOVING OUT

1. For other accounts of the period of Schumpeter's life covered in much of this
chapter, see Richard Swedberg, *Schumpeter: A Biography* (Princeton, N.J.: Princeton University Press, 1991), pp. 13–17; and Robert Loring Allen, *Opening Doors:
The Life & Work of Joseph Schumpeter,* two vols. (New Brunswick, N.J.: Transaction, 1991), I, pp. 56–71.

2. John Maynard Keynes, *The Economic Consequences of the Peace* (New York: Harcourt, Brace and Howe, 1920), pp. 11–12; Arthur Smithies, "Memorial: Joseph Alois Schumpeter, 1883–1950," in Seymour E. Harris, ed., *Schumpeter, Social Scientist* (Cambridge, Mass.: Harvard University Press, 1951), p. 11.

3. Schumpeter to John Bates Clark, May 2 and June 6, 1907, in Ulrich Hedtke and Richard Swedberg, eds., *Joseph Alois Schumpeter, Briefe/Letters* (Tübingen: J. C. B. Mohr, Paul Siebeck, 2000), pp. 39–41.

4. Schumpeter to George Stocking, September 19, 1949, in Hedtke and Swedberg, eds., *Briefe,* p. 389.

5. Schumpeter, *History of Economic Analysis* (New York: Oxford University Press, 1954), pp. 831–832; Schumpeter treats Marshall extensively on pp. 833–840.

6. Some of Marshall's insights as a theorist, Schumpeter later wrote, "are the results of his tireless and sympathetic observation of contemporaneous business life which he understood as few academic economists ever did. In its very nature the latter achievement implies certain limitations. The practice of the middle-sized English business firm of his time no doubt absorbed a greater share of the attention of the analyst than it should have done in an exposition making large claims to generality. But within those limits a realism was attained which greatly surpasses that of Adam Smith—the only comparable instance. This may be one of the reasons why no institutionalist opposition rose against him in England." See "Alfred Marshall," in *Ten Great Economists: From Marx to Keynes* (New York: Oxford University Press, 1951), p. 94, an essay originally published in 1941.

7. Carrington & Co. to Schumpeter, August 13, 1907, Schumpeter Papers, HUG(FP)—4.7, Correspondence and other misc. papers ca. 1920s-1950, box 3, folder C 1940, HUA. By some accounts Gladys was 23 years old at this time, by others 36. See Swedberg, *Schumpeter: A Biography,* p. 253n31. Two prominent scholars may be found on opposite sides of the question: Professor Christian Seidl has evidence that Gladys was 23, while Professor Yuichi Shionoya has reproduced the marriage certificate, which lists Schumpeter's age as 24 and Gladys's as 36.

8. Over the long term, Gladys's chief contribution was improving his facility with English, which they spoke to each other wherever they were living.

9. Allen, *Opening Doors,* I, pp. 67–69.

10. The book, whose German title is *Das Wesen und der Hauptinhalt der theoretischen Nationalökonomie* (The Nature and Content of Theoretical Economics), appeared under the imprint of von Duncker and Humblot, an established Leipzig publishing firm.

11. Schumpeter, *History of Economic Analysis,* p. 850.

12. Quoted and translated by Erich Schneider, "Schumpeter's Early German Work, 1906–1917," in Harris, ed., *Schumpeter, Social Scientist,* p. 54.

13. Instead, Schumpeter continued, he believed "that there was a source of energy

within the economic system which would of itself disrupt any equilibrium that might be attained." This did not mean that he devalued Walras' work on equilibrium theory, which he continued to believe was the single greatest contribution any economist ever made to the discipline. See Schumpeter, "Preface to the Japanese edition of *The Theory of Economic Development*" (Tokyo: Iwanami Shoten, 1937), printed in Schumpeter, *Essays on Entrepreneurs, Innovation, Business Cycles, and the Evolution of Capitalism,* Richard V. Clemence, ed. (first published by Addison-Wesley, 1951, new edition by Transaction, New Brunswick, N.J. 1989, with an introduction by Richard Swedberg), p. 166. See also the three flattering letters Schumpeter wrote to Walras, a man 50 years his senior: October 9 and November 6, 1908, and June 7, 1909, in Hedtke and Swedberg, eds., *Briefe,* pp. 43, 44, 47.

14. The word "innovation" does not make its first appearance in Schumpeter's writings in English until 1928, although the idea is implicit in many of his prior works in German. See A. C. Taymans, "Tarde and Schumpeter: A Similar Vision," *Quarterly Journal of Economics* 64 (November 1950), pp. 613–615 (Taymans misdates the relevant article, "The Instability of Capitalism," as 1927). The circular flow was not original to Schumpeter. Sir William Petty and Richard Cantillon had adumbrated the idea in the seventeenth and early eighteenth centuries, and the French Physiocrats elaborated on it at length in the mid-eighteenth century.

15. John B. Clark, *Political Science Quarterly* 24 (December 1909), pp. 721–724. Schumpeter had written to Clark, with whom he had corresponded before, to say how "delighted" he was "to hear that my book will have the honor of being reviewed by you." The main purpose of the letter was to discuss revisions of an article, "On the Concept of Social Value," which Schumpeter was preparing for the *Quarterly Journal of Economics,* where it appeared in volume 23 (1909), pp. 213–232. Schumpeter to Clark, December 3, 1908. See also Schumpeter to Clark, March 25, 1909, both in Hedtke and Swedberg, eds., *Briefe,* pp. 45, 46.

16. Schumpeter, *Das Wesen und der Hauptinhalt der theoretischen Nationalökonomie,* p. vi, quoted passage translated by Benjamin Hett.

17. Schumpeter, "*Neue Erscheinungen auf dem Gebiete der Nationalökonomie,*" (Recent Publications in the Field of Economics), *Zeitschrift für Sozialpolitik und Verwaltung,* 20 (1911), p. 241; Schumpeter, "*Meinungsäusserung zur Frage des Werturteils*" (Comment on the Question of Value Judgment), in *Äusserungen zur Werturteildiskussion im Ausschuss des Vereins für Socialpolitik,* pp. 49–50, printed in Schumpeter, *Aufsätze zur Tagespolitik* (Essays on Current Policy), Christian Seidl and Wolfgang F. Stolper, eds. (Tübingen: J. C. B. Mohr, Paul Siebeck, 1993), pp. 127–128. Quoted material translated by Benjamin Hett.

18. Schumpeter, "*Die 'positive' Methode in der Nationalökonomie,*" *Deutsche Literaturzeitung* ("The 'Positive' Method in Economics," *German Literary Times*), 34, 1914, reprinted in Schumpeter, *Aufsätze zur Ökonomische Theorie* (Essays on

Economic Theory), Erich Schneider and Arthur Spiethoff, eds. (Tübingen: J. C. B. Mohr, Paul Siebeck, 1952), p. 549. First quoted passage translated by Benjamin Hett. Second quoted passage translated by Erich Schneider, "Schumpeter's Early German Work, 1906–1917," p. 58.

19. Schumpeter to the Office of the University of Vienna, October 21, 1907 (asking that his diploma certify what he had done and that it be issued in Latin), in Hedtke and Swedberg, eds., *Briefe,* p. 42; Allen, *Opening Doors,* I, ch. 5 *passim.*

20. Some of the German-speakers' ancestors had been forcibly relocated to the east in order to strengthen the Austrians' hold on the area. The founding of the German-language university in which Schumpeter taught was part of the same goal. After World War I the city became part of Romania and was renamed Cernauti. Following the Molotov-Ribbentrop negotiations, Germany forced Romania in 1940 to cede much of Bukovina to the Ukrainian Soviet Socialist Republic, which in turn was part of the Soviet Union. The Russian name for the city was Chernovtsy. These kinds of shifts were common in the aftermaths of both World Wars, with their redefinitions of national borders. Statistics on Czernowitz's changing Jewish population may be found in Peter Pulzer, *The Rise of Political Anti-Semitism in Germany & Austria* (London: Peter Halban, 1988), p. 335.

5: CAREER TAKEOFF

1. Lincoln's remarks, and their context, appear in David Herbert Donald, *Lincoln* (New York: Simon and Schuster, 1995), pp. 80–82. Giving the first strong indication of the depth of his own ambition in what became known as his Lyceum speech, Lincoln was lamenting that for the previous generations of Americans, "all that sought celebrity and fame, and distinction, expected to find them in the success of that [national] experiment," whereas Lincoln's own generation confronted the transcendent issue of slavery: "If possible, it will have [distinction], whether at the expense of emancipating slaves, or enslaving freemen."

2. Robert Loring Allen, *Opening Doors: The Life & Work of Joseph Schumpeter,* two vols. (New Brunswick, N.J.: Transaction, 1991), I, pp. 97–98. See also Gottfried Haberler, "Joseph Alois Schumpeter, 1883–1950," in Seymour E. Harris, ed., *Schumpeter, Social Scientist* (Cambridge, Mass.: Harvard University Press, 1951), p. 27.

3. Allen, *Opening Doors,* pp. 98–99. Schumpeter had taken fencing lessons as an undergraduate at the University of Vienna, but he was far from being an expert with the sword.

4. In German, the book is titled *Theorie der wirtschaftlichen Entwicklung* (Leipzig: Duncker & Humblot, 1912 [the book actually appeared in 1911]). The English translation was titled *The Theory of Economic Development* (Cambridge, Mass.: Harvard University Press, 1934). Schumpeter later said that he would have pre-

ferred "Evolution" to "Development" (*Entwicklung* can be translated either way). In academic economics, the word "development" came to be associated primarily with countries beginning to undergo economic growth, but Schumpeter had intended his book to be a universal analysis of the capitalist process. In the analysis of the book presented below, I have used for the sake of convenience primarily the English language edition, which appeared in 1934 and was based on the revised German editions of 1926 and 1931. As described later in this book, Schumpeter had much shortened the original version of *Theorie der wirtschaftlichen Entwicklung,* and he and his translator shortened the text for the English edition even more.

In Marx's writings, entrepreneurs sometimes appear as effective agents of economic growth, but as exploitative capitalists still. In *Theorie der wirtschaftlichen Entwicklung,* by contrast, Schumpeter distinguished between innovative entrepreneurs and the capitalists who supplied them with funds.

5. So "steady" was Schumpeter's theoretic state that he defined both interest and profits out of the system altogether. These assertions, though not invalid in the restricted way he stated them, came back to haunt him. Not long after the book appeared, he became involved in a conspicuous controversy with his former mentor Eugen von Böhm-Bawerk over the zero interest rate, and the controversy continued in economic writings by other authors long afterward. See, for example, Paul A. Samuelson, "Paradoxes of Schumpeter's Zero Interest Rate," *Review of Economics and Statistics* 53 (November 1971), pp. 391–392, which is itself a rejoinder to an objection by another author to a prior argument by Samuelson.

6. In his introduction to the Hungarian translation of *The Theory of Economic Development,* A. Madarász aptly observes that "the inner tension of Schumpeter's work derives from the centuries old dilemma of political economics and economic theory that is due to the relationship between abstract logical analysis and the historical and sociological approach." Madarász, "Schumpeter's *Theory of Economic Development,*" *Acta Oeconomica* 25 (1980), pp. 337–367 (this is a separate publication of the author's introduction to the Hungarian translation). Erik S. Reinert makes a similar point in "Schumpeter in the Context of Two Canons of Economic Thought," *Industry and Innovation* 9 (April/August 2002), pp. 23–39.

7. *The Theory of Economic Development,* pp. 75–78.

8. Ibid., pp. 78, 81.

9. Ibid., pp. 91–94. In "Schumpeter 1911: Farsighted Visions on Economic Development," *American Journal of Economics and Sociology* 61 (April 2002), pp. 387–403, Markus C. Becker and Thorbjorn Knudsen argue that Schumpeter accorded the entrepreneur an even more central economic role in the 1911 edition of his book than in the English translation of 1934.

10. *The Theory of Economic Development,* pp. 91–94. In other writings, Schumpeter made clear that the kind of person he was discussing was not confined to the

business world but could be present "even in a primitive tribe or in a socialist community"; Schumpeter, *Business Cycles: A Theoretical, Historical, and Statistical Analysis of the Capitalist Process,* two vols. (New York: McGraw-Hill, 1939), I, p. 223. See also Harry Dahms, "The Entrepreneur in Western Capitalism: A Sociological Analysis of Schumpeter's Theory of Economic Development," diss., New School for Social Research, 1993. An influential treatment of entrepreneurship by a later leader of the Austrian school of economics is Israel Kirzner, *Competition and Entrepreneurship* (Chicago: University of Chicago Press, 1973). An important corrective to the emphasis many writers have loosely ascribed to what they represent at Schumpeter's "heroic" entrepreneur is in Nicolò De Vecchi, trans. Anne Stone, *Entrepreneurs, Institutions and Economic Change: The Economic Thought of J. A. Schumpeter (1905–1925)* (Aldershot, U.K.: Edward Elgar, 1995). De Vecchi highlights the institutional and financial components of Schumpeter's thought. A different view is expressed in Maria T. Brouwer, "Weber, Schumpeter and [Frank] Knight on Entrepreneurship and Economic Development," *Journal of Evolutionary Economics* 12 (2002), pp. 83–105, which does ascribe Nietzchean characteristics to Schumpeter's entrepreneur.

11. *The Theory of Economic Development,* pp. 155–156. In the increasingly rich literature on family capitalism, see especially Geoffrey Jones and Mary Rose, eds., *Family Capitalism* (Philadelphia: Taylor and Francis, 1994); and Harold James, *Family Capitalism: Wendels, Haniels, Falcks, and the Continental European Model* (Cambridge, Mass.: Harvard University Press, 2006).

12. *The Theory of Economic Development,* p. 86. Many other writers have made similar points about overthrowing conventional ways of thinking. Examples are John Maynard Keynes in *The General Theory of Employment, Interest and Money* (New York: Harcourt, Brace, 1936), and Thomas Kuhn in *The Structure of Scientific Revolutions* (Chicago: University of Chicago Press, 1962). For economic institutions, the point is elaborated at length by Mancur Olson in *The Rise and Decline of Nations* (New Haven: Yale University Press, 1982).

13. *The Theory of Economic Development,* pp. 86, 87, 133.

14. Schumpeter does not mention these entrepreneurs by name. His portrait in *The Theory of Economic Development* is largely of an ideal type, not of particular individuals. This would change in his book *Business Cycles* (1939), in which he identifies numerous specific firms and entrepreneurs.

15. *The Theory of Economic Development,* p. 65.

16. Ibid., p. 66; for an example of another major scholar's use of this definition many years later, see Alfred D. Chandler, Jr., *Scale and Scope: The Dynamics of Industrial Enterprise* (Cambridge, Mass: Harvard University Press, 1990), pp. 830–831n1.

17. *The Theory of Economic Development,* pp. 66, 137. S. M. Kanbur has properly pointed out that Schumpeter's comment about risk bearing leaves out the entre-

preneur's opportunity cost; see "A Note on Risk Taking, Entrepreneurship, and Schumpeter," *History of Political Economy* 12 (Winter 1980), pp. 489–498.

18. It is true, Schumpeter adds, that the buying and selling of stocks and bonds in secondary markets (that is, among securities traders rather than between investors and entrepreneurs) receive widespread publicity, as in daily Wall Street stock quotations. But he calls these trades "intermediate maneuvers which may easily veil the fundamental thing." In actual business, "the main function of the money or capital market is trading in credit for the purpose of financing development." *The Theory of Economic Development*, pp. 126–127.

19. Ibid., pp. 116, 126. Schumpeter later commented that many readers missed this key aspect of his argument: when *The Theory of Economic Development* first appeared, "criticism was mainly directed against certain points of credit creation which have become commonplace by now. The really controversial proposition which turns on the relation of credit creation to innovation was then not discussed at all. Nor has it really been discussed since, for the arguments from the classical theory of banking to the effect of what banks finance is precisely not innovation but current commodity transactions, miss the salient point entirely." Schumpeter, *Business Cycles,* p. 109n1. Yet he had made the point clearly in the first place. The traditional doctrine of credit and banking, he writes in *The Theory of Economic Development* (p. 68), "always refers merely to saving and to the investment of the small yearly increase attributable to it. In this it asserts nothing false, but it entirely overlooks much more essential things."

For an empirical test supporting Schumpeter's proposition in *The Theory of Economic Development* that financial intermediaries are essential for technological innovation and economic growth, see Robert G. King and Ross Levine, "Finance and Growth: Schumpeter Might Be Right," *Quarterly Journal of Economics* 108 (August 1993), pp. 717–737.

20. *The Theory of Economic Development*, pp. 70–74.

21. Schumpeter, "Recent Developments of Political Economy," a lecture given in 1931 in Osaka, reprinted in ch. 5 of Richard Swedberg, ed., *Joseph A. Schumpeter: The Economics and Sociology of Capitalism* (Princeton, N.J.: Princeton University Press, 1991), p. 296. For additional analysis of Schumpeter's emphasis on money and credit in economic development, see Wolfgang F. Stolper, *Joseph Alois Schumpeter: The Public Life of a Private Man* (Princeton, N.J.: Princeton University Press, 1994), pp. 46–51 and *passim*.

When he emphasized the role of banks in economic development, Schumpeter had in mind European and especially German institutions more than British or American ones. In contrast to major British banks such as Lloyds and Baring Brothers, which invested most of their capital overseas, German banks specialized in the home market. They sometimes underwrote new domestic ventures and, much more often, provided funds for innovative companies such as the electrical giant Siemens. A few German banks evolved into very large "universal" financial houses that combined commercial banking (loans to businesses and sometimes to individuals) with investment banking (the underwriting of stocks and bonds). Examples were the Deutsche Bank and the Dresdner Bank.

Even so, in their emphasis on entrepreneurship and the creation of credit, the ideas in *The Theory of Economic Development* apply with uncanny force to the historical experience of the United States. When Schumpeter finished his book in 1911, he had not yet visited the U.S., and was less familiar with its financial system than he became later on. In the history of American capitalism, banks took a smaller role in economic development than they did in Europe, despite the prominence of individual investment houses such as J. P. Morgan and Goldman Sachs. A major reason was the extreme decentralization of the U.S. banking system, a reflection of the country's distrust of concentrated economic power and its longtime prohibition against branch banking. One reviewer of *The Theory of Economic Development,* B. M. Anderson of Harvard, noticed this point and mentioned it in his review. See Anderson, "Schumpeter's Dynamic Economics," *Political Science Quarterly* 30 (December 1915), pp. 645–660.

This did not mean that the United States was any less entrepreneurial, of course. It was the most entrepreneurial country on earth, but not because of its banks. Substantial new businesses were funded less through bank loans than through "equity" (common stock) investments by wealthy families—and, especially in the case of railroads, from "debt" (mostly in the form of bonds, which were sold all over the world). As the new companies began to grow in the hothouse atmosphere of booming American prosperity, they financed themselves mostly through retained earnings. During the late nineteenth century and the entire twentieth, the overwhelming source of corporate funds for large firms was retained earnings that were plowed back into the company for further development.

There were two important corollaries to this general pattern. The first was the vast increase during the 1970s and 1980s of the issuance of high-yield ("junk") bonds to finance development in relatively new firms. The second was the even more important role of venture capitalists in funding startup companies and providing big infusions of cash into established firms developing new products. Beginning in the 1950s and multiplying their activities in subsequent decades, venture capitalists financed hundreds of high-tech businesses, most conspicuously in California's Silicon Valley. They also underwrote numerous biotechnology companies located near major research universities throughout the country. Much of the exploding American economic growth of the 1990s derived from the investments made by venture capitalists. This was an era of extraordinary entrepreneurship, and by no coincidence the time when Schumpeter's phrase "creative destruction" came into much more common usage. A thorough analysis of the role of venture capital may be found in Paul Gompers and Joshua Lerner, *The Money of Invention: How Venture Capital Creates New Wealth* (Boston: Harvard Business School Press, 2001).

22. Because of its title, it might reasonably be inferred that *The Theory of Economic Development* had, or should have had, a powerful influence on the strategies of developing countries. This has not been the case. Schumpeter believed, as he later wrote in *Business Cycles,* that industrially advanced countries were far preferable for analyzing the capitalist process, and this was his own method. Also, as noted earlier, Schumpeter would have preferred that *Entwicklung,* in the original title, be translated as "evolution" rather than "development."

There is a modest literature on the relevance of Schumpeter's ideas to developing countries, but on the whole this work is disappointing. Two of the best articles are P. S. Laumas, "Schumpeter's Theory of Economic Development and Underdeveloped Countries," *Quarterly Journal of Economics* 76 (November 1962), pp. 653–659; and R. C. Wiles, "Professor Joseph Schumpeter and Underdevelopment," *Review of Social Economy* 25 (September 1967), pp. 196–208.

23. In 1934, Schumpeter wrote to Harvard University Press, which was about to bring out the English-language edition, that "When this book first appeared in 1911 . . . it met almost universal hostility." Schumpeter to David T. Pottinger, June 4, 1934, in Ulrich Hedtke and Richard Swedberg, eds., *Joseph Alois Schumpeter, Briefe/Letters* (Tübingen: J. C. B. Mohr, Paul Siebeck), p. 270. This was not true, and Schumpeter went on to say in this same letter that his arguments had gained influence and that the book was being translated into several other languages.

24. B. M. Anderson, "Schumpeter's Dynamic Economics"; J. B. Clark, *American Economic Review* 2 (December 1912), pp. 873–875. In his review, Anderson added that Schumpeter's "sharp contrast between the timid, static masses and the few rare, dynamic spirits, is doubtless truer of Europe than of America. The enterpriser has found much sympathy and cooperation among the mass of men with us." Overall, Anderson judged Schumpeter to have done a great service: "The economist has too long been content with static theory," and Schumpeter's emphasis on constant change "is full of significance for the better understanding of economic life." Anderson did chide Schumpeter for writing a treatise about economic *evolution* while failing to mention Charles Darwin and Herbert Spencer.

25. Alvin Hansen, *Journal of Political Economy* 44 (August 1936), pp. 560–563.

26. For reflections on both *The Theory of Economic Development* and Schumpeter's general influence, see John E. Elliott, "Schumpeter and the Theory of Capitalist Economic Development," *Journal of Economic Behavior and Organization* 4 (December 1983), pp. 277–308.

27. Christian Seidl, "Joseph Alois Schumpeter: Character, Life and Particulars of His Graz Period," in Seidl, ed., *Lectures on Schumpeterian Economics* (Berlin:

Springer-Verlag, 1984), pp. 193–195 [cited hereafter as Seidl, "Schumpeter's Graz Period"]; see also Allen, *Opening Doors,* I, pp. 117–119.

28. Seidl, "Schumpeter's Graz Period," p. 194. The translation is Seidl's.

29. Ibid., pp. 193–195; Allen, *Opening Doors,* I, pp. 117–119.

30. Seidl, "Schumpeter's Graz Period," pp. 193–195; Allen, *Opening Doors,* I, pp. 117–119.

31. Schumpeter to John Bates Clark, March 10, 1912, in Hedtke and Swedberg, eds., *Briefe,* pp. 48–49.

32. Seidl, "Schumpeter's Graz Period," pp. 195–196; Allen, *Opening Doors,* I, pp. 123–127.

33. Seidl, "Schumpeter's Graz Period," p. 196; Allen, *Opening Doors,* I, pp. 123–127.

34. Allen, *Opening Doors,* I, pp. 125–127.

35. The following account of Schumpeter's sojourn in the United States is based primarily on Allen, *Opening Doors,* I, pp. 129–135.

36. Seligman to Nicholas Murray Butler, quoted in Allen, *Opening Doors,* I, p. 130.

37. Schumpeter to Seligman, November 23, 1913. Despite Seligman's initial enthusiasm for Schumpeter, he soon grew to dislike him. As he wrote to Frank Fetter of Princeton, "between ourselves, if I were you I should not think of putting up with a bore like him for two days [on a proposed train trip]. We are by this time absolutely disgusted with him." Seligman to Fetter, December 19, 1913. Both letters are printed in Hedtke and Swedberg, eds., *Briefe,* pp. 53–54.

38. Schumpeter, "The United States of America in Politics and Culture," *Neue Freie Presse,* October 21, 1919, in Schumpeter, *Aufsätze zur Tagespolitik* [Essays on Current Policy], eds. Christian Seidl and Wolfgang F. Stolper (Tübingen: J. C. B. Mohr, Paul Siebeck, 1993), pp. 128–132. See also Schumpeter, *Capitalism, Socialism and Democracy* (New York: Harper & Brothers, 1942), p. 331; and Felix Somary, trans. A. J. Sherman, *The Raven of Zürich: The Memoirs of Felix Somary* (New York: St. Martin's Press, 1986), p. 34.

39. Schumpeter to Hollander, November 11, 1913, Jacob Harry Hollander Papers, Ms. 59, Special Collections, Milton S. Eisenhower Library, The Johns Hopkins University.

40. Schumpeter to Fetter, March 21, 1914, quoted in Allen, *Opening Doors,* I, pp. 131–134. On the same day, he sent similar letters to others he had visited. To Jacob Hollander of Johns Hopkins, he wrote, "I leave America a confirmed admirer of the men as well as the methods of your universities and I am afraid that I shall feel never again as happy as a teacher and as a colleague as I have here." Schumpeter to Hollander, March 21, 1914, Jacob Harry Hollander Papers, Ms. 59, Special Collections, Milton S. Eisenhower Library, The Johns Hopkins University.

6: WAR AND POLITICS

1. Of the numerous histories of World War I, some of the most readable and important are Barbara Tuchman, *The Guns of August* (New York: Bantam Books,

1976); Paul Fussell, *The Great War and Modern Memory* (Oxford: Oxford University Press, 1989); Hanson W. Baldwin, *World War I: An Outline History* (London: Hutchinson, 1963); John Keegan, *The First World War* (New York: Knopf, 1999); David Stevenson, *Cataclysm: The First World War as Political Tragedy* (New York, Basic Books, 2004), and Hew Strachan, *The First World War* (New York: Viking, 2004). See also the profusely illustrated *World War I*, by Susanne Everett, introduction by John Keegan (London: Hamlyn, 1980).

2. Even though Germany's many constituent parts included important old states such as Prussia, Saxony, and Bavaria, the German Empire (Second *Reich,* the first *Reich* being the Holy Roman Empire) was unified only in 1871. For statistics on production, see Jeffrey Fear, "German Capitalism," in Thomas K. McCraw, ed., *Creating Modern Capitalism: How Entrepreneurs, Companies, and Countries Triumphed in Three Industrial Revolutions* (Cambridge, Mass.: Harvard University Press, 1997), p. 141.

3. Italy changed sides and entered the war in 1915 as a member of the Allies.

4. See in particular Keegan, *The First World War,* and Stevenson, *Cataclysm: The First World War as Political Tragedy.*

5. Karen Barkey and Mark von Hagen, eds., *After Empire: Multiethnic Societies and Nation Building. The Soviet Union and the Russian, Ottoman, and Habsburg Empires* (Boulder, Col.: Westview Press, 1997). On the Middle Eastern settlement, see David Fromkin, *A Peace to End All Peace: Creating the Modern Middle East* (New York: Henry Holt, 1989).

6. Baldwin, *World War I: An Outline History,* pp. 156–157; Everett, *World War I,* p. 249; John Horne, ed., *State, Society and Mobilization in Europe during the First World War* (Cambridge: Cambridge University Press, 1997). István Deák, *Beyond Nationalism: A Social and Political History of the Habsburg Officer Corps* (New York: Oxford University Press, 1990), gives slightly lower figures for casualties and takes due note of the Magyar-speaking as well as the German-speaking officer corps.

7. Helmut Gruber, *Red Vienna: Experiment in Working-Class Culture, 1919–1934* (New York: Oxford University Press, 1991).

8. Gladys Schumpeter to Hollander, November 16, 1915, Jacob Harry Hollander Papers, Ms. 59, Special Collections, Milton S. Eisenhower Library, The Johns Hopkins University.

9. Hollander to Gladys Schumpeter, December 6, 1915; Hollander to Joseph Schumpeter, December 7, 1915; Joseph Schumpeter to Hollander, January 7, 1916 [typewritten copy]; Gladys Schumpeter to Hollander, January 16, 1916; Hollander to Gladys Schumpeter, February 21, 1916 (forwarding Joseph Schumpeter's letter); all in ibid.

10. Robert Loring Allen, *Opening Doors: The Life & Work of Joseph Schumpeter,* two vols. (New Brunswick, N.J.: Transaction, 1991), I, p. 139.

11. On the proposed journal and other options, see Schumpeter to Paul Siebeck, May 14, 1916, June 16 (two letters), August 5, 1916, and August 10, 1916. In the last letter Schumpeter agrees to become co-editor of an existing journal. See Ulrich Hedtke and Richard Swedberg, eds., *Joseph Alois Schumpeter, Briefe/Letters* (Tübingen: J. C. B. Mohr, Paul Siebeck, 2000), pp. 61–71.

One example of his pleas for tolerance appears in Schumpeter, "*Die 'positive' Methode in der Nationalökonomie*" (The "Positive" Method in Economics), *Deutsche Literaturzeitung* 35 (1914), pp. 2101–08.

The assignment to write the book on the history of economic thought had come from the great German scholar Max Weber, the book appearing as volume one of a series Weber edited on the foundations of sociology and economics. Many years later, it formed part of the basis for Schumpeter's masterly *History of Economic Analysis,* which, at about 800,000 words, was the longest of all his works. Weber's series was *Grundriss der Sozialökonomik* (Foundations of Social Economics). Schumpeter's contribution is titled *Epochen der Dogmen- und Methodengeschichte* (Tübingen: J. C. B. Mohr, 1914). For details of the writing of this book, see Schumpeter to the publishing company, September 18, 1912, in Hedtke and Swedberg, eds., *Briefe,* pp. 49–51. Forty years after its initial appearance, the book was translated into English by R. Aris and published as *Economic Doctrine and Method: An Historical Sketch* (New York: Oxford University Press, 1954).

12. In one of his two letters to Siebeck of June 16, 1916, Schumpeter lays out what amounts to a long-term plan, and asks Siebeck's advice. This important letter is extremely candid about Schumpeter's interests and intentions (translation by Benjamin Hett):

> The "literary" situation in which I find myself is the following: above all two great works (along with the running work of articles etc.) must be taken care of, which in the framework of "complete works" have been firmly promised and are already bound in every respect. After and among these I want to work further on the subjects of my deepest interest, on which I can perhaps speak another time. But third works come to me in connection with teaching and other activities, which are rather lost labor in the auditoriums within and without the university which Graz and even Vienna have to offer, and by the presentation of which I often regret that they cannot be made accessible to a wider circle, above all since in their form they would really be suitable for such an audience. Thus the idea comes to me to work them up by and by and to publish them. They are the following:
>
> > 1.) for the sake of completeness I mention our plan [already underway] of the complete publication of an outline of the intellectual

history, which would come into consideration as soon as I have
held a colloquium on the subject.

2.) I have presented in lectures and speeches sketches of a money-
theory and currency-policy work, which have been published
nowhere . . . thus in one volume the most important theoretical,
practical, legal questions of money and the nature of credit at the
present day.

3.) years ago I began to work on the problem of social classes, then I
presented my theory of social classes in Czernowitz and New York
in lectures. Now I have come back to it and am holding a colloquium on it this semester. This work could be brought to a provisional close in a few months and likewise published in a volume of
15–20 quires.

4.) To the things that most "hold" me belong parts of my financial
lectures, which the listeners always like and perhaps would be suit-
able for publication because of their liveliness and current interest—likewise in a small volume with the title "Lectures on Financial Policy."

5.) the elements of a sociological history of political ideas have assembled around me, which could also form a whole work, and which
I would gladly free from the prison of a colloquium volume.

6.) My speeches on the most various subjects, which always disappear
into the abyss of nothingness although I am always concerned to
bring my thoughts out in them and they always have success in
the auditorium, would fill about two volumes, one on subjects
concerning the woman question, and one de omnibus rebus et
quibusdam aliis, whereby the wish for publication may be excused
by the fact that they all cost me so much work . . .

If the gods treat me well, I could, since the main work on all subjects
has been done, probably from 1918 on (because the coming year will
probably be rather lost to me because of the deanship) take care of one
such volume per year, but interruptions for pressingly necessary experi-
mental-psychological and other studies must be reckoned with.

I have still not spoken to anyone about these plans (and I ask for discretion), neither to colleagues nor to publishers."

Siebeck's response, in a long letter dated July 1, 1916, is encouraging as to
Siebeck's own interest in publishing the proposed volumes, and full of advice on
the sequence of publication of the several projects. Both letters are in the
Schumpeter Papers, HUG(FP)—4.7, Correspondence and other misc. papers,
ca. 1920s-1950 [sic], box 8, folder Mohr-Siebeck, HUA. The long letter of July 1,

1916 from Schumpeter to Siebeck is published in Hedtke and Swedberg, eds., *Briefe,* pp. 64–71.

13. Allen, *Opening Doors,* I, p. 145.

14. Schumpeter to Count Otto von Harrach, January 25, 1916, printed in Schumpeter, *Politische Reden* (Political Addresses), eds. Christian Seidl and Wolfgang F. Stolper (Tübingen: J. C. B. Mohr, Paul Siebeck, 1992), pp. 361–363. The translated portions of the letter are from Wolfgang F. Stolper, *Joseph Alois Schumpeter: The Public Life of a Private Man* (Princeton, N.J.: Princeton University Press, 1994), p. 189.

15. Schumpeter to Count Otto von Harrach, February 1, 1916, in Schumpeter, *Politische Reden* (Political Addresses), eds. Seidl and Stolper, p. 364, translation by Christopher Hall. Schumpeter wrote at least 12 letters to Harrach, all of which are published in *Politische Reden.* He addresses Harrach as "Your Illustriousness," and then refers to a Habsburg prince as "His Radiance"—marks of contemporary aristocratic custom.

16. Stolper, *Joseph Alois Schumpeter,* pp. 268–269n3 provides an overview of the movement for unification with Germany as it evolved during the first third of the twentieth century.

17. Schumpeter to Count Otto von Harrach, January 25, 1916, translated in Stolper, *Joseph Alois Schumpeter,* p. 190. Similar letters to Harrach, dated February 1, 1916; January 14, February 9, May 7, June 25, July 6, 1917; and February 7 and 19, 1918; all are printed in the original German in Hedtke and Swedberg, eds., *Briefe,* pp. 55–59, 71–72, 74–81, 82, and 84. See also Schumpeter to Angelo Franz Viktor Eisner von Eisenhof, January 14, 1917, in ibid., pp. 72–74.

18. Schumpeter to Lammasch, February 21, 1916, translated in Stolper, *Joseph Alois Schumpeter,* p. 173, and printed in the original German in Hedtke and Swedberg, eds., *Briefe,* pp. 59–61. See also Allen, *Opening Doors,* I, pp. 152–153.

19. This memorandum is printed in Schumpeter, *Aufsätze zur Wirtschaftspolitik* (Essays on Economic Policy), eds. Christian Seidl and Wolfgang F. Stolper (Tübingen: J. C. B. Mohr, Paul Siebeck, 1985), pp. 251–272. The quoted phrase is on p. 271.

20. The second memo is printed in Schumpeter, *Aufsätze zur Wirtschaftspolitik* (Essays on Economic Policy), eds. Seidl and Stolper, pp. 272–289. The translated passages appear in Stolper, *Joseph Alois Schumpeter,* pp. 180–181.

21. Schumpeter to Count Otto von Harrach, May 7, 1917, in Schumpeter, *Politische Reden* (Political Addresses), eds. Seidl and Stolper, p. 368. Translation by Christopher Hall.

22. Stolper, *Joseph Alois Schumpeter,* p. 179n22. Stolper was himself a student and longtime friend of Schumpeter's; Schumpeter to Count Otto von Harrach, July 16, 1917, in Schumpeter, *Politische Reden* (Political Addresses), eds. Seidl and Stolper, p. 372. Translation by Christopher Hall.

23. See, for example, Schumpeter to Otto von Harrach, February 9, 1917: "We can

perhaps succeed in making this publication the leading one in Austria and of thus creating an instrument that rides the crest of the times, and can fulfill the great task of using the modern technique of mastering public opinion to serve old Austrian ideas and interests . . . The audience—and with it the circle of influence—of the paper must extend from bishop to businessman. It must offer them all as much information as any other, in order to be able to serve the further aim of carrying conservative views bit by bit into circles where they have been unfamiliar until now . . . The specifically Catholic viewpoint must be emphasized throughout, something which can only be beneficial to the success of the paper, since this viewpoint often exists latently in the Austrians' subconscious, even where it does not explicitly emerge. And this paper could pave the way for a successful government policy." See Schumpeter, *Politische Reden* (Political Addresses), eds. Seidl and Stolper, pp. 366–367. Translation by Christopher Hall and Alison Fleig Frank. Other letters to Harrach on the same subject, dated June 4, 1917 and February 19, 1918, are printed in the same book, pp. 369–370 and 374–375.

24. The third memo, which unlike the first two has a title ("The Political Situation and the Interests of the Monarchy"), is printed in Schumpeter, *Aufsätze zur Wirtschaftspolitik* (Essays on Economic Policy), eds. Seidl and Stolper, pp. 289–310. All three of Schumpeter's memoranda are analyzed in Stolper, *Joseph Alois Schumpeter,* pp. 177–188, and the passage quoted in this paragraph is on p. 184. Schumpeter used contacts such as Count Otto von Harrach to get his memo into the hands of the Foreign Minister. See Schumpeter to Harrach, May 7 and May 17, 1917, in Schumpeter, *Politische Reden* (Political Addresses), eds. Seidl and Stolper, p. 368.

25. Schumpeter's comments about the United States' reasons for entering the war were published in his newspaper article, "The United States of America in Politics and Culture," *Neue Freie Presse,* October 20, 1919, printed in Schumpeter, *Aufsätze zur Tagespolitik* (Essays on Current Policy), eds. Christian Seidl and Wolfgang F. Stolper (Tübingen: J. C. B. Mohr, Paul Siebeck, 1993), p. 132. Translation by Christopher Hall and Alison Fleig Frank.

26. Schumpeter to Count Otto von Harrach, June 25, 1917 and February 7, 1918: "Only the coronation in Prague, adequate concessions toward the South Slavs, and a very decisive posture toward the German Reich can save the situation; and the stimulus to do so can only come from the conservative party and from a conservative government." See Schumpeter, *Politische Reden* (Political Addresses), eds. Seidl and Stolper, pp. 370–371 (first letter), pp. 373–374 (second letter); Schumpeter worried about the behavior of Parliament and the press: "We have created these democratic institutions," he wrote in still another letter to Harrach on July 6, 1917, "but in contrast to English society we do not understand how to use them," ibid., p. 371. Translations by Christopher Hall. See also Schumpeter

to Angelo Franz Viktor Eisner von Eisenhof, January 14, 1917; February 2 and 8; and August 22, 1918 for additional political opinions and maneuverings, all printed in Hedtke and Swedberg, eds., *Briefe*, pp. 72–74, 81–83, and 85–86. Other useful information is in Allen, *Opening Doors*, I, pp. 154–155; and Stolper, *Joseph Alois Schumpeter*, pp. 173–174.

27. Redlich is quoted in Christian Seidl, "Joseph Alois Schumpeter: Character, Life and Particulars of His Graz Period," in Seidl, ed., *Lectures on Schumpeterian Economics* (Berlin: Springer-Verlag, 1984), pp. 203–204. Translation by Seidl.

28. Felix Somary, trans. A. J. Sherman, *The Raven of Zürich: The Memoirs of Felix Somary* (New York: St. Martin's Press, 1986), pp. 120–121.

29. Schumpeter also wrote a second seminal piece at about the same time, which is also still taught in universities. Called "The Sociology of Imperialisms," it covers 98 printed pages in English translation, and was republished in 1955 in a small book, together with a second piece on social classes, for use in university courses. See *Imperialism, Social Classes: Two Essays by Joseph Schumpeter*, trans. Heinz Norden (New York: Meridian Books, 1955). The discussion below is based primarily on pp. 23–54, 73, and 89. See also Richard Swedberg, *Schumpeter: A Biography* (Princeton, N.J.: Princeton University Press, 1991), pp. 98–102.

In "The Sociology of Imperialisms," Schumpeter argues that capitalism is fundamentally anti-imperialist, a statement that went against the received wisdom of the time—including the orthodox Marxist interpretation—and is still hotly debated. In one passage that he chose to italicize, Schumpeter writes: *"It is a basic fallacy to describe imperialism as a necessary phase of capitalism, or even to speak of the development of capitalism into imperialism."*

He roots his argument in a careful reading of history, noting that imperialism had appeared in several different forms—hence the plural "imperialisms" in his title. His analysis begins with the recent British and German empires, then ranges backward to those of ancient powers such as Persia, Egypt, and Rome. These old empires were so constituted that they could not support themselves at home. They therefore raided and annexed other areas in expeditions of plunder designed to keep their domestic economies going. Once underway, "The policy of conquest inevitably led to situations that compelled further conquests." It ended only at the point where the expanding power overreached itself, its territories becoming too far-flung to administer.

By contrast, Schumpeter argues, a capitalist economy operates in exactly the opposite way. Its preoccupation with entrepreneurship and credit leaves little time and no taste for military adventurism. (He discounts familiar arguments that colonial powers used their empires to lock in supplies of raw materials and provide captive markets.) Capitalism's superior productivity generates more than enough goods and services for the home market, and a successful capitalist country is much more likely to export to other societies than to raid them.

Most recent research has confirmed the basics of Schumpeter's analysis, at least on the narrow issue that colonies usually cost the home country more in administrative and defense expenses than they bring in as revenue-producers. Of course, economic cost-benefit analysis does not address the questions of national hubris and rivalrous empire-building. Nor can it say much about policymakers' perceptions. Contests based on relative prestige and military advantage had been hallmarks of the imperial adventures of France, Germany, and Britain throughout the long buildup to World War I. In a later (1946) commentary on the connection between capitalism and imperialism, Schumpeter wrote, of the view that he himself opposed, that even though the objections to it are obvious, "three points, however, must be recorded in its favour": it is a thorough theory, taking in "the whole of the economic, political, and cultural pattern" since 1898, the year in which the United States itself embarked on imperialistic adventures in connection with the Spanish-American war; second, it is superficially "verified" by events, i.e., the imperialistic behavior of powerful capitalist countries; and "third, whatever may be wrong with its facts and interpretations, it certainly starts from a fact that is beyond challenge, the tendency toward industrial combination and the emergence of largest scale concerns." That is, imperialism had increased along with the development of big businesses and their quest for markets abroad, even as their home countries closed their own markets. But despite these trends of the first half of the twentieth century, Schumpeter had not changed his mind. And the rise of free trade and "globalization" during the second half of the century supports his original views. See Schumpeter, "Capitalism," in *Encyclopaedia Britannica* (New York: Encyclopaedia Britannica, 1946), pp. 801–887, reprinted in Richard V. Clemence, ed., *Joseph A. Schumpeter: Essays on Entrepreneurs, Innovations, Business Cycles, and the Evolution of Capitalism* (Cambridge, Mass.: Addison-Wesley, 1951), pp. 189–210. The quoted passage is on p. 197.

30. Schumpeter, "The Crisis of the Tax State," in Richard Swedberg, ed., *The Economics and Sociology of Capitalism* (Princeton, N.J.: Princeton University Press, 1991), pp. 100–101. A more descriptive title of this essay would be "The Management of Taxes in a Capitalist Economy, with Special Reference to the Current Austrian War Crisis." It originated as a lecture to the Sociological Society of Vienna, and first appeared in print in 1918. In the piece, Schumpeter gives due credit to the sociologist Rudolf Goldscheid for having "laid proper stress on this way of looking at fiscal history: to have broadcast the truth that 'the budget is the skeleton of the state stripped of all misleading ideologies.'"

31. Ibid., pp. 99, 113.

32. Ibid., pp. 114–116.

33. As Schumpeter saw the Austrian dilemma as of 1918, the fiscal "crisis" of his title would come in a predictable sequence. First the war itself would overwhelm Austria's finances. Meanwhile, its politics would disintegrate because of Czech, Serbian, and Hungarian nationalisms, and the resulting political ferment would feed

anti-capitalist movements. For Austria to get on with any kind of normal existence would require the rebuilding of its economy and the discharge of its war debts. The government would have to spend huge sums "for disablement payments, demobilization cost, reconstruction of devastated areas, and war damage compensation proper." Ibid., pp. 117–120.

34. Ibid., pp. 120–131.

35. Ibid., pp. 122–125.

36. The Commission was chaired by the well-known socialist Karl Kautsky. Felix Somary reported that "Hilferding often told me of his astonishment at Schumpeter's radicalism [in the Socialization Commission]; but Schumpeter was not radical at all, he merely followed through to the appropriate conclusions, given the premises. He felt that if socialism were to be introduced at the end of the war, it should be in a consistent way." See Somary, *The Raven of Zurich*, p. 120.

According to Schumpeter's Harvard colleague Gottfried Haberler, he liked to joke of his role: "If a man wants to commit suicide, it is a good thing if a doctor is present." But one of his fellow members of the Socialization Commission later wrote that this remark did not characterize his behavior at all.

> Certainly Schumpeter's presence added much brilliance and interest to our internal discussions and our very informal conversations outside the Committee Room. In fact Schumpeter sided mostly with the more extreme propagators of immediate and integral socialization, i.e., more with Lederer who, at that time, was rather radical and doctrinaire . . . as against Hilferding, who—as always on practical matters—was more compromising and willing to yield to the arguments of his opponents. In a private conversation with Schumpeter and some other members, after the official close of a session, I expressed a certain surprise about his position, whereupon he answered: "I don't know whether or not Socialism is a practical possibility, but I am convinced that it is impossible if not applied integrally. At any rate, it will be a[n] interesting experiment to try it out."

See Theodor H. Vogelstein, "Joseph A. Schumpeter and the *Sozialisierungskommission:* An Annotation to Gottfried Haberler's Memoir of Schumpeter," unpublished memo, n.d., quoted in Allen, *Opening Doors,* I, p. 180, notes 3 and 4. See also Stolper, *Joseph Alois Schumpeter,* ch. 11.

37. Bauer, one of the top leaders of the Social Democratic Party, also headed the Austrian Socialization Commission, which was patterned on the German model. Karl Renner once again led the Austrian government after World War II.

38. For an interpretation of Schumpeter's tenure as Finance Minister, see Eduard März, *Joseph Schumpeter: Scholar, Teacher and Politician* (New Haven: Yale University Press, 1991), ch. 9.

39. See Wolfgang F. Stolper, *Joseph Alois Schumpeter,* pp. 255–256. Stolper goes on to say that the plan in all its details "is vintage Schumpeter. It recognizes facts as they are, not as he would like them to be: there is no ideological bias in his solutions . . . [It] is vintage Schumpeter also in taking a developmental view based on a long-term analysis . . . The plan stresses the intimate connection between fiscal and monetary policy which at the time was certainly not common." Its provisions in many ways resembled the enlightened policies that were followed under American and British sponsorship years later in Germany and Japan, the losers of World War II.

40. For a further discussion of the *Finanzplan* and of the pseudo-scandals that dogged Schumpeter, see Stolper, *Joseph Alois Schumpeter,* pp. 217–293. Stolper provides a few more details in "Schumpeter's Ministerial Days," *History of Economic Ideas* 3 (1995), pp. 93–103.

41. *Neue Freie Presse,* April 14, 1919, in Schumpeter, *Politische Reden* (Political Addresses), eds. Seidl and Stolper, p. 42. The furnace comment comes from Vienna newspaper reports of March 21, 1919, quoted in Allen, *Opening Doors,* I, p. 171. The newspapers may have taken this quotation from a speech Schumpeter had made to the Sociological Society of Vienna and published in 1918. The wording is similar to phrases Schumpeter used in the article deriving from this speech, which is reprinted as "The Crisis of the Tax State," in Swedberg, ed., *The Economics and Sociology of Capitalism,* pp. 125–126. Many of Schumpeter's speeches and newspaper articles, along with public reports about his tenure in the finance ministry and as a banker, have been published in German in three volumes edited by Christian Seidl and Wolfgang F. Stolper: *Aufsätze zur Wirtschaftspolitik* (Essays on Economic Policy) (1985), *Politische Reden* (Political Addresses) (1992), and *Aufsätze zur Tagespolitik* (Essays on Current Policy) (1993). All were published in Tübingen: J. C. B. Mohr, Paul Siebeck.

42. See Stolper, *Joseph Alois Schumpeter,* pp. 18–20; and März, *Joseph Schumpeter: Scholar, Teacher and Politician,* pp. 151–163.

43. On May 31, 1919, Bauer wrote to Chancellor Karl Renner, "I shall do nothing for the time being, but after the conclusion of the peace treaty it will be inevitable to force [Schumpeter's] resignation." See März, *Joseph Schumpeter: Scholar, Teacher and Politician,* p. 157. A balanced account of the disagreements between Schumpeter and Bauer appeared in the *Neue Freie Presse,* October 9, 1919; an anti-Schumpeter version was published in another (socialist) newspaper, *Arbeiter Zeitung,* October 10, 1919. Both are printed in Schumpeter, *Politische Reden* (Political Addresses), eds. Seidl and Stolper, pp. 273–277. See also Christian Seidl, "The Bauer-Schumpeter Controversy on Socialization," *History of Economic Ideas* 2 (1994), pp. 41–69. Schumpeter's comment about the wishes of the population toward unification with Germany appear in Schumpeter to Victor E. Heller, April 30, 1943, printed in Hedtke and Swedberg, eds., *Briefe,* p. 342. On the dreadful food situation in Vienna during the war, see Maureen Healy, *Vienna*

and the Fall of the Habsburg Empire: Total War and Everyday Life in World War I (Cambridge: Cambridge University Press, 2004), especially ch. 1.

44. Among its other provisions, the Treaty of St. Germain (signed on September 10, 1919), which was the counterpart of the Treaty of Versailles that pertained specifically to Austria, greatly weakened the economic viability of Austria. As the Austrian delegation commented on the draft treaty, "What remains of German Austria could not live. Our territory would merely consist of Alpine districts and the Capital, Vienna, which with its two million inhabitants out of a total of six million, suffers far more than any other part of the Empire by its separation from the rest of the former Monarchy. This new State could only produce one-quarter of the food necessary for its population; the other three-quarters would have to be imported from abroad; it would moreover be obliged to purchase 12,000,000 tons of coal abroad each year, while its own output would not even amount to 2,000,000 tons." See Karl R. Stadler, *Austria* (London: Ernest Benn, 1971), p. 117. The quoted letter was written by Gustav Stolper and is quoted in Allen, *Opening Doors*, I, pp. 178–179. Stolper later became one of Schumpeter's closest friends.

45. Wieser's diary entries of March 15, March 19, and May 30, 1919, printed in Schumpeter, *Politische Reden* (Political Addresses), eds. Seidl and Stolper, pp. 10–11. Translation by Christopher Hall. See also Stolper, *Joseph Alois Schumpeter,* p. 293. In May, 1919, Ignaz Seipel, a prominent anti-unification conservative politician, wrote to Heinrich Lammasch, "I am in close contact with Schumpeter, who is very brave" in opposing Otto Bauer. Quoted in März, *Joseph Schumpeter: Scholar, Teacher and Politician,* p. 155.

46. See Fromkin, *A Peace to End All Peace: Creating the Modern Middle East, 1914–1922.*

47. Stolper, *Joseph Alois Schumpeter,* pp. 221, 233, 240, 247, 263n.

48. Poland's final borders were not settled for a few more years. In the case of Yugoslavia, the initial name of the new country was the Kingdom of the Serbs, Croats and Slovenes. Parliamentary debates became so divisive that in 1928 a Serbian member shot and killed the leader of the Croat Peasant Party. Partly in response to this event, King Alexander in 1928 proposed to rename the country the Kingdom of Yugoslavia (which means Land of the South Slavs). In 1934 Croat nationalists assassinated King Alexander.

49. Under the terms of the treaty, unification of Austria with Germany was not forbidden outright, but it had to be done with the approval of the League of Nations, which was a very unlikely prospect.

7: GRAN RIFIUTO

1. Schumpeter, "Should the Reserve Bank Be Established?" *Die Börse,* September 21, 1922, in Schumpeter, *Aufsätze zur Tagespolitik* (Essays on Current Policy), eds.

Christian Seidl and Wolfgang F. Stolper (Tübingen: J. C. B. Mohr, Paul Siebeck, 1993), pp. 53–54. Translation by Christopher Hall. In these remarks, Schumpeter was commenting on the role of central banks, and one of his points was that a stronger reserve bank, while essential, could not begin to do the entire job. The article as a whole anticipates many of the complex developmental issues of the 1990s that beset the post-communist Russian economy and other Eastern Bloc countries undergoing "shock therapy."

2. On the Berlin offer, see Schumpeter to Max Apt, August 24 and November 24, 1919, and June 29 and July 28, 1920; and Schumpeter to Arthur Spiethoff, September 2, 1921, all in Ulrich Hedtke and Richard Swedberg, eds., *Joseph Alois Schumpeter, Briefe/Letters* (Tübingen: J. C. B. Mohr, Paul Siebeck, 2000), pp. 89–91, 94.

   Two of the best sources on Schumpeter's activities during the 1919–1925 period, apart from the primary material cited in this chapter, are Wolfgang F. Stolper, *Joseph Alois Schumpeter: The Public Life of a Private Man* (Princeton, N.J.: Princeton University Press, 1994), chs. 20 and 21; and Robert Loring Allen, *Opening Doors: The Life & Work of Joseph Schumpeter* (New Brunswick, N.J.: Transaction, 1991), I, ch. 10.

3. For related correspondence, see Schumpeter to Finance Councillor Berman, February 13, 1921, and Schumpeter to Arthur Spiethoff, September 2, 1921, both in Hedtke and Swedberg, eds., *Briefe*, pp. 92–95.

4. Allen, *Opening Doors*, I, pp. 184–186.

5. "Conversation with Former State Secretary Dr. Schumpeter," *Die Börse*, November 11, 1920, in Schumpeter, *Aufsätze zur Tagespolitik* (Essays on Current Policy), eds. Seidl and Stolper, pp. 20–22, translation by Christopher Hall. Allen, *Opening Doors*, I, p. 186. Stolper, *Joseph Alois Schumpeter*, p. 307n3, gives a breakdown of shareholdings for the Biedermann Bank as of 1923, showing that the businessman Gottfried Kumwalt, who was closely connected to the conservative Christian Social political party, was the largest stockholder, with 95,000 shares. Schumpeter had probably received about 25,000 shares as part of the compensation for his concession, and by 1923 had acquired an additional 65,000 from his earnings. The third largest stockholder, with 85,000 shares, was the Anglo-Austrian Bank, an affiliate of the Bank of England and likely the most reliable source of cash for the Biedermann Bank. Artur Klein was fourth, with 76,000 shares.

6. Schumpeter himself wrote a somewhat technical contemporary piece about this subject. See Schumpeter, "Procedural Difficulties Raise the Costs of the Banking Business," *Die Börse*, October 23, 1924, printed in Schumpeter, *Aufsätze zur Tagespolitik* (Essays on Current Policy), eds. Seidl and Stolper, pp. 60–63.

   In a subsequent analysis, Schumpeter wrote that "It is generally known how this [type of inflation] accounts for a period of sham prosperity, during which peace and order were substantially preserved and much suffering avoided, mitigated, or deferred *at the expense of the holders of [depreciated] crowns or of claims payable in crowns.*" See Schumpeter, "The Currency Situation in Austria," in United States Senate, Commission of Gold and Silver Inquiry, Foreign Currency and Exchange Investigation Serial 9, *European Currency and Finance* (1925), printed in Schumpeter, *Aufsätze zur Tagespolitik* (Essays on Current Policy), eds. Seidl and Stolper, pp. 63–70; the quotation is on p. 64. On the experience of the Deutsche Bank, see David A. Moss, "The Deutsche Bank," in Thomas K. McCraw, ed., *Creating Modern Capitalism: How Entrepreneurs, Companies, and Countries Triumphed in Three Industrial Revolutions* (Cambridge, Mass.: Harvard University Press, 1997), p. 243.

7. Allen, *Opening Doors,* I, pp. 186–187.

8. "Bank President Schumpeter—The Girardi [a contemporary comedic singer/actor] of the Financial World," *Die Börse,* April 28, 1921, in Schumpeter, *Aufsätze zur Tagespolitik* (Essays on Current Policy), eds. Seidl and Stolper, p. 17. Translation by Christopher Hall and Alison Fleig Frank.

9. Shortly before, he had written that Austria had "retrieved itself from the situation of two years ago, and while safe harbor is not yet within reach, it is within sight." Schumpeter, "Recapitalization and Monetary Value Policy," *Neue Freie Presse,* January 30, 1924, in Schumpeter, *Aufsätze zur Tagespolitik* (Essays on Current Policy), eds. Seidl and Stolper, p. 55. Translation by Christopher Hall.

10. Stolper, *Joseph Alois Schumpeter,* p. 307. In 1926, two years after Schumpeter's departure, the Biedermann Bank itself ceased operations, ending 133 years of doing business. According to Stolper, the bank "did *not* go bankrupt, the difference being that all creditors were eventually paid in full." Schumpeter's comment about his own repayments is quoted in Stolper, p. 317, and Stolper's own remark about honor on p. 315n22.

11. See "A Lawsuit against the Former Finance Minister Dr. Schumpeter," *Neue Freie Presse,* July 11, 1925, in Schumpeter, *Aufsätze zur Tagespolitik* (Essays on Current Policy), eds. Seidl and Stolper, pp. 95–96. This newspaper article reports a court judgment against Schumpeter and his acquaintance Richard M. Braun-Stammfest (the real villain in Schumpeter's financial problems) in a suit brought by the Wiener Kaufmannsbank (of which Schumpeter was a member of the board of directors) in the glass company recapitalization (Schumpeter also sat on this firm's board). A loan of 1.9 billion Kronen was at issue, and the lawsuit was prompted by non-repayment with interest. Since Schumpeter had left the syndicate well before payment was due and the suit was brought, the judgment against him was only 199,000 crowns plus 8% interest for his participation in the acquisition of the original debt.

12. Wolfgang Stolper deals with these matters thoroughly in *Joseph Alois Schumpeter,* pp. 306–325; the quotation from Schumpeter about complete financial ruin is on p. 316. The details of this episode were sufficiently convoluted to blemish his rep-

utation not only for good business judgment but also for probity. See, for example, "Involuntary Resignation of President Dr. Schumpeter," *Die Neue Wirtschaft,* September 11, 1924, in Schumpeter, *Aufsätze zur Tagespolitik* (Essays on Current Policy), eds. Seidl and Stolper, pp. 94–95. This is an article critical of Schumpeter's behavior in the Braun-Stammfest scandal, published in a newspaper that was often unreliable. "From the beginning," the article erroneously stated, "Dr. Schumpeter has granted his intimate friend every possible encouragement. For a time, he even procured for him membership on the administrative council of the Biedermann Bank, and actively supported all his attempts to turn the Biedermann Bank into the source of funding for the formation of his bogus companies." The piece went on to report, somewhat more accurately, that "The weight of the Schumpeter name was decisive in enabling these phony business ventures to find financial help, if not from the Biedermann Bank, then from other credit institutions . . . The situation became even worse for Dr. Schumpeter when he got involved in ill-fated speculations in francs, not only with the Biedermann Bank, but also with other banks, in particular the Handelskreditbank. Although the [bank] president's debit balance at the Biedermann Bank has since been cleared, one can certainly speculate with good reason that this equalization [of debt] is part of the settlement that was granted to the institution's departing leader" (p. 94). Translation by Alison Fleig Frank.

13. Even at this time, when he was working almost exclusively on his business affairs, Schumpeter occasionally published academic writings into which he would insert, directly or indirectly, his preference for young, innovative companies. See, for example, Schumpeter, "*Angebot*" (Supply), in *Handworterbuch der Staatswissenschaften* (Dictionary of Political Science), fourth edition, vol. 1 (Jena: Gustav Fischer, 1923), pp. 299–303, in Schumpeter, *Aufsätze zur Tagespolitik* (Essays on Current Policy), eds. Seidl and Stolper, pp. 132–139. This is a succinct entry in a handbook. Schumpeter discusses supply curves, the effects of elasticities, and other conventional tools of economics. But he finds a way to imply that new and entrepreneurial firms are better for the overall economy than are traditional established ones.

14. Schumpeter, *Capitalism, Socialism and Democracy* (New York: Harper & Brothers, 1942), pp. 73–74.

15. Alfred North Whitehead, *Dialogues of Alfred North Whitehead, as Recorded by Lucien Price* (Boston: Little, Brown, 1954).

16. Long before he lost his own fortune, Schumpeter wrote about the venomous economic effects of the war: "The demands of the working class, the radical excesses, and the will to strike are not the cause, but rather the result of the situation and the endurance test that the war has forced on [our] nerves and social organization." See Schumpeter, "World Economic Crisis," excerpted in *Die Börse,* April 7, 1921, in Schumpeter, *Aufsätze zur Tagespolitik* (Essays on Current Policy), eds.

Seidl and Stolper, pp. 29–32. See also Schumpeter, "Financial Policy and the League of Nations," *Neue Freie Presse,* March 23, 1922, in ibid., pp. 39–42. He went on to say in a broader analysis a little later, "The unemployment, the capital losses, the breakdowns of this post-war time are manifestations of the war's devastation, the impoverishment of many countries, the current social tension and on top of everything the sudden, necessary structural changes in the industries of all nations from wartime to peacetime production." See Schumpeter, "Old and New Bank Policy," *Economic-Statistical Reports,* 1925, in ibid., pp. 78–93. Translations by Christopher Hall and Alison Fleig Frank.

17. Schumpeter, "World Economic Crisis," excerpted in *Die Börse,* April 7, 1921, in Schumpeter, *Aufsätze zur Tagespolitik* (Essays on Current Policy), eds. Seidl and Stolper, pp. 29–32. Translation by Christopher Hall and Alison Fleig Frank.

Elaborating on this theme, he insisted that the crisis was not basically a monetary one, as many of his contemporaries were arguing. Instead, it involved all elements of business, and could not be remedied through financial tinkering alone. Continuing the analysis he had begun in *The Theory of Economic Development,* he now drew on his own business experience as well. As he wrote in 1925, "What is characteristic of a period of prosperity is not just greater economic activity and more intense speculation along the usual channels. The essence of the phenomenon lies much more in striking new paths. New men with new goals appear, [and] the productive powers of the economy are applied to new facilities and production methods. To an overwhelming degree, innovations are implemented in new enterprises, they do not necessarily emerge in the most closely related existing companies, but rather arise alongside of these and compete with them . . . it is technologically and psychologically very difficult to undertake something new." Schumpeter, "Old and New Bank Policy," *Economic-Statistical Reports,* 1925, in Schumpeter, *Aufsätze zur Tagespolitik* (Essays on Current Policy), eds. Seidl and Stolper, p. 87. Schumpeter added in this same passage some comments about the business cycle: "The meaning and function of recurring depressions is the reabsorption and digestion of new creations in the normal cycle. Since every period of prosperity revolves around a limited number of new points of view, the impulse loses strength in a few years. And since the newly created is concretely limited, the period of depression always accomplishes its task within a few years." Translation by Christopher Hall and Alison Fleig Frank. Parts of these quotations reappear almost verbatim in *Business Cycles,* Schumpeter's book of 1939.

18. "When one undertakes something new," he wrote, "which the economic cycle had previously not known (or if one erects a new enterprise, introduces new production methods, etc.), then normally correspondent financial resources which were the outcome of prior periods are not available. One thus relies on credit, but not credit in the sense in which it can occur in the static cycle, where it

fulfills exclusively a technical market function in the sphere of circulation, but in a completely different fundamental sense." See Schumpeter, "Old and New Bank Policy," *Economic-Statistical Reports,* 1925, in Schumpeter, *Aufsätze zur Tagespolitik* (Essays on Current Policy), eds. Seidl and Stolper, p. 88. Translation by Christopher Hall.

19. "One could say," he added, "that the whole State follows the *politics of the cab driver,* who, should he get his hands on a paying passenger, charges him so much for a single ride that the customer avoids all cab stands in the future." Schumpeter, "Austria's Credit Problems," *Die Börse,* April 7, 1921, in Schumpeter, *Aufsätze zur Tagespolitik* (Essays on Current Policy), eds. Seidl and Stolper, pp. 29–32, quotation on p. 31. Translation by Christopher Hall and Alison Fleig Frank. Schumpeter, "The Currency Situation in Austria," in United States Senate, Commission of Gold and Silver Inquiry, Foreign Currency and Exchange Investigation Serial 9, *European Currency and Finance* (1925), printed in ibid., p. 69.

20. Schumpeter, "Current Economic Problems," *Die Börse,* December 15, 1921, in Schumpeter, *Aufsätze zur Tagespolitik* (Essays on Current Policy), eds. Seidl and Stolper, p. 38. This is the report of an interview with Schumpeter "about the debate over real value versus earning-capacity value of securities," i.e., whether investors should prefer assets such as real estate to stock in companies during a time of inflation; Schumpeter, "Financial Policy and the League of Nations," *Neue Freie Presse,* March 23, 1922, in Schumpeter, *Aufsätze zur Tagespolitik* (Essays on Current Policy), eds. Seidl and Stolper, pp. 39–42, quotation on p. 41. Translations by Christopher Hall.

21. Schumpeter, "The Currency Situation in Austria," in United States Senate, Commission of Gold and Silver Inquiry, Foreign Currency and Exchange Investigation Serial 9, *European Currency and Finance* (1925), printed in Schumpeter, *Aufsätze zur Tagespolitik* (Essays on Current Policy), eds. Seidl and Stolper, p. 70.

22. In 1922, Schumpeter wrote in a newspaper article that Vienna was in danger of losing its place as a financial center, and that the country must pin its hopes on the reawakening of the world economic cycle. Schumpeter, "The Big Question Marks," *Die Börse,* May 4, 1922, in Schumpeter, *Aufsätze zur Tagespolitik* (Essays on Current Policy), eds. Seidl and Stolper, pp. 42–47. The postwar economic policies of successor Habsburg states are concisely summarized in Rawi Abdelal, *National Purpose in the World Economy: Post-Soviet States in Comparative Perspective* (Ithaca and London: Cornell University Press, 2001), pp. 155–170.

23. Abdelal, *National Purpose in the World Economy,* pp. 155–170; Alice Teichova, *The Czechoslovak Economy, 1918–1980* (London: Routledge, 1988), pp. 3–18; Teichova, "Czechoslovakia: The Halting Pace to Scope and Scale," in Alfred D. Chandler, Jr., Franco Amatori, and Takashi Hikino, eds., *Big Business and the Wealth of Nations* (Cambridge: Cambridge University Press, 1997), pp. 433–434, 439–441.

24. Schumpeter's Diary, February 13, 1944, notebook entry, Schumpeter Papers, HUG(FP)—4.1, Brief Daily Records, notes and diaries, ca. 1931–1948, box 4, folder 1943–1944, HUA.

8: ANNIE

1. See the typescript in the Schumpeter Papers, HUG(FP)—66.90, Publisher and Estate Correspondence, box 4, folder titled "The Diaries of Anna Reisinger-Schumpeter: A Report," by Erica Gerschenkron, HUA, hereinafter cited as Gerschenkron, "A Report." Pp. 20–26 of this document, "Summary of Mrs. Anna Schumpeter's Diaries," constitute an excellent chronology and analysis of Annie's life. This document is the necessary starting point for research in the diaries, because of their very idiosyncratic organization. The diaries themselves are in ten small leather-bound volumes, and are copies by Joseph Schumpeter himself of Annie's originals, which he made repeatedly over a number of years. An explanation appears on pp. 2–6 of Gerschenkron, "A Report." Robert Loring Allen, *Opening Doors: The Life & Work of Joseph Schumpeter,* two vols. (New Brunswick, N.J.: Transaction, 1991), I, pp. 192–198, provides an account of Schumpeter's relationship with Annie, based primarily on the Gerschenkron Report but supplemented with interviews.

2. Gerschenkron, "A Report," pp. 20–22.

3. Diary of Anna Reisinger Schumpeter, Schumpeter Papers, HUG (FP)—4.2, Mostly extracts from Annie's diary, vol. IV, June 15, 1919, HUA. Cited hereinafter as Annie's Diary. All shorthand entries in Annie's Diary are as deciphered by Erica Gerschenkron in "A Report," Appended Transcripts I, pp. 27–41, and II, pp. 52–118. All translations of Annie's Diary in this chapter are by Holger Frank, with the exception of a few by Ms. Gerschenkron, as noted.

    The *New York Times* of June 17, 1919 contains the following account of the riot in Vienna: "The trouble began when 6,000 demonstrants attempted to obtain the release from prison of Communist leaders arrested Saturday. The police fired volleys into the air and then into the crowd. The Demonstrants succeeded in releasing the Communist leaders . . . The disturbance today was, perhaps, the most serious from a political point of view in Vienna since last November . . . Today was the first time that the local Communists had risen against the Government." On the poverty and upheavals in Vienna during and just after the war, see Maureen Healy, *Vienna and the Fall of the Habsburg Empire: Total War and Everyday Life in World War I* (Cambridge: Cambridge University Press, 2004).

4. Gerschenkron, "A Report," pp. 21–24.

5. Annie's Diary, vol. II, dates noted. Annie's spelling and punctuation are sometimes erratic. In almost all quotations, I have kept to the original, but on a very few occasions I have filled in blanks to clarify her meaning. See also

Gerschenkron, "A Report," p. 21n++ (Ms. Gerschenkron's footnotes are entered in plus signs: the first one on a page as +, the second as ++, and so on.) Other sample entries:

June 4, 1920, vol. IV: Schum wrote from Graz. He's looking forward to Monday . . . I'm nervous about Monday.

June 26, vol. II: Wrote Schum.

July 1, vol. I: Responded to Schum['s letter].

July 6, vol. I: Got another letter from Schumy.

July 22, vol. I: Left the office, met Schum; is he insulted because I didn't respond? I don't care.

July 26, vol. I: In the office congratulations on my name day [the feast of Anna Christa, Annie's patron saint; one's *Namentag* was an important occasion for Austrian and German Catholics]. Those from whom you expect some attention don't [give it]—was very sad that neither Schum nor Hansl wrote me at least . . . In the evening at home. Schum very repulsive. Won't forget that.

6. One of these boys, named Egon, was especially taken with her. Annie records both her continued relationship with Egon, which ended when her father put a stop to it, and her occasional contact with Schumpeter. See Annie's Diary, vol. II, August 6, 9, 16, 22, 23, 29, and September 1 and 22, 1920.
7. Annie's Diary, vol. I, September 4, 28, 30, and October 1, 1920. Annie's "rude" letter, October (n.d.), 1920, is in the Schumpeter Papers, HUG(FP)—4.4, Personal letters, miscellany, box 1, folder Personal letters—Annie (wife) ca. 1923–1926, HUA.
8. Annie's Diary, vol. III, October 3, 1920.
9. Annie's Diary, vol. I, October 7, 9, 11, 13, 22, 28, 30, and November 5 and 19, 1920.
10. Gerschenkron, "A Report," pp. 21–22; Annie's Diary, vol. II, entries for late 1920 and early 1921, *passim;* see also Allen, *Opening Doors* I, pp. 192–198.
11. Gerschenkron, "A Report," p. 22.
12. Annie's Diary, vol. I, November 9, 1922; vol. II, June 6, 1923, and July 19, 1923. See also Allen, *Opening Doors,* I, pp. 193–197.
13. Gerschenkron, "A Report," pp. 22–23; Allen, *Opening Doors,* I, pp. 192–198.
14. Quoted in Gerschenkron, "A Report," p. 23n++. Annie's Diary, vol. IV, April 5, 1924.
15. Gerschenkron, "A Report," pp. 23–24. Annie's Diary, vol. I, September 10, 1924;

vol. III, September 29, October 14, 15, 23, and 31, 1924. See also vol. IV, February 9, 1925, quoted in Gerschenkron, "A Report," p. 24n+++.

16. Gerschenkron, "A Report," pp. 23–24. Annie's Diary, vol. III, October 23, 26, 27, 28, 29, 30, 1924.

17. Annie's Diary, vol. III. In addition to the dates noted in the text, see also the entries for October 15, 23, 26, 27, 28, and 30, and November 4, 7, and 9, 1924.

18. Annie's Diary, vol. IV, dates noted. In addition, see entries for May 12 and 19, 1925. See also Gerschenkron, "A Report," p. 24n++++, for diary entry of April 25, 1925.

19. Annie's Diary, vol. I, dates noted. The addition by Schumpeter was made in 1933, as he recalled this day some eight years afterward. Gerschenkron, "A Report," Appended Transcripts I, p. 40. Details about their discussion of Gerhard L. are mentioned in Gerschenkron, "A Report," p. 25. In addition to the dates in Annie's Diary already mentioned, see the entries in vol. II, May 23, 24, 25, 28, and 29; June 1, 2, 4, 5, 12, 20, 21, 27, 28, and 30; and July 1, 1925. The letter from Annie of August 7, 1925 is in the Schumpeter Papers, HUG(FP)—4.4, Personal letters, miscellany, folder Personal letters from Annie ca. 1923–1926, HUA, translation by Benjamin Hett. Whether Annie told Schumpeter before their marriage of her abortion is unknowable for certain, but his own comment on her diary entry for October 25, 1925 suggests that she did tell him. He knew about it after he read her diary later on, and in his annotations makes no negative or judgmental comment. See the last entry in note 20 below.

20. Annie's Diary, vol. I, dates noted. In 1933, in a separate entry annotating Annie's Diary, vol. I, September 4, 1925, Schumpeter wrote "The first night together."
    Further samples from Annie's Diary, vol. I, during this period:

> *September 6, 1925:* [Illegible]; The path to the Baumgartnerhaus [little house in the mountains] back with Schneebergbahn—Buchberg—Vienna. Ate together again. Goodbye.

> *September 9:* Rendezvous at 11:00 o'clock; mass; J. is very quiet and tired; in the evening for a walk with mother.

> *September 11:* With Milli [her sister, whose name she sometimes spelled "Milly"] and J. in the Burgkino [movie theater] the path to power and beauty [probably the movie title], then in the Volksgarten.

> *September 12:* Trip with J. and Milli [listing places they visited].

> *September 16:* [Schumpeter himself writes at some length here, recording his reflections on September 16, 1933 (Gerschenkron, "A Report," Appended Transcripts I, p. 41):] Nothing in the little book [her diary], but I visited Annie in Doblhofgasse [where both of them grew up in the

apartment building], we went to the seamstress; in the evening together again and had dinner at Imperial [hotel]—lots of splendor and *immeasurably beautiful.*

[At the heading of this entry Schumpeter has recorded a series of thoughts that amount to a kind of poem, very poignant:]

Joyful tidings and such an infinite amount of splendor.
We kiss each other, when we demand it, but farewell and welcome . . .
We have to pay our creditors . . .
If, God forbid, something were to happen to you . . .
We seem to me to be like a student and his girl.

And from Annie's Diary, vol. III:

October 1, 1925: Jozsi leaves for Berlin [for his interview with the Ministry of Art, Science and Public Education.]

October 5: Joy. "*Bonn Erobert!*" Father's birthday. 50 years. Cooked, schnitzel, salad, apple strudel.

October 26, 1925: [Shorthand notes added later by Schumpeter. The day before, October 25, he wrote at the head of the entry, "Disclosure!" On this day, October 26, the 1924 entry in Annie's diary suggests she went to Linz for an abortion. See that reference above, n. 19.]

21. Schumpeter to Arthur Spiethoff, June 30, August 10, September 9, 1925, all in Ulrich Hedtke and Richard Swedberg, eds., *Joseph Alois Schumpeter, Briefe/Letters* (Tübingen: J. C. B. Mohr, Paul Siebeck, 2000), pp. 100–104; see also Allen, *Opening Doors,* I, pp. 193–198, 270. The invitation to teach at Tokyo Imperial University likely came from the initiative of Professor Kotaro Araki, who had visited Schumpeter in Vienna.
22. Annie's Diary, vol. III, October 5, 1925.
23. Annie's Diary, vol. III, dates noted. See also Gerschenkron, "A Report," pp. 23–24.
24. Gladys's attitude became clear when she learned of what had happened and began writing threatening letters to Schumpeter in Bonn.
25. Annie's Diary, vol. III, November 8, 13, 14, 15, 16, and 17, 1925; Allen, *Opening Doors,* I, pp. 194–198. Hans Kelsen was a distinguished constitutional lawyer not only in Austria but also in Weimar Germany. He occasionally kept in touch with Schumpeter over the years, writing in 1940, for example, on behalf of Franz X. Weiss, "for whose further fate I have the greatest fears under the present [Nazi] circumstances." Kelsen asked Schumpeter to recommend Weiss to Alvin Johnson of the New School for Social Research, whose University in Exile gave employ-

ment to displaced European scholars, especially Jewish refugees. See Kelsen to Schumpeter, September 12, 1940, Schumpeter Papers, HUG(FP)—4.7, Correspondence and other misc. papers, box 1, folder Unidentified 1920, HUA. Translation by Benjamin Hett.

26. Allen, *Opening Doors,* I, pp. 192–198.

27. Ibid., pp. 192–197.

9: HEARTBREAK

1. Numerous entries in the Diary of Anna Reisinger Schumpeter, Schumpeter Papers, HUG(FP)—4.2, vols. I, III, and IV, HUA, recount their days before and after the move to the University of Bonn; hereinafter cited as Annie's Diary. Secondary accounts are in Robert Loring Allen, *Opening Doors: The Life & Work of Joseph Schumpeter,* two vols. (New Brunswick, N.J.: Transaction, 1991), I, pp. 201–207; and Richard Swedberg, *Schumpeter: A Biography* (Princeton, N.J.: Princeton University Press, 1991), pp. 69–70.

2. On the two men's relationship, see, for example, Schumpeter to Spiethoff, September 2 and October 19, 1921; June 14, 1922, and April 17, 1924, all in Ulrich Hedtke and Richard Swedberg, eds., *Joseph Alois Schumpeter, Briefe/Letters* (Tübingen: J. C. B. Mohr, Paul Siebeck, 2000), pp. 94–97, 99–100.

3. Schumpeter to Spiethoff, April 17, 1924, and June 30, 1925, in Hedtke and Swedberg, eds., *Briefe,* pp. 99–101. Translation by Holger Frank. See also Schumpeter to Spiethoff, March 20, 1925, in the Spiethoff Papers at the Universitätsbibliothek Basel, Handschriftenabteilung. This collection contains 18 letters from Schumpeter to Spiethoff over the period 1918–1925, classified as HA NR 301: Spiethoff. Eight of these letters are included in the Hedtke-Swedberg collection. I will cite those that are not, plus letters from Spiethoff about Schumpeter, as Spiethoff Papers, UB Basel.

4. Spiethoff to the Ministry, July 2, 1925, Spiethoff Papers, UB Basel. Translation by Holger Frank.

5. Schumpeter to Spiethoff, June 30, August 10, and September 9, 1925, all in Hedtke and Swedberg, eds., *Briefe,* pp. 100–104. Schumpeter's suggestions for references are listed at the bottom of pp. 102 and 103. See also Schumpeter to Spiethoff, August 4, September 26, September 28 (telegram), and October 6, 1925, all in Spiethoff Papers, UB Basel.

6. Spiethoff to the Ministry, July 4, 1925, Spiethoff Papers, UB Basel. This is a long and thorough letter, an interim report. Translation by Holger Frank.

7. Stolper and his siblings were the first native German-speakers in their family. He once wrote Schumpeter that "I am of Jewish descent and I would never consider trying to hide that fact from anti-Semites." But he professed no religion himself, and his first wife was a Protestant. This sort of history was not unusual in Vi-

enna, whose Jewish citizens came from many different places under various circumstances and pursued diverse kinds of goals. Gustav Stolper, for example, strongly opposed Zionism. In addition to his own voluminous writings, the best source on Stolper is the biography prepared by his second wife: Toni Stolper, *Ein Leben in Brennpunkten unserer Zeit, Vien Berlin New York: Gustav Stolper 1888–1947* (A Life in the Hot Spots of Our Time: Vienna, Berlin, New York) (Tübingen: Rainer Wunderlich Verlag, Hermann Leins, 1960). This book contains many references to Schumpeter and his relationship with Stolper.

At the Nachlass Gustav und Toni Stolper, N 1186/31, Bundesarchiv Koblenz, is a collection of 112 letters from Schumpeter to Gustav Stolper (or Toni, or both), dating from 1918 to 1937. Thirty-four of these letters, not including the one quoted below, are printed in Hedtke and Swedberg, eds., *Briefe*. Schumpeter's initial letter, dated June 4, 1918 and written shortly after the two men first met, reports that he is having to give lectures in Graz to soldiers on furlough, and goes on to say that he would like to see Stolper again, because "in Austria interesting characters aren't so widespread that one can easily abandon one of them." Translation by Holger Frank.

8. Spiethoff to Gustav Stolper, August 14, 1925, quoted in Wolfgang Stolper, *Joseph Alois Schumpeter: The Public Life of a Private Man* (Princeton, N.J.: Princeton University Press, 1994), p. 310. Wolfgang Stolper was Gustav's son.

9. Gustav Stolper to Arthur Spiethoff, August 22, 1925, quoted in Wolfgang Stolper, *Joseph Alois Schumpeter,* pp. 310–311, where the letter is printed in full, translation by Wolfgang Stolper.

10. Gustav Stolper to Arthur Spiethoff, August 22, 1925, quoted in Wolfgang Stolper, *Joseph Alois Schumpeter,* p. 310, translation by Wolfgang Stolper.

11. Schumpeter to "St" (Gustav Stolper), November 11, 1925, printed in Eduard März, *Joseph Alois Schumpeter—Forscher, Lehrer und Politiker* (Scholar, Teacher and Politician) (Munich: R. Oldenbourg Verlag, 1983), appendix. Translation by Holger Frank.

12. Erich Schneider, trans. W. E. Kuhn, *Joseph A. Schumpeter: Life and Work of a Great Social Scientist* (Lincoln: University of Nebraska Bureau of Business Research, 1975), p. 29. Schneider himself was one of Schumpeter's students at Bonn. Spiethoff, "Josef Schumpeter in Memoriam," *Kyklos* 3 (1949) [sic; Schumpeter died in 1950], p. 290.

13. Schneider, *Joseph A. Schumpeter,* p. 29.

14. M. Ernst Kamp and Friedrich H. Stamm, *Bonner Gelehrte—Beiträge zur Geschichte der Wissenschaften in Bonn: Staatswissenschaften* (Bonn: H. Bouvier and Co. Verlag/Ludwig Röhrscheid Verlag, 1969), p. 55, cited and translated in Swedberg, *Schumpeter: A Biography,* p. 71.

15. Schumpeter to "St. . ." (Gustav Stolper), November 11, 1925, printed in März, *Joseph Alois Schumpeter,* appendix. Translation by Holger Frank.

16. Schumpeter to the Ministry of Art, Science and Public Education, February 25, 1926, in Hedtke and Swedberg, eds., *Briefe,* pp. 108–109.

17. Entries from Annie's Diary, vols. I and II, provide a vivid picture of their daily life, especially of their close friendship with the Spiethoffs. These and all other translations in this chapter from Annie's Diary are by Holger Frank.

   From vol. I:

   November 16, 1925: Prof. Spiethoff at our place.

   November 17: At Spiethoffs'—gramophone—danced, very funny.

   From vol. II:

   June 13: (Sunday) Volks, Spiethoffs, Schulzens and Husserl at our place.

   June 23: To the movies, visit from the Schulz family, Mrs. Spiethoff very nice . . .

   June 30, 1926: With J. in the motorboat to Godesberg [Bad Godesberg, along the Rhine next to Bonn], had dinner in the 9 Uhr Hof [9 o'clock yard restaurant]. We met Beckerat [Beckerath, another professor of economics], Kerns and von Ratz.

   July 10: Steamer trip with Spiethoffs to Remagen and back. Very hot.

18. Schumpeter to H[einrich Hoefflinger], January 1, 1926, in März, *Joseph Alois Schumpeter,* appendix. Translation by Holger Frank. The letter from Gladys, along with most of Schumpeter's other pre-1933 papers, did not survive. He may have kept this letter and other correspondence, but the place near Bonn where he stored his books and papers was bombed by the U.S. Army Air Forces in 1944.

19. Annie's Diary, vol. IV, April 4, 1926, quoted in Gerschenkron, "A Report," p. 26, n++; Allen, *Opening Doors,* I, pp. 216–217.

20. Allen, *Opening Doors,* I, pp. 208–210, 217–218, 219n33–34.

21. The entries from Annie's Diary on June 18, 21, and 22, 1926 are all from vol. II.

22. Annie's letter is in the Schumpeter Papers, HUG (FP)—4.4, Personal letters, miscellany, box 1, folder Personal letters—Annie (wife), ca. 1923–25, HUA. Translation by Benjamin Hett. The letter is dated "Wednesday," which would make it June 23, 1926. The nickname Go-Go is in the original.

23. Annie's Diary, vol. II, dates noted.

24. Mia Stöckel to Schumpeter, October 22, 1938, quoting a remark he had made to her on the occasion of her own mother's death, in Schumpeter Papers, HUG(FP)—4.5, Letters from Mia, 1932–1940, box 2, folder 1938, HUA. Translation by Benjamin Hett.

25. Annie's Diary, vol. II, dates noted. Schumpeter to Stolper, August 1, 1926, in Hedtke and Swedberg, eds., *Briefe,* pp. 117–120.

26. Schumpeter to Ottilie Jäckel, August 3, 1926, in Hedtke and Swedberg, eds., *Briefe*, p. 120. Translation by Robert Loring Allen and Florian Müller.

27. Schumpeter to "St" (Gustav Stolper), n.d. ("August 1926"), printed in März, *Joseph Alois Schumpeter—Forscher, Lehrer und Politiker*, appendix. Translation by Holger Frank. Schumpeter to Ottilie Jäckel, August 22, 1926, in Hedtke and Swedberg, eds., *Briefe*, pp. 121–122. Translation by Florian Müller.

28. Schumpeter to Ottilie Jäckel, August 22, 1926, in Hedtke and Swedberg, eds., *Briefe*, pp. 121–122. Translation by Robert Loring Allen and Florian Müller; Schumpeter to Ottilie Jäckel, n.d. ("Friday, 1926"), printed in März, *Joseph Alois Schumpeter*, appendix. Translation by Holger Frank. The quotation about the first day back is from Schumpeter's annotation of Annie's Diary, vol. 1, August 7, 1933 (see Gerschenkron, "A Report," Appended Transcripts I, p. 39). Translation by Holger Frank.

29. Allen, *Opening Doors*, I, pp. 223–224.

30. Schumpeter to Wesley C. Mitchell, August 30, 1926, in Hedtke and Swedberg, eds., *Briefe*, pp. 126–127.

31. Schumpeter to Stolper, August (?), 1926, Nachlass Gustav und Toni Stolper, N 1186/31, Bundesarchiv Koblenz. Translation by Holger Frank.

PART II PROLOGUE: WHAT HE HAD LEARNED

1. Schumpeter had long been interested in the social and cultural aspects of capitalism. Some of his articles during the years before 1926 are as much sociological as economic in nature, and as early as 1914, during his American sojourn, one of his hosts included in Schumpeter's seminar introduction (a document probably composed by Schumpeter himself), the following statement: "In recent years Professor Schumpeter's interest has been largely in the field of sociology, but he has not yet published anything in this department." See Jacob Hollander to Schumpeter, February 7, 1914, Jacob Harry Hollander Papers, Ms. 59, Special Collections, Milton S. Eisenhower Library, The Johns Hopkins University. Also, in 1941, he wrote about himself as a young man, "Dropping early sociological and historical interests I became an economic theorist." Schumpeter to Lloyd S. Huntsman, May 26, 1941, in Ulrich Hedtke and Richard Swedberg, eds., *Joseph Alois Schumpeter, Briefe/Letters* (Tübingen: J. C. B. Mohr, Paul Siebeck, 2000), p. 333.

   I am not arguing here that any sudden break from economics to sociology occurred in 1926, but the shift of emphasis is clear, as the following chapters of this book will show. See also Richard Swedberg, *Schumpeter: A Biography* (Princeton, N.J.: Princeton University Press, 1991); Yuichi Shionoya, *Schumpeter and the Idea of Social Science: A Metatheoretical Study* (Cambridge: Cambridge University Press, 1997); and David Reisman, *Schumpeter's Market: Enterprise and Evolution*

(Cheltenham, U.K.: Edward Elgar, 2004), especially ch. 3. Much of what Schumpeter wrote during this next phase of his life may be compared to the approach taken by his fellow Viennese Karl Polanyi in his influential book *The Great Transformation: The Political and Economic Origins of Our Time* (New York: Rinehart, 1944), which integrates history, economics, and sociology.

2. Arthur Young, *Political Essays concerning the Present State of the British Empire* (London, 1772), pp. 20–21. Robert Fogel, Stanley Engerman, and others have published informative works on the costs of slavery in the United States; here I am referring to much broader categories of opportunity costs throughout the world, over thousands of years of time.

3. The roots of welfare capitalism stretch back for several centuries, in provisions such as Britain's Poor Laws. The first broadly modern form was Germany's in the time of Bismarck, when many firms were required to provide housing and other amenities to members of their workforce. Britain and other European countries, often responding to socialist pressures, followed suit in varying degrees.

   The outlier in this process was the United States, which was notably late in enacting laws to restrain business and provide for the welfare of child laborers, unemployed citizens, and the elderly. The movement in America began during the Progressive Era (1901–1916), but bore little fruit until Franklin D. Roosevelt's New Deal (1933–1938). Together with measures enacted during and after World War II, and especially during the 1960s, this legislation ushered in the modern American mixed economy. Similar mixed economies evolved in nearly all modern industrialized countries during the twentieth century. Even so, to say merely that all systems of capitalism are not identical is an extreme understatement.

4. Carl N. Degler, *Out of Our Past: The Forces That Shaped Modern America* (New York: Harper, 1959), p. 1.

5. See *World Development Report* (New York: Oxford University Press for The World Bank), annual editions, 1996 to the present.

10: NEW INTELLECTUAL DIRECTIONS

1. Schumpeter's worries about his debts are vividly set forth in two dozen letters, mostly to Ottilie Jäckel, printed in Eduard März, *Joseph Alois Schumpeter—Forscher, Lehrer und Politiker* (Scholar, Teacher and Politician) (Munich: R. Oldenbourg Verlag, 1983), appendix. The comment about damaging him as a professor is from a letter dated January 27, 1927, translation by Holger Frank. See also Wolfgang Stolper, *Joseph Alois Schumpeter: The Public Life of a Private Man* (Princeton, N.J.: Princeton University Press, 1994), several chapters of which cover in copious detail Schumpeter's financial dealings and their aftermath.

2. The word he uses is *Tobsuchtszelle* (cell with padded walls), Schumpeter to

Gustav Stolper, August 25, 1926, in Ulrich Hedtke and Richard Swedberg, eds., *Joseph Alois Schumpeter, Briefe/Letters* (Tübingen: J. C. B. Mohr, Paul Siebeck, 2000), pp. 122–125. Translation by Holger Frank.

3. Appeals fill Schumpeter's transcriptions of Annie's Diary for years after the deaths of the *Hasen;* and "H s D" appears frequently in his lecture notes. Schumpeter Papers, HUG(FP)—4.2, Mostly extracts from Annie's diary, and HUG(FP)—4.62, Lecture notes, 1930–1949, *passim,* HUA.

4. He also renewed his concern with the life of the spirit, dormant since his Catholic boyhood. The Schumpeter Papers in the Harvard University Archives contain numerous sketches and photos of cathedrals. See, for example, HUG(FP)—4.3, Misc. personal writings and notes, box 1, folder Notebook, HUA.

5. There was also a fourth German edition, published in 1935. See Yuichi Shionoya, "Schumpeter's Preface to the Fourth German Edition of *The Theory of Economic Development," Journal of Evolutionary Economics* 14 (2004), pp. 131–142, which contains an English translation of much of the new preface.

6. Oscar Morgenstern, in the *American Economic Review* 17 (June 1927), pp. 281–282. [Morgenstern's first name is spelled "Oskar" in some other publications.] In his revision, Schumpeter eliminated one of the original seven chapters, and tightened the other six. He completely reorganized chapter 2, "The Fundamental Problem of Economic Development." This is the analytical heart of the book, and he subdivided it into three sections, making his argument clearer. He deleted chapter 7, which mainly concerns the sociology of culture. He did this not because he wasn't interested in the topic (he was, and frequently wrote about it), but because he thought that for this book it distracted readers from his main messages about economic development.

In chapter 6, he added material comparing his own views with those of other economists and paid tribute to the thinking of Arthur Spiethoff on business cycles. Spiethoff, he writes, has provided "the most thorough effort in this field." He goes on to say that both he and Spiethoff date the origins of modern capitalism to 1821 in Britain and the 1840s in Germany, the times during which alternating situations of prosperity and recession began to occur regularly. In other words, both he and Spiethoff were beginning to define capitalism in part by the existence of its characteristic business cycles. Schumpeter develops this theme fully in *Business Cycles,* published in 1939.

7. Taussig to Fabian Franklin, December 31, 1930, Frank W. Taussig Papers, HUG 4823.5, box 4, folder F 1930–31, HUA. The history of the English translation is a bit complicated. In a letter to Allen & Unwin, London publishers, dated June 18, 1931, Schumpeter wrote that Macmillan had assured him that Allen & Unwin would publish the translated version, and that he now sought clarification and possible release from any obligation:

For some years past I have had several offers from translators and publishers of different countries both for that and another book. None of
these suggestions have been followed up by me, partly because I
thought of rewriting both books partly because, being absorbed in other
work, I felt unable to bestow on the matter the amount of attention
which would have been necessary . . . I have not kept copies of my answers but what I meant to convey was in both cases that the matter
should be put off until I should have found the time to rewrite the
book. Here the matter would have rested probably for ever, if my eminent friend Prof. Taussig had not, during my stay in Harvard in 1930,
encouraged me to have the book translated as it is. He went even further, and with unparalleled kindness undertook to find and test translators, to enter into correspondence with publishers and so on, while I
was travelling in Japan and the Dutch Indies . . . I gratefully put the
matter in Professor Taussig's hands, who naturally opened negotiations
with firms with whom he is himself connected. I am quite sure that if
he had known what I know now by your letter, which I am sending on
to him he would have been just as pleased to communicate with your
firm, the name of which he would agree with me in considering second
to none. As it is, it may be too late, but I shall write to you as soon as I
hear from him.

This letter, written in English, is printed in Hedtke and Swedberg, eds., *Briefe*,
p. 193. Taussig allocated $700 for the translation. Throughout the process of
bringing out the translation of *The Theory of Economic Development,* the British
publisher Allen & Unwin remained dissatisfied, and had reason to be unhappy
when Harvard University Press's prior arrangement with Oxford University Press
for British rights to the books in its economics series trumped the interests of Allen & Unwin. See, among much correspondence, the letter from managing director Stanley Unwin to Harvard University Press, July 19, 1933 ("There are few
books about which we have spent so much time writing lengthy letters explaining a situation for which we are in no way responsible. We have, in fact, become
so tired of the whole matter than when we last wrote to Dr. Redvers Opie we left
him to make his own arrangements with an American publisher"); and Taussig to
Unwin, February 13, 1934; in UAV 349.11, Department of Economics, Correspondence and Records, 1930–1961, box Robertson-Schumpeter, folder Joseph A.
Schumpeter, HUA.

8. Opie to Schumpeter, November 21, 1932, in Schumpeter Papers, HUG(FP)—
4.7, Correspondence and other misc. papers, ca. 1920s-1950, box 8, folder R1930,
HUA; Schumpeter to Gottfried Haberler, August 6, 1931, in Hedtke and

Swedberg, eds., *Briefe,* pp. 196–198; Robert Loring Allen, *Opening Doors: The Life & Work of Joseph Schumpeter, two vols. (New Brunswick, N.J.: Transaction), I, p. 278.*

9. Schumpeter, *The Theory of Economic Development: An Inquiry into Profits, Capital, Credit, Interest, and the Business Cycle* (Cambridge, Mass.: Harvard University Press, 1934), preface.

10. The original article was published in *Archiv für Sozialwissenschaft* 44 (1917), pp. 627–715. It appeared in English, translated by Schumpeter's friend Arthur Marget under the title "Social Product and Money Calculations," in *International Economic Papers* 3 (1953), pp. 148–211. Schumpeter also wrote a series of papers in Dutch during the 1920s arguing against the use of certain types of monetary management to achieve price stability. These papers influenced the Dutch economist J. G. Koopmans. See M. M. G. Fase, "The Rise and Demise of Dutch Monetarism; or, the Schumpeter-Koopmans-Holtrop Connection," *History of Political Economy* 26 (1994), pp. 21–38.

11. Schumpeter to Stolper, April 2, 1930, Nachlass Gustav und Toni Stolper, N 1186/31, Bundesarchiv Koblenz. Schumpeter to Gottfried v. Haberler, March 20, 1933, in Hedtke and Swedberg, eds., *Briefe,* p. 239.

Some of Schumpeter's admirers did see to the money book's partial publication in 1970. But by that time the theory of money had progressed so far that Schumpeter's arguments were mostly obsolete. His book has many merits, but he probably made the right decision in not publishing a work with which he himself was so dissatisfied. The book was published in 1970 under the title *Das Wesen des Geldes (The Nature of Money),* ed. Fritz Karl Mann (Göttingen: Vandenhoeck and Ruprecht).

On the 1970 version of the book, see Erich Schneider, "The Nature of Money: On a Posthumous Publication by Joseph A. Schumpeter," *German Economic Review* 8 (1970), pp. 348–352; Parth J. Shah and Leland B. Yeager, "Schumpeter on Monetary Determinacy," *History of Political Economy* 26 (1994), pp. 443–464; and especially Marcello Messori, "The Trials and Misadventures of Schumpeter's Treatise on Money," *History of Political Economy* 29 (1997), pp. 639–673, which provides a thorough history of the money book. See also Marcello Messori, "Credit and Money in Schumpeter's Theory," in Richard Arena and Neri Salvadori, eds., *Money, Credit and the Role of the State: Essays in Honour of Augusto Graziani* (Aldershot, U.K.: Ashgate, 2004), pp. 175–200. As late as November 1949, two months before he died, Schumpeter was still thinking of writing about the subject: "Within a year or two I hope to write a book on money that will give my latest views." Schumpeter to René Roux, November 8, 1949, in Hedtke and Swedberg, eds., *Briefe,* p. 391.

12. Richard Musgrave, one of Schumpeter's graduate students at Harvard, is the source for Schumpeter's belief that Keynes "had stolen some of his ideas on mon-

etary theory" from Schumpeter's article of 1917. Musgrave interview with my then-research associate Benjamin Hett, September 30, 2000.

In his letter to Keynes, Schumpeter added that the book was a *"tour de force, and must cause you the most intense satisfaction. I believe it will ever stand as a landmark in its field."* A little later, Schumpeter wrote Keynes that he had discussed *A Treatise on Money* with a well-read classics professor during a long ocean voyage. This man "delighted in classifying the scientists of his time, whether Greek scholars or not, and in the first class he included but two names, yours and Einstein's. Do not despise this. It is true vox populi." See Schumpeter to Keynes, November 29, 1930 and October 22, 1932, in Hedtke and Swedberg, eds., *Briefe,* pp. 180–181, 224–225.

Schumpeter's later judgment was that Keynes's book had "somehow missed fire . . . he had failed to convey the essence of his own personal message." See Schumpeter, "Keynes, the Economist," in Seymour E. Harris, ed., *The New Economics: Keynes' Influence on Theory and Public Policy* (New York: Knopf, 1947), p. 89. This essay was first published in the *American Economic Review* 36 (September 1946).

13. Schumpeter himself described Keynes as "the most influential theorist of our epoch." See Schumpeter, "Keynes and Statistics," *Review of Economic Statistics* 28 (November 1946), pp. 194–196.

14. Schumpeter to Gottfried v. Haberler, March 20, 1933, in Hedtke and Swedberg, eds., *Briefe,* p. 239. Schumpeter's context here was what he called "aggregative [macroeconomic] analysis," Keynes's chief legacy to economic theory. Schumpeter to David McCord Wright, quoted in Wright, "Schumpeter and Keynes," in *Weltwirtscharfliches Archiv* 65 (1950), pp. 188–189; Schumpeter to Werner Richter, February 28, 1929, in Hedtke and Swedberg, eds., *Briefe,* p. 165. More generally, see Herbert von Beckerath, "Joseph A. Schumpeter as a Sociologist," *Weltwirtscharfliches Archiv* 65 (1950), pp. 200–214; and the overall argument of Richard A. Swedberg, *Schumpeter: A Biography* (Princeton, N.J.: Princeton University Press, 1991).

15. A useful history of the Harvard Economics Department is Edward S. Mason, "The Harvard Department of Economics from the Beginning to World War II," *Quarterly Journal of Economics* 97 (August 1982), pp. 384–433.

16. Schumpeter, *"Gustav v. Schmoller und die Probleme von heute,"* Schmollers *Jahrbuch für Gesetzgebung, Verwaltung und Volkswirtschaft im Deutschen Reich* 50 (1926), vol. I, pp. 337–388. For a thorough discussion of the significance of this piece, see Swedberg, *Schumpeter: A Biography,* pp. 82–89. Schumpeter's close association with Schmoller's former pupil Arthur Spiethoff, his best friend in Bonn, likely helped to confirm his new way of thinking.

17. Schumpeter, *"Die Tendenzen unserer sozialen Struktur"* (The Tendencies of Our Social Structure), in *Die Chemische Industrie* 51/52 (December 24, 1928), printed

in Schumpeter, *Aufsätze zur Tagespolitik* (Essays on Current Policy), eds. Christian Seidl and Wolfgang F. Stolper (Tübingen: J. C. B. Mohr, Paul Siebeck, 1993), pp. 177–193. Schumpeter argues that a country can change one of these structures as a way to preserve something cherished in another. As an example, he cites Britain's 1846 repeal of its famous Corn Laws (high tariffs on imported grain). This repeal, he says, stopped economic subsidies to large landowners, but its real aim was to preserve the nation's social and political structures. Repeal of the Corn Laws would make food cheaper, and would thereby prevent urban riots that would undermine the established order, which the British Parliament wanted to sustain.

18. Schumpeter goes on to say, somewhat obscurely, that the peasantry, producing children at a disproportionately large rate, "is currently finding itself in an especially advantageous situation" in supplying urban and professional workers. But the rural mindset has persisted long after the peasants' move to cities, and this has become a source of political stability. Ibid. Translation by Florian Müller.

19. Ibid. Translation by Florian Müller. Schumpeter adds here that the increasingly powerful socialists were forward-looking in their acceptance of industrialization. But even if the socialists were not certain to win politically, the old craft culture was certain to lose.

20. In the latter case, Schumpeter was referring to the new industrial proletariat; in the former, to the emerging *Mittelstand* tradition of small firms: "It is not unimportant that the number of German businesses employing 6–50 persons has increased from about 160,000 in 1907 to 206,000 in 1925." Ibid. Translation by Florian Müller.

21. As Schumpeter puts it, in the finance sector, "The 'money lender,' the actual capitalist, is mainly represented first by the banker and second by the 'investing public,' the purest form of which is the retiree. This latter type was not only badly affected by the inflation, he is also more and more deprived of his rights as a shareholder." Ibid. Translation by Florian Müller. What Schumpeter was saying here applied not just to Germany, of course, but to any modern economy. As the American critic Edmund Wilson once wrote, "Above all, Marx did not know the United States." See *To the Finland Station: A Study in the Writing and Acting of History* (New York: Harcourt, Brace, 1940), p. 376.

22. Schumpeter, *"Die Tendenzen unserer sozialen Struktur"* (The Tendencies of Our Social Structure). Translation by Florian Müller.

23. Ibid. Translation by Florian Müller.

24. Ibid. Translation by Florian Müller.

25. Schumpeter, trans. Heinz Norden, "Social Classes in an Ethnically Homogeneous Environment," in *Imperialism, Social Classes: Two Essays by Joseph Schumpeter* (New York: Meridian Books, 1955). Schumpeter had worked on this article intermittently for more than 15 years, having begun it as a series of lectures

at Czernowitz in 1910. "Subsequently," as he himself recalled, "at Columbia University in the winter of 1913–1914, I presented it at length in a course entitled 'The Theory of Social Classes.'" He refined it still further for a 1926 lecture at the University of Heidelberg on "Leadership and Class Formation." He then published it in 1927 under the general title "Social Classes in an Ethnically Homogeneous Environment" (pp. 106–108). A more descriptive title of the essay would be "The Growing Fluidity at the Top of Society in the Age of Industrialization."

26. Ibid., pp. 109–110.

27. But since some form of social class has always been prevalent among human beings, there is no specific date of origin. The only real origin of social class is the family. It, "not the physical person, is the true unit of class and class theory." Blood relationship being the test, the family can be extended to the clan or tribe in the analysis of classes. Ibid., pp. 111–113.

  The resulting economic mobility—indeed any sort of success—"presupposes shrewd and often ruthless exploitation of existing sources of revenue and rational utilization of their yield." In the end, "the fortunes of dynasties rose and fell in keeping with the success or failure of their policies" in achieving whatever goals their societies valued most highly. This was a key to the evolution of many aspects of western society: the feudal system; the development of aristocracies through military exploits; and even selection for high office in the Catholic Church, especially in countries such as Italy. Ibid., pp. 114–117.

28. Ibid., p. 119.

29. Ibid., pp. 120–122.

30. Ibid., emphasis added.

31. Ibid., pp. 120–123.

32. Ibid., pp. 123–124.

33. In Britain, far more than in Austria, one could rise into the aristocracy through merit or the accumulation of wealth. And at least some *hereditary* aristocrats had adapted themselves to tasks immediately at hand. At crucial moments, big landowners had been ready to take on agricultural improvements, and "even in our own times many outstanding presidents of English railway companies have been members of the court nobility."

  "The English," Schumpeter goes on to say, "always seemed able to find some way to keep *talented* nobles productively occupied." But if they could not perform, they lost their positions. Military ranks preserved for nobles, for example, "were abolished during Gladstone's second ministry" during the late nineteenth century. He added that the English nobility persisted in their status longer than those in other countries primarily because "it became an agent rather than a ruler." It seemed to remain "free of all economic activity" without degenerating into partisanship, as nobles elsewhere did. Once industrialism took hold in the nineteenth century, the old pattern of inherited estates perpetuating classes could not continue, because history was speeding up. The new "high bourgeoisie" of leading businesspeople had to keep at it if they were to continue on top. "The feudal master class was once—and the bourgeoisie was never—the supreme pinnacle of a uniformly constructed social pyramid." Thus, "The failing bourgeois family drops out of the class so swiftly that the class itself always consists of families which are normally equal to their function." Ibid., pp. 152–163.

34. Ibid., pp. 160–163.

35. The essay's overall style resembles that of Schumpeter's book *Business Cycles,* published a decade later: discursive, reflective, confident without being offensive, and ready in its concession that much remains to be learned about the subject. There is a also a direct line of thinking from his book *The Theory of Economic Development* to this essay on social classes. Schumpeter himself specifically mentions that tie with his earlier work. See "Social Classes in an Ethnically Homogeneous Environment," p. 177n4.

36. Schumpeter, "The Instability of Capitalism," *Economic Journal* 38 (September 1928), pp. 361–386. This essay is reprinted in Richard V. Clemence, ed., *Joseph A. Schumpeter: Essays on Entrepreneurs, Innovation, Business Cycles, and the Evolution of Capitalism* (Cambridge, Mass: Addison-Wesley, 1951). In this volume the article covers pp. 47–72, and the passage quoted below in this note is on pp. 71–72. Schumpeter adds that one cannot assume that capitalism will last forever. No other economic or social system has ever done so, and capitalism may be a transitional phase in a broad movement toward a more egalitarian order.

In the closing sentence of the article, Schumpeter offers a bold prediction: "Capitalism, whilst economically stable, and even gaining in stability, creates, by rationalizing the human mind, a mentality and a style of life incompatible with its own fundamental conditions, motives and social institutions, and will be changed, although not by economic necessity and probably even at some sacrifice of economic welfare, into an order of things which it will be merely [a] matter of taste and terminology to call Socialism or not." This provocative statement is not the real theme of the article, and it seems tacked on as something of an afterthought. But it foreshadows a very thorough development of the same idea in Schumpeter's great book of 1942, *Capitalism, Socialism and Democracy.* Schumpeter had been "correspondent" (local professional contact) for the *Economic Journal* in Austria for the years 1920–26, and in Germany from 1927 to 1932.

His article of 1928 is heavily footnoted, and it makes numerous references to the work of leading economists throughout the world. He and Keynes exchanged several letters during the revision of the article. Schumpeter thanked Keynes for his "unexampled generosity and kindness" in suggesting improvements in the draft, and went on to say that he feels "greatly honored by any writing of mine having been the object of as much care from an economist, whom I consider my superior by far, and I am most grateful both for your approval of the drift of the argument—an approval duly prized by me—and for your criticisms." See Schumpeter to Keynes, May 28, July 7, and August 16, 1928, in Hedtke and Swedberg, eds., *Briefe,* pp. 146–150, 153–154, 176n6.

37. Existing theory, he adds, defines economic progress as industrial expansion and population growth, both of which unfold in more or less predictable fashion. But these two phenomena, by themselves, fail to show how a capitalist "order" actually evolves. "For expansion is *no* basic fact, capable of serving in the role of a cause, but is itself the result of a more fundamental 'economic force.'" Schumpeter, "The Instability of Capitalism," pp. 61n2, 62. At about the same time, he wrote in a private letter to a young economist, "Of course, the building up of a qualitative theory of the economic process is the great task of this generation. And just as we have to fit our data for theoretic treatment, so we have to fit our theory to the task before it." Schumpeter to Arthur Marget, August 30, 1928, Schumpeter Papers, HUG(FP)—4.7, Correspondence and other misc. papers, ca. 1920s-1950, box 7, folder M1920, HUA.

38. Schumpeter, "The Instability of Capitalism," pp. 63–64.

39. Ibid., pp. 64–66.

40. Ibid., pp. 67–68.

41. Ibid., pp. 69–70.

42. Ibid., pp. 70–71.

43. Milly Reisinger to Schumpeter, May 28 and June 30, 1930, Schumpeter Papers, HUG(FP)—4.7.5, Miscellaneous correspondence, box 1, folder Miscellaneous Correspondence Received, HUA. Translations by Benjamin Hett. On December 13, 1938, Milly, now married, wrote Schumpeter still again, thanking him for "all of the monthly transfers" of money for the Reisinger family. Ibid.

44. Schumpeter, "Ships in the Fog," Schumpeter Papers, HUG(FP)—4.3, Miscellaneous personal writings and notes, box 1, folder Material for Ships in the Fog, HUA.

11: POLICY AND ENTREPRENEURSHIP

1. According to Robert Loring Allen, Schumpeter first hired Mia in mid-1927. See Allen, *Opening Doors: The Life & Work of Joseph Schumpeter,* two vols. (New Brunswick, N.J.: Transaction, 1991), I, pp. 233–235. But one of Mia's letters in the Schumpeter Papers, HUG(FP)—4.5, Letters from Mia, 1932–1940, HUA, makes it clear that her original work with him began in January 1926, about eighteen months earlier, and seven months before Annie's death.

2. Numerous photographs of Mia are in the Schumpeter Papers, HUG (FP)—4.5, Letters from Mia, 1932–1940, box 1, folder Photos of Mia and family, HUA. Mia's efficiency is evident in references to their work that she makes in her letters to Schumpeter, many of which are excerpted in chapter 16 below.

3. During his first year in Bonn, his most important "scientific" publications for academic journals were an article on the control of credit, and a tribute to the work of the English economist Francis Y. Edgeworth, the longtime editor of the *Economic Journal*. See Schumpeter, *"Kreditcontrolle," Archiv für Sozialwissenschaft* 55 (1925), pp. 289–328. The article on Edgeworth appeared in *Weltwirtschaftliches Archiv* 22 (1925), pp. 183–202. Schumpeter also worked on an economics textbook, but never found the time to finish it.

4. Schumpeter to Ottilie Jäckel, January 25 [1929] (the year is not given), printed in März, *Joseph Alois Schumpeter—Forscher, Lehrer und Politiker* (Scholar, Teacher and Politician) (Munich: R. Oldenbourg Verlag, 1983), appendix. Translation by Holger Frank.

5. Schumpeter to Ottilie Jäckel, September 22, 1928, in Ulrich Hedtke and Richard Swedberg, eds., *Joseph Alois Schumpeter, Briefe/Letters* (Tübingen: J. C. B. Mohr, Paul Siebeck, 2000), pp. 154–155. Translation by Holger Frank.

6. Stolper began his Berlin career on the editorial staff of the *Berliner Börsen-Courier* (Berlin Financial Journal) before founding *Die deutsche Volkswirt* (The German Economist). The sequence of Schumpeter's early contributions to both of these journals can be traced in his letters to Stolper on the following dates: December 17, 1925; February 14 and 25, March 2, May 29, June 24, August 1, August 25, September 7, October 8, November 3, 1926; March 5, March 21, March 27, April 6, May 15, May 24, and June 22, 1927, all printed in Hedtke and Swedberg, eds., *Briefe*, pp. 105–108, 110–120, 122–125, 128–132, 133–140. In addition to these letters, dozens of others from Schumpeter to Stolper—mostly pertaining to *Die deutsche Volkswirt*—are in the Nachlass Gustav und Toni Stolper, N 1186/31, Bundesarchiv Koblenz.

7. Schumpeter, "The Future of Gold," address before the Economic Club of Detroit, April 14, 1941, printed in Schumpeter, *Aufsätze zur Tagespolitik* (Essays on Current Policy), eds. Christian Seidl and Wolfgang F. Stolper (Tübingen: J. C. B. Mohr, Paul Siebeck, 1993), p. 71. He went on to say that "These problems are largely political and it is up to you to say what you want to do and to fight for it, to say what you will extol and what you will destroy. The economist has no particular qualification to speak about that aspect of any subject."

8. Schumpeter to Ottilie Jäckel, September 22, 1928, in Hedtke and Swedberg, eds., *Briefe*, p. 155; also to Ottilie Jäckel, n.d. (1928?; year is not given), printed in März, *Joseph Alois Schumpeter—Forscher, Lehrer und Politiker*, appendix. Translations by Holger Frank.

9. The reparations issue, which played a very significant and controversial role in Weimar politics, dragged on into the early 1930s. After Germany's default on its reparations in January 1923, adjustments in the payments schedule and its administrative details were worked out under the Dawes Plan of 1924, named for committee chairman Charles G. Dawes, an American. Still another adjustment

derived from the Young Plan of 1929 (named for Owen D. Young, like Dawes an American businessman/politician), which went into effect in May 1930. Within Germany, politicians and the electorate were deeply divided on how best to use the American loans: whether to rebuild the infrastructure with public works and support social welfare programs, or whether to channel the money into business enterprises—and, in the case of the latter choice, which kinds of enterprises. Schumpeter was correct in arguing that in the end, too much of the money went into established industries such as coal and steel, and too little into entrepreneurial firms.

10. Divisions in the Austro-Hungarian Parliament had been based primarily on ethnicity and incipient nationalism. Those in Germany's *Reichstag* were based more on class, region, and ideology—the latter of sometimes hair-splitting fineness. The historical literature on Weimar Germany is exceptionally thorough, and more than a little contentious. See, among many works, Harold James, *The Reichsbank and Public Finance in Germany, 1924–1933: A Study of the Politics of Economics during the Great Depression* (Frankfurt am Main: Fritz Knapp Verlag, 1985); William C. McNeill, *American Money and the Weimar Republic: Economics and Politics on the Eve of the Great Depression* (New York: Columbia University Press, 1986); Harold James, *The German Slump: Politics and Economics, 1924–1936* (New York: Oxford University Press, 1986); Larry Eugene Jones, *German Liberalism and the Dissolution of the Weimar Party System, 1918–1933* (Chapel Hill: University of North Carolina Press, 1988); Eberhard Kolb, *The Weimar Republic* (London: Unwin Hyman, 1988); Ian Kershaw, ed., *Weimar: Why Did German Democracy Fail?* (New York: St. Martin's, 1990); Detlev J. K. Peukert, trans. Richard Deveson, *The Weimar Republic: The Crisis of Classical Modernity* (New York: Hill and Wang, 1992); Theo Balderston, *The Origins and Course of the German Economic Crisis, November 1923 to May 1932* (Berlin: Haude and Spende, 1993); Hans Mommsen, trans. Elborg Forster and Larry Eugene Jones, *The Rise and Fall of Weimar Democracy* (Chapel Hill: University of North Carolina Press, 1996); Sheri Berman, "Civil Society and the Collapse of the Weimar Republic," *World Politics* 49 (1997), pp. 401–429; and Peter C. Caldwell, *Popular Sovereignty and the Crisis of German Constitutional Law: The Theory and Practice of Weimar Constitutionalism* (Durham, N.C.: Duke University Press, 1997).

11. In addition to the works cited in note 10 above, a quick overview of these voting results, together with basic economic statistics, may be found in Hermann Kinder and Werner Hilgemann, trans. Ernest A. Menze, *The Penguin Atlas of World History, Vol. 2: From the French Revolution to the Present* (New York: Penguin Books, 2003), pp. 148–151, 183–185.

12. Jeffrey Fear, "German Capitalism," in Thomas K. McCraw, ed., *Creating Modern Capitalism: How Entrepreneurs, Companies, and Countries Triumphed in Three Industrial Revolutions* (Cambridge, Mass.: Harvard University Press, 1997), p. 158.

In most countries today, including Germany and the United States, these standards are administered primarily by industry associations. Sometimes they have been used defensively, as non-tariff barriers against competition from other countries.

13. Fear, "German Capitalism," in McCraw, ed., *Creating Modern Capitalism*, pp. 180–182. For an argument that Mittelstand firms retain very great importance in the German economy, see Hartmut Berkhoff, "The End of Family Business? The Mittelstand and German Capitalism in Transition, 1949–2000," *Business History Review* 80 (Summer 2006), pp. 263–295.

14. Schumpeter's view of trustification (and other issues as well) appears to have been influenced by the writings of the German economist Robert Liefmann. See Liefmann, *Kartelle und Trusts und die Weiterbildung der volkswirtschaftlichen Organisation* (Stuttgart, 1910). On the specifics of trustification in Germany, see, among many other works, Wilfried Feldenkirchen, "Big Business in Interwar Germany: Organizational Innovation at Vereinigte Stahlwerke, IG Farben, and Siemens," *Business History Review* 61 (Autumn 1987), pp. 417–451; Jeffrey Fear, *Organizing Control: August Thyssen and the Construction of German Corporate Management* (Cambridge, Mass.: Harvard University Press, 2005), chs. 13–16; Fear, "German Capitalism," in McCraw, ed., *Creating Modern Capitalism,* fig. 6.2, p. 220; and Alfred D. Chandler, Jr., *Scale and Scope: The Dynamics of Industrial Capitalism* (Cambridge, Mass.: Harvard University Press, 1990), appendix C.2, pp. 705–713.

In addition to "rationalization," mergers also could be used to exploit temporary business distress, especially during Germany's period of inflation during the first years of the 1920s. The industrialist and "inflation king" Hugo Stinnes, for example, bought up numerous firms and stripped their assets, in addition to acquiring dozens of newspapers that soon began to propagate his right-wing views.

15. See, for example, Mary Nolan, *Visions of Modernity: American Business and the Modernization of Germany* (New York: Oxford University Press, 1994).

16. Schumpeter, *"Kreditpolitik und Wirtschaftslage"* (Lending Policy and the Economic Situation) in *Berliner Börsen-Courier* 58/603 (December 23, 1925), printed in Schumpeter, *Aufsätze zur Tagespolitik* (Essays on Current Policy), eds. Seidl and Stolper, pp. 154–158, quotation on p. 158. Translation by Holger Frank. Schumpeter's argument here is a prescient formula for what the Japanese and Koreans, in their post-World War II economic miracles, called "window guidance": the selection of high-potential growth industries as preferential recipients of loans and grants—awarded under the condition that the receiving companies meet prescribed performance criteria.

In a similar piece, Schumpeter again analyzes subsidy policies, mentioning not only postwar Germany but France, Britain, and Italy as well. He says that there is no universal cure-all, but rather that specific national circumstances must be taken into account. Again he is looking toward the long term, and emphasizing

entrepreneurial development of new businesses. See Schumpeter, *"Sub-
ventionspolitik"* (Subsidy Policy)," in *Handelsblatt von Berliner Börsen-Courier,
Beilage 3* (third supplement), February 21, 1926, printed in Schumpeter,
Aufsätze zur Tagespolitik (Essays on Current Policy), eds. Seidl and Stolper,
pp. 158–162.

17. He finds one cause of fiscal problems in the Weimar constitution, which encouraged the formation of multiple minority parties with different agendas. He says
that the cabinet lacks the support of Parliament because Parliament itself is
merely the agent of a few leaders at the very top of the numerous parties. These
leaders control the way the cabinet is put together, leaving the prime minister little influence in assembling groups that can cooperate within Parliament.
Schumpeter holds out some hope that in the future new electoral laws will increase Parliament's effectiveness. See Schumpeter, *"Finanzpolitik und
Kabinettsystem"* (Fiscal Policy and the Cabinet System), in *Der deutsche Volkswirt* 1
(1926), pp. 865–869, printed in Christian Seidl and Wolfgang F. Stolper, eds.,
Aufsätze zur Wirtschaftspolitik (Essays on Economic Policy), (Tübingen: J. C. B.
Mohr, Paul Siebeck, 1985), pp. 70–76. In addition, see Schumpeter,
"Finanzpolitik" (Fiscal Policy), also in *Der deutsche Volkswirt* 1 (1926/27), printed
in ibid., pp. 63–70.

He also points out that in practice, the success of any fiscal policy depends on
how its details are communicated to and perceived by the public. Political and
social psychology are involved. But in Germany, the requisite perception as of
1926 has not been well developed among public administrators, business leaders,
or the public. Taxpayers should have more rights in order to make sure that the
state's claims can be appealed. That is, taxpayers should have more legal security
than they now possess in regard to what assets and funds are actually taxable. See
Schumpeter, *"Geist und Teknik der Finanzverwaltung"* (Spirit and Technique of
Fiscal Administration), in *Der deutsche Volkswirt*, 1 (1926), pp. 1028–1031, printed
in *Aufsätze zur Wirtschaftspolitik* (Essays on Economic Policy) eds. Seidl and
Stolper, pp. 77–83. Hereinafter I will give only the English translations of the
titles of these economic essays.

Schumpeter goes on to say that the generic problem of all central governments
is how to create an "equilibrium" in which local governments can exercise policies appropriate to their own regions with a minimum of friction and a just allotment of funds. He asserts that Britain, France, and other countries do this well.
But Germany cannot, because of the historic independence of its many parts
(Prussia, Saxony, Hannover, Bavaria, and so on) prior to the unification of 1871,
and the current popular perception in Germany that the central government has
too much power. He warns that spirited opposition will appear, as it always does
with any important change. See Schumpeter, "Fiscal Equilibrium," I, in *Der
deutsche Volkswirt* 1 (1926/1927), printed in *Aufsätze zur Wirtschaftspolitik* (Essays
on Economic Policy), eds. Seidl and Stolper, pp. 84–91.

At the time of Schumpeter's writing, Germany's government was (as it still remains), a federal system less centralized than the governments of Britain or France. And it still has serious problems of competing claims on tax moneys. In Germany today, this practice is known as "the principle of subsidiarity," and it resembles somewhat the division of functions in the United States among federal, state, and local governments. Schumpeter, "Fiscal Equilibrium," II, in *Der deutsche Volkswirt* 1 (1926/1927), printed in ibid., pp. 92–99. See also Schumpeter, "The Power to Tax and the National Future," in *Der deutsche Volkswirt* 1 (1926/1927), printed in ibid., pp. 55–63.

18. Schumpeter says that the state *(Länder)* governments can also increase their taxes on alcoholic beverages. See "Fiscal Equilibrium," II, in *Der deutsche Volkswirt* 1 (1926/1927), printed in Schumpeter, *Aufsätze zur Wirtschaftspolitik* (Essays on Economic Policy), eds. Seidl and Stolper, pp. 92–99. He also argues for an increase in the general sales tax from 1% to at least 1.5%. This, he says, will yield ample additional funds without harming consumers, who don't change their buying habits because of small sales-tax hikes. And domestic sales taxes will have no effect on export prices, which are vital for export-dependent Germany. Overall, he concludes, sales taxes hinder a nation's development less than other taxes because they do not take away funds that entrepreneurs need for capital investment. See Schumpeter, "Whom Does the Turnover Tax Hit?" in *Der deutsche Volkswirt* 3 (1928/1929), pp. 203–208, printed in Schumpeter, *Aufsätze zur Wirtschaftspolitik* (Essays on Economic Policy), eds. Seidl and Stolper, pp. 107–112.

19. A companion approach would be to exempt from taxation that portion of people's incomes that is not used for consumption, which would result in a quick growth of private capital. For a rich country this kind of policy might in fact be unfair, but for a developing nation, or one in as much trouble as Germany, Schumpeter recommends it as the right path, assuming that nobody is actually starving. Schumpeter, "What Could a Financial Reform Do?" in *Der deutsche Volkswirt* 4 (1929/1930), pp. 75–80, printed in Schumpeter, *Aufsätze zur Wirtschaftspolitik* (Essays on Economic Policy), eds. Seidl and Stolper, pp. 113–122. How fiscal policy can accomplish these ends, says Schumpeter, was explained by Gustav Stolper in a series of other articles. Stolper had proposed a limitation of future expenses by some industries, the introduction of a tobacco monopoly to raise funds, and increases in alcohol taxes.

20. Many people in Germany, Schumpeter argues, regard income taxes as "modern robber-barondom." Not only are high rates unfair to individuals, they also reduce savings and therefore investment—an especially untimely effect when innovative projects require heavy infusions of capital, as they did in Germany when Schumpeter was writing. See Schumpeter, "Economics and Sociology of the Income Tax," in *Der deutsche Volkswirt* 4 (1929/1930), pp. 380–385, printed in

Schumpeter, *Aufsätze zur Wirtschaftspolitik* (Essays on Economic Policy), eds. Seidl and Stolper, pp. 123–132. On the evolution of the U.S. income tax, see W. Elliot Brownlee, *Federal Taxation in America: A Short History* (New York: Cambridge, University Press, 1996).

21. Schumpeter, "Inheritance Tax," in *Der deutsche Volkswirt* 3 (1928/1929), pp. 110–114, printed in Schumpeter, *Aufsätze zur Wirtschaftspolitik* (Essays on Economic Policy), eds. Seidl and Stolper, pp. 99–107.

22. Schumpeter, "World Crisis and Fiscal Policy," in *Der deutsche Volkswirt* 6 (1931–32), pp. 739–742, printed in Schumpeter, *Aufsätze zur Wirtschaftspolitik* (Essays on Economic Policy), eds. Seidl and Stolper, pp. 143–150.

23. Schumpeter, "If the Finance Reform Fails," in *Der deutsche Volkswirt* 4 (1929/1930), pp. 695–699, printed in Schumpeter, *Aufsätze zur Wirtschaftspolitik* (Essays on Economic Policy), eds. Seidl and Stolper, pp. 133–143.

Schumpeter underscored his constant theme of the need for additional domestic investment, which could only come from savings, and by simple logic mostly from the wealthier classes. The German situation at this time differed from what happened a few years later in Britain and especially the United States, where ample capital existed but business did not want to invest it because of slack demand. That situation was accurately diagnosed by Keynes as a "liquidity trap," and would not have been helped by the kinds of policies Schumpeter was advocating for Germany in 1929. But far less liquidity was available in Germany than in Britain or the United States.

24. Schumpeter, "Unemployment," in *Der deutsche Volkswirt* 1 (1926/27), pp. 729–732, printed in Schumpeter, *Aufsätze zur Wirtschaftspolitik* (Essays on Economic Policy), eds. Seidl and Stolper, pp. 153–160.

25. Referring to the standard economic theorem of the equilibrium wage, Schumpeter reminded his audience that back-and-forth movements in the supply and demand of labor tend to stabilize wages. Against this movement toward equilibrium, only "progress" in new production technologies and other innovations could lead to higher productivity, lower prices, and therefore higher real wages. The opposing argument—that mechanization and better organization of business produces higher unemployment—describes a temporary phenomenon and therefore is not a valid basis for long-term policy. Ultimately, consumer demand will catch up with higher production and lower costs, and will stimulate the hiring of more workers. He went on to say that in a few instances, wage increases have bolstered productivity, as tended to happen in the U.S. automobile industry. But in most industries this does not occur. Wage gains without increased productivity damage the overall economy. Schumpeter summarizes by saying that all policies that foster economic development can have a positive effect on the wage level. But policies aimed solely at increasing wages as a tool of development cannot work in the long run. See Schumpeter, "Wage

Configuration and Economic Development," in *Der Arbeitgeber* 18 (1928), pp. 479–482, printed in Schumpeter, *Aufsätze zur Wirtschaftspolitik* (Essays on Economic Policy), eds. Seidl and Stolper, pp. 173–185.

26. Hermann Dahl, quoted in Gerald D. Feldman, *The Great Disorder: Politics, Economics, and Society in the German Inflation, 1914–1924* (New York: Oxford University Press, 1993), p. 811.

27. Then, too, he went on to say, in actual practice a small *in*crease in the wage level usually led to a relatively higher increase in unemployment. Conversely, a small *de*crease often led to a proportionally higher gain in new jobs. Schumpeter, "The Limits of Wage Policy," in *Der deutsche Volkswirt* 3 (1928/29), pp. 847–851, printed in Schumpeter, *Aufsätze zur Wirtschaftspolitik* (Essays on Economic Policy), eds. Seidl and Stolper, pp. 192–201. The distinctive German custom of co-determination in the governance of business, in which labor has a virtually equal voice with management, had already begun when Schumpeter was writing.

28. Schumpeter, "Unemployment," in *Der deutsche Volkswirt* 1 (1926/27), pp. 729–732, printed in *Aufsätze zur Wirtschaftspolitik* (Essays on Economic Policy), eds. Seidl and Stolper, pp. 153–160.

Schumpeter's recognition of the need for temporary protection of infant industries anticipates measures followed in Japan during its "economic miracle" of 1953–1973: for steel, automobiles, machinery, electronics, and other industries in which Japan came to lead the world. As he later wrote, "I feel strongly that nothing but confusion and misunderstanding can result from any analysis of the effects of protective tariffs from purely economic considerations." Other issues must be taken into account: a nation's drive for independence, and the particular circumstances "into which its lot is cast." In an ideal world, universal commitments to free trade—a fundamental tenet of orthodox economics—are wholly correct. "But there seems to be little point in losing contact with reality for their sake." See Schumpeter, "The Influence of Protective Tariffs on the Industrial Development of the United States," *Proceedings of the Academy of Political Science,* 29 (May 1940), p. 2; and Schumpeter, "English Economists and the State-Managed Economy," *Journal of Political Economy* (October 1949), pp. 371–382, reprinted in Richard V. Clemence, ed., *Joseph A. Schumpeter: Essays on Entrepreneurs, Innovations, Business Cycles, and the Evolution of Capitalism* (Cambridge, Mass.: Addison-Wesley, 1951), p. 320.

In the years since he wrote these words, many countries have used protectionism, but most have failed in their aims—India and Brazil during the 1960s and 70s, to take two prominent examples. Most governments have lacked the discipline to execute their programs well: specifically, to require high economic performance as a condition of continued protection from imports. But Japan possessed this discipline during its miracle years, and so did Germany during the years before World War I. And the pattern of high U.S. tariffs during the nineteenth century, Schumpeter says, "presents an almost ideal case" of the infant-industry argument for economic development. In his eyes, both German and American economic history showed that protection did not necessarily stifle innovation. As Schumpeter well knew, Germany's industrial rise during an earlier period (1879–1913) had depended on—or, at the very least, coincided with—protectionist policies. The comments on the role of protectionism in American industrial history appear in Schumpeter, "The Influence of Protective Tariffs on the Industrial Development of the United States," p. 4.

29. Schumpeter adds that research on business cycles—perhaps the hottest topic in the economics profession at the time he was writing—should be especially relevant for businesspeople who are trying to think analytically about the future. He identifies the six-to-eleven-year swings characteristic of business cycles during the decades before World War I. But he goes on to note that these "normal" swings are invariably disrupted by extraordinary events. He mentions the Great War, the postwar inflation, and political and societal crises such as those then going on in Germany. The most sophisticated analyses of these situations as a whole, against the background of all the other data, are best done by those working on the economic theory of crises. That theory merges naturally with research on business cycles. See Schumpeter, "*Konjunkturforschung,*" (Research on the Economic Situation or Cycle, two parts), *Berliner Börsen-Courier,* 58/137, *Beilage 4* (Supplement 4, April 4, 1926); and ibid., 58/159, *Beilage 2* (Supplement 2, April 7, 1926), both printed in Schumpeter, *Aufsätze zur Tagespolitik* (Essays on Current Policy), eds. Seidl and Stolper, pp. 163–173.

Schumpeter makes little explicit mention of psychological factors here—the expectations that both consumers and business managers have about the future. But it is clear that he has them in mind. For example, he points out that the German economy is so dependent on exports that its businesspeople must pay close attention to subtle changes in international markets. Under the fluid conditions of modern capitalism, managers and investors can no longer rely solely on their intuitive "businessman's nose" (as he calls it). Because of constant innovation, they need detailed statistical data. Schumpeter mentions five types of meaningful indicators: (1) Financial data, including bank interest rates, the shares and reserves of Central Banks as percentages of total funds, and quotations from stock exchanges and money markets; (2) International data from various countries, showing their imports and exports, price levels, and similar indicators; (3) Information on levels of industrial production, especially by key industries such as steel, coal, copper, and cotton; (4) Data concerning the emergence of new kinds of industries; and (5) Different national policies regarding trade, taxes, and monetary affairs. He points out that these are the most rudimentary kinds of information that businesspeople need to manage well under capitalist systems. If one wished to tap more sophisticated sources of data, then elaborate statistical and theoretical tools were available in new economic models developed at Harvard University, the Cambridge Economic Service in the U.K., and the new German Institute for the Analysis of the Economic Situation. Schumpeter himself used data gathered by the latter Institute, which was located in Berlin. It offered a wealth of information of a type that had been helpful in other countries, notably in the form developed by American firms such as Babson and Brookmire. Small businesses and private investors, he writes, should make much more use of this kind of data. Up to then, systematic data-gathering in Germany had been done mostly by banks. It had not been used very much by other businesses even when they have had access to it. Schumpeter's also discusses the "economic barometers" that might prove useful in anticipating crises. He debates the merits of yardsticks such as the Harvard Index, the Babson system, the Spiethoff Index (developed by his close friend, and emphasizing steel production), and others. He then presents a simplified model of a typical business cycle. Ibid.

30. Schumpeter, "Change in the World Economy," in *Der deutsche Volkswirt* 4 (1929/ 30), pp. 1729–1733, printed in Schumpeter, *Aufsätze zur Wirtschaftspolitik* (Essays on Economic Policy), eds. Seidl and Stolper, pp. 218–225. Schumpeter here asks whether there might be a rise in socialism because of this progress. He says that perhaps the tendency away from traditional forms of ownership (that is, the shift from real assets such as land and equipment to paper ones such as stocks and bonds) would create a state of the world which to call socialist or capitalist would be purely a matter of taste. He was fond of making provocative statements such as this one, and he used similar language in many other writings, all the way to the 1940s.

31. Recent research on Americans' development of their natural resource endowment has provided much support for Schumpeter's argument. See Gavin Wright, "The Origins of American Industrial Success, 1879–1940," *American Economic Review* 80 (September 1990), pp. 651–688. Schumpeter goes on to contest the idea that the U.S. holds an effective monopoly on some of the raw materials that would make it possible for Europe to be competitive. This, he says, rests on a misapprehension of what a monopoly really is. A genuine monopoly over a material such as cotton would actually damage U.S. businesses and consumers as much as European ones. As long as there is no war, the U.S. endowment of raw materials is not a significant inhibitor of European growth. In any case, Europe itself possesses vast deposits of the most important industrial raw materials, so the whole argument is invalid.

He also expresses the view that American industry and its infrastructure are very efficient, whereas its government, on practically all levels, is badly managed and inordinately expensive. See, on all of these points, Schumpeter, "Change in the World Economy," in *Der deutsche Volkswirt* 4 (1929/30), pp. 1729–1733, printed in Schumpeter, *Aufsätze zur Wirtschaftspolitik* (Essays on Economic Policy), eds. Seidl and Stolper, pp. 218–225.

32. Here, ten years in advance of his great book *Capitalism, Socialism and Democracy,* Schumpeter comes close to articulating his famous theory of creative destruction. Schumpeter, "Enduring Crisis," in *Der deutsche Volkswirt* 6 (1931/32), pp. 418–421, printed in Schumpeter, *Aufsätze zur Wirtschaftspolitik* (Essays on Economic Policy), eds. Seidl and Stolper, pp. 202–210.

33. Schumpeter, "The Function of Entrepreneurs and the Interest of the Worker," in *Der Arbeitgeber* 17 (1927), pp. 166–170, printed in Schumpeter, *Aufsätze zur Wirtschaftspolitik* (Essays on Economic Policy), eds. Seidl and Stolper, pp. 160–173.

34. Ibid.

35. Ibid.

36. Ibid., p. 168. Schumpeter uses the same saying two years later in "The Entrepreneur in the National Economy Today," in Bernhard Harms, ed., *Strukturwandlungen der Deutschen Wirtschaft* (Structural Changes in the German National Economy), 2nd ed. (Berlin: Reimar Hobbing, 1929), pp. 306–326, reprinted in Schumpeter, *Aufsätze zur Wirtschaftspolitik* (Essays on Economic Policy), eds. Seidl and Stolper, p. 235, where he calls it an English saying. See also Schumpeter, trans. Heinz Norden, "Social Classes in an Ethnically Homogeneous Environment," in *Imperialism, Social Classes: Two Essays by Joseph Schumpeter* (New York: Meridian Books, 1955), p. 129.

37. Schumpeter, "The Function of Entrepreneurs and the Interest of the Worker," in *Der Arbeitgeber* 17 (1927), pp. 166–170, printed in Schumpeter, *Aufsätze zur Wirtschaftspolitik* (Essays on Economic Policy), eds. Seidl and Stolper, pp. 160–173.

38. Schumpeter, "The Entrepreneur in the National Economy Today," in Harms, ed., *Strukturwandlungen der Deutschen Wirtschaft,* printed in *Aufsätze zur Wirtschaftspolitik* (Essays on Economic Policy), eds. Seidl and Stolper, pp. 226–247.

39. Ibid. Schumpeter does not mention antitrust explicitly, but it is obviously what he had in mind.

40. There is a third powerful clue as well—his frequent praise of the Victorian statesman William E. Gladstone, "the most representative as well as the most brilliant exponent" of British liberalism. As he later wrote of Gladstone,

> The principle of leaving individuals to themselves and of trusting their free interaction to produce socially desirable results cannot be better expressed than it was by the three rules which sum up [his] policy: that public expenditure should be limited to the minimum required for the essential services ("retrenchment"); that budgets should not only balance

but display a surplus to be applied to the reduction of the national debt; and that taxation should serve no other purpose than that of raising the necessary revenue, and exact as little effect as possible on the distribution of income and on the channels of trade, from which it followed that it must be light. The income tax was an essential part of this program; but it was not less essential that it should be so low as to constitute a minor item.

Gladstone, who served as Prime Minister during four different periods, was also known for his sympathies for the poor, and a good deal of social legislation went along with his fiscal program. See Schumpeter, "Capitalism," in *Encyclopaedia Britannica* (New York: Encyclopaedia Britannica, 1946), pp. 801–87, reprinted in Clemence, ed., *Joseph A. Schumpeter: Essays on Entrepreneurs , Innovations, Business Cycles, and the Evolution of Capitalism,* pp. 189–210. The quoted passage is on p. 193.

41. Many Japanese economists have shown a special affinity for Schumpeter's works. Economic growth has been almost a national obsession in Japan since the Meiji Restoration of 1868, and Schumpeter's *Theory of Economic Development* (1911) was one of the first real classics of growth theory. It was not by chance that universities in Tokyo were the first to offer him employment in 1925, after his misadventures at the Biedermann Bank. In 1931, he made a triumphal tour of Japan, delivering numerous lectures and receiving wide media coverage. As his personal letters make clear, he felt a special kinship with Japanese academics, several of whom he taught at Bonn and Harvard. After his death, Hitotsubashi University in Tokyo purchased his library, and still displays it in a special room. See, generally, Jean-Pascal Bassino, "The Diffusion and Appropriation of Schumpeter's Economic Thought in Japan," *History of Economic Ideas* 6 (1998), pp. 79–105.

Of the eleven books Schumpeter wrote that appeared during his lifetime or shortly afterward, ten have been translated into Japanese. (The eleventh is a brief co-authored text on mathematics for economists that he updated for a course at Harvard.) In no other language, not even German or English, are so many of his books available. Among Schumpeter scholars in Japan, one of the best known is Yuichi Shionoya, both for his analytical works and for his presidency of the International Schumpeter Society. Perhaps the most prolific is Motoi Kanazashi, one of many Japanese scholars listed in the very thorough *Joseph Alois Schumpeter: A Reference Guide,* by Massimo M. Augello (Berlin: Springer-Verlag, 1990), which is 353 pages long. See also Augello's bibliographical essay in Swedberg, ed., *Joseph A. Schumpeter: The Economics and Sociology of Capitalism,* pp. 445–481. Of the substantial Japanese-language literature on Schumpeter, an example is the special issue of *Kei Seminar* 541 (February 2000), which is devoted to his works and its relevance to recent economic problems in Japan.

Of course, no national economy is ever purely Keynesian, Marxist, Schumpeterian, or Hayekian. But there is no mistaking the Schumpeterian core of the Japanese system during the 1953–1973 miracle growth period, the heavy hand of government notwithstanding. The most important Schumpeterian elements were these six: an unprecedented outburst of entrepreneurship, a relatively cooperative system for setting wages, a fiscal structure that emphasized consumption taxes and encouraged savings, an exceedingly high rate of investment, the support of industries with high growth potential, and the generous dispensing of domestic credit, including a strict prevention of capital flight. All six of these policies are consistent with Schumpeter's premise that innovation, creative destruction, and the expansion of credit are the keys to economic growth. And all six were promoted with single-minded energy by both government and business. One of the most important of the six was Japanese entrepreneurship, to which many analysts have paid far too little attention.

42. Schumpeter to Ottilie Jäckel, February 5, 1927, printed in März, *Joseph Alois Schumpeter—Forscher, Lehrer und Politiker* (Scholar, Teacher and Politician), appendix. On the Freiburg offer, Schumpeter wrote Gustav Stolper that the kindness of the faculty exceeded anything to be found in Prussia—"the first time in my life that everything was delightful without exception." Schumpeter to Stolper, February 9, 1927, Nachlass Gustav und Toni Stolper, N 1186/31, Bundesarchiv Koblenz. Translation by Holger Frank.

43. Schumpeter to Ottilie Jäckel, February 5, 1927, printed in März, *Joseph Alois Schumpeter—Forscher, Lehrer und Politiker* (Scholar, Teacher and Politician), appendix.

44. Ibid.; See also Schumpeter to Ottilie Jäckel, July 26, 1927 and n.d. [August 1927], in ibid. Translation by Holger Frank. Schumpeter to the Ministry of Science, Art and Public Administration, Berlin, August 3, 1927, in Hedtke and Swedberg, eds., *Briefe*, p. 142.

12: THE BONN-HARVARD SHUTTLE

1. Taussig to Schumpeter, November 27, 1912, responding to a letter from Schumpeter about the state of economics, in Schumpeter Papers, HUG(FP)—4.7, Correspondence and other misc. papers, ca. 1920s to 1950, box 9, folder T 1910; Taussig to Lowell, October 22, 1913, UAI.5.160, Presidential Papers of A. Lawrence Lowell, box Series 1909–1914, folder 413, Economics Department—Taussig (Chairman). All in HUA.

2. Schumpeter, Arthur H. Cole, and Edward S. Mason, "Frank William Taussig, 1859–1940," *Quarterly Journal of Economics* 55 (May 1941), pp. 337–363, reprinted in Schumpeter, *Ten Great Economists: From Marx to Keynes* (New York: Oxford University Press, 1951), pp. 191–221; Bernard Baruch to Allyn Young, December 19, 1925, UAV 349.10.5, Department of Economics—Correspondence of A. A.

Young, Chairman 1925–1927, Departmental Correspondence, 1925–1926, folder 1, HUA.

3. Schumpeter, *History of Economic Analysis* (New York: Oxford University Press, 1954), p. 870; Edward S. Mason, "The Harvard Department of Economics from the Beginning to World War II," *Quarterly Journal of Economics* 97 (August 1982), pp. 393–394, 408.

4. Schumpeter, Cole, and Mason, "Frank William Taussig, 1859–1940," in Schumpeter, *Ten Great Economists,* pp. 191–207. Although co-authored, this piece was written almost entirely by Schumpeter. For 40 years, from 1896 to 1936, Taussig edited the prestigious *Quarterly Journal of Economics.* Of Taussig, Schumpeter wrote in 1931 that he was "not an elegant young little Jew, but the famous 72 year old economist, who made the economics department of Harvard maybe the first garden of this science in the world and who taught there almost 50 years." Schumpeter to Ottilie Jäckel, January 5, 1931, printed in Eduard März, *Joseph Alois Schumpeter—Forscher, Lehrer und Politiker* (Scholar, Teacher and Politician) (Munich: R. Oldenbourg Verlag, 1983), appendix. Translation by Holger Frank.

   In the United States, as in Europe, one's Jewishness was seldom a simple matter, and Frank Taussig chose not to identify himself with Jewish affairs or causes. (See, for example, Taussig's revealing eight-page summary of his own career, which is preserved in the Taussig Papers, HUG 4823.5, box 12, folder Taussig, Frank W., HUA.) But it seems unlikely that Schumpeter, who lived with Taussig for five years and had innumerable conversations with him, knew nothing of his friend's background. For one thing, Taussig's sister had married Alfred Brandeis, the brother of Louis Brandeis, the first Jewish member of the Supreme Court.

5. Schumpeter, Cole, and Mason, "Frank William Taussig, 1859–1940," in Schumpeter, *Ten Great Economists,* pp. 206, 207, 217. Taussig's book *Origins of American Business Leaders* was written in collaboration with C. S. Joslyn.

6. On enrollment for the coming year, see Allyn Young to Dean Clifford H. Moore, June 6, 1927, UAV 359.10.5, Correspondence of A. A. Young, Chairman 1925–1927, Departmental Correspondence 1926–1927. On the official appointment of Schumpeter, see ibid.; also Moore to Lowell, July 8, 1927; Lowell to Young, July 19, 1927, UAI.5.160, Presidential Papers of A. Lawrence Lowell, box Series 1925–1928, folder 668, Economics Department—Budget for 1927–8. A total of 13 letters are in the file to and from the parties at Harvard, including members of the governing "Corporation." Nearly all of the letters are pro forma. The Economics Department's minutes (January 11, 1927) report the decision as follows: "The question of bringing some distinguished European economist to Harvard for the next year, or, possibly for the next three years, was discussed. The Department expressed itself as favoring a one-year arrangement. The names of Professors Schumpeter of Bonn, Cassel of Stockholm, and Cannan of London were pre-

sented and discussed. It appeared to be the opinions [sic] of the Department that no steps should be taken at this time toward the calling to Harvard of any American economist." Economics Department Meeting Minutes/Records, UAV 349.3, box 1, folder Economics Dept. Records 1920–27. All sources in HUA.

7. Harvard hinted that if Schumpeter declined, it would invite Gustav Cassell, a prominent Swedish economist. Schumpeter told his friend Gustav Stolper that he did not really want to go, but neither did he want Cassell to get the post. Schumpeter to Stolper, June 22 and July 9, 1927, in Ulrich Hedtke and Richard Swedberg, eds., *Joseph Alois Schumpeter, Briefe/Letters* (Tübingen: J. C. B. Mohr, Paul Siebeck, 2000), pp. 140, 141. Allyn Young to secretary directing the sending of a telegram to Schumpeter, typewritten note, May 12, 1927, UAV 349.11, Department of Economics Correspondence and Records, 1930–1961, box Robertson-Schumpeter, folder Joseph Alois Schumpeter, HUA; Schumpeter to Young, telegrams, May 31 and June 15, 1927, ibid. In Schumpeter's course on Money and Banking, he emphasized the theory and mechanics of credit creation, as he had done at Bonn.

8. Taussig to the Executive Committee of the Colonial Club, October 19, 1927: "He is a distinguished writer and scholar, and his present year's service at Harvard University adds to our prestige as well as to his. He is, also, a most attractive gentleman." UAV 349.11, Department of Economics Correspondence and Records, 1930–1961, box Robertson-Schumpeter, folder Joseph Alois Schumpeter, HUA.

9. Schumpeter to Ottilie Jäckel, October 29, 1927, printed in März, *Joseph Alois Schumpeter,* appendix. Translation by Holger Frank. Mason, "The Harvard Department of Economics from the Beginning to World War II," p. 413. The actual number of graduate students during the 1925–26 academic year was 75, of undergraduate "concentrators" (majors) 324. See Confidential Report on Long-Range Plans for the Department of Economics (Revised Edition), typescript, February 25, 1948, HUG 4795.5, Sumner H. Slichter Personal Papers, box 1, Correspondence Relating to Harvard, Special Folders: A-F, folder Harvard Correspondence, Old, HUA. See also Paul H. Buck, Provost of Harvard University, to Slichter, March 27, 1948, UAV 349.208, Department of Economics, Budget, folder Budget 1940/41–1945/46, HUA, relating that the Report was adopted by the Executive Committee of the Department on March 9, 1948.

10. Schumpeter to Ottilie Jäckel, November 20, 1927, printed in März, *Joseph Alois Schumpeter,* appendix. Translation by Holger Frank.

11. Ibid. See also Robert Loring Allen, *Opening Doors: The Life & Work of Joseph Schumpeter,* two vols. (New Brunswick, N.J.: Transaction, 1991), I, p. 245.

12. Schumpeter to Harold Burbank (Chairman of the Economics Department), April 9, 1928; Burbank to Dean Clifford Moore, April 13, 1928; Moore to Burbank, April 16, 1928 ("I regret his withdrawal but think it would be unwise to object now"); Burbank to Schumpeter, April 17, 1928, all in UAV 349.10, Depart-

ment of Economics, Correspondence and Records, box 7, folder Correspondence S, HUA.

13. Schumpeter to Stolper, April 26, 1928, in Hedtke and Swedberg, eds., *Briefe,* p. 143.

14. Mia Stöckel to Schumpeter, January 11, 1934, Schumpeter Papers, HUG(FP)—4.5, Letters from Mia, 1932–1940, box 1, folder 1934, HUA. Translation by Benjamin Hett.

15. Mia's frequent attention to Annie's grave is evident in many letters from Mia to Schumpeter during the 1930s, all in ibid., boxes 1 and 2.

16. Later, after Schumpeter's move to Harvard, this changed, and he took three long summer vacations with Mia.

17. Allen, *Opening Doors,* I, pp. 281–283.

18. Ibid., pp. 282–283.

19. Quoted in Barbara Wood, *E. F. Schumacher: His Life and Thought* (New York: Harper & Row, 1984), cited in Allen, *Opening Doors,* I, p. 258.

20. Quoted in Allen, *Opening Doors,* I, p. 258.

21. Schumpeter to Ottilie Jäckel, n.d. (September 1929), and November 30, 1929, printed in März, *Joseph Alois Schumpeter,* appendix. Translations by Holger Frank.

22. H. H. Burbank to Schumpeter, December 21, 1928, UAV 349.10, Department of Economics, Correspondence and Records, box 7, folder Correspondence S, HUA; Mason, "The Harvard Department of Economics from the Beginning to World War II," p. 413. Burbank's letter went on to say: "It is not necessary to expand upon our need for you as we talked of this many times last year. The senior professors are now well along in years. The new department must be built largely around new men, Allyn Young, we hope, and you . . . I wish fervently that I could picture your need for us as vividly as I can depict our need for you. But I do think—for what it is worth—that with our unusual abilities and accomplishments Harvard has not a little to offer you. It is only a matter of time before we will have adequate departmental endowment that will furnish all the necessary facilities for research and will make it possible both to increase largely our staff and to decrease teaching requirements. Also shortly, salaries should be on a considerably higher level. These material advantages are easily overemphasized. They do, however, lead to the end that Harvard should be able to advance steadily in influence and accomplishment. I am sure that this perspective makes it appeal to you. I can only hope that the appeal is irresistibly strong."

23. Schumpeter to Burbank, March 31, 1929, ibid. He goes on to say: "You have been so generous as to emphasize what you thought I might do for Harvard, but of course Harvard would mean much more than that to me. It could be just the atmosphere I want to work and teach in and I doubt whether I can, outside of America, carry out my present plan of research at all: ideas I want to follow up

will be sterile here, whilst, on the other hand, I am entirely lacking in precisely those methods of handling statistical material, which I could have at my disposal with you. To carry on Harvard's great tradition and to take a hand in developing or helping to develop the line of quantitative theory, has been my ardent wish ever since Harvard's invitation to join her offered me the chance. I need not add that, above all, to live and work in so congenial an environment and among so eminent colleagues would have been as near to happiness for me as anything can be."

24. Schumpeter to Burbank, March 31, 1929, ibid.

25. Lowell to Schumpeter, April 15, 1929, UAI.5.160, Presidential Papers of A. Lawrence Lowell, box Series 1928–30, folder 476, Economics Department—Schumpeter, HUA. Appealing to Schumpeter's cross-disciplinary preoccupations, Lowell also wrote in this letter, "I am wondering whether the filling of this gap may appeal to you, for it offers a very great chance of rendering a great service to the cause of economic knowledge . . . Moreover, an interest is arising here in questions that connect physiology [sic; the typist likely meant psychology] on one side and industry on the other, with many aspects of human life. We are still hoping to obtain funds for carrying on research of this kind, and if we succeed I think you will be interested in it." Schumpeter to Lowell, May 8, 1929, ibid. The text of Schumpeter's letter also includes the following: "My dear friend Taussig—or Mr. Burbank—has probably explained the reasons, by which I have, much against my wishes, felt compelled to arrive at the conclusion that I could not, without failing in my duty, accept the invitation to join Harvard for good. It would be impossible for me to go back on that decision at the present moment," but through the new proposal that he visit Harvard on a regular basis he hopes "to become pars parva of the great scientific community over which you preside."

26. Burbank to Schumpeter, May 4, 1929: "We are hopeful that many of the difficulties will be removed by the possibility of being in residence for only a half of each year . . . You will be interested in the developments here in quantitative theory. Our funds will be forthcoming presently, and under the senior staff the work will be launched and we hope will go far. But this is a venture of unlimited possibilities . . . Your point of view and your abilities are very necessary if this work is to attain the significant position we hope for it . . . It would be helpful to us if you could manage it for either half of 1929–30, but if this is out of the question we will do the best we can in the expectation that you will be here the following year." See also Taussig and Burbank to Schumpeter, telegram, dated "5/29," both in UAV 349.10, Department of Economics, Correspondence and Records, box 7, folder Correspondence S, HUA.

27. Schumpeter to Burbank, May 8 and December 5, 1929, February 25, 1930 (telegram), and March 4, 1930; Burbank to Schumpeter, June 4, 1929 and January 20 and March 31, 1930, all in ibid. In proposing to "rechristen" the first course,

Schumpeter wrote: "the idea being to discuss those tools of economic analysis, which are, or may be expected to become, useful of 'quantitative economics' and to go over the leading controversies of our day." Schumpeter to Burbank, March 4, 1930; Burbank to Schumpeter, March 31, 1930, both in ibid.

28. Burbank told Schumpeter that the new House system "may result in nothing more than a highly desirable change in living conditions; it may prove revolutionary in undergraduate education, not only here but throughout the endowed institutions in this country" (Burbank to Schumpeter, March 31, 1930). See also Taussig to Chester N. Greenough (Master of Dunster House), May 16, 1930; and Greenough to Schumpeter, May 24, 1930, all in ibid.

29. Schumpeter to Burbank, December 5, 1929; Burbank to Schumpeter, January 20, 1930, both in ibid. See also Greenough to A. Lawrence Lowell, November 17, 1932: "Many thanks for your letter of November 4 about Professor Schumpeter. I am happy to have him connected with Dunster House in any relation." Presidential Papers of A. Lawrence Lowell, UAI.5.160, box Series 1930–1933, folder 45: Economics Department—Schumpeter, HUA. Schumpeter to Ottilie Jäckel, September 17, 1930, printed in März, *Joseph Alois Schumpeter,* appendix. Translation by Holger Frank.

30. Schumpeter to the ministry, January 30, 1930. See also Schumpeter to Gustav Stolper, July 1 and August 30, 1930; and Schumpeter to Keynes, September 9, 1930, all in Hedtke and Swedberg, eds., *Briefe,* pp. 170–171, 174, 175–177.

31. Schumpeter to Ottilie Jäckel, October 18, 1930, printed in März, *Joseph Alois Schumpeter,* appendix. Translation by Holger Frank.

32. Schumpeter to Gottfried Haberler, November 30, 1939, in Hedtke and Swedberg, eds., *Briefe,* pp. 181–182; Burbank to Schumpeter, December 8 and 15, 1930; Schumpeter to Burbank, December 12, 1930, all in UAV 349.10, Department of Economics, Correspondence and Records, box 7, folder Correspondence S; Burbank, *Memoranda* [sic], typescript, December 22, 1930, UAV 349.11, Department of Economics, Correspondence and Records, 1930–1961, box Robertson-Schumpeter, folder Joseph Alois Schumpeter: "H. H. B. [Burbank] talked with Schumpeter on December 21. He stated definitely his intention to return in 1932–33," and gave specific details about what he would teach. HUA.

33. At the end of the conference, Schumpeter bade farewell to his Harvard colleagues, and made a pitch for Harvard's hiring of Ragnar Frisch. As he wrote Burbank from Cleveland, "Again I have been greatly impressed by Frisch. This is, indeed, a man of such immense [illeg.] gifts and of such single-minded devotion to science, that, loving Harvard as I do, I cannot help urging once more the importance of having him, for a time at least." Schumpeter to Burbank, January 1, 1931, UAV 349.10, Department of Economics, Correspondence and Records, box 7, folder Correspondence S, HUA.

A history of the Econometric Society, together with annual reports of membership and finances, is on the society's website, http://www.econometricsociety.org/, accessed June 3, 2006. Schumpeter's article is titled "The Common Sense of Econometrics," *Econometrica* 1 (January 1933), pp. 5–12. In the twenty-first century, membership in the Econometric Society is about 2,300, and is concentrated in highly industrialized countries, especially the United States (the home of about two-thirds of its members), the U.K., Germany, and Japan.

34. Schumpeter to Arthur Spiethoff, January 8, 1931, from La Playa Hotel, Carmel-by-the-Sea, in Hedtke and Swedberg, eds., *Briefe*, pp. 183–186.

35. Schumpeter to Clifford Moore, February 13, 1931, in Hedtke and Swedberg, eds., *Briefe*, p. 186.

36. Schumpeter to Toni and Gustav Stolper, February 24, 1931; Schumpeter to Seiichi Tobata, a young Japanese economist, March 17, 1931, both in Hedtke and Swedberg, eds., *Briefe*, pp. 187–189. See also Allen, *Opening Doors*, I, pp. 271–272.

37. Schumpeter to Ottilie Jäckel, March 13, 1931, printed in März, *Joseph Alois Schumpeter*, appendix. Translation by Holger Frank.

38. Schumpeter to Ottilie Jäckel, April 31, 1931, printed in ibid., appendix. Translation by Holger Frank. Schumpeter to Gustav Stolper, September 14, 1931, in Hedtke and Swedberg, eds., *Briefe*, pp. 199–200.

39. Schumpeter to Gustav Stolper, May 8, 1931, in Hedtke and Swedberg, eds., *Briefe*, pp. 189–192. Translation by Holger Frank.

40. Quoted in Allen, *Opening Doors*, I, p. 290.

41. This controversy is laid out in detail in a series of letters from Schumpeter: to Gustav Stolper, May 8, July 30, and September 14, 1931; February 22 and July 8, 1932; to Stolper reconstructing an earlier letter to Werner Richter of the education ministry, March 26, 1932; and three letters to Emil Lederer, July 5 and 6, 1932—all in Hedtke and Swedberg, eds., *Briefe*, pp. 189–192, 194–196, 200, 203–204, 206–211, and 216–219. See also Schumpeter to Stolper, August 2 and 5, 1931, July 5 and 6, 1932, and n.d. (summer 1932), Nachlass Gustav und Toni Stolper, N 1186/31, Bundesarchiv Koblenz. Translation by Holger Frank.

42. Schumpeter to Gustav Stolper, May 8 and September 23, 1931, in Hedtke and Swedberg, eds., *Briefe*, pp. 189–192 and 200–201. Translation by Holger Frank. Lederer, a socialist and a Jew, was dismissed from his post in the Hitler purges of April 1933 and left Germany for the United States.

43. Schumpeter to Richard Thoma, March 31, 1932, in ibid., pp. 211–213.

44. Singer is quoted in Allen, *Opening Doors*, I, pp. 282. For the comment on German politics, see Schumpeter to Haberler, August 3, 1932, in Gottfried Haberler Collection, box 31, folder: Schumpeter, Joseph, Hoover Institution Archives. Schumpeter, "The Whence and Whither of Our Science," in Erich Schneider and Arthur Spiethoff, eds., *Aufsätze zur ökonomischen Theorie* (Essays on Economic Theory) (Tübingen: J. C. B. Mohr, 1952). This was Schumpeter's long farewell address to his students in Bonn, given in April 1932.

Some critics have used part of the speech as evidence of sympathy for Nazism and anti-Semitism, and their view is understandable.

> We stand before a powerful movement that is unique in history. Never has an organization succeeded in opposing the established parties. This powerful apparatus of strength is like a monster of infinite impulse, and *it can mean catastrophe or glory for the German people,* depending on how it is used. But *how important would it be if this colossus were advised correctly in economic matters; and if among them there were people that felt national-socialist and still didn't disregard economic technique—what unbelievable subjective possibilities for a young man!*
>
> One only means something where nothing has been thought through yet. That one must turn to parties that have irrational programs is something that all important politicians have known. Benjamin Disraeli became a conservative because these lovely gentlemen, who provide the right following for a man of substance, stood behind it.

All translations by Holger Frank. The italicized part in the speech is in the original notes, taken by Cläre Tisch and August Lösch, on which the published version is based. Both Tisch and Lösch were Jews, and were two of Schumpeter's favorite students, quite devoted to him. His comments likely struck them as odd, at the very least, and perhaps the more so because of his use of Disraeli as a parallel.

Schumpeter's remarks about not foreseeing Hitler's rise and about his reasons for emigration are contained in a letter he wrote on February 5, 1943, to Waldemar Gurian, another European émigré, then editor of the *Review of Politics,* printed in Hedtke and Swedberg, eds., *Briefe,* p. 339. Although Schumpeter feared a "laborite" drift in Germany, the incumbent Weimar government had actually begun to move not to the left but to the authoritarian right in 1930, with the replacement of Chancellor Müller by Chancellor Brüning.

45. The most damning evidence against Schumpeter that I have seen is a diary entry from 1932, written several months before Hitler came to power, and at a time when Schumpeter knew that he himself was moving to the United States: "I have to leave. Everyone who is close to me and with whom I could work stand on one side. And what I feel in my innermost self is around Hitler. But is it really so?" See Allen, *Opening Doors,* I, pp. 285–288. Through the years, Schumpeter's diaries contains dozens of Hamlet-like statements like this, on many different subjects. He would write out some assertion, often the reverse of what he actually thought, and then try to figure out his true feelings. On this occasion, however, the sentiment is simply inexcusable, regardless of the context (30 percent unemployment, weak German governments for many years, and so on).

46. Burbank to Schumpeter, February 1, 1932, UAV 349.11, Department of Econom-

ics, Correspondence and Records, 1930–1961, box Robertson-Schumpeter, folder Joseph Alois Schumpeter, HUA. Leontief wrote to Schumpeter on August 10, 1931, asking his help in finding a job in the United States. Soon Leontief was in the United States, and on October 7, 1931, wrote Schumpeter again, this time under the letterhead of the National Bureau of Economic Research, then based at Columbia: "Recently I spent three days at Harvard. All the economists were extraordinarily nice to me. That is certainly a place where one could really work. Unofficially I was asked if I would perhaps be agreeable to giving a few lectures on methodological questions." Both letters are in the Schumpeter Papers, HUG(FP)—4.7, Correspondence and other misc. papers, ca. 1920s-1950, box 6, folder Leontief Only, HUA. Translations by Benjamin Hett.

Similarly, Gottfried Haberler sought career advice from Schumpeter, and received numerous letters suggesting which posts to consider in Europe and, ultimately, how to deal with Harvard, whose faculty Haberler joined in the mid-1930s. See Schumpeter to Haberler, August 25, 1930; August 3, 1932; March 20 and May 24, 1933; July 23, November 2, and winter (n.d.), 1934; and April 5, 1935, all in Gottfried Haberler Collection, Box 31, folder: Schumpeter, Joseph, Hoover Institution Archives.

47. Schumpeter to Burbank, March 9, 1932; Burbank to Schumpeter, May 26 and June 13, 1932, all in UAV 349.11, Department of Economics, Correspondence and Records, 1930–1961, box Robertson-Schumpeter, folder Joseph Alois Schumpeter, HUA. Schumpeter to Stolper, May 13, 1932, Nachlass Gustav und Toni Stolper, N 1186/31, Bundesarchiv Koblenz. Translation by Holger Frank.

48. Schumpeter's Diary, quoted in Allen, *Opening Doors,* I, pp. 293–295. In *Persuasion,* her novel of 1818, Jane Austen has one of her female characters sarcastically say something very similar: "You [men] have difficulties, and privations, and dangers enough to struggle with. You are always labouring and toiling, exposed to every risk and hardship. Your home, country, friends, all quitted. Neither time, nor health, nor life, to be called your own. It would be too hard, indeed . . . if woman's feelings were to be added to all this."

49. Schumpeter, "The Whence and Whither of Our Science." Translation by Holger Frank.

50. Schumpeter to the Ministry of Art, Science and Public Education, Berlin, May 13, 1932; to minister Adolph Grimme, June 2, 1932; to Toni and Gustav Stolper, September 12, 1932, all in Hedtke and Swedberg, eds., *Briefe,* pp. 214–215, 219–221. Translation by Holger Frank.

13: HARVARD

1. See the lavishly illustrated *Harvard University: An Architectural Tour,* by Douglass Shand-Tucci (New York: Princeton Architectural Press, 2001). As of 2006, Har-

vard's endowment was about $26 billion. The exact amount, like that of almost all nonprofit institutions, varies with the current market price of securities and other assets.

2. In addition to its undergraduate programs, Harvard's nine professional schools were in law, medicine, business, public health, government, education, divinity, dentistry, and design. Together with the Graduate School of Arts and Sciences, these professional schools had an enrollment well above the undergraduate total of about 6,500. The aggregate number of full-time students at all levels in the early twenty-first century was about 18,000. Data on the Class of 2010 are from *Harvard Gazette,* March 30, 2006.

3. Of the students from prep schools, one third came from just four: Exeter, Andover, St. Paul's, and Milton Academy. Almost half of Harvard's undergraduates (versus only 1.5 percent nationally) came from families whose annual incomes exceeded $7,500, which was a substantial sum during the Great Depression. See Morton and Phyllis Keller, *Making Harvard Modern: The Rise of America's University* (New York: Oxford University Press, 2001), ch. 2.

4. On anti-New Deal sentiment, see *Harvard Magazine* 107 (November–December 2004), p. 63. On anti-Semitism, see Keller and Keller, *Making Harvard Modern,* pp. 47–51 and *passim.* It is possible that anti-Semitism was stronger at Harvard than it had been at the University of Bonn during Schumpeter's years there.

5. Keller and Keller, *Making Harvard Modern,* pp. 51–59 and *passim.* Schumpeter to Stolper, 1937 (n.d.), Nachlass Gustav und Toni Stolper, N 1186/31, Bundesarchiv Koblenz.

6. Keller and Keller, *Making Harvard Modern,* p. 110. The survey covered 28 academic disciplines.

7. When I was a young professor, the former Dean of the Faculty of Arts and Sciences, John Dunlop, said to me, "Being a prima donna is not a barrier to tenure at this university. It may even be a prerequisite."

8. Schumpeter's relationship with Parsons continued for many years, and was doubly significant because of Parsons' future influence on Alfred D. Chandler, Jr., the pioneer of modern business history (see Chapter 15 below). Schumpeter well understood both the significance and the limitations of Parsons' work. For all his merits, Parsons had a notoriously difficult writing style. In Schumpeter's evaluation of Parsons' manuscript "Sociology and the Elements of Human Action," prepared at the request of Harvard's Committee on Research in the Social Sciences and dated December 23, 1936, he recommends publication and praises the work's many virtues in bringing the insights of Max Weber and Emile Durkheim to English-speaking audiences. But he goes on to say that the manuscript is too prolix and "would considerably gain by being shortened." Also, Parsons "has in fact so deeply penetrated into the German thicket as to lose in some places the faculty of writing clearly in English about it, and some turns of phrase become

fully understandable only if translated into German." Committee on Research in the Social Sciences, UAV 737.32, Combined Correspondence, General and Subject File, 1929–1949, box 6, folder Parsons' Mss: Criticisms of Readers, HUA. Several years later, Schumpeter and Parsons organized a faculty group for the study of rationality.

9. This transformation is a major theme of Keller and Keller, *Making Harvard Modern*. See also Richard Norton Smith, *The Harvard Century: The Making of a University to a Nation* (New York: Simon and Schuster, 1986).

10. Taussig to Department Chairman Harold Burbank, July 15, 1930, enclosing extracts from a letter from Schumpeter to Taussig, June 19, 1930: "I have just had a long letter from Schumpeter, and he speaks of his plans for next winter and for later days. There are a couple of passages in the letter which I think it just as well for you to see. They bear upon some Department problems which we have to think about. Please consider them confidential for the present." UAV 349.10, Department of Economics, Correspondence and Records, box 7, folder Correspondence S, HUA.

Schumpeter knew neither Lowell nor Conant well, but with his preference for the well-born, he had a higher opinion of Lowell than of Conant, despite his respect for the latter's meritocratic policies.

11. Schumpeter to Lowell, October 29, 1932; Lowell to Schumpeter, October 31, 1932, Presidential Papers of A. Lawrence Lowell, UAI.5.160, box Series 1930–1933, folder 45, Economics Department—Schumpeter, HUA.

12. In 1932, when he arrived as a permanent member of the faculty, this was the scale: full professors: $8,000–12,000; associate professors: $6,000–7000; assistant professors: $4,000 plus annual increase of $300 if renewed; instructors: maximum $3,000. See Final Revised Budget 1932–33, UAV 349.208, Department of Economics Budget, folder Budget 1930/31–1939/40, HUA.

13. Moore to Lowell, October 7, 1930; Lowell to Moore, December 9, 1930, Presidential Papers of A. Lawrence Lowell, UAI.5.160, box Series 1930–1933, folder 45, Economics Department—Schumpeter, HUA. Source for exchange rates: *Global Financial Data,* an Internet database, accessed in September 2004, for rates prevailing on December 31, 1930.

14. Moore to Lowell, December 10, 1930; Lowell to Moore, December 29, 1930; Moore to Lowell, January 3, 1931, Presidential Papers of A. Lawrence Lowell, UAI.5.160, box Series 1930–1933, folder 45, Economics Department—Schumpeter, HUA. Taussig, pushing his advocacy to the absolute limit, also tried to get Schumpeter a regular excused absence during Harvard's "Reading Period" between the end of classes in early December and examinations in mid-to-late January. This would save a faculty member six to eight weeks each year for travel or other activity. Schumpeter received one exemption so that he could begin his tour of east Asia, and Taussig himself received it quite often. But here President

Lowell drew the line, writing Taussig: "I think you are giving him an impression of freer leave of absence in the Reading Periods than is the fact. Of course a man of your age is treated in a way a younger man would not be. I fear that you have given him the impression that ordinarily he would be permitted to go, whereas, ordinarily, I think he would not; but it would be merely an occasional matter for some special reason." See Taussig to Lowell, September 28, 1931, raising this question, enclosing copy of memo from Taussig to Schumpeter; Lowell to Taussig, October 1, 1931, ibid.

When Schumpeter learned of these arrangements, he was still on his trip to Japan. From there he wrote to the dean, "I have just left Kobe, where I have yesterday received your letter of January 15 [1931]. I beg to thank you and the President and Fellows of Harvard College for this additional token of good-will, all the more pleasant as it came to me as a surprise, not being contained in the terms as offered . . . you are correct in assuming that it will equalize retirement arrangements with those in Germany." Schumpeter to Moore, February 13, 1931, in Ulrich Hedtke and Richard Swedberg, eds., *Joseph Alois Schumpeter, Briefe/Letters* (Tübingen: J. C. B. Mohr, Paul Siebeck), 2000), p. 186.

15. In constant dollars, a 1932 salary of $12,000 was the equivalent of about $170,000 in the early twenty-first century, not considering higher tax rates, which would reduce the latter salary by a much greater proportion. In the meantime, however, professorial salaries at Harvard considerably escalated. In the early twenty-first century, a person of Schumpeter's stature would receive much more than the straight equivalent in constant dollars—likely in excess of $300,000. If he wished, he could augment this pay with lucrative speaking fees. But given Schumpeter's feelings about "prostitution" he might be less prone to do this than are most high-profile professors of the present day. In the much more prosperous times of the early twenty-first century, his base salary would be nine or ten times the average per capita pre-tax income—extremely generous compensation, but nothing like the multiple of thirty Schumpeter enjoyed in 1932. These numbers come from the Bureau of Labor Statistics for the relevant years, plus my own knowledge of compensation at Harvard. On monthly living expenses, see Schumpeter to Gottfried Haberler, November 30, 1930, in *Briefe,* pp. 181–182.

16. Schumpeter to Burbank, July 6, 1932, UAV 349.11, Department of Economics, Correspondence and Records, 1930–1941, in box Robertson-Schumpeter, folder Joseph Alois Schumpeter, HUA; Schumpeter to Lowell, August 5, 1932; Lowell to Schumpeter, August 20, 1932. See also Taussig to Dean Kenneth B. Murdock, March 18, 1932, forwarded by Murdock to Lowell, March 21, 1932; Schumpeter to F. W. Hunnewell (Secretary of the University), May 3, 1932; Hunnewell to Schumpeter May 13, 1932, all in Presidential Papers of A. Lawrence Lowell, UAI.5.160, box Series 1930–1933, folder 45, Economics Department—Schumpeter, HUA.

17. He was tied in 1932/33 and 1933/34 with Taussig (24 years his senior) and C. J. Bullock (14 years his senior), who specialized in public finance. Taussig then retired. In 1934/35, he was tied with Bullock, who retired at the end of that year. In 1935/36, he was tied with Edwin Gay (16 years Schumpeter's senior, an economic historian and former dean of the Business School, who retired at the end of that year). After that, Schumpeter alone made $12,000, the highest salary in the department. See UAV 349.208, Department of Economics, Budget, folders Budget 1930/31–1939/40, and Budget 1940/41–1945/46, HUA.

In 1932/33, total Departmental salaries were $104,528, with an additional $25,000 or so paid from other sources for people with other duties. Chairman Harold Burbank, for example, earned $8,000 plus $2,000 for tutorials—as one of nine staff members, most very junior to him, who were paid additionally for this close work with students.

During the Great Depression, Harvard was by some accounts the only university in the United States not to reduce its faculty salaries. But during the inflationary 1940s, the faculty's purchasing power declined because President Conant was notoriously stingy with raises. Harvard did increase the compensation it gave to its junior faculty, but kept a ceiling of $12,000 for full professors until raising it to $14,000 (which Schumpeter received) in the late 1940s. See Robert Loring Allen, *Opening Doors: The Life & Work of Joseph Schumpeter,* two vols. (New Brunswick, N.J.: Transaction, 1991), I, p. 234.

18. Paul A. Samuelson, "Schumpeter as a Teacher and Economic Theorist," in Seymour E. Harris, ed., *Schumpeter, Social Scientist* (Cambridge, Mass.: Harvard University Press, 1951), p. 48; Allen, *Opening Doors: The Life & Work of Joseph Schumpeter,* II, p. 45; the comment about the plane crash is in a handwritten letter from Schumpeter to Harold Burbank, January 13, 1937, UAV 349.11, Department of Economics, Correspondence and Records, 1930–1961, box Robertson-Schumpeter, folder Joseph Alois Schumpeter, HUA.

19. John Kenneth Galbraith, *A Life in Our Times: Memoirs* (Boston: Houghton Mifflin, 1981), pp. 48–49.

20. Samuelson, "Schumpeter as a Teacher and Economic Theorist," pp. 50–51.

21. Richard Musgrave, interview with my then-research associate Benjamin Hett, September 30, 2000; Samuelson, "Schumpeter as a Teacher and Economic Theorist," pp. 50–52.

22. Schumpeter's extremely chaotic files survive in the 132 boxes in the collection of his Papers, HUG (FP)—4.1 through 4.66–90, HUA. On his own disorganized system, see Schumpeter's comment about himself in his essay, "John Maynard Keynes," in Schumpeter, *Ten Great Economists* (New York: Oxford University Press, 1951), p. 273n14.

23. See, for example, Schumpeter to H. H. Burbank, February 18, 1933, in Hedtke and Swedberg, eds., *Briefe,* pp. 231–233, listing eleven graduate students and find-

ing something good to say about nearly all of them. Paul Samuelson, among others, often commented on Schumpeter's undue generosity in grading.

24. All excerpts are from Schumpeter's Weekly Review pages in Diary of Anna Reisinger Schumpeter, Schumpeter Papers, HUG(FP)—4.2, Mostly extracts from Annie's diary, vol. I, October 9–15 and 25–31, 1933, HUA. Shorthand deciphered by Erica Gerschenkron; see Gerschenkron, "A Report," Appended Transcripts II, p. 66. For this period the diary contains weekly entries, though a few months are missing. Here Schumpeter wrote mostly in German, but occasionally included English words and phrases. Translations by Holger Frank.

25. Schumpeter's endless lunches and dinners with students and colleagues are noted throughout his diaries, particularly for the period 1933–1936. For an example of his concern with graduate students' activities, see Schumpeter to Harold Burbank, December 4, 1935, UAV.349.11, Department of Economics, Correspondence and Records, 1930–1961, box Robertson-Schumpeter, folder Joseph A. Schumpeter 1933–1942, HUA. The quotation is from Paul M. Sweezy, "Schumpeter on 'Imperialism and Social Classes,'" in Harris, ed., *Schumpeter, Social Scientist*, p. 124.

26. In 1934, the Wise Men published, for limited circulation, a short volume called *The Economics of the Recovery Program*, a critique of the Roosevelt Administration's early efforts. In its early economic policies, the New Deal went off in so many different directions that there was much to criticize on grounds of intellectual incoherence. But the book's appearance was premature, an ill-advised venture by over-enthusiastic young critics. Schumpeter was not closely involved with the book, nor was his contribution a characteristic performance, since he disliked dabbling in political discourse and no longer had the severe press of debt repayment to draw him into journalism. "The book was not a great success, and it was not a good book," Harris, "Introductory Remarks," in Harris, ed., *Schumpeter, Social Scientist*, p. 5.

27. Allen, *Opening Doors*, II, pp. 4, 27, 62. The "Nobel Prize" in economics is separate from the prizes established in the will of Alfred Nobel in 1901 for literature, chemistry, physics, medicine or physiology, and peace. The economics award is called the Central Bank of Sweden Prize in Economic Science in Memory of Alfred Nobel. It was established in 1968 and is funded by the Bank. For convenience I will refer to it in this book as the Nobel Prize in economics, although that designation is not strictly correct.

28. Harris, "Introductory Remarks," in Harris, ed., *Schumpeter, Social Scientist*, pp. 5–7.

29. Ibid., p. 6.

30. Schumpeter to Keynes, December 3, 1932 and April 19, 1933, in Hedtke and Swedberg, eds., *Briefe*, pp. 230, 245.

31. Gottfried Haberler, "Joseph Alois Schumpeter, 1883–1950," in Harris, ed.,

Schumpeter, Social Scientist, p. 39; Harris, "Introductory Remarks," in ibid., p. 6; Schumpeter to Henry Owen Tudor, September 28, 1937, UAV 349.11, Department of Economics, Correspondence and Records, 1930–1961, box Robertson-Schumpeter, folder Joseph A. Schumpeter, 1933–1942, HUA.

32. Harris, "Introductory Remarks," in Harris, ed., *Schumpeter, Social Scientist,* p. 6. See also Arthur Smithies, "Memorial: Joseph Alois Schumpeter, 1883–1950," in ibid., pp. 14–15: Schumpeter was "profligate in the time he would spend with any student with the merest spark of an idea."

He continued to try to improve himself as a teacher. Early in 1933, he wrote Joan Robinson, a prominent economist at Cambridge University: "I have to confess that in my old age I am getting interested much more than I used to be in the problems of the teaching of our science." He asked Mrs. Robinson to send him a copy of her "sort of memorandum on the teaching of economics," which another Cambridge economist had told him about. Schumpeter to Joan Robinson, March 20, 1933, in Hedtke and Swedberg, eds., *Briefe,* p. 242.

33. For the weekly summary, see note 24 above. To the economist Adolph Löwe in Frankfurt, he wrote: "I feel quite happy at Harvard which in fact is an old love of mine and really my research work is so far going on at the desired rate of velocity and much quicker than it ever did on the charming borders of the Rhine. But I have now definitely found out the fact that there is no such thing as light teaching duties for if students are really interested in what one has to tell them they will take a terrible amount of time and energy even if the official amount of teaching work is ever so small. And yet I should not like to miss it." Schumpeter to Löwe, November 19, 1932. See also Schumpeter to Irving Fisher, February 25, 1933, in the context of not wishing to be the next president of the Econometric Society: "What energy I have is entirely absorbed by the exigencies of an inexorable research program"; and to Gottfried Haberler in Vienna, March 20, 1933: "It is always the same tale with me. My inexorable program of work takes out of me what steam I have and then there is hardly anything left for other things." All in Hedtke and Swedberg, eds., *Briefe,* pp. 226, 235, 239.

34. Fritz Machlup, "Schumpeter's Economic Methodology," in Harris, ed., *Schumpeter, Social Scientist,* pp. 95–96; Ragnar Frisch, "Some Personal Reminiscences on a Great Man," in ibid., p. 8. Frisch had used similar language in a letter to Schumpeter, October 13, 1939: "let me tell you that I have never met a person with your ability to and eagerness to understand the other fellows [sic] point of view and to do him justice." Frisch wrote this letter from Oslo, on a "sad morning" when the future of Norway was in doubt because of Nazi actions and the Russo-Finnish war. Schumpeter Papers, HUG(FP)—4.7, Correspondence and other misc. papers, ca. 1920s-1950, box 4, folder F1930, HUA.

35. Schumpeter thought so highly of Frisch's work that he tried to learn Norwegian so that he could read it in the original. He especially admired Frisch's mathemati-

cal ability. See, for example, Schumpeter to Gustav Stolper, October 25, 1930, in Hedtke and Swedberg, eds., *Briefe,* pp. 179–180, praising the work of Frisch, who at the time was visiting at Yale. Schumpeter also mentioned Frisch to his Harvard colleagues as a potential hire. On Frisch's invention of the word "econometrics," see Schumpeter, *History of Economic Analysis* (New York: Oxford University Press, 1954), p. 209n2. With typical sensitivity to language, Schumpeter goes on to say that "the term is exposed to objection on philological grounds: it ought to be either Ecometrics or Economometrics."

Econometricians were not unanimous in their acceptance of Schumpeter's professed stance. Disagreeing with Ragnar Frisch, Jan Tinbergen wrote that in view of Schumpeter's comments in the inaugural paper for *Econometrics,* "It is striking, therefore, that upon a careful study of his own largest publication since then—*Business Cycles*—one finds a mental attitude vis-à-vis econometric work which is not only rather critical, but to some extent alien to it." Tinbergen, "Schumpeter and Quantitative Research in Economics," in Harris, ed., *Schumpeter, Social Scientist,* p. 59.

36. Schumpeter, "The Common Sense of Econometrics," *Econometrica* 1 (January 1933), pp. 5–6. For a partial attempt to mathematize Schumpeter's theories and reconcile them with Samuelson's work, see H. W. Ursprung, "Schumpeterian Entrepreneurs and Catastrophe Theory, or a New Chapter to the Foundations of Economic Analysis," *Zeitschrift für Nationalökonomie,* supplement 4 (1984), pp. 39–69. Among other arguments (especially pp. 53–55), Ursprung observes that "it is small wonder that the principal advocate of the mathematical method in the German speaking countries at the beginning of the century had to be content with a verbal formulation of his ideas. The mathematical tools which existed at that time were simply of no use for Schumpeter's purposes." See also the very important work pioneered by Richard R. Nelson and Sidney G. Winter, *An Evolutionary Theory of Economic Change* (Cambridge, Mass.: Harvard University Press, 1982), and numerous subsequent articles by Nelson, Winter, their students, and others. One good example is Sidney G. Winter, "Schumpeterian Competition in Alternative Technological Regimes," *Journal of Economic Behavior and Organization* 5 (September–December 1984), pp. 287–320.

37. Schumpeter, "The Common Sense of Econometrics," pp. 8–9, 11.

38. Schumpeter to E. B. Wilson, May 24, 1934, in Hedtke and Swedberg, eds., *Briefe,* pp. 268–269. Schumpeter also worked with his colleague W. L. Crum, and later updated a short text Crum had prepared for economics graduate students on the use of math. In some years, Wassily Leontief taught the course.

39. Schumpeter to Wilson, May 24, 1934, and May 19, 1937, in *Briefe,* pp. 268–269, 306; Paul A. Samuelson, "How *Foundations* Came to Be," *Journal of Economic Literature* 36 (September 1998), p. 1376. Schumpeter attended Wilson's course in 1935, 1937, and perhaps other years as well.

40. Haberler, "Joseph Alois Schumpeter, 1883–1950," in Harris, ed., *Schumpeter, Social Scientist,* p. 24; Samuelson, "Schumpeter as a Teacher and Economic Theorist," in ibid., pp. 50–52; Tinbergen, "Schumpeter and Quantitative Research in Economics," in ibid., p. 59. Comments about Samuelson's correcting Schumpeter, and the latter's reaction, come from an interview by my then-research associate Benjamin Hett of Richard Musgrave (another prominent Schumpeter student), September 30, 2000. Schumpeter's reference to Samuelson's intellectual superiority is in a letter to Dean George D. Birkhoff, February 1, 1937, Schumpeter Papers, HUG(FP)—4.8, carbons of JAS's correspondence, 1932–1949, box 2, folder B, HUA.

41. He went on to say, "I give an advanced course on Theory where mathematics comes in a very cautious and mild way and yet frightens the audience to the bone. And besides I have a little circle in the evenings, meeting once a fortnight, [in] which I read with them and interpret for them Cournot. This is obviously not enough." He then posed a series of questions to Schultz. Should senior professors establish an association of teachers who would emphasize math? Should the Econometric Society be involved? Should math be in every course, or in separate ones of its own? Although most people seemed to think it should be reserved for the most advanced students, "Myself I think on the contrary that the very beginners could be easily familiarized with the fundamental concepts and methods and that this would be no more difficult than teaching them Physics where they must also from the beginning take to some exact notions." He concluded by saying that in Germany his former student Erich Schneider has tried this second method "in a Gymnasium and met with very great success: all his youngsters of fourteen and fifteen constructing demand curves furiously after a few weeks." He wondered whether "it is an advisable thing to suggest, not I mean either at Chicago or at Harvard, but with the hope that other universities might do the same?" Schumpeter to Henry Schultz, March 9, 1933, in Hedtke and Swedberg, eds., *Briefe,* pp. 236–238.

42. Schumpeter to Haberler, March 20, 1933, in ibid., p. 240. Schumpeter went on to say that a hundred years before, practitioners of math and of physics had been mutually suspicious, speaking a sort of nonsense to each other. But now, physics without mathematics would be all but useless, and economists owed it to themselves to learn how to incorporate math into their science as physicists had done.

43. Sweezy, "Schumpeter on 'Imperialism and Social Classes,'" in Harris, ed., *Schumpeter, Social Scientist,* pp. 119; Samuelson, "Schumpeter as a Teacher and Economic Theorist," in ibid., p. 53. Schumpeter championed Sweezy's career as well as Samuelson's. In 1945, he wrote to Harvard's Dean Paul H. Buck that Sweezy should be promoted to an associate professorship over John Dunlop, a labor economist who would fill an important void. Schumpeter argued that the

void was less than had been represented, and that there were other reasons to prefer Sweezy: "Any lack of balance that may result from this is amply compensated by increased vitality and originality of performance. When I try to form an idea of how the Department will look in twenty years if the point of view is allowed to prevail . . . concerning the supposed necessity of an appointment in the labor field, I arrive at results that are melancholy indeed." In an accompanying memo on Sweezy's merits, Schumpeter writes that the candidate's "latest book, published only a short time before he joined the armed forces, is entitled 'The Theory of Capitalist Development,' 1942. It is a masterly exposition of the Marxian system of thought. This task, which has been attempted by dozens of economists of all countries, has never before been done so well." Dunlop was promoted over Sweezy, and went on to a distinguished career as professor, Dean of the Faculty, and U.S. Secretary of Labor. But as a pure scholar he was not Sweezy's equal. Schumpeter to Buck, May 19, 1945, in Schumpeter Papers, HUG(FP)—4.7, Correspondence and other misc. papers, ca. 1920s-1950, box 5, folder 1943–49, Miscellaneous correspondence through department secretary, HUA.

44. Sweezy, "Schumpeter on 'Imperialism and Social Classes,'" in Harris, ed., *Schumpeter, Social Scientist;* Harris, "Introductory Remarks," in ibid., p. 5. In 1933, a disillusioned Schumpeter wrote to a friend that "Still more bitterly I feel that there is no more and never will be any room on this earth for that cultivated conservativism [sic] which would command my allegiance." In another letter, dated 1937, he wrote to the same friend that "no satisfactory exposition of the rationale of conservativism exists . . . It is one of the humors of the situation that conservativism has never satisfactorily defined itself." See Wolfgang F. Stolper, *Joseph Alois Schumpeter: The Public Life of a Private Man* (Princeton, N.J.: Princeton University Press, 1994), p. 35.

14: SUFFERING AND SOLACE

1. As suggested earlier, the problem with the money book was one that marked some of Schumpeter's other works, sometimes to their advantage: a disinclination to simplify arguments and a penchant for excessive detail. Also, few of Schumpeter's writings lent themselves easily to mathematical notation, which is often essential in technical discussions of money.

2. Robert Loring Allen, *Opening Doors: The Life & Work of Joseph Schumpeter,* two vols. (New Brunswick, N.J.: Transaction, 1991), II, p. 43.

3. Schumpeter to Fisher, March 19, 1936, in Ulrich Hedtke and Richard Swedberg, eds., *Joseph Alois Schumpeter, Briefe/Letters* (Tübingen: J. C. B. Mohr, Paul Siebeck), 2000), p. 282.

4. Schumpeter's Diary, October 19, 1936, loose sheet, HUG(FP)—4.1, Brief Daily Records, notes and diaries, ca. 1931–1948, box 7, folder ca. 1936–1937, HUA,

hereinafter cited as Schumpeter's Diary; Schumpeter to Fisher, March 19, 1936, in Hedtke and Swedberg, eds., *Briefe,* p. 282.

5. Schumpeter's annotations of Diary of Anna Reisinger Schumpeter, Schumpeter Papers, HUG(FP)—4.2, Mostly extracts from Annie's diary, vol. II, May 21–27, 1934; vol. IV, February 11–17 and May 5–12, 1935; vol. VI, October 19–25, 1936, HUA. Cited hereinafter as Schumpeter's annotations of Annie's Diary. Schumpeter to Gottfried Haberler, December 9, 1935, Haberler Papers, box 31, folder: Joseph Schumpeter, Hoover Institution Archives. Translations by Holger Frank. Seymour E. Harris, "Introductory Remarks," in Harris, ed., *Schumpeter, Social Scientist* (Cambridge, Mass.: Harvard University Press, 1951), p. 6.

6. Schumpeter to Flexner, May 8, 1934, in Hedtke and Swedberg, eds., *Briefe,* pp. 261–262.

7. Schumpeter to Frisch, May 10, 1935, in Hedtke and Swedberg, eds., *Briefe,* pp. 278–279.

8. Schumpeter to Conant, December 7, 1936, in Hedtke and Swedberg, eds., *Briefe,* pp. 287–288. Both the Schumpeter Papers, HUG(FP)—4.7, and the Department of Economics, Correspondence and Records, UAV 349.160 and 349.11, HUA, contain a very large number of his recommendations for women as well as men, for fellowships and faculty positions. See, as three examples among many, Schumpeter to the Secretary of the Committee on Fellowship Awards, American Association of University Women, November 27, 1935, concerning Betty Goldwasser ("a serious and capable student and worthy of all help you may be able to render her"); December 9, 1936, on Selma Fine ("I cannot too strongly urge that Miss Fine has exceptional claims to consideration. She is an excellent economist and her work promises to be a significant contribution to our knowledge"); and Schumpeter to Bernice Cronkhite, Dean of Radcliffe College, February 11, 1937: "This is to support Miss Marion Crawford's application for a fellowship . . . She proves her ability by the fact that, being a senior, she takes graduate courses with the utmost ease, and in fact much better than most of the graduates, whether male or female." All in UAV 349.11, Department of Economics, Correspondence and Records, 1930–1961, box Robertson-Schumpeter, folder Joseph A. Schumpeter, 1933–1942, HUA.

9. Schumpeter to Conant, December 7, 1936, in Hedtke and Swedberg, eds., *Briefe,* pp. 287–288.

10. Ibid., p. 289.

11. Schumpeter to Mrs. Pauline R. Thayer, Division of Immigration and Americanization, State House, Boston, February 24, 1933, in Hedtke and Swedberg, eds., *Briefe,* p. 234. Schumpeter's Diary, n.d. (1936), box 7, folder Ca. 1935–1936.

12. Schumpeter to Keynes, December 3, 1932, in Hedtke and Swedberg, eds., *Briefe,* p. 230. Another example emerged at the founding of the Econometric Society. As Schumpeter and his fellow planners were deciding whom to invite to join,

Ragnar Frisch wrote that some of Schumpeter's objections seemed to point toward excluding socialists and perhaps Jews—in particular Jacob Marschak, an economist who had come to Germany from Russia. Schumpeter replied: "No. You do me an injustice . . . If I did take political opinion into consideration I should be much in favor of including socialists in our lists of fellows. In fact, I should consider it good policy to do so. Nor am I [nor] have I ever been an anti-Semite." But Marschak "is both a Jew and a socialist of a type which is probably unknown to you": a knee-jerk partisan whose "allegiance to people answering these two characteristics is so strong that he will . . . not be satisfied until we have a majority of them, in which case he will disregard all other qualifications. This is in the nature of a difficulty. But personally I like him immensely and I think a lot of him." Schumpeter to Ragnar Frisch, December 3, 1932, ibid., pp. 227–228.

Schumpeter wrote this letter in December 1932, a month before Hitler came to power. He was influenced by a letter he had received two weeks earlier from Mia Stöckel. Mia, who was still in an anti-Semitic phase that she later rejected, reported to Schumpeter on a recent meeting of economists in Paris at which Marschak "must really have behaved very impertinently. That annoys me. I don't know why it is, I have the feeling that these Jews want to lead or rule the Society, which has scarcely come into being, and that really won't do." Erich Schneider, one of Schumpeter's former students, had written Mia about the Paris Conference and his concern about the formation of the Econometric Society, and Mia had concluded "that the Jews want to play the leading role and you should try to get away from Marschak's influence." Mia Stöckel to Schumpeter, November 1, 1932, Schumpeter Papers, HUG(FP)—4.5, Letters from Mia, 1932–1940, box 1, folder 1932, HUA. Translation by Benjamin Hett.

In later years, Schumpeter warmly supported Marschak, in recommendations to many correspondents, including Alvin Johnson for the University in Exile. To Tracy B. Kittredge of the Rockefeller Foundation, Schumpeter wrote in 1938 that when Marschak "came from Russia to Germany he was a mere tiro [sic]," but had made great progress since. "After the advent of the Hitler regime he went to Oxford where he did much to organize the institute of statistics which seems to be managing with success. His program of observing methods of political research and of studying time series analysis and the application of functional calculus to economics are of course the fashionable items of the day and do not convey any specific aim." For Schumpeter, this was high praise, and evidence of a change of mind about the socialist instrumentalism of Marschak's scholarship. Schumpeter to Kittredge, n.d. (September 1938), UAV 349.11, Department of Economics, Correspondence and Records, 1930–1961, box Robertson-Schumpeter, folder Joseph Alois Schumpeter, HUA. Later, in a letter to the Harvard economist Sumner H. Slichter, he recommended that Marschak (rather than two other candidates) be chosen to give a paper at the joint meeting of the

Econometric Society and the American Economic Association. Schumpeter to Slichter, October 14, 1941, ibid. Marschak went on to a distinguished career in the United States, as one of the leading mathematical economists of his generation.

13. Stolper to Schumpeter, January 31, 1933, in Schumpeter Papers, HUG(FP)—4.7, Correspondence and other misc. papers, ca. 1920s-1950, box 8, folder S, HUA.

14. On reflation and other issues, see Hansjörg Klausinger, "Schumpeter and Hayek: Two Views of the Great Depression Re-Examined," *History of Economic Ideas* 3 (1995), pp. 93–127. Schumpeter and Hayek took slightly different positions, but both believed that neither reflation or price stabilization would be effective.

15. Schumpeter to Irving Fisher, February 25, 1933, in Hedtke and Swedberg, eds., *Briefe,* p. 235. In 1934, Schumpeter wrote that "although there would have been a crisis anyway, it is non-economic causes which account for the depth of the depression." In his view, the interaction of politics and economics had vastly complicated the question, especially through very bad monetary policy. Even so, because of the historic pattern of more or less automatic recoveries, he believed governmental "reflation" to be unnecessary. See Schumpeter to Seiichi Tobata, June 16, 1934, ibid., p. 272. Schumpeter also believed, as he wrote in 1939, that even the Hitler government had been very reluctant to reflate, because of Germany's earlier experience with hyperinflaton. "The common man still remembers what happened in 1923." So, "Powerful as that [National Socialist] government is, it was in its first years afraid to tamper with the currency, because this would have in Germany meant a tremendous loss of prestige." Schumpeter to H. B. Ellison of the *Christian Science Monitor,* February 2, 1939, ibid., p. 314.

16. Schumpeter to Haberler, March 20, 1933, in Hedtke and Swedberg, eds., *Briefe,* p. 241.

17. Many of these scholars, especially if they were Jews, saw that this was the end of their careers in Germany. They began making plans to emigrate as soon as possible. Others stayed on for a few months or years, hoping for the best. See F. M. Scherer, "The Emigration of German-Speaking Economists after 1933," *Journal of Economic Literature* 38 (September 2000), pp. 614–626. Among the non-economists close to Schumpeter was the eminent constitutional lawyer Hans Kelsen, a Jew who had been best man at his wedding to Annie in 1925. Schumpeter's letter to Mitchell is dated April 22, 1933, and appears in Hedtke and Swedberg, eds., *Briefe,* pp. 249–251.

18. Schumpeter to Fosdick, April 19, 1933, in Hedtke and Swedberg, eds., *Briefe,* pp. 243: "Your name has been suggested to me in connection with my plan for forming a Committee to take care of some of those German scientists who are now being removed from their chairs by the present government on account of their Hebrew race or faith . . . In order to avoid what would be a very natural misunderstanding, allow me to state that I am a German citizen but not a Jew or

of Jewish descent . . . My conservative convictions make it impossible for me to share in the well-nigh unanimous condemnation the Hitler Ministry meets with in the world at large. It is merely from a sense of duty towards men who have been my colleagues that I am trying to organize some help for them which would enable them to carry on quiet scientific work in this country should necessity arise." Schumpeter to Mitchell, April 19, 1933, ibid., pp. 246. The letter continues: "Enclosed please find that list of Hebrew colleagues in Germany which we talked about. I have dictated it from memory" but can supply additional details. "I did on purpose not include any distinctly weak brothers. Of course there are great differences between them. By far the most remarkable men being Stolper, Marschak, and, in his own particular line, Mannheim. But this you know just as well as I do." Schumpeter's list includes Gustav Stolper, Jacob Marschak, Hans Neisser, Karl Mannheim, Emil Lederer, Adolph Löwe, Gerhart Colm, Karl Pribram, and Eugen Altschul, all of whom except Altschul escaped, most of them in 1933 to the United States.

19. Schumpeter to Hansen, April 19, 1933, in Hedtke and Swedberg, eds., *Briefe,* pp. 244. Schumpeter adds that he himself does not agree with Mannheim's approach to the discipline, but that Mannheim "is the outstanding exponent of his line of thought." See also Schumpeter to Day, May 2, 1933, ibid., pp. 251–252.

20. Schumpeter to Johnson, May 2, 1933, in Hedtke and Swedberg, eds., *Briefe,* pp. 252–254.

21. Schumpeter to Mitchell, May 2, 1933, in ibid., pp. 254–255.

22. Schumpeter to Mitchell, April 19, 1933: praising Stolper highly, Schumpeter noted that he had founded *The German Economist,* had served in the German Parliament, and spoke good English—altogether, "A very remarkable man who three years ago was in measurable distance of taking office as German Minister of Finance. Can be useful in many ways. Will be, although more than prosperous, probably without means if he has to leave the country against the will of the government." See also Schumpeter to Edmund A. Day of the Rockefeller Foundation, May 2, 1933; and to Alvin Johnson, May 2, 1933, all in Hedtke and Swedberg, eds., *Briefe,* pp. 246–253. Schumpeter to Thomas Lamont, April 19, 1933, Schumpeter Papers, HUG(FP)—4.7, Correspondence and other misc. papers, ca. 1920s-1950, box 4, folder Jobs or recommendations, HUA.

Stolper had written to Schumpeter on April 2, 1933: "Heartfelt thanks for your lines. Your suggestion for the start-up there is topical in the most literal sense of the word. I ask you urgently to do immediately everything required in connection with the stipend." Stolper was discussing arrangements beyond his own rescue, either funding for other scholars or for a startup of another magazine. He says that from his publishing experience, "for the matter to be funded unshakably, is $150,000. I will also naturally mobilize my connections here, in order to bring in the most considerable share of this sum. But there lies the decisive and most difficult point. Couldn't Prof. Taussig be helpful to you. I hold the personnel question, with the extensive connections that I have anyway in America, relatively easy to solve." He goes on to ask that Schumpeter try to find a place for his son and Schumpeter's Bonn student Wolfgang, "somewhere in Boston (bank or something like that), so that he can cover his necessary expenses and thereby stay under your wings." Stolper to Schumpeter, April 2, 1933, Schumpeter Papers, HUG(FP)—4.7, Correspondence and other misc. papers, ca. 1920s-1950, box 31, folder Unidentified 1930 [sic], HUA.

23. Schumpeter to Haberler, September 25, 1933, Gottfried Haberler Collection, box 31, folder: Schumpeter, Joseph, Hoover Institution Archives; Schumpeter to Esther Lowenthal (Smith College) and Susan M. Kingsbury (Bryn Mawr), May 26, 1933; Schumpeter to John A. Ryan (Catholic University), October 15, 1934; all in Hedtke and Swedberg, eds., *Briefe*, pp. 257, 275.

24. Schumpeter to Donald Young, April 2, 1935, in Hedtke and Swedberg, eds., *Briefe*, p. 277; Zassenhaus's wife was Jewish, but Schumpeter does not mention it in his letter. Schumpeter received not only appeals for help, but thank-you letters afterwards. For example, a former colleague wrote him from Cologne-Braunsfeld: "I send you these lines in memory of our common work on the Rhine. They are to thank you for giving support to my grand-nephew Georg Halm in so friendly and effective a manner, so that he could build a new existence. Without your help it would certainly have been more difficult for him to find his feet in the United States and to carry on a fruitful teaching activity." ___? Eckert to Schumpeter, May 31, 1937, HUG(FP)—4.7, Correspondence and other misc. papers, ca. 1920s-1950, box 3, folder E 1930, HUA. Translation by Benjamin Hett.

25. Alvin Johnson, *Pioneer's Progress: An Autobiography* (New York: Viking, 1952), pp. 332–348. Schumpeter tried throughout the 1930s and 1940s to assist displaced European scholars, always giving a candid assessment of their abilities. See Schumpeter to William L. Langer, May 3, 1939, on behalf of the Austrian jurist Oskar Pisko; to Alvin Johnson, November 21, 1940, concerning the French economist Gaëtan Pirou and the Austrian economist and sociologist Edgar Salin; to Edward S. Mason, November 23, 1940, on behalf of the Austrian economist Victor Heller, all in Hedtke and Swedberg, eds., *Briefe*, pp. 317–318, 325, 327.

When Alvin Johnson, during a fund drive, asked him for an endorsement of the work of the University in Exile, Schumpeter sent an enthusiastic letter praising both the effort itself and the work of the scholars being supported. See Schumpeter to Johnson, February 12, 1937, UAV 349.11, Department of Economics Correspondence and Records, 1930–1961, box Robertson-Schumpeter, folder Joseph A. Schumpeter 1933–1942, HUA. For other examples of recommendations for particular persons, see Schumpeter to the President, Vassar College, April 13, 1938, recommending the German philosopher Julius Kraft; Schumpeter to Robert Calkins, Chairman of the Economics Department, University of California at Berkeley, May 18, 1938, recommending Wolfgang Stolper; Schumpeter to R. T. Sharpe, Secretary for the [Harvard] Committee on Scholarships, May 20, 1938, recommending Johannes Schulz, son of a prominent law professor in Berlin who had been dismissed because his wife was Jewish, all in ibid. On Harvard's own tentative steps, see Schumpeter to S. v. Ciriacy-Wentrup of the University of California, Berkeley, January 4, 1939, in ibid. Schumpeter took little part in this effort, which was managed by Harvard deans, on behalf of senior European scholars.

26. Scherer, "The Emigration of German-Speaking Economists after 1933," pp. 614–616, interpreting results derived primarily from Harald Hagemann and Claus-Dieter Krohn, eds., *Biographisches Handbuch der deutschsprachigen wirstschaftswissenschaftlichen Emigration nach 1933* (Biographical Handbook on the Emigration of German-Speaking Economists after 1933), two vols. (Munich: K. G. Saur, 1999). I have limited these numbers to "first-generation" emigrants. Several had children who also became economists.

27. As early as 1930, Schumpeter had expressed dismay at the quality of economists appointed to the faculty at Graz. At that time he still regarded Vienna as the leading center of economic thinking among German-speaking universities. See Schumpeter to Gottfried Haberler, May 27 and August 25, 1930. By the summer of 1933, he wrote Haberler that "Your attitude toward a German appointment [that it was a move up the academic ladder from Geneva in prestige] does you credit, but is a disservice to our science—this opinion is also shared by the expelled Germans (Lederer and his circle) whom I met in London." Schumpeter to Haberler, July 21, 1933. All in Gottfried Haberler Collection, Box 31, folder: Schumpeter, Joseph, Hoover Institution Archives.

28. Schumpeter to S. Colum Gilfillan, May 18, 1934, in Hedtke and Swedberg, eds., *Briefe,* p. 265. Many other letters and entries in Schumpeter's diaries track his summer months in Europe during these three years.

29. Robbins, "Schumpeter's History of Economic Analysis," *Quarterly Journal of Economics* 69 (February 1955), p. 22.

30. Schumpeter's travels are fully chronicled in his Weekly Reviews for 1933–35, Annie's Diary, vols. I-IV. On Spa, see Schumpeter to Gottfried Haberler, August 25, 1935, Gottfried Haberler Collection, box 31, folder: Schumpeter, Joseph, Hoover Institution Archives.

31. Elizabeth's college career is summarized in the 1920 edition of the *Radcliffe Year Book,* p. 36. Chronologies and other details of her life are documented in her papers at the Schlesinger Library, Radcliffe Institute, Harvard University. Particularly helpful are the lengthy employment forms she filled out in applications

for work with the Federal Government during and after World War II. See also Elizabeth Waterman Gilboy, "Elizabeth Boody Schumpeter, 1898–1953," a memoir and preface to Elizabeth Boody Schumpeter, *English Overseas Trade Statistics, 1697–1808* (Oxford: Oxford University Press, 1960), n.p. On "Romaine Boody," see John Donovan to Irving Sargent, January 25, 1939, in R. Elizabeth Boody Schumpeter Papers, 1938–1953, A-43, Schlesinger Library, Radcliffe Institute, Harvard University. Hereinafter cited as Elizabeth Boody Schumpeter Papers.

32. Application for Federal Employment, n.d. (1950), four pages, and Personal History Statement, n.d. (1950), thirteen pages, with addendum of twelve pages, both in Elizabeth Boody Schumpeter Papers. The information contained in the two forms overlaps to a great extent. They appear to have been completed at the same time.

33. Page 8 of addendum to Personal History Statement, ibid.

34. Page 10 of Personal History Statement, ibid. See also Allen, *Opening Doors,* II, pp. 29–30.

35. A portion of her dissertation was published in 1960 as *English Overseas Trade Statistics 1697–1808* (Oxford: Oxford University Press), with an introduction by T. S. Ashton. The pages of this brief, oversized book look like a large spreadsheet, noteworthy in that most of its thousands of numerical entries are neatly entered in Elizabeth's own hand, not in typeface.

36. Gilboy, "Elizabeth Boody Schumpeter, 1898–1953," n.p. Elizabeth Boody's height and weight in about 1950 are listed in the Application for Federal Employment, n.d. (1950), p. 1, and Personal History Statement, n.d. (1950), p. 2, both in Elizabeth Boody Schumpeter Papers.

37. Addendum to Personal History Statement, p. 4, Elizabeth Boody Schumpeter Papers.

38. Mia's protests are evident in her correspondence from this period, Schumpeter Papers, HUG(FP)—4.5, Letters from Mia 1932–1940, box 1, folder Letters from Mia 1932–1936, HUA. For references to Elizabeth and Taconic, see Schumpeter's Weekly Review pages in Annie's Diary, vol. VI; and Schumpeter's Diary, box 7, folders ca. 1936 and ca. 1936–37.

39. Schumpeter's Diary, n.d. (April 6, 1937), box 7, folder ca. 1936–1937. Another entry at about the same time also takes poetic form (ibid.):

> Waiting weary through my day
> like a cab horse tired of trotting
> everything is grey and low
> and my plans are lying rotting
> stream of energy won't flow
> I am far from being gay

But the day wears on and on
and one task goes with another
why should after all I bother. . .
And its [sic] not so bad!
Dizzy

40. Elizabeth Boody Firuski to Schumpeter, July 8 and July 12, 1937, Schumpeter Papers, HUG(FP)—4.4, Personal letters, miscellany, folder Letters from EBF—summer 1937, HUA.

41. Elizabeth Boody Firuski to Schumpeter, July 12, 1937, ibid.

42. Schumpeter's Diary, *passim.* Elizabeth mentions her illness in a letter to Schumpeter from the Cosmopolitan Club in New York in the summer of 1937, dated "Thursday morning": "The doctor I saw yesterday does not think I should have a child. It is possible, but she does not advise it. This is because of my Diabetes and not because of my age. In all other ways, I am an excellent healthy specimen. Shall we mind very much? We need not, of course, take this opinion as final. I thought I should tell you, however, because I had so much the other impression from my doctor in Lakeville" [near Taconic]. Elizabeth Boody Firuski to Schumpeter, n.d. (1937), Schumpeter Papers, HUG(FP)—4.7.5, Miscellaneous Correspondence, folder E-J, HUA.

43. Elizabeth Boody Firuski to Schumpeter, undated (summer 1937); and July 12, 1937, Schumpeter Papers, HUG(FP)—4.4, Personal letters, Miscellany, folder Letters from EBF, HUA.

44. Elizabeth Boody Firuski to Schumpeter, undated (summer 1937), ibid.

45. Elizabeth Boody Firuski to Schumpeter, undated (summer 1937), ibid.

46. Elizabeth Boody Firuski to Schumpeter, undated (summer 1937), ibid.

47. Elizabeth Boody Firuski to Schumpeter, undated letters (summer 1937), Schumpeter Papers, HUG(FP)—4.7.5, Miscellaneous correspondence, folder E-J, HUA. Engraved wedding announcement, August 16, 1937, Schumpeter Papers, HUG(FP)—4.7, Correspondence and other misc. papers, ca. 1920s-1950, box 9, folder wedding announcement, HUA. See also Allen, *Opening Doors,* II, p. 47.

PART III PROLOGUE: HOW AND WHY HE EMBRACED HISTORY

1. Henrik Wilm Lambers, "The Vision," in Arnold Heertje, ed., *Schumpeter's Vision: Capitalism, Socialism and Democracy after 40 Years* (New York: Praeger, 1981), p. 114.

2. Jacob Viner, "Schumpeter's *History of Economic Analysis:* A Review Article," *American Economic Review,* 44 (December 1954), p. 895.

3. Schumpeter, *History of Economic Analysis* (New York: Oxford University Press, 1954), pp. 12–13. At a 1949 conference of the National Bureau of Economic Re-

search, he told his fellow economists much the same thing: "If the good fairies
will allot you only one of *economic history* or *mathematical econometrics,* then to
become an outstanding economist, master the corpus of economic history." See
Paul A. Samuelson, "Reflections on the Schumpeter I Knew Well," *Journal of
Evolutionary Economics* 13 (2003), p. 465. One of Schumpeter's Harvard colleagues, the distinguished economic historian A. P. Usher, commented that "The
vital question for history is 'How do things happen?'" and added that this was
Schumpeter's approach to the theory of economic development. See Usher, "Historical Implications of the Theory of Economic Development," in Seymour E.
Harris, ed., *Schumpeter, Social Scientist* (Cambridge, Mass.: Harvard University
Press, 1951), p. 125. Usher went on to say that Schumpeter's attempt to fuse theory, history, and statistics was extremely original. Almost no others had tried it
except Marxists, who "sacrificed history to theory." As Schumpeter's former graduate student Wolfgang F. Stolper later wrote, his "sense of history and his unique
combination of history and economic theory" marked all of his writings. Stolper,
"The Schumpeterian System," *Journal of Economic History* 11 (1951), pp. 273–274.
In his important book, *Schumpeter and the Endogeneity of Technology: Some American Perspectives* (New York: Routledge, 2000), Nathan Rosenberg argues that
Schumpeter himself was fundamentally an economic historian.

15: BUSINESS CYCLES, BUSINESS HISTORY

1. The full title of the book is *Business Cycles: A Theoretical, Historical, and Statistical Analysis of the Capitalist Process* (New York: Macmillan, 1939). In a diary entry
of January 2, 1939, Schumpeter wrote, "On dec. [sic] 9, I finished my Cycle ms!
. . . laying aside Money in the summer of 1934, I hoped to get the business cycle
[book] done in another year and that I planned accordingly. That may have been
foolish to hope, yet I am now, with ref. to that program, late by (academically
counting) 3 1/2 years which otherwise would possibly have given me a chance,
which now has passed through the ivory gate. For this I shall never be able to
make up—and the periodic misery, laziness, idiocy from which I suffer must be
accepted as a fact." Quoted in Robert Loring Allen, *Opening Doors: The Life &
Work of Joseph Schumpeter,* two vols. (New Brunswick, N.J.: Transaction, 1991),
II, pp. 71–72. Schumpeter's Weekly Review in his transcriptions of his late wife's
diary for several years preceding 1939 is full of similar self-flagellation about his
delays. See folder titled Gerschenkron, "The Diaries of Anna Reisinger
Schumpeter, A Report," Appended Transcripts II, pp. 176–190, in Schumpeter
Papers, HUG(FP)—66.90, Publisher and Estate Correspondence, box 4, HUA.
2. Schumpeter to the Committee on Research in the Social Sciences, June 16, 1937,
UAV 737.18, box P-Z, folder Prof. Schumpeter (Economics), HUA; Schumpeter
to Burbank, January 17, 1938, UAV 349.11, Department of Economics Records

and Correspondence, 1930–1961, box Robertson-Schumpeter, folder Joseph A. Schumpeter, HUA.

Examples of contemporary large projects include the two big sociological books on "Middletown" (Muncie, Indiana), done under the direction of Robert and Helen Lynd; the federal government's multi-volume *Social Trends,* published during the Hoover Administration; and a thorough study of the American economy completed in the late 1930s by the Temporary National Economic Committee of Congress.

In Schumpeter's time, Harvard had a Committee on Economic Research, and this small bureau provided faculty members with some support, including pay for assistants helping with their research. But the scale of funds was never remotely adequate to what Schumpeter was attempting to do in *Business Cycles.* In the 1920s and 1930s, the fledgling National Bureau of Economic Research (NBER), then headquartered at Columbia University and directed by Schumpeter's friend Wesley Clair Mitchell, collected economic statistics and moved toward a program of systematic publication. Today the NBER itself, among other organizations, sponsors the kinds of team-oriented projects necessary for the type of work Schumpeter was doing almost entirely by himself.

3. Schumpeter to Mitchell, May 6, 1937; Schumpeter to Oscar Lange, February 24, 1937, both in Ulrich Hedtke and Richard Swedberg, eds., *Joseph Alois Schumpeter, Briefe/Letters* (Tübingen: J. C. B. Mohr, Paul Siebeck, 2000), pp. 295, 301, 303. Schumpeter had written about cycles several times before. See, for example, Schumpeter, *"Über das Wesen der Wirtschaftskrisen"* (On the Nature of Economic Crises), *Zeitschrift für Volkswirtschaft, Socialpolitik und Verwaltung* 19 (1910), pp. 79–132; *The Theory of Economic Development* (whose subtitle is *An Inquiry into Profits, Capital, Credit, Interest, and the Business Cycle*); Schumpeter, "The Explanation of the Business Cycle," *Economica* 7 (December 1927), pp. 286–311 (essentially a review article on A. C. Pigou's book, *Industrial Fluctuations* (1927); Schumpeter, "The Analysis of Economic Change," *Review of Economic Statistics* 17 (May 1935), pp. 2–10 (which is a partial preview of the argument in *Business Cycles*); and Harald Hagemann, "Schumpeter's Early Contributions on Crises Theory and Business-Cycle Theory," *History of Economic Ideas* 9 (2003), pp. 47–67 (which mainly concerns Schumpeter's 1910 essay).

4. *Business Cycles,* I, p. v.

5. Ibid., I, pp. 169, 173–174. At times in the book he wrote not just of three cycles but of five; and in fact there could be many more than that, as innumerable stock-market analysts have tried to show. But the overall point was the one he made in his preface: cycles are of the essence in capitalism; and it follows that depressions are an inescapable and even beneficial phase in its evolution.

In a letter to the American scholar Paul Homan, which he wrote as he was finishing the book, Schumpeter elaborated a bit: "For if one thinks of business cycles as the typical form of capitalistic evolution and if one looks upon those long

time movements, which are sometimes called industrial revolutions, as one species of business cycles, it is but natural to link up with the cyclical phenomenon
practically the whole of the economics and sociology of capitalist society."
Schumpeter to Homan, April 2, 1938, in Hedtke and Swedberg, eds., *Briefe,*
p. 309.

6. *Business Cycles,* I, p. 299. Samuelson, "Joseph A. Schumpeter," *Dictionary of
American Biography,* Supplement Four, 1946–1950 (New York: Scribner, 1974),
p. 299. This is not to say that the cycle scheme has no value at all, or that it is
necessarily deterministic. See, for example, Nathan Rosenberg and C. R.
Frischtak, "Technological Innovation and Long Waves," *Cambridge Journal of
Economics* 8 (March 1984), pp. 7–24; Walt W. Rostow, "Kondratieff, Schumpeter,
and Kuznets: Trend Periods Revisited," *Journal of Economic History* 35 (December
1975), pp. 719–753; Allen Oakley, *Schumpeter's Theory of Capitalist Motion: A
Critical Exposition and Reassessment* (Aldershot, U.K.: Edward Elgar, 1990);
Christopher Freeman, "Schumpeter's *Business Cycles* Revisited," in Arnold
Heertje and Mark Perlman, eds., *Evolving Technology and Market Structure:
Studies in Schumpeterian Economics* (Ann Arbor: University of Michigan Press,
1990), pp. 17–38; William R. Thompson, "Long Waves, Technological Innova-
tion, and Relative Decline," *International Organization* 44 (Spring 1990),
pp. 201–203; Maria Brouwer, *Schumpeterian Puzzles: Technological Competition
and Economic Evolution* (New York: Harvester Wheatsheaf, 1991), esp. ch. 1;
Roger Lloyd-Jones and M. J. Lewis, "The Long Wave and Turning Points in
British Industrial Capitalism: A Neo-Schumpeterian Approach," *Journal of European Economic History* 29 (2000), pp. 359–401; and Mümtaz Keklik, *Schumpeter,
Innovation and Growth: Long-cycle Dynamics in the Post-WWII American Manufacturing Industries* (Aldershot, U.K.: Ashgate, 2003).

7. Schumpeter to Mitchell, May 6, 1937, in Hedtke and Swedberg, eds., *Briefe,*
pp. 301–303; *Business Cycles,* I, p. 174.

8. J. Marschak, *Journal of Political Economy* 48 (December 1940), p. 893;
Schumpeter, *Business Cycles,* I, p. v.

9. Obviously, there is a great deal to say on this subject; but in what Schumpeter
liked to call a spirit of "desperate brevity," I will limit my comments to two paragraphs:

In 1927 the Harvard Business School established a chair in business history,
endowed by the family of Isidor Straus, the guiding entrepreneur of Macy's Department Store who had died in the 1912 sinking of the *Titanic.* The first occu-
pant of this chair was Norman S. B. Gras, a Canadian economist who had
trained under Edwin F. Gay, a professor in Harvard's Department of Economics
and later the founding dean of the university's Business School. Gras, one year
younger than Schumpeter, wrote a number of useful books in economic history.
In the same year Schumpeter's *Business Cycles* appeared, Gras brought out a textbook, *Business and Capitalism: An Introduction to Business History* (New York:

Crofts, 1939); and, together with his skillful colleague Henrietta Larson, an immense *Casebook in American Business History* (New York: Crofts, 1939).

A curious circumstance is that there was little or no communication between them and Schumpeter, whose office was just across the Charles River, and who later spent innumerable hours in the Kress Library of rare books (located inside the Business School's Baker Library) doing research for his monumental *History of Economic Analysis* (New York: Oxford University Press, 1954). I have found no correspondence between Schumpeter and Gras in the private papers of either man, or any other evidence of personal contact. On Gras, Larson, and their approaches to business history, see Barry E. C. Boothman, "A Theme Worthy of Epic Treatment: N. S. B. Gras and the Emergence of American Business History," *Journal of Macromarketing* 21 (June 2001), pp. 61–73; and Mary A. Yeager's analysis of the work of Larson: "Mavericks and Mavens of Business History: Miriam Beard and Henrietta Larson," *Enterprise and Society* 2 (December 2001), pp. 687–768. During the late 1940s, Alfred D. Chandler, Jr.—the key figure in the development of *modern* business history—was a graduate student at Harvard, and met Schumpeter; but Chandler was influenced by him mostly through his own teacher Talcott Parsons, who had worked directly with Schumpeter. For the rich potential of Parsons' work for business history, see Louis Galambos, "Parsonian Sociology and Post-Progressive History," *Social Science Quarterly* 50 (June 1969), pp. 25–45.

10. I am generalizing broadly here, and obvious exceptions come to mind: the work of members of the German Historical School, who produced numerous studies of industries and firms; and N. S. B. Gras and Henrietta Larson of Harvard Business School. Still, in all of these examples, the kind of theoretical rigor characteristic of Schumpeter's work was largely absent. In the United States, the empirical studies of a few economists senior to Schumpeter, such as Jeremiah Jenks, Eliot Jones, William Z. Ripley, Arthur Hadley, and Frank Taussig, were better grounded theoretically than those of the others listed. But it would be too much of a stretch to call the work of these scholars business history.

11. Schumpeter to Edna Lonegan, a student at Brooklyn College, February 16, 1942, in Hedtke and Swedberg, eds., *Briefe*, pp. 339–340. The intellectual connections between the work of Schumpeter and Alfred D. Chandler, Jr. (and other scholars as well, including Marx), are discussed in William Lazonick, *Business Organization and the Myth of the Market Economy* (Cambridge: Cambridge University Press, 1991), ch. 4.

One of the first scholars to make a connection between *Business Cycles* and the subdiscipline of business history was Robert J. Wolfson, in "The Economic Dynamics of Joseph Schumpeter," *Economic Development and Cultural Change* 7 (October 1958), p. 52n4: "In addition to this work of [Fritz] Redlich [a German émigré who directly influenced Chandler], the whole field of business history which has grown up during the last ten years or so is clearly traceable to

Schumpeter." Among other relevant commentaries, see Yuichi Shionoya's discussion of the connection between *Business Cycles* and Schumpeter's *Theory of Economic Development,* in "Schumpeter's Preface to the Fourth German Edition of *The Theory of Economic Development,*" *Journal of Evolutionary Economics* 14 (2004), pp. 131–142; Shionoya, *Schumpeter and the Idea of Social Science: A Metatheoretical Study* (Cambridge: Cambridge University Press, 1997); and Mário da Graça Moura, "Schumpeter on the Integration of Theory and History," *European Journal of the History of Economic Thought* 10 (Summer 2003), pp. 279–301.

12. *Business Cycles,* I, pp. 72–73, 84–102. Here Schumpeter recurs to his categories of innovation first set forth in *The Theory of Economic Development* (1911). He also anticipates his article, "The Creative Response in Economic History," *Journal of Economic History* 7 (November 1947), pp. 149–159, which had a significant influence on business historians.

13. *Business Cycles,* I, pp. 100–102.

14. Ibid., I, pp. 102, 103. Schumpeter adds that "The outlines of an economic and social analysis of both types and both functions" appear in *The Theory of Economic Development,* chs. 2 and 4.

15. *Business Cycles,* I, pp. 103–104.

16. Ibid., I, p. 104. Among many examples of his preoccupation with class, see Schumpeter, "*Die Tendenzen unserer sozialen Struktur*" (The Tendencies of Our Social Structure), in *Die Chemische Industrie* 51/52 (December 24, 1928), printed in Schumpeter, *Aufsätze zur Tagespolitik* (Essays on Current Policy), eds. Christian Seidl and Wolfgang F. Stolper (Tübingen: J. C. B. Mohr, Paul Siebeck, 1993), pp. 177–193; and "Social Classes in an Ethnically Homogeneous Environment," originally published in 1927 and reprinted in *Imperialism, Social Classes: Two Essays by Joseph Schumpeter* (New York: Meridian, 1955), trans. Heinz Norden.

17. *Business Cycles,* I, pp. 104–107.

18. Ibid., I, pp. 105–108, 291.

19. Ibid., I, pp. 240–241. Schumpeter does not give it sufficient emphasis, but the use of the clock was a vital innovation in successive industrial revolutions. Rather than using sun time and toiling sporadically at home, workers gathered in one place and labored together under a rigid schedule. Even outside the factory, the clock changed the way people thought about life in general. See David S. Landes, *Revolution in Time: Clocks and the Making of the Modern World* (Cambridge, Mass.: Harvard University Press, 1983).

20. *Business Cycles,* I, p. 242. For elaborations of the advantages of cotton over wool, see David S. Landes, *The Wealth and Poverty of Nations: Why Some Are So Rich and Some So Poor* (New York: Norton, 1998). As noted earlier, scholars disagree on the appropriateness of the term "industrial revolution," but Schumpeter believed in it and often used it.

21. *Business Cycles,* I, p. 242.

22. Ibid., I, pp. 240–243.

23. Ibid., I, pp. 243, 244.

24. Ibid., I, pp. 240, 241, 244.

25. Ibid., I, p. 243. In *The Theory of Economic Development* (p. 65), Schumpeter had written that companies had to teach consumers to "want new things."

26. *Business Cycles,* II, p. 1035. On the importance of marketing, advertising, and selling in the American economy, see Roland Marchand, *Advertising the American Dream: Making Way for Modernity, 1920–1940* (Berkeley: University of California Press, 1985); Susan Strasser, *Satisfaction Guaranteed: The Making of the American Mass Market* (New York: Pantheon, 1989); Richard S. Tedlow, *New and Improved: The Story of Mass Marketing in America* (New York: Basic Books, 1990); Daniel Pope, *The Making of Modern Advertising* (New York: Basic Books, 1983); Pamela Walker Laird, *Advertising Progress: American Business and the Rise of Consumer Marketing* (Baltimore: Johns Hopkins Press, 1998); and Walter A. Friedman, *Birth of a Salesman: The Transformation of Selling in America* (Cambridge, Mass.: Harvard University Press, 2004).

27. *Business Cycles,* I, pp. 270–271. The word "calico" is a corruption of "Calcutta." The British later began to suppress production in India—which had been the world leader in cotton textiles—as a means of assisting exports of cloth from the mother country. The industry in India did not recover until the twentieth century.

28. Ibid., I, p. 271.

29. Ibid., I, pp. 271–272.

30. In analyzing economic development, "only confusion can result" from focusing on inventions instead of innovations. Ibid., I, pp. 84–85, 271–272. In later years this distinction became a foundation stone in the subdiscipline of the history of technology, as is evident in the perusal of almost any issue of the journal *Technology and Culture.* Two of the best books that treat this subject (among others) are David S. Landes, *The Unbound Prometheus: Technological Change and Industrial Development in Western Europe from 1750 to the Present* (Cambridge: Cambridge University Press, 1969); and Joel Mokyr, *The Lever of Riches: Technological Creativity and Economic Progress* (New York: Oxford University Press, 1990). Mokyr's book contains a particularly effective (and explicit) delineation of the Schumpeterian perspective on technology.

31. *Business Cycles,* I, p. 272.

32. Ibid., I, 272. The burgeoning demand for cotton made the American Eli Whitney's gin (1793) one of the most important inventions in history. This was true in many senses, because Whitney's breakthrough induced a tremendous expansion of slavery, which had been in decline on tobacco and rice plantations.

33. Ibid., I, pp. 272–273.

34. Ibid., I, p. 376. Many scholars have analyzed this process. See, for example, Wil-

liam Lazonick, *Competitive Advantage on the Shop Floor* (Cambridge, Mass.: Harvard University Press, 1990), chs. 3–5 and the notes to those chapters.

35. An immense literature on the evolution of the British textile industry, and particularly cotton, developed both before and after Schumpeter wrote this analysis.

36. Ibid., I, p. 357. Other aspects of the German story reinforce several of Schumpeter's themes. "The old silk industry revived in response to increasing wealth, but did not display any innovating activity until mechanized mass production." Meanwhile, "Linen decayed, being crowded out by cotton. Both in this respect and because of headway made by the factory and the power loom, this industry affords a particularly drastic example of how the New crowds out the Old." In wool, the pattern was similar, though the decline not as precipitous as in linen.

37. Ibid., I, pp. 433–434.

38. Ibid.

39. Ibid., I, p. 435. As it turned out, of course, rayon was only the first of a long list of synthetic fibers that emerged from the chemical industry. The most important was nylon, developed during the 1930s even as Schumpeter was writing *Business Cycles*. Afterward, there came a flood of other new synthetics, all produced either by chemical firms (especially DuPont), or by petrochemical subsidiaries of oil companies. The rise of rayon and nylon, and then a vast array of other synthetics (orlon, dacron, polyesters) completely transformed the "old" textile industry. And in every case, identifiable entrepreneurs led the way—New Men, but in this case working in established science-based companies. In the latter half of the twentieth century, petroleum-based synthetic materials ramified through the economies of all industrialized nations. They generated hundreds of new plastics and other products that replaced natural leather, rubber, wood, metals, paints, and adhesives. The petrochemical revolution was so pervasive that it invites comparison with the steam engine and the electric generator. It created disturbances not only in a group of industries, but cut wide swaths through entire economies. In the large literature on this subject, see especially David A. Hounshell and John Kenly Smith, *Science and Corporate Strategy: Du Pont R & D, 1902–1980* (Cambridge: Cambridge University Press, 1988); Peter H. Spitz, *Petrochemicals: The Rise of an Industry* (New York: Wiley, 1988); and Alfred D. Chandler, Jr., *Shaping the Industrial Century: The Remarkable Story of the Evolution of the Modern Chemical and Pharmaceutical Industries* (Cambridge, Mass.: Harvard University Press, 2005).

40. *Business Cycles,* I, pp. 291–292.

41. Ibid., I, p. 383.

42. Ibid., I, p. 327. Schumpeter mentions the telegraph elsewhere in the book, but gives too little attention to it.

43. Ibid., I, pp. 383–388. Schumpeter does not mention all the cities listed here.

44. Ibid., I, pp. 339–341.

45. Ibid., I, pp. 328–330. Schumpeter here takes the trouble to note that what he is saying is not controversial and "has often been emphasized and never been contested" by other scholars. His overall point was the vital importance of credit creation, which he often identified as one of the defining traits of capitalism.

46. Ibid., I, pp. 338–339, 383.

47. Ibid., I, pp. 303–304.

48. Ibid., I, p. 247.

49. Ibid., I, p. 246.

50. Ibid., I, pp. 244–247.

51. Ibid., I, pp. 244–247, 280, 307.

52. Schumpeter does not go into every detail covered here. But while he was composing *Business Cycles,* he wrote a fellow scholar who had studied joint stock companies in Britain during the 1830s that statistical time series were very helpful, but not sufficient. "Therefore we must turn to industrial and financial history in order to find out what has actually happened in the economic organism year by year, and it is only when we have done this that the true meaning of the fluctuations displayed by the time series reveals itself. This is why I think economic history of such paramount importance for the understanding of the business cycle and even of the most practical contemporaneous problems." Schumpeter to Bishop C. Hunt, June 13, 1935, Schumpeter Papers, HUG(FP)—4.7, Correspondence and other misc. papers, ca. 1920s-1950, box 5, folder H 1930s, HUA.

53. *Business Cycles,* I, pp. 402–403. The literature on American railroads is enormous. Good starting points are old sources such as John F. Stover, *American Railroads* (Chicago: University of Chicago Press, 1961); and especially Alfred D. Chandler, Jr., ed., *The Railroads: The Nation's First Big Business* (New York: Harcourt, Brace, 1965).

54. Schumpeter lays heavy emphasis on the merger movement, but he does not give the statistics quoted here. Nor does he mention the names of the firms listed. On merger waves, see Jesse Markham, "Survey of the Evidence and Findings on Mergers," in *Business Concentration and Price Policy* (Princeton, N.J.: Princeton University Press, 1955), especially p. 157; Ralph Nelson, *Merger Movements in American Industry, 1895–1956* (Princeton, N.J.: Princeton University Press, 1959); and Naomi R. Lamoreaux, *The Great Merger Movement in American Business, 1895–1904* (Cambridge: Cambridge University Press, 1985).

55. *Business Cycles,* I, pp. 403–404. In the history of American business, the period Schumpeter was discussing has seldom if ever been surpassed in the creation of important new companies. As later research disclosed, fully half of the firms that later were members of the *Fortune* 500 largest U.S. companies in the 1990s were founded during the 50-year period between 1880 and 1930. The majority of these

firms were entrepreneurial startups that grew into giants through internal expansion. Others (General Electric, United States Steel, General Motors, IBM) were formed by mergers of existing companies.

Over time, the largest corporate units prospered only in certain industries, most of which required big capital investments: oil, steel, automobiles, chemicals, heavy machinery, and others represented by the companies listed above. Big Business did not work well in most industries, such as furniture, housing construction, and jewelry. They were often ineffective throughout the service sector, including restaurants, hotels, and repair of all kinds. (A partial exception is franchised businesses, which began to grow rapidly during the 1960s, and which combine advantageous features of big and small firms.)

Also, for the period Schumpeter was writing about, many ill-advised entrepreneurs started down dead-end roads by forming mergers that had no chance of working—because the structures of the industries in question gravitated naturally toward small firms. Standard Oil is a familiar name, but Standard Rope and Twine rapidly disappeared. National Biscuit (RJR Nabisco) remains an important company today, but National Cordage, National Starch, National Salt, and National Novelty all dropped quickly from view. In 1901 United States Steel became the world's largest firm, but United States Button, whose promoters tried to "trustify" their industry in the same way, did not flourish.

The tendency of some industries to grow into big businesses while others do not has seldom been well understood, either today or during Schumpeter's time. Neither he nor the majority of scholars writing since his time have noted these important points about industry segmentation. (The most noteworthy exception is Alfred D. Chandler, Jr., *The Visible Hand: The Managerial Revolution in American Business* (Cambridge, Mass.: Harvard University Press, 1977.) But the historical record shows that except in communist countries, where governments forcibly collectivized both agriculture and industry into giant units, most of the world's labor force has never worked for large enterprises. The total employment of small and medium-sized firms has always far exceeded that of companies employing more than 1,000 persons. The economics literature on why firms grow large is very extensive, and often controversial.

56. This argument pervades many of Schumpeter's writings, and is implicit throughout the text of *Business Cycles*. The reference to the traveling salesman is on p. 405 of vol. I. In his earlier writings, as in *Business Cycles,* he frequently noted that entrepreneurs come from all social classes. Later, in *Capitalism, Socialism and Democracy,* he mounted a pointed attack on Americans' denunciations of big businesses as "monopolies." And he was especially displeased with what he regarded as his fellow economists' misunderstanding of the issue.

57. *Business Cycles,* I, 415–416. Alfred D. Chandler, Jr., ed., *Giant Enterprise: Ford,*

General Motors, and the Automobile Industry: Sources and Readings (New York: Harcourt, Brace, 1964), 1–2 and *passim.* The standard history of mass production in the United States, which contains much material on the automobile industry, is David A. Hounshell, *From the American System to Mass Production, 1800–1932: The Development of Manufacturing Technology in the United States* (Baltimore: Johns Hopkins University Press, 1984).

58. *Business Cycles,* I, p. 415. Alfred P. Sloan, Jr., *My Years with General Motors* (New York: Doubleday, 1964), ch. 9; Tedlow, *New and Improved: The Story of Mass Marketing in America,* ch. 3; Arthur J. Kuhn, *GM Passes Ford, 1918–1938: Designing the General Motors Performance-Control System* (University Park: Pennsylvania State University Press, 1986); Daniel M. G. Raff, "Making Cars and Making Money in the Interwar Automobile Industry: Economies of Scale and Scope and the Manufacturing behind the Marketing," *Business History Review* 65 (Winter 1991).

59. *Business Cycles,* I, p. 416n.

60. Ibid., I, p. 372.

61. Ibid., I, pp. 372–373.

62. Bessemer had relatively quick success, says Schumpeter—not against other steelmakers, "the enemy it had been his intention to attack, but over the producers of wrought iron." Ibid., I, p. 373.

63. Ibid., I, p. 373.

64. Ibid., I, pp. 373–374.

65. Ibid., I, p. 388; for details, see Harold C. Livesay, *Andrew Carnegie and the Rise of Big Business* (Boston: Little, Brown, 1975).

66. *Business Cycles,* I, pp. 397, 398, 412.

67. Ibid., I, pp. 412–413.

68. Ibid., I, p. 412.

69. Ibid., II, pp. 771–772. In absolute numbers, Schumpeter goes on to say that the number of installed telephones grew from 515,200 in 1897 to over 10 million in 1914. The number of "automatic" telephones increased from 12.7 million in 1919 to over 20 million by 1920. He does not, as one might have expected, devote much space to the American Telephone and Telegraph Company, which for many years was the world's largest private corporation.

70. Ibid., I, p. 413. For a detailed overview, see Alfred D. Chandler, Jr., *Scale and Scope: The Dynamics of Industrial Capitalism* (Cambridge, Mass.: Harvard University Press, 1990), pp. 212–221 and Appendix A.1, p. 642.

As he does throughout *Business Cycles,* Schumpeter compares one country's history of innovations with another's. In Germany, "The crux of electrical enterprise was 'power finance.'" Only the largest *manufacturing* companies could afford to enter the business of generating and transmitting electricity. They did so through allied financial subsidiaries ("banks") which underwrote local power systems as markets for the parent manufacturers. Three large concerns led the movement: first, the "bank" for Electrical Securities, headquartered in Berlin and allied with AEG (German General Electric, with no relationship to the American company GE); second, the Continental Company for Electrical Enterprises, a Siemens affiliate centered in Nuremberg; and third, the "bank" for Electrical Enterprises, which aimed at international business from the beginning, and was located in Zürich.

"But unlike America," Schumpeter points out, "Germany resorted to public enterprise, as well, at a comparatively early stage. Occasionally this led to conflicts but in general this form of 'municipal socialism'" did not offend the private sector. By the beginning of the twentieth century, most of Germany was supplied with electricity, even though by American standards the typical generating plants remained small.

Several German firms, replete with staff engineers, had a big advantage in their drive to capitalize on electricity. Schumpeter notes that in Germany, electrical technology had long since become "an applied science which it was possible to learn and to develop in laboratories and schools." The technical departments of established companies were so well stocked with New Men that it proved unnecessary to set up New Firms. In this advantageous situation, "the entrepreneurs being largely employees," German firms were by 1913 manufacturing about one-third of all electrical products in the world. No fewer than three of Germany's six biggest industrial companies produced electrical equipment: AEG, Siemens-Schuckert, and Siemens-Halske. For the quotations, and other aspects of the German story, see *Business Cycles,* I, pp. 439–441. The authoritative comparative history of electrification in the U.S., Germany, and Britain is Thomas Parke Hughes, *Networks of Power: Electrification in Western Society, 1880–1930* (Baltimore: Johns Hopkins University Press, 1983). See, for details on particular companies, Alfred D. Chandler, Jr., *Scale and Scope: The Dynamics of Industrial Capitalism,* pp. 463–474, and Appendix C.1, p. 703. The rankings are by assets.

In Britain, meanwhile, the making of electrical machinery lagged behind, and no British company competed effectively with the American and German giants. Most of the national market was supplied by imports from General Electric, Westinghouse, AEG, and the two Siemens firms, or by local subsidiaries of these four companies.

In the development of electric power systems, private entrepreneurship in Britain "signally failed in an obvious and purely economic task." So, in contrast to the United States, the government had to fill the void. By 1929, public agencies owned more than 70 percent of Britain's supply system. This "National Grid" turned out to be a useful model for public projects in other countries. But from the beginning Britain could not compete with the United States and Germany in the industries that supplied electrical equipment. See *Business Cycles,* II, pp. 757–

758. Detailed subsequent research confirmed Schumpeter's argument here. Whereas three of the top six German industrial firms made these products, and two of the top 17 American firms, the largest British electrical firm ranked number 50 among the nation's industrial companies, and the second largest ranked number 54. Neither produced much heavy equipment, specializing instead in light bulbs and other small items. The three next largest "British" electrical companies were local subsidiaries of the German and American giants. At the beginning of World War I, two-thirds of the output of electrical equipment in Britain came from subsidiaries of General Electric, Westinghouse, and the Siemens companies. After the disruption of trading patterns during World War I, British companies did somewhat better. But they did not catch up with the American and German giants. See Chandler, *Scale and Scope*, p. 276 and Appendix B.1, p. 671.

71. *Business Cycles*, II, pp. 907, 1033. The parenthetical word "endogenous" is in the original. Schumpeter went on to say that if an existing capitalist system did somehow stabilize, "There would be increasing reluctance to invest or even reinvest, a tendency to 'live on capital,' to hold on to balances, to recreate vanishing returns by all the shifts open to a class which, though by then economically functionless, yet would, like its feudal predecessor, for a time retain the powers acquired by and associated with the functions previously filled. Maladjustments, unemployment and underutilization of resources—though now of a different nature—and neutral, unstable, and subnormal equilibria might hence well stay with a nonexpanding world." This statement, unlike most of the rest of *Business Cycles,* has many elements in common with Keynes's *General Theory of Employment, Interest and Money.*

72. Neisser, *Annals of the American Academy of Political and Social Science* 208 (March 1940), pp. 205–206; Lange, *Review of Economic Statistics* 23 (November 1941), pp. 190–193; Rosenberg, *American Historical Review* 46 (October 1940), pp. 96–99. Rosenberg went on to say that despite the book's many merits, the evidence for some of Schumpeter's theories did not take them much beyond "stimulating working hypotheses." In the Schumpeter Papers, HUG(FP)—4.7, Correspondence and other misc. papers, ca. 1920s-1950, box 1, folder Business Cycles, n.d., HUA, are further commentaries on the book, likely written as reports for the publisher or intended as blurbs. One is from Oscar Lange, who later reviewed *Business Cycles:* "The most important parts are, in my opinion, 1) the historical parts of the book—this is really the first systematic and comprehensive account of the history of business cycles available in the English language . . . 2) The parts on how the capitalist system generates evolution and on the role of technical progress in the business cycle are also almost the only comprehensive treatment of the subject available in English, not to speak of its originality."

73. Simon Kuznets, *American Economic Review* 30 (June 1940), pp. 257, 266–271.

74. Richard Musgrave, interview with my then-research associate Benjamin Hett, September 30, 2000; Schumpeter to Haberler, September 30, 1942, UAV 349.11,

Department of Economics, Correspondence and Records, 1930–1961, box Robertson-Schumpeter, folder Joseph A. Schumpeter, 1933–1942, HUA. See also Wolfgang F. Stolper, "Reflections on Schumpeter's Writings," in Seymour E. Harris, ed., *Schumpeter, Social Scientist* (Cambridge, Mass.: Harvard University Press, 1951), p. 109n27.

75. If data were not adjusted for outside events, Schumpeter wrote, "it would also be inadmissible for a doctor to say: 'Organically this man is perfectly sound. If he is dying that is due to a brick which has fallen on his head.'" Schumpeter to Mitchell, May 6, 1937, in Hedtke and Swedberg, eds., *Briefe,* pp. 301. Again, this assertion makes perfect sense on its own terms. But it also vitiates exact economics, because there is no reliable guide for either the selection of outside events that require adjustment of the data, nor for the degree of adjustment. Both are inherently subjective. "I strongly feel," Schumpeter added in his letter to Mitchell, "that we must get thoroughly rid of the prejudice that our [cyclical] phenomena are simple and can be directly handled by simple methods either theoretical or statistical." This accurate insight represented a move away from exact economics.

Before Simon Kuznets published his review of *Business Cycles,* he corresponded with Schumpeter about the precise dates of the cycles described in the book. Schumpeter responded: "You will understand, however, that my dating is frankly experimental, and in many cases only approximate. For instance, I feel fairly confident that a new wave of development started in the three countries studied by me in the 80's of the eighteenth century . . . The phases of the Kondratieff [long cycles] of the Industrial Revolution I date as follows: [listed] Prosperity 1787–1800, Recession 1801–1813, Depression 1814–1827, Recovery 1828–1842. The phases of the bourgeois Kondratieff are: [listed] Prosperity 1843–1857, Recession 1858–1869, Depression 1870–1884/5, Recovery 1886–1897. The phases of the Neo-Mercantilist Kondratieff: [listed] Prosperity 1898–1911, Recession 1912–1924/5, Depression 1926–1938. I know that I have been sticking my neck out in being so positive about a doubtful matter, but I think I can say this for myself: wherever the scheme does not fit I am prepared to prove in detail the presence of disturbances which seem to me to be adequate to account for the deviations." Schumpeter to Kuznets, March 18, 1940, in Hedtke and Swedberg, eds., *Briefe,* pp. 321–322.

76. Jacob Viner, "Mr. Keynes on the Causes of Unemployment," *Quarterly Journal of Economics* 51 (1936), p. 147. Alvin Hansen later changed his mind and became Keynes's most influential American apostle.

77. Schumpeter, review of *The General Theory of Employment, Interest and Money,* in *Journal of the American Statistical Association* 31 (December 1936), p. 791.

78. Ibid., p. 792.

79. Ibid., pp. 794–795.

80. Ibid., pp. 794–795.

81. Schumpeter to Lange, February 24, 1937; on the same day, he wrote to another

economist, Arthur W. Marget: "I am more pessimistic about the future than you are—I do not believe that either dictators or any other people ever fail on the score of idiocy. For this is what humanity loves. In the particular case before us, I have been much struck by the fact that the majority of our very best young people are almost fanatically for Mr. Keynes's book, and this phenomenon seems to be fairly general." Both letters are printed in Hedtke and Swedberg, eds., *Briefe*, pp. 295–297.

82. *Business Cycles*, I, p. vi. Schumpeter goes on to say that he wishes "to make it clear that my analysis lends no support to any general principle of *laisser faire*."

83. E. Rothbarth, *Economic Journal* 52 (June–September 1942), p. 229; J. Marschak, *Journal of Political Economy* 48 (December 1940), p. 892.

84. Schumpeter sent Keynes a copy of *Business Cycles*, and received a cordial reply. He then wrote Keynes that "I cannot visualize you really wading through those two vols [sic]—or else I should apologize, not only for my egotistical concentration on my own tale (which you so generously forgive) but also that terrible size due to my wish to deal fully, historically and statistically, with 16 units of what I call the Juglar cycle, pointing laboriously in every instance to where my schema fits the facts and where it doesn't." Schumpeter to Keynes, October 3, 1939, in Hedtke and Swedberg, eds., *Briefe*, pp. 319–320.

85. In the acknowledgments to *Business Cycles*, Schumpeter thanks a few research assistants and, briefly, two of his Harvard colleagues, Seymour Harris and W. L. Crum, as well as "Professor Gordon, now of the University of California, and Dr. Clausing of the University of Bonn"; but not Elizabeth, nor the many friends and colleagues who could have given him useful advice.

86. Tobin, Foreword to Eduard März, *Schumpeter: Scholar, Teacher, Politician* (New Haven, Conn.: Yale University Press, 1991), p. ix.

87. *Business Cycles*, I, pp. v–vi.

88. Perkins also edited most of the work of F. Scott Fitzgerald and Ernest Hemingway. In addition to condensing *Look Homeward, Angel*, he cut Wolfe's *Of Time and the River* by about half, though perhaps more for legal reasons than artistic ones, since the excised portion, which dealt largely with Wolfe's affair with the formidable Aline Bernstein, might have subjected Scribner's to lawsuits. See David Herbert Donald, *Look Homeward: A Life of Thomas Wolfe* (New York: Little, Brown, 1987), pp. 202, 294–303; and the long discussion on pp. 464–484 of the controversial work of another editor (Edward Aswell) on Wolfe's posthumously published novels.

89. In 1964, the economist Rendigs Fels of Vanderbilt, a former student of Schumpeter's, condensed *Business Cycles* by about fifty percent, though not in the pattern I have described here. McGraw-Hill, the original publisher, brought out this abridged edition. It was not very successful.

90. If properly argued, a different method in *Business Cycles* might also have gone far

toward reconciling the Keynesian approach with Schumpeter's own. James Tobin once wrote that "I did not personally find Schumpeter and Keynes seriously contradictory. Keynes stressed the essential unpredictability of business investment, and Schumpeter gave important reasons why this should be so." See Tobin, Foreword to März, *Joseph Schumpeter,* p. ix.

Schumpeter himself, writing ten years after the publication of *Business Cycles,* argued that "the role of the econometric model (which includes the statistical element) is to implement the results of historical analysis of the phenomenon and to render the indispensable service of describing the mechanics of aggregates." He went on to call for detailed research on "the incessant historical change in production and consumption functions." He concluded that "the most serious shortcoming of modern business-cycle studies is that nobody seems to understand or even to care precisely how industries and individual firms rise and fall and how their rise and fall affects the aggregates and what we call loosely 'general business conditions.'" This was a very telling criticism. See Schumpeter, "The Historical Approach to the Analysis of Business Cycles," Universities-National Bureau Conference on Business Cycle Research, November 1949, printed in Richard V. Clemence, ed., *Joseph A. Schumpeter: Essays on Entrepreneurs, Innovation, Business Cycles, and the Evolution of Capitalism* (Cambridge, Mass.: Addison-Wesley, 1951), pp. 327, 329.

16: LETTERS FROM EUROPE

1. For a learned meditation on the period from 1920 to 1940, see William N. Parker, "Capitalistic Organization and National Response: Social Dynamics in the Age of Schumpeter," *Journal of Economic Behavior and Organization* 5 (March 1984), pp. 3–23.

2. On intellectuals' fascination with communism, see François Furet, trans. Deborah Furet, *The Passing of an Illusion: The Idea of Communism in the Twentieth Century* (Chicago: University of Chicago Press, 1999). During the 1930s, most intellectuals in nearly all countries, including the United States, were inclined toward a favorable view of left-wing politics, often even Soviet-style communism. The French in particular seemed reluctant to accept the truth about the murderousness of the Soviet regime. Paradoxically, numerous other French intellectuals were attracted to fascism. See David Carroll, *French Literary Fascism: Nationalism, Anti-Semitism, and the Ideology of Culture* (Princeton, N.J.: Princeton University Press, 1995).

3. Hermann Kinder and Werner Hilgemann, trans. Ernest A. Menze, *The Penguin Atlas of World History, Vol. 2: From the French Revolution to the Present* (New York: Penguin Books, 2003), p. 139; Mark Mazower, *Dark Continent: Europe's Twentieth Century* (New York: Knopf, 1998), p. 18.

4. Quoted in Mazower, *Dark Continent,* p. 16.

5. In Weimar Germany, Article 48 was used only 16 times from 1925 through 1930. Then, in 1931 alone, it was used 42 times compared with 35 laws passed by Parliament; and in 1932, 59 times compared with 5 Parliamentary acts. See Mazower, *Dark Continent,* p. 21. The right-leaning chancellor was Heinrich Brüning, who in the spring of 1930 replaced the left-leaning Social Democrat Hermann Müller. Brüning came from the right wing of the Catholic Center Party. Two of his main policies were to try to restore the Hohenzollern dynasty, and to convince the Western allies that Germany could not continue paying reparations. In pursuit of the latter policy (which in itself was a good idea), he tried the unwise policy of deflation, which would tend to worsen the depression.

6. Mazower, *Dark Continent,* p. 19. For one of many interesting contemporary views, see William E. Rappard, *The Crisis of Democracy* (Chicago: University of Chicago Press, 1938). For convenient historiographical surveys of the European situation, see the following four review articles, each of which covers several important books: John Hiden, "Hard Times—From Weimar to Hitler," *The Historical Journal* 32 (December 1989), pp. 947–962; Theo Balderston, "Coping with Catastrophes: Economic Policy, Performance and Institutions in Troubled Times, 1919–1955," *The Historical Journal* 36 (June 1993), pp. 455–468; Patricia Clavin, "The Impact of Inflation and Depression on Democracy: New Writing on the Inter-War Economy," *The Historical Journal* 38 (September 1995), pp. 749–757; and Omer Bartov, "Review Forum: Rewriting the Twentieth Century," *Kritika: Explorations in Russian and Eurasian History* 3 (Spring 2002), pp. 281–302. Of the large literature on the Great Depression, a convenient brief account is Charles Kindleberger, *The World in Depression, 1929–1939* (Berkeley: University of California Press, 1987). Keynes's *General Theory of Employment, Interest, and Money* (1936) is by far the most important of the many contemporary interpretations.

7. Kinder and Hilgemann, *The Penguin Atlas of World History,* vol. 2, p. 184.

8. Schumpeter to Oscar Lange, February 24 1937, in Ulrich Hedtke and Richard Swedberg, eds., *Joseph Alois Schumpeter, Briefe/Letters* (Tübingen: J. C. B. Mohr, Paul Siebeck, 2000), p. 295.

9. These arrangements are explicit in Mia's letters, in the Schumpeter Papers, HUG(FP)—4.5, Letters from Mia 1932–1940, *passim,* HUA. Unfortunately, only her side of the huge correspondence between her and Schumpeter is available because his letters were lost during World War II; but much of what he said in these letters is evident in her responses.

10. Schumpeter's remittances to Mrs. Reisinger are recorded in a series of letters in 1938 and 1939 between his secretary, Catharine S. Bunnell, and P. Firchow, Boston agent for the Hamburg-American Line and North German Lloyd, in the Schumpeter Papers, HUG(FP)—4.25, *Business Cycles* Correspondence, 1937–

1938, folder Correspondence re: Permissions for *Business Cycles*. See also Milly Reisinger Krassnigg to Schumpeter, June 30, 1930 and December 13, 1938, HUG (FP)—4.7.5, Miscellaneous correspondence, box 1, folder Miscellaneous correspondence received, all in HUA. The exchange rate varied considerably during this period, and Schumpeter sent checks for whatever amount would purchase 200 Marks. See also note 11 below.

11. All of these contributions, and many more, are mentioned in thank-you letters from Mia and her family in the Schumpeter Papers, HUG (FP)—4.5, Letters from Mia, 1932–1940, *passim,* HUA. The Schumpeter Papers also contain evidence of his gifts to the Reisingers, HUG(FP) 4.7.5., box 1, Miscellaneous correspondence, folder Miscellaneous correspondence received. See also copies of his letters making arrangements for sending money to Mia. For funding Mia's studies in Grenoble, see Schumpeter to the Consul of France, Cologne, Germany, October 9, 1935, UAV 349.11, Department of Economics, Correspondence and Records, 1930–1961, box Robertson-Schumpeter, folder Joseph A. Schumpeter 1933–1942. For Mia's wedding gift, see the letter of October 20, 1936, from Zimmermann & Foshay, Inc. Investment Securities to Schumpeter, saying that they had received his instructions and would send "the Wedding Gift [to Mia and Stojan in Germany] in the amount of approximately Rm 1500.00. This, however, can only be done through the medium of Scrips/Coupons which we can offer you today at the rate of Rm 3.33 per $1.00 or 30c per Mark." (This would equal $450, the equivalent of $6,135 in the year 2004. Bureau of Labor Statistics, at http://www.bls.gov, accessed October 6, 2004.) Schumpeter Papers, HUG(FP)—4.7, Correspondence and other misc. papers, ca. 1920s-1950s, box 9, folder XYZ.

12. Mia Stöckel to Schumpeter, October 3, 1933, Schumpeter Papers, HUG (FP)—4.5, Letters from Mia, 1932–1940, box 1, folder 1933, HUA. Translation by Benjamin Hett.

13. Schumpeter Papers, HUG(FP)—4.5. Box 1 contains letters from 1932 to 1936 except for one letter from Mia's father in 1947; box II those from 1937 and later. The great majority of translations of the following letters are by Benjamin Hett. For most of 1936 and much of 1937, Mia wrote in French, and those letters are translated by Felice Whittum.

14. Schleicher was the last of a series of short-term chancellors, serving in December and January before Hitler's appointment as chancellor by the 84-year-old Otto von Hindenburg. (Schleicher was murdered by the Nazis during the Roehm purge of 1934.) There had been presidential elections in the spring of 1932, won by Field Marshall von Hindenburg running against Hitler. In the two Reichstag elections of 1932, the Nazis won about 38% of the vote in July, more than any other party; in November they won about 33%. The accession of Hitler as his party was losing ground was the final instance of the Weimar Constitution's inherent flaws. The Communist Party gained slightly: 14.3 percent in July, 16.6 per-

cent in November. See Volker Berghahn, *Modern Germany: Society, Economy, and Politics in the Twentieth Century* (Cambridge: Cambridge University Press, 1982), pp. 113, 184.

15. It is not clear which article Mia is referring to here. It might have been any one of several Schumpeter published before he left Germany in September 1932, including one in which he wrote, almost as an aside, that Hitler had little understanding of economics. See Schumpeter to Richard Thoma, March 31, 1932, in Hedtke and Swedberg, eds., *Briefe*, pp. 211–213.

16. The German word *Schwanz*, which Mia uses here, can mean either tail, as I have indicated, or penis, which she perhaps intended.

17. Mia's suspicions were unfounded. Schumpeter tried repeatedly to get a Rockefeller Fellowship for Stojan. Schumpeter to Tracy Kittredge, n.d. (September 1938), UAV 349.11, Department of Economics, Correspondence and Records, 1930–1961, box Robertson-Schumpeter, folder Joseph A. Schumpeter, 1933–1942, HUA. In addition to his appeals to Tracy Kittredge, who administered the grants, see Schumpeter to Oscar Anderson of the University of Sofia, Bulgaria, who was in charge of recommendations from Bulgaria and Serbia, April 13, 1938, in ibid.

18. The letter of February 8, 1941, unlike the others in this series of excerpts, is in the Schumpeter Papers, HUG(FP)—4.7, Correspondence and other misc. papers, 1920s-1950, box 1, folder unidentified 1940, HUA.

19. Otto Stöckel to Schumpeter, May 1, 1947, Schumpeter Papers, HUG(FP)—4.5, box 1, folder Letter on Mia's death. Schumpeter received a few more communications from members of the Stöckel family, mainly thanking him for his continuing generosity. See, for example, HUG (FP)—4.7, Correspondence and other misc. papers, ca. 1920s-1950, box 1, folders unidentified 1930, unidentified 1940, and unidentified no date, all in HUA. For example, Otto Stöckel to Schumpeter, March 2, 1948 (ibid., box 8, folder S):

> Yesterday I had my 77th birthday. When I look back, my life was just trouble, work, and through the loss of my wife, Mia, Stojan and Toni, great suffering. Nonetheless I am satisfied with my lot; Mia's two children keep me young and healthy, they replace their parents. They are highly gifted and beautiful children. Zora was 10 on February 4 and Vlado will be 7 on May 29.
>
> I want to leave the children my house and garden. The house has been badly damaged and must be restored. The building permit and the materials are difficult to obtain from the city. It is well known that Jülich was very heavily bombed on November 16, 1944, and the city was 97% destroyed.

Similarly, Otto Stöckel to Schumpeter, May 29, 1948 (ibid.): "Although I sleep badly, because I always think about my wife, Mia, Stojan and Toni, still I am always fresh and strong in the morning . . . The two children of Mia's progress well . . . In the last few days the third packet arrived from you. My most sincere thanks for this heavenly gift."

Treschen Stöckel (Frau Dautzenberg) to Schumpeter, from Jülich, March 13, 1949: "Your kind shipments, with which you have once again blessed us this week, prove to me that you are still alive. In the name of the whole family I would like to express to you my most heartfelt thanks. You are really the true savior in a time of need . . . Recently we heard once more a lecture on the radio about you." She enclosed a photo of Mia's two children, taken in March 1949. Ibid. All translations by Benjamin Hett.

17: TO LEAVE HARVARD?

1. For the first nine months of their marriage, the Schumpeters lived at 15 Ash Street, just around the corner from Acacia Street. The dates of residence at these addresses appear in Elizabeth's Personal History Statement, n.d. (1950), p. 9, in the R. Elizabeth Boody Schumpeter Papers, 1938–1953, A-43, at Schlesinger Library, Radcliffe Institute, Harvard University, cited hereinafter as Elizabeth Boody Schumpeter Papers. The purchase of the Acacia Street house is recorded at the Middlesex County Registry of Deeds, Cambridge, under the names of both Elizabeth and Joseph. Elizabeth sold the house on June 22, 1950, after her husband's death in January of that year.

2. Elizabeth Schumpeter to J. C. Roraback, June 2, 1939, Elizabeth Boody Schumpeter Papers. The controversy had begun in 1938, after Elizabeth sold a portion of her property. Elizabeth goes on to say that her neighbors, Mr. and Mrs. Deknatel, could easily accommodate her wishes. She is also concerned about landscaping. "I had the impression from you last year [when she sold one of the two houses on the estate to the Deknatels] that the existing planting and landscaping could be disturbed only with my consent."

3. In addition, Elizabeth devoted much energy to improving the grounds of Windy Hill. She also operated a small commercial nursery for parts of several years, both during her marriage to Firuski and after she married Schumpeter. Robert Loring Allen, *Opening Doors: The Life & Work of Joseph Schumpeter*, two vols. (New Brunswick, N.J.: Transaction, 1991), II, p. 32.

4. He went on to say, "Let me thank you for all I feel I personally owe to your contributions to, and leadership in, the discussions of our group. I am all for going on with the work of developing and coordinating the material we have so far—and for venturing further on too." Schumpeter to Parsons, June 12, 1940, in Ulrich Hedtke and Richard Swedberg, eds., *Joseph Alois Schumpeter, Briefe/Letters* (Tübingen: J. C. B. Mohr, Paul Siebeck, 2000), p. 324. Parsons was 19 years Schumpeter's junior. The original draft proposal about the rationality group is in Schumpeter's handwriting: "T. Parsons and J. Schumpeter propose to start a dis-

cussion group on The Meaning of Rationality in Action and cordially invite you to join. First meeting, Friday, 27th, at 4 P.M. in Mr. Parsons' rooms, G23 Adams House: Schumpeter on The Role of Rationality in the Interpretation of Economic Phenomena. *Please answer* & give [illegible]." Most of Schumpeter's paper was published posthumously in 1984, in a German journal. The full text, titled "The Meaning of Rationality in the Social Sciences," appears in Richard Swedberg, ed., *Joseph A. Schumpeter: The Economics and Sociology of Capitalism* (Princeton, N.J.: Princeton University Press, 1991), pp. 316–337. It is not completely clear whether the essay was written in 1939 or 1940. The draft of the invitation is not dated, and is located in a folder containing correspondence of the Economics Department dated 1939. The addressees of the invitation were: Dr. Overton Taylor, Dr. Paul M. Sweezy, Professor Leontief, Professor Haberler, Mr. A. Bergson, Mr. Dunlop [then a line separating the economists above from others below], Prof. Crane Brinton, Mr. Lincoln Gordon, and Dr. Pettie [at least two of whom were in the Department of Government]." UAV 349.11, Department of Economics, Correspondence and Records, 1930–1961, box Robertson-Schumpeter, folder Joseph Alois Schumpeter, HUA.

5. Schumpeter, *History of Economic Analysis* (New York: Oxford University Press, 1954), p. 801n5.

6. Schumpeter to Conant, October 24, 1938, Schumpeter Papers, HUG(FP)—4.8, Carbons of JAS's correspondence, 1932–1949, box 2, folder C, HUA.

7. Conant to Schumpeter, October 25, 1938, Schumpeter Papers, HUG(FP)—4.7, Correspondence and other misc. papers, ca. 1920s-1950, box 3, folder C1940, HUA.

8. Schumpeter's Diary, n.d. (late 1930s), quoted in Robert Loring Allen, *Opening Doors*, II, p. 94. Schumpeter believed that the Samuelson issue, in addition to likely anti-Semitism, hinged on the candidate's obvious intellectual superiority to members of the old guard. See ibid., pp. 94–95, and Richard Swedberg, *Joseph Schumpeter: A Biography* (Princeton, N.J.: Princeton University Press, 1991), p. 139. Samuelson took a position at the nearby Massachusetts Institute of Technology, where he proceeded to help build one of the world's leading departments of economics. In the meantime, with the sponsorship of Schumpeter and others, he became a Junior Fellow at Harvard—a three-year appointment with no duties except his own research and writing. It was during these years that Samuelson wrote his seminal *Foundations of Economic Analysis*.

9. Schumpeter's Diary, January, 1940, quoted in Allen, *Opening Doors*, II, p. 94.

10. Aristotle's comment is from the *Politics*, c. 340 B.C.

11. Furniss to Schumpeter, May 1, 1940, Schumpeter Papers, HUG(FP)—4.1, Brief Daily Records, notes, and diaries, ca. 1931–1948, box 4, folder 1940, HUA. Yale's purpose, Furniss continued, "is primarily to strengthen the work of the Graduate School." Furniss offered to come to Cambridge at any time to talk things over.

12. Furniss to Schumpeter, May 18, 1940, ibid.

13. Schumpeter to Furniss, May 20, 1940, ibid.

14. Ibid. Allen, in *Opening Doors,* II, p. 95, reports that "In June 1940, he notified Harvard of his intent to resign." I have found no record of an official notification, but other evidence suggests that Schumpeter did indicate his intent in some way. Irving Fisher was still an active scholar in 1940. For many years before his retirement from the Yale faculty in 1935, he had taken a minimal role in the Economics Department. He taught very little, focusing instead on his many research programs. He ran these projects—which went on simultaneously—from his large house in New Haven, where his many research assistants worked.

15. They included Edward H. Chamberlin, Wassily Leontief, Edwin Frickey, John D. Black, William L. Crum, E. B. Wilson, Alvin Hansen, A. E. Monroe, O. H. Taylor, A. P. Usher, J. H. Williams, Edward S. Mason, Sumner H. Slichter, H. H. Burbank, Seymour E. Harris, and Gottfried Haberler. Their letter, dated June 3, 1940, is in the Schumpeter Papers, HUG(FP)—4.7, Correspondence and other misc. papers, ca. 1920s-1950, box 5, folder Harvard Department Business, 1935–1940, HUA.

16. This letter is also dated June 3, 1940, and is in ibid. It was signed by Samuelson, Tobin, Wolfgang F. Stolper, Abram Bergson, Robert L. Bishop, John D. Wilson, Maxine Yaple Sweezy, John T. Dunlop, Richard A. Musgrave, Daniel Vandermeulen, Sidney Alexander, Benjamin Higgins, Shigeto Tsuru, Laughlin McHugh, Herbert Wooley, Marion C. Samuelson, Richard E. Slitor, Heinrich Heuser, Paul M. Sweezy, R. M. Goodwin, Russell A. Nixon, Lloyd Metzler, Julian Holley, William Salant, Wendell Hance, and P. D. Bradley.

17. Schumpeter to his colleagues, June 8, Schumpeter Papers, HUG(FP)—4.7, Correspondence and other misc. papers, ca. 1920s-1950, box 9, folder Yale Decision, 1940, HUA.

18. Quoted in Allen, *Opening Doors,* II, p. 97.

19. Furniss to Schumpeter, June 22, 1940, Schumpeter Papers, HUG(FP)—4.7, Correspondence and other misc. papers, ca. 1920s-1950, box 9, folder XYZ 1940; Seymour to Schumpeter, September 7, 1940, Schumpeter Papers, HUG(FP)—4.1, Brief Daily Records, notes and diaries, ca. 1931–1948, box 4, folder 1940, HUA.

20. Chamberlin to Schumpeter, September 13, 1940, Schumpeter Papers, HUG(FP)—4.7, Correspondence and other misc. papers, ca. 1920s-1950, box 3, folder C 1940; Ferguson to Schumpeter, September 16, 1940, ibid., box 9, folder XYZ 1940, HUA.

18: AGAINST THE GRAIN

1. Schumpeter, *Capitalism, Socialism and Democracy* (New York: Harper & Row, 1950), p. 404.

2. Ibid., p. 399.

3. Schumpeter to Jean Paul Hutter, April 22, 1937, in Ulrich Hedtke and Richard Swedberg, eds., *Joseph Alois Schumpeter, Briefe/Letters* (Tübingen: J. C. B. Mohr, Paul Siebeck, 2000), pp. 299–300.

4. The quotation in poetic form is from Schumpeter's Diary, loose sheet, Schumpeter Papers, HUG(FP)—4.1, Brief Daily Records, notes and diaries, ca. 1931–1948, box 4, folder 1940, n.d. (1940), HUA; hereinafter cited as Schumpeter's Diary. The ellipsis at the close is in the original. The other two quotations are from Schumpeter's Diary, box 7, folder Taconic 9IV39–5II40 [i.e. April 9, 1939-May 5, 1940], n.d.; this box and folder are also the sources for notes 5 and 6 below.

5. Ibid., September 1, 1939, notebook entry.

6. Ibid., n.d. (September 1939), notebook entry, and n.d. (October 1940), loose sheet.

7. Among many books on America's preference for neutrality, see Wayne S. Cole's authoritative *Roosevelt and the Isolationists, 1932–45* (Lincoln: University of Nebraska Press, 1983); and Justus D. Doenecke, *The Battle against Intervention, 1939–1941* (Malabar, Fla.: Kreiger, 1997), a brief volume containing an interpretive essay and a collection of original documents. Roosevelt's 1940 speech was delivered in Boston on October 30, 1940, a few days before the election.

8. This is made clear in Morton and Phyllis Keller, *Making Harvard Modern: The Rise of America's University* (New York: Oxford University Press, 2001); and Richard Norton Smith, *The Harvard Century: The Making of a University to a Nation* (New York: Simon and Schuster, 1986). Thornton Bradshaw went on to write, "Many of my classmates raised funds to provide an ambulance for the loyalist forces. None, to my knowledge, left to join the [American volunteer] Lincoln Brigade" to fight against the dictator Franco, who was supported by the fascists. See Jeffrey L. Lant, *Our Harvard: Reflections on College Life by Twenty-two Distinguished Graduates* (New York: Taplinger, 1982), pp. 116, 117, 137.

9. There is only partial consensus among historians and economists about the causes of the Great Depression, despite a flood of studies. The one point on which nearly all authorities agree is the dreadful performance of the Board of Governors of the Federal Reserve System in the United States, whose monetary policies made the depression very much worse than it might have been. In addition to the sources on the New Deal cited below, all of which treat the Depression in some detail, see the following works: Michael A. Bernstein, *The Great Depression: Delayed Recovery and Economic Change in America, 1929–1939* (New York: Cambridge University Press, 1987); Lester V. Chandler, *America's Greatest Depression, 1929–1941* (New York: Harper & Row, 1970); Milton J. Friedman and Anna Schwartz, *A Monetary History of the United States, 1867–1960* (Princeton, N.J.: Princeton University Press, 1960); John Kenneth Galbraith, *The Great Crash: 1929*

(Boston: Houghton Mifflin, 1955); John Maynard Keynes, *The General Theory of Employment, Interest and Money* (New York: Macmillan, 1936); Peter Temin, *Lessons from the Great Depression* (Cambridge, Mass.: MIT Press, 1989); Barry Eichengreen, *Golden Fetters: The Gold Standard and the Great Depression, 1919–1939* (New York: Oxford University Press, 1992); and Robert M. Collins, *The Business Response to Keynes: 1929–1964* (New York: Columbia University Press, 1981).

During Roosevelt's initial Hundred Days as President, he called Congress into special session and secured the enactment of fifteen major new laws. These included banking and securities legislation (to halt the financial slide), the Agricultural Adjustment Act (to raise farm prices), relief and public employment programs (to put money into the pockets of consumers), development laws such as the Tennessee Valley Authority Act (to help distressed regions), and the National Industrial Recovery Act (a broad measure to facilitate the cartelization of industries, the unionization of workers, and the construction of public works projects). Most of this outburst of legislation required deficit spending on a moderate scale.

In 1935, during a Second Hundred Days, the Roosevelt Administration sponsored another flood of new laws, which set the framework for much of American government for years to come. The two most important laws were the National Labor Relations Act, which strengthened the labor movement; and the Social Security Act, which became the cornerstone for a mild form of welfare state. In addition, the Second Hundred Days produced the Works Progress Administration, which created hundreds of thousands of new public jobs; the Rural Electrification Administration, which brought electric power to millions of farms; and the Public Utility Holding Company Act, which put the electric power industry under greater federal regulation.

The literature on the New Deal is very large. A representative sample includes: William E. Leuchtenberg, *Franklin D. Roosevelt and the New Deal, 1932–1940* (New York: Harper & Row, 1963); Arthur M. Schlesinger, Jr.'s trilogy, *The Age of Roosevelt* (Boston: Houghton Mifflin, 1957–1960): *The Crisis of the Old Order, The Coming of the New Deal,* and *The Politics of Upheaval;* Ellis W. Hawley, *The New Deal and the Problem of Monopoly: A Study in Economic Ambivalence* (Princeton, N.J.: Princeton University Press, 1966); Harvard Sitkoff, ed., *Fifty Years Later: The New Deal Evaluated* (New York: Knopf, 1985), which includes Thomas K. McCraw, "The New Deal and the Mixed Economy" (pp. 37–67), a survey of economic policies and the thinking behind them; Lizabeth Cohen, *Making a New Deal: Industrial Workers in Chicago* (Cambridge: Cambridge University Press, 1990); Colin Gordon, *New Deals: Business, Labor, and Politics in America, 1920–1935* (Cambridge: Cambridge University Press, 1994); Alan Brinkley, *The End of Reform: New Deal Liberalism in Recession and War* (New York: Knopf, 1995); and Jason Scott Smith, *Building New Deal Liberalism: The*

Political Economy of Public Works, 1933–1956 (Cambridge: Cambridge University Press, 2006). For a broad view of the entire period from the thirties through World War II, see David M. Kennedy, *Freedom from Fear: The American People in Depression and War, 1929–1945* (New York: Oxford University Press, 1999).

10. Schumpeter's Diary, n.d. (June 1939), notebook entry, box 7, folder Taconic 9IV39–5II40. This folder contains entries written in the late 1930s as well as on the dates noted.

11. Schumpeter to Gottfried Haberler, November 7, 1934 and August 15, 1935, Gottfried Haberler Collection, Box 31, folder: Schumpeter, Joseph, Hoover Institution Archives, Stanford University. Schumpeter's Diary, n.d., box 4, folder 1941–1942 [sic]. Some scholars of the New Deal believe that Roosevelt was a master politician, but that his economic policies and philosophy of government were so flexible as to approach incoherence. For a concise statement of this view, see Paul K. Conkin, *The New Deal*, 3rd. ed. (Wheeling, Ill.: Harlan Davidson, 1992). An interesting comparison of Schumpeter's views with those of other contemporary theorists—especially Alvin Hansen and Gardiner Means—may be found in Theodore Rosenof, *Economics in the Long Run: New Deal Theorists and Their Legacies, 1933–1993* (Chapel Hill: University of North Carolina Press, 1997).

12. Schumpeter's Diary, June 24, 1939, notebook entry, box 7, folder Taconic 9IV39–5II40.

13. Schumpeter's close friend Gottfried Haberler, a reliable source, wrote that Schumpeter "actually recommended a $9 billion emergency government spending programme, a very large sum by the standard of the time." Haberler, "Schumpeter's *Capitalism, Socialism and Democracy* after Forty Years," in Arnold Heertje, ed., *Schumpeter's Vision: Capitalism, Socialism and Democracy after 40 Years* (New York: Praeger, 1981), p. 77n; see also David McCord Wright, "Schumpeter and Keynes," *Weltwirtschaftliches Archiv* 65 (1950), p. 195n17 (quoting a communication from Haberler); and Robert Loring Allen, *Opening Doors: The Life & Work of Joseph Schumpeter,* two vols. (New Brunswick, N.J.: Transaction, 1991), II, pp. 21, 33n4, which cites similar comments by Schumpeter to other colleagues.

14. The Lowell Lectures are printed in Richard Swedberg, ed., *Joseph A. Schumpeter: The Economics and Sociology of Capitalism* (Princeton, N.J.: Princeton University Press, 1991), pp. 339–400. In a book of conventional size, their total length would be about 100 pages.

15. Lowell Lecture no. 1, in ibid., p. 340. Schumpeter went on to say that there was a consensus that "taxation should be kept within such limits that business and private life should develop in much the same way as they would have done if there had been no taxation at all. That roughly was the principle of Gladstonian finance," a system he had always admired.

16. Lowell Lecture no. 1, in ibid., pp. 341, 343.

17. Lowell Lecture no. 1, in ibid., pp. 343–345.

18. Lowell Lecture no. 2, in ibid., pp. 345–347.

19. Lowell Lecture no. 3, in ibid., pp. 348–351.

20. Lowell Lecture no. 3, in ibid., pp. 349–351.

21. Lowell Lecture no. 3, in ibid., pp. 351–352.

22. Lowell Lecture no. 3, in ibid., p. 353.

23. Lowell Lecture no. 3, in ibid., pp. 353–354.

24. Part of Schumpeter's antipathy toward the New Deal arose from its tax system. "Ladies and gentlemen, don't say the speaker is a reactionary or an economic royalist. I don't want to be misunderstood." His complaint was not about taxes per se, but about "discrimination against saving." In his eyes, this was a mortal sin, and he had denounced Keynes's *General Theory* for the same offense. Lowell Lectures no. 4 and 5, in ibid., pp. 362, 366–368, 370.

25. Politicians, Schumpeter continued, have always been tempted to pursue aggression abroad as a way to strengthen their popularity at home. "Foreign policy is domestic policy. Domestic policy is foreign policy." Economic sanctions imposed from abroad tended to unite people in the targeted countries. That had happened in Germany, where the punitive sanctions of the Versailles Treaty had imposed real grievances for politicians to exploit. "For instance, most of the measures of the Hitler government, most of its attempt to create a new national spirit, was [sic] prompted by the aim of national success." Lowell Lecture no. 7, in ibid., pp. 382–383, 386–387, 391.

26. Lowell Lecture no. 7, in ibid., pp. 387–388.

27. Lowell Lecture no. 8, in ibid., p. 391. Schumpeter did not know it, but Hitler's foreign minister Joachim von Ribbentrop had written to Joseph Stalin in 1940 that their two countries "were animated in the same degree by the desire for a New Order in the world as against the congealed plutocratic democracies." Quoted in Richard Overy, *The Dictators: Hitler's Germany and Stalin's Russia* (New York: Norton, 2004).

28. If the war should last for "not one or two but ten years," then the social and economic strains would severely test American democracy. One particular danger was that pressures for inflation would become almost irresistible. Schumpeter quotes Lenin's famous remark: "In order to destroy bourgeois society you must debauche [sic] its money," then goes on to say that inflation would bring a unique degree of "moral breakdown" in the United States, the most bourgeois of all countries. Having personally witnessed the disastrous effects of inflation in Austria and Germany, Schumpeter then listed a series of policies designed to minimize inflation in the U.S.: encouragement of savings, control over wages, rationing and price controls, higher taxes, and prohibition of installment plans and

other forms of consumer credit. Though a conservative on most issues, Schumpeter was very far from being a free-market fundamentalist. He advocated these strong anti-inflationary measures—and, contrary to his skepticism about the willingness of Congress to legislate them, almost all were enacted during 1942 and 1943, after the U.S. entered the war. Lowell Lecture no. 8, in Swedberg, ed., *Joseph A. Schumpeter: The Economics and Sociology of Capitalism,* pp. 394–396.

29. Lowell Lecture no. 8, in ibid., p. 397.

30. Lowell Lecture no. 8, in ibid., pp. 397–399. The comment about a Roosevelt dictatorship is in Schumpeter to Charles C. Burlingham, May 21, 1941, Hedtke and Swedberg, eds., *Briefe,* p. 332. Schumpeter's Diary, n.d. (May–June 1940), two loose sheets, box 4, folder 1940.

19: THE COURAGE OF HER CONVICTIONS

1. E. B. Schumpeter, ed., *The Industrialization of Japan and Manchukuo, 1930–1940: Population, Raw Materials and Industry* (New York: Macmillan, 1940). See, in addition to her book, the following articles by Elizabeth Boody Schumpeter: "Manchoukuo [sic], the Key to Japan's Foreign Exchange Problem," *Far Eastern Survey* 6 (May 12, 1937), pp. 107–112; "Politics and the Yen," *Far Eastern Survey* 6 (May 26, 1937); "Japanese Economic Policy and the Standard of Living," *Far Eastern Survey* 7 (January 19, 1938), pp. 13–20; "The Problem of Sanctions in the Far East," *Pacific Affairs* 12 (September 1939), pp. 245–262; "The Policy of the United States in the Far East," *Annals of the American Academy of Political and Social Science* (July 1940), pp. 98–106. During this same period, Elizabeth also published an important historical article based on her dissertation: "English Prices and Public Finance, 1660–1822," *Review of Economic Statistics* 20 (February 1938), pp. 21–37. In this note and those that follow, I have listed Elizabeth's name in the form in which it appears in the particular documents cited.

2. For convenience, I will use in this chapter modern English spelling of words such as Beijing, rather than the contemporary "Peking" or the westerners' preference of the time, "Peiping." Hence, Mao Zedong rather than Mao Tse-Tung, and so on. The one exception will be Nanking, because of the contemporary expression "rape of Nanking," which was used all over the world.

3. Elizabeth Boody Schumpeter wrote that most of her articles "were submitted to Herbert Feiss [sic] of the State Department before they were published and I gather that they had the approval of the Department in a period when it was rather more cautious." Elizabeth Schumpeter to David Lawrence, editor of *United States News* (later *U.S. News and World Report*), October 10, 1940. See also Elizabeth Schumpeter to Charles A. Beard, February 9, 1940: "Professor [A. Whitney] Griswold of Yale and I have very much the same point of view about our Far Eastern problems and we have been co-operating with one another to some extent in the last year"; Beard to Elizabeth Schumpeter, February 12, 1940,

thanking her for the update and praising her articles; Walter Lippmann to Elizabeth Schumpeter, n.d. (February 13, 1940), agreeing that things "are drifting from bad to worse for us"; Elizabeth Schumpeter to Lippmann, February 14, 1940; to John D. Rockefeller, Jr., September 5, 1939; to David Rockefeller, March 28, 1940; David Rockefeller to Elizabeth Schumpeter, March 24, 1940. All in R. Elizabeth Boody Schumpeter Papers, 1938–1953, A-43, Schlesinger Library, Radcliffe Institute, Harvard University. Hereinafter cited as Elizabeth Boody Schumpeter Papers.

Elizabeth Schumpeter also wrote to John Foster Dulles, then a partner at the prestigious New York law firm Sullivan & Cromwell. Dulles replied, March 8, 1940, "I agree very much with your views, and from the impressions which I gained in Japan, when there two years ago, feel that an embargo by us would be a mistake. Action by ourselves alone would not be effective. It would consolidate the people in back of the army, as they are exceedingly sensitive to, and resistant of, pressure from the western powers, and it might very well serve as a pretext for extending Japanese aggression in the east." Ibid.

4. *Fortune,* September 1936. It was here that the term "Japan, Inc." made its first appearance, on p. 176. Later treatments of Japanese economic expansion in Asia include Peter Duus, Ramon H. Myers, and Mark Peattie, eds., *The Japanese Informal Empire in China, 1895–1937* (Princeton, N.J.: Princeton University Press, 1989); Christopher Howe, *Origins of Japanese Trade Supremacy: Development and Technology in Asia from 1540 to the Pacific War* (Chicago: University of Chicago Press, 1996). A flood of books and articles on the Japanese economy appeared during and after the "economic miracle" of 1953–1973. For a concise and thoroughly footnoted account of Japanese business history in general, see Jeffrey Bernstein, "Japanese Capitalism," in Thomas K. McCraw, ed., *Creating Modern Capitalism: How Entrepreneurs, Companies, and Countries Triumphed in Three Industrial Revolutions* (Cambridge, Mass.: Harvard University Press, 1997), pp. 441–489.

5. Elizabeth Boody Schumpeter, "Japanese Economic Policy and the Standard of Living," p. 20; Elizabeth Boody Schumpeter, "The Problem of Sanctions in the Far East," p. 262.

6. Elizabeth Boody Schumpeter, "The Problem of Sanctions in the Far East," p. 262. Elizabeth Schumpeter to Frederick V. Field, August 12, 1938 and October 4, 1939, in Elizabeth Boody Schumpeter Papers.

7. Elizabeth Boody Schumpeter, "The Policy of the United States in the Far East," pp. 99–100.

8. Ibid., pp. 100–104.

9. Ibid., pp. 104–105.

10. Ibid., pp. 105–106.

11. Ibid.; George H. Gallup, *The Gallup Poll: Public Opinion 1935–1971,* two vols. (New York: Random House, 1972), I, p. 388.

12. Elizabeth Boody Schumpeter, "The Problem of Sanctions in the Far East," a separate 17-page typescript response sent to the editor of *Pacific Affairs* in 1940, Elizabeth Boody Schumpeter Papers. The quotations are on pp. 16–17.

13. E. B. Schumpeter, ed., *The Industrialization of Japan and Manchukuo, 1930–1940.* In addition to Elizabeth Schumpeter's six chapters, the book contains contributions by E. F. Penrose (7 chapters), G. C. Allen (11 chapters), and M. S. Gordon (4 chapters). Of the four co-authors, Allen was the best qualified, having spent much time in Japan himself.

14. E. B. Schumpeter, ed., *The Industrialization of Japan and Manchukuo, 1930–1940,* p. vii.

15. Ibid., p. 861.

16. Generally favorable reviews were written by H. F. Angus of the University of British Columbia in the *Canadian Journal of Economics and Political Science* 8 (February 1942), pp. 116–119; D. H. Buchanan of the University of North Carolina in the *Journal of Economic History* 1 (May 1941), pp. 102–103; J. B. Condliffe of the University of California in the *American Economic Review* 31 (March 1941), pp. 126–129; and A. J. Brown, in *International Affairs Review Supplement* 19 (June 1941), pp. 285–286.

17. See the reviews by John E. Orchard of the School of Business, Columbia University, April 1940, in *Pacific Affairs* 14 (June 1941), pp. 240–246; and Kenneth Colegrove of Northwestern, in the *American Political Science Review* 37 (February 1943), pp. 161–162.

18. C. R. Fay, review in the *Economic Journal* 52 (March 1942), pp. 88–90.

19. Elizabeth Boody Schumpeter to David Lawrence, October 10, 1940, Elizabeth Boody Schumpeter Papers.

20. Elizabeth Schumpeter to David Rockefeller, March 28, 1940. Elizabeth Schumpeter to Senator David I. Walsh, October 23, 1941: "I may say that the Japanese periodicals show that the Japanese liberals and moderates have been made powerless by the belief that this country does not want any kind of compromise settlement in the Far East but is merely stalling until we have a two ocean navy. They don't want war with us but they now believe that the United States and the British Empire are determined to crush them eventually, and, as a consequence, they may acquiesce in a desperate gamble because there seems to be no alternative for them. It seems to me that we should be permitted to know what these people are thinking even if they are mistaken"; she adds that she is sending the same information to Senator Arthur Vandenberg. See also Elizabeth Schumpeter to O. K. Armstrong, November 18, 1941. All letters in Elizabeth Boody Schumpeter Papers.

21. Elizabeth Boody Schumpeter to Frederick Lewis Allen, December 15, 1941, Elizabeth Boody Schumpeter Papers. She knew Allen, and adds that she has been trying to tell the American people and government "for years that they were under-

rating the Japanese economically." Among several books on Japan's brutal war in South Asia, see especially Christopher Bayly and Tim Harper, *Forgotten Armies: The Fall of British Asia, 1941–1945* (Cambridge, Mass.: Harvard University Press, 2005).

22. Chamberlin review, *New York Times,* February 2, 1942.

23. Elizabeth Boody Schumpeter to George Pettee, December 15, 1941, Elizabeth Boody Schumpeter Papers.

20: ALIENATION

1. All references to and quotations of the FBI files in this chapter come from the Bureau's dossier on the Schumpeters: Federal Bureau of Investigation, Freedom of Information/Privacy Acts Section, Subject: *Joseph Alois Schumpeter,* File Number *100-HQ-32226.*

2. The typewritten "Howard" University was changed at some point, corrected by hand to read "Harvard."

3. On May 18, 1950, four months after her husband's death, the FBI again interviewed Elizabeth about her views. According to the FBI report, she told questioners that she "had felt throughout the Thirties that the United States was greatly underestimating the Japanese potential for war. She stated that she had publicly expressed her opinions with the result that many people had felt that she was pro-Japanese. She complimented the Bureau for having conducted a discreet and non-embarrassing investigation of her. She noted, however, that she had been aware of the investigation throughout the time when it was conducted . . . at this time [she] points out that her estimation of the Japanese being a strong foe had been proven correct by history."

   In 1951, Elizabeth was summoned before the McCarran Committee of Congress to testify in executive session, for even more questioning about "un-American activities." Her testimony, given on July 3, appears in vol. 65, pp. 1–18 of the McCarran Committee's report. It adds nothing to the prior record except further evidence of misguided inquiries on the part of the U.S. government.

4. Nor, of course, were they alone. The FBI investigated several thousand immigrants during the war years. J. Edgar Hoover expanded the number of Special Agents assigned to this kind of duty from about 300 during the middle 1930s to 5,000 by 1945. He hired an additional 7,000 employees to process reports.

   The literature on this program is extensive. See, for example, Alexander Stephan, trans. Jan van Huerck, *"Communazis": FBI Surveillance of German Emigré Writers* (New Haven: Yale University Press, 2000), which is especially thorough on the extensive investigation of Thomas Mann and his family. See also the relevant portions of the following works: Athan G. Theoharis and John Stuart Cox, *The Boss: J. Edgar Hoover and the Great American Inquisition* (Philadelphia: Temple University Press, 1988); William W. Keller, *The Liberals and J. Edgar Hoover: Rise and Fall of a Domestic Intelligence State* (Princeton, N.J.: Princeton University Press, 1989); William S. Graebner, *The Age of Doubt: American Thought and Culture in the 1940s* (Boston: Twayne, 1990); and Athan G. Theoharis, ed., *The FBI: A Comprehensive Reference Guide* (Phoenix, Ariz.: Oryx, 1999).

5. Andreas Predohl to Schumpeter, May 28, 1940, in Schumpeter Papers, HUG(FP)—4.7, Correspondence and other misc. papers, ca. 1920s to 1950, box 8, folder P1940. Translation by Benjamin Hett. Schumpeter's Diary, December 28–30, 1941, Schumpeter Papers, HUG(FP)—4.1, Brief Daily Records, notes and diaries, ca. 1931–1949, box 4, folder Taconic 6XI41-Taconic 9VIII42, cited hereinafter as Schumpeter's Diary. All in HUA.

6. Schumpeter to Opie, who was working at the British Embassy in Washington, June 13, 1941, in Ulrich Hedtke and Richard Swedberg, *Joseph A. Schumpeter: Briefe/Letters* (Tübingen: J. C. B. Mohr, Paul Siebeck, 2000), p. 334.

7. The Schumpeter Papers contain twelve boxes of lecture notes, filed by year: HUG(FP)—4.62, Lecture notes 1930–1949, HUA. His annual practice was to prepare each course anew and write an outline of every lecture, often in full detail. When the time came to go to his class, he would leave his notes in his office and then deliver the lecture in a manner that appeared to his audience extemporaneous.

8. Schumpeter to William O. Weyforth, December 11, 1940, in Hedtke and Swedberg, eds., *Briefe*, p. 328; Schumpeter's Diary, n.d. (1941), box 7, folder 1941–1942. Schumpeter's teaching schedule for the academic year 1941/42 was typical for him:

> Economics 103: Advanced Economic Theory. 10:00 A.M., Tuesday, Thursday, Saturday.
>
> Economics 113B: History and Literature of Economics after 1776 (second term), MWF 11:00 A.M.
>
> Economics 145a: Business Cycles and Economic Forecasting (first term) Tuesday, Thursday, 2–3:30 P.M.
>
> Economics 145b: Seminar on Business Cycles and Economic Forecasting, with Gottfried Haberler. (second term); hours to be announced.

This schedule was sent to Schumpeter in Taconic by a departmental secretary, in a letter dated September 9, 1941. Department of Economics, Correspondence and Records, 1930–1961, UAV 349.11, box Robertson-Schumpeter, folder Joseph Alois Schumpeter, HUA.

9. Schumpeter's Diary, September 4, 1940, quoted in Robert Loring Allen, *Opening*

Doors: The Life & Work of Joseph Schumpeter, two vols. (New Brunswick, N.J.: Transaction, 1991), II, pp. 99–100.

10. Schumpeter to Montgomery D. Anderson, College of Business Administration, University of Florida, Gainesville, November 5, 1941, in Hedtke and Swedberg, eds., *Briefe,* pp. 336–337. Among Schumpeter's unopened correspondence is the final letter of many he received from his former Bonn student Cläre Tisch, sent just before Tisch was seized by the Nazis and sent to her death. Tisch to Schumpeter, November 8, 1941, Schumpeter Papers, HUG(FP)—4.7, Correspondence and other misc. papers, ca. 1920s-1950, box 9, folder T 1940, HUA.

11. Schumpeter to Canfield, April 14, 1942, Department of Economics, Correspondence and Records, 1930–1961, UAV 349.11, box Robertson-Schumpeter, folder Joseph A. Schumpeter 1933–1942, HUA.

21: CAPITALISM, SOCIALISM AND DEMOCRACY

1. Many of Schumpeter's prior writings foreshadow themes developed more fully in *Capitalism, Socialism and Democracy.* The list could be long, but I will mention only the following: his analysis of entrepreneurship proceeds from the work he did in *The Theory of Economic Development* (1911), from many articles he wrote during the late 1920s, and from *Business Cycles* (1939); his comments on the decline of capitalism, from his articles "The Crisis of the Tax State" (1919) and "The Instability of Capitalism" (1928); his sociological analyses, from his article "Social Classes" (1927); his dissection of big business, from *Business Cycles.* Most recently, his Lowell Lectures (1941) adumbrated several arguments of the book.

2. Schumpeter, *Capitalism, Socialism and Democracy* (New York: Harper & Brothers, 1942, 2nd ed., 1947; 3rd ed., 1950). The pagination of all three editions is the same, except that the second and third editions contain one extra chapter each. The length of the third edition reaches 431 pages, 50 more than the original.

3. Ibid., pp. 32, 44. For an elaboration of these issues, see John E. Elliott, "Marx and Schumpeter on Capitalism's Creative Destruction: A Comparative Restatement," *Quarterly Journal of Economics* 95 (August 1980), pp. 45–68.

4. *Capitalism, Socialism and Democracy,* pp. 15, 16, 24. Schumpeter believed that the source of Marx's emphasis on the working class could be found in the circumstances of Marx's personal history: as a failed 1848 revolutionary and an exile in England, it was unlikely that he could influence groups other than the workers and his fellow uprooted intellectuals. And Schumpeter accounted similarly for Marx's internationalism: "Having no country himself he readily convinced himself that the proletariat had none." Ibid., p. 312.

5. Ibid., pp. 35, 38.

6. Ibid., pp. 36–37, 66–67. As Schumpeter observes later in the book, "What ac-

tually increases is labor's stake in the capitalist system." (Ibid., p. 310.) Marx and Engels distrusted the British trade unions, "realizing the danger that this class might acquire bourgeois standing and adopt a bourgeois attitude." (Ibid., p. 315.) In recent years, especially since the 1980s, workers' percentage share in total national income has begun a slow decline in many industrialized countries, most notably the United States. But Schumpeter was correct at the time he was writing.

7. Ibid., pp. 32–37.

8. Ibid., pp. 6, 48.

9. Ibid., pp. 49, 63, 64. Schumpeter wrote in many other places of the failure of banks as the key to the severity of the Great Depression. The American financial system, with about 30,000 mostly independent banks, was unusually decentralized (by law)—more so than that of any other industrialized country. In 1949, Schumpeter wrote that "The virulence of the banking epidemics was due to the existence of a host of inefficient Lilliput banks and to mismanagement in some of the big banks." See Schumpeter, "The Historical Approach to the Analysis of Business Cycles," *Universities-National Bureau Conference on Business Cycle Research,* November 25–27, 1949, reprinted in Richard V. Clemence, ed., *Joseph A. Schumpeter: Essays on Entrepreneurs, Innovations, Business Cycles, and the Evolution of Capitalism* (Cambridge, Mass.: Addison-Wesley, 1951), p. 324. Like almost all other analysts, Schumpeter also placed heavy blame on the policies of the Board of Governors of the Federal Reserve System.

10. *Capitalism, Socialism and Democracy,* p. 61. Schumpeter had used this phraseology before. In a presentation to members of the Department of Agriculture on January 18, 1936, he had titled his speech "Can Capitalism Survive?" His opening line was "No, ladies and gentlemen, it cannot." His subsequent comments in that speech foreshadow some of the arguments in *Capitalism, Socialism and Democracy.* For the text of his presentation, see Richard Swedberg, ed., *Joseph A. Schumpeter: The Economics and Sociology of Capitalism* (Princeton, N.J.: Princeton University Press, 1991), pp. 298–315.

11. *Capitalism, Socialism and Democracy,* p. 61. After making what many writers have called his famous "prediction" about the inability of capitalism to survive, Schumpeter immediately qualifies his meaning: "Analysis, whether economic or other, never yields more than a statement about the tendencies present in an observable pattern. And these never tell us what *will* happen to the pattern but only what *would* happen if they continued to act as they have been acting in the time interval covered by our observation and if no other factors intruded. 'Inevitability' or 'necessity' can never mean more than this. What follows must be read with that proviso." Schumpeter was fond of startling statements, and his oft-quoted question and answer may simply have been his way of getting the reader's full attention.

Wolfgang F. Stolper, a former student of Schumpeter's, notes that following his opening statement, Schumpeter also "suggested that capitalism had at least fifty more years to do its good work. That was at the time a rather courageous statement to make, even if the number fifty is taken literally instead of simply meaning a long time. The world was then in the throes of war economics with its widespread controls," in addition to the dominance of fascism and communism in continental Europe. See Stolper, *Joseph Alois Schumpeter: The Public Life of a Private Man* (Princeton, N.J.: Princeton University Press, 1994), p. 105.

12. *Capitalism, Socialism and Democracy,* p. 63. In his chapter titled "Plausible Capitalism" (pp. 72–79), Schumpeter carefully answers the question of whether it is justifiable to attribute to capitalism the enormous rise in output that occurred between 1840 and 1940.

13. Ibid., pp. 67, 68.

14. Tobin, foreword to Eduard März, *Joseph Schumpeter: Scholar, Teacher and Politician* (New Haven, Conn.: Yale University Press, 1991), p. xiii. Tobin went on to say that in the body of his work Schumpeter presented a rich menu of theories: "of the state, of social classes, and of imperialism, all with explanations contrary to those of Marx. Like Marx, Schumpeter pretended to scientific objectivity, telling us history and the immutable future, not telling us his own hopes and preferences." Many other scholars, including Max Weber in the early twentieth century and Walt Rostow in the 1960s, have purported to turn Marx "upside down." The quotation from Schumpeter is in *Capitalism, Socialism and Democracy,* p. 81.

15. *Capitalism, Socialism and Democracy,* p. 83. U.S. Steel, Schumpeter's example in this passage, well illustrated the consolidation movement he was discussing. As a model of efficiency, however, the company was a less apt choice than, say, General Motors, Standard Oil, or Procter and Gamble would have been. U.S. Steel had steadily lost market share after its creation in 1901 through a merger of Carnegie Steel (an extremely efficient firm and a giant in its own right), Federal Steel, and many other companies. Part of U.S. Steel's loss of market share had been deliberate, as a defense in its antitrust prosecution. See Thomas K. McCraw and Forest Reinhardt, "Losing to Win: U.S. Steel's Pricing, Investment Decisions, and Market Share, 1901–1938," *Journal of Economic History* 49 (1989), pp. 593–619.

One scholar, Michael Perelman, has written that the American economist David A. Wells anticipated Schumpeter's ideas about creative destruction in his book of 1889, *Recent Economic Changes.* From the text of Perelman's article, the reader gets the impression that the author believes (although he does not quite say), that Schumpeter owed more to Wells than he acknowledged. Although the argument is plausible, it remains true that Schumpeter was one of the most generous of all economists in acknowledging and praising the work of others, especially his own predecessors. See Perelman, "Schumpeter, David Wells, and Creative Destruction," *Journal of Economic Perspectives* 9 (Summer 1995), especially pp. 195–196.

16. *Capitalism, Socialism and Democracy,* pp. 83–84. See also David L. McKee, *Schumpeter and the Political Economy of Change* (New York: Praeger, 1991).

17. *Capitalism, Socialism and Democracy,* pp. 83–84.

18. Schumpeter did not coin the term "business strategy," but his use of it here was quite important in popularizing the idea. One of the very first appearances of the term was by A. C. Miller, in "Theory of Collective Bargaining: Discussion," *American Economic Association Quarterly,* 3rd ser. 10 (April, 1909), p. 42. Over the next three decades the term occasionally reappeared, as in R. H. Tawney's review of Henry Hamilton's book, *English Brass and Copper Industries to 1800* (London: Longmans, 1926), published in the *English Historical Review* 42 (April 1927), p. 293; T. J. Kreps, "Joint Costs in the Chemical Industry," *Quarterly Journal of Economics* 44 (May 1930), pp. 428, 447, 454; in a long review article by the same author, Kreps, called "Profits and Prices in Prosperity and Depression: Paton, Epstein, Mills," *Quarterly Journal of Economics* 51 (August 1937), p. 689; Ben W. Lewis, "The Government as Competitor: The Effect on Private Investment," *American Economic Review* 29 (June 1939), p. 296; S. R. Dennison, "Vertical Integration and the Iron and Steel Industry," the *Economic Journal* 49 (June 1939), p. 256; E. G. Nourse, "The Meaning of 'Price Policy,'" *Quarterly Journal of Economics* 55 (February 1941), pp. 175, 190; and Sidney Weintraub, "Price Cutting and Economic Warfare," *Southern Economic Journal* 6 (January 1942), p. 312. The phrase "strategic factors" also occurs in a business context in Chester Barnard's important book, *The Functions of the Executive* (Cambridge, Mass.: Harvard University Press, 1938), pp. 204–205, and Schumpeter was familiar with that book. The phrase "corporate strategy" also appeared occasionally in economic writings, but not as often as business strategy.

In the cited sources, the essence of the term evolved toward Schumpeter's meaning particularly in the two articles by Kreps and in the pieces published from 1939 through 1942, when *Capitalism, Socialism and Democracy* itself appeared. It is almost certain that in discussing business strategy along with entrepreneurs, Schumpeter was using a military analogy. As he wrote in 1946, "In my youth, I did, for instance, under a man who was considered an authority, some work in the history of strategy and tactics. The one thing that still stands out in my memory is that there is no unitary type of 'military man' or 'great general' and that the attempt to construct such a type only falsifies our picture of military history." See Schumpeter, "Comments on a Plan for the Study of Entrepreneurship," unpublished memo (1946) printed in Swedberg, ed., *Joseph A. Schumpeter: The Economics and Sociology of Capitalism,* p. 426n14.

Since 1960, three of the most influential books on strategy have been Alfred D. Chandler, Jr., *Strategy and Structure: Chapters in the History of the Industrial En-*

terprise (Cambridge, Mass.: MIT Press, 1962); Kenneth Andrews, *The Concept of Corporate Strategy* (Homewood, Ill: Irwin, 1971); and Michael E. Porter, *Competitive Strategy: Techniques for Analyzing Industries and Competitors* (New York: Free Press, 1980). For an illuminating account of the explosive popularity of the term in business schools and consulting firms, see Pankaj Ghemawat, "Competition and Business Strategy in Historical Perspective," *Business History Review* 76 (Spring 2002), pp. 37–74, which mentions Chester Barnard's "strategic factors" but not Schumpeter's "business strategy" or the other sources cited above that appeared prior to *Capitalism, Socialism and Democracy.*

19. *Capitalism, Socialism and Democracy,* pp. 83, 104–106.

20. Ibid., p. 189.

21. Ibid., pp. 78–79.

22. Schumpeter, *History of Economic Analysis* (New York: Oxford University Press, 1954), p. 305; Schumpeter, *Capitalism, Socialism and Democracy,* p. 79. As Paul Samuelson and others later pointed out, approaches derived from game theory might be fruitful in a way that Schumpeter, writing in the early 1940s, could not have appreciated. The same is true of a few other mathematical techniques.

23. *Capitalism, Socialism and Democracy,* pp. 84–86.

24. Ibid., p. 106. For a fuller elaboration of this point, see Nathan Rosenberg, "Joseph Schumpeter, Radical Economist," in Rosenberg, *Exploring the Black Box: Technology, Economics, and History* (New York: Cambridge University Press, 1994), pp. 47–61.

25. *Capitalism, Socialism and Democracy,* pp. 93, 99, 100. Of Americans' inability to get monopoly off their minds, Schumpeter remarks that "Nothing is so retentive as a nation's memory." Many scholars have debated whether Schumpeter believed innovation to be helped or hindered by the rise of big business; and, much more importantly, about the facts of the proposition and their implications for antitrust policy. The answer to the first question is that Schumpeter himself could seem inconsistent; but beginning with some of his articles written during the late 1920s, more so in *Business Cycles,* then explicitly in *Capitalism, Socialism and Democracy* and several articles that appeared during the 1940s, he usually argued that size in and of itself does not preclude innovation, and can promote it in ways that would not occur in small business. He did not usually argue that small business was inherently less innovative, and he admired entrepreneurial startups throughout his career.

On the second question, about a score of useful articles have been published on the misnamed "Schumpeter hypothesis" that large firm size is more advantageous to innovation. Some of the best are F. M. Scherer, "Firm Size, Market Structure, Opportunity, and the Output of Patented Inventions," *American Economic Review* 55 (December 1965), pp. 1097–1125; Franklin Fisher and Peter Temin, "Returns to Scale in Research and Development: What Does the

Schumpeterian Hypothesis Imply?" *Journal of Political Economy* 81 (January–February 1973), pp. 56–70; Paul J. McNulty, "On Firm Size and Innovation in the Schumpeterian System," *Journal of Economic Issues* 8 (September 1974), pp. 626–632; A. Mayhew, "Schumpeterian Capitalism versus the Schumpeterian Thesis," *Journal of Economic Issues* 14 (June 1980), pp. 583–592; F. M. Scherer, "Schumpeter and Plausible Capitalism," *Journal of Economic Literature* 30 (September 1992), pp. 1416–1433; Mark Frank, "Schumpeter on Entrepreneurs and Innovation: A Reappraisal," *Journal of the History of Economic Thought* 20 (1998), pp. 505–516; and Tom Nicholas, "Why Schumpeter Was Right: Innovation, Market Power, and Creative Destruction in 1920s America," *Journal of Economic History* 63 (December 2003), pp. 1023–1058. Portions of this debate are analyzed in David Reisman, *Schumpeter's Market: Enterprise and Evolution* (Cheltenham, U.K.: Edward Elgar, 2004), ch. 5.

    An example of frequent misreadings of the "Schumpeter hypothesis" is J. B. Rosenberg, *Journal of Industrial Economics* 25 (December 1976), pp. 101–112: "Schumpeter believed that technological innovations are more likely to be initiated by large rather than small firms" (p. 101). This statement (and many like it by other authors), is inaccurate; but it is plausible, because of Schumpeter's sometimes contradictory statements and ambiguous language.

26. Schumpeter's Diary, November 6, 1943, Schumpeter Papers, notebook entry, HUG(FP)—4.1, Brief Daily Records, notes and diaries, ca. 1930–1948, box 4, folder 1943–1944, HUA.

27. *Capitalism, Socialism and Democracy,* pp. 101–102, 110. Schumpeter adds that making a distinction between capitalism and technological innovation, as many economists insist on doing, is "quite wrong—and also quite un-Marxian." Among his many comments on monopoly and government policy, one of the clearest appears in a letter to Professor George W. Stocking, September 19, 1949, in Ulrich Hedtke and Richard Swedberg, eds., *Joseph Alois Schumpeter, Briefe/Letters* (Tübingen: J. C. B. Mohr, Paul Siebeck), 2000), pp. 387–390. There, once more, it becomes clear that because of political considerations and economists' own fixation with the perfect-competition model, Schumpeter doubted the ability of antitrust authorities to take the kind of action that would help the economy in the long run.

28. *Capitalism, Socialism and Democracy,* pp. 129–130.

29. The argument as a whole is contained on pp. 124–157 of *Capitalism, Socialism and Democracy.*

30. Ibid., p. 128.

31. Ibid., pp. 129, 139.

32. Ibid., p. 138.

33. Ibid., pp. 138–139.

34. Ibid., p. 142. In a later chapter of the book, Schumpeter calls this phenomenon "Evaporation of the Substance of Property," p. 156.

35. Ibid., pp. 132–133. Many scholars have argued over what Schumpeter actually meant here: whether capitalism, or big business, was actually killing entrepreneurship, on the one hand, or only making it a collective function, on the other. His many other writings on this subject, notably *Business Cycles,* strongly suggest the latter—i.e., that the scope of the individual entrepreneur might be narrowing (never disappearing), but the entrepreneurial *function* remained very much alive in large companies, exercised mostly by top management.

36. *Capitalism, Socialism and Democracy,* p. 143.

37. Ibid., pp. 145–147. In a later article, published in Germany in 1948 and titled *"Der Kapitalismus und die Intellektuellen"* (Capitalism and the Intellectuals), Schumpeter expressed this same point rather bitterly—but in a way that many people who have spent time in universities will quickly recognize, regardless of their politics: the case for capitalism "contests its trial in front of judges who have the death sentence ready in their pockets." And "The atmosphere of enmity toward capitalism . . . makes it much more difficult than it otherwise would be to form a reasonable view of its economic and cultural accomplishments . . . the condemnation of capitalism and all of its works is a foregone conclusion—virtually a requirement of the etiquette of discussion . . . Any other position is held as not only crazy, but as anti-social, and is seen as a sign of immoral slavery." The article appeared in *Merkur: Deutsche Zeitschrift für Europäisches Denken* (Mercury: German Journal for European Thought) 2 (1948). The quoted passages appear on pp. 161–162. Translation by Benjamin Hett.

38. *Capitalism, Socialism and Democracy,* pp. 129–130.

39. Ibid., p. 331. The comparison could be extended. Except for Abraham Lincoln, no American president between Andrew Jackson, whose second term ended in 1837, and Theodore Roosevelt, who assumed office in 1901, was a truly impressive chief executive. The full list, in addition to those named, is Martin van Buren, William Henry Harrison, John Tyler, James K. Polk, Zachary Taylor, Millard Fillmore, Franklin Pierce, James Buchanan, Andrew Johnson, Ulysses S. Grant, James A. Garfield, Grover Cleveland, Benjamin Harrison, and William McKinley. By contrast, other prominent business leaders of the nineteenth century include Cornelius Vanderbilt, Jay Gould, J. Edgar Thomson, Jay Cooke, A. T. Stewart, H. J. Heinz, Marshall Field, J. Pierpont Morgan, Henry Clay Frick, Gustavus Swift, E. H. Harriman, and James J. Hill—in addition to inventor-businessmen such as Alexander Graham Bell, George Westinghouse, and Thomas A. Edison.

Schumpeter's point also illustrates one of his pet themes: that all societies suffer from a paucity of first-rate talent. He had written about this issue earlier in his career, and in the second (1947) edition of *Capitalism, Socialism and Democracy* itself, he argues that in contemporary business life, legal issues, labor problems, price controls, and antitrust prosecutions add up to a "drain on entrepreneurial and managerial energy." So much effort is expended on such issues that an executive often "has no steam left for dealing with his technological and commercial problems." One consequence is that except in very large companies, which can afford numerous specialists, "leading [management] positions tend to be filled by 'fixers' and 'trouble shooters' rather than by 'production men'" (p. 388).

40. *Capitalism, Socialism and Democracy,* p. 167. The theme of irony is well developed in Jerry Z. Muller, "Capitalism, Socialism, and Irony: Understanding Schumpeter in Context," *Critical Review: An Interdisciplinary Review of Politics and Society* 13 (1999), pp. 239–268; and "Schumpeter: Innovation and Resentment," ch. 11 of Muller, *The Mind and the Market: Capitalism in Modern European Thought* (New York: Knopf, 2002). Many otherwise insightful analysts of *Capitalism, Socialism and Democracy* have missed the irony in Schumpeter's treatment of socialism; a good example is Herbert Gintis, "Where Did Schumpeter Go Wrong?" *Challenge* 1 (January/ February 1991), pp. 27–33. The full title of Jonathan Swift's pamphlet is "A Modest Proposal for preventing the Children of poor People in Ireland, from being a Burden to their Parents or Country; and for making them beneficial to the Publick."

41. It was not coincidental that Jonathan Swift himself wrote at the dawn of British coffeehouse culture. Schumpeter's commentary on socialism also has much in common with a famous witticism delivered by the Earl of St. Vincent in Britain's House of Lords during the Napoleonic Wars. The Earl had been Admiral Jervis before his great naval victory off the Cape of St. Vincent won him his title. Later in the war, as Napoleon massed 250,000 troops for an amphibious assault on England, the old admiral rose in the House to reminded his countrymen of their Royal Navy's shield: "I do not say that [Napoleon] cannot come. I do say that he cannot come by sea." The only other route was by air, which of course was ridiculous at that time, as everyone knew.

42. Machlup, "Capitalism and Its Future Appraised by two Liberal Economists," *American Economic Review* 33 (June 1943), pp. 302, 318. Schumpeter's approach in *Capitalism, Socialism and Democracy* invites comparison with that of F. A. Hayek (still a third Austrian), in *The Road to Serfdom.* Hayek's book, published in 1944, became one of the most influential works of the late twentieth century—the Bible of Thatcherism in Britain and of many "Chicago School" economists in the United States. Hayek, unlike Schumpeter, eschews all subtlety and irony. He mounts a direct frontal assault on socialism—writing, in an easily readable style, a book less than half the length of *Capitalism, Socialism and Democracy.* Also, whereas Schumpeter says little about Nazi Germany and much about the Soviet Union, Hayek does the reverse. He was teaching at the London School of Economics at the time, and he later explained that his intended audience was the British public, whom he did not want to alienate from their wartime Soviet ally.

43. *Capitalism, Socialism and Democracy,* pp. 186–188.

44. Ibid., pp. 187, 200, 219ff. Marx, said Schumpeter, had "grafted" a "revolutionary ideology" onto his "fundamental doctrine," which was not unlike the gradualism of the Fabian socialists in England. (Ibid., p. 323.) But in Russia, Lenin had strayed from Marxism by introducing "socialization by *pronunciamiento* in an obviously immature situation," and effecting "emancipation" not by "the work of the proletariat itself but of a band of intellectuals officering the rabble." (Ibid., p. 330.)

45. Ibid., pp. 167, 170, 190–191. Later in the book, Schumpeter takes a harder line: under socialism, "the automatic restrictions imposed upon the political sphere by the bourgeois scheme of things" will no longer exist. "Lack of efficient management will spell lack of bread" (p. 299).

46. Ibid., pp. 170–171, 188.

47. Ibid., pp. 172, 188, 190. In his Chapter 16, "The Socialist Blueprint" (pp. 172–186), Schumpeter presents an extensive explanation of the ways in which a central authority could determine "what and how to produce," based on rules of rational behavior and on data available to it—including data from the preceding capitalist era. He refers to Enrico Barone as "the economist who settled the question" of whether it was possible to make such a determination, and cites many other scholars as well, among them Friedrich von Wieser, Vilfredo Pareto, Oscar Lange, A. P. Lerner, Fred M. Taylor, and Herbert K. Zassenhaus. Some of these economists were themselves socialists, and several were friends of Schumpeter. Wieser was his former teacher at the University of Vienna, and Zassenhaus his former student at the University of Bonn. The central argument Schumpeter pursues in his case for the workability of socialism resembles the favorable approach of Lange and Lerner (rooted in static allocation), far more than the critical logic of his fellow Austrians Mises and Hayek (dynamic allocation). The quotations are from pages 172 and 173. For additional analysis and critique of Schumpeter's treatment of socialism, see Reisman, *Schumpeter's Market: Enterprise and Evolution,* chs. 7–9 and *passim.*

48. *Capitalism, Socialism and Democracy,* pp. 186, 194, 202.

49. Ibid., p. 195.

50. Ibid., pp. 195–196.

51. Ibid., p. 196.

52. Ibid., p. 197–199.

53. Ibid., pp. 172–187, 200–201, 219ff, and *passim.*

54. Ibid., pp. 204–205.

55. Ibid., pp. 208–210. In the second edition of *Capitalism, Socialism and Democracy* (1946), Schumpeter writes that "The power and social position—which is one of the main reasons for valuing a high income—of the [Soviet] industrial manager, especially if leader of the local unit of the Bolshevik party, is far and away above that of an American industrialist." See p. 382n4.

56. Ibid., pp. 210–213.

57. Ibid., p. 214. In America, for example, by the mid-1930s employer discipline no longer had community backing. Government agencies had reversed their attitudes, in a three-step process. They had moved from a policy of supporting the employer, to one of neutrality, and finally to backing unions against both employers and individual workers who did not want to be union members. Here Schumpeter was obviously referring to the labor policies of the New Deal. He took little note that the changes had come decades after similar shifts in Germany, France, Britain, and other advanced industrial countries. The new American policies of the 1930s included not only a guarantee of labor's right to organize in unions and to bargain for wages and hours, but also—at long last—a minimum wage and the elimination of child labor.

58. Ibid., p. 215–218.

59. Ibid., p. 215–217.

60. Ibid., p. 218. Schumpeter does not cite the wave of show trials during 1937–1938, during which political and industrial officials deemed insufficiently authoritarian toward the labor force—or even those whose production quotas fell short—routinely "confessed" to the crime of being "wreckers" and were convicted in show trials. Large numbers were subsequently shot. Schumpeter mentions "wreckers" (p. 226), but it seems likely that he did not know the full extent of this practice, since he was writing this part of *Capitalism, Socialism and Democracy* in 1938, as he notes on p. 231. On "wrecking" and related show trials, see Roy Medvedev, *Let History Judge: The Origins and Consequences of Stalinism* (New York: Columbia University Press, 1989), pp. 452–453.

61. *Capitalism, Socialism and Democracy*, pp. 210, 218, 225.

62. Ibid., pp. 219–229. Schumpeter suggests that the United States, because of its big businesses, might have been "more ripe" for socialism than Britain or other countries, as early as about 1913. But he then cites the Germans of 1913 as having been far readier for a transition. They were long-since "state-broken, led and disciplined as they were by the best bureaucracy the world has ever seen." They also had much stronger trade unions than those in the United States.

   In saying "by now" with respect to Britain, Schumpeter makes clear that he wrote this part of *Capitalism, Socialism and Democracy* in 1938. He says he did not changed his text in response to changes during World War II, because he wanted to see the situation as it inherently was, and not as modified by the war, which would make some aspects of a transition to socialism easier, others more difficult.

63. Ibid., pp. 221–223.

64. Ibid., pp. 222–225.

65. Ibid., pp. 226–227.

66. Ibid., p. 226.

67. Ibid., pp. 228. Schumpeter closes his discussion with reflections on the condition of Britain in the late 1930s, and its likely drift toward socialism over the next 50 to 100 years. He judges that on the one hand, Britain's "industrial and commercial structure is obviously not ripe for successful one-stroke socialization, in particular because concentration of corporate control has not gone far enough." Also, "there is a lot of vital 'individualism' left," not only in the minds of capitalists and professional managers, but of workmen as well.

Against these barriers to socialism, however, Britain for several decades has exhibited "a perceptible slackening of entrepreneurial effort." Also, in part because of the war and welfare measures, "English [he almost surely meant British] people on the whole have become state-broken by now." Unions are strong. The civil service is capable. And the ruling class "wants to rule but it is quite ready to rule on behalf of changing interests." After all, for several centuries it has shown remarkable flexibility. It has managed industrialism just as it managed agrarianism. It has managed protectionism as well as free trade. It has succeeded in carrying out useful programs even when they were promoted by opposition parties and social outsiders. "And it possesses an altogether unrivaled talent for appropriating not only the programs of oppositions but also their brains." The British governing class "assimilated Disraeli" and "would have, if necessary, assimilated Trotsky himself."

Schumpeter therefore speculates that Britain could carry out a gradual move toward socialism. While leaving most industries alone for a time, it would nationalize basic sectors such as banking, insurance, inland transport, electricity, mining, iron and steel, and construction. After a long period of adjustment, other elements of the economy would migrate from the private to the public sector. Late in the discussion, Schumpeter makes it clear that he does not want any of this to happen. But as an imaginative foray into the future, he purports to see little reason why it cannot happen, and many reasons why it might. Ibid., pp. 228–231.

In note 4 on p. 231, Schumpeter says of his description of how socialism might be accomplished in Britain, and of his statement that "I have no objection to make as an economist," that "this is no place for airing personal preferences. Nevertheless I wish it to be understood that the above statement is made as a matter of professional duty and does not imply that I am in love with that proposal which, were I an Englishman, I should on the contrary oppose to the best of my ability."

68. Edgar Salin, "Einleitung," in Schumpeter, *Kapitalismus, Sozialismus und Democratie* (Bern: Verlag A. Francke, 1946), p. 8. Swift, preface to *The Battle of the Books* (1704).

69. This section of the book (Part IV) is 71 pages in length (pp. 232–303), and its structure is relevant to an analysis of the argument. Its chapter titles are "The Setting of the Problem" (ch. 20, 15 pp.); "The Classical Doctrine of Democracy"

(ch. 21, 19 pp.); "Another Theory of Democracy" (ch. 22, 15 pp.), and "The Infer-
ence" (ch. 23, 12 pp.). As in the rest of the book, each chapter has subtitles: two
to five each in this section, totaling 13 altogether.

70. *Capitalism, Socialism and Democracy,* pp. 235, 236, 238, 239.

71. Ibid., pp. 242–243. During a speech in the House of Commons in 1858, William
E. Gladstone, one of Schumpeter's few political idols, said something similar to
Schumpeter's comment about democracy's being a "method": "Decision by ma-
jorities is as much an expedient as lighting by gas."

72. *Capitalism, Socialism and Democracy,* pp. 240–242.

73. Ibid., p. 242.

74. Ibid., pp. 243–246.

75. Ibid., pp. 251, 256, 257.

76. Ibid., pp. 260–264. In a later essay, Schumpeter wrote that economists have acknowledged that "the business process must be seen from the businessman's interest . . . [but not] that the political process and hence political measures that
affect economic life must be understood from the politician's interest . . . [Many
economists still treat] political authority and especially government in the modern representative state as a kind of deity that strives to realize the will of the people and the common good." Marx had correctly identified this phenomenon, but
"he would have accepted my slogan—policy is politics—only for the vicious
bourgeois world." See "*The Communist Manifesto* in Sociology and Economics,"
Journal of Political Economy 57 (June 1949), pp. 199–212, reprinted in Richard V.
Clemence, ed., *Joseph A. Schumpeter: Essays on Entrepreneurs, Innovations, Business
Cycles, and the Evolution of Capitalism* (Cambridge, Mass.: Addison-Wesley, 1951).
The quotation is on pp. 300–301.

Schumpeter wrote something similar during the first week of 1950, in "American Institutions and Economic Progress," in his notes for the Walgreen Lectures
he was about to deliver when he died: "Every group exalts the policies that suit it
into eternal principles of a 'common good' that is to be safeguarded by an imagi-
nary kind of State. Nobody has attained political maturity who does not understand that policy is politics. Economists are particularly apt to overlook these
truths." See Swedberg, ed., *Joseph A. Schumpeter: The Economics and Sociology of
Capitalism,* p. 441.

77. *Capitalism, Socialism and Democracy,* pp. 296–298.

78. Ibid., pp. 297–298.

79. Ibid., pp. 299–300. Conspicuously absent from Schumpeter's presentation here is
reference to Nazi Germany. Hitler's "National Socialist" party was ardently nationalist, but hardly socialist at all by Schumpeter's (or Marx's) definition, since
the business system continued to function in private hands. The Nazi government did exercise tight supervision over the national economy, and implemented
many of the labor controls Schumpeter identified with socialism. But at the same

time, Hitler systematically expelled real socialists from the civil service and other responsible positions. At its roots, fascism—whether in Hitler's Germany, Mussolini's Italy, Franco's Spain, or Peron's Argentina—differed markedly from both capitalism and socialism.

80. Ibid., pp. 301–302: "The Minister of Production need not interfere more with the working of individual industries than English Ministers of Health or War interfere with the internal working of their respective departments." But socialist democracy "would be a perfectly hopeless task except in the case of a society that fulfills all the requirements of 'maturity' . . . including, in particular, the ability to establish the socialist order in a democratic way and the existence of a bureaucracy of adequate standing and experience." As his friend Wassily Leontief later remarked, Schumpeter's assessment of socialism "went far beyond the limits of technical economics." His comments about the momentum toward socialism were based "on a broad and penetrating analysis of the inner workings of our whole social and political system. Nothing reflects the intellectual stature of the man better than the fact that he made this prediction while despising the entire range of social and cultural values which the new society, according to his analytical conclusions, would necessarily inaugurate." In the end, however, there was little doubt about where Schumpeter himself stood. As Leontief goes on to say, "the pages of 'Can Socialism Work?' are peppered with barbs and ironies that unmistakably reveal the degree to which Schumpeter detested much of the preaching of socialism. There is not only his barb on p. 208 about penny stamps affixed to trousers as badges of prestige, but many other comments. On p. 212, for example, he writes that under socialism, 'every comrade will realize the true significance . . . of strikes . . . There would no longer be . . . any well-meaning bourgeois of both sexes who think it frightfully exciting to applaud strikers and strike leaders.'" Leontief, "Joseph A. Schumpeter (1883–1950)," *Econometrica* 18 (April 1950), pp. 103–110.

81. Hobsbawm's comment is in *Revolutionaries—Contemporary Essays* (New York: Pantheon, 1973), pp. 250–251. David McCord Wright, "Schumpeter's Political Philosophy," in Seymour E. Harris, ed., *Schumpeter, Social Scientist* (Cambridge, Mass.: Harvard University Press, 1951), pp. 130–135.

Schumpeter's arguments contributed to an outpouring of scholarship on the subject of democracy. Anthony Downs' classic *Economic Theory of Democracy* (New York: Harper & Row, 1957), one of the works that began the rational choice movement (which ultimately set off a virtual civil war within the discipline of political science), is explicit in its debt to Schumpeter. Yet Schumpeter's overall influence on the scholarship of rational choice and public choice was not profound. See W. C. Mitchell, "Schumpeter and Public Choice, Part I: Precursor to Public Choice?" *Public Choice* 42 (1984), pp. 73–88; and Mitchell, "Schumpeter and Public Choice, Part II: Democracy and the Demise of Capitalism: The Missing Chapter in Schumpeter," *Public Choice* 42 (1984), pp. 161–174. See also Manfred Prisching, "The Limited Rationality of Democracy: Schumpeter as the Founder of Irrational Choice Theory," *Critical Review* 9 (1995), pp. 301–324. On Schumpeter's influence on political thought in Latin America, see José Nun, trans. David Haskel and Guillermo Haskel, *Democracy: Government of the People or Government of the Politicians* (Lanham, Md.: Rowman & Littlefield, 2003).

For a largely unfavorable assessment of Schumpeter's stance toward democracy, see John Medearis, "Schumpeter, the New Deal, and Democracy," *American Political Science Review* 91 (December 1997), pp. 819–832; and Medearis, *Schumpeter's Two Theories of Democracy* (Cambridge, Mass.: Harvard University Press, 2001), which contains extensive citations both to Schumpeter's own writings on democracy and to the substantial secondary literature on those works.

82. Joan Robinson, review in the *Economic Journal* 53 (December 1943), pp. 161–175.

83. A. B. Wolfe, review in *Political Science Quarterly* 58 (June 1943), pp. 265–267; William S. Carpenter of Princeton wrote that the evidence with which Schumpeter supports his theses derived "almost wholly from European experience." Review in *American Political Science Review* 37 (June 1943), pp. 523–524.

84. Wootton to Schumpeter, October 2, 1943, Schumpeter Papers, HUG(FP)—4.1, Brief Daily Records, notes and diaries, ca. 1930–1948, box 4, folder 1943–1944, HUA.

85. Schumpeter to Wright, December 6, 1943, in Hedtke and Swedberg, eds., *Briefe*, p. 343.

86. Arthur M. Schlesinger, Jr., review in *The Nation*, April 26, 1947, pp. 489–491.

87. Arnold Heertje, ed., *Schumpeter's Vision: Capitalism, Socialism and Democracy after 40 Years* (New York: Praeger, 1981). Hendrik Wilm Lambers, "The Vision," in ibid., pp. 107–129. In this retrospective collection, Paul Samuelson led off by declaring that Schumpeter had written "a great book." Samuelson, "Schumpeter's *Capitalism, Socialism and Democracy*," p. 1. Schumpeter's friend and longtime Harvard colleague Gottfried Haberler wrote that although Schumpeter never said so in *Capitalism, Socialism and Democracy*, it was clear that his "real feeling" was "that capitalism or the 'bourgeois' society is very much worth fighting for." Schumpeter's forecast of capitalism's downfall "has shocked and puzzled many people. If all qualifications, reservations, and elucidations are given their proper attention, however . . . the demise of capitalism loses much of its inevitability." Then, too, Schumpeter's emphasis on rising resentment of taxation anticipated the American tax revolt that began in the 1970s, a movement of extraordinary importance (and one that continued into the twenty-first century). Haberler, "Schumpeter's Vision: *Capitalism, Socialism and Democracy* after Forty Years," in ibid., pp. 70, 71, 74–75, 83, 84, 89.

The economist Robert L. Heilbroner judged *Capitalism, Socialism and Democ-*

racy a profound and pathbreaking piece of work. A first-rate prose stylist himself, Heilbroner went on to evaluate the book partly on artistic grounds: "There is a great deal of attitudinizing . . . an open delight in *épater le bourgeois* and tweaking the noses of radicals. Yet the book remains full of "perceptive insights," such as Schumpeter's remark that "The evolution of the capitalist lifestyle is best described 'in terms of the genesis of the modern lounge suit,' a remark worthy of Thorstein Veblen." Heilbroner, "Was Schumpeter Right?" in ibid., pp. 95, 96, 99–100, 101–102, 106.

Arthur Smithies, a former student and colleague of Schumpeter's, saw *Capitalism, Socialism and Democracy* in part as a reaction against Keynesianism. Schumpeter had openly derided the "stagnation thesis" introduced in Keynes's *General Theory.* This thesis holds that as a country grows richer, investment opportunities shrink even as the propensity to save increases. Therefore, savings and investment balance only at high unemployment. "If valid," wrote Smithies, "the long-run Keynesian argument provided an impregnable case for socialism." Yet Schumpeter saw that the underpinnings of the stagnation thesis were the atypical conditions of the Great Depression. He "maintained his sanity" and insisted that such problems were not permanent but cyclical. As for Schumpeter's concern with inflation, in the 1940s Anglo-American economists had thought it "obsessive." But double-digit inflation throughout the world during the 1970s made Schumpeter's emphasis seem remarkably prescient. Smithies, "Schumpeter's Predictions," in ibid., pp. 130–132, 145–146.

In an earlier retrospective of Schumpeter's entire body of work, some of his Harvard colleagues, while praising it on the whole, were not so sure about particular analyses. For example, Edward S. Mason, who was 25 years younger than Schumpeter and his close friend, believed that the older man had offered "one of the most effective as well as most drastic critiques extant concerning traditional patterns of anti-trust thought." Schumpeter "plausibly undermines the two main pillars of the traditional ideology: first, that market power is the proper object of attack since power means the ability to exploit; and, second, that the preservation of competition, meaning the exclusion of positions of market power, will assure the efficient use of resources." Whereas in traditional American doctrine, market power is a bad thing per se, "the essence of Schumpeter's position is that market power is necessary to innovation and that innovation is the core of effective competition."

Yet, Mason adds, Schumpeter offers no really useful guide to policy. Granted that an ideal antitrust strategy would include all relevant issues, including a complete survey of the historical evolution of particular firms and market structures, such a process is much too cumbersome for the immediate decisions required of antitrust enforcers. Nor was Mason ready to accept Schumpeter's dictum that big business in general is good at innovation. Most empirical studies did not seem to bear this out, and Schumpeter's own stated preference for small startups, expressed many times during his career, seemed to point in another direction. In any case, innovation was not as automatic in large enterprises as Schumpeter makes it out to be in *Capitalism, Socialism and Democracy.* "Nevertheless," Mason concludes, "his powerful attack on the limitations of static economic analysis as an intellectual foundation for a public anti-monopoly policy is highly salutary and profoundly correct." See Mason, "Schumpeter on Monopoly and the Large Firm," in Harris, ed., *Schumpeter, Social Scientist,* pp. 89–94.

88. This quotation is sometimes attributed not to Talleyrand but to Clemenceau.

89. Schumpeter himself used this simile in his book *History of Economic Analysis* (New York: Oxford University Press, 1954), p. 975n9. The context is the definition of "competition": "The moral of this story is, of course, that dissecting a phenomenon into logical components and working out the pure logic of each may cause us to lose the phenomenon in the attempt to understand it: the essence of a chemical compound may be in the compound and not in any or all of its elements."

22: WAR AND PERPLEXITY

1. Disillusioned by the Great Depression and the uneven distribution of wealth and income in the United States, many American intellectuals joined the Communist Party. See, among the large number of works, *The God That Failed: A Confession* (New York: Harper & Row, 1950), a classic collection of first-person accounts by four Europeans and two Americans (Wright and Fischer); Harvey Klehr, *The Heyday of American Communism: The Depression Decade* (New York: Basic Books, 1984); Stephen Koch, *Double Lives: Spies and Writers in the Secret Soviet War of Ideas against the West* (New York: Free Press, 1994); Judy Kutulas, *The Long War: The Intellectual People's Front and Anti-Stalinism, 1930–1940* (Durham, N.C.: Duke University Press, 1995); Franklin Folsom, *Days of Anger, Days of Hope: A Memoir of the League of American Writers, 1937–1942* (Niwot, Col.: University Press of Colorado, 1994); and John Earl Haynes, "The Cold War Debate Continues: A Traditionalist View of Historical Writing on Domestic Communism and Anti-Communism," *Journal of Cold War Studies* 2 (Winter 2000), pp. 76–115.

2. Seymour E. Harris, "Introductory Remarks," in Harris, ed., *Schumpeter, Social Scientist* (Cambridge, Mass.: Harvard University Press, 1951), p. 7.

3. Haberler, "Joseph Alois Schumpeter, 1883–1950," in ibid., p. 138.

4. The September 1941 entry in Schumpeter's Diary is quoted in Robert Loring Allen, *Opening Doors: The Life & Work of Joseph Schumpeter,* two vols. (New Brunswick, N.J.: Transaction, 1991), II, p. 103. The other entries are from Schumpeter Papers, HUG(FP)—4.1, Brief Records, notes and diaries, ca. 1930–1948, box 4,

folder 1942–1943, notebook entries, April 25, 1943, and n.d. (July 17), 1943, HUA, cited hereinafter as Schumpeter's Diary.

5. George H. Gallup, *The Gallup Poll: Public Opinion 1935–1971,* two vols. (New York: Random House, 1972), I, p. 472.

6. Schumpeter, "The United States of America in Politics and Culture," *Neue Freie Presse,* October 21, 1919, printed in Schumpeter, *Aufsätze zur Tagespolitik* (Essays on Current Policy), eds. Christian Seidl and Wolfgang F. Stolper (Tübingen: J. C. B. Mohr, Paul Siebeck, 1993), p. 132. Translation by Christopher Hall and Alison Fleig Frank. Schumpeter's Diary, box 4, folder 1942–1943, notebook entry, n.d. (July 1943), HUA.

7. Schumpeter's Diary, box 5, folder 1945–1946, loose sheet, n.d. (1945), HUA; Gallup, *The Gallup Poll,* I, p. 337. Schumpeter's parallel with 1815 was questionable. The villain there was more Napoleon himself than the French nation, and the post–World War I treaties of Versailles and St. Germain took a much harsher stance toward the defeated countries than the Congress of Vienna had done in 1815.

8. Schumpeter, *Capitalism, Socialism and Democracy* (New York: Harper & Brothers, 1942), p. 360.

9. Schumpeter's Diary, notebook entries, November 1944, box 5, folder 1945 [sic]; April 14 and May 3–7, 1945, and n.d. (November 1945), folder 1945–46, HUA.

10. Schumpeter's Diary, May 11 and 14, 1945, notebook entries, box 5, folder 1945, HUA.

11. Schumpeter's Diary, May 3–7, 1945, notebook entries, box 5, folder 1945; n.d. (November 1945); box 5, folder 1945–1946; and n.d. (November 1944), box 5, folder 1945 [sic].

12. He was less accurate in predicting that the favored regimes would tilt toward the left in their domestic politics—that they would follow the "laborite" pattern that had emerged in Britain before the war and was being reinforced by socialists in Churchill's coalition government. That proved to be true for Britain, but less so for most other countries. Schumpeter, *Capitalism, Socialism and Democracy,* pp. 373–374.

13. Schumpeter's Diary, February 20 and 28, and March 16, 1944, notebook entries, box 4, folder 1943–1944; April 11, 1944, loose sheet, and May 11, 1945, notebook entry; and n.d. (October–November, 1943), loose sheet, folder 1943–1944, HUA.

14. Schumpeter's Diary, n.d. (February 1941), notebook entry, box 4, folder 1941–1942; and n.d. (January and February 1945), folder 1945, HUA.

15. Schumpeter's Diary, May 14 and 25, 1944, and n.d. (1944), notebook entries, box 5, folder 1944; and May 14, 1945, notebook entry, folder 1945, HUA.

16. "Area bombing" of cities eventually did take its toll in Germany's ability to produce munitions, but the extent of that toll remains controversial to this day. The Strategic Bombing Survey, conducted just after the war, found far less damage to

industrial production than had been expected. Other studies contested this verdict. But the reasoning that led to the campaign is sufficiently clear. As one of the most perceptive historians of World War II has written, "Admirals and generals pleaded with Roosevelt and Churchill to release the bombers [from urban raids] to help them overcome the armed power of the Axis at the battlefront. Without the urgent pressure of Soviet demands for a Second Front in 1942, which bombing was used to placate, even Churchill and Roosevelt might have given way. Strategic bombing emerged as a major commitment not from proven operational success but from political necessity. It was chosen by civilians to be used against civilians, in the teeth of strong military opposition." Richard Overy, *Why the Allies Won* (New York: Norton, 1995), p. 110. See also Mark A. Stoler, *The Politics of the Second Front: American Military Planning and Diplomacy in Coalition Warfare, 1941–1943* (Westport, Conn.: Greenwood Press, 1977).

17. Hermann Kinder and Werner Hilgemann, trans. Ernest A. Menze, *The Penguin Atlas of World History: Vol. 2: From the French Revolution to the Present* (New York: Penguin Books, 2003), p. 200. Otto Stöckel to Schumpeter, May 29, 1948, Schumpeter Papers, HUG(FP)—4.7, box 8, folder S, HUA.

18. Schumpeter's Diary, June 10 and n.d. (1945), notebook entries, box 5, folder 1945–1946, HUA. The remark about the dropping of the atomic bombs on Japan is quoted in Allen, *Opening Doors: The Life & Work of Joseph Schumpeter,* II, p. 155.

19. Schumpeter's Diary, n.d. (1944), notebook entry, box 4, folder 1945 [sic], HUA. The comment about democracy under American bombers is made in the context of the retreat of the West from India. His Ph.D. student James Tobin recalled that "One of the few passionate opinions I ever heard Schumpeter express was his condemnation of the American bombing of Hiroshima." Tobin, foreword to Eduard März, *Schumpeter: Scholar, Teacher, and Politician* (New Haven, Conn.: Yale University Press, 1991), p. xiii. On American military deaths, see *Historical Statistics of the United States,* two vols. (Washington, D.C.: Government Printing Office, 1970), II, p. 1140.

The bombing of civilians during World War II—called, variously, "area bombing," "strategic bombing," "carpet bombing," "saturation bombing," "mass bombing," and "obliteration bombing," is one of the most hotly contested of all questions associated with the war. There are many excellent books on the U.S. and British bombing campaigns, including Ronald Shaffer, *Wings of Judgment: American Bombing in World War II* (New York: Oxford University Press, 1985); Michael S. Sherry, *The Rise of American Air Power: The Creation of Armageddon* (New Haven, Conn.: Yale University Press, 1987); and Robert A. Pape, *Bombing to Win: Air Power and Coercion in War* (Ithaca, N.Y.: Cornell University Press, 1996). The number of Japanese civilians killed by American bombs is impossible to know with precision. My estimate in the text is a little less than that of some authorities, a little more than of others.

One of the most closely argued books on the subject (and one most critical of the Allies) is A. C. Grayling, *Among the Dead Cities: The History and Moral Legacy of the WWII Bombing of Civilians in Germany and Japan* (New York: Walker, 2006), which contains the quotation from Curtis LeMay (p. 171). Robert S. McNamara, later Secretary of Defense during the Vietnam War, had as a young man worked with LeMay and others in planning the Japanese bombing campaign. He too later said that if the United States had lost, he would have been tried as a war criminal. Grayling puts the total deaths from Allied area bombing of Germany and Japan at 800,000. (Some authorities claim significantly higher totals.) The 46-page appendix to his book recounts all British missions against Germany, and specifies estimates not only of deaths but also of the extensive homelessness brought by the bombing. For example, in the raids on Frankfurt on March 18 and 19, 1944, 421 people were killed, and 55,000 more were bombed out. The heaviest raids were against Hamburg, other port cities, Berlin, Cologne, Dresden, and the industrial cities in the Ruhr.

Overall, the strongest case in favor of civilian bombing is that it diverted enemy resources from munitions production, interrupted that production, and forced military personnel to staff thousands of anti-aircraft batteries rather than fight the Allies on the ground. The most damning aspect is that so much of the civilian devastation came so late in the war, after the ultimate outcomes in both Germany and Japan were certain. A. C. Grayling is a well-known philosopher, and his book engages the entire issue. While conceding that the atrocities of both the Germans and Japanese far overshadowed those of the Allies (what episode in all of history can compare with the Holocaust?), he nevertheless concludes: "Was area bombing necessary? No . . . Was it against the humanitarian principles that people have been trying to enunciate as a way of controlling and limiting war? Yes. Was it against moral standards of the kind recognized and agreed in Western civilization in the last five centuries, or even 2,000 years? Yes. Was it against what mature national laws provide in the way of outlawing murder, bodily harm, and destruction or property? Yes. In short and in sum: was area bombing wrong? Yes. Very wrong? Yes." This, of course, is a very controversial judgment. But it expresses almost perfectly the way Schumpeter felt in 1945.

20. The numbers cited here are from Williamson Murray and Allen R. Millett, *A War To Be Won: Fighting the Second World War* (Cambridge, Mass.: Harvard University Press, 2000), p. 558. As the authors state, their numbers may be on the low side, and other sources give higher figures, especially for the Soviet Union. Kinder and Hilgemann, *The Penguin Atlas of World History, Vol. 2: From the French Revolution to the Present*, p. 218, state the following: 13.6 million Soviets, 6.4 million Chinese (Communist as well as Nationalist), 4 million Germans, 1.2 million Japanese, and others bringing the total to about 26 million. Of many books on the Battle of Stalingrad, one of the best is Antony Beevor, *Stalingrad: The Fateful Siege, 1942–1943* (New York: Viking, 1998). On comparative infantry

casualties of the Soviets on the one hand and the British and Americans on the other—and the reasons for them—see Max Hastings, *Armageddon: The Battle for Germany, 1944–1945* (New York: Knopf, 2004).

21. Schumpeter, *Capitalism, Socialism and Democracy* (New York: Harper & Row, 1942), pp. 362n16, 373. In addition to lives lost, the war created the greatest refugee problem in history. Through expulsions and relocations, about 30 million "displaced persons" lost their homes and became hostage to starvation. Some 17 million were of German descent—expelled after the war from Russia, Poland, Czechoslovakia, and other countries. In like fashion, large numbers of Italians were evicted from Yugoslavia, and more than two million Japanese from Manchuria. Many hundreds of thousands of Poles and other eastern Europeans were abducted by the Red Army and sent to permanent concentration camps in Siberia. Meanwhile, the migration of surviving European Jews began in earnest, and the state of Israel was proclaimed in 1948. See Kinder and Hilgemann, *The Penguin Atlas of World History, Vol. 2: From the French Revolution to the Present,* pp. 221, 222; Mark Mazower, *Dark Continent: Europe's Twentieth Century* (New York: Knopf, 1998), p. 412. The huge total of Germans expelled from various countries and returned to Germany derived from several sources. In addition to the ethnic Germans sent by Hitler during the Third Reich to colonize eastern Europe under the *"Lebensraum"* policy, and those allocated after the Treaty of Versailles to the *"Sudetenland"* of the newly formed state of Czechoslovakia, this number includes those (and their progeny) who had been invited into tsarist Russia to disseminate modern practices of industry and civil government, or encouraged by the Habsburg government to seek their fortunes along the eastern frontier of the Austro-Hungarian Empire.

22. This sum has been estimated at $14 billion from 1945 to the death of Stalin in 1953. See Mazower, *Dark Continent: Europe's Twentieth Century,* p. 280.

23. Schumpeter's Diary, n.d. (March 1945), notebook entry, box 5, folder 1945, HUA.

24. Estimates of deaths and casualties from World War II vary from source to source, but all show colossal totals. The numbers cited here are from Murray and Millett, *A War To Be Won,* pp. 554–555, further details on pp. 556–559. See also Kinder and Hilgemann, *The Penguin Atlas of World History, Vol. 2: From the French Revolution to the Present,* p. 218, which lists about five million more military deaths but slightly smaller totals of civilian deaths. Large numbers of Jews from almost all European countries perished, the majority of the six million being Poles and Russians.

25. Robert Skidelsky, "Hot, Cold & Imperial," *New York Review of Books* 53 (July 13, 2006), p. 50.

26. On the very extensive role of academics in the OSS, see Barry M. Katz, *Foreign*

Intelligence: Research and Analysis in the Office of Strategic Services, 1942–1945 (Cambridge, Mass: Harvard University Press, 1989).

27. Among many books on these initiatives, see Elizabeth Borgwardt, *A New Deal for the World: America's Vision for Human Rights* (Cambridge, Mass.: Harvard University Press, 2005).

28. Schumpeter to Stolper, Easter 1942, Nachlass Gustav und Toni Stolper, Nl 1186/31, Bundesarchiv Koblenz. Gallup, *The Gallup Poll*, I, p. 478; seven percent of those polled had no opinion.

29. See U.S. Bureau of the Census, *Historical Statistics of the United States: Colonial Times to 1970*, II, p. 1141.

30. The American aircraft industry as a whole went from number 44 in value of national output in 1939 to number one in 1944. For details, see I. B. Holley, Jr., *Buying Aircraft: Matériel Procurement for the Army Air Forces* (Washington, D.C.: Government Printing Office, 1964); Jacob Vander Muelen, *The Politics of Aircraft: Building an American Military Industry* (Lawrence: University Press of Kansas, 1991); Robert D. Cuff, "Organizing U.S. Aircraft Production for War, 1938–1944: An Experiment in Group Enterprise," in Jun Sakudo and Takao Shiba, eds., *World War II and the Transformation of Business Systems* (Tokyo: University of Tokyo Press, 1994); Jonathan Zeitlin, "Flexibility and Mass Production at War: Aircraft Manufacture in Britain, the United States, and Germany, 1939–1945," *Technology and Culture* 36 (January 1995). For cross-national comparative figures, see Richard Overy, *Why the Allies Won* (New York: Norton, 1995).

31. Of the many public documents pertaining to American mobilization in World War II, the most thorough is U.S. Department of Commerce, Bureau of the Budget, *The United States at War: Development and Administration of the War Program by the Federal Government* (Washington, D.C.: Government Printing Office, 1946).

32. Robert D. Cuff, "Organizational Capabilities and U.S. War Production: The Controlled Materials Plan of World War II," (Boston: Harvard Business School Case no. 390116, 1997). The architect of the ingenious Controlled Materials Plan was the New York investment banker Ferdinand Eberstadt. See Calvin Lee Christman, "Ferdinand Eberstadt and Economic Mobilization for War, 1941–1943," Ph.D. diss. (history), Ohio State University, 1971; Robert C. Perez and Edward F. Willett, *The Will to Win: The Biography of Ferdinand Eberstadt* (New York: Greenwood Press, 1989).

33. For a general history of the United States during this period, see David M. Kennedy, *Freedom from Fear: The American People in Depression and War, 1929–1945* (New York: Oxford University Press, 1999). Standard studies of war mobilization, including the rationing programs, include Donald Nelson, *Arsenal of Democracy: The Story of American War Production* (New York: Harcourt, Brace, 1946), a first-

hand account by the head of the War Production Board; Eliot Janeway, *The Struggle for Survival: A Chronicle of Economic Mobilization in World War II* (New Haven, Conn.: Yale University Press, 1951), by a well-informed economic journalist; Richard Polenberg, *War and Society: The United States, 1941–1945* (Philadelphia: Lippincott, 1972), a concise interpretation by an academic historian; John Morton Blum, *V Was for Victory: Politics and American Culture during World War II* (New York: Harcourt Brace Jovanovich, 1976), by another well-known historian who was himself a war veteran; and Harold G. Vatter, *The U.S. Economy in World War II* (New York: Columbia University Press, 1985), a professional economist's account, especially strong on statistics.

34. Andrew H. Bartels, "The Office of Price Administration and the Legacy of the New Deal, 1939–1946," *Public Historian* 5 (Summer 1983), pp. 5–29; Harvey C. Mansfield, *Historical Reports on War Administration: Office of Price Administration,* vol. XV of which is *A Short History of OPA* (Washington, D.C.: Government Printing Office, 1947).

35. In 1936, the Roosevelt Administration sponsored an undistributed-profits tax, a very strong measure that levied progressive taxes on companies that retained parts of their earnings instead of distributing them to stockholders. This law alienated businesses as much as any other New Deal measure, and was repealed by legislation passed in 1938 and 1939.

36. W. Elliot Brownlee, *Federal Taxation in America: A Short History* (New York: Cambridge University Press, 1996); Carolyn C. Jones, "Class Tax to Mass Tax: the Role of Propaganda in the Expansion of the Income Tax during World War II," *Buffalo Law Review* 37 (Fall 1988/89) [sic].

37. Ibid. (both sources).

38. The literature on these topics is large. In addition to the studies of mobilization already cited, see, as a small sample, D'Ann Campbell, *Women at War with America: Private Lives in a Patriotic Era* (Cambridge, Mass.: Harvard University Press, 1984); Ruth Milkman, *Gender at Work: The Dynamics of Job Segregation by Sex during World War II* (Urbana: University of Illinois Press, 1987); Carl Abbott, *The New Urban America: Growth and Politics in Sunbelt Cities* (Chapel Hill: University of North Carolina Press, 1981); Ann Markusen, Scott Campbell, Peter Hall, and Sabina Deitrick, *The Rise of the Gunbelt: The Military Remapping of Industrial America* (New York: Oxford University Press, 1991); and Gerald D. Nash, *The American West Transformed: The Impact of the Second World War* (Bloomington: Indiana University Press, 1985).

39. In addition to the general histories of mobilization by Nelson, Janeway, Polenberg, Blum, and Vatter, see Robert Higgs, "Wartime Prosperity? A Reassessment of the U.S. Economy in the 1940s," *Journal of Economic History* 52 (March 1992); Hugh Rockoff, "From Plowshares to Swords: The American Economy in World War II," National Bureau of Economic Research Historical Paper 77 (De-

cember 1995); and U.S. Department of Commerce, Bureau of the Budget, *The United States at War.*

40. On American and Japanese racism, see John W. Dower, *War Without Mercy: Race and Power in the Pacific War* (New York: Pantheon, 1993).

41. *Review of Economic Statistics* 25 (February 1943), quotation on cover page. The issue, which contains exactly 100 pages, has thirteen articles. One is co-authored by the mathematicians E. B. Wilson and Jane Worcester, and twelve are written by single authors: Abram Bergson, R. M. Goodwin, Trygve Haavelmo, Oscar Lange, Fritz Machlup, Jacob Marshak, Lloyd A. Metzler, Paul A. Samuelson, Arthur Smithies, Hans Staehle, Wolfgang Stolper, and Paul M. Sweezy.

42. The pieces by Machlup, Samuelson, Stolper, and Sweezy are particularly interesting. Overall, there are more references to Schumpeter's *Theory of Economic Development* than to any of his other works. Some authors return to articles Schumpeter had written in German, and one refers in a footnote to *Capitalism, Socialism and Democracy,* which appeared too late for more general consideration, given the necessary lead time in journal publication. In most of the articles, the influence of Keynes is much in evidence; and one piece, by R. M. Goodwin, makes an explicit effort to reconcile Keynesian and Schumpeterian theories.

43. George H. Gallup, *The Gallup Poll,* I, p. 471.

44. Schumpeter's Diary, April 14, 1945, notebook entry, box 5, folder 1945, HUA.

45. Schumpeter, *Capitalism, Socialism and Democracy,* 2nd ed. (1947), pp. 398–399.

46. Ibid., pp. 398–399.

47. Ibid., p. 401. Schumpeter could not restrain himself from contrasting Americans' complacency with what the Soviets had done with their earlier fury at what the Nazis had attempted: "Those who are actuated by a passionate hatred of Germany or of the national-socialist regime are content. With the same arguments which they used to stigmatize as escapist, they now support the policy toward Russia which they used to stigmatize as appeasement in the case of Hitlerite Germany."

48. Ibid., p. 402.

49. Ibid., pp. 398–399n31, 402n32. Here Schumpeter analogizes the USSR with Standard Oil, which is now so well established that it no longer needs the genius of John D. Rockefeller.

50. Ibid., p. 403.

51. Ibid., pp. 404–405. In footnote 37 on p. 404, Schumpeter identifies fascism as "the political method of monopolistic vs. competitive leadership."

52. Of Japan and Spain, he remarks in a footnote that neither was economically "'totalitarian' in any meaningful sense of the term," although he admits that he had lost touch with Japanese economics after the start of World War II. *History of Economic Analysis* (New York: Oxford University Press, 1954), p. 1153n1.

53. Ibid., pp. 1155–1156.

54. Ibid., p. 1156. Robert Skidelsky confirms this judgment in the final chapters of *John Maynard Keynes: The Economist as Savior*, vol. 2 of *John Maynard Keynes: A Biography*, 3 vols. (New York: Viking, 1986–2001). See also George Garvy, "Keynes and the Economic Activists of Pre-Hitler Germany," *Journal of Political Economy* 83 (1975), pp. 391–406; and J. Backhaus, "Review Article: Theories and Political Interests: Scholarly Economics in Pre-Hitler Germany," *Journal of European Economic History* 12 (Winter 1983), pp. 661–667.

55. *History of Economic Analysis*, p. 1156. The persecution of Jews came later in Italy than in Germany, but it did come.

56. Ibid., p. 1157.

57. Ibid., p. 1157.

58. Ibid., p. 1158.

59. Martin Amis, *Koba the Dread: Laughter and the Twenty Million* (New York: Hyperion, 2002), pp. 97, 121. Amis cites the differential as 162 million versus 170 million. Robert Conquest, *Reflections on a Ravaged Century* (New York: Norton, 2000), p. 96, is the source of the quoted figures. Conquest attributes 10 million of the missing 15 million people to deaths by famine and deportation.

60. *History of Economic Analysis*, pp. 1158–1159.

61. Ibid., p. 1159n11.

62. The literature on this subject is growing rapidly. Among many excellent analyses, see Alec Nove, *An Economic History of the U.S.S.R., 1917–1991*, 3rd ed. (London: Penguin, 1992); Andrei Yu. [sic] Yudanov, "Large Enterprises in the USSR," in Alfred D. Chandler, Jr., Franco Amatori, and Takashi Hikino, eds., *Big Business and the Wealth of Nations* (Cambridge: Cambridge University Press, 1997), pp. 397–433, which is uncommonly clear on how the Soviet enterprise system worked; and Richard Overy, *The Dictators: Hitler's Germany and Stalin's Russia* (New York: Norton, 2005), which gives invaluable details on the administrative apparatus of the Soviet state as compared with that of the Nazis. On the magnitude of Stalinist horrors, see Roy Medvedev, ed. and trans. George Shriver, *Let History Judge: The Origins and Consequences of Stalinism* (New York: Columbia University Press, 1989); Robert Conquest, *The Great Terror: A Reassessment* (Oxford: Oxford University Press, 1990); Martin Malia, *The Soviet Tragedy: A History of Socialism in Russia, 1917–1991* (New York: Free Press, 1994); and Stéphane Courtois, et al., *The Black Book of Communism: Crimes, Terror, Repression* (Cambridge, Mass.: Harvard University Press, 1999).

23: INTROSPECTION

1. Schumpeter's Diary, October 9, 1942, notebook entry, Schumpeter Papers, HUG(FP)—4.1, Brief Daily Records, notes and diaries, ca. 1931–1948, box 4, folder 1942–1943; May 3–7, 1945, notebook entries, box 5, folder 1945, HUA. Hereinafter cited as Schumpeter's Diary. As he spent less time at Harvard and

more at Windy Hill, Schumpeter had to ask his Department's indulgence for some of his absences. In a typical letter in longhand to Chairman Harold Burbank, he wrote from Taconic, December 8, 1944:

> Ever so many thanks for thoughtfully inviting me to the dept meeting at which such important problems are to be discussed. I hope however that you will permit me to excuse myself and to enclose the short memo. in order to put you in possession of my views. For I am practically marooned here because of the gasoline shortage, and, moreover, can ill afford the two or three days of work it would cost me if I were to come up.
>
> It is not only in order to excuse myself that I now beg leave to report upon my work: both as friend and as chairman you are entitled to know about it; and you have so kindly encouraged me to keep you informed that I am glad to avail myself of this opportunity.

He then recounts in some detail the work he is doing. See Department of Economics, Correspondence and Records, 1930–1961, UAV 349.11, box Robertson-Schumpeter, folder Joseph Alois Schumpeter, HUA.

In succeeding years, Schumpeter's letters become less frequent, the tone of responses from the Department a little frostier, and he himself less concerned about his Harvard work and more about his writing. It was not a dramatic change; he had been drifting in this direction since about 1935. And there was no dropoff in his attention to teaching, as is evident from many sources. But a standoff developed between Schumpeter's dedication to his writing and Harvard's rules about required time on the campus. In a draft letter to Dean Paul Buck dated May 2, 1945, Schumpeter asks for a leave of absence during Harvard's "Reading Period," from May 31 to June 9. He explains that he is writing two books and indicates that he will again ask for leaves during the next year or two. There is a similar letter to Department Chairman Burbank on the same day, enclosing a copy of the draft letter to Buck, "which I herewith recommend to your benevolent consideration and support." Schumpeter adds that "The point is that absence means much more undisturbed and concentrated work than I can get here [in Cambridge] even if there are no lectures, and just now a fortnight more or less makes a lot of difference to me. Sometimes I feel as if you would never see that HISTORY [of economic analysis] finished in which you have expressed so much kind interest." Schumpeter Papers, HUG(FP)—4.7, box 5, folder 1943–1948, misc. corr. through Dept. Secretary, HUA.

Then comes a curt withdrawal of his request, addressed to "Mr. Chairman," also dated May 2, ibid. That Schumpeter's letters were sent through the secretary of the Economics Department suggests that Burbank, as indulgent as he was, had told Schumpeter that writing to Dean Buck just would not do. The whole issue of absence during the Reading Period arose many times (with Schumpeter and numerous other Harvard professors). Long before, in the original negotiations that brought Schumpeter from Bonn, it had been raised by Frank Taussig on Schumpeter's behalf and firmly turned down by President Lowell.

2. Schumpeter's Diary, September 6, 1941, notebook entry; n.d. (December 1941–January 1942); n.d. (1941–1942), loose sheet; January 5, October 30, and November 29, 1942, notebook entries; and n.d. (1942), loose sheet, all in box 4, folder 1941–42. The ellipses and the dash in the quotation are in the original.

3. Quoted in Robert Loring Allen, *Opening Doors: The Life & Work of Joseph Schumpeter,* two vols. (New Brunswick, N.J.: Transaction, 1991), II, p. 111.

4. Schumpeter's Diary, n.d. (October–November, 1942) and November 23, 1942, notebook entries, box 4, folder 1942–1943.

5. Samuelson, "Schumpeter as a Teacher and Economic Theorist," in Seymour E. Harris, ed., *Schumpeter, Social Scientist* (Cambridge: Harvard University Press, 1951), p. 50: "Schumpeter was a great showman. In all probability he spoke before more economists the world over than any other scholar in history," but "he was really at his best in his own classroom"; *Harvard Service News,* published by the *Harvard Crimson,* April 11, 1944, p. 1, quoting a senior telling a freshman about Schumpeter.

6. Schumpeter's Diary, dates noted, notebook entries and loose sheets, box 4, folders 1942–1943, 1943–1944, 1944, 1945. A list of 106 aphorisms, including some included here, is presented as Appendix I of Richard Swedberg, *Schumpeter: A Biography* (Princeton, N.J.: Princeton University Press, 1991), pp. 199–206.

7. Schumpeter's Diary, March 16, 1944, notebook entry, box 4, folder 1944.

8. Schumpeter, *History of Economic Analysis* (New York: Oxford University Press, 1954), p. 185.

9. Schumpeter did think about writing a counterpart to Keynes's *General Theory,* which would have presented his own system of economic thought in like fashion. But he seems to have viewed it as a complementary work rather than a rebuttal or refutation of what Keynes had written—even though he believed Keynes's *General Theory* to be full of flaws. See chapter 25 below; Schumpeter's Diary, n.d. (1947), notebook entries, box 5, folder 1947; and Allen, *Opening Doors,* II, p. 182.

10. As one close student of his career puts it, "Schumpeter was temperamentally indisposed toward the kinds of things an intellectual innovator normally does to gather a following and propagate his views . . . eschewal of 'schools' of thought combines intellectual integrity with a basic naiveté. In fact, there are schools of thought within social scientific disciplines, and with good cause." John E. Elliott, "Schumpeter and the Theory of Capitalist Economic Development," *Journal of Economic Behavior and Organization* 4 (December 1983), pp. 277–308, especially pp. 95–98.

11. George J. Stigler, review of *History of Economic Analysis,* in the *Journal of Political Economy* 62 (August 1954), pp. 344–345.

12. Schumpeter to Fisher, February 18, 1946, in Ulrich Hedtke and Richard Swedberg, eds., *Joseph Alois Schumpeter, Briefe/Letters* (Tübingen: J. C. B. Mohr, Paul Siebeck, 2000), p. 356. Sample entries from this period, Schumpeter's Diary, box 4, folder 1944, and box 5, folder 1945, notebook entries, dates noted:

> *2/28/44:* No Laune! [a German word meaning mood of good humor] This is just what I have not got!

> *2/29/44:* No Laune! . . . misery and disgust and sick of it all!

> *5/30/44:* Of course it is very nice here [in Taconic]—lovely even . . . but for me everything is overshadowed by this feeling of defeat.

> *7/28–31/1944:* I have not joy but peace[.] The fears and the griefs continue to worry me—but milder, further off

> *11/?/44:* My successes were due to concentration [.] My failures were due to lack of concentration.

> *1/21/45:* Looking back on these months and on the weeks that are still left, and looking back on my life in the process, three things stand out

> *1.)* always the same mistakes committed and the same type of strength and weakness displayed.

> *2.)* the story might be written in terms of lost opportunities (though of course that stands out to retrospect, there were those that were seized and promptly enough).

> *3.)* yet there is no regret—if I had used every one of those opportunities I should not have done a better job of it all—perhaps even on the contrary, for success up to the hilt with any one of them would have stuck me in the particular line and not only narrowed me [but] landed me in uncomfortable situations.

> *2/8/45 [his birthday]:* Good morning friend how does it feel to be 62— definitely old and definitely to feel old. One thing . . . humble thanks to U.S. . . . . No reprising, no sterile regrets or sorrow about this state of things: acceptance rather and a feeling: could be worse!

13. Schumpeter's Diary, April 3, 1946, notebook entry, box 5, folder 1945–1946.

24: HONORS AND CRISES

1. Schumpeter's articles are itemized by Massimo Augello in Richard Swedberg, ed., *Joseph A. Schumpeter: The Economics and Sociology of Capitalism* (Princeton, N.J.:

Princeton University Press, 1991), pp. 445–481; articles published or written from 1946 to 1948 are on pp. 477–480.

2. Oskar Morgenstern, "Obituary: Joseph A. Schumpeter, 1883–1950," *Economic Journal* (March 1951), pp. 197, 198; Arthur Smithies, "Memorial: Joseph Alois Schumpeter, 1883–1950," in Seymour E. Harris, ed., *Schumpeter, Social Scientist* (Cambridge, Mass.: Harvard University Press, 1951), p. 15.

3. Schumpeter to Harold Burbank, December 8, 1944, UAV 349.11, Department of Economics, Correspondence and Records, 1930–1961, box Robertson-Schumpeter, folder Joseph Alois Schumpeter, HUA. Also, in a letter of July 10, 1944 to his colleague John D. Black, Chairman of the Committee on Research in the Social Sciences at Harvard, Schumpeter mentions a "preliminary volume" to a "comprehensive work to be entitled 'The Analytic Apparatus of Economics,' which will still take years to complete." He was reporting to Black on the progress of his work, and estimating the research support he would need for the coming year. As he did throughout the 1940s, he predicts in this letter that his *History of Economic Analysis* "should be ready to go to press by the end of the current calendar year." See Ulrich Hedtke and Richard Swedberg, eds., *Joseph Alois Schumpeter, Briefe/Letters* (Tübingen: J. C. B. Mohr, Paul Siebeck, 2000), pp. 346–347.

4. Elizabeth Boody Schumpeter, *English Overseas Trade Statistics, 1697–1808* (Oxford: Oxford University Press, 1960), with an introduction by T. S. Ashton.

5. Schumpeter's Diary, Schumpeter Papers, HUG(FP)—4.1, Brief Daily Records, notes and diaries, ca. 1931–1948, boxes 4 and 5, *passim,* HUA, cited hereinafter as Schumpeter's Diary; Robert Loring Allen, *Opening Doors: The Life & Work of Joseph Schumpeter,* two vols. (New Brunswick, N.J.: Transaction, 1991), II, pp. 149–150, 193.

6. Quoted in Allen, *Opening Doors,* II, p. 234; Schumpeter to Therese Dautzenberg, May 20, 1948, in Hedtke and Swedberg, eds., *Briefe,* p. 361.

7. Quoted in Allen, *Opening Doors,* II, pp. 219–221; trying to absorb the initial shock, Schumpeter wrote in his diary that "Complete disorganization persists . . . but I must now see that nothing breaks *visibly* down." On the next day, "Brain chaotic," and then, as the date of Elizabeth's surgery approached, "I must pull myself together." Schumpeter's Diary, notebook entries, September 4, 5, and 13, 1948, box 5, folder 1948/2, HUA. The surgery was performed at the hospital in Sharon, Connecticut.

8. Quoted in Allen, *Opening Doors,* II, p. 221.

9. Schumpeter's Diary, notebook entry, June 25, 1947, box 5, folder 1947, HUA. Allen, *Opening Doors,* II, p. 182. Schumpeter to Tsuru, August 10, 1949, in Hedtke and Swedberg, eds., *Briefe,* pp. 386–387. Shigeto Tsuru had a very interesting background. A Marxist, he had married a cousin of Emperor Hirohito. Late in World War II, when the Japanese envoy seeking a path to peace with the United

States approached the Soviet Union for its good offices and was refused a hearing, Tsuru led a second mission, having been chosen by Japanese diplomats because they believed that his Marxism might gain him entree. The Soviets did receive Tsuru, but he did not succeed in his mission because his hosts wanted a part of the spoils of war themselves. I am indebted to F. M. Scherer for the story of this episode.

10. Allen, *Opening Doors,* II, pp. 161, 238. Allen himself was a graduate student during these years.

11. Samuelson, *Newsweek,* April 13, 1970; Allen, *Opening Doors,* II, pp. 170–171, citing the account Sweezy later gave to him.

12. Opinions of Returning Graduate Students in Economics, 1948, UAV 349.448, Department of Economics, HUA. Students did not rank their professors numerically. I have inferred rough rankings from the many comments in this long and informative document: Hansen first, Schumpeter second, J. H. Williams third, and Leontief fourth. I quote in the text all citations of Schumpeter contained in this section of the report. Two mentions occur in other sections:

> The professor was a very stimulating lecturer, with a broad background drawn from many fields of study. The material covered in the course was not so important as the opportunity to hear a very learned and unusually gifted individual.
>
> Professor Schumpeter—lecturer was interested in his subject, was thoroughly conversant with it, willing to discuss difficulties with students, and has an excellent mode of delivery.

The quotations come from pp. 36, 39, 41, 43, and 44 of the report.

13. Schumpeter, "Comments on a Plan for the Study of Entrepreneurship," unpublished memorandum (1946), printed in Richard Swedberg, ed., *Joseph A. Schumpeter: The Economics and Sociology of Capitalism* (Princeton, N.J.: Princeton University Press, 1991), pp. 426–427.

14. Allen, *Opening Doors,* II, pp. 172, 173.

15. Johnson told this story to Robert Loring Allen, who published it in *Opening Doors,* II, p. 194.

16. The one-third figure was down from one-half in the earlier period. Report on Long-Range Plans for the Department of Economics (Revised Edition), HUG 4795.5, Sumner H. Slichter, Personal Papers, Correspondence on matters relating to Harvard University, box 1, folder Harvard Correspondence—Old, p. 4, HUA. See also Paul H. Buck, Provost of Harvard, to Sumner H. Slichter, March 27, 1948, UAV 349.208, Department of Economics, Budget, folder Budget 1940/41–1945/46, HUA.

As was true in Economics, the number of undergraduate concentrators and graduate students in History and Government had also grown substantially during the period of the report:

	1930–1931	1947–1948
Economics		
Undergraduate	397	726
Graduate	82	264
History		
Undergraduate	254	327
Graduate	138	207
Government		
Undergraduate	130	763
Graduate	56	129

The establishment of Harvard's new Graduate School of Public Administration was one reason for the big rise in the number of graduate students in both Economics and Government.

17. Paul H. Buck to Sumner H. Slichter, March 27, 1948, UAV 349.208, Department of Economics, Budget, folder Budget 1940/41–1945/46, p. 6, HUA. The committee believed that Economics had taken on too many graduate students, and proposed a drop from 264 to 200, which would still be "twice the pre-war level."

   The authorized seventeenth member of the Department was to be Arthur Smithies, a close friend and former student of Schumpeter's who was born in 1907. Smithies was promoted to full professor in 1949. Ibid., pp. 15–16.

   One of the most striking aspects of the report is the relative seniority of the "permanent staff," whose birthdates the report listed (ibid., p. 2). Seven of the sixteen were past the age of 60, and four others past 50 (mandatory retirement age was 70). For the coming academic year, only two would be under 49: A. P. Usher b. 1/13/[18]83; J. A. Schumpeter 2/8/83; J. D. Black 6/6/83; A. E. Monroe 8/2/85; J. H. Williams 6/21/87; H. H. Burbank 7/3/87; A. H. Hansen 8/23/87; S. H. Slichter 1/8/92; E. Frickey 8/20/93; S. E. Harris 9/8/97; O. H. Taylor 12/11/97; E. S. Mason 2/22/99; E. H. Chamberlin 5/18/99; G. Haberler 7/20/[19]00; W. W. Leontief 8/5/05; J. T. Dunlop 7/5/14.

18. Allen, *Opening Doors,* II, p. 226. Allen was himself the graduate student, and here recounts Schneider's visit.

19. In 1948, Schumpeter spoke to students and faculty at Colby College in Maine, the University of Buffalo, and the MIT Graduate Students' Club in Cambridge. He also made presentations to the Boston Economic Club, and, at Harvard, to

the Graduate Students' Economic Club, the Social Relations Colloquy, and the Young Republicans. In 1949, he spoke to the Harvard Club of Philadelphia, the Boston Economic Club, the Choate Club, Radcliffe College, and the Yale Graduate Students' Club. He was invited to testify before Congress as a member of the Economists' National Committee on Monetary Policy, but—finding politics distasteful—he declined. Most of these activities are evident from Schumpeter's Diary. See also Allen, *Opening Doors,* II, pp. 187, 225.

20. The first Nobel Award in Economic Science was given in 1968, jointly to Jan Tinbergen and Schumpeter's good friend Ragnar Frisch. The second, in 1969, went to Schumpeter's former student Paul Samuelson.

25: TOWARD THE MIXED ECONOMY

1. "Capitalism in the Postwar World," in Seymour E. Harris, ed., *Postwar Economic Problems* (New York: McGraw-Hill, 1943), pp. 113–126, reprinted in Richard V. Clemence, ed., *Joseph A. Schumpeter: Essays on Entrepreneurs, Innovations, Business Cycles, and the Evolution of Capitalism* (Cambridge, Mass.: Addison-Wesley, 1951), pp. 175–188. The quotation is on p. 176.

2. Ibid., pp. 181, 182.

3. See *The Impact of the War on Civilian Consumption in the United Kingdom, the United States and Canada: A Report to the Combined Production and Resources Board from a Special Combined Committee on Nonfood Consumption Levels* (Washington, D.C.: Government Printing Office, 1945).

4. As Schumpeter put it in 1943, "The wants of impoverished households may be so urgent and so calculable that any postwar slump that may be unavoidable would speedily give way to a reconstruction boom. "Capitalism in the Postwar World," pp. 182, 183.

5. Ibid., pp. 183–185.

6. Ibid., pp. 186–187.

7. Ibid., p. 188.

8. Schumpeter, "Capitalism," in *Encyclopaedia Britannica* (New York: Encyclopaedia Britannica, 1946), pp. 801–87, reprinted in Clemence, ed., *Joseph A. Schumpeter: Essays,* pp. 209–210.

9. Schumpeter, trans. Michael G. Prime and David R. Henderson, "The Future of Private Enterprise in the Face of Modern Socialistic Tendencies," reprinted in Richard Swedberg, ed., *Joseph A. Schumpeter: The Economics and Sociology of Capitalism* (Princeton, N.J.: Princeton University Press, 1991), pp. 401–405. The quotations are on pp. 401, 402, and 403.

10. Ibid., p. 404.

11. Subsequent encyclicals on economic matters, notably those by Popes John XXIII and Paul VI, which were written in times of much greater affluence in advanced

industrial nations, tend toward a more critical view of business. They reaffirm the legitimacy of private property, but they emphasize the social obligations of capitalist systems.

12. See the commentary on *Quadragesimo Anno* by Swedberg in Swedberg, ed., *Joseph A. Schumpeter: The Economics and Sociology of Capitalism,* pp. 70–71.

13. Schumpeter, "The Future of Private Enterprise in the Face of Modern Socialistic Tendencies," in ibid., pp. 404–405.

14. Corporatist experiments in American history included railroad pools during the nineteenth century, agreements to fix prices and limit output in a variety of industries around the turn of the century (oil, gunpowder, coal), and widespread trade-association activity during the 1920s, effectively promoted by Secretary of Commerce Herbert Hoover. Each of these experiments had some success, but all tended to violate state and federal laws "in restraint of trade," and especially the antitrust legislation of state governments passed during the 1880s, the Sherman Antitrust Act of 1890, and the Federal Trade Commission Act of 1914. On the 1920s, see Robert F. Himmelberg, *The Origins of the National Recovery Administration: Business, Government, and the Trade Association Issue, 1921–1933,* 2nd ed. (New York: Fordham University Press, 1993); Ellis W. Hawley, "Three Facets of Hooverian Associationalism," in Thomas K. McCraw, ed., *Regulation in Perspective* (Boston: Harvard Business School Press, 1981); and, more generally, Ellis W. Hawley, "Society and Corporate Statism," in Mary K. Cayton, Elliott J. Gorn, and Peter W. Williams, eds., *Encyclopedia of American Social History* (New York: Scribner, 1993), pp. 621–636. On the 1930s, see Hawley, *The New Deal and the Problem of Monopoly: A Study in Economic Ambivalence* (Princeton, N.J.: Princeton University Press, 1966); and Donald R. Brand, *Corporatism and the Rule of Law: A Study of the National Recovery Administration* (Ithaca, N.Y.: Cornell University Press, 1988).

15. For discussions of corporatism and Schumpeter's Montreal speech, see Josef Solterer, "*Quadragesimo Anno:* Schumpeter's Alternative to the Omnipotent State," *Review of Social Economy* (March 1951), pp. 12–23; and the thoughtful analysis by Dale L. Cramer and Charles G. Leathers, "Schumpeter's Corporatist Views: Links among His Social Theory, *Quadragesimo Anno,* and Moral Reform," *History of Political Economy* 13 (Winter 1981), pp. 745–771.

The literature on corporatism in general is relatively large. A good introduction is Philippe Schmitter, "Still the Century of Corporatism?" in Frederick Pike and Thomas Stritch, eds., *The New Corporatism: Social-Political Structures in the Iberian World* (Notre Dame, Ind.: University of Notre Dame Press, 1974). See also Philippe Schmitter and Gerald Lembruch, eds., *Trends toward Corporatist Intermediation* (Beverly Hills, Calif.: Sage, 1979), and Peter J. Williamson, *Corporatism in Perspective: An Introductory Guide to Corporatist Theory* (Newbury Park, Calif.: Sage, 1989).

16. Schumpeter, *Capitalism, Socialism and Democracy*, 2nd ed. (New York: Harper, 1947), pp. 376, 384. He organized this 15-page section of the new chapter as follows:

> Economic Possibilities in the United States
> 1. Redistribution of Income through Taxation
> 2. The Great Possibility
> 3. Conditions for Its Realization
> 4. Transitional Problems
> 5. The Stagnationist Thesis
> 6. Conclusion

17. Ibid., pp. 382–384.

18. Ibid., pp. 385–387.

19. Ibid., pp. 384, 387–388, 389n13, 390n15.

20. Ibid., pp. 392–394. In a chapter section called "The Stagnationist Thesis," he wrote that "it remains to notice what to many economists is *the* postwar problem *par excellence:* how to secure adequate consumption." Schumpeter mentioned what he called the "salesman mentality of the country" during the period 1920–1940 as "all the explanation I can offer."

21. Ibid., p. 395. Schumpeter referred to the emotional effects of the Great Depression as "a psychological explanation of the Keynesian psychological law."

22. One of the sets of lectures is published in the outline form from which Schumpeter spoke in Swedberg, ed., *The Economics and Sociology of Capitalism*, pp. 429–437. The quoted material is on pp. 434–435.

23. Ibid., p. 436.

24. Schumpeter, "There Is Still Time to Stop Inflation," *Nation's Business*, June 1948, pp. 33–35, 88–91, reprinted in Clemence, ed., *Joseph A. Schumpeter: Essays*, pp. 241–253. This article may have been too recondite for a mass-audience business weekly. It has too many obscure references, does not relate to particular industries, does not contain enough statistics, and fails to specify the duration of the suggested remedies. The quoted passages are on pp. 241–244.

25. Ibid., pp. 241. Schumpeter had explained the anatomy of inflation (at unnecessary length) and shown how it applied to the current situation in the United States. His conclusion was the following:

> It is not possible to stop inflation in its tracks, without creating a depression that may be too much for our political system to withstand. But it *is* possible to make the inflationary process die out, and in such a way as to avoid a depression of unbearable proportions.
>
> Direct [wage and price] controls are futile, except as temporary measures in individual cases.

> Reduction in the mass of money, by Stalin's method [of forcibly taking currency out of circulation] or by a capital levy, is out of the question.
>
> Credit restriction is necessary to the extent indicated [in the text of the article] but not sufficient by itself. It must be supplemented by a pro-saving fiscal policy and by an attitude to public expenditures that is prepared to fight for every dollar.
>
> If we add the proviso "except for emergencies" then all we shall achieve is that politicians will style any occasion to spend as an emergency . . . One of the best things Lenin ever said was "In order to destroy bourgeois society you must debauch its money."

Ibid., p. 251. Except for the quotation from Lenin, which he had used in other writings, these summary paragraphs do not resemble Schumpeter's characteristic prose style, and were likely condensed from his drafts by the staff editors of *Nation's Business*.

26. Schumpeter, "Capitalism, Socialism and Democracy," in Christian Seidl and Wolfgang F. Stolper, eds., *Aufsätze für Tagespolitik* (Essays on Current Policy) (Tübingen: J. C. B. Mohr, Paul Siebeck, 1993), pp. 249–250, 251, 253. This was the Haddon House Lecture at the Institute of World Affairs, a program run by William Y. Elliott, a professor of government at Harvard (the site for the program was near Taconic). Imperialism as the last stage of capitalism was a basic tenet of Marxism, and had been developed by Lenin, Trotsky, and Schumpeter's own former classmates Otto Bauer and Rudolf Hilferding, among others.

27. Schumpeter, "English Economists and the State-Managed Economy," *Journal of Political Economy* 57 (October 1949), pp. 371–382, reprinted in Clemence, ed., *Joseph A. Schumpeter: Essays,* pp. 306–321. The quotations are on pp. 309, 312, and 319. For clarity, I have hyphenated Schumpeter's word, "bureausadism."

28. *Capitalism, Socialism and Democracy,* 3rd ed. (New York: Harper, 1950), pp. 418–419. In the book, the first sentence in this quotation is italicized. Elizabeth Schumpeter prepared her husband's address for publication, working from his handwritten draft and adding brief concluding paragraphs from her notes and what she heard him say on the occasion. See also Schumpeter's comment that "The provisional result [of current trends] is the halfway house of English laborism," in Schumpeter, "American Institutions and Economic Progress," notes made in late 1949 or early 1950 for the Walgreen Lectures he was about to deliver when he died, in Swedberg, ed., *Joseph A. Schumpeter: The Economics and Sociology of Capitalism,* p. 443.

29. *Capitalism, Socialism and Democracy,* 3rd ed. (1950), p. 419.

30. Ibid., p. 419. As he had done many times in the past—whether in Austria, Germany, or the United States—Schumpeter then pointed to chronic inflation as an

Achilles' heel of capitalist systems. He listed a set of remedies similar to the list he had presented in his magazine articles in 1920s Germany and in his 1948 piece for *Nation's Business:* a less steeply graduated income tax, a reduction in corporate taxes, and a greater emphasis on sales taxes. Ibid., p. 421–424, especially p. 423.

31. Of course, it has not been stable in the inner workings of its business system; Schumpeter was correct in saying that stabilized capitalism is a contradiction in terms.

26: HISTORY OF ECONOMIC ANALYSIS

1. The only rival of the Kress collection is at London University. The sets in both locations derive from the original Foxwell Collection, assembled in Britain by a private collector; both—particularly the Kress collection—have been much augmented by subsequent purchases. The quotation is from Schumpeter's Diary, July 20, 1943, HUG(FP)—4.1, Brief Daily Records, notes and diaries, c. 1931–1948, box 4, folder 1944, loose sheet, n.d. (summer 1944), HUA. Hereinafter cited as Schumpeter's Diary.

2. Schumpeter's Diary, quoted in Robert Loring Allen, *Opening Doors: The Life & Work of Joseph Schumpeter,* two vols. (New Brunswick, N.J.: Transaction, 1991), II, p. 99.

3. His fellow professors, he also noted, seemed to have doubts about "'this history of his.'" Schumpeter's Diary, box 4, folder 1942–43, notebook entries, April 25 and July 20, 1943; box 5, folder 1945, notebook entry, February 12, 1945. Schumpeter to William L. Crum, September 11, 1945; and to Edward S. Mason, August 10, 1949, in Ulrich Hedtke and Richard Swedberg, eds., *Joseph Alois Schumpeter, Briefe/Letters* (Tübingen: J. C. B. Mohr, Paul Siebeck, 2000), pp. 353, 386.

4. Elizabeth Schumpeter, introduction to Joseph Schumpeter, *History of Economic Analysis* (New York: Oxford University Press, 1954), p. v. The title of the 1914 book is *Epochen der Dogmen- und Methodengeschichte* (History of Doctrines and Methods), a volume of Weber's *Grundriss der Sozialwissenschaft.* Schumpeter's earlier book, Elizabeth continued, "was a long essay (about 60,000 words) of a little more than a hundred pages which was divided into four parts or chapters."

5. Elizabeth Schumpeter, introduction to Joseph Schumpeter, *History of Economic Analysis,* pp. v-vi. See also C. E. Staley, "Schumpeter's 1947 Course in the History of Economic Thought," *History of Political Economy* 15 (Spring 1983), pp. 25–37, which makes clear connections between the course and the book.

6. Elizabeth Schumpeter, editor's note to Joseph Schumpeter, *History of Economic Analysis,* p. 159. Working in the Kress had this kind of effect on me and many other scholars of my acquaintance. During the thorough remodeling of Baker Library in 2003–2005, the Kress was unfortunately reconfigured.

7. Elizabeth Schumpeter, introduction to Joseph Schumpeter, *History of Economic*

Analysis, p. vi. Schumpeter to Arthur Smithies, n.d. (1943), quoted in Smithies, "Memorial: Joseph Alois Schumpeter, 1883–1950," in Seymour E. Harris, ed., *Schumpeter, Social Scientist* (Cambridge, Mass.: Harvard University Press, 1951), p. 14.

8. Elizabeth Schumpeter, introduction to Joseph Schumpeter, *History of Economic Analysis,* pp. vii; see also p. 55.

9. Ibid., pp. vii–viii.

10. Ibid., pp. viii–ix.

11. The process of editing "could have gone on indefinitely," Elizabeth adds. She benefited from a gift from David Rockefeller and an additional grant from the Rockefeller Foundation, "which made possible much of the secretarial and editorial assistance outlined above." Elizabeth constructed most of the table of contents, which by itself runs to 15 pages of fine print. She also added a small amount of material to the text, placing it in brackets as a signal to the reader. Most of this is transitional matter from one section to the next. Several of her husband's friends and Harvard colleagues lent a hand as well, and she thanks them all. They include Arthur W. Marget, "the first person to read the entire *History* in typescript," who also advised her on editorial policy and put together the chapter on Value and Money; Gottfried Haberler, who read most of the typescript and helped check obscure references; and Paul Sweezy, who read the proofs for the entire book, "made many valuable suggestions, and caught several errors which had escaped me." Richard M. Goodwin, another of Schumpeter's former students, organized the final part of the book, which ends with the Keynesian Revolution. Other colleagues of Schumpeter thanked by Elizabeth include Alfred H. Conrad, William J. Fellner, Alexander Gerschenkron, and Frieda S. Ullian. See Elizabeth Schumpeter, introduction to Joseph Schumpeter, *History of Economic Analysis,* pp. ix–xiii.

Elizabeth's introduction is dated July 1952. In an additional note, the publisher adds that Elizabeth devoted most of her time from Schumpeter's death in January of 1950 "and up to the last weeks of her prolonged illness" to preparing the book for publication. When Elizabeth died in 1953, the body of the book was finished, and the author index (which contains the names of about 1,500 economic analysts) was almost done. Oxford University Press also notes that it is "deeply grateful to Professor Wassily Leontief for his help in making publication possible." This almost surely refers to a financial contribution to help underwrite the expensive initial printing of so very long a book.

12. *History of Economic Analysis,* pp. 6, 873. As in business, the task of understanding economic phenomena is constantly evolving. Economists have no cause for self-congratulation, Schumpeter adds, since "our performance is, and always was, not only modest but also disorganized." Nor do economists "trust one another to sum up 'the state of the science'" as is possible in physics and mathematics.

13. He goes on to say that in the history of economic thinking, many very good economic ideas have been proposed, then become lost in the shuffle. And this has harmed the discipline's ability to make cumulative progress, as physics does. It follows that the study of doctrinal history will turn up some of these lost ideas. Economics is in fact a science, but "a particularly difficult case, because common-sense knowledge goes in this field much farther relatively to such scientific knowledge as we have been able to achieve, than does common-sense knowledge in almost any other field." Ibid., pp. 6, 9.

14. Ibid., pp. 54–55.

15. Ibid., pp. 74, 92.

16. Ibid., pp. 181–182. The last comment perhaps says more about Schumpeter than Smith, and in any case is not quite correct. Smith's cousin Jane Douglas kept house for him over many years; and during a long sojourn in France during the 1760s, Smith made lasting friendships with several women who presided over salons.

17. Ibid., pp. 184–186.

18. Ibid., pp. 185, 186.

19. Even though it contained no theoretical advance "over even distant 'predecessors'" (whom Adam Smith did not generously acknowledge), Smith was unmatched "in heating the facts till they glow. The facts overflow and stumble over one another . . . Further facts have been amassed and theoretical technique has been improved but nobody has to this day succeeded in welding the two—plus a little political sociology—together as did A. Smith." *History of Economic Analysis,* pp. 186–187. Here Schumpeter is writing primarily about Book IV of *The Wealth of Nations,* where Smith discusses mercantilism and related topics.

20. *History of Economic Analysis,* pp. 193–194. Schumpeter mentions who these precursors were and enumerates their contributions. His knowledge of the publishing history of Smith's book came from the Kress Library at the Harvard Business School, which contains at least one copy of every known edition of *The Wealth of Nations* ever published, in any language—a collection now worth, by itself, millions of dollars.

21. *History of Economic Analysis,* p. 199. He also mentions Hamilton's associate Tench Coxe, the U.S. Commissioner of Revenue, whose collection of essays and addresses, *A View of the United States,* "comes near to actually being a systematic treatise."

22. *History of Economic Analysis,* p. 223.

23. Ibid.

24. Ibid., pp. 473–474.

25. Ibid., pp. 470, 473.

26. Ibid., pp. 473–474. Keynes is quoted in Phyllis Deane, *The Evolution of Economic Ideas* (Cambridge: Cambridge University Press, 1978), p. 83. Deane argues that

Keynes preferred Malthus because Malthus elevated moral concerns over the mathematical precision and simplifying assumptions of Ricardo (ibid., p. 80).

27. *History of Economic Analysis,* p. 382. Yet, Schumpeter goes on to say, the circumstances of all these positions "make it clear that the intent was not for lifetime tenure nor even that the posts should be held for very long."

28. Ibid., pp. 382–383.

29. Ibid., p. 397. Schumpeter might have added here that free trade and the tariff deeply divided American politics: the protectionist manufacturers of the Northeast versus the agrarian free-traders of the South and West. Aside from slavery, the battle between free traders and protectionists (who almost always won their battles in Congress) was the thorniest issue in the country for most of the nineteenth century. Schumpeter knew all of this, as his prior writings show.

30. Ibid., p. 771.

31. Ibid., pp. 771–772. Schumpeter does not name the modernists, of whom a long list could of course be compiled, from many countries.

32. Ibid., pp. 754–758. In Germany, "The Verein für Sozialpolitik [in sympathy with labor movements and labor reform] was founded in 1872, the American Economic Association in 1885 (the [American] Historical association in 1884), and the Royal Economic Society—to use the name it eventually adopted—in 1890." The Verein had a special purpose not purely scientific, and the American Economic Association's original statutes contained an article declaring that "We regard the State as an agency whose positive assistance is one of the indispensable conditions of human progress." This sentence, Schumpeter writes, "was intended to convey a principle of policy," but it was dropped in 1888, presumably in order to make the association less political and more scientific in nature.

   During this same period—mostly in the 1880s—economists founded new professional journals. Schumpeter names 12, including five in Germany, three in the United States, and one each in Britain, France, Italy, and Norway. And a few new institutions arose specifically to advance the science: "Let us salute the one that is by far the most important: the London School of Economics (1895)."

33. Ibid., pp. 764, 765–766, 769.

34. Ibid., pp. 801–802, 873. He mentions several others, but adds that they contributed essentially nothing to analysis "nor proved themselves masters of its use. I exemplify by the honored names of Henry C. Adams, [Richard T.] Ely, [Jacob Henry] Hollander, [J. Laurence] Laughlin, [Henry] Seager, and [E. R. A.] Seligman." This characterization is too harsh. Several of those named made significant contributions.

35. Ibid., pp. 514–515.

36. More broadly, he writes: "It is one of the major aims of this book to destroy the myth that there ever has been a time when economists as a body scorned research into historical or contemporaneous fact or when economics as a whole was

purely speculative or lacked its factual complement." Ibid., pp. 807–808.
Schumpeter acknowledges that much of the Historical School's work may have
been pedestrian. He notes that Henrik Ibsen, a master at conveying personalities
with a few quick strokes, portrays the colorless husband Dr. Tesman in *Hedda
Gabler* as having "just completed a work on the linen industry of Brabant in the
sixteenth century!" Ibid., p. 810.

37. Schumpeter adds that several members of the Historical School, and Schmoller
in particular, "who frankly admitted his error later on—associated theory [per se]
with 'Manchesterism,' that is, with unconditional laissez-faire." Ibid., pp. 809–
815, 849.

Schumpeter goes on to discuss the last three prominent members of the Historical School: his own close friend at Bonn, Arthur Spiethoff, who had worked
as Schmoller's assistant; Max Weber, one of the greatest of all social scientists;
and the controversial Werner Sombart, a well-known authority on capitalism
who later collaborated with the Nazis, and whom Schumpeter thoroughly disliked. Schumpeter writes of Sombart's book *Modern Capitalism* (first published
in 1902 and later brought out in a series of enlarged editions well into the 1920s),
that it "shocked professional historians by its often unsubstantial brilliance. They
failed to see in it anything that they would call real research—the material of the
book is in fact wholly second-hand and they entered protests against its many
carelessnesses. Yet it was in a sense a peak achievement of the historical school,
and highly stimulating even in its errors." In this damning with faint praise, it
becomes evident that Schumpeter has little respect for Sombart's loose generalizations; he writes that Sombart was the opposite of the careful Arthur Spiethoff in
every way. Without quite saying so, Schumpeter suggests that Sombart's international reputation is overrated. But he does concede that Sombart, like Weber, was
less hostile to economic theory than were most members of the Historical
School. Ibid., pp. 815–818. For a more favorable interpretation of Sombart than I
have given here, see Günther Chaloupek, "Long-term Economic Perspectives
Compared: Joseph Schumpeter and Werner Sombart," *European Journal of the
History of Economic Thought* 2 (1995), pp. 127–149. Chaloupek goes so far as to
imply that *Capitalism, Socialism and Democracy* was inspired in part by Sombart's
writings.

38. Schumpeter also goes on to quote Walras: "'If one wants to harvest quickly, one
must plant carrots and salads; if one has the ambition to plant oaks, one must
have the sense to tell oneself: my grandchildren will owe me this shade'—so he
once wrote to a friend." *History of Economic Analysis,* pp. 827–829.

39. Ibid., p. 773n5.

40. Ibid., pp. 10–11, 337n6. Schumpeter asserts that "'Special pleaders'—whether they
are paid or not—" are entitled to just as much a hearing as "'detached philosophers,' if the latter species does indeed exist."

41. Schumpeter commends F. A. Hayek for warning against indiscriminate borrowing from other disciplines, which Hayek called "Scientism." Ibid., pp. 15, 17, 19.

42. Ibid., pp. 19, 27. During the late twentieth and early twenty-first centuries, fusions of psychology and economics were often attempted—and in a few cases, including two Nobel Prize-winners—favorably recognized by economists. Schumpeter's treatment of the Austrian School, which had always been positive on balance, became noticeably more enthusiastic in *History of Economic Analysis* than in earlier works. See Lutz Beinsen, "Schumpeter's Perception of Austrian Economics: A Comparison between *Epochen der Dogmen- und Methodengeschichte* and the *History of Economic Analysis,*" *History of Economic Ideas* 6 (1988), pp. 55–77.

43. Ibid., pp. 41, 42. Schumpeter writes that Keynes's vision is summed up in chapter 18 of *The General Theory,* especially pp. 249–254.

44. *History of Economic Analysis,* pp. 42–43.

45. Ibid., pp. 42–43.

46. Ibid., pp. 561–562, 570.

47. Ibid., p. 570.

48. Ibid., pp. 571–572.

49. Ibid., pp. 572–573. In note 5 on p. 573, Schumpeter compares this phenomenon with the doctrine of class harmony as opposed to class antagonism. "The latter has been preached with unsurpassable force and, moreover, renders the radical intellectual's ideology. The former has never been put forcefully or even convincingly. And it does not suit the book of the radical intellectual. So he who holds it is likely to be sneered at as a sort of Caspar Milquetoast [a cartoon character of the time, presented in the comic strip "The Timid Soul"] and this is quite as effective as, or more so than, serious argument would be."

50. Ibid., pp. 573–574.

51. Ibid., pp. 893, 897–898.

52. Ibid., pp. 555–556. Schumpeter adds that "In Germany, the concept of the entrepreneur was a familiar element of the 'cameralist' tradition. And so was the corresponding term, *Unternehmer* [undertaker], which the economists of the period [the first half of the nineteenth century] continued to use."

53. Ibid., pp. 556–557.

54. Ibid., p. 897. Here Schumpeter is necessarily being rather technical, but the thought is sufficiently clear.

55. Ibid., pp. 893, 897–898.

56. Ibid., p. 545. He goes on to say, "And it stands to reason that the theorist's generalized description of economic behavior is greatly simplified by the assumption that the prices of all products and 'factors' cannot be perceptibly influenced by the individual household and the individual firm, and hence may be treated as given." Ibid., p. 972. In note 4, p. 973, Schumpeter adds that the term "pure

competition" was introduced by E. H. Chamberlin in *The Theory of Monopolistic Competition* (1932), following an idea in Chamberlin's Ph.D. thesis of 1927.

57. *History of Economic Analysis,* p. 1171. Schumpeter's chapter was still in longhand at the time of his death, having not even been typed, corrected, or edited. Yet he had written about Keynes many times, and this final statement, though published in first draft, was obviously the product of long reflection.

58. Ibid., p. 1171.

59. Ibid., pp. 1171–1172. Schumpeter adds that Keynes had a good deal of first-rate help in writing the *General Theory:* "Next we must record Keynes's acknowledgments of indebtedness, which in all cases can be independently established, to Mrs. Joan Robinson, Mr. R. G. Hawtrey, Mr. R. F. Harrod, but especially to Mr. R. F. Kahn, whose share in the historic achievement cannot have fallen very far short of co-authorship."

60. Yet in Schumpeter's view, Keynes's real radicalism lay elsewhere. Keynes's argument about the function in capitalist economies of *saving* broke decisively from a centuries-long orthodoxy. "His analysis seemed to restore intellectual respectability to anti-saving views; and he spelled out the implications of this in Chapter 24 of the *General Theory.* Thus, though his scientific message appealed to many of the best minds of the economic profession, it also appealed to the writers and talkers on the fringes of professional economics who gleaned nothing from the *General Theory* except the New Economics of Spending and for whom he brought back the happy times of Mrs. Marcet [Jane Marcet, author of an extremely popular economics textbook first published in 1816], when every schoolgirl, by learning the use of a few simple concepts, acquired competence to judge of all the ins and outs of the infinitely complex organism of capitalist society." In what was obviously in part a personal aside, Schumpeter adds in a footnote that "The old or even mature scholar may be not only the victim but also the beneficiary of habits of thought formed by his past work." Apart from policy preference, "there is such a thing as analytic experience. And in a field like economics, where training is often defective and where the young scholar very often simply does not know enough, this element in the case counts much more heavily than it does in physics where teaching, even though possibly uninspiring, is always competent." *History of Economic Analysis,* pp. 477n12, 1171, 1180–1181.

61. Ibid., p. 1181.

62. "His *General Theory,* in a sense, was a similar feat of leadership. It taught England, in the form of an apparently general analysis, his own personal view of her social and economic situation and also his own personal view of 'what should be done about it.'" *History of Economic Analysis,* p. 1170–1171.

63. Ibid., p. 1171. George J. Stigler review, *Journal of Political Economy* 62 (August 1954), p. 344.

64. Frank Knight review, *Southern Economic Journal* 21 (1955), p. 261. One of the

most thorough engagements of the book, containing practically a summary of its contents, was by H. Aufricht, "The Methodology of Schumpeter's *History of Economic Analysis*," *Zeitschrift für Nationalökonomie* 18 (December 1958), pp. 384–441. In 1994, the History of Economics Society devoted most of its annual meeting to the fortieth anniversary of the publication of *History of Economic Analysis*, and published the resulting papers as a book: Laurence S. Moss, ed., *Joseph A. Schumpeter, Historian of Economics: Perspectives on the History of Economic Thought: Selected Papers from the History of Economics Society Conference, 1994* (New York: Routledge, 1996).

65. Jacob Viner, "Schumpeter's *History of Economic Analysis:* A Review Article," *American Economic Review* 44 (December 1954), pp. 894–898. Viner goes on to say, however, that the author's preferences do stand out in *History of Economic Analysis.* "The importance of innate differences of abilities was one of Schumpeter's strongest convictions. I know of no one of consequence except Adam Smith who failed to point out as one of the services of division of labor that it enabled tasks to be assigned in accordance with aptitudes." Viner judges that "Schumpeter's 'Reader's Guide' to Adam Smith's *Wealth of Nations,* although unfinished, is an admirable outline of such theoretical structure or 'system' as there is in that book, and would make an extremely useful introduction to any new edition of it. Schumpeter does not like Smith, however, as theorist, as man, or with respect to his social views . . . It is not, I think, necessary to accept Adam Smith as a hero of our profession to conclude that Schumpeter's objectivity was somewhat undermined here by the conflict between Smith's and his own 'ideologies.'" Ibid., pp. 899, 904.

In another long essay, I. M. D. Little pronounces *History of Economic Analysis* "the most important [book] there has yet been for its subject." The index of authors "must contain about 1,500 names; and Schumpeter could and did evidently read almost every European language, ancient and modern, though he apologizes for his lack of Russian." Then, too, "he was himself an original theorist of the first rank," and "his views on monopoly, on the functions of profit and the entrepreneur, and on the declining motive power of capitalism, add up to a dynamic vision of the economic process which has enlightened many, and deserves the title of 'analysis', and yet . . . he keeps his own name strictly out of the book."

Little believed that Schumpeter was too fond of the "gadget aspect" of economic theory, as represented by mathematics, and not sufficiently respectful of practical contributions. Schumpeter's "fierce disapproval" of professionals who became deeply involved in politics "seems to me to stem from too idealistic a view of economic theory." In this sense, his mistrust of political economy led to his relatively unkind verdict on the British classical economists. In Little's opinion, "a very large part of economics vanishes if one is really to keep one's scientific conscience absolutely clean." Little makes the interesting observation that "Schumpeter's admiration for economists seems to have been inversely related to the success of their books, the width of audience reached, and their political influence. He could not appreciate anyone who scored so highly in all these ways." But this criticism can be only partly true, given the generally favorable treatment of Alfred Marshall and especially of Karl Marx, who reached a huge audience and had an immense political influence that was near its height in the Soviet Union, China, and other communist countries at the time Little was writing. See Little's review article, *Economic History Review* (2nd ser.) 8 (August 1955), pp. 91–98.

66. Kuznets, the *Journal of Economic History* 15 (September 1955), pp. 323–325. Kuznets adds that even though Schumpeter's stated goal was to treat only *analysis*, the book is actually "a history of economic thinking—much of it economic ideology and historical generalization and relatively little of value-free economic 'mechanics.' This is all the more fortunate, in my opinion." Politics and economics are so tied up with each other "that economic theories frequently emerge as ideologies; *i.e.*, crystallization of group positions that serve in the political struggle." Even though Kuznets did not credit the author's own statement that if starting afresh he would emphasize economic history over theory, "I do believe that Schumpeter was essentially a historian and social philosopher—and perhaps for that very reason tended to pay excessive homage to mathematical tools and formal theory."

Stigler, the *Journal of Political Economy* 62 (August 1954), pp. 344–345. Himself a historian of economic analysis, Stigler points out a few errors, and then, echoing Kuznets, goes on to say that "The only general dissent I would make . . . is that his admiration for the superior formal theorist [e.g., Walras] leads him to put this genre on too high a pedestal." Hayek, *Studies in Philosophy, Politics and Economics* (Chicago: University of Chicago Press, [1954], 1964), pp. 339–341. V. W. Bladen, a Canadian economist, agreed with Hayek's theme: "A very great book . . . He was a great economist and a great teacher: through this book he will go on teaching economics." Bladen, "Schumpeter's *History of Economic Analysis* and Some Related Books," *Canadian Journal of Economics and Political Science* 22 (February 1956), pp. 104, 111.

67. Richardson argues that in emphasizing an economist's "Vision," Schumpeter "accepts, with significant qualifications, Marx's doctrine of ideological bias, according to which mans' [sic] ideas and systems, while claiming objectivity, are in fact distorted by unconscious desires to justify, exalt, or further a particular nation, class, or interest." Speculating on Schumpeter's reservations about Keynes, Richardson says that "Keynes's frequently quoted dictum that 'ideas and not vested interests are in the long run dangerous for good and evil' might have seemed to him a shallow, rationalistic dichotomy, attributing as it does to ideas an auton-

omy and independence of our desires which they rarely acquire. Indeed the possession by most English economists of a relatively untroubled confidence in their working philosophy and moral ideas may have been felt by him to stem from provinciality and lack of depth, though he may have envied the more comfortable assurance which it was able to afford."

Richardson adds that it is clear from the text of *History of Economic Analysis* that Schumpeter's "personal approval" goes most strongly to those with the widest vision, "who impress us by the grandeur of their conception rather than by its immediate practical utility." Thus Marx and Walras are better treated than Ricardo, Marshall, and Keynes. Yet the breadth of vision so admired by Schumpeter, Richardson writes, tended to repel others. Keynes, for example, could find "nothing in [Marx] except out-of-date controversializing." Richardson, "Schumpeter's *History of Economic Analysis*," *Oxford Economic Papers* (new series) 7 (June 1955), pp. 136, 137, 139–140, 141, 150.

68. Robbins, "Schumpeter's History of Economic Analysis," *Quarterly Journal of Economics* 69 (February 1955), pp. 2–3, 4, 7, 20–21.

69. Smithies, "Schumpeter and Keynes," in Seymour E. Harris, ed., *Schumpeter, Social Scientist* (Cambridge, Mass.: Harvard University Press, 1951), p. 136. Schumpeter, "John Maynard Keynes, 1883–1946," *American Economic Review* 36 (September 1946), pp. 495–518; Schumpeter, "Keynes and Statistics—Four Views," *Review of Economic Statistics* 28 (November 1946), pp. 194–196.

70. Smithies, "Schumpeter and Keynes," p. 138.

71. Schumpeter, "Capitalism," in *Encyclopaedia Britannica* (New York: Encyclopaedia Britannica, 1946), reprinted in Richard V. Clemence, ed., *Joseph A. Schumpeter: Essays on Entrepreneurs, Innovations, Business Cycles, and the Evolution of Capitalism* (Cambridge, Mass.: Addison-Wesley, 1951), p. 204.

72. Smithies, "Schumpeter and Keynes," p. 139. Smithies goes on to say, however, that macroeconomic measures of the Keynesian variety (that is, monetary and fiscal policies that cut across all industries) may be the only workable measures for democratic governments, because they do not discriminate favorably or unfavorably toward particular industries. Overall, such policies may be "less anti-capitalistic in their import than any governmental policy that attempts to deal with a general economic problem on a specific industry basis," and that some of the early New Deal policies that did this were more radical than post-1938 macro measures. "It seems to me that aggregative policies are the only kind of policies that can be consistent with private enterprise in the vastly complex U.S. economy." Ibid., p. 140.

73. A brief comparison of Schumpeter's "vision" with Thorstein Veblen's—using Schumpeter's own definition of the term—is L. A. O'Donnell, "Rationalism, Capitalism, and the Entrepreneur: The Views of Veblen and Schumpeter," *History of Political Economy* 5 (Spring 1973), pp. 199–214.

27: A PRINCIPLE OF INDETERMINATENESS

1. Elizabeth Schumpeter, introduction to Joseph Schumpeter, *History of Economic Analysis* (New York: Oxford University Press, 1954), pp. v–vi. On the "preliminary volume," see also Schumpeter to John D. Black, July 10, 1944, in Ulrich Hedtke and Richard Swedberg, eds., *Joseph Alois Schumpeter, Briefe/Letters* (Tübingen: J. C. B. Mohr, Paul Siebeck, 2000). p. 347. The final work was to be called "The Analytic Apparatus of Economics."

2. Robert Loring Allen, *Opening Doors: The Life & Work of Joseph Schumpeter,* two vols. (New Brunswick, N.J.: Transaction, 1991), II, p. 163.

3. Schumpeter's Diary, Schumpeter Papers, HUG(FP)—4.1, Brief Daily Records, notes and diaries, c. 1931–1948, box 5, folder 1948/1, notebook entries, n.d. (1948); boxes 4 and 5 *passim,* HUA; Allen, *Opening Doors,* II, pp. 158, 190, 231. Gibrat's Law, which helps in explaining industry structures, had existed since 1931, and was an important foreshadowing of chaos theory, which is useful for some applications Schumpeter had in mind, as is game theory. The most significant applications of math to "Schumpeterian" topics began with Richard Nelson and Sidney Winter's very important book, *An Evolutionary Theory of the Firm* (Cambridge, Mass.: Harvard University Press, 1982), and the articles leading up to and following that book.

4. In the memorial volume edited by Seymour E. Harris, *Schumpeter, Social Scientist* (Cambridge, Mass.: Harvard University Press, 1951), Schumpeter's Harvard colleague Edward H. Chamberlin chides him for failing—for a time—to see that economics is indeterminate. Chamberlin's point of departure is his own work on oligopoly, which he erroneously believed Schumpeter did not understand or sufficiently appreciate. Chamberlin's real argument seems to be not with Schumpeter but with trends in the profession, which he accurately describes as follows: "To this extent economics simply is not an 'autonomous science' (p. 41 of *Business Cycles*) and will only lose in the end by pretending to be. It must seek out the indeterminate as well as the determinate, and carefully avoid the tempting expedient, currently so popular with the mathematicians, of adjusting the formulation of its problems with the *objective* of assuring a determinate answer." Chamberlin goes on to note that Schumpeter backed away from his stance in *Business Cycles* as early as in *Capitalism, Socialism and Democracy,* published only three years later. See Chamberlin, "Impact of Recent Monopoly Theory on the Schumpeterian System," pp. 84–85, 87.

5. Schumpeter, "*The Communist Manifesto* in Sociology and Economics," *Journal of Political Economy* 57 (June 1949), pp. 199–212, reprinted in Richard V. Clemence, ed., *Joseph A. Schumpeter: Essays on Entrepreneurs, Innovations, Business Cycles, and the Evolution of Capitalism* (Cambridge, Mass.: Addison-Wesley, 1951), pp. 293, 305.

Schumpeter pointed out here and elsewhere, as he had often done, that Marx and others had made a gross error in positing only two social classes—the capitalists and the workers. Instead, they should have seen a much wider range: "the co-operative and antagonistic interactions of, at least, the classes associated with the control of large, medium and small business; the farmers who differ so significantly from the other business classes that there is no point in including them with one of these; the *rentier* class ('capitalists' in a narrower but more useful sense); the professional class; the clerical ('white collar') class; the skilled workers; the unskilled workers." See Schumpeter, "Capitalism," in *Encyclopaedia Britannica* (New York: Encyclopaedia Britannica, 1946), pp. 801–87, reprinted in Clemence, ed., *Joseph A. Schumpeter: Essays* pp. 189–210. The quotation is on pp. 200–201. See also H. E. Jensen, "J. A. Schumpeter on Economic Sociology," *Eastern Economic Journal* 11 (July–September 1985), pp. 257–266; and especially Tom Bottomore, *Between Marginalism and Marxism: The Economic Sociology of J. A. Schumpeter* (New York: Harvester Wheatsheaf, 1992), which explores the sources of Schumpeter's own ideas, his attempt to fuse economics, history, and sociology, and his intellectual relationship with Marx.

6. Schumpeter, "Comments on a Plan for the Study of Entrepreneurship," unpublished paper in the Schumpeter Papers, HUA, printed in Swedberg, ed., *Joseph A. Schumpeter: The Economics and Sociology of Capitalism* (Princeton, N.J.: Princeton University Press, 1991), pp. 406–428. The quoted passage is on p. 409.

7. During this period, Schumpeter was extremely busy with his huge *History of Economic Analysis,* with writing articles, and with the organization of the December 1948 program of the American Economic Association, of which he was president. These tasks consumed most of his time during the 17 months between the Center's founding and his death in January 1950. In the early planning for the Center, Cole especially wanted Schumpeter's participation, and in his first projected budget suggested an annual $1,000 honorarium for him—a significant sum for that time. See Cole to Harvard Provost Paul H. Buck, September 2, 1947, enclosing a long proposal titled "Committee for Research in Entrepreneurial History." Papers of Arthur H. Cole, HUG 4290.507, Additional correspondence relating to the Research Center in Entrepreneurial History, 1940s and 1950s, box 1, folder Buck, Paul H., HUA.

The principal leaders of the Center were Cole, the sociologist Leland Jenks, the historian Thomas C. Cochran, and the European economic historian Fritz Redlich. The list of young scholars who participated in the Center's activities reads like an all-star team of historians over the next generation: Alfred D. Chandler, Jr., Bernard Bailyn, David S. Landes, Hugh G. C. Aitken, Douglass North, Henry Rosovsky, and John Sawyer, among others. See Ruth Crandall, *The Research Center in Entrepreneurial History at Harvard University, 1948–1958: A Historical Sketch* (Cambridge, Mass: The Center, 1960); Hugh G. C. Aitken, ed., *Ex-*

plorations in Enterprise (Cambridge, Mass.: Harvard University Press, 1965), especially pp. 8–11 and 24–26, which describe Schumpeter's role; and Steven A. Sass, *Entrepreneurial Historians and History: Leadership and Rationality in American Economic Historiography, 1940–1960* (New York: Garland, 1986). The quotation from Cole is in his memorial essay, "Joseph A. Schumpeter and the Center for Research in Entrepreneurial History," *Explorations in Entrepreneurial History* 2 (1950), p. 56.

8. Schumpeter, "The Historical Approach to the Analysis of Business Cycles," *Universities-National Bureau Conference on Business Cycle Research,* November 25–27, 1949, printed in Clemence, ed., *Joseph A. Schumpeter: Essays,* p. 327; Schumpeter, "Comments on a Plan for the Study of Entrepreneurship," p. 416.

   "Comments on a Plan. . ." was Schumpeter's main paper in furtherance of the establishment and the intellectual life of the Center. Arthur Cole called it "a vigorous polemic in favor of continued research in the area [of entrepreneurship] and particularly for the establishment of a central coordinating bureau or institute." See Crandall, *The Research Center in Entrepreneurial History,* p. 8. In his paper, Schumpeter mentions several existing studies, and especially praises Fritz Redlich's *History of American Business Leaders* (Ann Arbor, Mich: Edwards, 1941), and Arthur C. Cole and Harold F. Williamson's *The American Carpet Manufacture* (Cambridge, Mass.: Harvard University Press, 1941) as exemplars of entrepreneurial history. On October 7, 1948, Schumpeter delivered the Center's second paper (Cole had given the first), titled "Economic Theory and Entrepreneurial History," published by the Center itself in *Change and the Entrepreneur: Postulates and Patterns in Entrepreneurial History* (Cambridge, Mass., 1949), pp. 63–84.

9. Schumpeter, "Comments on a Plan for the Study of Entrepreneurship," pp. 408, 424.

10. Ibid., p. 408. Most histories of business remained atheoretical and immature until the appearance of the work of Alfred D. Chandler, Jr. In a series of pathbreaking books and articles that fused economics and sociology with history, Chandler firmly established the subdiscipline of business history, worldwide. The most creative and influential of his books are *Strategy and Structure: Chapters in the History of the American Industrial Enterprise* (Cambridge, Mass.: MIT Press, 1962); *The Visible Hand: The Managerial Revolution in American Business* (Cambridge, Mass.: Harvard University Press, 1977), which won both the Pulitzer Prize in History and the Bancroft Prize; and *Scale and Scope: The Dynamics of Industrial Capitalism* (Cambridge, Mass.: Harvard University Press, 1990), an 860-page comparative analysis of business as it evolved in the United States, Britain, and Germany).

   Chandler was born some 35 years after Schumpeter, and received his A. B. and Ph.D. at Harvard. The two men met a few times, but Chandler was more directly influenced by Talcott Parsons, one of the world's most prominent sociolo-

gist. As a graduate student during the 1930s, Parsons himself had been close to
Schumpeter and other economists at Harvard, before switching his interests to
sociology. Parsons later translated and popularized the work of Max Weber,
whose own writings had influenced Schumpeter several decades earlier. In this
way, several powerful strands of theoretical and empirical traditions came together in Chandler's great books. And those books have now taught the world as
much about the inner history of business—particularly big business—as the
work of any other scholar. Chandler has readily acknowledged that he himself is
"a Schumpeterian."

   On Chandler's career and influence, see Thomas K. McCraw, "The Intellectual Odyssey of Alfred D. Chandler, Jr.," introduction to McCraw, ed., *The Essential Alfred Chandler: Essays Toward a Historical Theory of Big Business* (Boston:
Harvard Business School Press, 1988). For a survey of the field of business history
with Chandler's work as a starting point, see Richard R. John, Jr., "Elaborations,
Revisions, Dissents: Alfred D. Chandler's *The Visible Hand* after Twenty Years,"
Business History Review 71 (Summer 1997). On some aspects of the relationship
between Chandler's work and Schumpeter's, see Richard Langlois, "Schumpeter
and Personal Capitalism," in Gunnar Eliasson and Christopher Green, eds.,
Microfoundations of Economic Growth: A Schumpeterian Perspective (Ann Arbor:
University of Michigan Press, 1998), pp. 57–82.

11. Schumpeter, "Comments on a Plan for the Study of Entrepreneurship," p. 411.

12. Ibid., p. 412. Schumpeter adds that a creative response obviously has "*something,*
be that much or little, to do (a) with quality of the personnel available in a society; (b) with relative quality of personnel, that is, with quality available to a particular field of activity relatively [sic] to quality available, at the same time, to
others; (c) with individual decisions, actions, patterns of behavior."

13. Ibid., pp. 419, 420. He adds that Veblen's "*Theory of the Leisure Class* exemplifies
well what I mean. It is brilliant and suggestive. But it is an impressionist essay
that does not come to grips with the real problems involved."

14. Schumpeter, "The Creative Response in Economic History," *Journal of Economic
History* 7 (1947), p. 149; this article is a condensation of his longer unpublished
paper "Comments on a Plan for the Study of Entrepreneurship." Schumpeter,
"Economic Theory and Entrepreneurial History," p. 75.

15. Schumpeter, "Comments on a Plan for the Study of Entrepreneurship," p. 412;
Schumpeter, "American Institutions and Economic Progress," late 1949, notes for
the Walgreen Lectures he was about to deliver when he died. Printed in
Swedberg, ed., *The Economics and Sociology of Capitalism*, p. 438–444. The
quoted passage is on p. 442.

16. Schumpeter, "American Institutions and Economic Progress," p. 442.

17. Schumpeter, "Science and Ideology," *American Economic Review* 29 (March
1949), pp. 345–359, reprinted in Clemence, ed., *Joseph A. Schumpeter: Essays*,
pp. 273–286. The quotations are on pp. 275–277.

18. Ibid., pp. 276–278.

19. Ibid., p. 277.

20. Ibid., pp. 277–278.

21. Ibid., pp. 278–279.

22. Ibid., pp. 279–281. Schumpeter adds that Smith's economics is dated (much of it is pre-industrial); and "There is some semiphilosophical foliage of an ideological nature but it can be removed without injury to his scientific argument."

23. Ibid., p. 281.

24. Ibid., p. 282.

25. Ibid., p. 282.

26. Ibid., pp. 282–283.

27. Ibid., p. 283.

28. Ibid., p. 283. In 1946, Schumpeter had written a concise account of how he believed this odd state of affairs had evolved: "So long as economists were practically unanimous in considering thrift or saving as the principal requisite for the expansion of the physical apparatus of industry (capital formation), or even for all economic progress, the most important, and indeed a decisive, economic argument for inequality was that the bulk of saving is done by the higher incomes and that equalisation by share-the-wealth policies would hence paralyse the very process that operates to raise the standard of life of the masses. But that practical unanimity does not longer exist . . . During the 1930s, an increasing number of economists adopted the opposite view, viz., that saving, withholding income elements from being expanded [sic] on consumers' goods, has a depressing effect on the economic process and thus impedes, instead of fosters, the expansion of plant and equipment." See Schumpeter, "Capitalism," in *Encyclopaedia Britannica*, reprinted in Clemence, ed., *Joseph A. Schumpeter: Essays*, p. 204.

29. "Science and Ideology," p. 283. In his article on "Capitalism" published in *The Encyclopaedia Britannica* in 1946, Schumpeter further describes the Keynesian vision of stagnationism or "capitalist maturity." It "may also be called the doctrine of vanishing investment opportunity, [and] is not intended to explain the economic and political pattern of modern capitalist society as a whole. It limits itself to the propositions: (1) that the capitalist system has reached maturity in the sense of having substantially exhausted its possibilities of growth, particularly its opportunities for new investments on a large scale, both for technological reasons and because of the decreasing rate of increase of population; (2) that the whole scheme of capitalist society, particularly its saving habits, being geared to the task of exploiting such opportunities, the permanent depression of anaemia will result from their gradual disappearance; (3) that in this state of maturity or stagnation, the capitalist process can be kept going only by incessant injections of purchasing power by means of government deficit spending. This theory, mainly framed to account for the unsatisfactory conditions that prevailed in the United States (and in France) during the 1930s, is not supported by any facts prior to 1932. Its wide

appeal is, however, understandable: the public and the economic profession are equally apt to be more impressed by the real or supposed peculiarities of their own problems and troubles than by any analogies with conditions half a century ago." See the reprint of the *Encyclopaedia Britannica* article in Clemence, ed., *Joseph A. Schumpeter: Essays,* p. 196.

30. "Science and Ideology," pp. 284–285.

31. Ibid.

32. Ibid., p. 285.

33. Ibid. An exceptionally well-researched (and sometimes overdrawn) interpretation is M. Gottlieb, "The Ideological Influence in Schumpeter's Thought," *Zeitschrift für Nationalökonomie* 19 (January 1959), pp. 1–42.

34. "Science and Ideology," p. 286.

35. Ibid., p. 286.

36. Many of the arguments Schumpeter set forth in "Science and Ideology" are insightfully discussed in Robert L. Heilbroner's essay marking the 1983 centennial of the death of Marx and the birth of Keynes and Schumpeter: "Economics and Political Economy: Marx, Keynes, and Schumpeter," *Journal of Economic Issues* 18 (September 1984), pp. 681–695. Rather than "vision," the word Schumpeter preferred, Heilbroner emphasizes politics. He writes of the different versions of economic life proffered by the three great economists that "each model serves all too plainly to underpin or substantiate the political values of its proponent." He also makes the interesting observation (which was shared by Schumpeter) that "So far as Keynes was concerned, Marx might as well have never lived." (Pp. 681–683.) Curiously enough, Heilbroner says nothing about "Science and Ideology," Schumpeter's presidential address, but takes his evidence from similar (and often fuller) statements in *History of Economic Analysis,* which Heilbroner mistakenly calls in his text *History of Economic Thought.* See also Heilbroner, "Was Schumpeter Right?" in Arnold Heertje, ed., *Schumpeter's Vision: Capitalism, Socialism and Democracy after 40 Years* (New York: Praeger, 1981), esp. pp. 95–106; and Heilbroner's revision and supplement of his earlier views in "Was Schumpeter Right After All?" *Journal of Economic Perspectives* 7 (Summer 1993), pp. 87–96.

37. Schumpeter's Diary, quoted in Allen, *Opening Doors,* II, p. 221.

28: L'ENVOI

1. Schumpeter to Herbert von Beckerath, January 24, 1949, in Ulrich Hedtke and Richard Swedberg, eds., *Joseph Alois Schumpeter, Briefe/Letters* (Tübingen: J. C. B. Mohr, Paul Siebeck, 2000), p. 367.

2. Schumpeter's Diary, February 8, 1949, quoted in Robert Loring Allen, *Opening*

Doors: The Life & Work of Joseph Schumpeter, two vols. (New Brunswick, N.J.: Transaction, 1991), II, p. 235.

3. The second was a long article on Vilfredo Pareto, the great Italian sociologist and economist; the third, Schumpeter's centennial re-evaluation of "The Communist Manifesto"; the fourth, a review article on "English Economists and the State-Managed Economy"; the fifth, a short piece in German, "*Der Democratische Kurs*" (The Democratic Course); the sixth, his long essay, "Economic Theory and Entrepreneurial History"; the seventh, "The Historical Approach to the Analysis of Business Cycles"; the eighth, an overview of economics ("Some Questions of Principle"), a prior draft for a section of *History of Economic Analysis,* published years later in an Italian retrospective; the ninth, an extensive obituary and appreciation of Wesley Clair Mitchell; the tenth, a piece on business cycles and forecasting, published by the *Journal of the American Statistical Association;* the eleventh, his paper "The March into Socialism." For bibliographical references, see Massimo M. Augello, comp., "Works by Schumpeter," in Richard Swedberg, ed., *Joseph A. Schumpeter: The Economics and Sociology of Capitalism* (Princeton, N.J.: Princeton University Press, 1991), pp. 479–481. The new preface to *Capitalism, Socialism and Democracy* was actually for the third English edition of 1949 but appears also in the American-imprint Harper edition of 1950.

4. Schumpeter, *Capitalism, Socialism and Democracy,* 3rd ed. (Harper, 1950), p. 416.

5. Ibid., pp. 412, 416.

6. Schumpeter's Diary, May 29, 1949 and n.d. (late 1940s), quoted in Allen, *Opening Doors,* II, pp. 199, 236.

7. Schumpeter's Diary, September 1949 (dated Labor Day), quoted in Allen, *Opening Doors,* II, p. 236.

8. Allen, *Opening Doors,* II, pp. 238–239. He titled the fifth of these six lectures "The Personal Element and the Element of Chance: A Principle of Indeterminateness"; see Swedberg, ed., *Joseph A. Schumpeter: The Economics and Sociology of Capitalism,* pp. 75, 438–444.

9. Schumpeter's death and his final days are described in Allen, *Opening Doors,* II, pp. 238–241; Allen examined the death certificate at the Town Hall in nearby Salisbury, Connecticut.

10. The minute was entered into the records of the Faculty of Arts and Sciences, and published in Seymour E. Harris, ed., *Schumpeter, Social Scientist* (Cambridge, Mass.: Harvard University Press, 1951), pp. ix–x.

11. Harris, ed., *Schumpeter, Social Scientist.* The May 1951 issue of the *Review of Economics and Statistics* was the second one of this quarterly dedicated to Schumpeter, the first having been in recognition of his 60th birthday in 1943. In the intervening years, its name had been changed from the *Review of Economic Statistics.*

12. Harris, "Introductory Remarks," in Harris, ed., *Schumpeter, Social Scientist,* pp. 1, 4, 7.

13. Haberler, "Joseph Alois Schumpeter, 1883–1950," in ibid., pp. 30, 47.

14. Smithies, "Memorial: Joseph Alois Schumpeter, 1883–1950," in ibid., pp. 14, 15.

15. Ibid., p. 16.

16. Ibid., pp. 14–15.

17. Ibid., pp. 21–22.

18. Ibid., pp. 21, 136. Smithies contributed not one but two articles to the final collection, *Schumpeter, Social Scientist.* The first appeared originally in the *American Economic Review.* In his second essay, "Schumpeter and Keynes," Smithies pressed the comparison as a way to clarify Schumpeter's faults and virtues; see in particular p. 136. Many writers had compared the two great economists, and many more were to do so in the future. But no effort has ever surpassed Smithies'.

   On Schumpeter as a precursor of macro theory, see Hansen, "Schumpeter's Contribution to Business Cycle Theory," in Harris, ed., *Schumpeter, Social Scientist,* p. 79: "Macro-economics began with monetary and business-cycle theory. Schumpeter was one of five Continental economists whose work on business cycles laid the foundation for modern macro-economics." The five "originated nearly all of the really basic ideas in modern business-cycle theory (the most significant omission being the multiplier and the consumption function)"; and Schumpeter was "one of the most brilliant and original" of the five. The other four were Wicksell, Spiethoff, Tugan-Baranowsky, and Aftalion.

19. Smithies, "Memorial: Joseph Alois Schumpeter, 1883–1950," in ibid., p. 15.

20. Ibid., p. 16.

21. Oskar Morgenstern, "Obituary: Joseph A. Schumpeter, 1883–1950," the *Economic Journal* (March 1951), pp. 201, 202.

22. Leontief's tribute, "Joseph A. Schumpeter (1883–1950)," appeared in neither the *Review of Economics and Statistics* nor in *Schumpeter, Social Scientist,* but in the journal of the Econometric Society: *Econometrica* 18 (April 1950), pp. 103–110. The quotations are on pp. 104, 109, and 110.

23. Morgenstern, "Obituary: Joseph A. Schumpeter, 1993–1950," p. 201; G. B. Richardson, "Schumpeter's *History of Economic Analysis,*" *Oxford Economic Papers,* New Series 7 (June 1955), p. 136.

EPILOGUE: THE LEGACY

1. Schumpeter, "Comments on a Plan for the Study of Entrepreneurship," in Richard Swedberg, ed., *Joseph A. Schumpeter: The Economics and Sociology of Capitalism* (Princeton, N.J.: Princeton University Press, 1991), pp. 425–426. The idea of

entrepreneurship in Schumpeter's writings tended to shift a bit over the course of his career from the role of a person to the function of an organization.

2. Hundreds of other entrepreneurs, from many countries, could of course be added to this list. On the point of small versus large business as the more natural home of entrepreneurial behavior, see the bibliographical discussion in note 25, ch. 21 above.

3. On the evolution of the term "business strategy," see note 18, ch. 21 above.

4. The spread of business schools and of Schumpeter's influence, along with a great deal of other information about entrepreneurship, is well analyzed in Amar V. Bhidé, *The Origin and Evolution of New Businesses* (Oxford: Oxford University Press, 2000), especially in the preface and ch. 13. The story of the introduction of entrepreneurship as a topic of formal study into one major institution may be traced in Jeffrey L. Cruikshank, *Shaping the Waves: A History of Entrepreneurship at Harvard Business School* (Boston: Harvard Business School Press, 2005).

5. In 1946, negotiators designed a new international monetary order: the Bretton Woods system, named after the New Hampshire resort where the conference took place. This system, marked by semi-fixed exchange rates for national currencies (the "gold exchange standard") lasted for one generation. It collapsed in 1971, and a regime of floating exchange rates took its place. The Japanese yen, for example, which had been deliberately undervalued by international monetary authorities so as to help promote Japanese exports and rebuild the economy as a bulwark against Soviet expansion, "floated" after 1971 from 360 to the dollar to about 100—a drastic realignment, but one that occurred over several decades. Meanwhile, the euro gradually replaced national currencies in the many nations of the European Union.

6. The evidence here could hardly be clearer. If one were to plot on a graph the ups and downs of the U.S. business cycle throughout the nation's history, the result would look radically different before World War II versus afterwards. For the 160 years between 1780 and 1940, the ups and downs were regularly violent. Significant recessions occurred very often, and major depressions dealt devastating blows during the 1780s, 1810s, 1830s, 1850s, 1870s, 1890s, 1907–08, 1920–21, and 1929–39. A graph depicting this pattern would resemble lines going wildly up and down in a polygraph test being administered to an unskillful liar.

After the 1940s, by contrast, the business cycle in the United States and other advanced industrial nations became much smoother. Economies continued to have recessions and upturns, of course, along with the occasional serious bout with inflation. But the business cycle as a whole was brought under greater control.

This is not to say, of course, that issues relating to business cycles are no longer of interest to scholars. Debates still go on, and numerous articles are published. For a specifically Schumpeterian treatment, see E. Montgomery and W. Wascher,

"Creative Destruction and the Behavior of Productivity over the Business Cycle," *Review of Economics and Statistics* 70 (February 1988), pp. 168–172, which examines the period 1953–1983 and employs a good deal of mathematical notation.

7. The literature on this subject is very large, but four examples will suffice, each written by an economist but from very different viewpoints: Robert M. Solow, "Economic History and Economics," *American Economic Review* 75 (May 1985), pp. 328–331; Donald N. McCloskey, *The Rhetoric of Economics* (Madison: University of Wisconsin Press, 1985); Philip Mirowski, *More Heat Than Light: Economics as Social Physics: Physics as Nature's Economics* (Cambridge: Cambridge University Press, 1989); and Douglass C. North, *Institutions, Institutional Change and Economic Performance* (Cambridge: Cambridge University Press, 1990). More recently, the incessant debates among economists may be sampled in David Warsh, *Economic Principals: Masters and Mavericks of Modern Economics* (New York: Free Press, 1993), and, in the twenty-first century, through Warsh's online newsletter "Economic Principals."

8. Arjo Klamer and David Colander, *The Making of an Economist* (Boulder, Col.: Westview Press, 1990), pp. 17–18. This survey was done in the late 1980s, but there is little reason to believe the situation has changed much since then.

9. Among many books on this subject, see ibid.; also Yuval Yonay, *The Struggle Over the Soul of Economics: Institutionalist and Neoclassical Economists in America between the Wars* (Princeton, N.J.: Princeton University Press, 1998), a sociologist's analysis that goes beyond the period specified in its title; and Michael A. Bernstein, *A Perilous Progress: Economists and Public Purpose in Twentieth-Century America* (Princeton, N.J.: Princeton University Press, 2001), a critique of economists for abandoning their social role in favor of an uncritical "scientific" praise of the "free market." An enlightening and unusually personalized account appears in E. Roy Weintraub, *How Economics Became a Mathematical Science* (Durham, N.C.: Duke University Press, 2002).

The relationship of economics to the other social sciences is a complex story with two main and rather paradoxical themes. In university departments of economics, there has been an ongoing de-emphasis (and frequent exclusion altogether) of courses in economic history, the history of economic thought, and similar topics—in favor of ever more refined mathematical technique. Meanwhile, similar mathematical methods, along with a general "imperialism" by economists (as many critics have called it), have invaded sister disciplines such as political science, sociology, and economic history. These trends can be easily seen by comparing today's professional journals in each discipline with issues of those same journals published a generation ago. In general, the content of today's journals is all but impenetrable for the non-specialist. A generation ago, it could be easily understood by most social scientists regardless of field. This same kind of phenomenon, of course, has appeared in one way or other in virtually all other academic disciplines, including the humanities.

10. Schumpeter, trans. Redvers Opie, *The Theory of Economic Development* (Cambridge, Mass.: Harvard University Press, 1934), pp. 91–94. A rare look at Schumpeter's own sense of how innovation should be studied (which was principally through historical analysis of industries and business leadership) appears in a long letter he wrote to Professor Rupert Maclaurin on July 17, 1944, printed in Ulrich Hedtke and Richard Swedberg, eds., *Joseph Alois Schumpeter, Briefe/Letters* (Tübingen: J. C. B. Mohr, Paul Siebeck), 2000), pp. 349–351.

It would not be difficult, of course, to list hundreds of other major entrepreneurs of the last half-century, from all market economies throughout the world. One could name at least a score from Silicon Valley alone. The literature on Schumpeter and innovation is large and rapidly becoming larger, both in journalistic treatments and academic scholarship. This work tends to be eclectic, uneven in its direct connection to Schumpeter, and of varying quality. The significance of the body of work as a whole is in its broad recognition of the centrality of innovation for economic growth, and there are some real gems. Examples of the academic literature, which I list in chronological order of appearance, include Universities-National Bureau Committee for Economic Research, *The Rate and Direction of Inventive Activity: Economic and Social Factors* (Princeton, N.J.: Princeton University Press, 1962), the report of a pioneering conference; Jonathan Hughes, *The Vital Few: The Entrepreneur and American Economic Progress* (New York: Oxford University Press, 1965); Edwin Mansfield, *Industrial Research and Technological Innovation* (New York: Norton, 1968); Nathan Rosenberg, *Technology and American Economic Growth* (New York: Harper & Row, 1972); Edwin Mansfield, John Rapoport, Anthony Romeo, Edmund Villani, Samuel Wagner, and Frank Husic, *The Production and Application of New Industrial Technology* (New York: Norton, 1977); F. M. Scherer, *Innovation and Growth: Schumpeterian Perspectives* (Cambridge, Mass.: MIT Press, 1984); Joel Mokyr, *The Lever of Riches: Technological Creativity and Economic Progress* (New York: Oxford University Press, 1990); Frederic M. Scherer and Mark Perlman, eds., *Entrepreneurship, Technological Innovation, and Economic Growth: Studies in the Schumpeterian Tradition* (Ann Arbor: University of Michigan Press, 1992); Mark Elam, *Innovation as the Craft of Combination: Perspectives on Technology and Economy in the Spirit of Schumpeter* (Linköping, Sweden: Dept. of Technology and Social Change, Linköping University, 1993); Yuichi Shionoya and Mark Perlman, eds., *Innovation in Technology, Industries, and Institutions: Studies in Schumpeterian Perspectives* (Ann Arbor: University of Michigan Press, 1994); David E. H. Edgerton, ed., *Industrial Research and Innovation in Business* (Cheltenham, U.K.: Edward Elgar, 1996); Clayton M. Christensen, *The Innova-*

tor's Dilemma: When New Technologies Cause Great Firms to Fail (Boston: Harvard Business School Press, 1997) (a book directed primarily toward business managers, and subsequently issued in several revised editions); Johannes M. Bauer, "Market Power, Innovation, and Efficiency in Telecommunications: Schumpeter Reconsidered," *Journal of Economic Issues* 31 (June 1997), pp. 557–565 (in which the author considers Schumpeter's potential influence on deregulation); F. M. Scherer, *New Perspectives on Economic Growth and Technological Innovation* (Washington, D.C.: Brookings Institution Press, 1999) (a brief book with unusually full references to related studies); Bruce McFarling, "Schumpeter's Entrepreneurs and Commons's Sovereign Authority," *Journal of Economic Issues* 34 (September 2000), pp. 707–721 (in which the author tries to combine Schumpeter's and John R. Commons's approaches to innovation); Nathan Rosenberg, *Schumpeter and the Endogeneity of Technology: Some American Perspectives* (New York: Routledge, 2000); John Cantwell, "Innovation, Profits, and Growth: Penrose and Schumpeter," in Christos Pitelis, ed., *The Growth of the Firm: The Legacy of Edith Penrose* (Oxford: Oxford University Press, 2002), pp. 215–248 (in which the author argues that Penrose incorporates Schumpeter's ideas about innovation into her own thinking, and modernizes them); Richard Arena and Cécile Dangel Hagnauer, eds., *The Contributions of Joseph Schumpeter to Economics: Economic Development and Institutional Change* (London: Routledge, 2002), a collection of essays by French scholars arguing, generally, that Schumpeter's economics was institutionalist as well as evolutionary, and thus not solely concerned with innovation and competition; Mümtaz Keklik, *Schumpeter, Innovation and Growth: Long-cycle Dynamics in the Post-WWII American Manufacturing Industries* (Ashgate, U.K.: Edward Elgar, 2003); Robert F. Lanzillotti, "Schumpeter, Product Innovation and Public Policy: The Case of Cigarettes," *Journal of Evolutionary Economics* 13 (2003), pp. 469–490; and Tom Nicholas, "Why Schumpeter Was Right: Innovation, Market Power, and Creative Destruction in 1920s America," *Journal of Economic History* 63 (December 2003), pp. 1023–1058. Although this list may seem long, it is actually only a brief sample of the vast literature on innovation.

11. Wolfgang F. Stolper, "Reflections on Schumpeter's Writings," in Harris, ed., *Schumpeter, Social Scientist,* p. 108.

12. Schumpeter, "Capitalism," in *Encyclopaedia Britannica* (New York: Encyclopaedia Britannica, 1946), pp. 881–887, reprinted in Richard V. Clemence, ed., *Joseph A. Schumpeter: Essays on Entrepreneurs, Innovations, Business Cycles, and the Evolution of Capitalism* (Cambridge, Mass.: Addison-Wesley, 1951), pp. 189–210. The quotation is on p. 190. John Kenneth Galbraith, *A View from the Stands of People, Politics, Military Power and the Arts* (Boston: Houghton Mifflin, 1986), p. 288.

13. Schumpeter, "Capitalism," in *Encyclopaedia Britannica,* reprinted in Clemence,

ed., *Joseph A. Schumpeter: Essays on Entrepreneurs, Innovations, Business Cycles, and the Evolution of Capitalism,* p. 204. Schumpeter had described this process most thoroughly in *Business Cycles.*

14. At the start of the twentieth century, fewer than a half-million Americans owned stocks. By 1929, ten million people were "in the market," an increase of 20-fold. By the end of the twentieth century, the figure exceeded 100 million—an multiple of 200 from the year 1900, or 20,000 percent. Most of these latter-day shareholders owned stocks through investments in pension funds or other retirement funds.

In 1929, the Dow-Jones Industrial Average had peaked at 381, only to lose almost 90 percent of its value by 1932, when it hit bottom at 41. (Medium-term gyrations of this magnitude are difficult to believe today, after more than six decades of a flatter business cycle.) After the Great Depression, the Dow began an erratic ascent, as trading volume gradually recovered. Even so, it took 34 years, until 1963, for the volume of shares traded to equal the 1929 figure. Trading then began to shoot upward, especially in the 1980s and 1990s; and with it the Dow-Jones Industrial Average: to 1,000 in the early 1980s, to 2,500 in 1987 (when another downward break of about 25 percent occurred), then to a sustained and dramatic rise during the 1990s, to a peak of over 11,000 in 1999. At that point it leveled off, partly because of the bursting of the dot.com bubble, and declined slightly over the next several years. It then reached 12,000 in 2006.

Meanwhile, the NASDAQ Composite Index had come into existence, expressing the rapid progress of high-tech firms in information technology and biotechnology—including several thousand new ones founded by entrepreneurs and backed by venture capitalists.

15. Peter F. Drucker, "Schumpeter and Keynes," *Forbes,* May 23, 1983, p. 124.

16. Herbert Giersch, "The Age of Schumpeter," *American Economic Review* 74 (May 1984), pp. 103–109; see also Herbert Giersch, "Economic Policies in the Age of Schumpeter," *European Economic Review* 31 (February/March 1987), pp. 35–52. Charles J. Whalen, "America's Hottest Economist Died 50 Years Ago," *Business Week,* December 11, 2000.

17. The German business journal *Wirtschaftswoche,* which is the lineal descendant of Gustav Stolper's *Deutsche Volkswirt,* finances this prize. Detailed information on the International Schumpeter Society may be found through its homepage, http://www.iss-evec.de. Sometimes the proceedings volumes of the Society pertain to topics Schumpeter promoted (such as technology and innovation), and sometimes to Schumpeter himself. A good example of the latter is Yuichi Shionoya and Mark Perlman, eds., *Schumpeter in the History of Ideas* (Ann Arbor: University of Michigan Press, 1994).

18. The *Journal of Evolutionary Economics* is printed in English and published in Germany. For other comments on Schumpeter's continuing influence, see Uwe

Cantner and Horst Hanusch, "On the Renaissance of Schumpeterian Econom-
ics," Working Paper No. 51, Universität Augsburg, Institut für
Volkswirtschaftslehre, 1991; Richard Swedberg, *Can Capitalism Survive?
Schumpeter's Answer and Its Relevance for New Institutional Economics* (Stockholm:
Stockholm University, Department of Sociology, 1992); and Jan Fagerberg,
"Schumpeter and the Revival of Evolutionary Economics: An Appraisal of the
Literature," *Journal of Evolutionary Economics* 13 (2003), pp. 125–159.

19. For the lecture series and other activities organized by the Graz Schumpeter Society, see http://homepage.univie.ac.at/Bernd.Brandl/schumpeter/
schumpeter.html. The first of the Schumpeter lectures, which apply less to
Schumpeter himself than to the subject of the resulting book's title, is J. Stanley
Metcalfe, *Evolutionary Economics and Creative Destruction* (Florence, KY:
Routledge, 1998). Subsequent lecture series, listed on the website above, have varied across a spectrum of topics—appropriately so, given Schumpeter's own broad
interests.

20. Douglass North's statement appeared in *The Wall Street Journal,* July 29, 1994,
p. B1. North later wrote that "Schumpeter had a strong influence upon me." See
"Douglass C. North," in William Breit and Roger W. Spencer, eds., *Lives of the
Laureates: Thirteen Nobel Economists,* 3rd ed. (Cambridge, Mass.: MIT Press,
1995), p. 254. North was a pioneer "cliometrician"—an economic historian who
used advanced mathematical techniques. Given a series of simplifying assumptions, proof *is* available in precisely specified economic propositions. The careful
use of techniques such as regression analysis and simultaneous equations can
bring a researcher much closer to economic precision than untested hypotheses
can, or back-of-the-envelope calculations. But in the end, even an infinite set of
statistics and a million equations cannot make exact determinate sense of a major
economic problem such as business cycles, the future course of an industry or a
national economy—or even of such an apparently simple question as the importance of leadership in a business situation. The number of variables in all of these
phenomena is almost limitless. The answer to any economic question depends
inherently not only on statistics and mathematics, but also on exogenous factors
(wars, droughts, the mindsets of participants); and, especially in capitalist economies, on the endogenous forces of continuous innovation.

21. In university departments of economics, instructors also speak of "stories." But
what they usually mean is stylized models of behavior. Even so, their most memorable generalizations almost always come in mini-narratives, often expressed as
metaphors: Adam Smith's "invisible hand," Marx's "reserve army of the unemployed," Schumpeter's "creative destruction," Thorstein Veblen's "conspicuous
consumption," Paul Samuelson's "revealed preference" (the best guide to what a
person wants is what that person does), Oliver Williamson's "bounded rationality" (nobody can know everything), Paul David's "path dependency" (inertia of-

ten prevents innovation), and Lawrence Summers' aphorism that "nobody ever washed a rented car." But even these formulations can become what Schumpeter called "slogans"—easy substitutes for the whole truth, potentially misleading if not tempered by the facts of particular situations.

22. A. P. Usher, "Historical Implications of the Theory of Economic Development," in Seymour E. Harris, ed., *Schumpeter, Social Scientist* (Cambridge, Mass.: Harvard University Press, 1951), p. 129; Paul A. Samuelson, "Schumpeter's *Capitalism, Socialism and Democracy*," in Arnold Heertje, ed., *Schumpeter's Vision: Capitalism, Socialism and Democracy after 40 Years* (New York: Praeger, 1981), p. 21; Sidney G. Winter, "Schumpeterian Competition in Alternative Technological Regimes," *Journal of Economic Behavior and Organization* 5 (September–December 1984), p. 287; Robert Heilbroner, *The Worldly Philosophers: The Lives, Times, and Ideas of the Great Economic Thinkers,* 6th ed. (New York: Hyperion Books, 1991), p. 291. Schumpeter is one of only five economists to whom Heilbroner devotes an entire chapter (the others being Adam Smith, Karl Marx, Thorstein Veblen, and John Maynard Keynes). The author goes on to say that economics has become too narrow to produce any more "worldly philosophers."

ACKNOWLEDGMENTS

My largest debt by far is to Susan McCraw, to whom this book is dedicated. Her insights and editorial skills, honed during years of legal practice, affected its every page, and her fine artist's eye the choice of every illustration. What cannot be evident here is her unwavering care for our family over many years—not to mention her sustained support of my work, often at the expense of her own. Goethe once wrote that "the sum which two married people owe one another defies calculation. It is an infinite debt, which can only be discharged through all eternity." For me that does not overstate the case in the slightest.

In writing the book, I've had marvelous opportunities to absorb knowledge about innovation and capitalism from numerous friends and fellow scholars—both in my own field of history and in a half-dozen others as well. But before I name those friends and scholars, I want to record that I've had the priceless good luck to learn just as much from my students. At the school where I teach, their average age is twenty-seven, and they've held jobs in almost every kind of industry and public agency throughout the world. Apart from my Ph.D. seminar, my typical class has contained ninety-five students from twenty-six countries, ranging from the rich nations to the very poor. Some of these students come from affluent families, but the majority do not. Their debates with one another about the history and nature of capitalism have been brisk, fervent, and sometimes angry. If one listens closely in this kind of setting—day after day, year after year—only the most obtuse instructor can fail to *be* instructed. As the Roman proverb has it, *Qui docet discet.* He who teaches learns.

The experience has been exhilarating, and the lessons profound. Long ago, during the breakup of the Soviet Union, I asked one of my classes to define capitalism. After the debate meandered for a while, a Russian student said, "It's a system in which you get to keep what you earn." In that brief sentence, this Soviet citizen identified two of the pillars of successful capitalist society: private property and the rule of law. In the years since, his words have rung truer than ever, as dozens of countries—including his own—have tried to install capitalist systems, with very mixed success.

Of the readings I've assigned, my students have most prized the work of Joseph Schumpeter, which is one of the reasons why I wrote this book. Their reaction to his analysis of capitalism—its benefits and costs, its creative and destructive effects in their own countries and elsewhere—has been "Yes, this is how it really is *out there.*" When I began to write about Schumpeter, I found that many people had said the same thing to him, to his great pleasure.

All contemporary students of Schumpeter's life and work owe a great deal to the scholars who went before them. Those predecessors number in the hundreds, and their appearance in my notes is itself an acknowledgment of my debt. Here, however, I wish to make further mention of five writers: Richard Swedberg, Ulrich Hedtke, Robert Loring Allen, Wolfgang Stolper, and Christian Seidl.

Professor Swedberg is a superb sociologist who has done as much as any other person in bringing Schumpeter's work to the attention of a wider public. He has written an excellent brief biography of Schumpeter, emphasizing his contributions to *Sozialökonomie*. He has also edited a collection of Schumpeter's articles and has co-edited with Ulrich Hedtke an invaluable collection of Schumpeter's letters. Professor Hedtke maintains from Berlin a website (www.Schumpeter.info), which is essential to any serious student of Schumpeter's work. The late Robert Loring Allen wrote another good biography, which—though often uneven in its documentation—is quite helpful in confirming what Schumpeter was doing when, and also in its use of interviews with persons now no longer living. The late Wolfgang Stolper wrote still a third biography, concentrating on Schumpeter's public life. Just as important, Professor Stolper—in collaboration with Professor Christian Seidl, a fifth perceptive interpreter of Schumpeter's life and work—located, collected, and coedited in three volumes a large body of Schumpeter's writings from the period before he came to the United States.

In addition to my fellow Schumpeter scholars, many economists (including at least twenty of my Ph.D. seminar students), helped me to avoid technical errors and to understand Schumpeter's unique place in their discipline. I can't name them all, but I extend special thanks to Mike Scherer of Harvard and Jack High of George Mason. Both are extremely perceptive veteran economists who read the entire manuscript and improved it immeasurably—Mike when the initial version was finished, and Jack in a long exchange of letters as it emerged chapter by chapter. Among political scientists, Rawi Abdelal was by far the most helpful. He too read the whole manuscript—large parts of it more than once—and made dozens of useful suggestions.

Three uncommonly talented young historians improved my understanding of the Austro-Hungarian Empire, Germany between the two world wars, and Central Europe in general. Alison Fleig Frank guided me through the vast and rich literature on the Dual Monarchy and on Vienna in particular. She also edited early versions of Parts I and II of the book and helped with some difficult translations. Benjamin Hett worked long and efficient hours during the earliest phase of the project. An experienced lawyer as well as a first-rate historian, Ben ferreted out crucial items from Schumpeter's early work and also from the Schumpeter Papers. He also helped me think through the initial plan of the book. A third young historian, Jeffrey Fear, read the entire manuscript and shared with me his deep understanding of German business history. Both before and during the composition of this book, I had numerous conversations with Jeff about innovation, industrial organization, and the nature of German-style capitalism.

Like almost everyone else who has worked in the subdiscipline of business history, I've learned more from Alfred D. Chandler, Jr., than from any other scholar. He has been a guide and close friend for more than thirty years, and I owe him a great deal, personally and professionally. The same is true of my three other longtime collaborators in the business history enterprise at Harvard: Richard S. Tedlow, with whom I've had scores of conversations about this book over the last six years; Richard H. K. Vietor, who offered useful criticism on early drafts of four chapters, and who worked with me for fifteen years under the inspired leadership of our former dean, John H. McArthur, in building a cross-disciplinary group for the study of business and government; and Walter A. Friedman, my former associate editor and coeditor of the *Business History Review.* Walter, who still holds the latter office, has been singularly thoughtful in his suggestions about how to improve this book—frequently taking time from his own writing to edit mine and to help locate obscure source materials.

Among my colleagues in our Entrepreneurial Management Unit, I owe most to Howard Stevenson, who founded and nurtured the group and commented on early drafts of the manuscript; to Bill Sahlman, a pioneer in the study of entrepreneurial finance—what Schumpeter called "credit creation"; to Tom Nicholas, a young economic historian who carefully edited chapter 3; to Teresa Amabile, a leading student of creativity who has chaired our Unit with scrupulous care; and to Geoffrey Jones, my good friend, successor as the Isidor Straus Professor of Business History, and one of the world's leading authorities on the history of international business.

I am grateful for the opportunity to present early versions of parts of this book in papers, comments, and articles in several venues: Harvard's Business History Seminar, sessions at the annual Business History Conference, The Historical Society, the Seminar on Austrian Economics at New York University, *The American Scholar,* the Economic History Association's commemoration of the twentieth century's best books in the field (www.eh.net.project2000), *SternBusiness,* the *Business History Review,* and the Berkley Center for Entrepreneurial Studies at the Stern School of Business, where I was the first Entrepreneurship Scholar-in-Residence.

For assistance in research and translations I thank most of all Holger Frank, who worked for more than two years with a mass of difficult materials from the Schumpeter Papers at Harvard. Holger is a native of Graz, where Schumpeter lived both as a boy and a professor, and he organized a research expedition that took us to places in Europe where Schumpeter lived and taught—from his birthplace in the Czech Republic, to Graz and Vienna, to Bonn, and to many sites along the way. Others who provided indispensable help with research, translations, or both were Kevin Burke, Rustin Gates,

Christopher Hall, Takashi Hikino, Susanna Kim, Phil Mead, Florian Müller, David Nickles, and Felice Whittum.

Five close friends of long standing—Jim Baughman, Bill Childs, Paul Glad, Hubert McAlexander, and Dick Walton—helped enormously at various stages of the book, reading draft chapters and giving astute advice. George Gibson and Michael Aronson, two of the wisest editors and publishers I've ever met, gave similarly valuable counsel.

In no aspect of this book was I more fortunate than in its editing. Besides the many friends and colleagues already mentioned, two genuine masters of the English language—Jeff Strabone and Susan Wallace Boehmer—read the draft manuscript with meticulous care and made hundreds of good suggestions. Susan also shepherded the book's progress from submission to publication and showed unerringly good judgment about both the big picture and the subtlest details.

Like all books based on manuscript collections, this one would have been impossible to write without the help of librarians and archivists. I thank, in particular, Robin McElheny of Harvard's Pusey Library, Ellen Shea of the Schlesinger Library (Radcliffe Institute), Margaret Burri of the Milton S. Eisenhower Library (Johns Hopkins), Dominick Hunger of the Universitätsbibliothek Basel, Carol Leadenham of the Hoover Institution Archives, Manuela Vack of the Bundesarchiv Koblenz, and the staff of the photographic section of the Österreichische Nationalbibliothek in Vienna. I also thank each of these institutions for permission to quote from or reproduce materials in their possession. The Division of Research of the Harvard Business School provided unfailingly generous support throughout the long period of research and writing.

All errors and infelicities that remain in the book are, of course, my own, and I take full responsibility for them.

ILLUSTRATION CREDITS

Page 48, bottom right: Reproduced by permission of the Österreichische Nationalbibliothek, Vienna

Page 48, bottom left: Reproduced by permission of the Österreichische Nationalbibliothek, Vienna

Page 61: Courtesy of Harvard University Archives, HUGB S276.90

Page 69: Reproduced by permission of the Österreichische Nationalbibliothek, Vienna

Page 78: Photograph by the author

Page 79: Photograph by the author

Page 99: Reproduced by permission of the Österreichische Nationalbibliothek, Vienna

Page 108: Reproduced by permission of the Österreichische Nationalbibliothek, Vienna

Page 118: Courtesy of Harvard University Archives, HUGB S276.90

Page 125: Courtesy of Harvard University Archives, HUGB S276.90

Page 127: Courtesy of Harvard University Archives HUGFP_4.5

Page 132, right: Courtesy of Bundesarchiv, Koblenz, Germany

Page 132, below: Courtesy of Universitäts- und Landesbibliothek, Bonn, Germany

Page 141: Courtesy of Bundesarchiv, Koblenz, Germany

Page 154: Photograph by Mia Stöckel, courtesy of Zora Recker, www.schumpeter.info

Page 180: Courtesy of Harvard University Archives, HUGB S276.90

Page 185: Courtesy of Harvard University Archives, HUP Taussig, Frank William (5a)

Page 190: Courtesy of Harvard University Archives, HUGB S276.90p

Page 195: Courtesy of Kevin Burke

Page 197: Courtesy of Harvard University Archives, HUGB S276.90

Page 198: Courtesy of Harvard University Archives, HUGB S276.90

Page 214, top left: Courtesy of Harvard University Archives, HUP Parsons, Talcott (1a)

Page 214, top right: Courtesy of Harvard University Archives, HUP Galbraith, John Kenneth, (1a)

Page 214, bottom left: Courtesy of Harvard University Archives, UAV 605.270.5p

Page 214, bottom right: Courtesy of Harvard University Archives, HUP Harris, Seymour Edwin (3)

Page 215, left: Courtesy of Harvard University Archives, HUP Leontief, Wassily W. (1)

Page 215, right: Courtesy of Bentley Historical Library, University of Michigan

Page 233: Courtesy of Harvard University Archives, HUGB S276.90

Page 238: Courtesy of Radcliffe Archives, Radcliffe Institute, Harvard University

Page 240: Courtesy of Radcliffe Archives, Radcliffe Institute, Harvard University, and Bachrach Photography, Boston, Mass.

Page 272, above: Courtesy of Harvard University Archives, HUD-343.04

Page 272, left: Courtesy of Library of Congress

Page 301: Courtesy of Harvard University Archives, HUGB S276.90

Page 304, top: Courtesy of Harvard University Archives, HUGB S276.90p

Page 304, bottom: Courtesy of Kevin Burke

Page 377, above: Courtesy of Harvard University Archives, HUGB S276.90

Page 377, left: Courtesy of Harvard University Archives, HUGB S276.90

Page 418, top: Courtesy of *Monthly Review*

Page 418, bottom: Courtesy of Harvard University Archives, HUV 175 (2–4)

Page 419: Courtesy of Harvard University Archives, HUGB S276.90

Page 439, left: Courtesy of MIT Museum

Page 439, bottom: Courtesy of Yale University Library, 10724

Page 440: Courtesy of Harvard University Archives, HUP Smithies, Arthur (2)

Page 462, top: Courtesy of Harvard University Department of Economics

Page 462, bottom: Courtesy of Harvard Archives, HUV 1467 (5–2)

Page 463: Courtesy of Harvard University Archives, HUGB S276.90

Page 472, left: Courtesy of Harvard University Archives, HUP Cole, Arthur H. (1)

Page 472, below: Courtesy of Harvard University Archives, HUGB S276.90

Page 480: Courtesy of Harvard University Archives, HUGB S276.90

INDEX